THE HUMAN RECORD

THE HUMAN RECORD

Sources of Global History

VOLUME II: *Since 1500*

ALFRED J. ANDREA

University of Vermont

JAMES H. OVERFIELD

University of Vermont

HOUGHTON MIFFLIN COMPANY   BOSTON

Dallas   Geneva, Illinois   Palo Alto   Princeton, New Jersey

Copyright © 1990 by Houghton Mifflin Company. All rights reserved.

Printed in the U.S.A.

Library of Congress Catalog Card Number: 89-80909

ISBN: 0-395-48400-6

ABCDEFGHIJ-B-9543210-89

We Dedicate This Book with Love and Thanks to
Juanita B. Andrea and Susan L. Overfield

CONTENTS

PART I   *The World at the Time of Western Expansion, 1500–1650*

C H A P T E R 1   Europe's Expansion: Consequences and Counterattacks . . . 4

GEOGRAPHIC CONTENTS

TOPICAL CONTENTS

International Relations

Politics

Religion

Christianity

Hinduism

Islam

Judaism

PREFACE

Many goals and principles have guided our work on *The Human Record*. We are committed to the proposition that students of history at all levels need to meet the challenge of analyzing primary sources. Involvement with the evidence of the past enables students to see that historical scholarship is primarily a process of drawing inferences from incomplete and often ambiguous clues, not of collecting, cataloguing, and memorizing immutable facts. Analysis of primary sources is also the basis for historical understanding; to discover what people thought and did and to organize this into a record of the human past, historians must search for evidence—for the sources of history. For the student of world history, who attempts to understand the development over time of human institutions and ways of thought, this search is essential to determine periods of significant historical change, as well as lines of continuity.

For these reasons, we have compiled a collection of sources that emphasizes the long and intricate course of human history and that reveals the differences and affinities among the world's cultures. Volume I follows the evolution of the cultures that most significantly influenced world history from 3500 B.C. to A.D. 1700, with particular emphasis on the major religious, social, and intellectual traditions of the Afro-Eurasian ecumene. It concurrently develops the theme of the growing interconnectedness of human societies down to the early modern age. Volume II traces the gradual emergence of the West to a position of global hegemony, the simultaneous historical development of other civilizations and societies around the world, the eventual anticolonial revolts of the twentieth century, and the emergence of today's "one world." We have taken care to group selections thematically, avoiding isolated sources that provide a "taste" of some culture or age but, by their dissociation, shed no light on the dual phenomena of historical change and continuity. Our objective is to present an overview of global history in mosaic form.

In selecting and placing the various pieces of our mosaic, we aimed to create a balanced picture of human history and to craft a book that reveals the contributions of all major geographic areas. In a similar vein, we attempted to give our readers a collection of sources representing a wide variety of perspectives and experiences. Believing that the study of history properly concerns every aspect of past human behavior, we sought sources that mirror the concerns and practices of all manner of persons and groups.

At the same time, most of the sources that appear in these two volumes reflect the actions and thoughts of history's great and near great. It cannot be otherwise in a book that seeks to cover the highpoints of over five millennia of history.

Our quest for historical balance also led us into the arena of nonverbal evidence. Although most historians center their research on documentary sources, the discipline obligates us to consider all of the clues surrendered by the past, and these include its artifacts. Moreover, we have discovered that students enjoy analyzing pictures of artifacts and seem to remember vividly the conclusions they draw from them. For these reasons, we have included a number of illustrations of works of art that we ask the users of this book to analyze as historical sources. We also took special care in selecting the artwork that opens each chapter. Each piece of art illustrates an important theme developed in the chapter, and we urge our readers to study these pictures as additional sources. All are identified at the rear of the volume.

For the introductory student, source analysis is often a daunting exercise. Therefore, to make these selections as accessible as possible, we have provided our readers with a variety of aids. First there is the Prologue, in which we explain, initially in a theoretical manner and then through concrete examples, how a student of history goes about the task of interpreting written and artifactual sources. Next we offer part, chapter, subchapter, and individual source introductions, all to help the reader place each selection into a meaningful context and to understand its historical role and significance.

Suggested questions for analysis also precede each source. The questions fall into three categories. Some are quite specific and are intended to assist the reader in picking out important pieces of information or in noticing something we consider especially suggestive. Answering concrete questions of this sort prepares the student researcher for the next, more significant level of analysis, drawing general inferences. Questions that demand such conclusions invariably follow. Finally, we offer questions that challenge the student to compare the individual or society that produced a particular source with an individual, group, or culture encountered earlier in the volume. We believe such comparisons help students fix more firmly in their minds the distinguishing cultural characteristics of the various societies they encounter in their brief survey of world history.

Another form of help we proffer is to gloss the sources, explaining in full those words and allusions that a first-year college student cannot reasonably be expected to know. To facilitate reading, these footnotes appear at the bottom of the page on which they are cited. Some documents also contain italicized interlinear notes that serve as transitions and suggest the main themes of the passages that follow. Used primarily in lengthier sources from the great thinkers, these notes help to guide students through the readings.

By virtues of its comprehensiveness, organization, and pedagogic features, some instructors may choose to use *The Human Record* as a replacement for a standard textbook. Most of our colleagues, however, will probably use it as a supplement to a standard text, and many will decide not to require their students to analyze every entry. To assist professors (and students) in selecting documents and artifacts that best suit their interests and needs, we have prepared two analytical tables of contents for each volume. The first lists readings and artifacts by geographic and cultural area, the second by topic. The two tables suggest to instructor and student alike the rich variety of material available within these pages, particularly for research papers in comparative history.

Specific suggestions for assignments and classroom activities are offered in the Instructor's Manual that accompanies *The Human Record*. In this manual, prepared by the editors, we also explain our reasons for choosing the sources that appear in these volumes and the insights we believe students should be capable of drawing from them. Further, we describe classroom strategies for eliciting thought and discussion on the various sources and offer bibliographic suggestions and a pronunciation guide. Much of the advice we present is the fruit of our own use of these sources in the classroom.

Our final duty is to thank the many professionals who offered their expert advice and assistance during the preparation of this book. Among our friends and colleagues at the University of Vermont, we must acknowledge the cheerful and competent help of Bridget M. Butler, the Department of History's Administrative Assistant, and the invaluable support of the entire Reference Department of Bailey-Howe Library, particularly Nancy Crane, its director, and Bonnie Ryan, head of interlibrary loan services. Scholars at UVM who generously shared their expertise with us include Robert V. Daniels, Constance McGovern, Kristin M. Peterson-Ishaq, Abubaker Saad, Wolfe W. Schmokel, Peter Seybolt, John W. Seyller, Marshall True, and Denise Youngblood. We wish to thank especially Peter D. Andrea, who drew the prototype for map 2 in Volume I.

We wish also to acknowledge the following instructors who read and commented on all or portions of our manuscript in its various stages of preparation. Their comments and suggestions helped us to see more clearly what we were doing and where we were headed. They forced us to rethink a number of our conclusions and general statements, and in several instances we deleted or added a particular text in response to excellent advice. Even on those occasions when we disagreed with their interpretations and suggestions, we benefited from the exchange of ideas.

Jerry Bentley, *University of Hawaii, Manoa*
Dan Binkley, *Hawaii Pacific College*
Robert Carlisle, *St. Lawrence University*

James Casada, *Winthrop College*
Allen Cronenberg, *Auburn University*
Stephen Englehart, *California Polytechnic State University, Pomona*
Lorraine Gesick, *University of Nebraska at Omaha*
Marc Gilbert, *North Georgia College*
Robert Gowen, *East Carolina University*
William Hamblin, *University of Southern Mississippi*
Craig Lockard, *University of Wisconsin—Green Bay*
Peter Mellini, *Sonoma State University*
Bruce Mouser, *University of Wisconsin—La Crosse*
Richard Porterfield, *Glassboro State College*
Kerry Spiers, *University of Louisville*

Special thanks are owed to the editors and staff of Houghton Mifflin. It has been a pleasure to work with a publishing firm that takes such pride in its professionalism.

Finally, our debt to our spouses is beyond payment, but the dedication of this book to them reflects in some small way how deeply we appreciate their support.

A. J. A.

J. H. O.

PROLOGUE: HOW TO READ THE EVIDENCE

1. What Is History?

Many students believe that studying history simply involves memorizing dates, names, battles, treaties, and countless similar facts. After all, so the argument goes, the past is over and done with. Historians know what has happened, and all students have to do is absorb that body of knowledge. But this notion is wrong. History, as is true of all branches of human understanding, involves discovery and interpretation. Historians are continually learning more about the past and shedding fresh light on its meaning. As you become involved in interpreting historical evidence, you will come to understand and appreciate the creative process that takes place as we explore the past.

The drive to understand what has gone before us is innately human and springs from our need to know who we are. History serves this function of self-discovery in a variety of ways. Its subject matter is universal, dealing with all aspects of past human activity and belief. Among the many issues historians face in interpreting our complex and variegated past, two are fundamental: continuity and change. How and why do things change over time, and how and why do certain values and practices endure throughout a society's history? Answers to these questions, no matter how partial or tentative, reveal the dynamics of a culture. When applied to the global community, historical perspective enables us to appreciate the richness of human experience and expression and the factors underlying the striking similarities and differences that exist among the world's peoples.

The collection of sources in this book will help you discover some of the principal lines of development within world history and understand the major cultural traditions and forces that have shaped history around the globe. We will not hand you answers, however: you will have to work for them, for hard work lies at the heart of historical study. The word *history*, which is Greek in origin, means "learning through inquiry," and that is precisely what historians do. They discover and interpet the past by asking questions and conducting research. Their inquiry revolves around an examination of evidence left by the past. For lack of a better term, historians call that evidence "primary source material."

2. Primary Sources: Their Value and Limitations

Primary sources for the most part are records that have been passed on in written form, thereby preserving the memory of past events. These written sources include, but are not limited to, official records, private correspondence, literature, religious texts, memoirs — the list goes on and on. None of these sources by itself contains unadulterated truth or the whole picture. Each gives us only a glimpse of reality, and it is the historian's task to fit these fragments of the past into a coherent picture.

Imagine for a moment that some historian in the late twenty-first century decides to write a history of your college class. Think about the primary sources that researcher would seek out: the school catalogue, the registrar's class lists, academic transcripts, and similar official documents; class lecture notes, course syllabi, exams, term papers, and textbooks; diaries and private letters; the school newspaper, yearbooks, and sports programs; handbills, posters, and even photographs of graffiti; recollections recorded by some of your classmates long after they have graduated. With some more thought you can add other items to the list, among them some important nonwritten sources, such as recordings of popular music and photographs and videotapes of student life and activity. But let us confine ourselves, for the moment, to written records. What do all these documentary sources have in common?

As we examine this list of sources, we realize that, though numerous, these records do not and cannot present the past in its entirety. Where do we see among them the long telephone calls home, the all-night study groups, the afternoons spent at the student union? Someone may have recorded memories of some of these events, but how complete and trustworthy is that evidence? Also keep in mind that all the documents available to our twenty-first-century historian will be fortunate survivors. They will represent only a small percentage of the vast bulk of written material generated during your college career. Thanks to the wastebasket, the delete key, the disintegration of materials, and the inevitable loss of life's memorabilia as years slip by, the evidence available to the future historian will be fragmentary. This is always the case with historical evidence. We cannot preserve the records of the past in their totality, nor do we wish to. Clearly, the more remote the past, the more fragmentary our documentary evidence. Imagine the feeble chance any particular document from the twelfth century had of surviving the wars, wastebaskets, and worms of the past 800 years.

Now let us consider those many individual pieces of documentary evidence relating to your class's history that have survived. As we review the list, we see that not one of those primary sources gives us a pure, unvarnished, and complete picture. Each has its perspective, value, and limitations.

You certainly know that every college catalogue presents an idealized picture of campus life. Despite its flaws, however, that catalogue can be an important piece of evidence because it reflects the values of the faculty and administrators who composed it and provides useful information by listing rules and regulations, courses, instructors, school organizations, and similar items. That information, however, is the raw material of history, not history itself, and certainly it does not reflect the full historical reality of your class.

What is true of the catalogue is equally true of the student newspaper and every other piece of evidence generated by or pertinent to your class. Each primary source is a part of a larger whole but, as we have already seen, we do not have all the pieces. Think of your historical evidence in terms of a jigsaw puzzle. Many of the pieces are missing, but it is possible to put most, though probably not all, of the remaining pieces together in a reasonable fashion to form a fairly accurate and coherent picture. The picture that emerges may not be complete, but it is useful and valid. The keys to fitting these pieces together are hard work and imagination. Each is absolutely necessary.

3. Examining the Sources

Hard work speaks for itself, but students are often unaware that a historian also needs an imagination to reconstruct the past. After all, many students ask, doesn't history consist of strictly defined and irrefutable dates, names, and facts? Where does imagination enter into the process of learning these facts? Again, let us consider your class's history and its documentary sources. Many of those documents provide factual data — dates, names, grades, statistics — and these data are important, but individually and collectively they have no historical meaning until they are interpreted. Your college class is not a collection of statistics and facts. It is a group of individuals who, despite their differences, share and help mold a collective experience. It is a community evolving within a particular time and space. Influenced by the larger environment in which it finds itself, it is, in turn, an influence on that world. Any valid or useful history must reach beyond a mere list of dates, names, and facts to interpret the historical characteristics and role of your class. What were its values? How did it change and why? What impact did it have? These are some of the important questions a historian asks of the evidence.

In order to arrive at answers, the historian must examine each and every piece of evidence as fully as possible and wring from that evidence as many *inferences* as possible. Facts may be the foundation stones of history, but inferences are its edifices. An inference is a logical conclusion drawn from evidence, and it is the inference that is the heart and soul of historical inquiry.

Every American schoolchild learns that Christopher Columbus "sailed the ocean blue in 1492." That fact is worthless, however, unless the student understands the motives, causes, and significance of this late fifteenth-century voyage. Certainly a historian must know when Columbus sailed west. After all, time is history's framework. Yet the questions historians ask go beyond simple chronology. Why did Columbus sail west? What factors made possible and almost inevitable Spain's involvement in such enterprises at this time? Why was Europe willing and able to exploit the "New World"? These are some of the significant questions whose inferential answers historians seek, and those answers can be found only in the evidence.

One noted historian, Robin Winks, has written a book entitled *The Historian as Detective*, and the image is appropriate, although inexact. Like the detective, the historian examines clues in order to reconstruct events. However, the detective is essentially interested in discovering what happened, who did it, and why, while the historian goes one step further and asks what it all means.

Like the detective interrogating witnesses, the historian also examines the testimony of sources, and both researchers ask similar questions. First and foremost, the historian must evaluate the *validity* of the source. Is it what it purports to be? Artful forgeries have misled many historians. Even if the source is authentic, and most are, it can still draw the historian into significant error. The possibility always exists that the source's author is lying or otherwise deliberately misrepresenting reality. Even if this is not the case, the historian can easily be led astray by not fully understanding the *perspective* reflected in the document. As any detective who has examined a number of eyewitnesses to an event knows, viewpoints differ radically due to a number of factors. The police detective has the opportunity to reexamine witnesses and offer them the opportunity to change their testimony in the light of new evidence and deeper reflection. The historical researcher is usually not so fortunate. Even when the historian attempts to establish a creative interchange with documentary evidence by studying it in a probing manner and comparing it with other evidence, there is no way to cross-examine it in detail. What is written is written. Given this fact, it is absolutely necessary for the historian to understand, as fully as possible, the source's perspective. Thus, the historian must ask several key questions. *What* kind of document is this? *Who* wrote it? For *whom* and *why*? *Where* was it composed and *when*?

The *what* is important, because understanding the nature of the particular source can save the historian a great deal of frustration. Many historical sources simply do not directly address the questions a historian would like to ask of them. That twenty-first-century historian would be foolish to try to learn much about the academic quality of your school's courses from a study of the registrar's class lists and grade sheets. Student and faculty class notes, copies of old syllabi, exams, papers, and textbooks would be far more fruitful sources.

Who, for *whom*, and *why* are equally important questions. The official school catalogue undoubtedly addresses some issues pertaining to student social life. But should this document, designed to attract potential students and to place the school in the best possible light, be read and accepted uncritically? Obviously not. It should be tested against student testimony, discovered in such sources as private letters, memoirs, posters, the student newspaper, and the yearbook.

Where and *when* are also important questions to ask of a primary source. As a general rule, distance in space and time from an event colors perceptions and can adversely affect the validity of a source's testimony. The recollections of a person celebrating a twenty-fifth class reunion may prove quite insightful and valuable. Conceivably this graduate now has a perspective and even information that were absent a quarter of a century earlier. Just as conceivably this person's memory might be playing tricks. It is possible for a source to be so close to or so distant from the event it deals with that its view is distorted or totally erroneous. Even so, the source is not necessarily worthless. Often the blind spots and misinformation within a source reveal to the researcher much about the author's attitudes and sources of information.

The historical detective's task is not easy. In addition to constantly questioning the validity and perspectives of available sources, the historical researcher must often use whatever evidence is available in imaginative ways. He or she must interpret these fragmentary and flawed glimpses of the past and piece together the resultant inferences as best as possible. While realizing that a complete picture of the past is never possible, the historian assumes the responsibility of re-creating a past that is valid and has meaning for the present.

4. You and the Sources

This book will involve you actively in the work of historical inquiry by asking you to draw inferences based on your careful analysis of primary-source evidence. This is not an easy task, especially at first, but it is well within your capability, and we will help you all along the way.

You will analyze two types of evidence, documents and artifacts. Each source will be authentic, so you will not need to worry about validating it. We will supply you with the information necessary to place each piece of evidence in its proper context, and we will suggest questions you legitimately can and should ask of each source. If you carefully read the introductions and notes, the questions, and the sources — and think about what you are doing — solid inferences will follow.

To illustrate how you should go about this task and what is expected of you, we have prepared a sample exercise, which we will take you through step by step. The exercise consists of a document written by Christopher Columbus and a reproduction of an early sixteenth-century woodcut. First we present the document just as it would appear in any of the chapters of this book: introduction, suggested analytical questions, and the source itself, with explanatory notes. Then we show you how to read that document. The exercise will not draw every possible insight and inference from the document, but it will demonstrate how to set about answering several of the more important questions you should ask of that source.

Following that, we introduce you to the art of "reading" a nonwritten piece of historical evidence. After a few general words on how a historian uses artifacts as evidence, we present the piece of evidence just as it would appear in the book. Then we show you what we read in this picture. By the end of this exercise, if you have worked closely with us, you should be ready to begin interpreting sources on your own.

Christopher Columbus

A LETTER CONCERNING RECENTLY DISCOVERED ISLANDS

There is no need to recount in detail the story of Christopher Columbus (1451–1506), a Genoese sea captain in the service of Isabella of Castile and Ferdinand of Aragon, who sailed westward over the Atlantic Ocean seeking a new route to the empires of East Asia. On October 12, 1492, his fleet of three ships dropped anchor at a small Bahamian island, which Columbus claimed for Spain, naming it San Salvador. The fleet then sailed to the major islands of Cuba, which he named Juana, and Hispaniola (where the modern nations of Haiti and the Dominican Republic are located), which he named Española. After exploring the two islands and establishing the post of Navidad del Señor on Española, Columbus departed for Spain in January 1493. On his way home, Columbus prepared a public account of his expedition to the "Indies" and posted it from Lisbon, Portugal, where he landed in early March. As intended, the letter preceded Columbus to the Spanish royal court, which he entered in triumph in April.

As you analyze the document, you should be aware of several facts. The admiral was returning with only two of his vessels. He had lost his flagship, the *Santa Maria*, when it was wrecked on a reef off present-day Haiti on Christmas Day. Also, many of Columbus's facts and figures reflect more his enthusiasm than dispassionate analysis. His estimate of the dimensions of the two main islands he explored exaggerates their sizes. His optimistic report of the wide availability of such riches as gold, spices, cotton, and mastic, an eastern Mediterranean aromatic gum, was not borne out by subsequent explorations and colonization. Gold was rare in the islands; the only indigenous "spice" proved to be the fiery chili pepper; the wild cotton was excellent but not plentiful; and mastic was nonexistent in the Caribbean.

Questions for Analysis

1. What evidence is there in the letter that allows us to judge Columbus's reliability as an objective reporter? To what extent can we trust his account?

2. What do the admiral's admitted actions regarding the natives and the ways in which he describes these people allow us to conclude about his attitudes toward these "Indians" and his plans for them?
3. What does Columbus's description of the physical attributes of the islands he explored suggest about some of the motives that underlay his voyage?
4. What does this letter tell us about the culture of the people of the Caribbean on the eve of European expansion into that region?

Knowing that it will afford you pleasure to learn that I have brought my undertaking to a successful termination, I have decided upon writing you this letter to acquaint you with all the events which have occurred in my voyage, and the discoveries which have resulted from it.

Thirty-three days after my departure . . . I reached the Indian sea, where I discovered many islands, thickly peopled, of which I took possession without resistance in the name of our most illustrious Monarch, by public proclamation and with unfurled banners. To the first of these islands, which is called by the Indians Guanahani, I gave the name of the blessed Savior[1] (San Salvador), relying upon whose protection I had reached this as well as the other islands; to each of these I also gave a name, ordering that one should be called Santa Maria de la Concepcion, another Fernandina, the third Isabella, the fourth Juana,[2] and so with all the rest respectively. As soon as we arrived at that, which as I have said was named Juana, I proceeded along its coast a short distance westward, and found it to be so large and apparently without termination, that I could not suppose it to be an island, but the continental province of Cathay.[3] . . .

In the meantime I had learned from some Indians whom I had seized, that that country was certainly an island: and therefore I sailed towards the east, coasting to the distance of three hundred and twenty-two miles, which brought us to the extremity of it; from this point I saw lying eastwards another island, fifty-four miles distant from Juana, to which I gave the name of Española. . . .

In Española there are mountains of very great size and beauty, vast plains, groves, and very fruitful fields, admirably adapted for tillage, pasture, and habitation. The convenience and excellence of the harbors in this island, and the abundance of the rivers, so indispensable to the health of man, surpass anything that would be believed by one who had not seen it. The trees, herbage, and fruits of Española are very different from those of

---

1. Jesus Christ.

2. Named for the daughter and heiress of Isabella and Ferdinand.

3. Technically, Cathay was that area of northern China ruled by the Khitan Mongols from 907 to 1101. Columbus understood Cathay to be the entire Chinese empire of the Great Khan, not realizing that the Chinese had expelled the Mongol khans in the mid-fourteenth century.

Juana, and moreover it abounds in various kinds of spices, gold, and other metals.

The inhabitants of both sexes in this island, and in all the others which I have seen, or of which I have received information, go always naked as they were born,[4] with the exception of some of the women, who use the covering of a leaf, or small bough, or an apron of cotton which they prepare for that purpose. None of them . . . are possessed of any iron, neither have they weapons, being unacquainted with, and indeed incompetent to use them, not from any deformity of body (for they are well-formed), but because they are timid and full of fear. They carry however in lieu of arms, canes dried in the sun, on the ends of which they fix heads of dried wood sharpened to a point, and even these they dare not use habitually; for it has often occurred when I have sent two or three of my men to any of the villages to speak with the natives, that they have come out in a disorderly troop, and have fled in such haste at the approach of our men, that the fathers forsook their children and the children their fathers. This timidity did not arise from any loss or injury that they had received from us; for, on the contrary, I gave to all I approached whatever articles I had about me, such as cloth and many other things, taking nothing of theirs in return: but they are naturally timid and fearful. As soon however as they see that they are safe, and have laid aside all fear, they are very simple and honest, and exceedingly liberal with all they have; none of them refusing any thing he may possess when he is asked for it, but on the contrary inviting us to ask them.

They exhibit great love towards all others in preference to themselves: they also give objects of great value for trifles, and content themselves with very little or nothing in return. I however forbad that these trifles and articles of no value (such as pieces of dishes, plates, and glass, keys, and leather straps) should be given to them, although if they could obtain them, they imagined themselves to be possessed of the most beautiful trinkets in the world. It even happened that a sailor received for a leather strap as much gold as was worth three golden nobles, and for things of more trifling value offered by our men, especially newly coined blancas, or any gold coins, the Indians would give whatever the seller required; as, for instance, an ounce and a half or two ounces of gold, or thirty or forty pounds of cotton. . . . Thus they bartered, like idiots, cotton and gold for fragments of bows, glasses, bottles, and jars; which I forbad as being unjust, and myself gave them many beautiful and acceptable articles which I had brought with me, taking nothing from them in return; I did this in order that I might the more easily conciliate them, that they might be led to become Christians, and be inclined to entertain a regard for the King and Queen, our Princes and all Spaniards, and that I might induce them to take an interest in seeking out, and collecting, and delivering to us such things as they possessed in abundance, but which we greatly needed.

They practice no kind of idolatry, but have a firm belief that all strength and

---

4. Marco Polo, whom Columbus had read, described a number of island folk in South Asia who went naked.

power, and indeed all good things, are in heaven, and that I had descended from thence with these ships and sailors, and under this impression was I received after they had thrown aside their fears. Nor are they slow or stupid, but of very clear understanding; and those men who have crossed to the neighboring islands give an admirable description of everything they observed; but they never saw any people clothed, nor any ships like ours. On my arrival at that sea, I had taken some Indians by force from the first island that I came to, in order that they might learn our language, and communicate to us what they knew respecting the country; which plan succeeded excellently, and was a great advantage to us, for in a short time, either by gestures and signs, or by words, we were enabled to understand each other. These men are still traveling with me, and although they have been with us now a long time, they continue to entertain the idea that I have descended from heaven; and on our arrival at any new place they published this, crying out immediately with a loud voice to the other Indians, "Come, come and look upon beings of a celestial race": upon which both women and men, children and adults, young men and old, when they got rid of the fear they at first entertained, would come out in throngs, crowding the roads to see us, some bringing food, others drink, with astonishing affection and kindness.

Each of these islands has a great number of canoes, built of solid wood, narrow and not unlike our double-banked boats in length and shape, but swifter in their motion: they steer them only by the oar. These canoes are of various sizes, but the greater number are constructed with eighteen banks of oars, and with these they cross to the other islands, which are of countless number, to carry on traffic with the people. I saw some of these canoes that held as many as seventy-eight rowers. In all these islands there is no difference of physiognomy, of manners, or of language, but they all clearly understand each other, a circumstance very propitious for the realization of what I conceive to be the principal wish of our most serene King, namely, the conversion of these people to the holy faith of Christ, to which indeed, as far as I can judge, they are very favorable and well-disposed. . . .

Juana . . . I can assert . . . is larger than England and Scotland united; . . . there are in the western part of the island two provinces which I did not visit; one of these is called by the Indians Anam,[5] and its inhabitants are born with tails.[6]. . . But the extent of Española is greater than all Spain from Catalonia to Fontarabia, which is easily proved, because one of its four sides which I myself coasted in a direct line, from west to east, measures five hundred and forty miles. This island is to be regarded with especial interest, and not to be slighted; for although as I have said I took possession of all these islands in the name of our invincible King, and the government of them is unreservedly committed to his said Majesty, yet there was one large town in Española of which especially I took possession, situated in a remark-

---

5. Havana.

6. Marco Polo reported the existence of tailed humans (possibly orangutans) in the islands of Southeast Asia.

ably favorable spot, and in every way convenient for the purposes of gain and commerce.

To this town I gave the name of Navidad del Señor,[7] and ordered a fortress to be built there, which must by this time be completed, in which I left as many men as I thought necessary, with all sorts of arms, and enough provisions for more than a year. I also left them one caravel,[8] and skillful workmen both in ship-building and other arts, and engaged the favor and friendship of the King of the island in their behalf, to a degree that would not be believed, for these people are so amiable and friendly that even the King took a pride in calling me his brother. But supposing their feelings should become changed, and they should wish to injure those who have remained in the fortress, they could not do so, for they have no arms, they go naked, and are moreover too cowardly; so that those who hold the said fortress, can easily keep the whole island in check, without any pressing danger to themselves, provided they do not transgress the directions and regulations which I have given them.[9]

As far as I have learned, every man throughout these islands is united to but one wife, with the exception of the kings and princes, who are allowed to have twenty:[10] the women seem to work more than the men. I could not clearly understand whether the people possess any private property, for I observed that one man had the charge of distributing various things to the rest, but especially meat and provisions and the like. I did not find, as some of us had expected, any cannibals amongst them,[11] but on the contrary men of great deference and kindness. Neither are they black, like the Ethiopians: their hair is smooth and straight: for they do not dwell where the rays of the sun strike most vividly. . . . Thus, as I have already said, I saw no cannibals, nor did I hear of any, except in a certain island called Charis, which is the second from Española on the side towards India, where dwell a people who are considered by the neighboring islanders as most ferocious: and these feed upon human flesh.[12] The same people have many kinds of canoes, in which they cross to all the surrounding islands and rob and plunder wherever they can; they are not different from the other islanders, except that they wear their hair long, like women, and make use of the bows and javelins of cane, with sharpened spear-points fixed on the thickest end, which I have before described, and therefore they are looked upon as ferocious, and regarded by the other Indians with unbounded fear; but I think no more of them than of the rest. These are

---

7. The Lord's Nativity (Christmas).

8. The wreck of the *Santa Maria,* which was totally useless to the garrison.

9. When Columbus returned in November 1493, he discovered that the entire garrison had been killed by the native inhabitants in reaction to intolerable abuses.

10. Marco Polo had described a number of polygamous customs in his Asiatic memoirs.

11. Both Polo's late thirteenth-century travelogue and the equally popular late fourteenth-century *Travels* of John Mandeville reported numerous instances of cannibalism.

12. These would be the Caribs, who shortly before the arrival of Columbus began to displace the peaceful Arawak people of the Lesser Antilles, the archipelago to the east and south of Hispaniola. Sixteenth-century Spanish writers unanimously agreed that the Caribs were cannibals. At least one modern historian has cast doubt on the Caribs' alleged cannibalism, but most accept the basic veracity of the Spanish accounts.

the men who form unions with certain women, who dwell alone in the island Matenin, which lies next to Española on the side towards India, these latter employ themselves in no labor suitable to their own sex, for they use bows and javelins as I have already described their paramours as doing, and for defensive armor have plates of brass, of which metal they possess great abundance.[13] They assure me that there is another island larger than Española, whose inhabitants have no hair,[14] and which abounds in gold more than any of the rest. I bring with me individuals of this island and of the others that I have seen, who are proofs of the facts which I state.

Finally, to compress into few words the entire summary of my voyage and speedy return, and of the advantages derivable therefrom, I promise, that with a little assistance afforded me by our most invincible sovereigns, I will procure them as much gold as they need, as great a quantity of spices, of cotton, and of mastic (which is only found in Chios),[15] and as many slaves for the service of the navy as their Majesties may require. I promise also rhubarb and other sorts of drugs, which I am persuaded the men whom I have left in the aforesaid fortress have found already and will continue to find. . . .

Although all I have related may appear to be wonderful and unheard of, yet the results of my voyage would have been more astonishing if I had had at my disposal such ships as I required. But these great and marvelous results are not to be attributed to any merit of mine, but to the holy Christian faith, and to the piety and religion of our Sovereigns; for that which the unaided intellect of man could not compass, the spirit of God has granted to human exertions, for God is wont to hear the prayers of his servants who love his precepts even to the performance of apparent impossibilities. Thus it has happened to me in the present instance, who have accomplished a task to which the powers of mortal men had never hitherto attained; for if there have been those who have anywhere written or spoken of these islands, they have done so with doubts and conjectures, and no one has ever asserted that he has seen them, on which account their writings have been looked upon as little else than fables.

Therefore let the king and queen, our princes and their most happy kingdoms, and all the other provinces of Christendom, render thanks to our Lord and Savior Jesus Christ, who has granted us so great a victory and such prosperity. Let processions be made, and sacred feasts be held, and the temples be adorned with festive boughs. Let Christ rejoice on earth, as he rejoices in heaven in the prospect of the salvation of the souls of so many nations hitherto lost. Let us also rejoice, as well on account of the exaltation of our faith, as on account of the increase in our temporal prosperity, of which not only Spain, but all Christendom will be partakers.

---

13. Columbus had read in Marco Polo of two islands, one inhabited solely by women, another exclusively by men. Mandeville, who probably never traveled to most of the Asiatic lands he so vividly described, wrote of the land of Amazonia, populated totally by warrior women. There is no evidence that this female society reported by Columbus ever existed in the Caribbean. Neither is there any evidence that the Caribbean Amerindians used metal to any significant degree.

14. John Mandeville described people with little body hair, and Marco Polo told of Buddhist monks whose heads and faces were shaved.

15. An island in the Aegean Sea (an arm of the Mediterranean, between Greece and Turkey).

5. Interpreting Columbus's Letter

This letter contains a number of interesting and potentially important facts. For example, the natives whom Columbus encountered on these islands were apparently homogeneous, were skilled sailors, and initially offered no resistance. Yet as fascinating as these facts are, knowing them does not make a person a historian. Similarly, garnering such isolated items from a source does not constitute analysis. Historical analysis consists of drawing as much inferential insight as possible from a source and trying to answer, at least in part, the central question of historical study: what does it all mean? This document allows us to do just that.

The historian uses no secret method or magic formula to draw historical insights from documentary evidence. All she or he needs are attention to detail, thoroughness, common sense, and a willingness to enter imaginatively into the mind of the document's author as fully and honestly as possible while trying to set aside momentarily personal values and perspectives. Anyone who is willing to work can profitably interpret written primary sources. To prove that point, let us answer the first three questions for analysis on pages P-6 and P-7.

The first question — What evidence is there in the letter that allows us to judge Columbus's reliability as an objective reporter? — strikes at the heart of historical inquiry. The researcher always has to evaluate the worth of each source, and this means understanding its point of view and reliability. In this letter, several points are obvious. Columbus believes he has discovered Asian islands. Marco Polo's *Travels* and other accounts of Asia have provided a number of reference points by which he can recognize the Orient, and he believes he has found many of them. Equally obvious is the fact that Columbus is trying to present his discoveries in the best possible light. He is sending this letter ahead to the court of Ferdinand and Isabella to ensure that he will be received on arrival with due honor.

His account contains exaggeration and error. As the introduction informs us, Columbus overestimates the size of several islands and, except for chilies, the spices he claims to have discovered proved eventually to be mirages.

We also find Columbus deliberately trying to mislead his reader. The *Santa Maria* has been lost, yet the admiral wants the reader to believe that he left the ship in seaworthy condition with the sailors who remained in the garrison at Navidad del Señor. Still, this is the only outright falsehood that we can discover in the letter. Generally, despite Columbus's enthusiasm and understandable tendency to exaggerate and to see what he wants to see, he seems to want to present a factual account.

Although he was prepared to encounter every sort of human monstrosity and undoubtedly would have enjoyed reporting such contacts, Columbus honestly notes that all the natives he has met are quite unmonstrous in appearance and temperament. He does report stories of people with tails, cannibals, and warlike women who live apart from men, but there is no good reason to believe that the admiral is deliberately misleading anyone. The fierce Caribs were real enough, although Columbus did not encounter any on his first voyage. Rumors of tailed people and latter-day Amazons might have been the result of the natives' efforts to please Columbus. It is not difficult to imagine the admiral inquiring after the location of those various human curiosities whom Polo and others had placed in the islands of the Indian Ocean, and the Amerindian natives agreeably pointing across the waters to other islands. All things considered, Columbus's letter may be accepted as a generally honest, if not totally accurate, account of his discoveries and experiences.

That basic honesty, tempered by an understandable enthusiasm and desire to present his accomplishments in a positive and attractive manner, comes through in his attempt to describe both the islands' physical qualities and the people he has encountered. The picture that emerges tells us a lot about the complex motives underlying his great adventure. Let us consider the second and third questions for analysis together, as they are closely related.

We notice that Columbus has matter-of-factly taken possession of these lands in the names of the monarchs of Spain and has even renamed the islands without once giving thought to anyone else's claims. Also, despite his avowed interest in protecting and winning over these native peoples, whom he apparently likes and admires, he thinks nothing of seizing some natives as soon as he arrives and of carrying several "Indians" back to Spain. Moreover, he remarks toward the end of his letter that he will procure from these islands as many slaves to serve in the navy as the monarchs of Spain desire. At the same time, and this may strike the modern student as curious, Columbus notes that he has acted kindly toward these natives so that they might become both Christians and loyal subjects of Ferdinand and Isabella. According to the admiral, the Indians' intelligence, timidity, naiveté, ignorance, sense of wonder at the Europeans, and ability to communicate freely among themselves make them prime candidates for conversion and subjugation. Is Columbus concerned with these people as humans, and is he interested in helping them achieve salvation through conversion? The tone of this letter suggests that he is, but there is a contrary note, which points up the tension that would exist within the entire Spanish colonial experience: Columbus believes it to be his and Catholic Spain's right and duty to rule and exploit these people.

Conquest of these people and their lands involved more than just a sense of divine mission and Christian altruism — as real as these motives were. Columbus, his royal patrons, and most others who joined overseas adventures expected to gain in earthly wealth as well. Even a superficial reading of his letter shows us the admiral's preoccupation with the riches of these islands. Gold, spices, cotton, aromatic mastic, and, of course, slaves are the material rewards that await Christian Europeans, and Columbus is fully interested in them.

Is he being cynical or hypocritical when, in his closing words, Columbus claims that Jesus Christ has provided this great victory to the Spanish monarchs, and, indeed, to all Christians, and from it will flow the dual benefits of worldly riches and the conversion of many people? It does not seem likely. Here was a man who saw no contradiction between spreading the faith and benefiting materially from that action, even if doing so meant exploiting those he had converted. He and most of his contemporaries generally perceived no inconsistency in converting a people to the freedom of an otherworldly faith and enslaving them in this world.

There are other questions we can ask of this source and other insights we can gather from it. Certainly it tells us a lot about this Amerindian culture, the issue raised in question 4 on page P-7. Despite his cultural blinders, his naiveté, and his tendency at times to see what he wanted to see, Columbus was an accurate and perceptive observer, and anyone interested in the culture of the Caribbean peoples, before Europeans had much chance to influence it, must necessarily look to this and similar accounts of first contacts. It would be good practice for you to try to answer question 4, which we have only briefly considered.

We trust that you now have a good idea of how a student of history should examine and mine a documentary source. Let us next look at an artifact.

6. Unwritten Sources

Historians distinguish between the prehistorical and historical past, and the chief characteristic of any historical culture is that it provides written records from which we can reconstruct its past. Without a large volume and variety of documentary sources it is impossible to write any society's history in detail. This is not to say that the unwritten relics of the past are worthless. The art and science of archeology proves the contrary, and historians, as we shall see, use such sources. As a rule of thumb, however, no matter how extensive its physical remains may be, if a culture has not left us records we can read, its history largely remains a closed book. The ancient civilizations of Harappan India and Minoan Crete, for example, knew and practiced the art of writing, but until we learn how to decipher their texts, we can draw only vague pictures of their respective histories.

Given the central role documents play in our reconstruction of the past, it should surprise no one to learn that most historians concentrate their research almost exclusively on written sources. Yet historians would be foolish to overlook *any* piece of evidence from the past. As we suggested earlier, photographs can be a rich source for anyone researching the history of your class. Our future historian might even want to study all the extant souvenirs and supplies sold in your school's bookstore. Examined properly, they probably could help fill in some gaps in the story of your class's cultural history.

Artifacts can be illuminating, particularly when used in conjunction with records. Coins tell us a lot about a society's ideals or its leaders' programs. Art in its many forms reveals the interests, attitudes, and modes of perception of various segments of society. More down-to-earth items, such as domestic utensils and tools, allow us to infer much about the lives of common individuals. In this book we concentrate on written sources, for reasons already outlined, but we also include some examples of important artifactual evidence. Let us look at an example and proceed to "read" it.

AN ANONYMOUS WOODCUT OF 1511

Columbus arrived in Barcelona in April 1493 to discover not only had his letter arrived, but it had already been published and publicly circulated. Within months the letter was translated into several languages, and the Latin translation alone went through nine editions, several of which were lavishly illustrated, before the end of 1494. Printers discovered that educated Europeans had an almost insatiable desire to learn about the peoples and lands Columbus and other explorers were "discovering," and they catered to that interest.

    Their clientele wanted not only to read about the fascinating peoples, flora, and

fauna of these lands — they wanted also to see them. Consequently, as books prolif-erated on the new explorations, so did the number of printed illustrations, many of which are quite fanciful and tell us more about the Europeans who created them than the peoples and regions they supposedly portrayed. The woodcut print we have chosen appeared in a popular English pamphlet of 1511.

Questions for Analysis

1. What scene has the artist set? What do each person's actions, dress, and de-meanor tell us about her or him? What has the artist placed to the immediate right of the standing man, and what function does it have in this scene?
2. What does this illustration tell us about popular European notions concerning the natives of the New World?

7. Interpreting the Woodcut

What a charming, even idyllic domestic scene. An attractive mother nurses an infant at her breast while amusing an older child with a feather. A well-muscled, equally attractive and proud father stands nearby, holding the tools of his trade while next to him the family's dinner is slowly cooking. Dinner, of course, may strike us as macabre, as these are cannibals, and it looks like roast European is on the menu. The tools of the father's trade are weapons. Both children are naked, and the parents are virtually nude, save for what appear to be leaves that cover their loins, decorative necklaces, armbands and anklets of some indeterminate material, and feathers in their hair.

What is the message? What we have is a reprise of the image provided by Colum-bus in his letter of 1493 — the "noble savage." These are fully human beings with human bonds and affections. Yet they are still "savages," as their clothing (or lack of it), decorations, weapons, and choice of food would have suggested to most six-teenth-century Europeans. Here, as Columbus and many of those who followed agreed, were a people who could become Christians but who also, by virtue of their backwardness, were to be subjugated. There is something appealing about their innocent savagery, but what of that poor fellow whose severed members are slowly roasting?

Have we read too much into the woodcut? It is arguable that we may have. The historian always faces this problem when trying to analyze an isolated piece of evi-dence, particularly when it is a nonverbal source. Yet this artifact is not completely isolated, for we brought to its analysis insight gained from documentary evidence — Columbus's letter. That is how we generally read the artifacts of historical cultures. We attempt to place them in the context of what we have already learned or inferred from documentary sources. Documents illuminate artifacts, and artifacts make more vivid and tangible the often shadowy world of words.

As you attempt to interpret the unwritten sources in this book, keep in mind what you have learned from the documents you have already read, your textbook, and class lectures. Remember that we have chosen these artifacts to illustrate broad themes and general trends. You should not find their messages overly subtle. As with the documents, always try to place each piece of nonverbal evidence into its proper context, and, in that regard, read the introductions and questions for analysis very carefully. We will do our best to provide you with all the information and clues you need.

Good luck and have fun!

The Human Record

PART I

The World at the Time of Western Expansion, 1500–1650

For many of the world's societies, but especially for the peoples of Eurasia, the period from 1500 to the mid-1600s was a time of significant change. In Japan, a century of civil war concluded around 1600, when a new regime under the Tokugawa clan ended disorder and established a government that maintained internal peace almost three centuries. In China, the Ming Dynasty, after ruling since 1368, was toppled and replaced in 1644 by invading Manchus, who established the Ch'ing Dynasty. The Russians, having broken free of Mongol domination in the late 1400s, struggled to establish political order and, despite chronic turmoil, initiated a campaign of eastward expansion that by 1700 gave them Eurasia's largest empire. The Ottoman Turks consolidated and expanded an empire that included North Africa, the Arabian peninsula, Asia Minor, central and southeastern Europe, and parts of the Ukraine. To their east, Ismail Safavi in 1502 established the Safavid Empire in the area of modern Iran and Iraq. Another upheaval took place in northern India, where Babur, grandson of the great Turkish conqueror Timur the Lame, founded the Mughal (the Persian word for Mongol) Empire, the third great Islamic empire in the Middle East and South Asia.

Yet none of these developments matched the significance of the changes experienced by the peoples who inhabited the far-western tip of Eurasia. Over many centuries, this sparsely populated area had played only a peripheral role in humankind's historical development. Beginning in the eleventh century, however, northwest Europeans began to experience wide-ranging transformations that prepared them for their revolutionary role in world history after 1500. Indeed, by 1500 this new European society had already begun to make its mark on the world. In the 1400s ships sailing the flag of the small kingdom of Portugal began to explore the waters of Africa's west coast in the hope of expanding trade and of contacting Prester John, the legendary Christian king believed to live in Africa. Although the Portuguese eventually made contact with the ancient Christian civilization of Ethiopia, they failed to convert it to Catholicism, and their missionaries were expelled in 1633. Portuguese commercial ventures, however, were enormously lucrative. Having reached India in 1498, the Malay coast in 1511, and

China in 1513, Portuguese ships were soon bringing back to Europe spices, silks, dyes, and other exotic items, which they sold at huge profits.

Witnessing the Portuguese success, other European nations began to seek new ocean routes to Asia. Columbus's voyage of 1492 was only the first of dozens that established Spanish domination not in Asia but in the Americas. The nations of northern Europe also joined the competition. The French, Dutch, English, Danes, and Swedes struck claims to lands in the western hemisphere, and the French, Dutch, and English successfully challenged the early Portuguese commercial monopoly in Asia.

This initial burst of European expansion had little effect on the ancient centers of civilization in South and East Asia. Rulers tolerated limited European trade but prevented Europeans from undermining their own political power and their subjects' cultural and religious traditions. In contrast, Spanish conquests, economic exploitation, and the introduction of new diseases obliterated the Amerindian civilizations of Central and South America. Indians of North America faced similar threats only after 1600, when European settlers began to arrive in substantial numbers. Here, Native Americans' loss of territory and identity was not so sudden, but the process was no less painful, and, in the end, the results were the same. Africa too was deeply affected by Europeans, even though they remained on the coast and relied on native merchants to bring them commodities for trade. Tragically, in addition to ivory, gold, and pepper, these commodities included human slaves, who at first were shipped to Europe, and then, in ever greater numbers, to the New World.

European society continued to transform in the sixteenth and seventeenth centuries. Profits from overseas trade fueled further economic development, accelerated the consolidation of nation-states, and strengthened the position of middle-class businessmen. Knowledge of new lands and peoples added to the intellectual ferment stimulated by the Renaissance, the Protestant Reformation, and the early Scientific Revolution. Europe by the end of the seventeenth century was far different from the Europe of 1500, and its continuing capacity for change made it unique among the world's civilizations.

1

Europe's Expansion:
Consequences and Counterattacks

Well before the legendary voyages of Columbus, Da Gama, and Magellan, well before the foundation of Spain's American empire, and well before the Portuguese establishment of a direct sea route to India and East Asia, western Europeans showed a propensity for expansion and conquest. As early as the eighth century, they began extending their frontiers when Charlemagne campaigned against the pagan Saxons of northeast Germany. Europe's first great age of overseas colonialism took place in the eleventh and twelfth centuries, when crusaders established states in the eastern Mediterranean lands conquered from the Muslims. Even before the crusades, the Norsemen of Scandinavia had pushed out into the Atlantic, establishing colonies in Iceland, Greenland, and, for a short while, North America.

Although aggressive expansion had been part of the dynamics of European civilization for over 700 years, its transoceanic explorations from the late fifteenth century onward mark a turning point in the history not only of the West but also of the entire world. Europeans created new patterns of trade; began an unprecedented exchange of animals, plants, and disease germs between the New World and the Old; brought about significant demographic shifts; and made the Americas an offshoot of European civilization. Most important, these explorations became the single most influential factor in the breakdown of regional isolation around the world. This European expansion laid the foundation for the global community of the late twentieth century.

Yet it would be a mistake to assume that European expansion suddenly raised Europe to the rank of the world's greatest power or made inevitable the Europeans' world dominance. Europeans by 1650 had managed to establish political control only over the Americas, a region of sparse population, political disunity, and unsophisticated technology. Meanwhile, they had been thrown out of Japan and Ethiopia, kept at a distance by the Chinese, restricted to only coastal trade in India and Africa, and lost large amounts of territory in central and southeastern Europe to the Ottoman Turks. Throughout Asia their products, ideas, religion, and manners were generally viewed with disdain. For every area into which Europeans were expanding their influence, there were others where they were retreating or were rebuffed.

The Portuguese in Africa

When the first Portuguese ships began pushing their way down the West African coast in the fifteenth century, they encountered peoples who were part of complex regional and international trade patterns that were 2,000 years old. Long before the birth of Christ, merchants from the Sudan — the vast plains region extending across north-central Africa — carried gold, ivory, pepper, copper, and slaves to North Africa on the trans-Saharan caravan routes or to the cosmopolitan cities of East Africa, where ships carried African products to Arabia, the Persian Gulf, India, and even Indonesia and China. When the merchants returned, they brought salt, horses, fabrics, jewelry, tempered steel, and other products. Profits from this trade produced wealthy individuals, helped support large kingdoms, and fostered the growth of urban centers whose independence and sophistication have been compared favorably to the cities of the European Renaissance.

Before the fifteenth century, European merchants were not involved directly with African trade and were only dimly aware of its richness and diversity. In 1415, however, the Portuguese, as part of their ongoing military campaign against the Muslims, conquered and held Ceuta, a Muslim naval base in Morocco, where they heard impressive accounts of lucrative sub-Saharan trade. They were especially excited about reports of gold, a commodity in increasingly short supply not only in Portugal but also throughout much of Europe. Thus, for the purposes of trade and a variety of other motives, the Portuguese began systematically to explore West Africa in 1418. In less than a century they not only had established themselves on the west coast of Africa, but also had sailed around the Cape of Good Hope to reach Mozambique, the east coast of Africa, the region of the Persian Gulf, India, and China.

The first document that follows offers insight into the motives for Portuguese expansion into Africa, revealing that trade was not the sole inspiration. The second document offers evidence concerning African reactions to the intrusion of the Portuguese.

Gomes Eannes de Azurara

THE CHRONICLE OF GUINEA

The driving force behind the early expeditions down the west coast of Africa was the third son of King John I of Portugal, known in history as Prince Henry the Navigator (1394–1460). Obsessed with the exploration of the African coast, he gathered on Cape St. Vincent, on the southwest corner of Portugal, cartographers, ship architects, instrument makers, artillery experts, and mariners to design, build, and outfit the ships that sailed out annually from home port into the south Atlantic. By the time of his death, Portuguese seamen had reached as far as Sierra Leone, and the foundation for Portugal's commercial empire was in place.

In 1452 Prince Henry commissioned Gomes Eannes de Azurara to write a history of his life and exploits. The result was *The Chronicle of Guinea*, completed in 1453, which described Portuguese exploration until 1448. When Azurara died sometime after 1472, he left unfinished a sequel that would have continued the story to 1460. In the following excerpts, he discusses Prince Henry's motives in sponsoring these expeditions and comments on the condition of the approximately 1,000 black West Africans who at the time of writing had been sold into slavery in Portugal.

Questions for Analysis

1. According to Azurara, what are the five reasons for Henry's interest in exploration?
2. On the basis of Azurara's comments, is it possible to infer which reasons were foremost in Henry's mind?
3. How does Azurara justify the Portuguese enslavement of the Africans?
4. How would you describe the tone of Azurara's defense of slavery? Does he seem wholly at ease with slavery's realities?
5. Does Azurara seem racially prejudiced against the Africans?

We imagine that we know a matter when we are acquainted with the doer of it and the end for which he did it. And since in former chapters we have set forth the Lord Infant[1] as the chief actor in these things, giving as clear an understanding of him as we could, it is meet that in this present chapter we should know his purpose in doing them. And you should note well that the noble spirit of this Prince, by a sort of natural constraint, was ever urging him both to begin and to carry out very great deeds. For which reason, after the taking of Ceuta he always kept ships well armed against the Infidel,[2] both for war, and because he had also a wish to know the land that lay beyond the isles of Canary and that Cape called Bojador, for that up to his time, neither by writings, nor by the memory of man, was known with any certainty the nature of the land beyond that Cape. Some said indeed that Saint Brandan[3] had passed that way; and there was another tale of two galleys rounding the Cape, which never returned. But this does not appear at all likely to be true, for it is not to be presumed that if the said galleys went there,

---

1. The reference is to Prince Henry. A *Lord Infant* was any son of a Portuguese king who was not heir to the throne.

2. Muslims.

3. A wandering Irish monk of the seventh century.

some other ships would not have endeavored to learn what voyage they had made. And because the said Lord Infant wished to know the truth of this, — since it seemed to him that if he or some other lord did not endeavor to gain that knowledge, no mariners or merchants would ever dare to attempt it — (for it is clear that none of them ever trouble themselves to sail to a place where there is not a sure and certain hope of profit) — and seeing also that no other prince took any pains in this matter, he sent out his own ships against those parts, to have manifest certainty of them all. And to this he was stirred up by his zeal for the service of God and of the King Edward his Lord and brother, who then reigned. And this was the first reason of his action.

The second reason was that if there chanced to be in those lands some population of Christians, or some havens, into which it would be possible to sail without peril, many kinds of merchandise might be brought to this realm, which would find a ready market, and reasonably so, because no other people of these parts traded with them, nor yet people of any other that were known; and also the products of this realm might be taken there, which traffic would bring great profit to our countrymen.

The third reason was that, as it was said that the power of the Moors[4] in that land of Africa was very much greater than was commonly supposed, and that there were no Christians among them, nor any other race of men; and because every wise man is obliged by natural prudence to wish for a knowledge of the power of his enemy; therefore the said Lord Infant exerted himself to cause this to be fully discovered, and to make it known determinately how far the power of those infidels extended.

The fourth reason was because during the one and thirty years that he had warred against the Moors, he had never found a Christian king, nor a lord outside this land, who for the love of our Lord Jesus Christ would aid him in the said war. Therefore he sought to know if there were in those parts any Christian princes, in whom the charity and the love of Christ was so ingrained that they would aid him against those enemies of the faith.

The fifth reason was his great desire to make increase in the faith of our Lord Jesus Christ and to bring to him all the souls that should be saved, — understanding that all the mystery of the Incarnation, Death, and Passion of our Lord Jesus Christ was for this sole end — namely the salvation of lost souls — whom the said Lord Infant by his travail and spending would fain bring into the true path. For he perceived that no better offering could be made unto the Lord than this; for if God promised to return one hundred goods for one, we may justly believe that for such great benefits, that is to say for so many souls as were saved by the efforts of this Lord, he will have so many hundreds of guerdons[5] in the kingdom of God, by which his spirit may be glorified after this life in the celestial realm. For I that wrote this history saw so many men and women of those parts turned to the holy faith, that even if the Infant had been a heathen, their prayers would have been enough to have obtained his salvation. And not only did I see the first captives,[6] but their chil-

---

4. Here, Muslims. The author also uses "Moor" in a more general sense to mean "African."

5. Rewards.
6. Slaves.

dren and grandchildren as true Christians as if the Divine grace breathed in them and imparted to them a clear knowledge of itself. . . .

How the Infant Don Henry Made Lançarote[7] a Knight

Although the sorrow of those captives was for the present very great . . . and although it chanced that among the prisoners the father often remained in Lagos, while the mother was taken to Lisbon,[8] and the children to another part (in which partition their sorrow doubled the first grief) — yet this sorrow was less felt among those who happened to remain in company. For as saith the text, the wretched find a consolation in having comrades in misfortune. But from this time forth they began to acquire some knowledge of our country; in which they found great abundance, and our men began to treat them with great favor. For as our people did not find them hardened in the belief of the other Moors; and saw how they came in unto the law of Christ with a good will; they made no difference between them and their free servants, born in our own country; but those whom they took while still young, they caused to be instructed in mechanical arts, and those whom they saw fitted for managing property; they set free and married to women who were natives of the land;[9] making with them a division of their property, as if they had been bestowed on those who married them by the will of their own fathers, and for the merits of their service they were bound to act in a

like manner. Yea, and some widows of good family who bought some of these female slaves, either adopted them or left them a portion of their estate by will; so that in the future they married right well; treating them as entirely free. Suffice it that I never saw one of these slaves put in irons like other captives, and scarcely any one who did not turn Christian and was not very gently treated.

And I have been asked by their lords to the baptisms and marriages of such; at which they, whose slaves they were before, made no less solemnity than if they had been their children or relations.

And so their lot was now quite the contrary of what it had been; since before they had lived in perdition of soul and body; of their souls, in that they were yet pagans, without the clearness and the light of the holy faith; and of their bodies, in that they lived like beasts, without any custom of reasonable beings — for they had no knowledge of bread or wine, and they were without the covering of clothes, or the lodgment of houses; and worse than all, through the great ignorance that was in them, in that they had no understanding of good, but only knew how to live in a bestial sloth.

But as soon as they began to come to this land, and men gave them prepared food and coverings for their bodies, their bellies began to swell, and for a time they were ill; until they were accustomed to the nature of the country; but some of them were so made that they were not able to endure it and died, but as Christians.

Now there were four things in these captives that were very different from the

---

7. The leader of a slave hunt who captured some 200 slaves in 1444.

8. Lagos is an African coastal city in modern Nigeria; Lisbon is the largest city in Portugal.

9. Portuguese.

condition of the other Moors who were taken prisoners from this part. First, that after they had come to this land of Portugal, they never more tried to fly, but rather in time forgot all about their own country, as soon as they began to taste the good things of this one; secondly, that they were very loyal and obedient servants, without malice; thirdly, that they were not so inclined to lechery as the others; fourthly, that after they began to use clothing they were for the most part very fond of display, so that they took great delight in robes of showy colors, and such was their love of finery, that they picked up the rags that fell from the coats of the other people of the country and sewed them on to their garments, taking great pleasure in these, as though it were matter of some greater perfection. And what was still better, as I have already said, they turned themselves with a good will into the path of the true faith; in the which after they had entered, they received true belief, and in this same they died. And now reflect what a guerdon should be that of the Infant in the presence of the Lord God; for thus bringing to true salvation, not only those, but many others, whom you will find in this history later on.

▓ Nzinga Mbemba (Afonso I)

LETTERS TO THE KING OF PORTUGAL

The largest state in central West Africa by 1500 was the kingdom of Kongo, stretching along the estuary of the Congo River in territory that today lies within Angola and Zaire. In 1483 the Portuguese navigator Diogo Cão made contact with Kongo and several years later visited its inland capital. When he sailed home he brought with him Kongo emissaries, whom King Nzinga Kuwu dispatched to Lisbon to learn European ways. They returned in 1491, accompanied by Portuguese priests, artisans, and soldiers who brought with them a wide variety of European goods, including a printing press. In the same year the king and his son, Nzinga Mbemba, were baptized into the Catholic faith.

Around 1506, Nzinga Mbemba, whose Christian name was Afonso, succeeded his father and ruled until about 1543. Afonso promoted the introduction of European culture into his kingdom by adopting Christianity as the state religion (although most of his subjects, especially those in the hinterlands, remained followers of the ancient ways), imitating the etiquette of the Portuguese royal court, and using Portuguese as the language of state business. His son Henrique was educated in Portugal and returned to serve as West Africa's first black Roman Catholic bishop. European firearms, horses, and cattle, as well as new foods from the Americas, became common in Kongo, and Afonso dreamed of achieving a powerful and prosperous state through cooperation with the Europeans. By the time of his death, however, his kingdom was on the verge of disintegration, in no small measure because of the Portuguese. As many later African rulers were to discover, the introduction of European products and customs unsettled the people and caused widespread dissension. Worse, the unceasing Portuguese pursuit of slaves undermined Afonso's authority and made his subjects restive. In 1526 the desperate king wrote the following three letters to King João III of Portugal, urging him to exercise greater control of his rapacious subjects. The documents are part of a collection of twenty-four letters that Afonso and his Portuguese-educated, native secretaries dispatched to the kings of Portugal on a variety of issues.

Questions for Analysis

1. According to King Afonso, how have the availability of Portuguese goods and the presence of slave traders affected Kongo society?
2. Does King Afonso see the Portuguese presence in his kingdom as a right or a privilege?
3. How has King Afonso attempted to control Portuguese activity?
4. How does King Afonso distinguish between legitimate and illegitimate trade in slaves?
5. What elements of Portuguese culture does he welcome? Why?

Sir, Your Highness should know how our Kingdom is being lost in so many ways that it is convenient to provide for the necessary remedy, since this is caused by the excessive freedom given by your factors [agents][1] and officials to the men and merchants who are allowed to come to this Kingdom to set up shops with goods and many things which have been prohibited by us, and which they spread throughout our Kingdoms and Domains in such an abundance that many of our vassals, whom we had in obedience, do not comply because they have the things in greater abundance than we ourselves; and it was with these things that we had them content and subjected under our vassalage and jurisdiction, so it is doing a great harm not only to the service of God, but the security and peace of our Kingdoms and State as well.

And we cannot reckon how great the damage is, since the mentioned merchants are taking every day our natives, sons of the land and the sons of our noblemen and vassals and our relatives, because the thieves and men of bad conscience grab them wishing to have the things and wares of this Kingdom which they are ambitious of; they grab them and get them to be sold; and so great, Sir, is the corruption and licentiousness that our country is being completely depopulated, and Your Highness should not agree with this nor accept it as in your service. And to avoid it we need from those (your) Kingdoms no more than some priests and a few people to teach in schools, and no

---

1. Throughout the text, words in brackets have been added as glosses by the editors. Brackets around glosses from the original sources have been changed to parentheses to distinguish them.

other goods except wine and flour for the holy sacrament. That is why we beg of Your Highness to help and assist us in this matter, commanding your factors that they should not send here either merchants or wares, because it is *our will that in these Kingdoms there should not be any trade of slaves nor outlet for them*.[2] Concerning what is referred above, again we beg of Your Highness to agree with it, since otherwise we cannot remedy such an obvious damage. Pray Our Lord in His mercy to have Your Highness under His guard and let you do for ever the things of His service.

. . .

Moreover, Sir, in our Kingdoms there is another great inconvenience which is of little service to God, and this is that many of our people, keenly desirous as they are of the wares and things of your Kingdoms, which are brought here by your people, and in order to satisfy their voracious appetite, seize many of our people, freed and exempt men, and very often it happens that they kidnap even noblemen and the sons of noblemen, and our relatives, and take them to be sold to the white men who are in our Kingdoms; and for this purpose they have concealed them; and others are brought during the night so that they might not be recognized.

And as soon as they are taken by the white men they are immediately ironed and branded with fire, and when they are carried to be embarked, if they are caught by our guards' men the whites allege that they have bought them but they cannot say from whom, so that it is our duty to do justice and to restore to the freemen their freedom, but it cannot be done if your subjects feel offended, as they claim to be.

And to avoid such a great evil we passed a law so that any white man living in our Kingdoms and wanting to purchase goods in any way should first inform three of our noblemen and officials of our court whom we rely upon in this matter, and these are Dom Pedro Manipanza and Dom Manuel Manissaba, our chief usher, and Gonçalo Pires our chief freighter, who should investigate if the mentioned goods are captives or free men, and if cleared by them there will be no further doubt nor embargo for them to be taken and embarked. But if the white men do not comply with it they will lose the aforementioned goods. And if we do them this favor and concession it is for the part Your Highness has in it, since we know that it is in your service too that these goods are taken from our Kingdom, otherwise we should not consent to this.

. . .

Sir, Your Highness has been kind enough to write to us saying that we should ask in our letters for anything we need, and that we shall be provided with everything, and as the peace and the health of our Kingdom depend on us, and as there are among us old folks and people who have lived for many days, it happens that we have continuously many and different diseases which put us very often in such a weakness that we reach almost the last extreme; and the same happens to our children, relatives and natives owing to the lack in this country of physicians and surgeons who might know how to cure properly such diseases. And as we have got neither dispensaries nor drugs which might help us in this for-

---

2. Emphasis appears in original letter.

lornness, many of those who had been already confirmed and instructed in the holy faith of Our Lord Jesus Christ perish and die; and the rest of the people in their majority cure themselves with herbs and breads and other ancient methods, so that they put all their faith in the mentioned herbs and ceremonies if they live, and believe that they are saved if they die; and this is not much in the service of God.

And to avoid such a great error and inconvenience, since it is from God in the first place and then from your Kingdoms and from Your Highness that all the good and drugs and medicines have come to save us, we beg of you to be agreeable and kind enough to send us two physicians and two apothecaries and one surgeon, so that they may come with their drug-stores and all the necessary things to stay in our kingdoms, because we are in extreme need of them all and each of them. We shall do them all good and shall benefit them by all means, since they are sent by Your Highness, whom we thank for your work in their coming. We beg of Your Highness as a great favor to do this for us, because besides being good in itself it is in the service of God as we have said above.

AN AFRO-PORTUGUESE SALTCELLAR

It is generally agreed that the peoples of sub-Saharan Africa have produced some of the world's greatest sculpture. Since at least 500 B.C. sculptors and artisans working in clay, wood, ivory, and bronze created a wide range of artistic works — masks, human and animal figures, ceremonial weapons, and religious objects — that played important roles in African society. In some regions bronze casting and ivory carving were royal monopolies carried on by highly trained professionals.

Such was the case in the coastal kingdom of Benin (modern Nigeria) when the Portuguese arrived in the fifteenth century. Impressed by the skills of the Benin ivory cutters, the Portuguese commissioned works such as condiment sets, utensils, and hunting horns. The ivory carving shown here was crafted in the sixteenth or seventeenth century and is usually identified as a *salerio*, or saltcellar, even though we are not sure how its two chambers were actually used. It depicts two Portuguese officials, flanked by two assistants. Above them is a Portuguese ship, with a man peering out of the crow's nest.

Questions for Analysis

1. Notice what hangs around the central standing figure's neck, what he holds in his hands, and his facial expression. What is the sculptor trying to communicate about this person?
2. What might we infer from this work about Portuguese-African relations as perceived by the artist?

Saltcellar from Benin

Europeans in the Americas

Perhaps as early as 50,000 B.C., the first ancestors of Native Americans migrated across a land bridge from east Asia to the area of modern Alaska. Hundreds of thousands followed them until the Pacific Ocean rose and submerged the land crossing under the Bering Sea around 10,000 B.C. After that, the peoples of the Americas lived in isolation from the outside world. Then, in the years following A.D. 1500, Europeans began to arrive. The first contacts between the two cultures raised immediate questions. The Native Americans had to decide whether to cooperate with the new arrivals or resist. The Europeans had to balance the conflicting religious, commercial, and imperialist aspirations that inspired colonization of the Americas. Were Native Americans brutish "savages" to be worked like slaves, deprived of their land, ruled with an iron hand, and even killed? Or should their customs be respected and honest efforts be made to "civilize" them and protect them from exploitation? In the end, European greed won out over altruism, and Native Americans lost their lands, self-government, and dignity. As the following documents show, however, in the 1500s and 1600s, European settlers and governments were still debating the treatment of the human beings they encountered in the Americas.

Bernardino de Sahagun

GENERAL HISTORY OF THE THINGS OF NEW SPAIN

Bernardino de Sahagun (ca 1499–1590) was one of the earliest Franciscan missionaries in Mexico, arriving from Spain in 1529. In addition to his deep piety, he possessed a thorough knowledge of the Aztec language, a love of the Mexican people among whom he worked, and a scientific curiosity. Around 1545 he began a systematic collection of oral and pictorial information on the culture of the Mexican people, which became the basis for his *General History of the Things of New Spain*. This history is regarded as the first important ethnographic work on any Native American society and remains today a principal source for the study of Mexican culture at the time of the Spanish conquest. In his own day, many Spaniards opposed Sahagun's work because they saw his efforts to preserve native culture as a threat to their policy of transforming the land and its people into a new Spain. Consequently, he suffered the indignity of seeing his studies and notes confiscated by royal decree in 1578. Anthropologists and historians had to wait until the nineteenth century to rediscover them.

The following selection comes from the twelfth and last book of the *General History*. Relying on the tales of natives who had experienced the conquest less than three decades earlier and on Aztec picture narratives that elderly storytellers interpreted for him, Sahagun vividly portrays initial native reactions to Cortes's arrival in

Mexico in 1519. The excerpt begins with the Aztec ruler Moctezuma (Montezuma) nervously awaiting news of the arrival from the sea of what he believes may be Topiltzin-Quetzalcóatl, a legendary fair-skinned, bearded god-king prophesied to reappear after five centuries in 1519.

Questions for Analysis

1. What do we learn about Aztec religious beliefs and practices from this source?
2. What led the Spaniards to think the natives of Mexico were "savages"?
3. Why did the Aztecs believe the Spaniards were gods?
4. How did the Aztecs regard blood sacrifice?
5. How did the Spaniards use native enmities to their advantage?
6. The Spanish expeditionary force was quite small, yet a number of factors favored it. How many can you discover in this excerpt?

Meanwhile Moctezuma had been unable to rest, to sleep, to eat. He would speak to no one. He seemed to be in great torment. He sighed. He felt weak. He could enjoy nothing. . . .

Then the five emissaries arrived. "Even if he is asleep," they told the guards, "wake him. Tell him that those he sent to the sea have returned."

But Moctezuma said, "I shall not hear them in this place. Have them go to the Coacalli building." Further he commanded, "Have two captives covered with chalk."[1]

So the messengers went to the Coacalli, the house of snakes.[2]

Moctezuma came later. In front of the messengers, the captives were killed — their hearts torn out, their blood sprinkled over the messengers; for they had gone into great danger; they had looked into the very faces of the gods; they had even spoken to them.

After this they reported to Moctezuma all the wonders they had seen, and they showed him samples of the food the Spaniards ate.

Moctezuma was shocked, terrified by what he heard. He was much puzzled by their food, but what made him almost faint away was the telling of how the great lombard gun,[3] at the Spaniards' command, expelled the shot which thundered as it went off. The noise weakened one, dizzied one. Something like a stone came out of it in a shower of fire and sparks. The smoke was foul; it had a sickening, fetid smell. And the shot, which struck a mountain, knocked it to bits — dissolved it. It reduced a tree to sawdust — the tree disappeared as if they had blown it away.

And as to their war gear, it was all iron. They were iron. Their head pieces were of iron. Their swords, their crossbows, their shields, their lances were of iron.

---

1. Slaves and captives were covered with chalk and feathers prior to sacrifice.

2. A reception hall for visiting dignitaries.

3. A ship deck gun, or cannon.

The animals they rode — they looked like deer — were as high as roof tops.

They covered their bodies completely, all except their faces.

They were very white. Their eyes were like chalk. Their hair — on some it was yellow, on some it was black. They wore long beards; they were yellow, too. And there were some black-skinned ones with kinky hair.

What they ate was like what Aztecs ate during periods of fasting: it was large, it was white, it was lighter than tortillas; it was spongy like the inside of corn stalks; it tasted as if it had been made of a flour of corn stalks; it was sweetish.

Their dogs were huge. Their ears were folded over; their jowls dragged; their eyes blazed yellow, fiery yellow. They were thin — their ribs showed. They were big. They were restless, moving about panting, tongues hanging. They were spotted or varicolored like jaguars.

When Moctezuma was told all this, he was terror-struck. He felt faint. His heart failed him.

Nevertheless, Moctezuma then again sent emissaries, this time all the doers of evil he could gather — magicians, wizards, sorcerers, soothsayers. With them he sent the old men and the warriors necessary to requisition all the food the Spaniards would need, the turkeys, the eggs, the best white tortillas, everything necessary. The elders and fighting men were to care well for them.

Likewise he sent a contingent of captives, so that his men might be prepared in case the supposed gods required human blood to drink. And the emissaries indeed so thought, themselves. But the sacrifice nauseated the Spaniards. They shut their eyes tight; they shook their heads. For Moctezuma's men had soaked the food in blood before offering it to them; it revolted them, sickened them, so much did it reek of blood.

But Moctezuma had provided for this because, as he assumed them to be gods, he was worshipping them as gods. So were the Mexicans.[4] They called these Spaniards "gods come from the heavens"; the Mexicans thought they were all gods, including the black ones, whom they called the dusky gods. . . .

As for the magicians, wizards, sorcerers, and soothsayers, Moctezuma had sent them just in case they might size up the Spaniards differently and be able to use their arts against them — cast a spell over them, blow them away, enchant them, throw stones at them, with wizards' words say an incantation over them — anything that might sicken them, kill them, or turn them back. They fulfilled their charge; they tried their skill on the Spaniards; but what they did had no effect whatsoever. They were powerless.

These men then returned to report to Moctezuma. "We are not as strong as they," was what they said as they described the Spaniards to him. "We are nothing compared to them.". . .

Moctezuma could only wait for the Spaniards, could only show resolution. He quieted, he controlled himself; he made himself submit to whatever was in store for him. So he left his proper dwelling, the great palace, so that the gods — the Spaniards — could occupy it, and moved to the palace he had originally occupied as a prince.

The Spaniards, pressing inland meanwhile to go through the city of Cempoalla, had with them a previously captured man known to have been a high warrior. He

---

4. That is, the Aztecs.

was now interpreting for them and guiding them, since he knew the roads and could keep them on the right ones.

Thus they came to reach a place called Tecoac, held by people of the Otomí tribe subject to the city of Tlaxcalla.[5] Here the men of Tecoac resisted; they came out with their weapons. But the Spaniards completely routed them. They trampled them down; they shot them down with their guns; they riddled them with the bolts of their crossbows. They annihilated them, not just a few but a great many.

When Tecoac perished, the news made the Tlaxcallans beside themselves with fear. They lost courage; they gave way to wonder, to terror, until they gathered themselves together and, at a meeting of the rulers, took counsel, weighed the news among themselves, and discussed what to do.

"How shall we act?" some asked. "Shall we meet with them?"

Others said, "The Otomís are great warriors, great fighters, yet the Spaniards thought nothing of them. They were as nothing. In no time, with but the batting of an eyelash, they annihilated our vassals."

"The only thing to do," advised still others, "is to submit to these men, to befriend them, to reconcile ourselves to them. Otherwise, sad would be the fate of the common folk."

This argument prevailed. The rulers of Tlaxcalla went to meet the Spaniards with food offerings of turkey, eggs, fine white tortillas — the tortillas of lords.

"You have tired yourselves, O our lords," they said.

The Spaniards asked, "Where is your home? Where are you from?"

"We are Tlaxcallans," they answered. "You have tired yourselves. You have come to your poor home, Quauhtlaxcalla." . . .

The Tlaxcallans led the Spaniards to the city, to their palace. They made much of them, gave them whatever they needed, waited upon them, and comforted them with their daughters.

The Spaniards, however, kept asking them "Where is Mexico? What is it like? Is it far?"

"From here it is not far," was the answer; "it is a matter of perhaps only three days' march. It is a very splendid place; the Mexicans are strong, brave, conquering people. You find them everywhere."

Now the Tlaxcallans had long been enemies of the people of Cholula.[6] They disliked, hated, detested them; they would have nothing to do with them. Hoping to do them harm, they inflamed the Spaniards against them, saying, "They are very evil, these enemies of ours. Cholula is as powerful as Mexico. Cholula is friendly to Mexico."

Therefore the Spaniards at once went to Cholula, taking the Tlaxcallans and the Cempoallans with them all in war array. They arrived; they entered Cholula. Then there arose from the Spaniards a cry summoning all the noblemen, lords, war leaders, warriors, and common folk; and when they had crowded into the temple courtyard, then the Spaniards and their allies blocked the entrances and every exit.

There followed a butchery of stabbing, beating, killing of the unsuspecting Cholulans armed with no bows and arrows,

---

5. Tlaxcalla was an independent state in the mountains east of the Aztec capital of Tenochtitlán.

6. A city allied with the Aztecs, some fifty miles east of Tenochtitlán.

protected by no shields, unable to contend against the Spaniards. So with no warning they were treacherously, deceitfully slain. The Tlaxcallans had induced the Spaniards to do this.

What had happened was reported quickly to Moctezuma: his messengers, who had just arrived, departed fleeing back to him. They did not remain long to learn all the details. The effect upon the people of Mexico, however, was immediate; they often rose in tumults, alarmed as by an earthquake, as if there were a constant reeling of the face of the earth. They were terrified.

After death came to Cholula, the Spaniards resumed their marching order to advance upon Mexico. They assembled in their accustomed groups, a multitude, raising a great dust. The iron of their lances and their halberds glistened from afar; the shimmer of their swords was as of a sinuous water course. Their iron breast and back pieces, their helmets clanked. Some came completely encased in iron — as if turned to iron, gleaming, resounding from afar. And ahead of them, preceding them, ran their dogs, panting, with foam continually dripping from their muzzles.

All this stunned the people, terrified them, filled them with fear, with dread.

THE LAWS OF BURGOS

Many of Christopher Columbus's dreams and promises for the lands he explored were never realized, but his vision that their inhabitants could be easily enslaved proved all too correct. Queen Isabella of Spain, who had supported Columbus's expeditions, was, by most accounts, disquieted by the idea of enslaving Native Americans, but forced labor came to the new Spanish colonies nevertheless. The first major vehicle for forced labor in New Spain was the *encomienda* system, in which the Crown granted a Spaniard (the *encomendero*) control of towns and their surrounding territory and the right to receive tribute and free labor from the natives. The encomendero in turn was supposed to be responsible for the spiritual and physical welfare of the local population.

In 1510 a group of Dominican priests arrived in the Caribbean (New Spain) to serve the spiritual needs of both colonists and natives. Shocked to discover what they perceived as the colonists' brutal callousness toward their native laborers, the priests launched a campaign to stir the Crown to eradicate these abuses. The result was a code of laws promulgated at Burgos, Spain on December 27, 1512, with a supplement of four amendments added the following July. The code comprises thirty-nine articles, which became the fundamental law governing Spanish–Native American relations for the next three decades. The laws are invaluable for the modern historian, because they reveal actual conditions in New Spain and early Spanish attitudes toward the natives.

Questions
for Analysis

1. How does the Spanish royal court justify the encomienda system, and what does its justification tell us about Spanish attitudes toward Native Americans?
2. Does the royal court see the encomienda as a permanent system or an intermediate step? If intermediate, what is the professed goal?
3. What specific abuses are the Laws of Burgos aimed at eradicating, and what protection do they theoretically afford the natives?
4. How does the Crown propose to ensure that the laws are obeyed? Does it seem likely that the laws will be effective?
5. Even if a landowner were to follow these laws to the letter, what would have been the status of the natives on the encomienda?
6. How does the basic philosophy of the Laws of Burgos compare with the views on slavery expressed by Gomes Eannes de Azurara in *The Chronicle of Guinea*?

Whereas, the King, my Lord and Father, and the Queen, my Mistress and Mother[1] (may she rest in glory!) always desired that the chiefs and Indians of the Island of Española be brought to a knowledge of our Holy Catholic Faith. . . .

Whereas, it has become evident through long experience that nothing has sufficed to bring the said chiefs and Indians to a knowledge of our Faith (necessary for their salvation), since by nature they are inclined to idleness and vice, and have no manner of virtue or doctrine, and that the principal obstacle in the way of correcting their vices and having them profit by and impressing them with a doctrine is that their dwellings are remote from the settlements of the Spaniards . . . because, although at the time the Indians go to serve them they are indoctrinated in and taught the things of our Faith, after serving they

return to their dwellings where, because of the distance and their own evil inclinations, they immediately forget what they have been taught and go back to their customary idleness and vice, and when they come to serve again they are as new in the doctrine as they were at the beginning. . . .

Whereas, it is our duty to seek a remedy for it in every way possible, it was considered by the King, my Lord and Father, and by several members of my Council and by persons of good life, letters, and conscience that the most beneficial thing that could be done at present would be to remove the said chiefs and Indians to the vicinity of the villages and communities of the Spaniards . . . and thus, by continual association with them, as well as by attendance at church on feast days to hear Mass . . . and by observing the conduct of

---

1. These laws were granted in the name of Queen Joanna of Castile, daughter of Isabella and Ferdinand. Queen Isabella of Castile had died in 1504, but because Joanna was considered insane, her father, Ferdinand, King of Aragon, served as regent of Castile and its colonial possessions in the New World.

the Spaniards, as well as the preparation and care that the Spaniards will display in demonstrating and teaching them, while they are together, the things of our Holy Catholic Faith, it is clear that they will the sooner learn them and, having learned them, will not forget them as they do now. And if some Indian should fall sick he will be quickly succored and treated, and thus the lives of many, with the help of Our Lord, will be saved who now die because no one knows they are sick; and all will be spared the hardship of coming and going, which will be a great relief to them, because their dwellings are now so remote from the Spanish communities, so that those who now die from sickness and hunger on the journey, and who do not receive the sacraments which as Christians they are obligated to receive, will not die [without the sacraments], because they will be given the sacraments in the said communities as soon as they fall sick; and infants will be baptized at birth; and all will serve with less hardship to themselves and with greater profit to the Spaniards, because they will be with them more continually. . . .

I

First, since it is our determination to remove the said Indians and have them dwell near the Spaniards, we order and command that the persons to whom the said Indians are given, or shall be given, in encomienda, shall at once and forthwith build, for every fifty Indians, four lodges of thirty by fifteen feet, and have the Indians plant 5,000 hillocks (3,000 in cassava[2] and 2,000 in yams), 250 pepper plants, and 50 cotton plants, . . . and as soon as the Indians are brought to the estates they shall be given all the aforesaid as their own property; and the person whom you[3] send for this purpose shall tell them it is for their own use and that it is given them in exchange for what they are leaving behind, to enjoy as their own property. And we command that the persons to whom they are given in encomienda shall keep it for them so that they may enjoy it as their own; and we command that this property shall not be sold or taken from them by any person to whom they may be given in encomienda, or by anyone else, but that it shall belong to the said Indians to whom it is assigned and to their descendants, even though this said person sell the estate in which they are, or the said Indians be removed from him; and we declare and command that the person to whom the said Indians are given in encomienda may utilize the goods that the said Indians abandon when they are brought to the estates of the Spaniards, each according to the number of Indians he has, in order to maintain them with such goods; and after the said persons have removed the said goods I command you, our said Admiral and judges and officers, to have the lodges of the said villages burned, since the Indians will have no further use for them: this is so that they will have no reason to return whence they have been brought. . . .

III

Also, we order and command that the citizen to whom the said Indians are given in encomienda shall, upon the land that is assigned to him, be obliged to erect a structure to be used for a church . . . and

---

2. A tropical American plant, with a large starchy root.

3. The person addressed is Columbus, governor of New Spain.

in this said church he shall place an image of Our Lady[4] and a bell with which to call the Indians to prayer; and the person who has them in encomienda shall be obliged to have them called by the bell at nightfall and go with them to the said church, and have them cross themselves and bless themselves, and together recite the *Ave Maria,* the *Pater Noster,* the *Credo,* and the *Salve Regina,*[5] in such wise that all of them shall hear the said person, and the said person hear them, so that he may know who is performing well and who ill, and correct the one who is wrong. . . .

IX

Also, we order and command that whoever has fifty Indians or more in encomienda shall be obliged to have a boy (the one he considers most able) taught to read and write, and the things of our Faith, so that he may later teach the said Indians, because the Indians will more readily accept what he says than what the Spaniards and settlers tell them; and if the said person has a hundred Indians or more he shall have two boys taught as prescribed. . . .

XIII

Also, we order and command that, after the Indians have been brought to the estates, all the founding (of gold) that henceforth is done on the said Island shall be done in the manner prescribed below: that is, the said persons who have Indians in encomienda shall extract gold with them for five months in the year and, at

the end of these five months, the said Indians shall rest forty days, and the day they cease their labor of extracting gold shall be noted on a certificate, which shall be given to the miners who go to the mines. . . . And we command that the Indians who thus leave the mines shall not, during the said forty days, be ordered to do anything whatever, save to plant the hillocks necessary for their subsistence that season; and the persons who have the said Indians in encomienda shall be obliged, during these forty days of rest, to indoctrinate them in the things of our Faith more than on the other days, because they will have the opportunity and means to do so. . . .

XVIII

Also, we order and command that no pregnant woman, after the fourth month, shall be sent to the mines, or made to plant hillocks, but shall be kept on the estates and utilized in household tasks, such as making bread, cooking, and weeding; and after she bears her child she shall nurse it until it is three years old, and in all this time she shall not be sent to the mines, or made to plant hillocks. . . .

XXIV

Also, we order and command that no person or persons shall dare to beat any Indian with sticks, or whip him, or call him dog,[6] or address him by any name other than his proper name alone; and if an Indian should deserve to be punished for something he has done, the said per-

---

4. The Virgin Mary.

5. Four prayers: the Hail Mary, the Lord's Prayer ("Our Father"), the Creed of Faith, and the Hail Holy Queen.

6. An especially degrading insult.

son having him in charge shall bring him to the visitor[7] for punishment, on pain that the person who violates this article shall pay, for every time he beats or whips an Indian or Indians, five pesos gold; and if he should call an Indian dog, or address him by any name other than his own, he shall pay one gold peso, to be distributed in the manner stated. . . .

AMENDMENTS

The King, my Lord and Father, and I were informed that, although the said ordinances were very useful, profitable, and necessary, as well as fitting, it was said that some of them had need of further elucidation and modification. . . .Therefore, having considered the said ordinances and listened to the religious who have knowledge of the affairs of the said Island and the conditions and habits of the said Indians, they, together with other prelates and members of our Council, amended and modified the said ordinances as follows.

I

First, we order and command that Indian women married to Indian men who have been given in encomienda shall not be forced to go and come and serve with their husbands, at the mines or elsewhere, unless it is by their own free will, or unless their husbands wish to take them; but the said wives shall be obliged to work on their own land or on that of their husbands, or on the lands of the Spaniards, who shall pay them the wages agreed upon with them or with their husbands. . . .

II

Also, we order and command that Indian children under fourteen years of age shall not be compelled to work at tasks (of adults) until they have attained the said age or more; but they shall be compelled to work at, and serve in, tasks proper to children, such as weeding the fields and the like, on their parents' estates (if they have parents); and those above the age of fourteen shall be under the authority of their parents until they are of age and married. . . .

IV

Also, we order and command that within two years (of the publication of this ordinance) the men and women shall go about clad. And whereas it may so happen that in the course of time, what with their indoctrination and association with Christians, the Indians will become so apt and ready to become Christians, and so civilized and educated, that they will be capable of governing themselves and leading the kind of life that the said Christians lead there, we declare and command and say that it is our will that those Indians who thus become competent to live by themselves and govern themselves, under the direction and control of our said judges of the said Island, present or future, shall be allowed to live by themselves and shall be obliged to serve (only) in those things in which our vassals in Spain are accustomed to serve, so that they may serve and pay the tribute which they (our vassals) are accustomed to pay to their princes.

---

7. A supervisor appointed by the governor.

■ **David Pieterzen DeVries**

VOYAGES FROM HOLLAND TO AMERICA

As a result of the efforts of Henry Hudson, who explored what is now New York Harbor and the Hudson River in 1609, the Dutch claimed New Netherlands, an area that included Long Island, eastern New York, and parts of New Jersey and Connecticut. To encourage colonization, the Dutch government granted wealthy Dutch colonists huge tracts of land, known as "patroonships," with the understanding that each patroon would settle at least fifty tenants on the land within four years. At first, relations with the Algonquins and Raritans in the area around New Amsterdam (modern New York City) were generally cordial, but they rapidly deteriorated after the arrival of the merchant Wilhelm Kieft as governor in 1642. He sought to tax the Algonquins to pay for the construction of a fort and attempted to force them off their land to create new patroonships, even though few existing patroonships had attracted even the minimum number of tenants. When the Algonquins resisted, he ordered the massacre described by David DeVries in the following excerpt from his work, *Voyages from Holland to America*. Born in Rochelle, France, in 1592 or 1593, DeVries spent most of his life as a merchant in the Netherlands before becoming a patroon in the Dutch colony in the early 1640s.

Questions
for Analysis

1. What are the main reasons DeVries opposed the governor's plan to attack the Algonquins? What does this suggest about DeVries's attitude toward the Amerindians?
2. How did the Algonquins react immediately after the massacre? What does their behavior suggest about their early relations with the Dutch?
3. What was the long-term result of the massacre?

*T*he 24th of February, sitting at a table with the Governor, he began to state his intentions, that he had a mind to *wipe the mouths* of the savages; that he had been dining at the house of Jan Claesen Damen, where Maryn Adriaensen and Jan Claesen Damen, together with Jacob Planck, had presented a petition to him to begin this work. I answered him that they were not wise to request this; that such work could not be done without the approbation of the Twelve Men;[1] that it could not take place without my assent, who was one of the Twelve Men; that more-

---

1. The board of directors responsible for governing New Netherlands.

over I was the first patroon, and no one else hitherto had risked there so many thousands, and also his person, as I was the first to come from Holland or Zeeland to plant a colony; and that he should consider what profit he could derive from this business, as he well knew that on account of trifling with the Indians we had lost our colony in the South River at Swanendael, in the Hoere-kil, with thirty-two men, who were murdered in the year 1630; and that in the year 1640, the cause of my people being murdered on Staten Island was a difficulty which he had brought on with the Raritan Indians, where his soldiers had for some trifling thing killed some savages. . . . But it appeared that my speaking was of no avail. He had, with his co-murderers, determined to commit the murder, deeming it a Roman deed,[2] and to do it without warning the inhabitants in the open lands that each one might take care of himself against the retaliation of the savages, for he could not kill all the Indians. When I had expressed all these things in full, sitting at the table, and the meal was over, he told me he wished me to go to the large hall, which he had been lately adding to his house. Coming to it, there stood all his soldiers ready to cross the river to Pavonia to commit the murder. Then spoke I again to Governor Willem Kieft: "Let this work alone; you wish to break the mouths of the Indians, but you will also murder our own nation, for there are none of the settlers in the open country who are aware of it. My own dwelling, my people, cattle, corn, and tobacco will be lost." He answered me, assuring me that there would be no danger; that some soldiers should go to my house to protect it. But that was not done. So

was this business begun between the 25th and 26th of February in the year 1643. I remained that night at the Governor's, sitting up. I went and sat by the kitchen fire, when about midnight I heard a great shrieking, and I ran to the ramparts of the fort, and looked over to Pavonia. Saw nothing but firing, and heard the shrieks of the savages murdered in their sleep. I returned again to the house by the fire. Having sat there awhile, there came an Indian with his squaw, whom I knew well, and who lived about an hour's walk from my house, and told me that they two had fled in a small skiff, which they had taken from the shore at Pavonia; that the Indians from Fort Orange had surprised them; and that they had come to conceal themselves in the fort. I told them that they must go away immediately; that this was no time for them to come to the fort to conceal themselves; that they who had killed their people at Pavonia were not Indians, but the Swannekens, as they call the Dutch, had done it. They then asked me how they should get out of the fort. I took them to the door, and there was no sentry there, and so they betook themselves to the woods. When it was day the soldiers returned to the fort, having massacred or murdered eighty Indians, and considering they had done a deed of Roman valor, in murdering so many in their sleep; where infants were torn from their mothers' breasts, and hacked to pieces in the presence of the parents, and the pieces thrown into the fire and in the water, and other sucklings, being bound to small boards, were cut, stuck, and pierced, and miserably massacred in a manner to move a heart of stone. Some were thrown into the river, and when the

---

2. A glorious deed in the manner of the ancient Romans.

fathers and mothers endeavored to save them, the soldiers would not let them come on land but made both parents and children drown — children from five to six years of age, and also some old and decrepit persons. Those who fled from this onslaught, and concealed themselves in the neighboring sedge, and when it was morning, came out to beg a piece of bread, and to be permitted to warm themselves, were murdered in cold blood and tossed into the fire or the water. Some came to our people in the country with their hands, some with their legs cut off, and some holding their entrails in their arms, and others had such horrible cuts and gashes, that worse than they were could never happen. And these poor simple creatures, as also many of our own people, did not know any better than that they had been attacked by a party of other Indians — the Maquas. After this exploit, the soldiers were rewarded for their services, and Director Kieft thanked them by taking them by the hand and congratulating them. At another place, on the same night, on Corler's Hook near Corler's plantation, forty Indians were in the same manner attacked in their sleep, and massacred there in the same manner. Did the Duke of Alva[3] in the Netherlands ever do anything more cruel? This is indeed a disgrace to our nation, who have so generous a governor in our Fatherland as the Prince of Orange,[4] who has always endeavored in his wars to spill as little blood as possible. As soon as the savages understood that the Swannekens had so treated them, all the men whom they could surprise on the farm-lands, they killed; but

we have never heard that they have ever permitted women or children to be killed. They burned all the houses, farms, barns, grain, haystacks, and destroyed everything they could get hold of. So there was an open destructive war begun. They also burnt my farm, cattle, corn, barn, tobacco-house, and all the tobacco. My people saved themselves in the house where I alone lived, which was made with embrasures, through which they defended themselves. Whilst my people were in alarm the savage whom I had aided to escape from the fort in the night came there, and told the other Indians that I was a good chief, that I had helped him out of the fort, and that the killing of the Indians took place contrary to my wish. Then they all cried out together to my people that they would not shoot them; that if they had not destroyed my cattle they would not do it, nor burn my house; that they would let my little brewery stand, though they wished to get the copper kettle, in order to make darts for their arrows; but hearing now that it had been done contrary to my wish, they all went away, and left my house unbesieged. When now the Indians had destroyed so many farms and men in revenge for their people, I went to Governor Willem Kieft, and asked him if it was not as I had said it would be, that he would only effect the spilling of Christian blood. Who would now compensate us for our losses? But he gave me no answer. He said he wondered that no Indians came to the fort. I told him that I did not wonder at it; "why should the Indians come here where you have so treated them?"

---

3. Spanish general in the service of Philip II of Spain responsible for carrying out harsh anti-Protestant measures in the Netherlands in the 1560s.

4. Frederick Henry, *stadholder* or elected executive and military commander of the Netherlands.

Europeans and the World of Islam

A cherished dream of Prince Henry the Navigator and other early proponents of European expansion was that the voyages of discovery would give Catholic Europe some unknown advantage in the struggle against its ancient enemies, the Muslims. Perhaps the Muslims could be outflanked, making them susceptible to rearguard attacks; perhaps their trade could be so damaged as to weaken their power; perhaps Europeans could combine forces with a Christian king such as Prester John; perhaps expansion would provide new opportunities for missionary activity. Although the Europeans cut into Muslim trade in Africa, the Middle East, and India, their hopes of gaining a significant military or political advantage over their foe were soon dashed. Europeans proved incapable of denting the political power of the Islamic kingdoms of Africa, let alone the mighty empires of the Middle East and India. As the first document shows, sixteenth-century Europeans stood in awe of the Ottoman Empire, which spread across North Africa, west Asia, and central and southeastern Europe. The second document reveals that the rulers of Mughal India tolerated but did not fear the newcomers. They allowed them to trade on a limited basis and found their ideas only mildly interesting.

Ogier Ghiselin de Busbecq

TURKISH LETTERS

It would have been a surprise to residents of central and southeastern Europe during the 1500s and 1600s to learn that future historians would refer to this period as the "age of European expansion." To them the term would have seemed more appropriate for the Ottoman Turks, who by the mid-sixteenth century had conquered much of the region and whose mighty armies were a constant source of apprehension. Their greatest conqueror was Sultan Suleiman the Magnificent (1520–1566), who captured Belgrade (in modern Yugoslavia) in 1521, took control of most of Hungary in 1526, and came close to capturing the Austrian city of Vienna in 1529. When Suleiman died while campaigning in Hungary in 1566, he left behind the largest and best-organized empire in western Eurasia. For the remainder of the sixteenth century and into the next, the Ottomans were Europe's greatest challenger, and it was never certain that the next time Turkish soldiers advanced on Vienna they would be checked. Indeed, the Ottoman siege of 1683 nearly succeeded.

Because Suleiman directly threatened the Austrian Hapsburgs' lands, and because he had entered into an alliance with their enemy, the French, in 1536, the Hapsburgs began in the 1540s to send permanent ambassadors to the Ottoman court at Constantinople. In 1555 this post fell to Ogier Ghiselin de Busbecq (1524–1590), a Flemish nobleman who spent most of his life in the service of the Hapsburgs, especially the Holy Roman Emperor Ferdinand I (1558–1564). Ferdinand sent Busbecq to Constantinople to represent Hapsburg interests in a dispute over the control of Transylvania, a region in Hungary (today a part of modern Rumania). After six years of discussion, the Hapsburgs and the Ottomans reached a compromise by which Transylvania became an independent state but would continue to pay annual tribute to the sultan.

During his seven years in Turkey, Busbecq recorded his observations and impressions and sent them in the form of four long letters, written in Latin, to a friend and fellow Hapsburg diplomat, Nicholas Michault. Although not intended for publication, all four letters were published in a Paris edition in 1589. Subsequently published in numerous Latin versions and translated into the major European languages, Busbecq's letters provide a wealth of insight and information about Ottoman society. In the following excerpts he describes the role of Suleiman in European affairs and suggests how to counter his power.

Questions for Analysis

1. It is known that Busbecq's experiences in Turkey convinced him that the Hapsburg government needed to undertake various reforms and strengthen its army if it wanted to repulse the Ottomans. Does it seem that his conviction colored Busbecq's evaluation of Suleiman and the Turkish menace?
2. How do Busbecq's views of slavery differ from those of Azurara's in *The Chronicle of Guinea*?
3. Does Busbecq see the Turks as an integral part of the European balance of power?
4. What policy toward the Turks does Busbecq believe would be most effective?

*A*fter a delay of fourteen days at Constantinople, for the purpose of recruiting my strength, I set out for Vienna. But the beginning of my journey was marked by an evil chance. Just as I left Constantinople I met some wagons of boys and girls who were being carried from Hungary to the slave market at Constantinople; this is the commonest kind of Turkish merchandise, and just as loads of different kinds of goods meet the traveller's eye, as he leaves Antwerp[1] so every now and then we came across unhappy Christians of all ranks, ages, and sexes who were being carried off to a horrible slavery; the men, young and old, were either driven in gangs or bound to a chain and dragged over the road in a long file, after the same

---

1. A major commercial port in the Flemish Netherlands (modern Belgium).

fashion as we take a string of horses to a fair. It was indeed a painful sight; and I could scarce check my tears, so deeply did I feel the woes and humiliation of Christendom. . . .

The Turks were much annoyed at the conclusion of peace between the Kings of Spain and France, which was by no means favorable to their interests;[2] especially as they found the treaty was not such as they had believed it to be at first, for they had been convinced that they would have been high in the list of those entitled to enjoy the benefits of the same peace. Accordingly, when they found themselves passed over, thinking that a bad return had been made them, though they dissembled their vexation, they sought an opportunity to give some hint that their feelings were no longer so friendly as they had been. Solyman [Suleiman] had written to the King of France to say he approved of the peace, but at the same time desired the King to remember that old friends do not easily become foes, or old foes friends. . . .

No one will deny that what I have said so far is true, but perchance some will regret that he has not paid more attention to warlike enterprises, and won his laurels on the battle-field. The Turks, such an one will say, have now for many years past been playing the tyrant in Hungary, and wasting the land far and wide, while we do not give any assistance worthy of our name. Long ago ought we to have marched against them, and allowed fortune by one pitched battle to decide which was to be master. Such persons, I grant, speak boldly, but I question if they speak

prudently. Let us go a little deeper into the matter. My opinion is that we should judge of the talents of generals or commanders rather from their plans than from results. Moreover, in their plans they ought to take into account the times, their own resources, and the nature and power of the enemy. If any enemy of an ordinary kind, with no great prestige, should attack our territories, I frankly confess it would be cowardly not to march against him, and check him by a pitched battle, always supposing that we could bring into the field a force equal to his. But if the enemy in question should be a scourge sent by the wrath of God (as was Attila[3] of yore, Tamerlane[4] in the memory of our grandfathers, and the Ottoman Sultans in our own times), against whom nothing can stand, and who levels to the ground every obstacle in his way; to oppose oneself to such a foe with but scanty and irregular troops would, I fear, be an act so rash as to deserve the name of madness.

Against us stands Solyman, that foe whom his own and his ancestors' exploits have made so terrible; he tramples the soil of Hungary with 200,000 horse, he is at the very gates of Austria, threatens the rest of Germany, and brings in his train all the nations that extend from our borders to those of Persia. The army he leads is equipped with the wealth of many kingdoms. Of the three regions, into which the world is divided, there is not one that does not contribute its share towards our destruction. Like a thunderbolt he strikes, shivers, and destroys everything in his way. The troops he leads are trained veterans, accustomed to his command; he

---

2. The Treaty of Cateau-Cambrésis of 1559, which ended the protracted war between the Hapsburgs and the French Valois, was signed by Henry II of France and Philip II of Spain.

3. A fifth-century leader of the Huns who devastated portions of the late Roman Empire.

4. Timur the Lame, a Turkish warlord, who between 1369 and 1405 ravaged Central Asia.

fills the world with the terror of his name. Like a raging lion he is always roaring around our borders, trying to break in, now in this place, now in that. On account of much less danger many nations, attacked by superior forces, have left their native lands and sought new habitations. When the peril is small, composure deserves but little praise, but not to be terrified at the onset of such an enemy, while the world re-echoes with the crash of kingdoms falling in ruins all around, seems to me to betoken a courage worthy of Hercules himself. Nevertheless, the heroic Ferdinand[5] with undaunted courage keeps his stand on the same spot, does not desert his post, and stirs not an inch from the position he has taken up. He would desire to have such strength that he could, without being charged with madness and only at his own personal risk, stake everything on the chance of a battle; but his generous impulses are moderated by prudence. He sees what ruin to his own most faithful subjects and, indeed, to the whole of Christendom would attend any failure in so important an enterprise, and thinks it wrong to gratify his private inclination at the price of a disaster ruinous to the state. He reflects what an unequal contest it would be, if 25,000 or 30,000 infantry with the addition of a small body of cavalry should be pitted against 200,000 cavalry supported by veteran infantry. The result to be expected from such a contest is shown him only too plainly by the examples of former times, the routs of Nicopolis and Varna, and the plains of Mohacs, still white with the bones of slaughtered Christians.[6]

Abul Fazl

AKBARNAMA

Between 1526 and his death in 1530, the Afghan chieftain Babur managed to subdue north-central India with a small, well-drilled army that enjoyed the advantage of European firearms. This new Muslim lord of Hindustan, a direct descendant of both the Mongol Genghis Khan and the Turk Timur the Lame, initiated India's Mughal Age and laid the base for the reign of his illustrious grandson, Jalal ad-Din Akbar (1556–1605), known simply as Akbar ("the Great"). A wise ruler and a successful military commander, Akbar was also an accomplished musician, a designer of artillery, a patron of the arts, and an intellectual with a keen interest in philosophy and theology. The most thorough description of Akbar's personality and exploits is derived from the *Akbarnama,* a long, laudatory history of his reign written by Abul Fazl (1551–1602), Akbar's chief adviser and confidant from 1579 until his murder. At the time of his assassination, instigated by the future Emperor Jahangir (1605–1627), Abul Fazl had covered only the first forty-six years of Akbar's life, but that was

---

5. Ferdinand I (1556–1564), Hapsburg Holy Roman Emperor.

6. These were all smashing defeats of Christian armies by the Turks that took place respectively in 1396, 1444, and 1526.

enough to ensure his work's standing as one of the masterpieces of Mughal literature. Although Western historians view the arrival of the Portuguese and other Europeans in sixteenth century India as an event of great significance, in the *Akbarnama*'s thousands of pages, there are few references to Akbar's or India's relations with *Faringis* (Franks), as Europeans were called at the Mughal court. This silence reveals the level of early Mughal concern with these foreigners. The following excerpts constitute the work's major references to Europeans in India.

Questions
for Analysis

1. What aspects of European culture most fascinate Akbar?
2. What do Akbar and Abul Fazl believe they can gain from these *Faringis*?
3. What do Akbar and Abul Fazl believe they can offer the Europeans?
4. How do Akbar and Abul Fazl regard the Portuguese coastal bases?
5. What does the discussion with Padre Radif (Father Rodolfo) tell us about Akbar and Abul Fazl's attitudes toward the teachings of Europe's Christian missionaries?
6. Jesuit missionaries to Akbar's court often believed they were on the verge of converting him to Catholic Christianity. What evidence strongly indicates that there was never any chance Akbar would have become a Christian?

One of the occurrences of the siege[1] was that a large number of Christians came from the port of Goa and its neighborhood to the foot of the sublime throne, and were rewarded by the bliss of an interview. Apparently they had come at the request of the besieged in order that the latter might make the fort over to them, and so convey themselves to the shore of safety. But when that crew saw the majesty of the imperial power, and had become cognizant of the largeness of the army, and of the extent of the siege-train, they represented themselves as ambassadors and performed the *kornish*.[2] They produced many of the rarities of their country, and the appreciative Khedive[3] received each one of them with special favor and made inquiries about the wonders of Portugal and the manners and customs of Europe. It seemed as if he did this from a desire of knowledge, for his sacred heart is a storehouse of spiritual and physical sciences. But his . . . soul wished that these inquiries might be the means of civilizing this savage race.[4]

One of the occurrences was the dispatch of Haji Habibullah Kashi to Goa.[5] At

---

1. The siege of the west coast port of Surat in 1573 during his campaign in Gujarat (note 6). This successful expedition gave Akbar access to the sea. Through his conquests, Akbar more than tripled the empire he had inherited.

2. The act of obeisance.

3. Akbar.

4. The Portuguese.

5. The chief Portuguese stronghold in India since 1510.

the time when the country of Gujrat became included among the imperial dominions, and when many of the ports of the country came into possession, and the governors of the European ports became submissive,[6] many of the curiosities and rarities of the skilled craftsmen of that country became known to His Majesty. Accordingly the Haji,[7] who for his skill, right thinking and powers of observation was one of the good servants of the court, was appointed to take with him a large sum of money, and the choice articles of India to Goa, and to bring for His Majesty's delectation the wonderful things of that country. There were sent along with him many clever craftsmen, who to ability and skill added industry, in order that just as the wonderful productions of that country (Goa and Europe) were being brought away, so also might rare crafts be imported (into Akbar's dominions). . . .

One of the occurrences was the arrival of Haji Habibullah. It has already been mentioned that he had been sent to the port of Goa with a large sum of money and skilful craftsmen in order that he might bring to this country the excellent arts and rarities of that place. On the 9th he came to do homage, attended by a large number of persons dressed up as Christians and playing European drums and clarions. He produced before His Majesty the choice articles of that territory. Craftsmen who had gone to acquire skill displayed the arts which they had

learnt and received praises in the critical place of testing. The musicians of that territory breathed fascination with the instruments of their country, especially with the organ. Ear and eye were delighted, and so was the mind. . . .

One night, the assembly in the 'Ibadatkhana[8] was increasing the light of truth. Padre Radif,[9] one of the Nazarene[10] sages, who was singular for his understanding and ability, was making points in that feast of intelligence. Some of the untruthful bigots[11] came forward in a blundering way to answer him. Owing to the calmness of the august assembly, and the increasing light of justice, it became clear that each of these was weaving a circle of old acquisitions, and was not following the highway of proof, and that the explanation of the riddle of truth was not present to their thoughts. The veil was nearly being stripped, once for all, from their procedure. They were ashamed, and abandoned such discourse, and applied themselves to perverting the words of the Gospels. But they could not silence their antagonist by such arguments. The Padre quietly and with an air of conviction said, "Alas, that such things should be thought to be true! In fact, if this faction have such an opinion of our Book, and regard the *Furqun* [the Qur'an] as the pure word of God, it is proper that a heaped fire be lighted. We shall take the Gospels in our hands, and the 'Ulama of that faith shall take their book, and then let us enter that

---

6. In 1573 Akbar conquered the northwest coastal region of Gujarat, where the Portuguese held the ports of Diu and Bassein. In theory, but not fact, these Portuguese bases were now under imperial control.

7. Haji Habibullah, who bore the title Haji since he had completed the hajj, or pilgrimage to Mecca.

8. The House of Worship, where Akbar held weekly Thursday night discussions on theological issues with Muslim, Hindu, Zoroastrian, and Christian religious teachers.

9. Father Rodolfo Acquaviva, a Jesuit missionary.

10. Christian.

11. Conservative Muslim *ulama* or religious teachers.

testing-place of truth. The escape of any one will be a sign of his truthfulness." The liverless and black-hearted fellows wavered, and in reply to the challenge had recourse to bigotry and wrangling. This cowardice and effrontery displeased his (Akbar's) equitable soul, and the banquet of enlightenment was made resplendent by acute observations. Continually, in those day-like nights, glorious subtleties and profound words dropped from his pearl-filled mouth. Among them was this: "Most persons, from intimacy with those who adorn their outside, but are inwardly bad, think that outward semblance, and the letter of Muhammadanism, profit without internal conviction. Hence we by fear and force compelled many believers in the Brahman (i.e. Hindu) religion to adopt the faith of our ancestors. Now that the light of truth has taken possession of our soul, it has become clear that in this distressful place of contrarities (the world), where darkness of comprehension and conceit are heaped up, fold upon fold, a single step cannot be taken without

the torch of proof, and that that creed is profitable which is adopted with the approval of wisdom. To repeat the creed, to remove a piece of skin (i.e. to become circumcised) and to place the end of one's bones on the ground (i.e. the head in adoration) from dread of the Sultan, is not seeking after God.". . .

One of the occurrences was the appointing an army to capture the European ports.[12] Inasmuch as conquest is the great rule of princes, and by the observance of this glory-increasing practice, the distraction of plurality[13] places its foot in the peacefulness of unity, and the harassed world composes her countenance, the officers of the provinces of Gujarat and Malwa were appointed to this service under the leadership of Qutbu-d-din Khan on 18 Bahman, Divine month (February 1580). The rulers of the Deccan were also informed that the troops had been sent in that direction in order to remove the Faringis who were a stumbling-block in the way of the pilgrims to the Hijaz.[14]

Chinese and Japanese Reactions to the West

Of all the areas Europeans reached during the sixteenth and seventeenth centuries, China and Japan were least affected. This was not for lack of European effort. Portuguese traders reached south China in 1513, opened trade at Canton in 1514, and established a permanent trading base in Macao in 1557. In 1542, the first Portuguese merchants reached Japan and soon were reaping healthy profits carrying goods

---

12. The ports of Diu and Bassein (note 6 above). This expedition was unsuccessful, and Abul Fazl tells us nothing else about it.

13. That is, the distraction of multiple rulers.

14. Many Muslims complained that, when embarking at Portuguese ports, they were

forced to accept letters of passage on which were printed images of Jesus and Mary. Orthodox Muslims consider such images blasphemous, and some Muslim teachers went so far as to argue that it was better to forego the pilgrimage than to be a partner to such sacrilege.

between Japan and China. Later in the century the Dutch and the English success-fully entered these East Asian markets.

Roman Catholic Europeans, especially the Portuguese, energetically supported missionary efforts in China and Japan, usually in cooperation with the newly founded religious order, the Society of Jesus, popularly known as Jesuits. Francis Xavier and other Jesuits began preaching in Japan in 1549, and, by the early 1600s, had won approximately 300,000 converts to Christianity. Catholic missionary activi-ties in China began later, in 1583, and followed a somewhat different strategy: the Jesuits did less preaching to the common people and instead sought to win the support of Chinese intellectuals, government officials, and members of the imperial court. The Jesuits were moderately successful, because they impressed Confucian scholars with their erudition, especially in mathematics and science, and the Chinese appreciated the missionaries' willingness to understand and respect China's culture.

For all their efforts, the economic benefits and religious gains the Europeans ob-tained were meager. Although the Chinese tolerated the learned and civilized Jesuit missionaries, they viewed European merchants as boorish, overly aggressive, and purveyors of shoddy goods. Preferring to deal with Arabs and other foreigners, they limited trade with Europeans to Canton and Macao and placed it under numerous restrictions. Missionary efforts resulted in some converts, but feuding among reli-gious orders, staunch opposition from many Chinese officials, and the unwilling-ness of most Chinese, even converts, to abandon ancient rites such as ancestor worship and veneration for the Chinese sage, Confucius, weakened the enterprise. When in 1742 Pope Benedict XIV decreed that Chinese Christians must abandon Confucianism, Emperor Ch'ien-lung expelled the missionaries and Chinese Christi-anity withered.

Although European efforts to trade and win converts had a more promising start in Japan, by the mid-seventeenth century the Japanese had suppressed Christianity and restricted European trade to only one Dutch ship per year. This turn of events resulted from attempts of Japanese leaders in the early 1600s to bring stability to Japan after a century of civil war and rebellion. Convinced that European merchants and missionaries had contributed to Japan's disorder, the government outlawed Christianity and essentially closed Japan to the outside world. Not until the nine-teenth century would the Japanese and Chinese again have to deal with serious threats and intrusions from the West.

Matteo Ricci

JOURNALS

The most celebrated of the Jesuit scholar-missionaries to work in China was the Italian Matteo Ricci, who arrived in 1583 and died there in 1610. Ricci dazzled

Chinese intellectuals with clocks, maps, and various types of scientific equipment, much of which he constructed himself. A gifted linguist, he composed over twenty-five works in Chinese on mathematics, literature, ethics, geography, astronomy, and, above all else, religion. He so impressed Confucian scholars that they accorded him the title "Doctor from the Great West Ocean." In 1601 Emperor Wan-li summoned Ricci to his court at Peking (modern Beijing) and provided him with a subsidy to carry on his study of mathematics and astronomy. When Ricci died, the emperor donated a burial site outside the gates of the imperial city as a special token of honor.

During his twenty-seven years in China, Ricci kept a journal, with no thought of publishing it. Shortly after his death, however, a Jesuit colleague edited and published the journal, into which he incorporated a number of other, more official sources, and it became one of Europe's primary stores of information about China until the late eighteenth century, when accounts by European travelers to the Middle Kingdom became more common. In the following selection from that diary, Ricci tells of charges brought against certain Jesuits working at Nan-ch'ang. Here we can see some of the cultural barriers and attitudes that frustrated the Jesuits' efforts to accommodate Christianity to Chinese civilization.

Questions
for Analysis

1. What most offended the Confucian officials who brought charges against the Jesuits and their religion?
2. The Jesuits' association with Father Ricci seems to have favored them in the course of events. Why? What was there about Ricci that gave his fellow Jesuits an aura of legitimacy?
3. Does Ricci see the outcome of the hearing as a Christian victory? If so, why? Is there another way of interpreting the Chief Justice's decision and its consequences? How do you think one of the Jesuits' Confucian opponents might describe this confrontation and its resolution?
4. If the Chief Justice prepared a report on this case, what do you think he would write?

During 1606 and the year following, the progress of Christianity in Nancian[1] was in no wise retarded. . . . The number of neophytes[2] [increased] by more than two hundred, all of whom manifested an extraordinary piety in their religious

1. Nan-ch'ang, in the southern province of Kiangsi.

2. Converts.

devotions. As a result, the reputation of the Christian religion became known throughout the length and breadth of this metropolitan city. . . .

Through the efforts of Father Emanuele Dias another and a larger house was purchased, in August of 1607, at a price of a thousand gold pieces. This change was necessary, because the house he had was too small for his needs and was situated in a flood area. Just as the community was about to change from one house to the other, a sudden uprising broke out against them. . . .

At the beginning of each month, the Magistrates hold a public assembly . . . in the temple of their great Philosopher.[3] When the rites of the new-moon were completed in the temple, and these are civil rather than religious rites,[4] one of those present took advantage of the occasion to speak on behalf of the others, and to address the highest Magistrate present. . . . "We wish to warn you," he said, "that there are certain foreign priests in this royal city, who are preaching a law, hitherto unheard of in this kingdom,[5] and who are holding large gatherings of people in their house." Having said this, he referred them to their local Magistrate . . . , and he in turn ordered the plaintiffs to present their case in writing, assuring them that he would support it with all his authority, in an effort to have the foreign priests expelled. The complaint was written out that same day and signed with twenty-seven signatures. . . . The content of the document was somewhat as follows.

"Matthew Ricci, Giovanni Soeiro, Emanuele Dias, and certain other foreigners from western kingdoms, men who are guilty of high treason against the throne, are scattered amongst us, in five different provinces. They are continually communicating with each other and are here and there practicing brigandage on the rivers, collecting money, and then distributing it to the people, in order to curry favor with the multitudes. They are frequently visited by the Magistrates, by the high nobility and by the Military Prefects, with whom they have entered into a secret pact, binding unto death.

"These men teach that we should pay no respect to the images of our ancestors, a doctrine which is destined to extinguish the love of future generations for their forebears. Some of them break up the idols, leaving the temples empty and the gods to be pitied, without any patronage. In the beginning they lived in small houses, but by this time they have bought up large and magnificent residences. The doctrine they teach is something infernal. It attracts the ignorant into its fraudulent meshes, and great crowds of this class are continually assembled at their houses. Their doctrine gets beyond the city walls and spreads itself through the neighboring towns and villages and into the open country, and the people become so wrapt up in its falsity, that students are not following their courses, laborers are neglecting their work, farmers are not cultivating their acres, and even the women have no interest in their housework. The whole city has become disturbed, and, where-

---

3. Confucius.

4. Ricci and his fellow Jesuits chose to regard all of the ceremonies of ancestor worship as purely "civil rites," thereby allowing their converts to continue to pay traditional devotion to deceased family members.

5. Ricci refers to China throughout his journal as a "kingdom" even though China had an emperor, not a king.

as in the beginning there were only a hundred or so professing their faith, now there are more than twenty thousand. These priests distribute pictures of some Tartar or Saracen,[6] who they say is God, who came down from heaven to redeem and to instruct all of humanity, and who alone according to their doctrine, can give wealth and happiness; a doctrine by which the simple people are very easily deceived. These men are an abomination on the face of the earth, and there is just ground for fear that once they have erected their own temples, they will start a rebellion. . . . Wherefore, moved by their interest in the maintenance of the public good, in the conservation of the realm, and in the preservation, whole and entire, of their ancient laws, the petition- ers are presenting this complaint and demanding, in the name of the entire province, that a rescript of it be forwarded to the King, asking that these foreigners be sentenced to death, or banished from the realm, to some deserted island in the sea.". . .

Each of the Magistrates to whom the in- dictment was presented asserted that the spread of Christianity should be prohib- ited, and that the foreign priests should be expelled from the city, if the Mayor saw fit, after hearing the case, and notify- ing the foreigners. . . . But the Fathers,[7] themselves, were not too greatly dis- turbed, placing their confidence in Divine Providence, which had always been pres- ent to assist them on other such danger- ous occasions. . . .

Father Emanuele is summoned before the Chief Justice.

Father Emanuele, in his own de- fense, . . . gave a brief outline of the Christian doctrine. Then he showed that according to the divine law, the first to be honored, after God, were a man's parents. But the judge had no mind to hear or to accept any of this and he made it known that he thought it was all false. After that repulse, with things going from bad to worse, it looked as if they were on the verge of desperation, so much so, indeed, that they increased their prayers, their sacrifices and their bodily penances, in pe- tition for a favorable solution of their diffi- culty. Their adversaries appeared to be triumphantly victorious. They were al- ready wrangling about the division of the furniture of the Mission residences, and to make results doubly certain, they stirred up the flames anew with added accusa- tions and indictments. . . .

The Mayor, who was somewhat friendly with the Fathers, realizing that there was much in the accusation that was patently false, asked the Magistrate Direc- tor of the Schools,[8] if he knew whether or not this man Emanuele was a companion of Matthew Ricci, who was so highly re- spected at the royal court, and who was granted a subsidy from the royal treasury, because of the gifts he had presented to the King. Did he realize that the Fathers had lived in Nankin[9] for twelve years, and

---

6. Tartars, or "tatars," were a Mongol-Turkic people who invaded central and western Asia and Europe in the Middle Ages. Saracens were originally a Syrian tribe, but by Ricci's day the word was a synonym for Arabs. The reference is to Jesus Christ.

7. The Jesuits.

8. The director of the local Confucian acad- emy was one of the Jesuits' chief opponents.

9. Nanking (modern Nanjing), the southern auxiliary capital.

that no true complaint had ever been entered against them for having violated the laws. Then he asked him if he had really given full consideration as to what was to be proven in the present indictment. To this the Director of the Schools replied that he wished the Mayor to make a detailed investigation of the case and then to confer with him. The Chief Justice then ordered the same thing to be done. Fortunately, it was this same Justice who was in charge of city affairs when Father Ricci first arrived in Nancian. It was he who first gave the Fathers permission, with the authority of the Viceroy, to open a house there. . . .

After the Mayor had examined the charges of the plaintiffs and the reply of the defendants, he subjected the quasi-literati[10] to an examination in open court, and taking the Fathers under his patronage, he took it upon himself to refute the calumnies of their accusers. He said he was fully convinced that these strangers were honest men, and that he knew that there were only two of them in their local residence and not twenty, as had been asserted. To this they replied that the Chinese were becoming their disciples. To which the Justice in turn replied: "What of it? Why should we be afraid of our own people? Perhaps you are unaware of the fact that Matthew Ricci's company is cultivated by everyone in Pekin, and that he is being subsidized by the royal treasury. How dare the Magistrates who are living outside of the royal city, expel men who have permission to live at the royal court? These men here have lived peacefully in Nankin for twelve years. I command," he

added, "that they buy no more large houses, and that the people are not to follow their law.". . .

A few days later, the court decision was pronounced and written out . . . [and] was then posted at the city gates as a public edict. The following is a summary of their declaration. Having examined the cause of Father Emanuele and his companions, it was found that these men had come here from the West because they had heard so much about the fame of the great Chinese Empire, and that they had already been living in the realm for some years, without any display of ill-will. Father Emanuele should be permitted to practice his own religion, but it was not considered to be the right thing for the common people, who are attracted by novelties, to adore the God of Heaven. For them to go over to the religion of foreigners, would indeed be most unbecoming. . . . It would therefore seem to be . . . [in] . . . the best interests of the Kingdom, to . . . [warn] . . . everyone in a public edict not to abandon the sacrifices of their ancient religion by accepting the cult of foreigners. Such a movement might, indeed, result in calling together certain gatherings, detrimental to the public welfare, and harmful also to the foreigner, himself, Wherefore, the Governor of this district, by order of the high Magistrates, admonishes the said Father Emanuele to refrain from perverting the people, by inducing them to accept a foreign religion. The man who sold him the larger house is to restore his money and Emanuele is to buy a smaller place, sufficient for his needs, and to live there

---

10. Literati, or "lettered ones," is the term Ricci used for Chinese government officials who had earned their positions by passing the civil service examinations held by the Chinese government. "Quasi-literati" was the term he used for those who had passed only the first examination level.

peaceably, as he has done, up to the present. Emanuele, himself, has agreed to these terms and the Military Prefects of the district have been ordered to make a search of the houses there and to confiscate the pictures of the God they speak of, wherever they find them. It is not permitted for any of the native people to go over to the religion of the foreigners, nor is it permitted to gather together for prayer meetings. Whoever does contrary to these prescriptions will be severely punished, and if the Military Prefects are remiss in enforcing them, they will be held to be guilty of the same crimes. To his part of the edict, the Director of the Schools added, that the common people were forbidden to accept the law of the foreigners, and that a sign should be posted above the door of the Fathers' residence, notify-

ing the public that these men were forbidden to have frequent contact with the people.

The Fathers were not too disturbed by this pronouncement, because they were afraid that it was going to be much worse. In fact, everyone thought it was rather favorable, and that the injunction launched against the spread of the faith was a perfunctory order to make it appear that the literati were not wholly overlooked, since the Fathers were not banished from the city, as the literati had demanded. Moreover it was not considered a grave misdemeanor for the Chinese to change their religion, and it was not customary to inflict a serious punishment on those violating such an order. The neophytes, themselves, proved this when they continued, as formerly, to attend Mass.

Tokugawa Iemitsu

"CLOSED COUNTRY EDICT OF 1635" AND "EXCLUSION OF THE PORTUGUESE, 1639"

When the first Europeans reached Japan in the mid-sixteenth century, they encountered a land plagued by civil war. The authority of the *shoguns,* military commanders who had ruled Japan on behalf of the emperor since the twelfth century, was in eclipse, as dozens of *daimyo* (great lords) fought for power. Turbulence ended at the close of the sixteenth century, when three military heroes, Oda Nobunaga (1534–1582), Toyotomi Hideyoshi (1536–1598), and Tokugawa Ieyasu (1543–1616), forced the daimyo to accept central authority. In 1603 the emperor recognized Tokugawa Ieyasu as shogun, and the era of the Tokugawa Shogunate, which lasted until 1867, had begun.

Between 1624 and 1641, Iemitsu, grandson of Ieyasu and shogun from 1623 to 1651, issued edicts that closed Japan to virtually all foreigners. This was the culmination of policies begun under Hideyoshi, who had sought to limit contacts between Japanese and foreigners, especially Catholic missionaries. He and his successors viewed the missionaries' aggressive proselytizing as a disturbing societal factor and a potential political threat. The first document, the most celebrated of Iemitsu's edits, is directed to the two *bugyo*, or commissioners, of Nagasaki, a port city in southwest Japan and a center of Japanese Christianity; the second more specifically deals with the pro-Catholic activities of the Portuguese.

Questions for Analysis

1. To what extent is the edict of 1635 directed against the activities of foreigners?
2. Much of the 1635 edict deals with trade issues. What do the various provisions suggest about the shogun's attitude toward trade?
3. What can one infer about the reasons for the promulgation of the 1639 edict?

CLOSED COUNTRY EDICT OF 1635

1. Japanese ships are strictly forbidden to leave for foreign countries.

2. No Japanese is permitted to go abroad. If there is anyone who attempts to do so secretly, he must be executed. The ship so involved must be impounded and its owner arrested, and the matter must be reported to the higher authority.

3. If any Japanese returns from overseas after residing there, he must be put to death.

4. If there is any place where the teachings of padres[1] is practiced, the two of you must order a thorough investigation.

5. Any informer revealing the whereabouts of the followers of padres must be rewarded accordingly. If anyone reveals the whereabouts of a high ranking padre, he must be given one hundred pieces of silver. For those of lower ranks, depending on the deed, the reward must be set accordingly.

6. If a foreign ship has an objection (to the measures adopted) and it becomes necessary to report the matter to Edo,[2] you may ask the Omura[3] domain to provide ships to guard the foreign ship. . . .

7. If there are any Southern Barbarians[4] who propagate the teachings of padres, or otherwise commit crimes, they may be incarcerated in the prison. . . .

8. All incoming ships must be carefully searched for the followers of padres.

9. No single trading city shall be permitted to purchase all the merchandise brought by foreign ships.

10. Samurai[5] are not permitted to purchase any goods originating from foreign ships directly from Chinese merchants in Nagasaki.

11. After a list of merchandise brought by foreign ships is sent to Edo, as before

---

1. Fathers, or priests, that is, Christians.
2. Modern Tokyo, the seat of the Tokugawa government.
3. The area around the city of Nagasaki.

4. Westerners.
5. Members of Japan's military aristocracy.

you may order that commercial dealings may take place without waiting for a reply from Edo.

12. After settling the price, all white yarns[6] brought by foreign ships shall be allocated to the five trading cities[7] and other quarters as stipulated.

13. After settling the price of white yarns, other merchandise (brought by foreign ships) may be traded freely between the (licensed) dealers. However, in view of the fact that Chinese ships are small and cannot bring large consignments, you may issue orders of sale at your discretion. Additionally, payment for goods purchased must be made within twenty days after the price is set.

14. The date of departure homeward of foreign ships shall not be later than the twentieth day of the ninth month. Any ships arriving in Japan later than usual shall depart within fifty days of their arrival. As to the departure of Chinese ships, you may use your discretion to order their departure after the departure of the Portuguese galeota.[8]

15. The goods brought by foreign ships which remained unsold may not be deposited or accepted for deposit.

16. The arrival in Nagasaki of representatives of the five trading cities shall not be later than the fifth day of the seventh month. Anyone arriving later than that date shall lose the quota assigned to his city.

17. Ships arriving in Hirado[9] must sell their raw silk at the price set in Naga-

saki, and are not permitted to engage in business transactions until after the price is established in Nagasaki

You are hereby required to act in accordance with the provisions set above. It is so ordered.

EXCLUSION OF THE PORTUGUESE, 1639

1. The matter relating to the proscription of Christianity is known (to the Portuguese). However, heretofore they have secretly transported those who are going to propagate that religion.

2. If those who believe in that religion band together in an attempt to do evil things, they must be subjected to punishment.

3. While those who believe in the preaching of padres are in hiding, there are incidents in which that country (Portugal) has sent gifts to them for their sustenance.

In view of the above, hereafter entry by the Portuguese galeota is forbidden. If they insist on coming (to Japan), the ships must be destroyed and anyone aboard those ships must be beheaded. We have received the above order and are thus transmitting it to you accordingly.

The above concerns our disposition with regard to the galeota.

Memorandum

With regard to those who believe in Christianity, you are aware that there is a pro-

---

6. Raw silk.

7. The cities of Kyoto, Edo, Osaka, Sakai, and Nagasaki.

8. A galleon, an oceangoing Portuguese ship.

9. A small island in the southwest, not too distant from Nagasaki.

scription, and thus knowing, you are not permitted to let padres and those who believe in their preaching to come aboard your ships. If there is any violation, all of you who are aboard will be considered culpable. If there is anyone who hides the fact that he is a Christian and boards your ship, you may report it to us. A substantial reward will be given to you for this information.

This memorandum is to be given to those who come on Chinese ships. (A similar note to the Dutch ships.)

The Realm of Mind and Spirit

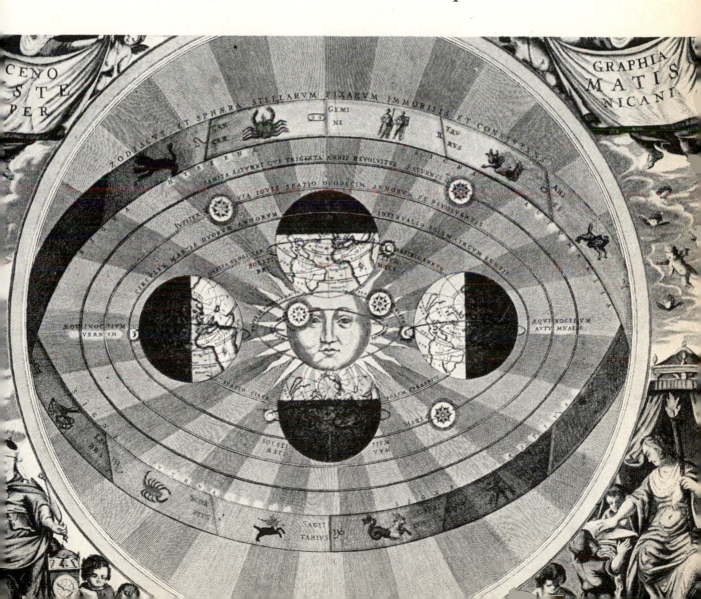

*A*t a remote point in history, men and women began to ponder the mysteries of their existence. What is the purpose of human life? What is the meaning of death? Who created the universe? What animates nature? How does one distinguish good from evil? How, if at all, can humans control their fate? When, to answer these questions, our distant ancestors developed a belief in supernatural powers who created and maintained the universe and demanded obedience and worship, the first religions were born. When our ancestors began to theorize systematically about the laws of nature, the origin of knowledge, and the principles of human conduct, philosophy came into existence. More than any other activities, religion and philosophy mark the human species as unique.

In the sixteenth and seventeenth centuries, as today, a wide variety of religious and philosophical beliefs characterized the world. Some of these, such as Hinduism and Judaism, had existed for thousands of years, while others, such as Islam, had begun as recently as the seventh century A.D. Some, such as Confucianism, affected the lives of millions of human beings throughout east Asia, while others, such as the religions of certain African and American tribes, commanded the allegiance of only a few thousand individuals.

Within the world's major religious and philosophical traditions, diversity was the norm. Hinduism had thousands of local variations in India, and Confucianism and Buddhism had many contending schools of interpretation and practice. Within the world of Islam, Shi'ites and Sunnis despised one another, and in western Eurasia rivalries among Christians — Orthodox, Roman Catholic, and Protestant — were intense.

A familiarity with the world's major religious and intellectual traditions is fundamental to an understanding of the history of the last 500 years. This chapter will provide insights into these crucial beliefs and practices.

Intellectual and Religious Ferment in Europe

Throughout history, most societies have feared change and resisted innovation, especially when basic religious beliefs and intellectual values have been involved. For this reason, times when traditional assumptions are scrutinized and rejected especially interest students of history.

The sixteenth and early seventeenth centuries were for Western Europe such a time of intellectual and religious upheaval. They saw the climax of the Renaissance, the onset of the Protestant and Catholic Reformations, and the beginning of the Scientific Revolution. The Renaissance opened the eyes of Europeans to the full range of ancient Greek and Roman thought and inspired a more worldly, secular approach to life and culture. The Protestant movement rejected traditional Catholic doctrine on the sacraments, salvation, religious authority, the status of the clergy, and much else. By the mid-sixteenth century, at least half of Western Europe was no longer Roman Catholic, and Europe's religious unity was shattered. Partly in response to Protestantism, the Catholic Church underwent its own reformation, marked by reform of abuses, new missionary vigor, and an affirmation of traditional beliefs and practices. Finally, the era saw the first serious challenge to the principles of ancient Greek science, a body of assumptions about nature that had defined humankind's place in the cosmos and provided the foundation for most medieval philosophy and theology. Taken together, these movements illustrate one of the most striking features of modern Western European civilization, namely, its willingness to challenge, debate, and, at times, discard values inherited from the past.

Niccolò Machiavelli

THE PRINCE

Niccolò Machiavelli (1469–1527), a contemporary of Botticelli, Leonardo da Vinci, and Michelangelo, lived when the artistic and intellectual creativity of the Italian Renaissance was at its peak. With his love and knowledge of ancient history and literature, Machiavelli himself was a product of the Renaissance and became one of its most celebrated spokesmen. He also lived at a time when the states of Italy were engulfed in political turmoil and gradually succumbed to the control of France and Spain. The immediate cause of Italy's political downfall was its invasion by King Charles VIII of France in 1494. As a diplomat in the service of the republic of Florence, Machiavelli was an active participant in the wars that followed and their victim. The Florentine republic was overthrown in 1512, and Machiavelli's political career was over. He retreated to his small country estate, read further in ancient history, and thought deeply about the reasons for Italy's political humiliation.

The first product of Machiavelli's rural exile was *The Prince*, which he essentially finished in 1514. Dedicated to the Florentine prince Lorenzo de Medici, *The Prince* was, in part, an effort by Machiavelli to impress the ruler and win back a job in the government. More broadly, the work represents Machiavelli's attempt to analyze, "from the wide experience of recent events and the constant reading of ancient classical authors," the factors behind political success and failure and to reduce his findings to a series of general principles. This handbook on the art of successful government expresses views about the realities of political life that had never before been so unambiguously articulated by a Western commentator.

Questions for Analysis

1. Consider Machiavelli's discussion of Agathocles the Sicilian and Oliverotto of Fermo. What point is he trying to make?
2. How does Machiavelli attempt to convince his readers that his assertions about politics are correct?
3. According to Machiavelli, how does morality in politics differ from morality in private life?
4. How does Machiavelli define "political virtue"? How does he define "good government"? In Machiavelli's view, what are the characteristics of an ideal prince?
5. How does Machiavelli's view of human nature affect his views of government?

VIII. THOSE WHO COME TO POWER BY CRIME

Agathocles, the Sicilian, not only from the status of a private citizen but from the lowest, most abject condition of life, rose to become king of Syracuse.[1] At every stage of his career this man, the son of a porter, behaved like a criminal; nonetheless he accompanied his crimes with so much audacity and physical courage that when he joined the militia he rose through the ranks to become praetor[2] of Syracuse. After he had been appointed to this position, he determined to make himself prince and to possess by force and without obligation to others what had been voluntarily conceded to him. He reached an understanding about this ambition of his with Hamilcar the Carthaginian, who was campaigning with his armies in Sicily. Then one morning he assembled the people and Senate of Syracuse, as if he meant to raise matters which affected the republic; and at a prearranged signal he had all the senators, along with the richest citizens, killed by his soldiers; and when they were dead he seized and held the government of that city, without encountering any other internal opposition. . . .

---

1. Agathocles was tyrant of Syracuse, a Greek city on the east coast of Sicily, from 217 to 289 B.C.

2. A high-ranking elected magistrate of a city, who usually had judicial powers.

In our own time, during the pontificate of Alexander VI,[3] there was Oliverotto of Fermo. Years before, he had been left fatherless as a small boy and was brought up by a maternal uncle called Giovanni Fogliani. In his early youth he was sent to serve as a soldier under Paulo Vitelli[4] so that he could win high command after being trained by him. When Paulo died, Oliverotto soldiered under Vitelozzo, his brother; and in a very short time, as he was intelligent, and a man of courage and audacity, he became Vitelozzo's chief commander. But he thought it was servile to take orders from others, and so he determined that, with the help of some citizens of Fermo[5] to whom the enslavement of their native city was more attractive than its liberty, and with the favor and help of the Vitelli, he would seize Fermo for himself. He wrote to Giovanni Fogliano saying that, having been many years away from home he wanted to come and see him and his city and to make some investigation into his own estate. He had worked for nothing else except honor, he went on, and in order that his fellow citizens might see that he had not spent his time in vain, he wanted to come honorably, with a mounted escort of a hundred companions and servants. He begged Giovanni to arrange a reception which would bring honor to Giovanni as well as to himself, as he was Giovanni's foster child. Giovanni failed in no duty of hospitality towards his nephew. He had him honorably welcomed by the citizens of Fermo and lodged him in his own mansion. There, after a few days had passed during which he waited in order to complete the secret arrangements for his future crime, Oliverotto prepared a formal banquet to which he invited Giovanni Fogliani and the leading citizens of Fermo. After they had finished eating and all the other entertainment usual at such banquets was done with, Oliverotto artfully started to touch on subjects of grave importance, talking of the greatness of Pope Alexander and of Cesare[6] his son, and of their enterprises. When Giovanni and the others began to discuss these subjects in turn, he got to his feet all of a sudden, saying that these were things to be spoken of somewhere more private, and he withdrew to another room, followed by Giovanni and all the other citizens. And no sooner were they seated than soldiers appeared from hidden recesses, and killed Giovanni and all the others. After this slaughter, Oliverotto mounted his horse, rode through the town, and laid siege to the palace of the governing council; consequently they were frightened into obeying him and into setting up a government of which he made himself the prince. And having put to death all who, because they would resent his rule, might injure him, he strengthened his position by founding new civil and military institutions. . . .

One might well wonder how it was that Agathocles, and others like him, after countless treacheries and cruelties, could live securely in his own country and hold foreign enemies at bay, with never a conspiracy against him by his countrymen, inasmuch as many others, because of their cruel behavior, have not been able to maintain their rule even in peaceful times, let alone in the uncertain times of war. I

---

3. Alexander VI (Rodrigo Borgia), pope from 1492 to 1503.

4. An Italian mercenary leader.

5. A central Italian city.

6. Cesare Borgia (1475–1507), the son of Pope Alexander VI, had been duke of the Romagna, a region of central Italy; earlier in *The Prince*, Machiavelli praises Cesare for his political boldness and vision.

believe that here it is a question of cruelty used well or badly. We can say that cruelty is used well (if it is permissible to talk in this way of what is evil) when it is employed once for all, and one's safety depends on it, and then it is not persisted in but as far as possible turned to the good of one's subjects. Cruelty badly used is that which, although infrequent to start with, as time goes on, rather than disappearing, grows in intensity. Those who use the first method can, with divine and human assistance, find some means of consolidating their position, as did Agathocles; the others cannot possibly stay in power. . . .

XV. The Things for Which Men, and Especially Princes, Are Praised or Blamed

It now remains for us to see how a prince must govern his conduct towards his subjects or his friends. I know that this has often been written about before, and so I hope it will not be thought presumptuous for me to do so, as, especially in discussing this subject, I draw up an original set of rules. But since my intention is to say something that will prove of practical use to the inquirer, I have thought it proper to represent things as they are in real truth, rather than as they are imagined. Many have dreamed up republics and principalities which have never in truth been known to exist; the gulf between how one should live and how one does live is so wide that a man who neglects what is actually done for what should be done learns the way to self-destruction rather than self-preservation. The fact is that a man who wants to act virtuously in every way necessarily comes to grief among so many who are not virtuous. Therefore if a prince wants to maintain his rule he must learn how not to be virtuous, and to make use of this or not according to need.

So leaving aside imaginary things, and referring only to those which truly exist, I say that whenever men are discussed (and especially princes, who are more exposed to view), they are noted for various qualities which earn them either praise or condemnation. Some, for example, are held to be generous, and others miserly. . . . Some are held to be benefactors, others are called grasping; some cruel, some compassionate; one man faithless, another faithful; one man effeminate and cowardly, another fierce and courageous; one man courteous, another proud; one man lascivious, another pure; one guileless, another crafty; one stubborn, another flexible; one grave, another frivolous; one religious, another sceptical; and so forth. I know everyone will agree that it would be most laudable if a prince possessed all the qualities deemed to be good among those I have enumerated. But, because of conditions in the world, princes cannot have those qualities, or observe them completely. So a prince has of necessity to be so prudent that he knows how to escape the evil reputation attached to those vices which could lose him his state, and how to avoid those vices which are not so dangerous, if he possibly can; but, if he cannot, he need not worry so much about the latter. And then, he must not flinch from being blamed for vices which are necessary for safeguarding the state. This is because, taking everything into account, he will find that some of the things that appear to be virtues will, if he practices them, ruin him, and some of the things that appear to be vices will bring him security and prosperity. . . .

XVI. Generosity and Parsimony

So, starting with the first of the qualities I enumerated above, I say it would be splendid if one had a reputation for generosity; nonetheless if you do in fact earn a reputation for generosity you will come to grief. This is because if your generosity is good and sincere it may pass unnoticed and it will not save you from being reproached for its opposite. If you want to acquire a reputation for generosity, therefore, you have to be ostentatiously lavish; and a prince acting in that fashion will soon squander all his resources, only to be forced in the end, if he wants to maintain his reputation, to lay excessive burdens on the people, to impose extortionate taxes, and to do everything else he can to raise money. This will start to make his subjects hate him, and, since he will have impoverished himself, he will be generally despised. As a result, because of this generosity of his, having injured many and rewarded few, he will be vulnerable to the first minor setback, and the first real danger he encounters will bring him to grief. When he realizes this and tries to retrace his path he will immediately be reputed a miser.

So as a prince cannot practice the virtue of generosity in such a way that he is noted for it, except to his cost, he should if he is prudent not mind being called a miser. In time he will be recognized as being essentially a generous man, seeing that because of his parsimony his existing revenues are enough for him, he can defend himself against an aggressor, and he can embark on enterprises without burdening the people. . . .

XVII. CRUELTY AND COMPASSION; AND WHETHER IT IS BETTER TO BE LOVED THAN FEARED, OR THE REVERSE

Taking others of the qualities I enumerated above, I say that a prince must want to have a reputation for compassion rather than for cruelty: nonetheless, he must be careful that he does not make bad use of compassion. Cesare Borgia was accounted cruel; nevertheless, this cruelty of his reformed the Romagna,[7] brought it unity, and restored order and obedience. On reflection, it will be seen that there was more compassion in Cesare than in the Florentine people, who, to escape being called cruel, allowed Pistoia to be devastated.[8] So a prince must not worry if he incurs reproach for his cruelty so long as he keeps his subjects united and loyal. By making an example or two he will prove more compassionate than those who, being too compassionate, allow disorders which lead to murder and rapine. These nearly always harm the whole community, whereas executions ordered by a prince only affect individuals. . . .

From this arises the following question: whether it is better to be loved than feared, or the reverse. The answer is that one would like to be both the one and the other; but because it is difficult to combine them, it is far better to be feared than loved if you cannot be both. One can make this generalization about men: they are ungrateful, fickle, liars, and deceivers, they shun danger and are greedy for profit; while you treat them well, they are yours. They would shed their blood for you, risk their property, their lives, their children, so long, as I said above, as danger is remote; but when you are in danger they turn against you. Any prince who has come to depend entirely on promises and has taken no other precautions ensures his own ruin; friendship which is bought with money and not with greatness and nobility of mind is paid for, but it does not last and it yields nothing. Men

---

7. A region of north-central Italy, in which Bologna is the major city; then part of the Papal States.

8. In 1501 Florence failed to act decisively in suppressing internal feuding in Pistoia, one of its subject cities.

worry less about doing an injury to one who makes himself loved than to one who makes himself feared. The bond of love is one which men, wretched creatures that they are, break when it is to their advantage to do so; but fear is strengthened by a dread of punishment which is always effective.

The prince must nonetheless make himself feared in such a way that, if he is not loved, at least he escapes being hated. For fear is quite compatible with an absence of hatred; and the prince can always avoid hatred if he abstains from the property of his subjects and citizens and from their women. If, even so, it proves necessary to execute someone, this is to be done only when there is proper justification and manifest reason for it. But above all a prince must abstain from the property of others; because men sooner forget the death of their father than the loss of their patrimony. . . .

XVIII. HOW PRINCES SHOULD HONOR THEIR WORD

Everyone realizes how praiseworthy it is for a prince to honor his word and to be straightforward rather than crafty in his dealings; nonetheless contemporary experience shows that princes who have achieved great things have been those who have given their word lightly, who have known how to trick men with their cunning, and who, in the end, have overcome those abiding by honest principles.

You must understand, therefore, that there are two ways of fighting: by law or by force. The first way is natural to men, and the second to beasts. But as the first way often proves inadequate one must needs have recourse to the second. . . .

So, as a prince is forced to know how to act like a beast, he must learn from the fox and the lion; because the lion is defenseless against traps and a fox is defenseless against wolves. Therefore one must be a fox in order to recognize traps, and a lion to frighten off wolves. Those who simply act like lions are stupid. So it follows that a prudent ruler cannot, and must not, honor his word when it places him at a disadvantage and when the reasons for which he made his promise no longer exist. If all men were good, this precept would not be good; but because men are wretched creatures who would not keep their word to you, you need not keep your word to them. And no prince ever lacked good excuses to color his bad faith.

A prince, therefore, need not necessarily have all the good qualities I mentioned above, but he should certainly appear to have them. I would even go so far as to say that if he has these qualities and always behaves accordingly he will find them harmful; if he only appears to have them they will render him service. He should appear to be compassionate, faithful to his word, kind, guileless, and devout. And indeed he should be so. But his disposition should be such that, if he needs to be the opposite, he knows how. You must realize this: that a prince, and especially a new prince, cannot observe all those things which give men a reputation for virtue, because in order to maintain his state he is often forced to act in defiance of good faith, of charity, of kindness, of religion. And so he should have a flexible disposition, varying as fortune and circumstances dictate. As I said above, he should not deviate from what is good, if that is possible, but he should know how to do evil, if that is necessary.

■ Martin Luther

TABLE TALK

The Protestant Reformation had many voices, but its first prophet was Martin Luther (1483–1546), whose "Ninety-Five Theses" of 1517 initiated the great anti-Catholic rebellion. Born into the family of a German miner and educated at the University of Erfurt, Luther was preparing for a career in law, when suddenly in 1505 he changed course and entered a cloister of Augustinian friars.

Because Luther and all Catholics believed that to God a monastic calling was the most pleasing vocation, Luther's decision reflected a deep concern over his salvation. His spiritual anxiety continued, however. Intensely conscious of his own weaknesses and inadequacies, he became convinced that he could never "earn" salvation by living up to the high standards of selflessness, charity, and purity prescribed by the Bible and the Catholic Church. He despaired of ever satisfying an angry God of Judgment and viewed with terror the prospect of eternal damnation in Hell.

After 1510, however, while he was a professor of theology at the University of Wittenberg, Luther found spiritual peace through the study of the scriptures. He learned that he could not earn salvation by performing the traditional pious acts enjoined by the established Church. Rather, salvation came only from God-implanted faith in Jesus as Savior.

As the Reformation spread to other parts of Europe, leadership of the Protestant movement passed to younger persons, such as John Calvin and John Knox. Luther remained at Wittenberg and, serving as pastor and university professor, poured forth hundreds of sermons and treatises in defense of his new religious vision. He and his wife, Katharina, a former nun, made their home in the Augustinian convent where Luther had once been a monk. Here they raised a family and entertained scores of reformers and students, with whom the gregarious Luther loved to discourse on the issues of the day. From 1522 to 1546, some of these guests recorded Luther's most notable sayings, as they remembered them, and from their journals we have what is known as Luther's *Tischreden*, or *Table Talk*.

Questions
for Analysis

1. What does Luther mean by "idolatry"?
2. What can a Christian accomplish without God's grace?
3. According to Luther, what is the importance of the Bible in a Christian's life? How had the Roman Catholic Church obscured the meaning and message of the Bible?
4. How does Luther define faith? Why is faith superior to external acts of devotion?
5. What are Luther's main objections to the pope and other officials of the Roman Catholic Church?
6. Luther's message is spiritual, but many of his followers found political and social implications in his teachings. How was that possible?

[*The Majesty and Power of God*]
All the works of God are unsearchable and unspeakable, no human sense can find them out; faith only takes hold of them without human power or aid. No mortal creature can comprehend God in his majesty, and therefore did he come before us in the simplest manner, and was made man, ay, sin, death, and weakness.

. . .

In all things, in the least creatures, and in their members, God's almighty power and wonderful works clearly shine. For what man, how powerful, wise, and holy soever, can make out of one fig a fig-tree, or another fig? or, out of one cherry-stone, a cherry, or a cherry-tree? or what man can know how God creates and preserves all things, and makes them grow.

. . .

Neither can we conceive how the eye sees, or how intelligible words are spoken plainly, when only the tongue moves and stirs in the mouth; all which are natural things, daily seen and acted. How then should we be able to comprehend or understand the secret counsels of God's majesty, or search them out with our human sense, reason, or understanding. Should we then admire our own wisdom? I, for my part, admit myself a fool, and yield myself captive.

. . .

Forasmuch as the everlasting, merciful God, through his Word and Sacraments,[1] talks and deals with us, all other creatures excluded, not of temporal things which pertain to this vanishing life, and which in the beginning he provided richly for us, but as to where we shall go when we depart hence, and gives unto us his Son for a Savior, delivering us from sin and death, and purchasing for us everlasting righteousness, life, and salvation, therefore it is most certain, that we do not die away like the beasts that have no understanding; but so many of us as sleep in Christ, shall through him be raised again to life everlasting at the last day, and the ungodly to everlasting destruction.

. . .

As lately I lay very sick, so sick that I thought I should have left this world, many cogitations and musings had I in my weakness. Ah! thought I, what may eternity be? What joys may it have? However, I know for certain, that this eternity is ours; through Christ it is given and prepared for us, if we can but believe. There it shall be opened and revealed; here we shall not know when a second creation of the world will be, seeing we understand not the first. If I had been with God Almighty before he created the world, I could not have advised him how out of nothing to make this globe, the firmament, and that glorious sun, which in its swift course gives light to the whole earth; how, in such manner, to create man and woman, etc., all which he did for us, without our counsel. Therefore ought we justly to give him the honor, and leave to his divine power and goodness the new creation of the life to come, and not presume to speculate thereon.

---

1. Although he rejected most of the Catholic Church's sacraments and "good works," Luther retained the sacraments of baptism and the eucharist.

[Faith Versus "Good Works"]

He that goes from the gospel to the law, thinking to be saved by good works, falls as uneasily, as he who falls from the true service of God to idolatry; for, without Christ, all is idolatry and fictitious imaginings of God, whether of the Turkish Koran, of the pope's decrees, or Moses' laws; if a man think thereby to be justified[2] and saved before God, he is undone.

. . .

When a man will serve God, he must look upon that which he does; not upon the work, but how it ought to be done, and whether God has commanded it or no; seeing, as Samuel[3] says, that "God hath more pleasure in obedience, than in burnt sacrifice."

. . .

Whoso hearkens not to God's voice, is an idolater, though he perform the highest and most heavy service of God. 'Tis the very nature of idolatry not to make choice of that which is esteemed easy and light, but of that which is great and heavy, as we see in the friars and monks, who have been constantly devising new worshipings of God; but, forasmuch that God in his Word has not commanded these, they are idolatry, and blasphemy.

. . .

I have often been resolved to live uprightly, and to lead a true godly life, and to set everything aside that would hinder this, but it was far from being put in execution; even as it was with Peter,[4] when he swore he would lay down his life for Christ.

. . .

I will not lie or dissemble before my God, but will freely confess, I am not able to effect that good which I intend, but await the happy hour when God shall be pleased to meet me with his grace.

. . .

A Christian's worshiping is not the external, hypocritical mask that our spiritual friars wear, when they chastise their bodies, torment and make themselves faint, with ostentatious fasting, watching, singing, wearing hair shirts, scourging themselves, etc. Such worshipping God desires not.

. . .

The pope and his crew can in nowise endure the idea of reformation; the mere word creates more alarm at Rome, than thunderbolts from heaven, or the day of judgment. A cardinal said, the other day: Let them eat, and drink, and do what they will; but as to reforming us, we think that is a vain idea; we will not endure it.

---

2. Justification for Luther meant being made "righteous" in God's eyes, that is, acceptable to God and therefore saved.

3. A Hebrew prophet and judge of the late eleventh century B.C., perhaps the author of the two biblical books named after him.

4. One of Jesus's twelve apostles; following Jesus's arrest by Roman soldiers before his crucifixion, Peter three times denied any relationship with Jesus, despite having vowed shortly before to lay down his life for his teacher. Eventually, Peter died a martyr's death in Rome.

Neither will we protestants be satisfied, though they administer the sacrament in both kinds, and permit priests to marry;[5] we will also have the doctrine of the faith pure and unfalsified, and the righteousness that justifies and saves before God, and which expels and drives away all idolatry and false-worshipping; these gone and banished, the foundation on which Popedom is built falls also.

[*The Bible*]

Great is the strength of the divine Word. In the epistle to the Hebrews,[6] it is called "a two-edged sword." But we have neglected and contemned the pure and clear Word, and have drunk not of the fresh and cool spring; we are gone from the clear fountain to the foul puddle, and drunk its filthy water; that is, we have sedulously read old writers and teachers, who went about with speculative reasonings, like the monks and friars.

. . .

Like as in the world a child is an heir only because it is born to inherit, even so, faith only makes such to be God's children as are born of the Word, which is the womb wherein we are conceived, born, and nourished, as the prophet Isaiah says. Now, as through such a birth we become God's children, (wrought by God without our help or doing), even so, we are also heirs, and being heirs, are freed from sin, death, and the devil, and shall inherit everlasting life.

. . .

I admonish every pious Christian that he take not offense at the plain, unvarnished manner of speech of the Bible. Let him reflect that what may seem trivial and vulgar to him, emanates from the high majesty, power, and wisdom of God. The Bible is the book that makes fools of the wise of this world; it is understood only of the plain and simple hearted. Esteem this book as the precious fountain that can never be exhausted. In it you find the swaddling-clothes and the manger whither the angels directed the poor, simple shepherds; they seem poor and mean, but dear and precious is the treasure that lies therein.

. . .

I did not learn my divinity at once, but was constrained by my temptations to search deeper and deeper; for no man, without trials and temptations, can attain a true understanding of the Holy Scriptures. St. Paul had a devil that beat him with fists, and with temptations drove him diligently to study the Holy Scripture. I had hanging on my neck the pope, the universities, all the deep-learned, and the devil; these hunted me into the Bible, wherein I sedulously read, and thereby, God be praised, at length attained a true understanding of it. Without such a devil, we are but only speculators of divinity, and according to our vain reasoning, dream that so and so it must be, as the monks and friars in monasteries do. The Holy Scripture of itself is certain and true: God grant me grace to catch hold of its just use.

---

5. Two of the many changes that the Protestant reformers called for were allowing all Christians to receive the sacrament of the Eucharist in the forms of bread and wine (in medieval Roman Catholic practice, only the priest drank the eucharistic wine) and allowing priests to marry. The principle behind both changes was Luther's teaching that all Christians are priests, that is, responsible for and capable of effecting their own salvation.

6. "Paul's Letter to the Hebrews," a part of the New Testament.

[*The Pope and the Roman Church*]

Kings and princes coin money only out of metals, but the pope coins money out of everything — indulgences, ceremonies, dispensations, pardons; 'tis all fish comes to his net. 'Tis only baptism escapes him, for children came into the world without clothes to be stolen, or teeth to be drawn.

. . .

In Italy, the monasteries are very wealthy. There are but three or four monks to each; the surplus of their revenues goes to the pope and his cardinals.

. . .

The cuckoo takes the eggs out of the linnet's[7] nest, and puts her own in their place. When the young cuckoos grow big, they eat the linnet. The cuckoo, too, has a great antipathy towards the nightingale. The pope is a cuckoo; he robs the church of her true eggs, and substitutes in their place his greedy cardinals, who devour the mother that has nourished them. The pope, too, cannot abide that nightingale, the preaching and singing of the true doctrine.

. . .

'Tis wonderful how, in this our time, the majesty of the pope is fallen. Heretofore, all monarchs, emperors, kings, and princes feared the pope's power, who held them all at his nod; none durst so much as mutter a word against him. This great god is now fallen; his own creatures, the friars and monks, are his enemies, who, if they still continue with him, do so for the sake of gain; otherwise they would oppose him more fiercely than we do.

. . .

In Popedom they make priests, not to preach and teach God's Word, but only to celebrate mass, and to gad about with the sacrament. For, when a bishop ordains a man, he says: Take unto thee power to celebrate mass, and to offer for the living and the dead. But we ordain priests according to the command of Christ and St. Paul, namely, to preach the pure gospel and God's Word. The papists in their ordinations make no mention of preaching and teaching God's Word, therefore their consecrating and ordaining is false and unright, for all worshipping which is not ordained of God, or erected by God's Word and command, is nothing worth, yea, mere idolatry.

. . .

The pope places his cardinals in all kingdoms — peevish milk-sops, effeminate and unlearned blockheads, who lie lolling in king's courts, among the ladies and women. The pope has invaded all countries with these and his bishops. Germany is taken captive by popish bishops, for I can count above forty bishoprics, besides abbeys and cathedrals, which are richer than the bishoprics. Now, there are in Germany but eight and twenty principalities, so that the popish bishops are far more rich and powerful than the princes of the empire.

---

7. A small songbird of the finch family.

Ignatius of Loyola

SPIRITUAL EXERCISES

Apart from arch-Catholic Spain's military power, the new Society of Jesus proved to be the Roman Catholic Church's most effective force in its campaign of renewal and resistance to Protestantism. The Jesuits, as they were popularly known, were founded by a Spanish soldier, Ignatius Loyola (1491–1556), who underwent a spiritual conversion while recuperating from a war wound suffered in 1521. Under Loyola's leadership, the Jesuits, who received papal approval in 1540, developed into a highly disciplined, broadly educated organization of priests and brothers who took a special vow of obedience to the pope. Their purpose was to fight heresy and unbelief by public preaching, acts of charity, mission work, and education of the young. They soon became recognized as the Roman Church's intellectual and spiritual elite.

A common experience for all Jesuits (and also many Catholic lay persons) is a month of prayer and self-examination based on the most famous of Loyola's writings, the *Spiritual Exercises*, first published in 1541. Based on Loyola's own spiritual experiences, the exercises he prescribed had the stated purpose of helping the individual in "seeking and discovering the Divine Will regarding the disposition of one's life, thus insuring the salvation of his soul." The following excerpt appears at the end of the *Exercises*, where Loyola offers instruction about the need to conform to the teachings of the Church.

Questions for Analysis

1. Historians debate whether the reforms of the sixteenth-century Catholic Church were reactions to the threat of Protestantism or the expression of a Catholic revival unrelated to Protestantism. What evidence does this selection provide on this issue?
2. In rule 14, Loyola seems to agree with Luther that no one can be saved without faith and unless it is predestined. How does he qualify his position later in the document?
3. Why does Loyola recommend "caution" when discussing predestination?
4. A major division between Protestants and Catholics is their view of religious authority. How do Loyola's views on this issue differ from Luther's in *Table Talk*?

RULES FOR THINKING WITH THE CHURCH

In order to have the proper attitude of mind in the Church Militant we should observe the following rules:

1. Putting aside all private judgment, we should keep our minds prepared and ready to obey promptly and in all

things the true spouse of Christ our Lord, our Holy Mother, the hierarchical Church.

2. To praise sacramental confession[1] and the reception of the Most Holy Sacrament once a year, and much better once a month, and better still every week, with the requisite and proper dispositions.

3. To praise the frequent hearing of Mass, singing of hymns and psalms, and the recitation of long prayers, both in and out of church; also the hours arranged for fixed times for the whole Divine Office, for prayers of all kinds and for the canonical hours.[2]

4. To praise highly religious life, virginity, and continence; and also matrimony, but not as highly as any of the foregoing.

5. To praise the vows of religion, obedience, poverty, chastity, and other works of perfection.[3] It must be remembered that a vow is made in matters that lead to evangelical perfection. It is therefore improper to make a vow in matters that depart from this perfection; as, for example, to enter business, to get married, and so forth.

6. To praise the relics of the saints by venerating them and by praying to these saints. Also to praise the stations, pilgrimages, indulgences, jubilees, Crusade indulgences, and the lighting of candles in the churches.[4]

7. To praise the precepts concerning fasts and abstinences, such as those of Lent, Ember Days, Vigils, Fridays, and Saturdays; likewise to praise acts of penance, both interior and exterior.

8. To praise the adornments and buildings of churches as well as sacred images, and to venerate them according to what they represent.

9. Finally, to praise all the precepts of the Church, holding ourselves ready at all times to find reasons for their defense, and never offending against them.

10. We should be more inclined to approve and praise the directions and recommendations of our superiors as well as their personal behavior. Although sometimes these may not be or may not have been praiseworthy, to speak against them when preaching in public or in conversation with people would give rise to murmuring and scandal rather than to edification. As a result, the people would be angry with their superiors, whether temporal or spiritual. Still, while it does harm to our superiors in their absence to speak ill of them in the presence of the people, it might be useful to speak of their bad conduct to those who can apply a remedy. . . .

13. If we wish to be sure that we are right in all things, we should always be ready to accept this principle: I will believe that the white that I see is black, if the hierarchical Church so de-

1. Protestants rejected auricular confession — confessing one's sins to God through a priest, who offers absolution in the name of God.

2. In his *Table Talk*, Martin Luther denies the merit of such "good works" as prayers, veneration of relics, and pilgrimages, claiming that external actions cannot earn God's grace. He argues that grace is a freely given gift that comes

only with a God-instilled faith in Jesus and the promise of salvation.

3. Arguing that all believers in Jesus are priests, all Protestant groups rejected a special priesthood of celibate ministers.

4. Many Protestant reformers considered images and decoration in churches a form of idolatry.

fines it. For, I believe that between the Bridegroom, Christ our Lord, and the Bride, His Church, there is but one spirit, which governs and directs us for the salvation of our souls, for the same Spirit and Lord, who gave us the Ten Commandments, guides and governs our Holy Mother Church.

14. Although it be true that no one can be saved unless it be predestined and unless he have faith and grace, still we must be very careful of our manner of discussing and speaking of these matters.

15. We should not make predestination[5] an habitual subject of conversation. If it is sometimes mentioned we must speak in such a way that no person will fall into error, as happens on occasion when one will say, "It has already been determined whether I will be saved or lost, and in spite of all the good or evil that I do, this will not be changed." As a result, they become apathetic and neglect the works that are conducive to their salvation and to the spiritual growth of their souls.

16. In like manner, we must be careful lest by speaking too much and with too great emphasis on faith, without any distinction or explanation, we give occasion to the people to become indolent and lazy in the performance of good works, whether it be before or after their faith is founded in charity.

17. Also in our discourse we ought not to emphasize the doctrine that would destroy free will.[6] We may therefore speak of faith and grace to the extent that God enables us to do so, for the greater praise of His Divine Majesty. But, in these dangerous times of ours, it must not be done in such a way that good works or free will suffer any detriment or be considered worthless.

18. Although the generous service of God for motives of pure love should be most highly esteemed, we should praise highly the fear of His Divine Majesty, for filial fear and even servile fear are pious and most holy things. When one cannot attain anything better or more useful, this fear is of great help in rising from mortal sin, and after this first step one easily advances to filial fear which is wholly acceptable and pleasing to God our Lord, since it is inseparable from Divine Love.

Nicholas Copernicus

ON THE REVOLUTIONS OF THE HEAVENLY SPHERES

Most historians date the beginning of Europe's Scientific Revolution from 1543, the year Nicholas Copernicus, a Polish Catholic cleric, published *On the Revolutions of the*

---

5. Luther, Calvin, and other reformers argued that because faith is given by God and not earned, persons are predestined to either salvation or damnation.

6. In his treatise of 1525, *On the Bondage of the Will,* Luther argued that on matters of salvation,

God's will completely controls the human will, that one is not free to accept or reject His gift of salvation. The Catholic position places the responsibility on the individual Christian to choose freely if he or she wants to live a meritorious life and thus earn salvation.

Heavenly Spheres. The significance of the book lay in its rejection of certain fundamental assumptions of ancient Greek science, most notably the idea that the earth was the center of the universe.

As a student at the Italian University of Padua, then the leading center for the study of Greek science, Copernicus became disenchanted with the ancient Greek cosmology as it was interpreted and taught. On his return to northern Europe, he painstakingly worked out a new mathematical model of a heliocentric universe, in which the earth revolved around the sun and turned on its axis.

Many of Copernicus's arguments and theories were wrong. He believed, for example, that planets orbited in perfect circles and at constant velocities. Nonetheless, his book was important as the first step away from Western European dependency on the authority of the ancient Greeks and the first step toward the basic new understanding of nature Europeans achieved in the seventeenth century.

In the following selection, the book's preface and dedication to Pope Paul III (1534–1549), Copernicus describes the genesis of his new theories.

Questions
for Analysis

1. Why did Copernicus delay the publication of his new theories about the universe for so long?
2. Why did Copernicus become dissatisfied with models of the universe accepted by his contemporaries?
3. What kind of research did he do to arrive at his new theories? Is this research "scientific" by modern standards?
4. What type of criticism does Copernicus expect of his book? How does he respond to it?

I can readily imagine, Holy Father, that as soon as some people hear that in this volume, which I have written about the revolutions of the spheres of the universe, I ascribe certain motions to the terrestrial globe, they will shout that I must be immediately repudiated together with this belief. For I am not so enamored of my own opinions that I disregard what others may think of them. I am aware that a philosopher's ideas are not subject to the judgment of ordinary persons, because it is his endeavor to seek the truth in all things, to the extent permitted to human reason by God. Yet I hold that completely erroneous views should be shunned. Those who know that the consensus of many centuries has sanctioned the conception that the earth remains at rest in the middle of the heaven as its center would, I reflected, regard it as an insane pronouncement if I made the opposite assertion that the earth moves. Therefore I debated with myself for a long time whether to publish the volume which I wrote to prove the earth's motion or rather to follow the example of the Pythagoreans[1] and certain others, who used to transmit philosophy's secrets only to kinsmen and friends, not in writing but by word of mouth. . . . When I weighed these considerations, the scorn which I had reason to fear on account of the novelty and unconventionality of my opinion almost induced me to abandon completely the work which I had undertaken.

But while I hesitated for a long time and even resisted, my friends drew me back. . . . They exhorted me no longer to refuse, on account of the fear which I felt, to make my work available for the general use of students of astronomy. The crazier my doctrine of the earth's motion now appeared to most people, the argument ran, so much the more admiration and thanks would it gain after they saw the publication of my writings dispel the fog of absurdity by most luminous proofs. Influenced therefore by these persuasive men and by this hope, in the end I allowed my friends to bring out an edition of the volume, as they had long besought me to do.

REVOLUTIONS

. . . I have . . . no desire to conceal from Your Holiness that I was impelled to consider a different system of deducing the motions of the universe's spheres for no other reason than the realization that astronomers do not agree among themselves in their investigations of this subject. For, in the first place, they are so uncertain about the motion of the sun and moon that they cannot establish and observe a constant length even for the tropical year. Secondly, in determining the motions not only of these bodies but also of the other five planets, they do not use the same principles, assumptions, and explanations of the apparent revolutions and motions. For while some employ only homocentrics, others utilize eccentrics and epicycles,[2] and yet they do not quite reach their goal. . . . On the contrary, their experience was just like some one taking from various places hands, feet, a head, and other pieces, very well depicted, it may be, but not for the representation of a single person; since these fragments would not belong to one another at all, a monster rather than a man would be put together from them. . . .

For a long time, then, I reflected on this confusion in the astronomical traditions concerning the derivation of the motions of the universe's spheres. I began to be annoyed that the movements of the world machine, created for our sake by the best and most systematic Artisan[3] of all, were not understood with greater certainty by

---

1. Followers of the Greek mathematician and philosopher Pythagoras (ca 580–ca 500 B.C.); they comprised a closed community, which jealously guarded their philosophical ideas.

2. In Aristotle's original theory, the orbits of the moon, planets, and stars are "homocentric," that is, they all have the same center, the earth. By the fifteenth century, astronomers, in order to explain the apparent erratic motion of the planets, had postulated "eccentric" (out-of-center) orbits and "epicycles." An eccentric orbit meant a planet might have a "center" that was not its circular orbit's true geometrical center or it might have two "centers," one for determining its velocity and another for calculating its circular orbit. An epicycle was a secondary orbital movement — a small circle, the center of which moved around the circumference of a larger circle, the center of which was the Earth. Only by such tinkering could astronomers retain the basics of the ancient Greek system.

3. A reference to God.

the philosophers, who otherwise examined so precisely the most insignificant trifles of this world. For this reason I undertook the task of rereading the works of all the philosophers which I could obtain to learn whether anyone had ever proposed other motions of the universe's spheres than those expounded by the teachers of astronomy in the schools. And in fact first I found in Cicero that Hicetas supposed the earth to move.[4] Later I also discovered in Plutarch[5] that certain others were of this opinion. I have decided to set his words down here, so that they may be available to everybody:

> Some think that the earth remains at rest. But Philolaus the Pythagorean believes that, like the sun and moon, it revolves around the fire in an oblique circle. Heraclides of Pontus and Ecphantus the Pythagorean make the earth move, not in a progressive motion, but like a wheel in a rotation from west to east about its own center.[6]

Therefore, having obtained the opportunity from these sources, I too began to consider the mobility of the earth. And even though the idea seemed absurd, nevertheless I knew that others before me had been granted the freedom to imagine any circles whatever for the purpose of explaining the heavenly phenomena. Hence I thought that I too would be readily permitted to ascertain whether explanations sounder than those of my predecessors could be found for the revolution of the celestial spheres on the assumption of some motion of the earth.

Having thus assumed the motions which I ascribe to the earth later on in the volume, by long and intense study I finally found that if the motions of the other planets are correlated with the orbiting of the earth, and are computed for the revolution of each planet, not only do their phenomena follow therefrom but also the order and size of all the planets and spheres, and heaven itself is so linked together that in no portion of it can anything be shifted without disrupting the remaining parts and the universe as a whole. . . .

Perhaps there will be babblers who claim to be judges of astronomy although completely ignorant of the subject and, badly distorting some passage of Scripture to their purpose, will dare to find fault with my undertaking and censure it. I disregard them even to the extent of despising their criticism as unfounded. For it is not unknown that Lactantius,[7] otherwise an illustrious writer but hardly an astronomer, speaks quite childishly about the earth's shape, when he mocks those who declared that the earth has the form of a globe. Hence scholars need not be surprised if any such persons will likewise ridicule me. Astronomy is written for astronomers.

---

4. Cicero (106–43 B.C.) was a Roman orator and statesman; Hicetas was a Pythagorean philosopher of the fourth century B.C.

5. Plutarch (ca A.D. 46–ca A.D. 119) was a Greek moralist and biographer. The work Copernicus cites, *Opinions of the Philosophers*, is no longer considered to be Plutarch's; its unknown author is now referred to as the "Pseudo-Plutarch."

6. Philolaus was a fifth-century B.C. philosopher who is credited with the theory that the energy of the universe is provided by a great fire at its center. Heraclides of Pontus (b. ca 390 B.C.) suggested that the earth rotates on its axis and that Venus and Mars revolve around the sun. Ecphantus, a fifth-century B.C. philosopher, is thought to have believed that the earth rotates on an axis.

7. Lactantius (A.D. 240–320), known as the "Christian Cicero" because of his elegant Latin style, wrote *Divine Precepts*, an antipagan tract.

Varieties of Religious Experience in West and South Asia

In the 1500s and 1600s, a broad swath of territory stretching from North Africa, through the Middle East, and all the way to northern India was dominated by three mighty empires, the Ottoman, Safavid, and Mughal, which are usually referred to as the three "Islamic" empires, since all of them had rulers who were Muslims, followers of the Islamic faith. One should not conclude, however, that religious unity characterized this huge region. The population of the Ottoman Empire, in North Africa, the Middle East, and southeastern and central Europe, was predominantly Muslim, but it also included numerous Jewish communities and many Christians, both Greek Orthodox and Roman Catholic. The Safavid Empire, in modern Iraq, Iran, and western Afghanistan, was more uniformly Muslim, but its rulers and the majority of its population adhered to a branch of Islam known as Shi'ism, which most Muslims, known as Sunnis, abhorred. Of the three empires, that of the Mughals, in north India and modern Pakistan, had the most conspicuous religious contrasts. Here the dominant Muslims ruled a population made up mostly of Hindus, adherents of India's ancient faith. Such diversity explains why the region's religious history was marked both by intolerance and by attempts at accommodation and understanding.

Islam, in both its Shi'ite and Sunni versions, originated in the seventh century A.D. and was based on the prophecies of Muhammad (570–632), whose revelations about Allah (Arabic for God) were recorded in Islam's most holy book, the Qur'an. Islam in Arabic means submission, and a Muslim is one who is submissive to God's will. Islam's basic creed is the simple statement that every follower must utter daily: "There is no God but God, and Muhammad is the Prophet of God." All Muslims are expected to accept the Qur'an as the word of God, perform works of charity, fast during the holy month of Ramadan, carry out daily prayers, and, if possible, make a pilgrimage to Mecca, the city on the Arab peninsula where Muhammad received his original revelation. Like Christianity, Islam teaches that at death each person will be judged by Allah, with the faithful rewarded by Heaven and the unfaithful damned to an eternity in Hell.

Almost from its very beginning, however, Islam has been divided by the Shi'ite-Sunni schism. Shi'ites believe that before his death Muhammad passed on secret teachings to his son-in-law, Ali, who was the fourth caliph, or "successor," to the Prophet. Shi'ites believe that before Ali and his son, Hussain, were murdered, they passed on these teachings to twelve *imams* (the secret true heads of Islam), the last of whom disappeared in the ninth century but who is expected to reappear sometime in the future. Sunni Muslims reject this belief, claiming that Ali had no special revelation and that the truths of Islam were revealed once and for all in the Qur'an and early Islamic traditions and law codes.

Potential for religious conflict was also high in the Mughal Empire, where a minority of Muslims, at best 30 percent of India's total population, ruled a majority that adhered to India's ancient religion, Hinduism. It would be hard to imagine two religions as different as Islam and Hinduism. Hinduism, which slowly evolved over many centuries, has no single creed, set of rituals, holy book, or organized church. Unlike Judaism, Christianity, and Islam, whose followers believe in the existence of only one supreme God, Hinduism includes many thousands of gods and goddesses in its pantheon, although all are believed to be manifestations of the creator deity, called Brahma. Hindus believe there are many paths to religious enlightenment, and Hinduism thus encompasses a wide range of faiths and forms of worship.

Islam, with its affirmation that all believers are equal before God, is far removed from the Hindu caste system, a religiously sanctioned order of social relationships that can be traced back to the beginnings of Indian civilization between 1500 and 1000 B.C. A person's caste, into which he or she is born for life, determines social and legal status, restricts marriage partners to other caste members, limits an individual to certain professions, and, in effect, minimizes contacts with members of other castes. The English word *caste* is derived from the Portuguese word *casta*, meaning "pure." Hindus use two different words for caste, *varna* (color) and *jati* (birth). *Varna* refers only to the four most ancient and fundamental social-religious divisions: Brahmans (priests and teachers), Kshatriyas (warriors, nobles, and rulers), Vaisyas (landowners, merchants, and artisans), and Sudras (peasants and laborers). A fifth group, the "untouchables," are outside the varna system and relegated to such despised tasks as gathering manure, sweeping streets, and butchering animals. Each of the four major castes is further divided into *jatis*, local hereditary occupational groups that during the 1500s and 1600s probably numbered around 3,000.

Hindu belief in caste is related to belief in the transmigration of souls. Also known as reincarnation, this is the belief that each individual soul, or *atman*, a dislocated piece of the universal soul, or Brahman, strives through successive births to reunite with Brahman and win eternal release from the chains of material existence. Reincarnation is based on one's *karma*, the fruit of one's actions, or the soul's destiny, which is decided by how well or poorly a person has conformed to *dharma*, another Hindu concept connected with the caste system. *Dharma* is the specific duty to be performed by members of each *jati*. If a person fulfills his or her *dharma*, in the next reincarnation he or she will move up the cosmic ladder, closer to ultimate reunion with the One.

Sultan Selim I

LETTER TO SHAH ISMAIL I OF PERSIA

In 1514, the Ottoman sultan, Selim I (1512–1520), led an army into Persia to crush his religious enemies, who were not Christians or Jews but Shi'ite Muslims, despised enemies of the Muslim majority, the Sunnis. Sunni-Shi'ite conflict heightened in the early sixteenth century, when the Safavid Dynasty, under Ismail I, established a strong Shi'ite state in Persia that persecuted Sunni Muslims and threatened the Ottoman Empire to the west. This was the reason for Selim I's invasion of Persia. After the Ottomans decisively defeated the Safavids at the Battle of Chaldrian in 1514, Persia remained under Safavid control, and thus committed to Shi'ism, but it no longer was a threat to the Ottoman regime.

The following document is a letter written by Selim I to his adversary, Ismail I, shortly before the Ottoman invasion.

Questions
for Analysis

1. How does Selim I perceive his place within the Islamic world?
2. Why does he condemn Ismail?
3. What does this letter tell us about Shi'ite beliefs? About Sunni beliefs?

The Supreme Being who is at once the sovereign arbiter of the destinies of men and the source of all light and knowledge, declares in the holy book[1] that the true faith is that of the Muslims, and that whoever professes another religion, far from being hearkened to and saved, will on the contrary be cast out among the rejected on the great day of the Last Judgment; He says further, this God of truth, that His designs and decrees are unalterable, that all human acts are perforce reported to Him, and that he who abandons the good way will be condemned to hellfire and eternal torments. Place yourself, O Prince, among the true believers, those who walk in the path of salvation, and who turn aside with care from vice and infidelity. May the purest and holiest blessings be upon Muhammad, the master of the two worlds, the prince of prophets, as well as upon his descendants and all who follow his Law!

I, sovereign chief of the Ottomans, master of the heroes of the age . . . I, the exterminator of idolators, destroyer of the enemies of the true faith, the terror of the tyrants and pharaohs of the age; I, before whom proud and unjust kings have humbled themselves, and whose hand breaks the strongest sceptres; I, the great Sultan-Khan, son of Sultan Bayezid-Khan, son of Sultan Muhammad-Khan, son of Sultan Murad-Khan, I address myself graciously to you, Amir Isma'il, chief of the troops of Persia, comparable in tyranny to Sohak and Afrasiab,[2] and predestined to perish . . . in order to make known to you that the works emanating from the Almighty are not the fragile products of caprice or folly, but make up an infinity of mysteries impenetrable to the human mind. The Lord Himself says in his holy book: "We have not created the heavens and the earth in order to play a game" [Qur'an, 21:16]. Man, who is the noblest of the

---

1. The Qur'an.
2. Legendary kings of Central Asia.

creatures and the summary of the marvels of God, is in consequence on earth the living image of the Creator. It is He who has set up Caliphs[3] on earth, because, joining faculties of soul with perfection of body, man is the only being who can comprehend the attributes of the divinity and adore its sublime beauties; but he possesses this rare intelligence, he attains this divine knowledge only in our religion and by observing the precepts of the prince of prophets, the Caliph of Caliphs, the right arm of the God of Mercy; it is then only by practising the true religion that man will prosper in this world and merit eternal life in the other. As to you, Amir Isma'il, such a recompense will not be your lot; because you have denied the sanctity of the divine laws; because you have deserted the path of salvation and the sacred commandments; because you have impaired the purity of the dogmas of Islam; because you have dishonored, soiled and destroyed the altars of the Lord, usurped the sceptre of the East by unlawful and tyrannical means; because coming forth from the dust, you have raised yourself by odious devices to a place shining with splendor and magnificence; because you have opened to Muslims the gates of tyranny and oppression; because you have joined iniquity, perjury and blasphemy to your sectarian impiety; because under the cloak of the hypocrite, you have sowed everywhere trouble and sedition; because you have raised the standard of irreligion and heresy; because yielding to the impulse of your evil passions, and giving yourself up without rein to the most infamous disorders, you have dared to throw off the control of Muslim laws and

to permit lust and rape, the massacre of the most virtuous and respectable men, the destruction of pulpits and temples, the profanation of tombs, the ill-treatment of the *ulama*, the doctors and amirs[4] descended from the Prophet, the repudiation of the Qur'an, the cursing of the legitimate Caliphs. Now as the first duty of a Muslim and above all of a pious prince is to obey the commandment, "O, you faithful who believe, be the executors of the decrees of God!" the *ulama* and our doctors have pronounced sentence of death against you, perjurer and blasphemer, and have imposed on every Muslim the sacred obligation to arm in defense of religion and destroy heresy and impiety in your person and that of all your partisans.

Animated by the spirit of this *fetwa*,[5] conforming to the Qur'an, the code of divine laws, and wishing on one side to strengthen Islam, on the other to liberate the lands and peoples who writhe under your yoke, we have resolved to lay aside our imperial robes in order to put on the shield and coat of mail, to raise our ever victorious banner, to assemble our invincible armies, to take up the gauntlet of the avenger, to march with our soldiers, whose sword strikes mortal blows, and whose point will pierce the enemy even to the constellation of Sagittarius. In pursuit of this noble resolution, we have entered upon the campaign, and guided by the hand of the Almighty, we hope soon to strike down your tyrannous arm, blow away the clouds of glory and grandeur which trouble your head and cause you fatal blindness, release from your despotism your trembling subjects, smother you

---

3. Deputies, or successors, of the Prophet Muhammad, who led the Muslim community on earth.

4. *Ulama* were bodies of religious teachers and interpreters of Muslim law; doctors here

means teachers; amirs are military commanders and princes.

5. Religious decree.

in the end in the very mass of flames which your infernal *jinn*[6] raises everywhere along your passage, accomplishing in this way on you the maxim which says: "He who sows discord can only reap evils and afflictions." However, anxious to conform to the spirit of the law of the Prophet, we come, before commencing war, to set out before you the words of the Qur'an, in place of the sword, and to exhort you to embrace the true faith; this is why we address this letter to you.

We all have a different nature, and the human race resembles mines of gold and silver. Among some, vice is deeply rooted; these are incorrigible, and one could no more draw them to virtue than one could whiten a Negro's skin; among others, vice has not become second nature; they retract their errors when they wish, by a serious return, to mortify their senses and repress their passions. The most efficacious means of remedying evil is to search the conscience deeply, to open one's eyes to faults, and to ask pardon of the God of Mercy with true sorrow and repentance. We urge you to look into yourself, to renounce your errors, and to march towards the good with a firm and courageous step; we ask further that you give up possession of the territory violently seized from our State and to which you have only illegitimate pretensions, that you deliver it back into the hands of our lieutenants and officers; and if you value your safety and repose, this should be done without delay.

But if, to your misfortune, you persist in your past conduct; if, puffed up with the idea of your power and your foolish bravado, you wish to pursue the course of your iniquities, you will see in a few days your plains covered with our tents and inundated with our battalions. Then prodigies of valor will be done, and we shall see the decrees of the Almighty, Who is the God of Armies, and sovereign judge of the actions of men, accomplished. For the rest, victory to him who follows the path of salvation!

▓ Abul Fazl

AKBARNAMA

Given the number of differences between Islam and Hinduism, it is not surprising that many Muslim rulers in India excluded Hindus from government positions, taxed them at discriminatory rates, and ordered the destruction of Hindu temples and art. Grudging toleration was the most Hindus could hope for from their Muslim overlords.

This policy changed during the reign of the early Mughal emperors, who sought to win support for their new dynasty by ending acts of intolerance against Hindus. Acceptance of Hinduism reached new heights during the reign of Akbar (1556–1605), whose views of Europeans Abul Fazl described in Chapter 1. Akbar brought Hindus into his administration, took a Hindu woman as his prime mistress, and

---

6. Supernatural spirit.

allowed Hindus to openly practice their ceremonies at court. He encouraged discussions with learned Hindus and even considered sponsoring his own religion, a blend of Muslim and Hindu beliefs. All this was disturbing to many orthodox Muslims, who were shocked to see their emperor encourage Hindu unbelief.

One must read the following excerpt, from the fourth book of Abul Fazl's *Akbarnama*, with this background in mind. As noted in Chapter 1, Abul Fazl was Akbar's closest adviser and thoroughly in sympathy with his master's religious views. Thus, in his discussion of the Hindu faith, Abul Fazl deals directly with the concerns of orthodox Muslims: that Hindus were guilty of the two greatest sins any human could commit against the majesty and Oneness of God, idolatry (the worship of idols) and polytheism (the belief in many gods).

Because of the system's antiquity, few Indian writers of the 1500s and 1600s commented on caste, simply accepting it as one of life's givens. To a non-Hindu, such as Abul Fazl, however, caste was one of the extraordinary features of Indian life, and he describes it at length here.

Questions for Analysis

1. How does Abul Fazl counter the charge that Hindus are polytheists? Do you find his arguments convincing?
2. How does he blunt the charge that they are idol worshipers?
3. Why does the Hindu Supreme Being periodically assume various bodily forms?
4. Abul Fazl is obviously attempting to make Hinduism more acceptable to Muslims, but this does not necessarily invalidate what he writes. If we accept what he tells us as basically true, what conclusions can we reach about the ways Hindus perceive and relate to Divine Reality?
5. In what way do caste and karma provide a moral understanding of the universe?
6. What do the dharmas of the castes reveal about the Hindu hierarchy of values?
7. Where do women fit into the structure of the ladder of reincarnation? What does this suggest about their status in Hindu society?

*T*hey one and all believe in the unity of God, and as to the reverence they pay to images of stone and wood and the like, which simpletons regard as idolatry, it is not so. The writer of these pages has exhaustively discussed the subject with many enlightened and upright men, and it became evident that these images . . . are fashioned as aids to fix the mind and keep the thoughts from wandering, while the worship of God alone is required as indispensable. In all their ceremonial observances and usage they ever implore the favor of the world-illumining sun and regard the pure essence of the Supreme Being as transcending the idea of power in operation.

Brahma . . . they hold to be the Creator;

Vishnu, the Nourisher and Preserver; and Rudra,[1] called also Mahadeva, the Destroyer. Some maintain that God who is without equal, manifested himself under these three divine forms, without thereby sullying the garment of His inviolate sanctity, as the Nazarenes hold of the Messiah.[2] Others assert that these were human creatures exalted to these dignities through perfectness of worship, probity of thought and righteousness of deed. The godliness and self-discipline of this people is such as is rarely to be found in other lands.

They hold that the world had a beginning, and some are of opinion that it will have an end. . . . They allow of no existence external to God. The world is a delusive appearance, and as a man in sleep sees fanciful shapes, and is affected by a thousand joys and sorrows, so are its seeming realities. . . .

Brahman is the Supreme Being; and is essential existence and wisdom and also bliss. . . .

Since according to their belief, the Supreme Deity can assume an elemental form without defiling the skirt of the robe of omnipotence, they first make various idols of gold and other substances to represent this ideal and gradually withdrawing the mind from this material worship, they become meditatively absorbed in the ocean of His mysterious Being. . . .

They believe that the Supreme Being in the wisdom of His counsel, assumes an elementary form of a special character[3] for the good of the creation, and many of the wisest of the Hindus accept this doctrine. . . .

TORTOISE-INCARNATION

In the *Satya Yuga* in the light half of the month of *Karttika* (Oct.-Nov.), on the twelfth lunar day, the Creator manifested himself in the shape of a tortoise. They relate that the deities wished to obtain the water of immortality after the manner of butter by churning the ocean of milk. Instead of a churning-stick, they used the largest of the mountains, *Mandara*. From its excessive weight the mountain sunk into the ocean, and great were their difficulties. The Deity assumed this shape and bore up the mountain on his back and the gods obtained their desire.

By this miraculous act, fourteen priceless objects were brought up from the sea: — (1). *Lakshmi*, the goddess of fortune, appeared as a bride and thus a source of happiness to all creatures was obtained. (2). *Kaustubha-mani* or the wonderful jewel *Kaustubha*, of extraordinary lustre and in value beyond price. (3). *Parijataka-vriksha*, the miraculous tree *Parijataka* whose flowers never fade and whose fragrance fills the universe. Some say that it grants all desires. It is called also *Kalpavriksha*. (4). *Sura*, (the goddess of) wine. (5). *Dhanvantari*, the physician (of the gods) who could heal the sick and raise the dead to life. In his right hand, he held a leech and in his left (a branch of) the myrobalan tree. His Majesty considers that these two should be regarded separately and the number of treasures be accounted sixteen. (6). *Ohandra-mani*, the (moon-gem or) world-illumining moon. (7). *Kama-dhenu*, the miraculous cow which gave forth from her udders the gratification of every wish.

---

1. Also known as Shiva.

2. Abul Fazl draws two comparisons here. He compares this Hindu trinity with both the Christian (Nazarene) Holy Trinity (three divine and fully separate persons in one God) and with the incarnation of Jesus Christ (the Messiah), the Second Person of the Holy Trinity. His Muslim audience would have known basic Christian beliefs.

3. That is, the Hindu Supreme Being assumes various bodies. These incarnations are known as *avatara*.

(8). *Airavata*, the white elephant (of Indra) with four tusks. (9). *Sankha*, the white conch-shell of wondrous sound that bestowed victory on whomsoever possessed it. (10). *Visha*, deadly poison. (11). *Amrita*, the water of life. (12) *Rambha*, the nymph, beautiful and sweet-dispositioned. (13) *Asea*, the horse with eight heads. (14). *Sarangadhanus*, or the bow *Saranga* of which the unerring arrow carried to any distance.

After producing these inestimable treasures, the tortoise descended into the earth and is believed still to exist.

INCARNATION AS KRISHNA[4]

More than four thousand years ago, Ugrasena of the Yadu race bore away in his capital of Mathura. His son Kansa rebelled and dethroning his father ruled with a persecuting hand, while at the same time Jarasandha, Sisupala and other princes of the Daityas exorcised unbounded tyranny. The afflicted earth assuming the form of a cow, hastened with Brahma to Vishnu and implored their destruction. The prayer was granted and the divine commission was entrusted to Krishna. They say that the astrologers foretold to Kansa that a child would shortly be born and that his reign would be at an end. He thereupon ordered the slaughter of all infants and thus each year the blood of many innocent children was shed until his sister Devaki married Vasudeva of the Yadu race. Now Kansa heard a report that Devaki's eighth son would be the cause of his death. He therefore confined them both in prison and put to death every son that was born to them. In the beginning of the *Kali Yuga*, on the eighth lunar day of the dark half of the month of *Bhadrapada* (Aug.-Sept.), in the city of Mathura near the metropolis of Agra, the child was born while the guards were negligent. The fetters fell off and the doors were opened and the child spoke thus. "On the other side of the Jamuna, a girl has even now been born in the house of the cowherd Nanda, and the family are asleep. Take and leave me there and bring the girl hither." As Vasudeva set out to fulfil this injunction, the river became fordable and the command was obeyed. Krishna in his ninth year killed Kansa, released Ugrasena from prison and seated him on the throne. He also engaged the other tyrants and overthrew them.

He lived one hundred and twenty-five years and had 16,108 wives, each of whom gave birth to ten sons and one daughter, and each wife thought that she alone shared her husband's bed. . . .

CASTE

The Hindu philosophers reckon four states of auspiciousness which they term *varna*. 1. *Brahman*. 2. *Kshatriya*. 3. *Vaisya*. 4. *Sudra*. Other than these are termed *Mlechchha*.[5] At the creation of the world the first of these classes was produced from the mouth of Brahma, a brief account of whom has already been given: the second, from his arms; the third, from his thigh and the fourth from his feet; the fifth from the cow *Kamadhenu*, the name of Mlechchha being employed to designate them.

The *Brahmans* have six recognized duties. 1. The study of the Vedas[6] and other sciences. 2. The instruction of others (in the sacred texts). 3. The performance of

---

4. Krishna, an avatar of Vishnu the Preserver, is the most popular of all Hindu divine incarnations.

5. The "outcastes" of Hindu society.

6. The four collections of ancient poetry that are essential sacred texts among Hindus.

the *Jag,* that is oblation of money and kind to the Devatas.[7] 4. Inciting others to the same. 5. Giving presents. 6. Receiving presents.

Of these six the *Kshatriya* must perform three. 1. Perusing the holy texts. 2. The performance of the Jag. 3. Giving presents. Further they must, 1. Minister to Brahmans. 2. Control the administration of worldly government and receive the reward thereof. 3. Protect religion. 4. Exact fines for delinquency and observe adequate measure therein. 5. Punish in proportion to the offense. 6. Amass wealth and duly expend it. 7. Supervise the management of elephants, horses, and cattle and the functions of ministerial subordinates. 8. Levy war on due occasion. 9. Never ask an alms. 10. Favor the meritorious and the like.

The *Vaisya* also must perform the same three duties of the Brahman, and in addition must occupy himself in: 1. Service. 2. Agriculture. 3. Trade. 4. The care of cattle. 5. The carrying of loads. . . .

The Sudra is incapable of any other privilege than to serve these three castes, wear their cast-off garments and eat their leavings. He may be a painter, goldsmith, blacksmith, carpenter, and trade in salt, honey, milk, butter-milk, clarified butter and grain.

Those of the fifth class, are reckoned as beyond the pale of religion, like infidels, Jews and the like.[8] By the inter-marriages of these, sixteen other classes are formed. The son of Brahman parents is acknowledged as a Brahman. If the mother be a Kshatriya, (the father being a Brahman) the progeny is called *Murdhavasikta.* If the mother be a Vaisya, the son is named *Ambastha,* and if a Sudra girl, *Nishada.* If

the father and mother are both Kshatriya, the progeny is Kshatriya. If the mother be a Brahman, (and the father a Kshatriya) the son is called *Suta.* If the mother be a Vaisya, the son is *Mahisya.* If the mother be a Sudra, the progeny is *Ugra.* If both parents be Vaisya, the progeny is Vaisya. If the mother be a Brahman, (which is illicit) the progeny is *Vaideha* but if she be a Kshatriya, which also is regarded as improper, he is *Magadha.* From the Vaisya by a Sudra mother is produced a *Karana.* When both parents are Sudra, the progeny is Sudra. If the mother be a Brahman, the progeny is *Chandala.* If she be a Kshatriya, it is called *Chatta.* From a Sudra by a Vaisya girl is produced the *Ayogava.*

In the same away still further ramifications are formed, each with different customs and modes of worship and each with infinite distinctions of habitation, profession, and rank of ancestry that defy computation. . . .

KARMA

Or the ripening of actions. This is a system of knowledge of an amazing and extraordinary character, in which the learned of Hindustan concur without dissenting opinion. It reveals the particular class of actions performed in a former birth which have occasioned the events that befall men in this present life, and prescribes the special expiation of each sin, one by one. It is of four kinds.

The first kind discloses the particular action which has brought a man into existence in one of the five classes into which mankind is divided, and the action which occasions the assumption of a male or female form. A *Kshatriya* who lives conti-

---

7. Hindu deities.

8. Abul Fazl is drawing an analogy for his Muslim readers. Just as Muslims consider all

nonbelievers to be outside the community of God, so Hindus regard the Mlechchha as outside the community.

nently, will, in his next birth, be born a *Brahman*. A *Vaisya* who hazards his transient life to protect a Brahman, will become a *Kshatriya*. A *Sudra* who lends money without interest and does not defile his tongue by demanding repayment, will be born a *Vaisya*. A *Mlechchha* who serves a *Brahman* and eats food from his house till his death, will become a *Sudra*. A *Brahman* who undertakes the profession of a *Kshatriya* will become a *Kshatriya*, and thus a *Kshatriya* will become a *Vaisya*, and a *Vaisya* a *Sudra*, and a *Sudra* a *Mlechchha*. Whosoever accepts in alms . . . the bed on which a man has died[9] . . . will, in the next birth, from a man become a woman. Any woman or *Mlechchha*, who in the temple . . . sees the form of *Narayana*,[10] and worships him with certain incantations, will in the next birth, if a woman, become a man, and if a *Mlechchha*, a *Brahman*. . . .

The second kind shows the strange effects of actions on health of body and in the production of manifold diseases.

Madness is the punishment of disobedience to father and mother. . . .

Pain in the eyes arises from having looked upon another's wife. . . .

Dumbness is the consequence of killing a sister. . . .

Colic results from having eaten with an impious person or a liar. . . .

Consumption is the punishment of killing a *Brahman*. . . .

The third kind indicates the class of actions which have caused sterility and names suitable remedies. . . .

A woman who does not menstruate, in a former existence . . . roughly drove away the children of her neighbors who had come as usual to play at her house. . . .

A woman who gives birth to only daughters is thus punished for having contemptuously regarded her husband from pride. . . .

A woman who has given birth to a son that dies and to a daughter that lives, has, in her former existence, taken animal life. Some say that she had killed goats. . . .

The fourth kind treats of riches and poverty, and the like. Whoever distributes alms at auspicious times, as during eclipses of the moon and sun, will become rich and bountiful (in his next existence). Whoso at these times, visits any place of pilgrimage . . . and there dies, will possess great wealth, but will be avaricious and of a surly disposition. Whosoever when hungry and with food before him, hears the supplication of a poor man and bestows it all upon him, will be rich and liberal. But whosoever has been deprived of these three opportunities, will be empty-handed and poor in his present life.

Nanak

ADI-GRANTH

Emperor Akbar was not the only person in sixteenth-century India who dreamed of combining elements of Hinduism and Islam into a new religious faith. Such a proc-

---

9. An "unclean" object.

10. The personification of solar and cosmic energy underlying creation.

ess was going on during his reign and resulted in the founding of Sikhism, a religion that now has approximately 9 million followers, mostly in the northwest Indian state of East Punjab. The founder of Sikhism and its first guru, or teacher, was Nanak, who lived from 1469 to 1539. Born into a Hindu family in modern Pakistan, as a young man Nanak sought out the teaching of Muslim and Hindu mystics and holy men. At the age of thirty, he began to wander through India searching for disciples who would accept his message of love and reconciliation between Hindus and Muslims. He taught that external religious acts such as making the pilgrimage to Mecca or bathing in the sacred Ganges River are worthless before God unless inward sincerity and true morality accompany them. As a strict and uncompromising monotheist, he declared that love of God alone suffices to free anyone of any caste from the law of Karma, bringing an end to reincarnation and resulting in absorption into the One.

The following poems come from the holy book of Sikhism, known as the *Adi-Granth,* or *Granth Sahid.* Compiled by Arjan (1563–1606), the fifth guru, it consists mostly of hymns and poetry composed by Nanak and other early gurus. It attained its final form in 1705–1706, when the tenth and last guru, Gobind Singh (1666–1708) added a number of hymns and declared that from then on the *Adi-Granth* itself, not any individual, was Sikhism's one true guru. The following excerpts are poems by Nanak.

Questions
for Analysis

1. What Muslim elements can be found in Nanak's message? What Hindu elements? What Hindu and Muslim practices does he reject?
2. Which religion seems to have had the stronger impact on Nanak's religious visions?
3. Once Sikhism was established Hindu and Muslim authorities persecuted it. Why would the Sikhs' religion constitute such a serious challenge to both Muslim and Hindu societies?
4. What parallels can you discover between Nanak's message and Martin Luther's? What differences?

*T*here is one God,
Eternal Truth is His Name;
Maker of all things,
Fearing nothing and at enmity with
    nothing,
Timeless is His Image;
Not begotten, being of His own Being:

By the grace of the Guru, made known to
    men.

. . .

It is not through thought that He is to be
    comprehended

Though we strive to grasp Him a
    hundred thousand times;
Nor by outer silence and long deep
    meditation
Can the inner silence be reached;
Nor is man's hunger for God appeasable
By piling up world-loads of wealth.
All the innumerable devices of worldly
    wisdom
Leave a man disappointed; not one
    avails.

How then shall we know the Truth?
How shall we rend the veils of untruth
    away?
Abide thou by His Will, and make thine
    own,
His will, O Nanak, that is written in thy
    heart.

.   .   .

He cannot be installed like an idol,
Nor can man shape His likeness.
He made Himself and maintains Himself
On His heights unstained for ever;
Honored are they in His shrine
Who meditate upon Him.

.   .   .

Those who have inner belief in the
    Name,
Always achieve their own liberation,
Their kith and kin are also saved.
Guided by the light of the Guru
The disciple steers safe himself,
And many more he saves;
Those enriched with inner belief
Do not wander begging.

Such is the power of His stainless Name,
He who truly believes in it, knows it.

.   .   .

There is no counting a men's prayers,
There is no counting their ways of
    adoration.
Thy lovers, O Lord, are numberless;
Numberless those who read aloud from
    the Vedas;[1]
Numberless those Yogis[2] who are
    detached from the world;

Numberless are Thy Saints
    contemplating,
Thy virtues and Thy wisdom;
Numberless are the benevolent, the
    lovers of their kind.

Numberless Thy heroes and martyrs[3]
Facing the steel of their enemies;
Numberless those who in silence
Fix their deepest thoughts upon Thee;

.   .   .

Pilgrimages, penances, compassion and
    almsgiving
Bring a little merit, the size of sesame
    seed.
But he who hears and believes and loves
    the Name
Shall bathe and be made clean
In a place of pilgrimage within him.

.   .   .

When in time, in what age, in what day
    of the month or week

---

1. The sacred books of the Aryans and basic Hindu texts.

2. Persons with occult powers achieved through discipline of the body.

3. Muslim warriors.

In what season and in what month did'st
   Thou create the world?
The Pundits[4] do not know or they would
   have written it in the Puranas;[5]
The Qazis[6] do not know, or they would
   have recorded it in the Koran;[7]
Nor do the Yogis know the moment of
   the day,
Nor the day of the month or the week,
   nor the month nor the season.
Only God Who made the world knows
   when He made it.

. . .

The Vedas proclaim Him,
So do the readers of the Puranas;
The learned speak of Him in many
   discourses;
Brahma and Indra[8] speak of Him,
Sivas[9] speak of Him, Siddhas[10] speak of
   Him,
The Buddhas[11] He has created, proclaim
   Him.

. . .

Maya, the mythical goddess,[12]
Sprang from the One, and her womb
   brought forth
Three acceptable disciples of the One:
Brahma, Visnu and Siva.
Brahma, it is said bodies forth the world,
Visnu it is who sustains it;

Siva the destroyer who absorbs,
He controls death and judgment.

God makes them to work as He wills,
He sees them ever, they see Him not:
That of all is the greatest wonder.

. . .

I have described the realm of *dharma*,
Now I shall describe the realm of
   Knowledge;

How many are the winds, the fires, the
   waters,
How many are the Krishnas[13] and Sivas,
How many are the Brahmas fashioning
   the worlds,
Of many kinds and shapes and colors;
How many worlds, like our own there
   are,
Where action produces the consequences.

. . . How many adepts, Buddhas and
   Yogis are there,
How many goddesses and how many
   images of the goddesses;
How many gods and demons and how
   many sages;

How many hidden jewels in how many
   oceans,
How many the sources of life;
How many the modes and diversities of
   speech,

---

    4. Brahmans learned in Hindu religion and
law.

    5. A collection of popular Hindu books that
contain stories of the gods.

    6. Muslim judges.

    7. The Qur'an.

    8. The name of the war-god of the Aryans
and the embodiment of strength, courage, and
leadership; Indra figures prominently in the
Vedas.

    9. Shiva, the god of destruction.

    10. A class of demigods.

    11. Those who have been enlightened.

    12. A Hindu goddess who symbolizes mate-
rial creation, because matter is the veil that covers the reality of the Spirit.

    13. The most popular of Vishnu's incar-
nations.

How many are the kings, the rulers and
the guides of men;
How many the devoted there are, who
pursue this divine knowledge,
His worshipers are numberless, saith
Nanak.

Confucianism in China and Japan

No person in history has influenced the lives of more human beings than the great Chinese philosopher Confucius, the Latinized name of K'ung fu-tzu. Born in 551 B.C., Confucius was deeply distressed by the political chaos into which China had fallen. He concluded that the troubles were caused by a lack of sense of proper conduct by society's members, especially its leaders. He reasoned that if leaders were virtuous, the people would learn from them and follow their example. When every-one behaved properly, society would achieve order and stability.

Proper conduct for Confucius meant actions that conformed to the standards of a glorified past, when all society was harmoniously structured along lines of authority and courtesy that paralleled those of the family. Each individual had a proper role in society and was expected to fulfill it without question. As Confucius succinctly stated, "Let the ruler be a ruler and the subject a subject; let the father be a father and the son a son." Because the wisdom and practices of ancient sages were so central to his teaching, it followed that his disciples could become virtuous only by carefully studying the literature, history, and rituals of the past. Education in tradi-tional values and behavior was the pathway to gentility, the quality of knowing what was proper and good and acting accordingly.

Although Confucius's philosophy competed with many other schools of thought in his own time, during the Han Dynasty (206 B.C.– A.D. 220) it was established as the officially sanctioned program of studies for anyone who wished to serve as an official in the imperial Chinese government. Mastery of the Confucian classics and their many commentaries was the only path to success in the civil service examina-tions, by which China filled its imperial administration. China became a country administered by a literary elite, all devoted to the principles and practices of Confucius.

During the sixteenth and seventeenth centuries, in China and elsewhere, interpre-tation of Confucianism depended for the most part on the work of scholars who had flourished during the Song Dynasty (960–1279). These scholars are referred to as Neo-Confucianists, because they brought new energy, influence, and scholarly rigor to Confucianism after several centuries in which its stature had declined. The great-est of the Neo-Confucianists was Chu Hsi (1130–1200), who presided over a huge project of historical research and wrote detailed commentaries on most of the Con-fucian classics. His commentaries came to be viewed as the orthodox version of Confucianism and served as the official interpretation for China's civil service examinations from the fourteenth century to 1905, when the examinations were abolished.

Confucianism's influence was not limited to China. Although it had to compete with Buddhism and with other indigenous religious practices, Confucianism deeply affected the ethics, political theory, legal precepts, and educational practices of Korea, Vietnam, and Japan.

Matteo Ricci

JOURNALS

As noted in Chapter 1, the *Journals* of the Jesuit missionary Matteo Ricci (1552–1610) provide invaluable insight into Chinese life and culture in the late sixteenth and early seventeenth centuries. The Chinese system of civil service examinations intrigued Ricci, and early in his diary he wrote down a thorough description of the way they were administered. Excerpts from his description follow.

Questions for Analysis

1. What was the primary objective of education in Ming China?
2. What values did this society appear to hold in highest regard?
3. Ming China has been characterized as a self-satisfied society. Is there any strong evidence in Ricci's *Journal* to support that judgment?
4. In 1644 the Ming Dynasty collapsed in the face of domestic rebellions and invaders from Manchuria seized the imperial throne, establishing the Ch'ing Dynasty (1644–1912). Can you discover in this account any factors that may have contributed to that sequence of events?

*T*he most renowned of all Chinese philosophers was named Confucius. This great and learned man was born five hundred and fifty-one years before the beginning of the Christian era, lived more than seventy years, and spurred on his people to the pursuit of virtue not less by his own example than by his writings and conferences. His self-mastery and abstemious ways of life have led his countrymen to assert that he surpassed in holiness all those who in times past, in the various parts of the world, were consid-

ered to have excelled in virtue. Indeed, if we critically examine his actions and sayings as they are recorded in history, we shall be forced to admit that he was the equal of the pagan philosophers and superior to most of them. He is held in such high esteem by the learned Chinese that they do not dare to call into question any pronouncement of his and are ready to give full recognition to an oath sworn in his name, as in that of a common master. . . .

It is evident to everyone here that no

one will labor to attain proficiency in mathematics or in medicine who has any hope of becoming prominent in the field of philosophy. The result is that scarcely anyone devotes himself to these studies, unless he is deterred from the pursuit of what are considered to be the higher studies, either by reason of family affairs or by mediocrity of talent. The study of mathematics and that of medicine are held in low esteem, because they are not fostered by honors as is the study of philosophy, to which students are attracted by the hope of the glory and the rewards attached to it. This may be readily seen in the interest taken in the study of moral philosophy. The man who is promoted to the higher degrees in this field, prides himself on the fact that he has in truth attained to the pinnacle of Chinese happiness.

I think it will be as interesting as it is new to the reader to treat somewhat more fully of this phase of their studies. Confucius . . . compiled four volumes of the works of more ancient philosophers and wrote five books of his own.[1] These five he entitled "The Doctrines," and they contain the ethical principles of right living, precepts governing the conduct of political life, customs, and examples of the ancients, their rites and sacrifices, and even samples of their poetry and other subjects of this nature. Besides these five books there is another one composed of the precepts of the great philosopher and of his disciples and compiled without particular arrangement.[2] These are chiefly directions for proper moral proceedings, in the light of human reason, with a view to virtuous conduct on the part of the individual, of the family and of the kingdom in general. This volume, being a summary in excerpts from the four books mentioned, is called the Tetrabiblion. The nine books of Confucius, making up the most ancient of Chinese libraries, of which all others are a development . . . present a collection of moral precepts for the future good and development of the kingdom.[3]

There is a law in the land, handed down from ancient kings and confirmed by the customs of centuries, stating that he who wishes to be learned, and to be known as such, must draw his fundamental doctrine from these same books. In addition to this it is not sufficient for him to follow the general sense of the text, but what is far more difficult, he must be able to write aptly and exactly of every particular doctrine contained in these books. To this end he must commit the entire Tetrabiblion to memory, so as to be a recognized authority thereon. . . .

In the field of philosophy there are three degrees, conferred upon those who pass

---

1. The nine books central to Confucianism are divided into the Five Classics and the Four Books. The Classics consist of the *I-Ching*, or *Classic of Changes*, a work of divination; the *Classic of Writings*, a disjointed collection of statements attributed to China's earliest kings and their ministers; the *Classic of Songs*, a collection of China's earliest poetry; the *Spring and Autumn Annals*, a chronicle of events covering from 722 to 481 B.C.; and the *Classics of Rituals*, three books of descriptions of supposedly early forms of governmental organization and human conduct. Although all five classics are ascribed to Confucius, his role in their creation was probably negligible. The Four Books are the *Analects*, or *Collected Sayings*, of Confucius; the *Meng-tzu*, or Book of Mencius; and two short essays, *The Great Learning* and *The Doctrine of the Mean*. All were composed well after Confucius's time, and even the *Analects*, which includes aphorisms that Confucius undoubtedly did utter, contains a good deal of much later material.

2. Apparently Ricci means the *Analects*.

3. As noted in Chapter 1, Ricci refers to China as a "kingdom," even though it was ruled by an emperor.

the written examinations assigned for each degree. The first degree is awarded in the larger cities and in a public academy, by some prominent scholar, appointed by the emperor for that purpose. . . . [Those who pass the examination for the first degree] . . . are . . . then known as academic bachelors,[4] a distinguished class representing the advanced citizenry of their particular town, and their company is cultivated by all who hope to attain to the same dignity. . . . In their home cities they enjoy a great many civil privileges and are looked upon as inferior to none, save the chancellor and the four city prefects. . . .

The second degree of the Chinese literati[5] . . . may be compared to our licentiate. This degree is conferred with considerable solemnity in each metropolitan province but only every third year. . . .

The same three days are set aside for this examination throughout the kingdom, namely — the ninth, the twelfth, and fifteenth of the eighth moon. Those taking part in the examinations are permitted to write from dawn to sunset, behind locked doors, and they are served with light meals, prepared the day before at public expense. When the candidate bachelors are admitted to the palace, they are carefully searched to see that they have no book or written matter in their possession. Entering the examination, they are allowed to have several brushes for writing, the writer's palette, and also ink and paper. Their clothes and even the brushes and palettes are carefully examined lest they should contain anything deceitful, and if fraud of any kind is discovered they are not only excluded from the examination but are severely punished as well. . . .

The first day of examination consists of the candidates writing essays on seven selected passages from the nine Confucian texts.

These seven written papers must show evidence not only of proper use of words but also of a proper appreciation of the ideas contained in the doctrines and a strict observance of the rules of Chinese rhetoric. No dissertation should exceed five hundred characters, corresponding to as many words in our usage.

On the second day of examination, after two days of rest, and behind closed doors as formerly, topics are offered for examination relative to things that have happened in the past, to the annals of the ancients, and to events which may be expected to happen in the near future. . . .

On the third day three difficulties or arguments are offered for examination, which are drawn from possibilities that might arise in planning the direction of public administration. Papers are written in triple copy, and each one explains the judgment he wishes to offer in settlement of the argument he has chosen to discuss. . . .

The degree of licentiate is far superior to that of bachelor and carries with it more dignity and more notable privileges. He who holds a licentiate degree is supposed to continue his studies and to go on to the doctorate, and if he declines to do so he is ineligible for even an inferior public office.

When the examinations are over and the ceremonies described at an end, the royal examiners publish a book which is distributed throughout the whole empire, containing the results of the examinations,

---

4. Ricci is applying terms from European universities to Chinese practices. In Europe a bachelor's degree is the lowest degree in any field of study. Later Ricci refers to other more advanced degrees, the licentiate and the doctorate.

5. A Latin term meaning those well versed in "letters," that is, literature; learned ones.

the names of the new licentiates, and the outstanding manuscripts on the various subjects treated in the examinations. . . .

The third literary degree among the Chinese is . . . equivalent to our doctorate. This degree is also conferred every third year but only in the province of Pekin.[6] The year for doctorate is always the one next following that for licentiate. No more than three hundred degrees are conferred at a time, for the entire country. Those holding licentiate degrees from any province are free to take this examination as often as they wish.

When this examination is over, the results are announced in the same manner and in the same place as already described. The only added feature is that the new doctors all adjourn to the royal palace and here, in presence of the Chief Magistrates of the court and at times of the Emperor also, they write a treatise on a given subject. The results of this contest determine to which of the three grades of the magistracy the doctors will be assigned. This is a celebrated examination, and it consists entirely of a rather brief written dissertation. . . .

The new doctors immediately adorn their special garb and particular hat and leggings, with the other insignia of the magistrate, and are promoted to the richer and more elevated benefices of the magistracy. From that time on they belong to a social order superseding that of the licentiates, and are counted among the ranking citizens of the kingdom. It is difficult for a stranger to appreciate how superior their rank is to that of their colleagues of the day before, who always cede them the place of honor and greet them with the most flattering titles and courtesy. . . .

Another remarkable fact and quite worthy of note as marking a difference from the West, is that the entire kingdom is administered by the Order of the Learned, commonly known as The Philosophers. The responsibility for orderly management of the entire realm is wholly and completely committed to their charge and care. The army, both officers and soldiers, hold them in high respect and show them the promptest obedience and deference, and not infrequently the military are disciplined by them as a schoolboy might be punished by his master. Policies of war are formulated and military questions are decided by the Philosophers only, and their advice and counsel has more weight with the King than that of the military leaders. In fact very few of these, and only on rare occasions, are admitted to war consultations. Hence it follows that those who aspire to be cultured frown upon war and would prefer the lowest rank in the philosophical order to the highest in the military, realizing that the Philosophers far excel military leaders in the good will and the respect of the people and in opportunities of acquiring wealth. What is still more surprising to strangers is that these same Philosophers, as they are called, with respect to nobility of sentiment and in contempt of danger and death, where fidelity to King and country is concerned, surpass even those whose particular profession is the defense of the fatherland. Perhaps this sentiment has its origin in the fact that the mind of man is ennobled by the study of letters. Or again, it may have developed from the fact that from the beginning and foundation of this empire the study of letters was always more acceptable to the people than the profession of arms, as being more suitable to a people who had little or no interest in the extension of the empire.

6. Peking (modern Beijing), the seat of the emperor.

Yamazaki Ansai

PREFACE TO THE COLLECTED COMMENTARIES ON CHU HSI'S REGULATIONS FOR THE WHITE DEER SCHOOL

Yamazaki Ansai (1619–1682) was one of Confucianism's most outstanding proponents in seventeenth-century Japan. After abandoning his parents' Buddhism in his twenties, he dedicated himself to the propagation of the philosophy of the Chinese Neo-Confucian Chu Hsi, many of whose works he edited and published. Yamazaki also founded schools in Kyoto and Edo (modern Tokyo), where he taught Confucianism to as many as 6,000 students.

The early Tokugawa rulers of Japan strongly supported the work of Confucian scholars such as Yamazaki because they believed that widespread acceptance of Confucianism would encourage social order and cohesiveness among their subjects. The excerpt that follows is from the preface he wrote to an edition of one of Chu Hsi's regulations for the White Deer School, where a generation of twelfth-century Chinese students gained instruction in the maxims of Neo-Confucianism.

Questions for Analysis

1. The Chinese and Japanese Neo-Confucian systems traced their origins to Chu Hsi and Confucius, and each aimed at developing educated rulers and administrators. Yet there are some striking differences between the two systems. How does Yamazaki's preface illustrate some of these differences and similarities?
2. What elements of Yamazaki's Neo-Confucian program are aimed at preserving order and stability in society?
3. What elements may have potentially prepared Japan for playing, at a later date, a major role in world affairs?

The philosopher Chu, styled Hui-an[1] was conspicuously endowed with intellectual leadership. Following in the line of (the Sung philosophers) Chou Tun-i and the Ch'eng brothers, he advanced the cause of Confucianism in both elementary education and higher education. For the guidance of his students he established these regulations, but they failed to gain wide acceptance in his own time because of opposition from vile quarters. . . .

It would seem to me that the aim of education, elementary and advanced, is to clarify human relationships. In the elementary program of education the various human relationships are made clear, the

---

1. Chu Hsi.

essence of this education in human relationships being devotion to (or respect for) persons. The "investigation of things" in advanced studies (as set forth in the *Great Learning*)[2] simply carries to its ultimate conclusion what has already been learned from elementary instruction. . . .

Chu Hsi's school regulations list the Five Human Relationships as the curriculum, following an order of presentation which complements the curriculum of advanced education (as found in the *Great Learning*). Studying, questioning, deliberating and analyzing — these four correspond to the "investigation of things" and "extension of knowledge" in advanced education. The article dealing with conscientious action goes with the "cultivation of one's person." From the emperor to the common people, the cultivation of one's person is essential, including both "making the thoughts sincere" and "rectifying the mind." The "managing of affairs" and "social intercourse'" (in Chu's Regulations) refer to "regulating the family," "governing the state" and "establishing peace" (in the *Great Learning*). These Regulations thus contain everything, and they should be used for instruction together with the *Book of Elementary Instruction* and the *Book of Advanced Education* (*Great Learning*). But so far they have gone almost unnoticed among the items in Chu's collected works, scarcely attracting any attention from scholars. I have taken the liberty, however, of bringing them out into the light of day by mounting and hanging them in my studio for constant reference and reflection. More recently I have found a detailed discussion of these regulations in *Some Reflections of Mine* by the Korean scholar Yi T'oege. It convinced me more than anything else that

these Regulations are the true guide to education. . . .

[*Signed*] Yamazaki Ansai
Keian 3 [1650]: Twelfth Month, 9th Day

REGULATIONS FOR THE SCHOOL OF THE WHITE DEER CAVE

(*The Five Regulations*)

Between parent and child there is intimacy.

Between lord and minister there is duty.

Between husband and wife there is differentiation.

Between elder and junior there is precedence.

Between friend and friend there is fidelity.

These five articles of teaching are what (the sage-kings) Yao and Shun commanded Ch'i, the Minister of Education, solemnly to promulgate as the five subjects of teaching. All that the student should study is contained in these five regulations, but in studying them he should follow five steps, as given below:

Study widely.
Question thoroughly.
Deliberate carefully.
Analyze clearly.
Act conscientiously. . . .

In speech be loyal and true; in action be conscientious and reverent. Subdue ire and stifle passion. Change yourself for the better; do not hesitate to correct your errors. These things are essential to personal culture.

Do not do to others what you do not care for yourself. When action fails to

---

2. *Great Learning* was one of the four basic Neo-Confucian books; it was written during the Han Dynasty (202 B.C.–A.D.220).

get results, seek the reason for failure in yourself. These are important in social intercourse.

The aim of teaching and guidance given by ancient sages and scholars, it seems to me, is nothing more than to set forth moral principles, in order, first, to culti-vate them in one's own person, and then to extend them to others. Simply to accumulate knowledge and learn to write well in order to gain fame and a well-paid position, is far from being the true function of education. Nevertheless that is what most men pursue learning for today.

Sun Worship and Divine Royalty in Peru and West Africa

The phenomena of adoration of the sun as the source of all life and service to a divine ruler who is perceived as the incarnation of that sun deity go back to the world's first civilizations and are common to many societies, most notably that of ancient Egypt. There is no reason to believe that the Egyptians ever exported sun worship and divine royalty to the Americas or the coast of West Africa. This form of religious expression seems to have risen independently in many widely scattered regions.

The following selections illustrate the ways sun worship and the cult of divine monarchy were intimately tied together in the Peruvian kingdom of the Incas and the African kingdom of Benin. These peoples' religious attitudes by no means dominated all sub-Saharan Africa or the Americas, but, with many variations, such beliefs were widespread.

Garcilaso de la Vega

ROYAL COMMENTARIES ON THE INCAS

Garcilaso de la Vega (1539–1616) was the son of a Spanish noble who had been one of the original conquerors of Peru and an Inca princess. His mother, Chimpa Ocllo, was baptized into the Catholic Church, but many of her royal relatives remained faithful to the old religion of the sun. De la Vega received a solid education in the European classics and learned the history and ways of his Inca ancestors from the tales his mother's relatives told him. In 1566 de la Vega went to Spain, where he became a captain in the army of King Philip II. Upon retiring from active service, he devoted himself to literary and historical pursuits. His greatest enterprise, *Royal Commentaries on the Incas*, was a detailed account of the civilization of the Incas and their conquest by the Spanish. It relied not only on stories he had learned from his relatives but on his own memories of Inca ceremonies, the notes of missionaries, and the research of a number of contemporary Spanish historians. Completed in 1609, it is the most complete and authoritative early history of Inca civilization.

Questions for Analysis

1. What religious meaning does each of the following elements of the festival have: (a) the preparatory fast, (b) *Canca* cakes, (c) the drinking of beverage, (d) the special roles played by the Inca and his relatives in this festival, (e) the sacrifice of a black lamb and the reading of its internal organs, (f) the lighting of the new fire, and (g) the festive meal?
2. On the basis of your analysis of each of these rites, how would you characterize this religion? Does it appear to have monotheistic tendencies? Was it likely to have been an ethical religion?

The word *Raymi* is equivalent to our word Easter. Among the four festivals which the Inca kings celebrated . . . the most solemn was that in honor of the Sun, during the month of June. It was called the "Solemn Feast of the Sun" . . . , and look place in the June solstice.

They celebrated this festival of the Sun in acknowledgment that they held and adored Him as the sole and universal God who, by his light and power, creates and sustains all things on earth; and that He was the natural father of first Inca[1] Manco Ccapac and of his wife Mama[2] Ocllo Huaco, and of all their descendants, who were sent to this earth for the benefit of all people. For these reasons, as they themselves say, this was their most solemn feast. . . .

All prepared themselves for the *Raymi* of the Sun by a rigorous fast; for, in three days they ate nothing but a little unripe maize, and a few herbs, with plain water. During this time no fire was lighted throughout the city, and all men abstained from sleeping with their wives.

After the fast, in the evening before the festival, the Inca sacrificial Priests prepared the sheep and lambs for sacrifice, and got ready the other offerings of food and drink that were to be offered to the Sun. All these offerings had been provided by the people who came to the feast. . . .

The women of the Sun[3] were engaged, during the night, in preparing an immense quantity of maize pudding called *Canca*. This was made up into small round cakes, about the size of an apple. . . .

The flour for this bread, especially for what was intended for the Inca and those of the blood royal, was ground by the cho-

---

1. Inca means "sovereign lord," and in its strictest sense should be used only to refer to this civilization's god-kings. De la Vega at times uses the term loosely to refer to anyone who shared royal blood, himself included. The tribe from which the Incas came was the Quechua.

2. Mother. The queen was the divine mother of her people. As eldest sister and wife of the Inca, she was *Mama-quilla*, or mother moon.

3. Virgins of royal blood who spent their lives in perpetual seclusion, serving the Sun, to whom they were symbolically married.

sen virgins of the Sun, who cooked all the other food for this feast; that it might appear to be given rather by the Sun to his children than by his sons to him; and it was therefore prepared by the virgins, as women of the Sun. . . .

The necessary preparations having been made, the Inca came forth at dawn, on the day of the festival, accompanied by all his relations marching according to their age and dignity. They proceeded to the great square. . . . Here they waited for sunrise, all of them being barefooted, and all watching the east with great attention. As soon as the sun appeared, they all bent down, resting on their elbows (which, among these Indians, is the same as going down on the knees), with the arms apart and the hands raised. Thus they worshiped, and kissed the air . . . and they adored with much fervor and devotion, looking upon the Sun as their god and natural father. . . .

Presently the King rose to his feet, the rest being still prostrate, and took two great cups of gold, full of the beverage that they drink. He performed this ceremony as the first-born, in the name of his father, the Sun, and, with the cup in his right hand, invited all his relations to drink. . . .

Having given the invitation to drink, the Inca emptied the vase in his right hand, which was dedicated to the Sun, into a jar of gold, whence the liquor flowed down a stone conduit of very beautiful masonry from the great square to the temple of the Sun, thus being looked upon as drunk by the Deity. . . .

———————— ❧ ————————

The royal procession then entered the temple of the sun.

———————— ❧ ————————

The Inca offered to the Sun the golden vases with which he had performed the ceremony, and the other members of his family gave their cups to the Inca priests, who were set apart for that office; for persons who were not priests, even if they were of the royal blood, were not allowed to perform the priestly office. . . .

As soon as the offerings were made . . . the priests came out with many lambs, ewes, and rams of all colors, for the native sheep of that country are of different colors, like the horses in Spain. All this flock was the property of the Sun. They took a black lamb, for among the Indians this color was preferred for the sacrifices, as more sacred. For they said that a black beast was black all over, while a white one, though its body might be white, always had a black nose, which was a defect, and caused it to be less perfect than a black beast. For this reason also, the Kings generally dressed in black. . . .

This first sacrifice of a black lamb was made to predict the omens of the festival. For they almost always sacrificed a lamb before undertaking any act either of peace or war, in order to see, by examining the heart and lungs, whether it was acceptable to the Sun, that is to say, whether it would be successful or the reverse. In order to seek an omen to tell them whether a harvest would be good; for some crops they used a lamb, for others a ram, for others a sterile ewe; but they never killed a fruitful sheep even to eat, until it was past bearing.

They took the lamb or sheep, and placed it with the head towards the east. They did not tie its feet, but three or four Indians held it, and it was cut open on the left side while still alive. They then forced their hands in, and pulled out the heart with the lungs and gullet up to the mouth, and the whole had to be taken out entire, without being cut. . . .

If the sacrifice of the lamb did not furnish good auguries, they made another sacrifice of a sheep, and if this was also unpropitious they offered up another. But, even if the third sacrifice was unlucky, they did not desist from celebrating the festival, though they did so with inward sorrow and misgiving, believing that their father, the Sun, was enraged against them for some fault or negligence that they must have unintentionally committed against his service. . . .

After the sacrifice of the lamb, they brought a great quantity of lambs and sheep for a general sacrifice, and they did not cut these open while they were alive, but beheaded them first. The blood and hearts of all these, as well as of the first lamb, were preserved and offered to the Sun, and the bodies were burnt until they were converted to ashes.

It was necessary that the fire for the sacrifice should be new, and given by the hand of the Sun, as they expressed it. For this purpose they took a large bracelet. . . . This was held by the high priest. It was larger than usual, and had on it a highly polished concave plate, about the diameter of an orange. They put this towards the Sun, at an angle, so that the reflected rays might concentrate on one point, where they had placed a little cotton wool well pulled out, for they did not know how to make tinder; but the cotton was soon lighted in the natural way. With this fire, thus obtained from the hands of the Sun, they consumed the sacrifice, and roasted all the meat on that day. Portions of the fire were then conveyed to the temple of the Sun, and to the convent of virgins, where they were kept in all the year, and it was an evil omen if they were allowed to go out.

A Portuguese Pilot

VOYAGE FROM LISBON TO THE ISLAND OF SÃO TOMÉ

De la Vega relates that upon the death of an Inca or his queen, the body was embalmed, seated on a golden throne, and hidden away, surrounded by treasure, as befit a deity. The following excerpt, taken from the anonymous account of a Portuguese pilot writing around 1540, describes the burial rites accorded the divine kings of Benin, one of the major states along the Guinea coast in Africa.

Questions
for Analysis

1. What are the reasons for the apparent eagerness of the late king's favorites to commit suicide?
2. What possible political benefits might the new king gain from the ceremonies described in this document?
3. Do these ceremonies indicate a belief in a life after death?

*T*o understand the negro traffic, one must know that over all the African coast facing west there are various countries and provinces, such as Guinea, the coast of Melegete, the kingdom of Benin, the kingdom of Manicõgo, six degrees from the equator and towards the south pole. There are many tribes and negro kings here, and also communities which are partly Muslim and partly heathen. These are constantly making war among themselves. The kings are worshipped by their subjects, who believe that they come from heaven, and speak of them always with great reverence, at a distance and on bended knees. Great ceremony surrounds them, and many of these kings never allow themselves to be seen eating, so as not to destroy the belief of their subjects that they can live without food. They worship the sun, and believe that spirits are immortal, and that after death they go to the sun. Among others, there is in the kingdom of Benin an ancient custom, observed to the present day, that when the king dies, the people all assemble in a large field, in the centre of which is a very deep well, wider at the bottom than at the mouth. They cast the body of the dead king into this well, and all his friends and servants gather round, and those who are judged to have been most dear to and favored by the king (this includes not a few, as all are anxious for the honor) voluntarily go down to keep him company. When they have done so, the people place a great stone over the mouth of the well, and remain by it day and night. On the second day, a few deputies remove the stone, and ask those below what they know, and if any of them have already gone to serve the king; and the reply is, No. On the third day, the same question is asked; and some-one then replies that so-and-so, mentioning a name, has been the first to go, and so-and-so the second. It is considered highly praiseworthy to be the first, and he is spoken of with the greatest admiration by all the people, and considered happy and blessed. After four or five days all these unfortunate people die. When this is apparent to those above, since none reply to their questions, they inform their new king; who causes a great fire to be lit near the well, where numerous animals are roasted. These are given to the people to eat, and he with great ceremony is declared to be the true king, and takes the oath to govern well.

CHAPTER

3

The Power of Rulers; the Duty of Subjects

*H*owever much they differed in social status, language, religious beliefs, and vocations, all human beings in the sixteenth and seventeenth centuries shared one common experience: they all were part of some sort of political order. In China, the Middle East, Russia, and parts of India, Africa, and the Americas, the political order took the form of large empires in which numerous officials carried out the policies of more or less authoritarian rulers. In Europe, political organization was much more diverse and decentralized; here existed emerging nation-states, republics, independent cities, and territories ruled by Roman Catholic churchmen, including the pope. In Australia and some regions of the Americas and Africa, political organization centered around the tribe, a relatively small group of as few as 100 individuals who had a common lineage and were ruled by a chief.

Despite their diversity, the thousands of political regimes and their millions of subjects faced common issues that were as old as government itself. On what basis, for example, could political power be justified? Did it rest on divine sanction, custom, consent of the subjects, or naked force? Under what circumstances, if any, could subjects disobey a ruler? What were the criteria for becoming a government official? What voice, if any, should subjects have in shaping policy? To what extent should ethical principles rather than expediency determine government policy? Who pays for government?

The selections included in this chapter illustrate how various peoples answered these questions during the sixteenth and seventeenth centuries. Although they lived hundreds of years ago, they faced political issues no different from those challenging humankind today.

Authority and Liberty in Early Modern Europe

In the sixteenth and seventeenth centuries, it was unclear if Europe's political future lay in the development of relatively large, centralized, and coherent states or if, as actually happened in Germany and Italy, political authority would become diffuse and localized. Among some groups and in some regions, support grew for what is known as absolutist monarchy, a type of government in which a hereditary monarch commanded unquestioned obedience and controlled legislation, the military, the judicial system, and administration. Many powerful nobles opposed these absolutist tendencies because they correctly saw strong monarchy as a threat to their local authority and independence. In western Europe the religious divisions created by the Protestant Reformation further complicated the situation. Did Protestants under a Catholic monarch or Catholics under a Protestant ruler have the right to resist their king, convinced as each side was, that theirs and theirs alone was the one true faith? Such issues were debated throughout Europe, but with special intensity in sixteenth-century France, a country deeply divided by religion and with traditions of both strong monarchy and a proud and assertive nobility.

Jean Bodin

SIX BOOKS OF THE COMMONWEALTH

One of the leading intellectuals of sixteenth-century France, Jean Bodin was born in 1529 or 1530, the son of a well-to-do master tailor. He studied philosophy, rhetoric, history, Latin, and Greek at the University of Paris and later earned a law degree from the University of Toulouse. From the 1560s until his death in 1596, he practiced law, wrote books on history, coinage, witchcraft, and politics, and held a number of government posts, including counselor for the Duke of Alençon, the brother of King Charles IX.

His political writings reflect the despair he felt over his country's devastation during the French Wars of Religion (1562–1593). Bodin, a Catholic who sympathized with certain Protestant ideas, was convinced that only the establishment of a strong monarchy and the acceptance of religious toleration could save France from disintegration. He expressed these views in his *Six Books of the Commonwealth*, published in 1576. Written in French rather than the scholarly Latin language, he hoped to convince France's political leaders, clergy, and educated laypersons that France's salvation lay in absolutism. His book was among the earliest statements of absolutist theory, and its discussion of sovereignty made an important contribution to the vocabulary of political philosophy.

Questions
for Analysis

1. According to Bodin, what are the major characteristics of sovereignty?
2. What limitations are there to the sovereign's power?
3. What is the origin of the power of kings?
4. How does Bodin's approach to the problems of political theory differ from that of Machiavelli in *The Prince* (Chapter 2)?

CONCERNING SOVEREIGNTY

Sovereignty is that absolute and perpetual power vested in a commonwealth which in Latin is termed *majestas* . . . The term needs careful definition, because although it is the distinguishing mark of a commonwealth, and an understanding of its nature fundamental to any treatment of politics, no jurist or political philosopher has in fact attempted to define it. . . .

I have described it as *perpetual* because one can give absolute power to a person or group of persons for a period of time, but that time expired they become subjects once more. Therefore even while they enjoy power, they cannot properly be regarded as sovereign rulers, but only as the lieutenants and agents of the sovereign ruler, till the moment comes when it pleases the prince or the people to revoke the gift. The true sovereign remains always seized of his power. . . .

Let us now turn to the other term of our definition and consider the force of the word *absolute*. The people or the magnates of a commonwealth can bestow simply and unconditionally upon someone of their choice a sovereign and perpetual power to dispose of their property and persons, to govern the state as he thinks fit, and to order the succession in the same way that any proprietor[1] . . . can freely and unconditionally make a gift of his property to another. Such a form of gift, not being qualified in any way is the only true gift, being at once unconditional and irrevocable. Gifts burdened with obligations and hedged with conditions are not true gifts. Similarly sovereign power given to a prince charged with conditions is neither properly sovereign, nor absolute, unless the conditions of appointment are only such as are inherent in the laws of God and of nature. . . .

If we insist however that absolute power means exemption from all law whatsoever, there is no prince in the world who can be regarded as sovereign, since all the princes of the earth are subject to the laws of God and of nature, and even to certain human laws common to all nations. . . .

It is the distinguishing mark of the sovereign that he cannot in any way be subject to the commands of another, for it is he who makes law for the subject, abrogates law already made, and amends obsolete law. No one who is subject either to the law or to some other person can do this. That is why it is laid down in the civil law that the prince is above the law, for the word *law* in Latin implies the command of him who is invested with sovereign power. . . .

As for laws relating to the subject,

---

1. Property owner.

whether general or particular, which do not involve any question of the constitution, it has always been usual only to change them with the concurrence of the three estates, either assembled in the States-General[2] of the whole of France, or in each bailliwick[3] separately. Not that the king is bound to take their advice, or debarred from acting in a way quite contrary to what they wish, if his acts are based on justice and natural reason. . . . Only that which it pleases the prince to assent to or dissent from, to command or to forbid, has the force of law and is embodied in his edict or ordinance. . . .

THE TRUE ATTRIBUTES OF SOVEREIGNTY

Because there are none on earth, after God, greater than sovereign princes, whom God establishes as His lieutenants to command the rest of mankind, we must enquire carefully into their estate, that we may respect and revere their majesty in all due obedience, speak and think of them with all due honour. He who contemns his sovereign prince, contemns God whose image he is. . . .

The first attribute of the sovereign prince . . . is the power to make law binding on all his subjects in general and on each in particular. But to avoid any ambiguity one must add that he does so without the consent of any superior, equal, or inferior being necessary. If the prince can only make law with the consent of a superior he is a subject; if of an equal he shares his sovereignty; if of an inferior, whether it be a council of magnates or the people, it is not he who is sovereign.

All the other attributes and rights of sovereignty are included in this power of making and unmaking law, so that strictly speaking this is the unique attribute of sovereign power. It includes all other rights of sovereignty, that is to say of making peace and war, of hearing appeals from the sentences of all courts whatsoever, of appointing and dismissing the great officers of state; of taxing, or granting privileges of exemption to all subjects, of appreciating or depreciating the value and weight of the coinage, of receiving oaths of fidelity from subjects and liegevassals alike, without exception of any other to whom faith is due. . . .

But because *law* is an unprecise and general term, it is as well to specify the other attributes of sovereignty comprised in it, such as the making of war and peace. This is one of the most important rights of sovereignty, since it brings in its train either the ruin or the salvation of the state. This was a right of sovereignty not only among the ancient Romans, but has always been so among all other peoples. . . .

The third attribute of sovereignty is the power to institute the great officers of state. It has never been questioned that the right is an attribute of sovereignty, at any rate as far as the great officers are concerned. I confine it however to high officials, for there is no commonwealth in which these officers, and many guilds and corporate bodies besides, have not some power of appointing their subordinate officials. . . .

The fourth attribute of sovereignty, and one which has always been among its principal rights, is that the prince should

---

2. The French representative assembly, the Estates General, met for the first time in 1302 and included representatives from the first estate (clergy), second estate (nobles), and third estate (commoners).

3. Province.

be the final resort of appeal from all other courts. . . .

Faith and homage are also among the most important attributes of sovereignty, as was made clear when the prince was described as the one to whom obedience was due without exception.

As for the right of coinage, it is contained within the law-making power, for only he who can make law can regulate currency. . . .

The right of levying taxes and imposing dues, or of exempting persons from the payment of such, is also part of the power of making law and granting privileges.

Philippe de Mornay

DEFENSE OF LIBERTY AGAINST TYRANTS

Philippe de Mornay (1549–1623) was born into an aristocratic family that converted to Protestantism in 1559. After traveling in Italy and studying at the German Protestant University of Heidelberg, Mornay returned to France early in the Wars of Religion and became a close adviser to Henry of Navarre, the Protestant leader. Throughout the conflict, he faithfully served the Protestant cause as a diplomat, publicist, and soldier. Bitterly disappointed when Henry converted to Catholicism in 1593, just four years after becoming King Henry IV, Mornay withdrew from politics and devoted the rest of his life to scholarship and the establishment of Protestant schools. He is best known today for his *Defense of Liberty Against Tyrants*, probably completed in 1574 although not published until 1579. Written in Latin for a learned audience but subsequently published in French, *Defense of Liberty* sought to justify and encourage Protestant and aristocratic resistance to the reigning French king.

Questions
for Analysis

1. Mornay, like Bodin, asserts that power is given to kings by the people. In what respects do the two writers interpret this "gift" differently? What does Mornay mean by a "compact"?
2. How do Mornay and Bodin differ on the relationship between the king and the "law"?
3. What views does Mornay have on the relationship between royal power and private property?
4. How does Mornay justify resistance to a tyrant? Which of his arguments is most convincing?
5. According to Mornay, what is the ultimate purpose of government? How do his ideas compare with those of Bodin? Of Machiavelli?

KINGS ARE CREATED BY THE PEOPLE

. . . We have already shown that it is God who makes kings, gives kingdoms, and selects rulers. And now we say that it is the people that establishes kings, gives them kingdoms, and approves their selection by its vote. For God willed that every bit of authority held by kings should come from the people, after Him, so that kings would concentrate all their care, energy, and thought upon the people's interests. And kings are not to think that they are of a higher nature than the rest of men and rule as men rule over cattle. Born the same as all the rest of men, they are always to remember that they were raised up from below to their estates, upon all others' shoulders, as it were, so that thereafter the burdens of the commonwealth should fall, for the most part, upon theirs. . . .

And since no one is born a king, and no one is a king by nature; and since a king cannot rule without a people, while a people can rule itself without a king, it is clear, beyond all doubt, that the people is prior to the king and that kings were originally established by the people. By adhering to the virtues of their forebears, the sons and relatives of kings sometimes seem to have rendered a kingdom hereditary, and in certain regions the right of free elections almost seems no longer to exist. And yet in all properly constituted kingdoms, the practice still remains inviolate. . . . They are not kings by birth, or by inheritance, but become kings only when they have received the office, together with the sceptre and the crown, from those who represent the people's majesty.

Since kings, then, are created by the people, it seems to follow that the people as a whole is greater than the king. This is an implication of the term itself, since one who is created by another is considered his inferior. . . .

THE REASON FOR CREATING KINGS

Kings, then, are established by the people. . . .

Let kings obey the law, then, and acknowledge law to be their queen. . . . Law is like an instrument, divinely given, through which human societies are ordered for the best and directed to a blessed end. A king who finds obedience to the law demeaning is therefore as ridiculous as a surveyor who considers the rule and compass and other instruments of skilled geometers to be disgraceful and absurd, or a captain who takes fancy as his guide and prefers to zigzag off in all directions rather than steer by the mariner's compass. . . .

MAY KINGS MAKE NEW LAWS?

Should kings, then, not even be permitted to repeal laws and make additions? The duty of a king is not only to stop violations of the law, but also to prevent evasion. He should, therefore, see that the law is free of omissions and redundancies; and that it does not grow obsolete and fade into oblivion, forgotten and unnoticed. If he sees something that ought to be repealed, replaced, or modified, he should convoke the people, or the notables of the people, either in ordinary or extraordinary assembly, advise them of the need, and request the legislation he proposes. But he may not enact anything as law until the assembly has deliberated and approved it. Once he has enacted it, moreover, it is too late for him to change his mind, for he is now obliged to keep it. . . .

DOES THE KING OWN EVERYTHING?

Nowadays the courts of princes are full of people who say that the king owns everything, that what he takes from his subjects is so far from theft that anything he leaves them is a temporary gift. . . .

We should always remember that kings were created for the people's benefit, that rulers are called "kings" when they promote the people's interest and are called "tyrants," as Aristotle[1] says, when they seek only to promote their own. Since each man loves his own and many men even covet the property of others, what kind of ruler were they most likely to have sought—a prince on whom to bestow all they had acquired by their labor, or one who would assume responsibility for guaranteeing the property of each, of the poor man no less than of the rich; a prince who would look on everything as his, or one who would render to each his own; a prince who would squander the fruits of other people's labor like a drone, or one who would keep their honey safe; a prince, finally, who would invade their properties himself, or one who would try to keep out invaders from abroad? . . .

If, therefore, men did not surrender all their property to kings when they created them, but entrusted them with its protection, what title, other than the law of pirates, can justify the claim of kings to everything? . . .

THE COMPACT BETWEEN THE KING AND THE PEOPLE

. . . This compact created the king. For the people made the king, not the king the people. . . . The people asked, by way of stipulation, whether the king would rule justly and according to the law. He then promised to do so. And the people, fi-

nally, replied that they would faithfully obey, as long as his commands were just. Hence, the promise of the king was absolute, that of the people was conditional; and if he does not perform, the people, by the same principle of civil law, are released from any obligation.

By the first covenant,[2] or compact, religious piety becomes an obligation; by the second, justice. In the first the king promises to obey God religiously, in the second, to rule the people justly; in the former, to maintain God's glory, in the latter, to preserve the people's welfare. . . . If the king does not perform the conditions of the first, God is properly the avenger, while the whole people may lawfully punish non-performance of the second. . . .

THE OBLIGATION TO RESIST A TYRANT

The next question is whether a tyrant may be lawfully resisted and, if so, by whom and by what means. . . .

In the first place, nature instructs us to defend our lives and also our liberty, without which life is hardly life at all. If this is the instinct of nature implanted in dogs against the wolf, in bulls against the lion, in pigeons against the falcon, and in chickens against the hawk, how much stronger must it be in man against another man who has become a wolf to man. To fight back is not only permitted, but enjoined, for it is nature herself that seems to fight here.

Next, there is the law of peoples, which distinguishes countries and establishes boundaries that everyone is obligated to

---

1. Greek philosopher (384–322 B.C.)

2. Earlier in the treatise, Mornay describes a covenant between a people and God in which

God promises to maintain the people as long as they offer proper worship.

defend against any person whatsoever. If an Alexander[3] invades a people over which he has no claim and which has not done him injury, it is as lawful to resist him and his mighty fleet. . . .

Last and most important is the civil law, which is the legislation that societies establish for their particular needs, so that here is one and there another kind of government, some being ruled by one man, others by a few, and still others by all. Some peoples deny political authority to women, others admit them; with some, kings are chosen from a particular line, among others the choice is free; and so forth. If anyone tries to break this law through force or fraud, resistance is incumbent upon all of us, because the criminal does violence to that association to which we owe everything we have, because he subverts the foundations of the fatherland to which we are bound — by nature, by the laws, and by our oath. Therefore, if we do not resist, we are traitors to our country, deserters of human society, and contemners of the law.

Giles Fletcher

ON THE RUSSE COMMONWEALTH

The Englishman Giles Fletcher was one of several western Europeans who published accounts of their visits to sixteenth-century Russia. Though historians must keep in mind these authors' biases, such writings are valuable sources, especially because the largely illiterate Russians produced few historical records themselves. Born in 1549, Fletcher was a professor of Greek at Cambridge until the 1580s, when he was elected to Parliament and entered the service of Queen Elizabeth I. In 1588 the queen sent him to Moscow to protect English commercial interests and to resolve certain problems between the Russian government and some resident Englishmen. On his return to England in late 1589, he began to write a treatise on Russia and after two years published it under the title *On the Russe Commonwealth*. It is generally regarded as the most complete and accurate extant portrait of sixteenth-century Russia.

Fletcher visited Russia just four years after the death of Tsar Ivan IV (1533–1584), one of Russia's most notable tsars. A fierce and determined warrior, Ivan added vast new territories to the Russian state with conquests of the Mongol khanates of Kazan and Astrakhan. He also increased the tsar's control of the Russian state and people. Most important, he smashed the political and economic power of the Russian landowning aristocracy, the *boyars*. Thousands of boyars were executed, and their lands were taken over by the state, which redistributed them to a new class of service nobility, whose property and titles were contingent on service in the tsar's army or

---

3. Alexander the Great (356–323 B.C.) of Macedon, who conquered the Persians and forged an empire that stretched from Greece to India.

administration. Commoners also felt Ivan's heavy hand. He limited the peasants' rights to move from one estate to another and prevented urban merchants and craftsmen from moving or changing jobs so he could tax them more easily.

In this document, Fletcher describes the foundations of an authoritarian, autocratic Russian state in which the powers of the tsars exceeded those of even the most powerful absolutist kings of western Europe.

Questions
for Analysis

1. How close do the powers of the tsar, as described by Fletcher, come to the ideals of "the sovereign" as described in Bodin's *Six Books of the Commonwealth*?
2. In western Europe, the nobility provided the main resistance to the establishment of absolutist government. What, in Fletcher's account, explains why the Russian nobility played no such role?
3. To what extent was local government an extension of the tsar's power?
4. Why, according to Fletcher, was there little chance of changing the Russian system of government?
5. Fletcher, an Englishman, came from a country with a strong representative assembly, the Parliament, extensive local self-government, and a legal tradition of protecting individual rights. Are there places in his description of Russian politics where he shows his bias for the English system?
6. Fletcher states that he saw no way in which the Russian political system could be altered. Yet shortly after having published his account, the Russian state was reduced to temporary chaos during the so-called Time of Troubles. On the basis of his description, what can you guess about possible causes of this political breakdown?

CHAPTER 7. THE STATE OR FORM OF THEIR GOVERNMENT

The manner of their government is much after the Turkish fashion, which they seem to imitate as near as the country and reach of their capacities in politic affairs will give them leave to do.

The state and form of their government is plain tyrannical, as applying all to the behoof[1] of the prince . . . as well for the keeping of the nobility and commons in an under proportion and far uneven balance in their several degrees, as also in their impositions and exactions[2] wherein they exceed all just measure without any regard of nobility or people, [except that] it gives the nobility a kind of injust and unmeasured liberty to command and exact upon the commons and baser sort of people . . . specially in the place where their lands lie or where they are appointed by the emperor to govern under him. . . . Wherein, notwithstanding, both nobility and commons are but storers[3] for the

---

1. Benefit.
2. Taxes.

3. Providers.

prince, all running in the end into the emperor's coffers, as may appear by the practice of enriching his treasury and the manner of exactions set down in the title of his customs and revenues.

Concerning the principal points and matters of state wherein the sovereignty consists, as the making and annulling of public laws, the making of magistrates, power to make war or league with any foreign state, to execute or to pardon life, with the right of appeal in all matters both civil and criminal, they do so wholly and absolutely pertain to the emperor, and his council under him, as that he may be said to be both the sovereign commander and the executioner of all these. For as touching any law or public order of the realm, it is ever determined of before any public assembly or parliament be summoned. . . .

Secondly, as touching the public offices and magistracies of the realm, there is none hereditary, neither any so great nor so little in that country, but the bestowing of it is done immediately by the emperor himself. . . .

Thirdly, the like is to be said of the jurisdiction concerning matters judicial, specially such as concern life and death. Wherein there is none that has any authority or public jurisdiction that goes by descent or is held by charter, but all at the appointment and pleasure of the emperor, and the same practiced by the judges with such awe and restraint as that they dare not determine upon any special matter, but must refer the same wholly up to Moscow to the emperor's council. To show his sovereignty over the lives of his subjects, the late emperor Ivan Vasil'evich[4] in his walks or progresses, if he had misliked the face or person of any man whom he met by the way, or that looked upon him, would command his head to be struck off, which was presently done, and the head cast before him.

Fourthly, for the sovereign appeal and giving of pardons in criminal matters to such as are convicted, it is wholly at the pleasure and grace of the emperor. . . .

CHAPTER 9. OF THE NOBILITY, AND BY WHAT MEANS IT IS KEPT IN AN UNDER PROPORTION AGREEABLE TO THAT STATE

The degrees of persons or estates of Russia, besides the sovereign state or emperor himself, are these in their order. First, the nobility, which is of four sorts, whereof the chief for birth, authority, and revenue are called . . . the exempt or privileged dukes. These held . . . jurisdiction and absolute authority within their precincts, much like unto the states or nobles of Germany, but afterwards . . . they yielded themselves to this house . . . when it began to wax mighty and to enlarge itself by overmatching their neighbors. Only they were bound to serve the emperor in his wars with a certain number of horse. But the late emperor Ivan Vasil'evich, father to this prince, being a man of high spirit and subtle in his kind, meaning to reduce his government into a more strict form, began by degrees to clip off their greatness and to bring it down to a lesser proportion till in the end he made them not only his vassals but his kholopy, that is, his very villeins or bondslaves, for so they term and write themselves in any public instrument or private petition which they make to the emperor. So that now they hold their authorities, lands, lives, and all at the emperor's pleasure, as the rest do. . . .

The second degree of nobility is of the boyars. These are such as the emperor

---

4. Ivan IV, known as "Ivan the Terrible" (1583–1584).

honors, besides their nobility, with the title of counselors. The revenue of these
two sorts of their nobles rises out of their
lands assigned them by the emperor and
held at his pleasure (for of their own inheritance there is little left them as was
said before). . . .

In the third rank are the *voevody* or such
nobles as are or have been generals in the
emperor's wars, which deliver the honor
of their title to their posterities also, who
take their place above the other dukes and
nobles that are not of the two former
sorts . . . his boyars.

The fourth and lowest degree of nobility with them is of such as bear the name
of kniaz'ia or dukes but come of the
younger brothers of those chief houses
through many descents and have no inheritance of their own, save the bare
name or title of duke only. . . .

CHAPTER 10. OF THE GOVERNMENT OF THEIR PROVINCES AND SHIRES

*In the first part of this chapter, Fletcher de-
scribes the administrative system in the Russian provinces.*

This manner of government of their
provinces and towns, if it were as well set
for the giving of justice indifferently to all
sorts as it is to prevent innovations by
keeping of the nobility within order and
the commons in subjection, it might seem
in that kind to be no bad nor unpolitic
way for the containing of so large a commonwealth of that breadth and length as
is the kingdom of Russia. But the oppression and slavery is so open and so great
that a man would marvel how the nobility
and people should suffer themselves to
be brought under it while they had any
means to avoid and repulse it, or being so

strengthened as it is at this present, how
the emperors themselves can be content
to practice the same with so open injustice
and oppression of their subjects, being
themselves of a Christian profession.

By this it appears how hard a matter it
were to alter the state of the Russian government as now it stands. First, because
they have none of the nobility able to
make headway. As for the lords of the
four chetverti or tetrarchies, they are men
of no nobility but are advanced by the emperor, depending on his favor and attending only about his own person. And for
the dukes that are appointed to govern
under them, they are but men of . . . no
power, authority, nor credit save that
which they have out of the office for the
time they enjoy it, which does purchase
them no favor but rather hatred of the
people, for as much as they see that they
are set over them not so much for any care
to do them right and justice as to keep
them under in a miserable subjection and
to take the fleece from them, not once in
the year (as the owner from his sheep) but
to pull and clip them all the year long. Besides, the authority and rule which they
bear is rent and divided into many small
pieces, being several of them in every
great shire, limited besides with a very
short time which gives them no scope to
make any strength nor to contrive such an
enterprise if happily they intended any
matter of innovation. As for the common
people, besides their want of armor and
practice of war (which they are kept from
of purpose), they are robbed continually
both of their hearts and money (besides
other means), sometimes by pretense of
some service to be done for the common
defense, sometimes without any show at
all of any necessity of commonwealth or
prince, so that there is no means either for
nobility or people to attempt any innovation so long as the military forces of the
emperor (which are the number of 80,000
at the least in continual pay) hold them-

selves fast and sure unto him and to the present state. Which needs they must do, being of the quality of soldiers and enjoying withal that free liberty of wronging and spoiling of the commons at their pleasure, which is permitted them of purpose to make them have a liking of the present state. As for the agreement of the soldiers and commons, it is a thing not to be feared, being of so opposite and contrary practice much one to the other. This desperate state of things at home makes the people for the most part to wish for some foreign invasion, which they suppose to be the only means to rid them of the heavy yoke of this tyrannous government.

Political Diversity in Sub-Saharan Africa

As had been true for many centuries, diversity characterized the politics of sub-Saharan Africa in the 1500s and 1600s. This vast region consisted of a mosaic of kingdoms, empires, city-states, and tribal regimes, which ruled territories that often did not have clearly delineated boundaries. This political diversity resulted from the region's climatic and ecological variety, the difficulty of transportation and communication, the low population levels, and the large numbers of distinct ethnic and linguistic groups.

The absence of written sources has made it difficult to trace the development of political institutions in early Africa except in the vaguest terms. Thus, visitors' observations of African practices are valuable, even though they are often from the perspective of an Arab or a European. Two visitors' accounts follow. They can offer only a hint of Africa's rich political mosaic.

Leo Africanus

THE HISTORY AND DESCRIPTION OF AFRICA

Al-Hassan ibn-Muhammad al-Wazzan al-Fasi was born around 1494 in Granada, a district of southern Spain, but was raised in Fez (in modern north-central Morocco), to which his family emigrated several years after the Catholic armies of Ferdinand and Isabella of Spain captured the last outpost of Muslim power in their country. Educated in Muslim law, the young man served in various commercial and diplomatic missions for the sultan of Fez, including two trips to sub-Saharan West Africa. In 1518 he was captured by Christian pirates and brought to Rome, where he was presented as a slave to Pope Leo X (1513–1521), who persuaded him to accept Christianity and bestowed upon him his own name, Giovanni Leone (John Leo).

While in Rome, in 1526 John Leo completed in Italian his most famous work, *Description of Africa*, probably on the basis of an early Arab version. It recounts his travels and experiences in Africa north of the equator and became a principal source for European knowledge of Islam. By virtue of this work, he became known as Leo Africanus (Latin for Leo the African). Little is known of the rest of his life, except that in 1530 he returned to Africa and died a Muslim in Tunis sometime after 1554.

In the following excerpt, Leo describes the two largest cities of the Songhai Empire, Timbuktu and Gao. Gao was the capital of this empire, which controlled the region of the Niger River between 1460 and 1591. Here resided its emperor, Muhammad Askia (1493–1528), who claimed the title Caliph of the Blacks. Timbuktu, the larger of the two cities, was ruled by a governor in the name of the emperor but was Gao's economic and cultural rival.

Questions for Analysis

1. How deeply does Islam seem to have penetrated Songhai society?
2. What are the bases of the emperor's power?
3. What factors seem to threaten the stability of this empire?
4. In 1591 Moroccan raiders destroyed the Songhai Empire. Why would they be attracted to this distant region across the desert, and what advantages would they have had in their war against Songhai?

THE KINGDOM OF TIMBUKTU

The name was imposed upon this kingdom in our day, as some believe, from the name of a certain town which, according to tradition, King Mansa Suleiman founded in the year of the Hijira 610 [A.D. 1213–1214].[1] . . .

All its houses are . . . cottages, built of chalk and covered with thatch. However, there is a most stately mosque to be seen, whose walls are made of stone and lime, and a princely palace also, constructed by the highly skilled craftsmen of Granada. Here there are many shops of artisans and merchants, especially of those who weave linen and cotton, and here Barbary [North African] merchants bring European cloth. The inhabitants, and especially resident aliens, are exceedingly rich, since the present king[2] married both of his daughters to rich merchants. Here are many wells, containing sweet water. Whenever the Niger River overflows, they carry the water into town by means of sluices. This region yields great quantities of grain, cattle, milk, and butter, but salt is very scarce here, for it is brought here by land from Tegaza, which is five hundred miles away. When I was there, I saw one camel-load of salt sold for eighty ducats.[3]

The rich king of Timbuktu has many plates and scepters of gold, some of which

1. Evidence suggests that Timbuktu was founded around 1106.

2. The king of Timbuktu was probably a tributary vassal of Muhammad Askia. Timbuktu, the capital of the earlier empire of Mali (ca 1250–ca 1460), had been incorporated recently into the loosely governed Songhai Empire, and its lord probably retained a great deal of local power.

3. One Venetian ducat was approximately a week's wage for a skilled craftsman in contemporary Italy.

weigh 1,300 pounds, and he keeps a magnificent and well-furnished court. When he travels anywhere, he rides upon a camel, which is led by some of his noblemen. He does so likewise when going to war, and all his soldiers ride upon horses. Whoever wishes to speak to this king must first of all fall down before his feet and then taking up earth must sprinkle it on his own head and shoulders. . . . [The king] always has under arms 3,000 horsemen and a great number of foot soldiers who shoot poisoned arrows. They often skirmish with those who refuse to pay tribute and whomever they capture they sell to the merchants of Timbuktu. Here very few horses are bred. . . . Their best horses are brought out of Barbary. As soon as the king learns that any merchants have come to the town with horses, he commands that a certain number be brought before him. Choosing the best horse for himself, he pays a most liberal price for it. He so hates all Jews that he will not admit any into the city, and he confiscates the goods of all Barbary merchants whom he learns have any dealings with the Jews.

Here are great numbers of religious teachers, judges, scholars and other learned persons, who are bountifully maintained at the king's expense. Here too are brought various manuscripts or written books from Barbary, which are sold for more money than any other merchandise.

The coin of Timbuktu is gold, without any stamp or inscription, but in matters of small value they use certain shells from the kingdom of Persia. Four hundred of these are worth a ducat, and six pieces of Timbuktu's golden coin weigh two-thirds of an ounce.

The inhabitants are gentle and cheerful and spend a great part of the night in singing and dancing throughout the city streets. They keep large numbers of male and female slaves, and their town is greatly vulnerable to fire. At the time of my second visit, almost half the town burned down in the space of five hours.

THE TOWN AND KINGDOM OF GAO

The great town of Gao . . . lies almost four hundred miles south of Timbuktu. Its houses are humble, except for those in which the king and his courtiers reside.

Here are very rich merchants and to here journey continually large numbers of Negroes who purchase here cloth from Barbary and Europe. The town abounds in grain and meat but lacks wine, trees and fruits. However, there are plenty of melons, lemons and rice. Here there are many wells, which also contain very sweet and wholesome water. Here also is a certain place where slaves are sold, especially upon those days when merchants assemble. A young slave of fifteen years of age is sold for six ducats, and children are also sold.

The king of this region has a certain private palace in which he keeps a large number of concubines and slaves, who are watched by eunuchs. To guard his person he maintains a sufficient troop of horsemen and foot soldiers. Between the first gate of the palace and the inner part, there is a walled enclosure wherein the king personally decides all of his subjects' controversies. Although the king is most diligent in this regard and conducts all business in these matters, he has in his company counsellors and such other officers as his secretaries, treasurers, stewards and auditors.

It is a wonder to see the quality of merchandise that is daily brought here and how costly and sumptuous everything is. Horses purchased in Europe for ten ducats are sold here for forty and sometimes fifty ducats apiece. There is not European cloth so coarse as to sell for less than four ducats an ell [about 45 inches]. If it is anywhere near fine quality, they will give fifteen ducats for an ell, and an ell of the scarlet of Venice or of Turkish cloth is here worth thirty ducats. A sword is here valued at three or four crowns, and likewise are spears, bridles and similar commodities, and spices are all sold at a high rate. However, of all other items, salt is the most expensive.

The rest of this kingdom contains nothing but villages and hamlets inhabited by herdsmen and shepherds, who in winter cover their bodies with the skins of animals, but in summer they go naked, save for their private parts. . . . They are an ignorant and rude people, and you will scarcely find one learned person in the space of a hundred miles. They are continually burdened by heavy exactions, to the point that they scarcely have anything left on which to live.

John dos Santos

ETHIOPIA ORIENTAL

John dos Santos was a Portuguese Dominican priest who resided in Portuguese-dominated Mozambique between 1585 and 1591. To seek out missionary opportunities, and to explore for exploring's sake, he traveled widely up and down the east coast of Africa. In 1590, he journeyed some 600 miles up the Zambezi River, where he observed the political and religious customs of the people who inhabited the Kingdom of Kiteve. On his return to Europe, he published in 1609 a memoir of his experiences, *Ethiopia Oriental*, hoping to inform other educated Europeans of the customs of the peoples he encountered. His account is the major source of information about conditions in eastern Africa during the late sixteenth century.

Questions for Analysis

1. What insights does this source offer about the African view of kingship?
2. What does this source tell us about the position of women in the Kingdom of Kiteve?
3. What seems to be the basis of the king's authority in his realm?

The king of these parts is of curled hair, a gentile,[1] which worships nothing, nor hath any knowledge of God; yea, rather he carries himself as God of his countries, and so is holden and reverenced of his vassals. He is called Kiteve, a

---

1. A pagan.

title royal and no proper name, which they exchange for this so soon as they become kings. The Kiteve hath more than one hundred women all within doors, amongst which one or two are his queens, the rest as concubines. Many of them are his own aunts, cousins, sisters, and daughters, which he no less useth, saying that his sons by them are true heirs of the kingdom without mixture of other blood. When the Kiteve dies, his queens must die with him to do him service in the other world; who accordingly at the instant of his death take a poison (which they call *lucasse*) and die therewith. The successor succeeds as well to the women as the state. None else but the king may, upon pain of death, marry his sister or daughter. This successor is commonly one of the eldest sons of the deceased king, and of his great women or queens; and if the eldest be not sufficient, then the next, or if none of them be fit, his brother of whole blood. The king commonly, while he lives, makes the choice, and trains up him to affairs of state, to whom he destines the succession. While I lived there . . . the king had above thirty sons, and yet showed more respect to his brother, a wise man, than to any of them, all honoring him as apparent heir.

The same day the king dies, he is carried to a hill where all the kings are interred. And early the next morning, he whom the king had named his successor goes to the king's house where the king's women abide in expectation, and by their consent he enters the house, and seats himself with the principal of them in a public hall where the king was wont to sit to hear causes, in a place drawn with curtains or covered with a cloth, that none may see the king nor the women with him. And thence he sends his officers, which go through the city and proclaim festivals to the new king, who is now quietly possessed of the king's house, with the women of the king deceased, and that all should go and acknowledge him for the king: which is done by all the great men then in court, and the nobles of the city, who go to the palace now solemnly guarded, and enter into the hall by licence of the officers, where the new king abides with his women; entering some, and some creeping on the ground till they come to the middle of the hall, and thence speak to the new king, giving him new obeisance, without seeing him or his women. The king makes answer from within, and accepts their service: and after that draws the curtains, and shows himself to them; whereat all of them clap their hands, and then turn behind the curtains, and go forth creeping on the ground as they came in. And when they are gone, others enter and do in like sort. In this ceremony the greatest part of the day is spent with feasting, music, and dancing through the city. They next day the king sends his officers through the kingdom to declare this his succession, and that all should come to the court to see him break the bow. . . .

Before the new king begins to govern, he sends for all the chiefs in the kingdom, to come to the court and see him break the king's bow, which is all one with taking possession of the kingdom. In those courts is a custom then also to kill some of those lords or great men, saying they are necessary for the service of the deceased king; whereupon they kill those of whom they stand in fear or doubt, or whom they hate, in place of whom they make and erect new lords. This custom causes such as fear themselves to flee the land. Anciently the kings were wont to drink poison in any grievous disasters, as in a contagious disease, or natural impotency, lameness, the loss of their fore-teeth, or other deformity; saying that kings ought to have no defect. Which if it happened, it was honor for him to die, and go to better himself in that better life, in which he should be wholly perfect. But the Kiteve which reigned while I was there, would not follow his predecessors herein; but having lost one of his fore-teeth, sent to proclaim through his kingdom that one of his teeth were fallen out, and (that they might not be ignorant when they saw him want it) that if his predecessors were such fools, for such causes to kill themselves, he would not do so, but await his natural death, holding his life necessary to conserve his estate against his enemies, which example he would commend to posterity.

If the Kaffirs[2] have a suit, and seek to speak with the king, they creep to the place where he is, having prostrated themselves at the entrance, and look not on him all the while they speak, but lying on one side clap their hands all the time (a rite of obsequiousness in those parts), and then, having finished, they creep out of the doors as they came in. For no Kaffir may enter on foot to speak to the king, nor eye him in speaking, except the familiars and particular friends of the king. . . .

The Kiteve has two or three hundred men for his guard, which are his officers and executioners, . . . and go crying, "Inhama, inhama," that is "Flesh, flesh." He has another sort called *marombes*, jesters, which have their songs and prose in praise of the king, whom they call, Lord of the Sun and Moon, King of the Land and Rivers, Conqueror of his Enemies, in everything great, great thief, great witch, great lion; and all other names of greatness which they can invent, whether they signify good or bad, they attribute to

them. When the king goes out of doors, these *marombes* go round about him with great cries of this argument. He has others which are musicians in his hall, and at the court gates, with divers instruments resounding his praises. Their best musical instrument is called *ambira*, much like to our organs. . . .

They use three kinds of oath[3] in judgment most terrible, in accusations wanting just evidence. The first is called *Lucasse*, which is a vessel full of poison, which they give the suspected, with words importing his destruction and present death if he be guilty, his escape if innocent. The terror whereof makes the conscious confess the crime. But the innocent drink it confidently without harm, and thereby are acquitted of the crime. And the plaintiff is condemned to him whom he falsely had accused; his wife, children, and goods being forfeited, one moiety to the king, and the other to the defendant.

The second oath they call *xoqua*, which is made by iron heated red hot in the fire, causing the accused to lick it being so hot with his tongue, saying, that the fire shall not burn him if he be innocent; otherwise it shall burn his tongue and mouth. . . .

The third oath they call Calano, which is a vessel of water made bitter with certain herbs which, they put into it, whereof they give the accused to drink, saying that if he be innocent he shall drink it all off at one gulp without any stay, and cast it all up again at once without any harm. If guilty he shall not be able to get down one drop without gargling and choking.

---

2. A term for Bantu-speaking peoples, who in the fifteenth century moved into the Mozambique region in large numbers.

3. The Kiteve "oaths" were trials to determine the guilt or innocence of individuals accused of crimes.

Power and Splendor in the Ottoman and Mughal Empires

Chapters 1 and 2 introduced two of the mightiest states of the 1500s and 1600s, the Ottoman Empire, centered in Asia Minor, and the Mughal Empire of India. Although each empire had populations that were quite different, Ottoman and Mughal politics were similar in several respects.

Both were "gunpowder" empires established by armed conquest. Ottoman expansion began around 1300, and by the sixteenth century resulted in an empire including northern Africa, Asia Minor, the Arab Middle East, and central and southeastern Europe. The Mughal Empire was founded in the sixteenth century as a result of the conquests of Babur, an adventurer from a small state in central Asia, and his grandson Akbar, who ruled from 1556 to 1605. Once established, both empires maintained large and disciplined armies, outfitted with European guns and artillery.

Rulers in both empires faced the problem of ruling populations divided by religion. For the Mughals, the division was between Muslims, most of whom lived in the northwest, and Hindus, a majority of the population. The Ottoman Empire was largely Muslim, but it also included many thousands of Christian subjects in Europe and numerous Christian and Jewish communities scattered throughout northern Africa and the Middle East.

In both empires ultimate political power was exercised by an emperor who determined policy, controlled the army, and directed a large administration. Given the emperors' enormous power, the effectiveness of government and the overall "success" of the regime was to a great extent determined by their abilities. Thus, in the early sixteenth century, when Ottoman power was at its peak, two tough and hard-working warriors, Selim I and his son, Suleiman I, reigned. Conversely, when in the seventeenth century Ottoman power began to wane, sultans were often self-indulgent, indolent, and foolish. The Mughal Empire reached its height during the period 1550 to 1650, when it too was ruled by capable emperors like Akbar and Jahangir, who worked hard at governing and pursued a tolerant policy toward their Hindu subjects. The empire declined during the reign of Aurangzeb (1658–1707), a devout Muslim who abandoned toleration for persecution of the Hindus.

Ogier Ghiselin de Busbecq

TURKISH LETTERS

Ogier de Busbecq (1522–1590) was a Flemish nobleman who spent most of his life in the service of the Hapsburgs, especially Ferdinand I, the archduke of Austria, king of Hungary and Bohemia, and from 1556 to 1564 Holy Roman Emperor. In 1555,

Ferdinand sent Busbecq to Constantinople to represent Hapsburg interests in a dispute over control of Transylvania, a region that had been part of Hungary and today is a region in Rumania. Both the Hapsburgs and the Ottomans wanted control of the region, but after six years of discussion, they devised a compromise by which Transylvania became an independent state but continued to pay annual tribute to the sultan.

As noted in Chapter 1, during his seven years in Turkey, Busbecq recorded his observations and impressions and sent them in the form of four long Latin letters to a friend and fellow Hapsburg diplomat, Nicholas Michault. Later Busbecq agreed to their publication, and all four letters appeared in a Parisian edition in 1589. Subsequently published in numerous Latin versions and translated into the major European languages, Busbecq's letters provide a wealth of insight and information about Ottoman society.

Questions for Analysis

1. What characteristics of Suleiman's administration particularly impress Busbecq?
2. What sort of attitude does Suleiman display toward Busbecq and his entourage?
3. How is Turkish society arranged, according to Busbecq?
4. What does Busbecq see as the main difference between Turkish and European social attitudes?
5. What, according to Busbecq, are the major differences between European and Turkish troops?

On our arrival . . . we were taken to call on Achmet Pasha (the chief Vizier) and the other pashas[1] — for the Sultan himself was not then in the town — and commenced our negotiations with them touching the business entrusted to us by King Ferdinand. The pashas . . . did not offer any strong opposition to the views we expressed, and told us that the whole matter depended on the Sultan's pleasure. On his arrival we were admitted to an audience; but the manner and spirit in which he [the Sultan] listened to our address, our arguments, and our message, was by no means favorable.

The Sultan was seated on a very low ottoman, not more than a foot from the ground, which was covered with a quantity of costly rugs and cushions of exquisite workmanship; near him lay his bow and arrows. His air, as I said, was by no means gracious, and his face wore a stern, though dignified, expression.

On entering we were separately conducted into the royal presence by the chamberlains,[2] who grasped our arms. . . . After

---

1. Pasha was an honorary title for a high-ranking military or government official; a vizier served the sultan as an adviser or provincial governor.

2. An official of the royal court involved in matters connected with the king's household.

having gone through a pretence of kissing his hand, we were conducted backwards to the wall opposite his seat, care being taken that we should never turn our backs on him. The Sultan then listened to what I had to say; but the language I used was not at all to his taste, for the demands of his Majesty breathed a spirit of independence and dignity, which was by no means acceptable to one who deemed that his wish was law; and so he made no answer beyond saying in an impatient way, "Giusel, giusel," i.e. well, well. After this we were dismissed to our quarters.

The Sultan's hall was crowded with people, among whom were several officers of high rank. Besides these there were all the troopers of the Imperial guard,[3] and a large force of Janissaries;[4] but there was not in all that great assembly a single man who owed his position to anything save his valor and his merit. No distinction is attached to birth among the Turks; the respect to be paid to a man is measured by the position he holds in the public service. There is no fighting for precedence; a man's place is marked out by the duties he discharges. . . . It is by merit that men rise in the service, a system which ensures that posts should only be assigned to the competent. Each man in Turkey carries in his own hand his ancestry and his position in life, which he may make or mar as he will. Those who receive the highest offices from the Sultan are for the most part the sons of shepherds or herdsmen, and so far from being ashamed of their parentage, they actually glory in it, and consider it a matter of

boasting that they owe nothing to the accident of birth; for they do not believe that high qualities are either natural or hereditary, nor do they think that they can be handed down from father to son, but that they are partly the gift of God, and partly the result of good training, great industry, and unwearied zeal; arguing that high qualities do not descend from a father to his son or heir, any more than a talent for music, mathematics, or the like. . . . Among the Turks, therefore, honors, high posts, and judgeships are the rewards of great ability and good service. If a man is dishonest, or lazy, or careless, he remains at the bottom of the ladder, an object of contempt; for such qualities there are no honors in Turkey!

This is the reason that they are successful in their undertakings, that they lord it over others, and are daily extending the bounds of their empire. These are not our ideas, with us there is no opening left for merit; birth is the standard for everything; the prestige of birth is the sole key to advancement in the public service. . . .

The Turkish monarch going to war takes with him over 40,000 camels and nearly as many baggage mules, of which a great part, when he is invading Persia,[5] are loaded with rice and other kinds of grain. These mules and camels also serve to carry tents and armor, and likewise tools and munitions for the campaign. The territories, which bear the name of Persia . . . are less fertile than our country, and even such crops as they bear are laid waste by the inhabitants in time of invasion in hopes of starving out the en-

---

3. The Imperial Guard under Suleiman consisted of approximately 4,000 men who camped around his tent at night and served as his personal bodyguard in battle.

4. An elite military force in the service of the sultan, whose ranks originally were filled by young sons of Christian families who were converted to Islam and given over completely to

military training. Ideally, they lived according to a strict code of absolute obedience, abstinence from luxury, religious observance, celibacy, and confinement to barracks.

5. The Shi'ite empire of Persia was the bitter enemy of the Ottoman sultans throughout the sixteenth century.

emy, so that it is very dangerous for an army to invade Persia, if it is not furnished with abundant supplies. The invading army carefully abstains from encroaching on its supplies at the outset, as they are well aware that, when the season for campaigning draws to a close, they will have to retreat over districts wasted by the enemy, or scraped as bare by countless hordes of men and droves of baggage animals, as if they had been devastated by locusts; accordingly they reserve their stores as much as possible for this emergency. . . .

From this you will see that it is the patience, self-denial, and thrift of the Turkish soldier that enable him to face the most trying circumstances, and come safely out of the dangers that surround him. What a contrast to our men! . . .

. . . For each man is his own worst enemy, and has no foe more deadly than his own intemperance, which is sure to kill

him, if the enemy be not quick. It makes me shudder to think of what the result of a struggle between such different systems must be; one of us must prevail and the other be destroyed, at any rate we cannot both exist in safety. On their side is the vast wealth of their empire, unimpaired resources, experience and practice in arms, a veteran soldiery, an uninterrupted series of victories, readiness to endure hardships, union, order, discipline, thrift, and watchfulness. On ours are found an empty exchequer, luxurious habits, exhausted resources, broken spirits, a raw and insubordinate soldiery, and greedy generals; there is no regard for discipline, license runs riot, the men indulge in drunkenness and debauchery, and, worst of all, the enemy are accustomed to victory, we, to defeat. Can we doubt what the result must be?

Jahangir

MEMOIRS

In addition to patronizing the work of many gifted writers and poets, Jahangir, Mughal emperor from 1605 to 1627, himself contributed to the literature of his age by writing a readable and informative memoir. Intended to glorify himself and instruct his heirs, his memoir covered the first thirteen years of his reign.

Questions
for Analysis

1. Other than to glorify the person of the emperor, what possible political purposes might have been served by the elaborate coronation ceremonies described by Jahangir?
2. What are Jahangir's and Akbar's attitudes toward the Hindus? What are their reasons for allowing them to practice their religion?
3. What do the episodes concerning Mirza Nour and the Afghan bandits reveal about Jahangir's view of his responsibilities?
4. To what extent do Jahangir's views of government agree with the ideas Machiavelli expresses in *The Prince* (see Chapter 2)?

[*The Splendor of the Mughals*]

For a memorial of sundry events incidental to myself, I have undertaken to describe a small portion, in order that some traces thereof may be preserved on the records of time.

On Thursday, then, the eighth of the latter month of Jammaudy, of the year of the Hidjera one thousand and fourteen,[1] the metropolis of Agrah, and in the forenoon of the day, being then arrived at the age of thirty-eight, I became Emperor, and under auspices the most felicitous, took my seat on the throne of my wishes. . . . As at the very instant that I seated myself on the throne the sun rose from the horizon, I accepted this as the omen of victory, and as indicating a reign of unvarying prosperity. Hence I assumed the titles of Jahangir Padshah, and Jahangir Shah: the world-subduing emperor; the world-subduing king. I ordained that the following legend should be stamped on the coinage of the empire: "Stricken at Agrah by that . . . safeguard of the world; the sovereign splendor of the faith, Jahangir, son of the imperial Akbar."

On this occasion I made use of the throne prepared by my father, and enriched at an expense without parallel, for the celebration of the festival of the new year. . . . In the fabrication of the throne a sum not far short of ten krours of ashrefies,[2] was expended in jewels alone. . . .

For the convenience of removal from place to place the throne was, moreover, so constructed, that it could be easily taken to pieces, and again put together at pleasure. The legs and body of the throne were at the same time loaded with fifty maunds of ambergris,[3] so that wherever it might be found expedient to put it together, no further perfumes were necessary, for an assemblage of whatever magnitude.

Having thus seated myself on the throne of my expectation and wishes, I caused also the imperial crown, which my father had caused to be made after the manner of that which was worn by the great kings of Persia, to be brought before me, and then, in the presence of the whole assembled Emirs,[4] having placed it on my brows, as an omen auspicious to the stability and happiness of my reign, kept it there for the space of a full . . . hour. On each of the twelve points of this crown was a single diamond . . . the whole purchased by my father with the resources of his own government, not from any thing accruing to him by inheritance from his predecessors. At the point in the centre of the top part of the crown was a single pearl . . . and on different parts of the same were set altogether two hundred rubies, . . . each of the value of six thousand rupees.

For forty days and forty nights I caused the . . . great imperial state drum, to strike up, without ceasing, the strains of joy and triumph; and . . . around my throne, the ground was spread by my directions with the most costly brocades and gold embroidered carpets. Censers[5] of gold and silver were disposed in different directions for the purpose of burning

---

1. October 10, 1605, according to the Muslim calendar, dated from the Hegira, Muhammad's flight from Mecca to Medina.

2. Krour is a measurement of weight, and an ashrefy is a unit of money. Although it is impossible to determine the exact value of ten "krours of ashrefies," it is an enormous sum.

3. A maund was a unit of weight, which could vary from as little as 10 pounds to as much as 160; ambergris, a waxy substance secreted by sperm whales and found floating in tropical seas, is used as a perfume.

4. High government officials.

5. A container for burning incense.

odoriferous drugs, and nearly three thousand camphorated wax lights, . . . in branches of gold and silver perfumed with ambergris, illuminated the scene from night till morning. Numbers of blooming youth, . . . clad in dresses of the most costly materials, woven in silk and gold, with zones and amulets sparkling with the lustre of the diamond, the emerald, the sapphire, and the ruby, awaited my commands, rank after rank, and in attitude most respectful. And finally, the Emirs of the empire, . . . covered from head to foot in gold and jewels, and shoulder to shoulder, stood round in brilliant array, also waiting for the commands of their sovereign. . . .

[*Policy Toward the Hindus*]

I am here led to relate that at the city of Banaras[6] a temple had been erected [in which] . . . the principal idol . . . had on its head a tiara or cap, enriched with jewels. . . . He had placed in this temple, moreover, as the associates and ministering servants of the principal idol, four other images of solid gold, each crowned with a tiara, in the like manner enriched with precious stones. It was the belief of these non-believers that a dead Hindu, provided when alive he had been a worshiper, when laid before this idol would be restored to life. As I could not possibly give credit to such a pretense, I employed a confidential person to ascertain the truth; and, as I justly supposed, the whole was detected to be an impudent imposture. . . .

On this subject I must however acknowledge, that having on one occasion asked my father the reason why he had forbidden any one to prevent or interfere with the building of these haunts of idola-try, his reply was in the following terms: "My dear child," said he, "I find myself a powerful monarch, the shadow of God upon earth. I have seen that he bestows the blessing of his gracious providence upon all his creatures without distinction. . . . With all of the human race, with all of God's creatures, I am at peace: why then should I permit myself, under any consideration, to be the cause of molestation or aggression to any one? Besides, are not five parts in six . . . either Hindus or aliens to the faith; and were I to be governed by motives of the kind suggested in your inquiry, what alternative can I have but to put them all to death! I have thought it therefore my wisest plan to let these men alone. Neither is it to be forgotten, that the class of whom we are speaking . . . are usefully engaged, either in the pursuits of science or the arts, or of improvements for the benefit of mankind, and have in numerous instances arrived at the highest distinctions in the state, there being, indeed, to be found in this city men of every description, and of every religion on the face of the earth."

. . .

In the practice of being burnt on the funeral pyre of their husbands,[7] as sometimes exhibited among the widows of the Hindus, I had previously directed, that no woman who was the mother of children should be thus made a sacrifice, however willing to die; and I now further ordained, that in no case was the practice to be permitted, when compulsion was in the slightest degree employed, whatever might be the opinions of the people. In other respects they were in no wise to be

---

6. A city on the Ganges River.

7. The reference is to the Hindu practice of sati.

molested in the duties of their religion, nor exposed to oppression or violence in any manner whatever.

. . .

The Rai Rayan had for some time held the appointment of Diwan under my father Akbar, and is one of his oldest dependents; he is now far advanced in years, and in proportion possessed of the most extensive experience, not less in the regulations of civil policy than in the management of martial discipline, on which he may be said to be master. . . . Together with his experience, he accumulated under my father treasure to an immense amount, in gold; so great, indeed, that even among the Hindus of his class he has not his equal in wealth, since he is known, at the period in which I am writing, to have at a time, in the hands of certain merchants of his caste in the city, no less than ten krours of ashrefies. . . .

[*The Duties of the Emperor*]
I am now about to relate an occurrence, from which the struggle between private friendship and the sense of public duty, occasioned considerable pain to my mind. Mirza Nour, the son of Khaun-e-Auzem, was brought before me on a charge of homicide. This young man had possessed an extraordinary share in my father's friendship, was as much beloved by him as if he had been his own child, and who made considerable sacrifices to gratify and indulge him. In these circumstances, I directed that he should be taken, together with his accusers, immediately before the . . . minister of justice, who received my injunctions, according to what might be proved in evidence, to fulfill with regard to him the dictates of the law. In due

time a report was laid before me from these officers of justice, declaring that Mirza Nour, the son of Khaun-e-Auzem, had been found guilty of the wilful murder of a man, and that, according to the law of Muhammad, "blood alone was the compensation for blood." Notwithstanding my extreme regard for the son, and the respect which I bore for the father, I found it impossible to act in contravention to the ordinances of God, and I therefore, with whatever reluctance, consigned him to the hands of the executioner.

For a month afterwards, however, I endured for his death the most consuming grief, deeply regretting the loss of one so young, and possessed of so many elegant and engaging qualifications. But, however repugnant, there cannot in these cases be any alternative: for should we omit to discharge ourselves of this our irksome duty, every aggrieved person would seize his opportunity of time and place to avenge himself in his adversary's blood. To bring, therefore, to prompt punishment the man who violates the laws of his country, is an alternative with which no person intrusted with the reins of power is authorized to dispense.

. . .

It had been made known to me that the roads about Kandahar[8] were grievously infested by the Afghans, who by their vexatious exactions rendered the communications in that quarter extremely unsafe for travellers of every description. . . .
Lushker Khan . . . was despatched by my orders towards Kabul for the purpose of clearing the roads in that direction, which had been rendered unsafe by the outrages of licentious bandits. It so happened that when this commander had

---

8. A city in Afghanistan.

nearly reached the point for which he was destined he found opposed to him a body of mountaineers, in manners and intellect not much better than wild beasts or devils, who had assembled to the number of forty thousand, horse and foot and matchlockmen, had shut up the approaches against him, and prevented his further advance. . . . A conflict thus commenced, which continued with unabated obstinacy from dawn of day until nearly sunset. The enemy were however finally defeated, with the loss of seventeen thousand killed, a number taken prisoners, and a still greater proportion escaping to their hiding-places among the mountains. The prisoners were conducted to my presence yoked together, with the heads of the seventeen thousand slain in the battle suspended from their necks. After some deliberation as to the destiny of these captives, I resolved that their lives should be spared, and that they should be employed in bringing forage for my elephants.

The intercourse with Kabul, so long interrupted by the atrocities of these robbers, was now by the effect of Lushker Khan's victory completely re-established, and the communication so well secured, that every description of fruit the produce of that province may at present be procured at Lahore[9] every other day, although neither very cheap nor in great abundance. The shedding of so much human blood must ever be extremely painful; but until some other resource is discovered, it is unavoidable. Unhappily the functions of government cannot be carried on without severity, and occasional extinction of human life: for without something of the kind, some species of coercion and chastisement, the world would soon exhibit the horrible spectacle of mankind, like wild beasts, worrying each other to death with no other motive than rapacity and revenge. God is witness that there is no repose for crowned heads. There is no pain or anxiety equal to that which attends the possession of sovereign power, for to the possessor there is not in this world a moment's rest. . . .

If indeed, in contemplation of future contingencies, I have been sometimes led to deal with thieves and robbers with indiscriminate severity, whether during my minority or since my accession to the throne, never have I been actuated by motive of private interest or general ambition. The treachery and inconstancy of the world are to me as clear as the light of day. Of all that could be thought necessary to the enjoyment of life I have been singularly fortunate in the possession. In gold, and jewels, and sumptuous wardrobes, and in the choicest beauties the sun ever shone upon, what man has ever surpassed me? And had I then conducted myself without the strictest regard to the honor and happiness of God's creatures consigned to my care, I should have been the basest of oppressors.

Political Decline and Recovery in East Asia

In contrast to the strength and stability of the west and south Asian empires, political decline and disorder characterized the politics of East Asia during the 1500s and early

---

9. A city in modern Pakistan.

1600s. From Korea to Indonesia, and from Japan to the interior of China, ineffectual leadership, civil war, and corruption spread like a plague. But in the 1600s political recovery came to most of the region. New leadership brought stability to Japan and China, and in southeast Asia a few small but strong kingdoms emerged that were able to offer staunch resistance to the Portuguese and Dutch.

During the sixteenth century, civil war and rebellion reduced Japan to a state of political disintegration. Emperors reigned from the imperial capital in Kyoto, but their function was purely ceremonial. Actual political authority was supposedly in the hands of a military commander known as the *shogun*, who attempted to rule Japan by commanding the obedience and service of powerful aristocratic warriors who owned most of the land. This Japanese version of feudalism collapsed in the sixteenth century, when the most powerful lords, the *daimyo*, indulged in a bloody struggle for land and power. In these conflicts the daimyo enlisted both *samurai*, lesser members of Japan's feudal aristocracy, and commoners, whom they trained and armed for war.

Feudal anarchy ended in Japan as a result of the achievements of three men. Oda Nobunaga (1534–1582) abolished the shogunate and brought about half of Japan under his rule before a treacherous vassal assassinated him. His successor, Toyotomi Hideyoshi (1536–1598), continued this work of consolidation, which was completed by Tokugawa Ieyasu (1542–1616), who conquered his rivals and had himself declared shogun in 1603. The political system he established brought stability to Japan and served as the basis of Japanese government until the nineteenth century.

For China, political deterioration came later. In the late 1500s and early 1600s, the Ming Dynasty, having presided over a long and impressive era of orderly rule, lost its grip on the government and administration. Irresponsible emperors, factionalism, peasant discontent, corruption, and bankruptcy paved the way for rebellion, the collapse of the dynasty, and foreign invasion. In 1644, a rebel bandit leader, Li Tzu-ch'eng (1605–1645), captured the Ming capital of Peking (modern Beijing), and in despair the last Ming emperor hanged himself. Within months, however, Li Tzu-ch'eng was driven from the city by invading Manchus, a Mongoloid people from the north of China, who in the previous several decades had built a strong military organization in the region of the Amur River.

In the next twenty years the Manchus extended their authority over all China and breathed new life into the Chinese imperial system. They established China's last imperial dynasty, known in Chinese as Ch'ing, meaning "clear" or "pure." Until foreign pressure and internal decay undermined Ch'ing government and society in the nineteenth century, the dynasty presided over a state that in its size and efficiency inspired awe in all who knew it.

Political problems also beset the East Indies, the large group of islands in the Malay Archipelago, which separates Asia from Australia. The geography of the area discouraged the establishment of large kingdoms or empires, although in the fourteenth century the Kingdom of Majapahit, centered in Java, managed to establish its authority in parts of Sumatra, Borneo, and other islands. With Majapahit's disintegration in the late fourteenth century, the Sultanate of Malacca, centered in this important trading city on the Malay coast, seemed on the verge of establishing an empire of its own, but in 1511 it was conquered by the Portuguese.

For a time, it appeared that this area, much of it recently converted to Islam, had no state or ruler powerful enough to withstand further Portuguese inroads. In the sixteenth century, however, a number of such states emerged, the most important of which was the Sultanate of Acheh. Centered on the northern shore of the island of Sumatra, Muslim Acheh in the sixteenth century launched a series of "holy wars" against non-Muslims on Sumatra, until by mid-century it had subdued most of the island. Throughout the sixteenth and seventeenth centuries, the sultanate proved a formidable commercial and military rival to the Portuguese and Dutch and was the major center of Islamic culture in the region.

Tokugawa Hidetada

LAWS GOVERNING THE MILITARY HOUSEHOLDS

After defeating his enemies among the daimyo, Tokugawa Ieyasu became shogun in 1603. Three years later, to ensure an orderly succession, he conferred the office on his son, Hidetada. Ieyasu continued to dominate the government, however, and it was his decision to appoint a committee of scholars to draw up a code of behavior for members of Japan's feudal aristocracy. The result was the following system of laws presented to the shogun's major vassals in 1615.

Questions
for Analysis

1. What provisions of this edict are meant to ensure the shogun's control of his vassals?
2. What does this document reveal about the Tokugawa rulers' thoughts on the reasons for Japan's social and political disintegration in the sixteenth century?
3. Where is it possible to detect the influence of Confucian principles in this document?
4. What view of human nature serves as the basis for this document?

1. The study of literature and the practice of the military arts, archery and horsemanship, must be cultivated diligently. . . .

From of old the rule has been to practice "the arts of peace on the left hand, and the arts of war on the right"; both must be mastered. Archery and horsemanship are indispensable to military men. Though arms are called instruments of evil, there are times when they must be resorted to. In peacetime we should not be oblivious to the danger of war. Should we not, then, prepare ourselves for it?

2. Drinking parties and wanton revelry should be avoided.

In the codes that have come down to us this kind of dissipation has been severely proscribed. Sexual indulgence and habitual gambling lead to the downfall of a state.

3. Offenders against the law should not be harbored or hidden in any domain.

Law is the basis of social order. Reason may be violated in the name of the law, but law may not be violated in the name of reason. Those who break the law deserve heavy punishment.

4. Great lords (daimyo), the lesser lords, and officials should immediately expel from their domains any among their retainers or henchmen who have been charged with treason or murder.

Wild and wicked men may become weapons for overturning the state and destroying the people. How can they be allowed to go free?

5. Henceforth no outsider, none but the inhabitants of a particular domain, shall be permitted to reside in that domain.

Each domain has its own ways. If a man discloses the secrets of one's own country to another domain or if the secrets of the other domain are disclosed to one's own, that will sow the seeds of deceit and sycophancy.

6. Whenever it is intended to make repairs on a castle of one of the feudal domains, the (shogunate) should be notified. The construction of any new castles is to be halted and stringently prohibited.

"Big castles are a danger to the state."[1] Walls and moats are the cause of great disorders.

7. Immediate report should be made of innovations which are being planned or of factional conspiracies being formed in neighboring domains.

"Men all incline toward partisanship; few are wise and impartial. There are some who refuse to obey their masters, and others who feud with their neighbors."[2] Why, instead of abiding by the established order, do they wantonly embark upon new schemes?

8. Do not enter into marriage privately (i.e., without notifying the shogunate authorities).

Marriage follows the principle of harmony between yin and yang,[3] and must not be entered into lightly. In the *Book of Changes*[4], . . . it says, "Marriage should not be contracted out of enmity (against another). Marriages intended to effect an alliance with enemies (of the state) will

---

1. The quotation is a paraphrase from one of the Confucian Classics, "The Tradition of Tso," originally a commentary on one of the other Classics, "The Spring and Autumn Annals."

2. From the Seventeen Article Constitution of Prince Shotuku (573–621). While serving as regent for his aunt, Empress Suiko, the prince drew up seventeen principles of government designed to strengthen central authority and end disorder. He drew heavily on Confucian principles.

3. Yin and yang are the two fundamental forces, tendencies, or elements in Chinese philosophy that since ancient times have been used to explain change in natural processes of all sorts. Yin suggests qualities that are female, weak, dark, cold, and connected with the moon; Yang suggests qualities that are male, strong, warm, bright, and connected with the sun.

4. *The Book of Changes*, a treatise on divination, and *The Book of Poetry*, a collection of songs, are among the oldest of the Confucian Classics.

turn out badly." The Peach Blossom ode in *The Book of Poetry* also says that "When men and women are proper in their relationships and marriage is arranged at the correct time; then throughout the land there will be no loose women." To form an alliance by marriage is the root of treason.

9. Visits of the *daimyo* to the capital are to be in accordance with regulations.

The *Chronicles of Japan, Continued*[5] contains a regulation that "Clansmen should not gather together whenever they please, but only when they have to conduct some public business; and also that the number of horsemen serving as an escort in the capital should be limited to twenty. . . ." Daimyo should not be accompanied by a large number of soldiers. Twenty horsemen shall be the maximum escort for daimyo with an income of from one million to two hundred thousand *koku* of rice.[6] For those with an income of one hundred thousand *koku* or less, the escort should be proportionate to their income. On official missions, however, they may be accompanied by an escort proportionate to their rank.

10. Restrictions on the type and quality of dress to be worn should not be transgressed.

Lord and vassal, superior and inferior, should observe what is proper to their station in life. (Then follows an injunction against the wearing of fine white damask or purple silk by retainers without authorization.)

11. Persons without rank shall not ride in palanquins.[7]

From of old there have been certain families entitled to ride in palanquins without special permission, and others who have received such permission. Recently, however, even the ordinary retainers and henchmen of some families have taken to riding about in palanquins, which is truly the worst sort of presumption. Henceforth permission shall be granted only to the lords of the various domains, their close relatives and ranking officials, medical men and astrologers, those over sixty years of age, and those ill or infirm. In the cases of ordinary household retainers or henchmen who willfully ride in palanquins, their masters shall be held accountable.

Exceptions to this law are the court families, Buddhist prelates, and the clergy in general.

12. The samurai of the various domains shall lead a frugal and simple life.

When the rich make a display of their wealth, the poor are humiliated and envious. Nothing engenders corruption so much as this, and therefore it must be strictly curbed.

13. The lords of the domains should select officials with a capacity for public administration.

Good government depends on getting the right men. Due attention should be given to their merits and faults; rewards and punishments must be properly meted out. If a domain has able men, it

---

5. *Nihon shoki, The Chronicle of Japan,* written in A.D. 720, is the oldest official history of Japan, covering the mythical age of the gods up to the time of the Empress Jito, who reigned from A.D. 686 to 697. This quote comes from a sequel to *The Chronicle,* written in 697, called the *Shoku nihongi.*

6. One *koku* equaled about five bushels; a person's rank was determined by the amount of rice his lands produced.

7. Enclosed carriages, or litters, usually for one person, borne on the shoulders of several men by means of poles.

flourishes; if it lacks able men it is doomed to perish. This is the clear admonition of the wise men of old.

The purport of the foregoing should be conscientiously observed.

▓ K'ang-hsi

SELF-PORTRAIT

Among the most illustrious and successful Ch'ing emperors was K'ang-hsi, who after inheriting the throne in 1661 at the age of seven, reigned until 1722. During this sixty-one-year reign, he suppressed internal rebellion, invaded Mongolia, toured the country no less than six times, maintained public works, and, on the basis of the Ming civil service examination system, established an efficient administration. He also left behind a rich store of poems, essays, aphorisms, edicts, and sayings that reveal his thinking about life and politics. In 1974, the American historian Jonathan Spence drew on these writings and statements to compile a self-portrait of K'ang-hsi. The following excerpts, on justice and on the civil service examination system, are the emperor's own words.

Questions
for Analysis

1. What seems to be K'ang-hsi's view of the emperor's duties and responsibilities?
2. According to K'ang-hsi, what considerations determined his decisions about the punishment of wrongdoers? How do his views compare with those of Jahangir, the Mughal emperor?
3. How do K'ang-hsi's views of politics compare with those of Machiavelli (Chapter 2)?
4. What problems does the emperor see in the system of civil service examinations? What are his solutions?
5. Compare the emperor's views of the civil service examinations with those of Matteo Ricci in Chapter 2. The views of Ricci, a foreigner, seem much more favorable to the examination system than those of K'ang-hsi. What might explain this?
6. Compare Jahangir's and K'ang-hsi's descriptions of their treatment of prisoners. What seems to have been their motives? Which approach was more successful?

Giving life to people and killing people — those are the powers that the emperor has. He knows that administrative errors in government bureaus can be rectified, but that a criminal who has been executed cannot be brought back to life any more than a chopped string can be joined together again. He knows, too, that sometimes people have to be persuaded into morality by the example of an execution. In 1683, after Taiwan had been captured, the court lecturers and I discussed the image of the fifty-sixth hexagram in the *Book of Changes*,[1] "Fire on the Mountain": the calm of the mountain signifies the care that must be used in imposing penalties; the fire moves rapidly on, burning up the grass, like lawsuits that should be settled speedily. My reading of this was that the ruler needs both clarity and care in punishing: his intent must be to punish in order to avoid the need for further punishing.

Hu Chien-ching was a subdirector of the Court of Sacrificial Worship whose family terrorized their native area in Kiangsu, seizing people's lands and wives and daughters, and murdering people after falsely accusing them of being thieves. When a commoner finally managed to impeach him, the Governor was slow to hear the case, and the Board of Punishments recommended that Hu be dismissed and sent into exile for three years. I ordered instead that he be executed with his family and in his native place, so that all the local gentry might learn how I regarded such behavior. Corporal Yambu was sentenced to death for gross corruption in the shipyards. I not only agreed to the penalty

but sent guards officer Uge to supervise the beheading, and ordered that all shipyard personnel from generals down to private soldiers kneel down in full armor and listen to my warning that execution would be their fate as well unless they ended their evil ways. . . .

The final penalty of lingering death[2] must be given in cases of treason, as the Legal Code requires. . . . I awarded the same punishment to the rebel Wang Shih-yüan, who had claimed to be Chu San T'ai-tzu, the surviving Ming claimant to the throne, so that the Ming prince's name should be invoked no more as a rallying point for rebels, as had been done too many times before. When Ilaguksan Khu-tuktu, who had had his spies in the lamas' residences so that they would welcome Galdan's[3] army into China, and had plotted with Galdan and encouraged him in his rebellion, was finally caught, I had him brought to Peking and cut to death in the Yellow Temple, in the presence of all the Manchu and Mongol princes, and the senior officials, both civil and military. All that was left of Galdan were the ashes, but these we exposed to the public outside the Forbidden City. . . .

But apart from such treason cases, when there are men who have to be executed immediately . . . or when one is dealing with men like those who plotted against me in the Heir-Apparent crisis[4]

---

1. Also known as the *I ching*, or *Classic of Changes*, this is one of the Confucian Classics; it is a handbook for telling the future based on the study of eight trigrams (figures made up of three lines) and sixty-four hexagrams (figures made up of six lines).

2. A slow, painful, and humiliating punishment in which a person died from the administration of numerous cuts on the body.

3. A lama was a Buddhist priest, or monk, in Tibet, Mongolia, and western China. Galdan

was a leader of a Western Mongol tribe who in the late seventeenth century conquered much of Chinese Turkestan and Outer Mongolia; when he threatened Peking (modern Beijing), Emperor K'ang-hsi raised an army and crushed him in 1696.

4. One of several plots designed to bring the Ming back to power in China.

and had to be killed immediately and secretly without trial, I have been merciful where possible. For the ruler must always check carefully before executions, and leave room for the hope that men will get better if they are given the time. In the hunt one can kill all the animals caught inside the circle, but one can't always bear to shoot them as they stand there, trapped and exhausted. . . .

Of all the things that I find distasteful, none is more so than giving a final verdict on the death sentences that are sent to me for ratification. . . . Though naturally I could not go through every case in detail, I nevertheless got in the habit of reading through the lists in the palace each year, checking the name and registration and status of each man condemned to death, and the reason for which the death penalty had been given. Then I would check through the list again with the Grand Secretaries and their staff in the audience hall, and we would decide who might be spared. . . .

Each year we went through the lists, sparing sixteen out of sixty-three at one session, eighteen out of fifty-seven at another, thirty-three out of eighty-three at another. For example, it was clear to me that the three cases of husbands killing wives that came up . . . were all quite different. The husband who hit his wife with an ax because she nagged at him for drinking, and then murdered her after another domestic quarrel — how could any extenuating circumstances be found? But Pao-erh, who killed his wife for swearing at his parents; and Meng, whose wife failed to serve him properly and used foul language so that he killed her — they could have their sentences reduced. . . . At other times what looked like a lighter crime proved to be serious: thus Liu-ta had killed Ma-erh with a stone, but as the Grand Secretaries explained, the victim had been struck twelve times in all, and

his brains had burst out onto the ground. Liu-ta was obviously an experienced killer and should be executed. . . .

It's a good principle to look for the good points in a person, and to ignore the bad. If you are always suspicious of people they will suspect you too; that was why, when Dantsila was brought to my tent, although he was Galdan's nephew and had been fleeing to Tibet with the ashes of Galdan's body before he despaired and surrendered, I showed my trust by having him sit near me, and offered him a knife with which to cut his meat. Later I gave him a prince's title, and he served me faithfully. Though the Russians had been killing our people on the northern frontier, I ordered that the Russian prisoners should be given new suits of clothes and be released just as we began the siege of Albazin, and after the second siege in 1687 I ordered that the sick Russians be treated personally by my own doctors and sent home. So thirty years later the Uriang-hai people submitted to us without a battle, because they remembered our clemency to the Russians long before.

. . .

There are too many men who claim to be pure scholars and yet are stupid and arrogant; we'd be better off with less talk of moral principle and more practice of it. Even in those who have been the best officials in my reign there are obvious failings. . . . P'eng P'eng was always honest and courageous — when robbers were in his district he simply put on his armor, rode out, and routed them — but when angry he was wild and vulgar in his speech, and showed real disrespect. Chao Shen-ch'iao was completely honest, traveled with only thirteen servants and no personal secretaries at all, but was too fond of litigation and was constantly getting the common people involved in complex cases. Shih Shih-lun was an official of complete integrity, but he swung too much in favor of the poor — in any lawsuit when a commoner was involved with a junior degree holder he'd favor the commoner, and when a junior degree holder was involved with a member of the upper gentry he'd favor the junior degree holder. . . . And Chang P'eng-ko, whom I praised so often and kept in the highest offices, could write a memorial so stupid that I ordered it printed up and posted in major cities so that everyone could read it — for he claimed that the drop in the river's level was due to a miracle performed by the spirit of the waters, when the real reason was that no rain had fallen for six months in the upper reaches of the Yellow River. . . .

This is one of the worst habits of the great officials, that if they are not recommending their teachers or their friends for high office then they recommend their relations. This evil practice used to be restricted to the Chinese: they've always formed cliques and then used their recommendations to advance the other members of the clique. Now the practice has spread to the Chinese Bannermen[5] like Yü Ch'eng-lung; and even the Manchus, who used to be so loyal, recommend men from their own Banners, knowing them to have a foul reputation, and will refuse to help the Chinese. . . .

In 1694 I noted that we were losing talent because of the ways the exams were being conducted: even in the military exams most of the successful candidates were from Chekiang and Chiangnan, while there was only one from Honan and one from Shansi.[6] The successful ones had often done no more than memorize old examination answer books, whereas the best *should* be selected on the basis of riding and archery. Yet it is always the strong men from the western provinces who are eager to serve in the army, while not only are troops from Chekiang and Chiangnan among the weakest, they also pass on their posts to their relatives who are also weak.

Even among the examiners there are those who are corrupt, those who do not understand basic works, those who ask detailed questions about practical matters of which they know nothing, those who insist entirely on memorization of the *Classics*[7] and refuse to set essays, those who put candidates from their own geographical area at the top of the list, or those who make false claims about their abilities to select the impoverished and deserving. . . . As to the candidates, not only are there few in the Hanlin Academy who can write a proper eulogy, there are many whose calligraphy is bad and who can't even punctuate the basic history books. . . . Other candidates hire people to sit the exams for them, or else pretend to be from a province that has a more liberal quota than their own. It's usually easy enough to check the latter, since I've learnt to recognize the accents from thirteen provinces, and if you watch the person and study his voice you can tell where he is really from. As to the other problems, one can overcome some of them by holding the exams under rigorous armed supervision and then reading the exam papers oneself.

---

5. Minor members of the noble class, usually provided with land and a small stipend by the government.

6. Chekiang and Chiangnan were southeast coastal regions of China; Honan and Shansi were north-central provinces with no seacoast.

7. A clearly specified set of books associated with China's Confucian tradition.

HISTORY OF ACHEH

The anonymous *History of Acheh*, dating from the 1620s or 1630s, was written to praise the accomplishments of Sultan Iskanadar Muda (1607–1636), Acheh's most illustrious ruler. In 1613 he gathered a military force and came close to driving the Portuguese from Malacca. The following excerpt describes the experiences of two of his predecessors, who ruled during the 1590s and early 1600s, a turbulent period marked by several assassinations and coups d'état.

Questions for Analysis

1. In what ways does the story of Sultan Seri 'Alam prove or disprove the points Machiavelli makes in *The Prince* (Chapter 2) concerning frugality and generosity?
2. What seems to have been the main motive behind the assassination of Zainal-'Abidin?
3. What does this excerpt tell us about the powers and the limits to the authority of the Acheh sultans?
4. After the death of Iskanadar Muda in 1636, the Sultanate of Acheh declined. What does this excerpt suggest about the possible reasons for the weakening of Acheh?

After the kingdom of Acheh with all its subject territories had been handed over to Sultan Seri 'Alam, he acted very generously. He would sit in state in the Friday annex[1] every day from midday until almost sunset.

Then the various rulers, judges, important chiefs, lawyers, courtiers . . . and all their attendants would stand paying homage in the courtyard of the royal palace. While they were all paying homage, Sultan Seri 'Alam would endow them with gold, silver and luxurious clothing, according to each one's rank. Thus they became rich because of the Sultan's many gifts.

Now it happened at that time that the Maharaja,[2] the judges and prominent persons did not approve of this behavior in the Sultan. So one day the various rulers, judges and important chiefs gathered. Maharaja az-Zahir said, "Oh chiefs, why are we permitting our lord to behave like this, daily taking money from the State treasury and throwing it away on the undeserving? After all we do not know what may happen next. Only Almighty God knows that. If at any time an enemy should come from the west or the east, what could we spend on the military operations, because our lord Sultan Seri 'Alam is as lacking in wisdom and counsel

---

1. Presumably an annex to a mosque.
2. A term for a powerful prince, or chief.

as a queen? We and the chiefs, on the other hand, must think hard before all the money has been used up on gifts for the rulers and chiefs in the land of Fansur.[3] The chiefs and prominent men replied, "We and the senior chiefs are all in the same boat, and if it sinks we shall all go down together. So we will agree to whatever you both propose." Maharaja az-Zahir said, "It is our opinion that we should depose our lord Seri 'Alam, and that we should transfer the kingship to our lord Sultan Zainal, son of Sultan Ghori, in order to preserve the continuity of succession in the kingdom of Acheh from the line of Sayyid al-Marhum."[4]

Then Sultan Seri 'Alam was deposed and Sultan Zainal was installed. . . .

After the kingdom of Acheh and all its subject territories had been handed over to Sultan Zainal-'Abidin, he would always go out on to the arena and would have rutting[5] elephants as well as ones which were not rutting charge each other, and as a result several people were gored to death by them, and the Bunga Setangkai palace was rammed and then collapsed in ruins together with its annexes. He pitted very small elephants against each other, and had buffaloes and bullocks fight, as well as rams. When he had the buffaloes fight a number of people were either killed, had bones broken, or were crippled or blinded. He would order men to beat each other and to duel with staves and shields, and would order Achehnese champion fencers to compete with Indian ones, so that several of the Achehnese and Indian fencers were killed and some were wounded. And he would order men to wrestle and to throw each other to the ground and to practice *penchak* (a dance

consisting of a stylized representation of the movements of combat). He would order men to do war-dances, and some had their faces smashed and their cheeks blown out. He would order men . . . to fight with the long *kris* (Indonesian dagger), and some of them were injured. He would order Javanese to fight with lances, to perform *wayang* (shadow-theatre) and play the *gender* (Javanese xylophone-like musical instrument), and others to dance Javanese dances and Sundanese dances, and he would always be ordering people to sing, play the *harbab* (violin-like instrument), *kechapi* (four-stringed lute) and *bangsi* (flageolet), and give all kinds of performances.

This was the Sultan's constant practice: whether he was seated in state in the Bunga Setangkai palace in the square or was leaving for the river, if he saw a buffalo or bullock he ordered it to be cut down, and if he saw a sheep or a goat he would order that too to be killed. He would even instruct the Bujang Khayyal Allah and Bujang Dandani to catch a dog if it should happen to pass by while the Sultan was sitting in state in the Bunga Setangkai palace. But if they could not find it, he would become angry with them as a result; when he ordered people to hunt deer or pigs, if these should escape from anyone's reach this person would also fall into disfavor.

If the Sultan were holding audience in a certain place all the chiefs were instructed to sit in homage in the hot sun or in the rain without distinction between the good or the evil.

If the Sultan should spur on his horse when setting out and the chiefs could not keep up with it and were left behind, then

---

3. A town on the east coast of Sumatra.

4. Presumably the founder of the Achehnese royal dynasty.

5. Male elephants in a state of heightened sexual excitement.

they too would incur his wrath.

When the chiefs noticed these habits of the Sultan, and observed that they were growing worse day by day, they said to each other, "What should we do about our lord, for if his oppression of us is like this while he is still young, what will it be like when he is older? According to us, if he continues to be ruler everything will certainly fall in ruins about our ears." Then Sharif al-Muluk Maharaja Lela said, "If that is how it is, it would be best for us to depose our lord the Sultan."

After the chiefs had reached agreement on this matter, one evening the Sultan summoned persons to recite texts in praise of God, and the chiefs were summoned along with them. On that occasion they were reciting texts in the Friday annex. The Sultan was then put on an elephant and was taken to Makota 'Alam. When he arrived at Makota 'Alam . . . he was done to death. . . . In the same year Sultan 'Ala ad-Din Ri'ayat Shah Marhum Sayyid al-Mukkamil was installed.

4

Economic Patterns and Social Attitudes

*A*lthough the "simplicity" of traditional societies is often compared to the "complexity" of modern life, a glance at the world in the 1500s and 1600s shows that economic and social patterns were neither simple nor lacking in variety. In economics, the vast majority of human beings, as had been true for millennia, engaged in agricultural or pastoral pursuits, mainly geared for local consumption. But tremendous variation characterized the world's agrarian societies in farming methods, patterns of land ownership, economic decision-making, marketing, and crops and animals. Furthermore, in some areas of the world, agricultural products such as spices, cotton, and wool were important items of international trade. Most manufacturing was carried out on a small scale, usually by individual artisans, and geared for a local market. But the methods and organization of such enterprises showed much variation, and some manufactured goods such as weapons, textiles, jewelry, and glassware entered world trade networks.

International commerce, involving complicated trade routes, extensive government regulation, and elaborate forms of business organization, was the most complex economic activity, even though comparatively few individuals engaged in it. Unlike agriculture and manufacturing, international trade changed fundamentally during the 1500s and 1600s. Beginning with the Spanish discovery of the Americas and the Portuguese arrival in India, European merchants opened new transatlantic trade routes involving Africa and the Americas and became serious competitors in Indian Ocean and east Asian trade.

Worldwide social structures and attitudes in the sixteenth and seventeenth centuries also showed much variation. The preponderance of agriculture meant that the world's population was overwhelmingly rural and that large landowners composed the wealthiest, most privileged, and most powerful class in most societies. World societies were also male-dominated. Women were considered inferior to men and had few rights. After these broad generalizations, however, the diversity of human social relationships becomes apparent. Child-rearing, gender roles, marriage, family patterns, attitudes toward the elderly, vocational status, and the degree of social mobility are just some of the areas in which the customs of the world's peoples showed marked heterogeneity.

Asian Commercial Activity and Attitudes

Carrying surplus goods from one area and selling them elsewhere for a profit has been one of humankind's oldest economic activities. By the 1500s, both the Old and New Worlds were crisscrossed by hundreds of thousands of miles of overland and water routes on which a vast variety of goods were transported and sold. None of them, however, rivaled the volume or profitability of the commerce centered in south and southeast Asia. The region itself was traversed by dozens of routes that linked China, Japan, the Philippines, the major islands of Indonesia, the Malay Peninsula, Indochina, and India. In addition, a strong market existed throughout western Eurasia and Africa for Asian products. Merchants carried east Asian spices, silks, porcelain, precious jewels, and medicines on pack animals or in the holds of ships to India, Africa, and Europe, where they commanded high prices. India itself produced spices, dyes, and fabrics sold in European, African, and east Asian markets. African merchants were able to exchange slaves, ivory, and animal skins for some of Asia's products, but for the most part Africans and Europeans paid for Asian commodities with gold and silver.

Chinese merchants had been involved in this regional and international commerce for many centuries, and they also bought and sold salt, manufactured goods, and agricultural products in the huge Chinese domestic market. Every indication suggests that during the early years of the Ming Dynasty (1368–1644), Chinese foreign and domestic trade steadily increased, thus enriching merchant families and raising substantial revenues for the imperial government. China had the capacity to become one of the world's premier maritime and commercial powers. But it failed to do so.

One of the reasons for this failure was the disdain of China's ruling class for commercial activity. This attitude was deeply rooted in Confucianism, which viewed merchants as exploiters and placed them at the bottom of the social hierarchy, below scholars, farmers, and artisans. Such views were widespread among Chinese government officials, mostly drawn from the landed gentry and thoroughly Confucian in their training. Late Ming emperors discouraged long-distance foreign trade and hampered commercial growth by heavily taxing merchant wealth. By default, control of the east Asian oceans and ultimately Chinese coastal trade fell into the hands of foreigners — for a time the Japanese and later the Europeans and Americans.

Tomé Pires

ACCOUNT OF THE EAST

Little is known about the early life of Tomé Pires, who sailed from Portugal to India in 1511, just thirteen years after his countryman Vasco da Gama became the first European to reach India by sailing around the Cape of Good Hope, on the southern tip of Africa. Born in 1468 in Lisbon, Pires served as the apothecary for the Portuguese royal family and was sent to India in 1511 to purchase medicinal drugs for King Manuel I. After spending several months in southern India, he was sent to Malacca, the port city on the west coast of the Malay peninsula that the Portuguese had conquered in 1511. Malacca was an important center of Asian trade, and while there Pires, a careful observer, gathered a wealth of information about commercial practices. He also visited the island of Java and other areas of southeast Asia. In 1517 he completed for King Manuel a report on Asian commerce, known as the *Suma Oriental*, or *Account of the East.* Having amassed a sizable fortune in trading ventures, he hoped at this point to return to Portugal. Instead, at his king's behest, he traveled to China, where he became the first Portuguese ambassador to the imperial Chinese court in Peking (modern Beijing). There he died in 1540.

While reading this document, consult the map on page 130, where many of the places mentioned by Pires are identified.

Questions
for Analysis

1. What is Pires's estimate of the capabilities of the Asian merchants? Which merchants does he admire the most? Why?
2. Does Pires find any noticeable differences or similarities between Asian and European merchants?
3. What types of goods comprised the trade of the region? What might one guess about who would be the major consumers of such goods?
4. Are there any signs of European involvement in the region's trade before the arrival of the Portuguese?
5. What seem to be Pires's assumptions about the future of Portuguese involvement in the region?

GUJARAT[1]

I now come to the trade of Cambay. These (people) are (like) Italians in their knowledge of and dealings in merchandise. All the trade in Cambay is in the hands of the heathen.[2] Their general designation is Gujaratees. . . . There is no doubt that these people have the cream of the trade. They are men who understand merchandise; they are so properly steeped in the sound and harmony of it, that the Gujara-

tees say that any offence connected with merchandise is pardonable. There are Gujaratees settled everywhere. They work some for some and others for others. They are diligent, quick men in trade. They do their accounts with figures like ours and with our very writing. They are men who do not give away anything that belongs to them, nor do they want anything that belongs to anyone else; wherefore they have been esteemed in Cambay up to the pres-

1. Gujarat is the region on the northwest coast of India on the Arabian Sea, just to the south of modern Pakistan.

2. The reference is to Hindus.

ent, practising their idolatry, because they enrich the kingdom greatly with the said trade. There are also some Cairo merchants settled in Cambay, and many . . . from Aden and Ormuz, all of whom do a great trade in the seaport towns of Cambay; but none of these count in comparison with the heathens, especially in knowledge. Those of our people who want to be clerks and factors[3] ought to go there and learn, because the business of trade is a science in itself which does not hinder any other noble exercise, but helps a great deal.

They trade with the kingdom of the Deccan and Goa and with Malaba, and they have factors everywhere, who live and set up business — as the Genoese do in our part (of the world) — taking back to their own country the kind of merchandise which is valued there. And there is no trading place where you do not see Gujarat merchants. Gujarat ships come to these kingdoms every year, one ship straight to each place. The Gujaratees used to have large factories in Calicut.

The Cambay merchants make Malacca their chief trading centre. There used to be a thousand Gujarat merchants in Malacca, besides four or five thousand Gujarat seamen, who came and went. Malacca cannot live without Cambay, nor Cambay without Malacca, if they are to be very rich and very prosperous. All the clothes and things from Gujarat have trading value in Malacca and in the kingdoms which trade with Malacca; for the products of Malacca are esteemed not only in this world, but in others, where no doubt they are wanted. . . . If Cambay were cut off from trading with Malacca, it could not live, for it would have no outlet for its merchandise. . . .

SIAM[4]

Through the cunning (of the Siamese) the foreign merchants who go to their land and kingdom leave their merchandise in the land and are ill paid; and this happens to them all — but less to the Chinese, on account of their friendship with the king of China. And for this reason less people go to their port than would (otherwise) go. However, as the land is rich in good merchandise, they bear some things on account of the profit, as often happens to merchants, because otherwise there would be no trading.

There is a great abundance of rice in Siam, and much salt, dried salt fish, *oraquas*,[5] vegetables; and up to thirty

---

3. A business representative, or agent.

4. Former name of Thailand.

5. This is the first of numerous commodities mentioned by Pires that may be unfamiliar to most readers. They are listed here together:
Oraquas: A distilled spirit from the palm tree.
Lac: A resinous substance produced by females of the lac insect; used as a red dye and in the making of varnishes.
Benzoin: A resin produced by certain tropical trees; used as a medicine.
Brazil: Refers to brazilwood, any of several tropical trees whose wood produced a red dye.
Cassia fistula: Pods from an East Indian tree used as a mild laxative.

Quicksilver: Mercury.
Vermilion: A fragrant heartwood used as incense.
Cowries: Shells used for jewelry or, in some societies, money.
Borneo camphor: A compound derived from the camphor tree; used for medicinal purposes.
Alum: A compound used for making dyes and as a medicine.
Lignaloes: The wood of the aloes tree, burnt as incense.
Saltpeter: Potassium nitrate, used for making gunpowder.
Liquid storax: A solid resin obtained from a small tropical tree; used as a medicine and as a perfume.

junks[6] a year used to come to Malacca with these.

From Siam comes lac, benzoin, brazil, lead, tin, silver, gold, ivory, cassia fistula; they bring vessels of cast copper and gold, ruby and diamond rings; they bring a large quantity of cheap, coarse Siamese cloth for the poor people.

They say that the chief merchandise they take from Malacca to Siam are the male and female slaves, which they take in quantities, white sandalwood, pepper, quicksilver, vermilion, opium, cloves, mace, nutmeg, wide and narrow muslins,[7] camlets, rosewater, carpets, brocades from Cambay, white cowries, wax, Borneo camphor, and the merchandise they bring from China every year is also of value there. . . .

The Siamese trade in China — six or seven junks a year. They trade with Sunda and other islands. They trade with Cambodia, Cochin China,[8] and with Burma when they are at peace. . . .

CHINA

It certainly seems that China is an important, good and very wealthy country, and the Governor of Malacca[9] would not need as much force as they say in order to bring it under our rule, because the people are very weak and easy to overcome. And the principal people who have often been there affirm that with ten ships the Governor of India who took Malacca could take the whole of China along the seacoast. And China is twenty days' sail distant for our ships. They leave here at the end of June for a good voyage, and with a monsoon wind they can go in fifteen days. From China they have recently begun sailing to Borneo, and they say that they go there in fifteen days, and that this must have been for the last fifteen years.

The chief merchandise is pepper — of which they will buy ten junk-loads a year if as many go there — cloves, a little nutmeg . . . they will buy a great deal of incense, elephants' tusks, tin, apothecary's lignaloes; they buy a great deal of Borneo camphor, red beads, white sandalwood, brazil, infinite quantities of the black wood that grows in Singapore. . . . Pepper apart, they make little account of all the rest.

The said junks from Malacca go and anchor off the island of Tumon, twenty or thirty leagues[10] away from Canton. These islands are near the land of Nan-t'ou, a league to seaward from the mainland. Those from Malacca anchor there in the port of Tumon and those from Siam in the port of Hucham. Our port is three leagues nearer to China than the Siamese one,

---

Rosewater: A preparation consisting of water and the oil of roses; used as a perfume.

Madder: A plant whose root was used as a yellow dye.

6. Seagoing ships, primarily used in Chinese waters.

7. Pires mentions several types of fabrics. They include:

Muslins: Various kinds of cotton cloth, often dyed or printed.

Camlets: Rich fabrics made from camel's wool or angora wool.

Brocades: Fabrics with an elaborate raised design.

Damask: A reversible fabric, made of silk or linen.

Taffeta: A fine, rather stiff, silk cloth with a sheen.

8. A region in southern Vietnam.

9. The Portuguese governor of Malacca.

10. A measurement of length, varying in different countries and at different times, but usually thought to mean approximately three miles.

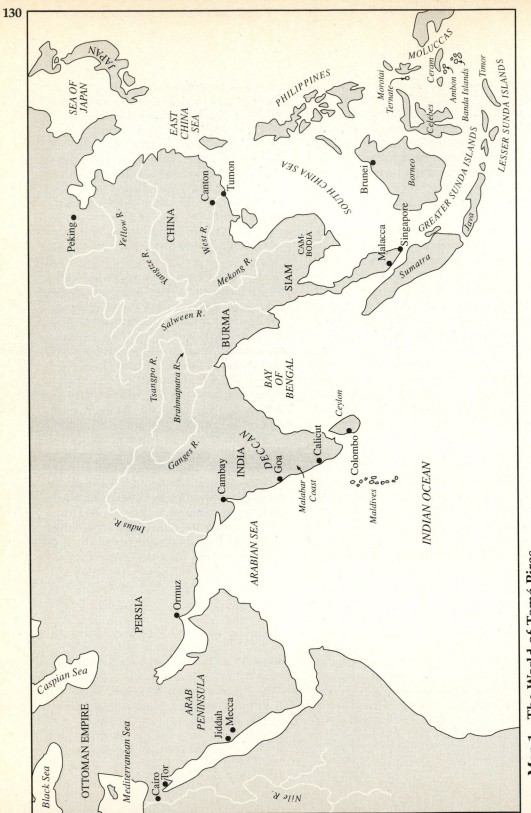

Map 1 The World of Tomé Pires

and merchandise comes to it rather than to the other.

As soon as the lord of Nan-t'ou sees the junks he immediately sends word to Canton that junks have gone in among the islands; the valuers from Canton go out to value the merchandise; they receive their dues; they bring just the amount of merchandise that is required: the country is pretty well accustomed to estimate it, so well do they know of you the goods you want, and they bring them. . . .

The chief merchandise from China is raw white silk in large quantities, and loose colored silks, many in quantity, satins of all colors, damask checkered in all colors, taffetas and other thin silk cloths and many other kinds of all colors; an abundance of seed-pearl in various shapes, mostly irregular; they also have some big round ones — this in my opinion is as important a merchandise in China as silk, although they count silk as the chief merchandise — musk in powder and in pods, plenty of this, and certainly good, apothecary's camphor in large quantities, alum, saltpetre, sulphur, copper, iron, rhubarb, . . . vases of copper, cast iron kettles, bowls, basins, quantities of these things, boxes, fans, plenty of needles of a hundred different kinds, some of them very fine and well made, these are good merchandise, and things of very poor quality like those which come to Portugal from Flanders, countless copper bracelets; gold and silver come and I did not see much, and many brocades of their kind, and porcelains beyond count. Of the things which come from China some are products from China itself and some from outside. . . .

Salt is a great merchandise among the Chinese. It is distributed from China to these regions; and it is dealt with by fifteen hundred junks which come to buy it, and it is loaded in China to go to other places. Traders in this are very rich and they say to one another among themselves, "Are you a salt merchant to speak of?"

THE MOLUCCAS

The chief island of all the five (Moluccas) is the island of Ternate. The king is a Mohammedan. He is called Sultan Bem Acorala. They say he is a good man. His island produces at least a hundred and fifty bahars[11] of cloves every year. Two or three ships can anchor in the port of this island; this is a good village. This king has some foreign merchants in his country. Gold comes from other islands. It has some little ivory; it has coarse native cloth. A great many parrots come from the islands of Morotai and the white parrots come from Ceram. . . .

Do not say that the navigation from Malacca to the Moluccas is dangerous, for it is a good route and convenient for our ships. . . . Our well-equipped ships . . . must go on to the Moluccas, especially anyone who has been able to learn and investigate how to come from Portugal to the Moluccas in such a short time; anyone will be able, as is known, when his turn comes and if he works — anyone who is zealous that things should be accomplished in the service of the King our lord — to make the journey of the Moluccas not by way of the coast of Java, but by Singapore, and from Singapore to Borneo and from Borneo to the island of Buton and then to the Moluccas. Anyone who

---

11. A measurement of weight, approximately 350 pounds.

has sailed to the Moluccas has always found this a very good way, in a monsoon, and quick. . . .

MALACCA

Finally, in the port of Malacca very often eighty-four languages have been found spoken, every one distinct, as the inhabitants of Malacca affirm; and this in Malacca alone, because in the archipelago which begins at Singapore . . . up to the Moluccas, there are forty known languages, for the islands are countless.

Because those from Cairo and Mecca and Aden cannot reach Malacca in a single monsoon.[12] as well as the Parsees[13] and those from Ormuz, Turks and similar peoples such as Armenians, at their own time they go to the kingdom of Gujarat, bringing large quantities of valuable merchandise; and they go to the kingdom of Gujarat to take up their companies in the said ships of that land, and they take the said companies in large numbers. They also take from the said kingdoms to Cambay, merchandise of value in Gujarat, from which they make much profit. Those from Cairo take their merchandise to Tor, and from Tor to Jidda, and from Jidda to Aden, and from Aden to Cambay, where they sell in the land things which are valued there, and the others they bring to Malacca, sharing as aforesaid.

Those from Cairo bring the merchandise brought by the galleasses of Venice, to wit, many arms, scarlet-in-grain, colored woollen cloths, coral, copper, quicksilver, vermilion, nails, silver, glass and other beads, and golden glassware.

Those from Mecca bring a great quantity of opium, rosewater and such like merchandise, and much liquid storax.

Those from Aden bring to Gujarat a great quantity of opium, raisins, madder, indigo, rosewater, silver, seed-pearls, and other dyes, which are of value in Cambay.

In these companies go Parsees, Turks, Turkomans and Armenians, and they come and take up their companies for their cargo in Gujarat, and from there they embark in March and sail direct for Malacca; and on the return journey they call at the Maldive Islands.

Four ships come every year from Gujarat to Malacca. The merchandise of each ship is worth fifteen, twenty, or thirty thousand *cruzados*,[14] nothing less than fifteen thousand. And from the city of Cambay one ship comes every year; this is worth seventy or eighty thousand *cruzados*, without any doubt.

The merchandise they bring is cloths of thirty kinds, which are of value in these parts; . . . they bring rosewater and opium; from Cambay and Aden they bring seeds, grains, tapestries and much incense; they bring forty kinds of merchandise.

The principal merchandise brought back is cloves, mace, nutmeg, sandalwood, seed-pearls, some porcelain, a little musk; they carry enormous quantities of apothecary's lignaloes, and finally some benzoin, for they load up with spices, and of the rest they take a moderate amount. And besides they take gold, enormous quantities of white silk, tin, much white damask — they take great pains to get this — colored silks, birds from Banda for plumes for Turks and Arabs, which are much prized there. These have the main Malacca trade. . . .

---

12. The time during the summer in the Indian Ocean and southern Asia when the wind blows from the southwest.

13. Indians of Persian descent.

14. A *cruzado* is a Portuguese gold coin.

It is an old custom in Malacca that as soon as the merchants arrive they unload their cargo and pay their dues or presents, as will be said. Ten or twenty merchants gathered together with the owner of the said merchandise and bid for it, and by the said merchants the price was fixed and divided amongst them all in proportion. And because time was short and the merchandise considerable, the merchants were cleared, and then those of Malacca took the merchandise to their ships and sold them at their pleasure; from which the traders received their settlement and gains, and the local merchants made their profits. And through this custom the land lived in an orderly way, and they carried on their business. And that was done thus orderly, so that they did not favor the merchant from the ship, nor did he go away displeased; for the law and the prices of merchandise in Malacca are well known.

Wang Tao-k'un

BIOGRAPHY OF CHU CHIEH-FU AND GENTLEMAN WANG

Wang Tao-k'un (1525–1593), whose father and grandfather were salt merchants, was a child prodigy who at the age of twenty began a long career as an official in the Chinese imperial bureaucracy. He served as governor of several provinces and filled important offices in the upper echelons of the Chinese army. In 1575 he abandoned his career as a public servant to care for his aged parents. Until his death in 1593 he occupied himself by writing treatises on a wide variety of subjects, among them card playing, drinking games, and proper sacrifices to the gods. He also wrote a series of biographies of Chinese merchants, which reveal the characteristics admirable merchants were expected to have in the eyes of a sixteenth-century Confucian scholar-official.

Questions for Analysis

1. What, according to Wang Tao-k'un are the virtues of Chu Chieh-fu and Gentleman Wang? To what extent do the two merchants represent different virtues?
2. What does this source suggest about Chinese attitudes toward elders? Toward political authority? Toward the proper use of wealth?
3. On the basis of these biographies, what may one infer about the status of women in Chinese society?
4. What do these biographies reveal about the Chinese government's attitudes and policies toward merchants? Does the author reveal any bias toward either the merchants or the government officials in their dealings with one another?

THE BIOGRAPHY OF CHU CHIEH-FU

Chu Chieh-fu . . . started as a Confucian scholar. He was from T'un-hsi . . . and his father . . . was a salt merchant who lived away from home at the Wu-lin. Hsing had taken Shao-chi of Wu-lin as his concubine[1] but she was barren. Later, when he returned home for his father-in-law's birthday, his primary wife became pregnant and gave birth to Chieh-fu. In his early childhood, Chieh-fu lived in Wu-lin with his father and went to school there. Shao-chi, relying on the father's favor, did not treat him as her son. Chieh-fu, however, served her respectfully and worked diligently in school. At the age of fourteen, he officially registered Wu-lin as his native place and was designated an official student of that place.[2] Shortly thereafter, his father died at Wu-lin. His concubine took the money and hid it with some of her mother's relatives and would not return to her husband's hometown. Chieh-fu wept day and night, saying, "However unworthy I may be, my late father was blameless." Finally the concubine arranged for the funeral and burial of her husband in his hometown. Thus, everything was done properly.

After the funeral, Chieh-fu was short of funds. Since for generations his family had been in commerce, he decided not to suffer just to preserve his scholar's cap. Therefore he handed in his resignation to the academic officials and devoted himself to the salt business. He thoroughly studied the laws on salt merchandising and was always able to talk about the strengths and weaknesses of the law. . . .

Therefore, all the other salt merchants respected him as their leader.

During the Chia-ching period (1522–1567), salt affairs were handled by the Central Law Officer,[3] who increased the taxes suddenly, causing great inconvenience for the merchants. They gathered in Chieh-fu's house and asked him to serve as their negotiator. Chieh-fu entered the office and stated the advantages and disadvantages of the new law eloquently in thousands of words. Leaning against his couch, the Central Law Officer listened to Chieh-fu's argument and finally adopted his suggestion.

At that time, the merchants suffered greatly from two scoundrels who often took them to court in the hopes of getting bribes from them. During tense moments at trials, the merchants usually turned to Chieh-fu as their spokesman. Being lofty and righteous, he always disclosed the soundrels' crimes and condemned them. The merchants thus esteemed Chieh-fu for his virtue and wanted to give him a hundred taels of gold as a birthday present. But he protested: "Even if my acts have not been at the lofty level of a knight-errant, I did not do them for the sake of money." Thus, the merchants respected him even more and no longer talked about giving him money.

When there was a dispute among the merchants which the officials could not resolve, Chieh-fu could always mediate it immediately. Even when one group would go to his house and demand his compliance with their views, he would still be able to settle the dispute by indirect and gentle persuasion. Hence, people both far and near followed each other, coming to ask him to be their arbitrator.

---

1. It was common for men to have concubines, in some cases, several of them, in addition to their legal wives. No legal impediments prevented children of concubines from inheriting their father's property.

2. This meant that Chu Chieh-fu was being groomed to take the Chinese civil service examinations for entry into the imperial bureaucracy.

3. An official of the imperial bureaucracy.

Yet, after settling a dispute, Chieh-fu would always step aside and never take credit himself.

The populace in T'un-hsi city where Chieh-fu lived was militant and litigious. When he returned home for his father's funeral, slanderous rumors were spread about him, but Chieh-fu humbled himself and never tried to get back at the instigators. Later, when he grew rich rapidly, people became even more critical. Chieh-fu merely behaved with even greater deference. When the ancestral shrine fell into disrepair, Chieh-fu on his own sent workmen to repair it. When members of his lineage started talking about it, he had the workmen work during the day and consulted with his relatives in the evening. Finally the whole lineage got together and shared the task with him.

Once Chieh-fu bought a concubine in Wu-lin who bore a child after only a few months. His family was about to discard the child but Chieh-fu upbraided them, saying, "I love my children dearly. How could I cause someone else's child to die in the gutter?" He brought the child up and educated him until he was able to support himself. . . .

Chieh-fu finally discontinued his salt business and ordered his son to pursue a different career. By that time he was already planning to retire to his hometown. Then in 1568 a Central Law Officer who was appointed to inspect the salt business started to encourage secret informants. Soon Chieh-fu was arrested, an enemy having laid a trap for him. However, the official could not find any evidence against him. But then Ho, whose son Chieh-fu had once scolded, came forward to testify. Consequently, Chieh-fu was found guilty. When the litigation against him was completed, he was sentenced to be a frontier guard at Ting-hai. The merchants said, in describing Chieh-fu's case: "Beating the drum, the official seized a

lamb and claimed it to be a tiger; pretending to net a big fish, he actually aimed at the big bird."

When Chieh-fu received his sentence to enter the army, he controlled his feelings and immediately complied. His son, fearing his father would acquire a bad name, suggested that he send a petition to the Emperor. Chieh-fu merely sighed and said, "Your father must have offended Heaven. The truth is that the Central Law Officer is a representative of his Heavenly Majesty, not that your father is falsely charged."

Frontier General Liu had heard of Chieh-fu and therefore summoned him to work in his own encampment. At that time, a friend of the General's moved to Hsin-tu upon his retirement. The General sent Chieh-fu to Hsin-tu as his personal messenger but within a short time Chieh-fu became seriously ill. He advised his son, Cheng-min: "Your father's name has been recorded in the official labor records. Now he is about to die as a prisoner. Never let your father's example stop you from behaving righteously. Remember this." Then, at the age of sixty-five, he died.

THE BIOGRAPHY OF GENTLEMAN WANG

. . . Mr. Wang lives in Shang-hai. Being open and confident he has attracted the respect of many capable and prosperous people who compete to attach themselves to him. At first, Mr. Wang's capital was no greater than the average person's. Later, as he grew more prosperous every day, the number of his associates also steadily increased. To accommodate his apprentices, Mr. Wang built buildings with doors on four sides. Whenever customers came, they could be taken care of from all four directions; thus, no one ever had to wait very long.

Mr. Wang set up the following guidelines for his associates: do not let anyone who lives in another county control the banking; when lending money, never harass law-abiding people unnecessarily or give them less than they need; charge low interest on loans; do not aim at high profit and do not ask for daily interest. These principles led customers to throng to him, even ones from neighboring towns and provinces. Within a short time, Mr. Wang accumulated great wealth; in fact, of all the rich people in that area he became the richest.

Mr. Wang liked to help people and to give assistance to the poor. If anyone among his kinsmen could not afford a funeral for his parents, Mr. Wang would always buy some land and build a tomb for him. As soon as he heard someone could not make ends meet, he would buy land to rent to him. Whenever he was out traveling and met some unburied spirit, he would bid his servants bury it and present some offerings.

During the Chia-ching period (1522–1567), there was a serious drought, and the Prefect[4] proposed opening the granary. Considering the hardship this would cause the people, Mr. Wang sent a written report to the Prefect, as follows:

This proposal will cause starving people to travel here from hundreds of *li*[5] away to wait for the distribution. Even if there are no delays en route, they may die before they get here. Yet if we make them stay home and wait for a pint of food, it will be like abandoning them to die in the gutters. I suggest that we exchange the grain for money and distribute it around the area. All the wealthy people ought to donate some money to help the poor. I myself will start with a donation of a hundred taels[6] of gold.

The Prefect accepted his suggestion and everyone said that this was much more convenient. Then Mr. Wang also prepared some food to feed people in his own county and caused similar actions to be taken throughout the whole of Shang-hai. Thus most people in this area survived. . . .

Whenever there was a dispute, Mr. Wang could always resolve it immediately, even if it was quite serious. When Magistrate Hsü was in charge of Shang-hai, he imprisoned someone named Chu, who died in jail. The victim's father then presented a petition to the Emperor which worried the Magistrate. The officials, elders, and local leaders were willing to offer the father a thousand taels of gold on the Magistrate's behalf, but on discussing it, they decided only Mr. Wang could settle the matter, and indeed he persuaded the father to accept the terms. Then the Magistrate was transferred to another position. Upon learning this fact, the officials, elders, and local leaders all quickly dispersed. Mr. Wang sighed and said, "It isn't easy to collect a thousand taels of gold but I will not break the promise made to the Magistrate in trouble." He then paid the thousand taels of gold and the Magistrate was out of his difficulties. Even when Magistrate Hsü was dismissed soon thereafter, Mr. Wang did not voice any concern, and after two years Hsü returned the thousand taels of gold to him. . . .

When Mr. Wang is at home he is always in high spirits. He likes to make friends with the chivalrous youths. In his later years he has become particularly fond of chess, often staying up all night until he either wins or loses a game. The youths say that Mr. Wang is no ordinary person, that he must have received instruction from Heaven.

---

4. Also an official of the imperial bureaucracy.

5. A Chinese measure of distance, approximately a third of a mile.

6. A coin, weighing approximately an ounce and a half.

Now Mr. Wang is almost one hundred years old. He has at least thirty sons and grandsons living at home with him.

It is said, "One who seeks perfection will attain it." This describes Mr. Wang perfectly.

Business Organization and State Planning in the European Economy

In 1500 even the best-informed observer could not have predicted Europe's revolutionary role in the world economy over the next several centuries. Europe was just recovering from a 150-year economic slump marked by population loss, industrial stagnation, and commercial decline. As it had for several centuries, the region suffered from an imbalance of trade caused by high European demand for Asian spices, cottons, and silks and by Asia's indifference to European manufactures and agricultural products. Having to pay for imports with cash, Europeans found their supplies of gold and silver shrinking to alarmingly low levels.

By 1700, however, Europe's economic situation had changed dramatically. During the sixteenth and seventeenth centuries, its population grew, its supplies of gold and silver were replenished, its manufacturing expanded, and its merchants emerged as the most aggressive and successful in the world. The causes of this striking economic growth might at first seem obvious. Clearly, overseas expansion, with its attending influx of American gold and silver, and its creation of lucrative new commercial opportunities, was the most important single factor. But what enabled Europeans to take advantage of these new resources and opportunities? The answer lies partly in the economic policies of the major European states and partly in the development of new forms of business organization.

During the 1500s and 1600s European governments pursued an economic policy known as *mercantilism*, the avowed purpose of which was to strengthen the state by encouraging the development of industry, the growth of commerce, and self-sufficiency in agriculture. Although governments had regulated economic activities since the Middle Ages, mercantilism was a new approach to regulation that reflected the growing competitiveness of the European state system. Mercantilism was viewed as economic warfare, in which each nation competed in the world market for economic advantages that would increase revenues, maintain high employment, and create a favorable balance of trade, all at the expense of its rivals. Later advocates of laissez-faire came to regard its doctrine of extensive government regulation of the nation's economy as counterproductive and unnecessary. During the 1500s and 1600s, however, government encouragement of commerce and manufacturing undoubtedly contributed to Europe's economic expansion.

In addition to governments, tens of thousands of individuals contributed to Europe's economic growth through their investment in joint stock companies. Ever since the Middle Ages, European merchants and bankers had pooled their money and talents to carry on commercial enterprises. These early arrangements proved incapable of generating the large amounts of capital necessary to finance the expensive and risky transoceanic ventures of the sixteenth and seventeenth centuries. The solution was a form of business organization known as the *joint stock company*. Having received a government monopoly to trade in a specific region, such as Russia or the East Indies, joint stock companies raised capital by issuing stock to individual investors, who would then share in the companies' profits or liabilities. Not all such companies were profitable, but those that were played an instrumental role in Europe's commercial expansion.

Jean Baptiste Colbert

"ON MARITIME COMMERCE" AND "MEMORANDUM TO KING LOUIS XIV ON ROYAL FINANCES"

Born into a family of merchants in Reims in 1619, Jean Baptiste Colbert was the best known and most powerful minister of King Louis XIV of France (1643–1715). During the 1660s Colbert held several positions in the royal administration, the most important of which was Controller General of Finance. No statesman better represents the policies of seventeenth-century mercantilism; for the French, the words mercantilism and "Colbertism" are synonymous. Colbert's goal was to strengthen the French economy so that Louis would have the resources to successfully fight his wars. In the following memoranda, addressed to his king, Colbert summarizes the theory and practice of mercantilism.

Questions
for Analysis

1. Why is Colbert convinced of the importance of maximizing the amount of silver circulating in France?
2. Why does Colbert feel it necessary for France to increase its foreign trade?
3. What specific measures does Colbert propose to reach his goal of a prosperous and economically competitive France?
4. What relationship does Colbert see between foreign trade and domestic output of manufactured and agricultural goods?
5. To what extent does Colbert seem concerned about the economic welfare of the French people?

[*On Maritime Commerce (1669)*]
There are two kinds of commerce in all states: that which is carried on within, and that which is carried on abroad by means of navigation of the seas. . . .

In regard to the second, as it is the most

important matter in the world, it is very necessary to understand well in what it consists. . . . Maritime commerce consists of five main parts: The first is the carrying of materials and merchandise from port to port and from one province to another in the same kingdom, for consumption within the country. The second is the bringing in from neighboring states of merchandise and material required for the consumption of the country, whether as necessities or luxuries. The third is the carrying of all the European manufactures needed by the Levant,[1] and the bringing back of all the products of the Levant which are needed for the manufacturing or consumption of all Europe. . . . The fourth (is) the commerce of the West Indies. . . . The fifth consists in carrying to the North all the said materials and merchandise which grow or are the manufactures of the states and kingdoms of Europe or the (West) Indies, and in taking back those special things which are found there, particularly wood, hemp, masts, copper, iron and other necessities of navigation. . . .

All these different kinds of commerce have always been pursued in Europe, with the distinction that while they are controlled by a single nation, consumption has been less and goods have always been more expensive. As a consequence commerce has drawn more money from other regions to enrich and give more wealth to that country controlling it. . . .

With this knowledge, and after close examination, one can say certainly that the commerce of all Europe is carried on by ships of every size to the number of 20,000, and that it is quite clear that this number cannot be increased, since the number of people in all the states remains the same and consumption likewise remains the same; and that, of this number,

20,000 ships, the Dutch have 15,000 to 16,000, the English about 3,000 to 4,000 and the French 500 to 600. . . .

An increase in commerce is possible only by giving employment to the vessels of one's country and by increasing their number. That increase can only proceed by the discovery of some new commercial opportunity, up to the present unknown, or by the diminution of the number of vessels of some one of the other nations. The discovery of new commerce is very uncertain. . . . It is necessary then that it be by the diminution of the number of vessels of one of the other nations. . . .

It should be added that commerce causes a perpetual battle in peace and war between the nations of Europe, as to who will win the best part of it. . . .

[Memorandum to King Louis XIV on Royal Finances (1670)]
Sire, the present state of Your Majesty's finances has obliged me to study them extensively, to search for the causes of the change I find, and then to present it to Your Majesty, in order that by his great prudence and his insight he may provide those remedies which he deems necessary and appropriate. . . .

The Dutch, the English, and other nations took from the realm wines, liqueurs, vinegar, linen, paper, a certain amount of clothing, and wheat in time of need, so that, of ten parts of commerce, the Dutch nevertheless carried on nine of them. But they brought us fabrics and other merchandise made of wool and hair; sugar, tobacco, and indigo from the American islands; all the spices, drugs . . . silks, cotton clothes, leathers, and an infinity of other merchandise from the Indies; the same merchandise from the Levant, through commerce with the port cities of the area; all the merchandise necessary for

---

1. The region of the eastern Mediterranean.

the construction of vessels, such as wood, masts, iron from Sweden and Galicia,[2] copper, tar, iron cannons, hemp, rope, tin and iron, brass, pilots' implements, bolts, iron, anchors, and generally everything which served in the construction of vessels and for the navy of both the king and his subjects. . . .

By all these means and an infinity of others which would be too long to enumerate, the Dutch, English, Hamburgers,[3] and other nations bringing into the realm a much greater quantity of merchandise than that which they carried away, withdrew the surplus in circulating money, which produced both their abundance and the poverty of the realm, and indisputably resulted in their power and our weakness.

We must next examine the means which were employed to change this destiny.

Firstly, in 1662 Your Majesty maintained his right to 50 sols[4] per ton of freight from foreign vessels, which produced such great results that we have seen the number of French vessels increase yearly; and in seven or eight years the Dutch have been practically excluded from port-to-port commerce, which is carried on by the French. . . .

At the same time, Your Majesty ordered work done to abolish all the tolls which had long been established on all the rivers of the kingdom, and he began from then on to have an examination made of the rivers which could be rendered navigable, in order to facilitate the [transportation] of commodities . . . to foreign lands. . . .

Finally, after having thoroughly studied this matter, Your Majesty ordered the tariff of 1664, in which the duties are regulated on a completely different principle, that is to say, that all merchandise and manufactured items of the realm were markedly favored and the foreign ones priced out of the market, though not completely; (for) having as yet no established manufactures in the realm, this increase in duties, had it been excessive, would have been a great burden for the people, because of their need for the aforesaid foreign merchandise and manufactured items; but this change began to provide means of establishing the same manufactures in the realm; and to this end:

The fabric manufacture of Sedan has been reestablished, and enlarged to 62 from the 12 looms there were then.

The new establishments of Abbéville, Dieppe, Fécamp, and Rouen have been built, in which there are presently more than 200 looms.

The factory for barracan was next established at La Ferté-sous-Jouarre, which is made up of 120 looms;

That of little damasks from Flanders, at Meaux, consisting of 80 looms;

That for carpeting, in the same city, made up of 20 looms;

For camlets, at Amiens and Abbeville, with 120 looms;

Dimities and twills of Bruges and Brussels, at Montmorin, St. Quentin, and Avranches, with 30 looms;

For fine Dutch linens, at Bresle, Louviers, Laval, and other places, with 200 looms;

Serge[5] of London, at Gournay, Auxerre, Autun, and other places, with 300 looms;

---

2. A region of east-central Europe, then controlled by the Austrian branch of the Hapsburg dynasty.

3. Merchants from Hamburg, an important German port on the North Sea.

4. A sol was a French coin, equal to 1/20 of a livre; Colbert here refers to the royal tariff of 1662.

5. Serge is a type of fabric, as are barracan, damask, camlet, dimities, and twills, all mentioned later in the text.

English woolen stockings, in the province of Beauce, at Provins, in Picardy, at Sens, Auxerre, Autun, and elsewhere, with a total of 32 cities or towns;

That for tin, in Nivernois;

That for French lace, in 52 cities and towns, in which more than 20,000 workers toil;

The manufacture of brass, or yellow copper, set up in Champagne;

That for camlet of Brussels, in Paris, which will become large and extensive;

Brass wire, in Burgundy;

Gold thread of Milan, at Lyons;

The manufacture of silks called *organzines*, in the same city.

In order to decrease the importation of cattle into the realm, import duties were markedly increased, and at the same time orders were given to prevent the seizure of cattle by the royal tax collector throughout the realm, which caused at the same time a decrease in leather imports.

Looms for silk stockings were established to a total of 100;

The search for saltpeter,[6] and at the same time the manufacture of powder;

That of match;

The establishment of the manufacture of muskets and of weapons of all sorts in Nivernois, and the reestablishment of the same in Forez;

The distribution of stud horses, which has produced and will certainly produce the reestablishment of stud farms and will considerably decrease the importation of foreign horses, if it does not prevent it completely.

And since Your Majesty has wanted to work diligently at reestablishing his naval forces, and since for that it has been necessary to make very great expenditures, since all merchandise, munitions and manufactured items formerly came from Holland and the countries of the North, it has been absolutely necessary to be especially concerned with finding within the realm, or with establishing in it, everything which might be necessary for this great plan.

To this end, the manufacture of tar was established in Médoc, Auvergne, Dauphiné, and Provence;

Iron cannons, in Burgundy, Nivernois, Saintonge, and Périgord;

Large anchors, in Dauphiné, Nivernois, Brittany, and Rochefort;

Sailcloth for the Levant, in Dauphiné;

Coarse muslin, in Auvergne;

All the implements for pilots and others, at Dieppe and La Rochelle;

The cutting of wood suitable for vessels, in Burgundy, Dauphiné, Brittany, Normandy, Poitou, Saintonge, Provence, Guyenne, and the Pyrenees;

Masts, of a sort once unknown in this realm, have been found in Provence, Languedoc, Auvergne, Dauphiné, and in the Pyrenees.

Iron, which was obtained from Sweden and Biscay, is currently manufactured in the realm.

Fine hemp for ropes, which came from Prussia and from Piedmont, is currently obtained in Burgundy, Mâconnais, Bresse, Dauphiné; and markets for it have since been established in Berry and in Auvergne, which always provides money in these provinces and keeps it within the realm.

In a word, everything serving for the construction of vessels is currently established in the realm, so that Your Majesty can get along without foreigners for the navy and will even, in a short time, be able to supply them and gain their money in this fashion. . . .

In addition, in order to prevent the Dutch from profiting from the American

---

6. Potassium nitrate, used in the manufacture of gunpowder.

islands,[7] of which they had gained control and from which they had excluded the French, which was worth at least a million in gold to them every year, Your Majesty formed and established the West Indian Company in which he has up until the present invested 4 million livres; but he has also had the satisfaction of having snatched from the Dutch that million in gold which served to nourish and maintain more than 4,000 of their subjects who continually navigated among the islands with more than 200 vessels.

Pieter van Dam

A DESCRIPTION OF THE DUTCH EAST INDIA COMPANY

The first joint stock company was the Moscow Company, chartered by the English Crown in 1553 for the purpose of trading with Russia. The most successful, however, was the Dutch East India Company, chartered by the government of the Netherlands in 1602 to trade with India, China, Japan, and the East Indies. During its heyday in the seventeenth century, stockholders often received annual returns of 20 percent on their investments.

The author of the following excerpt is Pieter van Dam (1621–1706), a lawyer who served as the chief legal official for the Dutch East India Company. On his retirement he wrote a history of the company's organization and accomplishments. Van Dam, like most of the Dutch, was proud of the achievements of the East India Company, and he had become a wealthy man as a result of his connection with it. His history, therefore, written in Dutch for the general reading public, glossed over some of the company's more unsavory actions in its dealings with Asian peoples and in its competition with the Portuguese. Even in his description of the company's origins, which is basically objective, signs of his Dutch patriotism are not completely lacking.

Questions
for Analysis

1. What historical conditions does van Dam describe that led to the formation of the Dutch East India Company?
2. What do you see as the main motive for forming the company?
3. What in van Dam's account illustrates the close ties between the Dutch government and the Dutch merchant community?
4. What powers did the Dutch government grant to the Dutch East India Company?
5. How did these powers differ from those of a modern corporation? What might account for these differences?

---

7. The Dutch West Indies.

*I*f Philip II, king of Spain,[1] had been capable of winking at the shipping and trade of the inhabitants of these [Dutch] provinces with Spain and Portugal and had permitted it to go on, it is very probable that they [the Dutch] would never have attempted to extend it any further, for it was only when he began to interfere with it that they started to look beyond, even to the East Indies.

So long as these lands remained under the dominion of Spain, even during the government of Emperor Charles V,[2] Netherlanders were not permitted to voyage either to the West Indies or the East Indies, lands belonging . . . to the first discoverers or to those who made the first journey to them in the East Indies, and hence assigned by the decree of Pope Alexander VI[3] to the kingdoms of Spain and Portugal, each receiving for its share lands and realms to possess, travel, and trade in, with all other nations excluded. Therefore those who lived in these provinces at that time had to be satisfied to send their trading ships only to Spain and Portugal and no further.

Besides, a very large trade to the Baltic and the adjacent lands had long been in existence, principally in grain and naval stores and timber, most of which was then re-exported from here to Spain and Portugal for the construction and repair of ships, especially the heavy carracks and galleons[4] of a burden of a thousand, twelve hundred, and even more tons; for warships and merchantmen needed cables and cordage, masts, anchors, sails, and sailcloth, as well as pitch, tar, and other naval stores which all had to be imported from abroad, in exchange for which they brought back silver, spices, and other wares which came from the East and West Indies. This trade continued for many years, even after this country declared its independence from the king of Spain.[5] . . .

Although this situation came to the attention of Philip II a number of times, he permitted it to continue unnoticed for some years in view of his own shortages and necessities, especially of naval stores, but also because it increased his revenues from customs tolls. It is also possible that he was afraid that if he interfered with this trade, the people of this country, who cannot survive without trade, industry, and shipping, would attempt to discover other distant lands and thereby cause him great harm and loss. But when various persons caused him to change his mind, he began, despite these considerations, to subject our shippers and crews to all kinds of vexations, which became more frequent and troublesome; ships were seized and detained under the pretext that the king needed their crews for his own service at very low pay. Then, declaring that they were rebels and heretics,[6] he threw them into jail, where they perished from hun-

---

1. Ruled from 1556 to 1598; the Netherlands at this time was a Spanish possession.

2. Philip's father; his rule of the Netherlands was considered more lenient than his son's.

3. Pope Alexander VI (1492–1503) proclaimed a line of demarcation in 1493 that essentially ceded to Spain all newly discovered territories in the Americas. A year later Portugal and Spain negotiated the Treaty of Tordesillas, which moved the line further west; as a result Brazil became a Portuguese possession.

4. Carracks were light vessels with a long stern, used mainly for trade; galleons were larger, often with three or four decks, capable for use both as warships and traders.

5. In 1581 seven northern Dutch provinces, led by Holland and Zeeland, declared their independence from Spain, forming the United Provinces of the Netherlands.

6. Those who have denounced the true faith, in this case, Protestants.

ger and other hardships; he confiscated their goods, turned some of them over to the Inquisition,[7] then finally he ordered a general seizure of all ships and goods belonging to Dutchmen to be found in his kingdoms of Spain and Portugal and had the rudders and sails removed. . . . We could not put any trust whatever in Spain where, after the death of King Philip II in the year 1598, his son[8] who succeeded him did not merely continue the cruel conduct of his father but treated our people even more harshly, throwing them into foul, stinking jails, putting some to death and sending others to the galleys, confiscating their ships and goods, and the like. Furthermore, because of the loss or obstruction of this trade it became necessary to find work and employment for the seamen, of whom there was now a large number. It became necessary therefore to seek out new trading routes to places as far as the East Indies, in order to buy and bring back the spices and other wares which otherwise we would have had to go to get from the Spaniards and the Portuguese, often at high prices, and then bring here for resale by our merchants in other countries. As a result, the first efforts were made to find a shorter route to these lands in the East Indies, to wit: China, Japan and others, by the northeastern route along Tartary,[9] although it had been investigated by other nations, especially the English, for many years and found unprofitable. Others chose the route around the Cape of Good Hope because, although it was estimated to be a good 2,000 miles longer than the

other, it was safer. Those who favored this route were nine in number, eminent merchants in Amsterdam, among them Hendrik Hudde, Reynier Pauw, and Pieter Dircksz Hasselaer, who were also members of the municipal government. They took the risk of sending out four ships on this voyage, including a yacht, all well-provided with cannon and ammunition for vigorous self-defense, as well as with the money and trading goods most wanted in those regions. This society was named the Company for Far Journeys. . . .

After various private merchants joined with others in the 1590s and after the turn of the century to form companies, first in Amsterdam and then in other cities of Holland and Zeeland, to open up and undertake travel and trade with the East Indies, and from time to time equipped and sent out many ships, which returned, on the average, with no small success, the State General[10] came to the conclusion that it would be more useful and profitable not only for the country as a whole but also for its inhabitants individually, especially all those who had undertaken and shared in navigation and trade, that these companies should be combined and this navigation and trade be placed and maintained on a firm footing, with order and political guidance. After much argument and persuasion, this union was worked out by Their High Mightinesses, in their own words, to advance the prosperity of the United Netherlands, to conserve and increase its industry and to bring profit to the Company and to the people of the country.

---

7. A church court controlled by the Spanish Crown, responsible for maintaining Catholic orthodoxy in Spanish lands.

8. Philip III (1598–1621),

9. Refers to Russia.

10. The Dutch States (or Estates) General was a representative assembly that loosely ruled the seven provinces of the United Netherlands; its members were known as "Their High Mightinesses."

Their High Mightinesses later, by an edict of September 19, 1606, acceded to vigorous requests of the Company and granted to it a charter for a period of twenty-one years, permitting it to voyage east of the Cape of Good Hope or through the Straits of Magellan and excluding all others, under penalty not only of confiscation of ships and cargo but also of fines and imprisonment.

Furthermore, the Company's charter authorized it to make alliances with princes and potentates east of the Cape of Good Hope and beyond the Straits of Magellan, to make contracts, build fortresses and strongholds, name governors, raise troops, appoint officers of justice, and perform other necessary services for the advancement of trade; to dismiss the said governors and officers of justice if their conduct was found to be harmful and disloyal, provided that these governors or officers could not be prevented from returning here to present such grievances or complaints as they think they might have to Their High Mightinesses. This was further confirmed by the eighth article of the instructions of the year 1617, approved and ratified by Their High Mightinesses, which established and regulated the government in the Indies in such a way that, as is easily seen, the Company after the date of this charter has made great progress in the Indies. It has captured a number of fortresses from the Spaniards and the Portuguese, its enemies, and has established trading posts at several places. It was decided as a consequence that it was desirable to establish a formal government in the Indies, with a Governor General and a Council, and to provide it with proper instructions, and this was done by the assembly of the XVII[11] and by Their High Mightinesses. . . .

The inhabitants of this country were permitted to invest as much or as little as they pleased in shares of the Company.

The subscription had to be made before September 1, 1602; the first part of the price had to be paid before October 1, with interest of 8 percent until the next April; the second third before October 1, 1603, and the remaining third before October 1, 1604, at the same rate of interest.

It was further agreed that a full third of the capital would be furnished for the equipment of the first fleet, the original paid-up capital amounting in all to 6,424,588 guilders 8 stivers[12] in which connection it is to be noted that according to the resolution of the assembly of August 12, 1603, the subscribed capital then amounted to 6,459,840 guilders.

Women in Traditional Societies

All the sources so far presented in this volume were written by males and mostly describe male activities — reflecting the uncontested fact that males dominated all the world's major societies in the sixteenth and seventeenth centuries. Although

---

11. Refers to the seventeen directors of the company.

12. Guilders and stivers were units of Dutch currency.

women provided much of the labor in the world's economy, especially in agriculture, through law and custom they were excluded from positions of political and religious leadership. Furthermore, because societies paid little attention to educating females, women had little chance of becoming intellectuals, artists, or creative writers.

At the personal level, women's lives were controlled by others — first by parents, then by husbands or male children, and always by the customs and taboos of their culture. In some instances, women's subservience resulted in physical abuse, as in China, where to please men the feet of young girls were broken and tightly bound to prevent growth, and even death, as in India, where in the practice of *sati*, some castes required a widow to commit suicide by throwing herself into the flames of her husband's funeral pyre. It is not an exaggeration to say that in the 1500s and 1600s, women made up the world's largest oppressed group.

Heinrich Kramer and Jakob Sprenger

MALLEUS MALEFICARUM (THE HAMMER OF WITCHES)

Many find it surprising that sixteenth- and seventeenth-century Europe, a society experiencing progress on many fronts, underwent a widespread and destructive hysteria over witchcraft. Common people and intellectuals alike were convinced that society was threatened by countless individuals, who, in return for pledging themselves to the devil, gained the ability to fly, change their shape, and cause crop failures, storms, shipwrecks, infertility, disease, and countless other misfortunes through their incantations and spells. Some 200,000 individuals were burned or hanged for witchcraft during these years, most of them having confessed their "crime" only after excruciating torture.

The alleged witches were overwhelmingly female, with the small number of executed males usually related in some way to accused female witches. Women, it was thought, were more likely to be snared by the devil because in every respect — intellectually, spiritually, morally, and physically — they were inferior to men.

Such was the argument of two German Dominican theologians, Heinrich Kramer and Jakob Sprenger, who in the late 1400s were involved in trying cases of supposed witchcraft and heresy in western Germany. Convinced that judges, churchmen, and the general public were not aware of witchcraft's terrible threat, in 1484 they published the *Malleus Maleficarum* to alert their readers to the growing satanic cult and to suggest ways to resist witchcraft. Their treatise, published in numerous editions well into the seventeenth century, was a blend of folk belief and theological erudition. Their views on women were extreme even by the standards of their day, but their book's success and the tragic facts of the persecutions show that many Europeans accepted and acted on their premises.

Questions
for Analysis

1. What kinds of evidence do the authors use to prove women's inferiority? What does this evidence suggest about attitudes toward women in past societies?
2. According to Kramer and Sprenger, in what areas are the women's weaknesses especially apparent?
3. What is there about Kramer and Sprenger's background that might explain their low regard for women?
4. If one accepted Kramer and Sprenger's premise about women, what implications does it have for women's overall place in society?

*A*s for the first question, why a greater number of witches is found in the fragile feminine sex than among men; it is indeed a fact that it were idle to contradict, since it is accredited by actual experience, apart from the verbal testimony of credible witnesses. And without in any way detracting from a sex in which God has always taken great glory . . . , let us say that various men have assigned various reasons for this fact, which nevertheless agree in principle. Wherefore it is good, for the admonition of women, to speak of this matter; and it has often been proved by experience that they are eager to hear of it, so long as it is set forth with discretion.

Now the wickedness of women is spoken of in *Ecclesiasticus* xxv.[1] There is no head above the head of a serpent: and there is no wrath above the wrath of a woman. I had rather dwell with a lion and a dragon than to keep house with a wicked woman. And among much which in that place precedes and follows about a wicked woman, he concludes: All wickedness is but little to the wickedness of a woman. Wherefore S. John Chrysostom[2]

says on the text, It is not good to marry (*S. Matthew* xix). What else is woman but a foe to friendship, an unescapable punishment, a necessary evil, a natural temptation, a desirable calamity, a domestic danger, a delectable detriment, an evil of nature, painted with fair colors! Therefore if it be a sin to divorce her when she ought to be kept, it is indeed a necessary torture; for either we commit adultery by divorcing her, or we must endure daily strife. Cicero[3] in his second book of *The Rhetorics* says: The many lusts of men lead them into one sin, but the one lust of women leads them into all sins; for the root of all woman's vices is avarice. . . .

Others again have propounded other reasons why there are more superstitious women found than men. And the first is, that they are more credulous; and since the chief aim of the devil is to corrupt faith, therefore he rather attacks them. See *Ecclesiasticus* xix: He that is quick to believe is light-minded, and shall be diminished. The second reason is, that women are naturally more impressionable, and more ready to receive the influence of a disembodied spirit; and that when they use this

---

1. A collection of proverbs written between 200 and 180 B.C.; considered part of the Old Testament by Catholics and Orthodox Christians, but not by Protestants.

2. Saint John Chrysostom (A.D. 347–407) was a Greek Church father, famous for his preaching, who served as Patriarch of Constantinople.

3. Cicero (106–43 B.C.) was a Roman lawyer, statesman, orator, and philosopher.

quality well they are very good, but when they use it ill they are very evil.

The third reason is that they have slippery tongues, and are unable to conceal from their fellow-women those things which by evil arts they know; and, since they are weak, they find an easy and secret manner of vindicating themselves by witchcraft. . . .

For as regards intellect, or the understanding of spiritual things, they seem to be of a different nature from men; a fact which is vouched for by the logic of the authorities, backed by various examples from the Scriptures. . . .

But the natural reason is that she is more carnal than a man, as is clear from her many carnal abominations. And it should be noted that there was a defect in the formation of the first woman, since she was formed from a bent rib, that is, a rib of the breast, which is bent as it were in a contrary direction to a man. And since through this defect she is an imperfect animal, she always deceives. . . . And all this is indicated by the etymology of the word: for *Femina* comes from *Fe* and *Minus*,[4] since she is ever weaker to hold and preserve the faith. And this as regards faith is of her very nature; although both by grace and nature faith never failed in the Blessed Virgin, even at the time of Christ's Passion, when it failed in all men.

Therefore a wicked woman is by her nature quicker to waver in her faith, and consequently quicker to abjure the faith, which is the root of witchcraft.

. . .

When the philosopher Socrates was asked if one should marry a wife, he an-swered: If you do not, you are lonely, your family dies out, and a stranger inherits; if you do, you suffer perpetual anxiety, querulous complaints, reproaches concerning the marriage portion, the heavy displeasure of your relations, the garrulousness of a mother-in-law, cuckoldom, and no certain arrival of an heir. This he said as one who knew. For S. Jerome[5] says: This Socrates had two wives, whom he endured with much patience, but could not be rid of their contumelies and clamorous vituperations. So one day when they were complaining against him, he went out of the house to escape their plaguing, and sat down before the house; and the women then threw filthy water over him. But the philosopher was not disturbed by this, saying, "I knew that the rain would come after the thunder."

There is also a story of a man whose wife was drowned in a river, who, when he was searching for the body to take it out of the water, walked up the stream. And when he was asked why, since heavy bodies do not rise but fall, he was searching against the current of the river, he answered: "When that woman was alive she always, both in word and deed, went contrary to my commands; therefore I am searching in the contrary direction in case even now she is dead she may preserve her contrary disposition."

And indeed, just as through the first defect in their intelligence they are more prone to abjure the faith; so through their second defect of inordinate affections and passions they search for, brood over, and inflict various vengeances, either by witchcraft, or by some other means. Wherefore it is no wonder that so great a number of witches exist in this sex.

Women also have weak memories; and

---

4. In Latin *Fe* means faith, *Minus* means less.

5. Saint Jerome (A.D. 347–419) was a Latin Church father best known for his translation of the Bible from Greek and Hebrew manuscripts into Latin.

it is a natural vice in them not to be disciplined, but to follow their own impulses without any sense of what is due; this is her whole study, and all that she keeps in her memory. . . .

Let us consider another property of hers, the voice. For as she is a liar by nature, so in her speech she stings while she delights us. Wherefore her voice is like the song of the Sirens,[6] who with their sweet melody entice the passers-by and kill them. For they kill them by emptying their purses, consuming their strength, and causing them to forsake God. . . .

To conclude. All witchcraft comes from carnal lust, which is in women insatiable. See *Proverbs* xxx: There are three things that are never satisfied, yea, a fourth thing

which says not, It is enough; that is, the mouth of the womb. Wherefore for the sake of fulfilling their lusts they consort even with devils. More such reasons could be brought forward, but to the understanding it is sufficiently clear that it is no matter for wonder that there are more women than men found infected with the heresy of witchcraft. And in consequence of this, it is better called the heresy of witches than of wizards[7] since the name is taken from the more powerful party. And blessed be the Highest Who has so far preserved the male sex from so great a crime: for since He was willing to be born and to suffer for us, therefore He has granted to men this privilege.

John Mayer

A PATTERN FOR WOMEN

Many paradoxes exist in the history of attitudes toward women in Western European society. One tradition, represented by Kramer and Sprenger, identifies women with spiritual weakness, sin, and depravity. Another, represented by such movements as medieval chivalry and the cult of the Virgin Mary, idealizes women as symbols of all that is noble, virtuous, and pure.

The following selection illustrates this second tradition. It is a eulogy written by an Anglican minister, John Mayer, to praise the virtue and piety of Lucy Thornton, who died in her thirties, leaving several children and her husband Roger. It offers an excellent picture of what sort of life a woman of the English upper middle class was expected to lead in the early 1600s. Mayer opens his eulogy by praising Lucy Thornton's great religious zeal and continues by describing her other virtues.

Questions for Analysis

1. Why, according to Mayer, does Lucy Thornton's life represent a "pattern" for other women to follow?

---

6. Sirens were half-bird, half-woman creatures who lured sailors to their destruction through the beauty of their songs.

7. The term "wizard" was sometimes used to describe male witches.

2. Even in his praise for Lucy, Mayer makes several points that suggest the subservience of women in English society. Can you identify them?
3. What does Mayer's eulogy reveal about women's place in the family?

*S*he was anointed with wisdom, as Abigail,[1] who is said to be of excellent understanding. . . . Such was her understanding as that she could readily recite fit texts of Scripture for any purpose and find them out; and for harder places, by singular labor she attained good skill herein. . . .

She was anointed with true love, causing in her plenty of good works; as in Dorcas,[2] her love was exceeding great both towards God and towards her neighbor. Of God, her love was so great as that she burnt with the fire of earnest zeal for his glory, stoutly (even beyond the strength of her sex) opposing sin and maintaining virtue in those that were about her. . . . For the love of God, she kept a continual watch over her ways, lest she should offend against his holy will; no child is more afraid of offending the father or master than she of offending God. Because that, notwithstanding all watches, sin cannot altogether be kept out, she was not a little troubled for her frailties and falls, being always glad when the Lord took the matter into his own hands by chastising her with sickness; for then, and in health time also, she did much complain of her sins and forgetfulness for which it was necessary to be corrected. . . .

Of her neighbor she had also a true love, not in word but in deed. She had love of almsdeeds, which she plentifully performed to the poor. . . . From her youth up, the poor were nourished up with her; their lives blessed her, for that they were kept warm with her fleeces. Whilst she lived, the hungry could not go unfed, the naked unclothed, the sick unvisited. . . . She showed love by admonishing the disorderly, instructing the ignorant, and exhorting the backward in religion, by all means provoking to love and good works.

She was anointed with humility, as Mary the blessed mother of Christ who, being so highly graced by God, yet acknowledgeth herself his humble handmaiden. . . . She despised the ornaments of vanity, which other women so much delight in; her outward habit did show the inward lowliness and modesty of her mind. She strove against the sharpness of her natural disposition, and by striving did attain a great measure of meekness and gentleness. . . .

She was anointed with due subjection to her own husband, as Sarah,[3] . . . promising that thus they become the daughters of Sarah, not being terrified with any fear. Wherefore, having this virtue also added, she was doubtless without fear steadfast in the faith of her salvation.

Unruly wives . . . have such a mist or dark cloud of black sins before their eyes as that they cannot see this salvation. They may have hope indeed, but their

---

1. One of the wives of King David (?1010–970 B.C.), the second king of Israel and the reputed author of many of the *Psalms*.

2. Dorcas, also known as Tabitha, was an early Christian convert mentioned in *Acts*. She was noted for her good works and charity.

3. The wife of the Old Testament patriarch Abraham; she represents loyalty, hope, and God's promise to people.

hope is presumption, the end of which is damnation.

Now as this elect servant of God was beautified with these graces in her health, so they remained in her without being dimmed in her last sickness.

For heavenly zeal, she gave a sure instance hereof in the beginning of this sickness by commanding her servants not to trouble her with any worldly affairs, for now she would wholly be settled to heaven. And indeed she lay in her sickbed as in heaven, full of heavenly speeches and of heavenly comfort. Now all her practice was praying, confessing of sins, singing Psalms, and godly conference.

For wisdom, when strength of body failed her, this was strong yet in her even unto the end; most wisely she spoke to everything, with much understanding producing sundry places of the holy Scriptures. Being much troubled for her sins and buffeted by the temptations of Satan, she said that she had yet much assurance because that "Come unto me," saith the Lord, "all you that are weary and heavy laden, and I will refresh you."

Olfert Dapper

DESCRIPTION OF AFRICAN AFFAIRS

Olfert Dapper (1636–1689) was a Dutch physician and author who wrote histories of Amsterdam and the Dutch East India Company and descriptive works on African and Asian government and society. Dapper never visited Africa, so what he says about the continent comes from secondhand sources, especially his fellow Dutchman, Samuel Blommaart, a merchant who lived and traveled in Africa for several years. Nonetheless, most experts accept Dapper's 1668 work as reliable. The following passages deal with the position of women in the Kingdom of Benin, centered at the mouth of the Niger River in modern Nigeria.

Questions
for Analysis

1. In what ways do Benin's laws of inheritance reveal the position of women in Benin society?
2. What does Dapper's account reveal about Benin family life and customs?

When a woman has had a son by her deceased husband she becomes the servant of the son and may not be given in marriage to another person without his permission, but must wait upon the son as a slave. Should it happen that any man desires such a widow he asks the son for permission to marry her and promises to provide a young woman as a wife instead who must then serve as a slave for as long as he requires. The man may not sell the old mother without the king's permission unless the son agrees.

A daughter is not given in marriage by her father until she is twelve or fourteen years old, after which time she is no longer his concern.

After a man dies all the wives with whom he has had sexual relations become the King's and are given again in marriage by him; but those with whom he has not slept go to the son who may keep them or remarry them to others. . . .

After a man's wife has been in childbed he has no sexual relations with her until the child is one-and-a-half years old and can walk. But if he comes to know that his wife has meanwhile been making shift with another he makes a complaint to the Fiadors.[1] . . .

In matters of inheritance they proceed in this way: the man takes all the goods which the wife leaves behind without let-ting the children keep anything unless the mother gave it to them during her life-time. But the wife in contrast, after her husband's death, cannot touch the least of his goods, since everything — wives and slaves as well as other things — goes to the King. If there are sons the King often makes the eldest the only heir to his fa-ther's slaves and property, and also to any wives with whom the father has not slept, because those with whom he has slept are given as wives to others.

The King has a great number of wives; the number would be well over a thou-sand, because with his father's death he inherits all the wives with whom his fa-ther has not slept. The others may by no means marry again, but are locked up to-gether in a cloister and guarded by eu-nuchs. Should one of these women try to escape with someone and be caught she must die directly with all her belongings.

■ **Ogier Ghiselin de Busbecq**

TURKISH LETTERS

It is a testimony to the authority and thoroughness of Ogier Ghiselin de Busbecq, Ferdinand I's ambassador to the Ottoman court in Constantinople between 1555 and 1561, that this volume contains three excerpts from the descriptive letters he wrote about his years in Turkey. See the introductions to Busbecq's *Turkish Letters* in Chap-ters 1 and 3 for details about his life.

Questions
for Analysis

1. According to Turkish custom, as described by Busbecq, what seems to have been the legal relationship between wives and concubines?
2. What does the Turkish custom of divorce say about women's status?
3. What conclusions can you draw about the legal status of women in Turkey and in Benin?

---

1. Judges in Benin society.

*T*he Turks are the most careful people in the world of the modesty of their wives, and therefore keep them shut up at home and hide them away, so that they scarce see the light of day. But if they have to go into the streets, they are sent out so covered and wrapt up in veils that they seem to those who meet them mere gliding ghosts. They have the means of seeing men through their linen or silken veils, while no part of their own body is exposed to men's view. For it is a received opinion among them, that no woman who is distinguished in the very smallest degree by her figure or youth, can be seen by a man without his desiring her, and therefore without her receiving some contamination; and so it is the universal practice to confine the women to the harem. Their brothers are allowed to see them, but not their brothers-in-law. Men of the richer classes, or of higher rank, make it a condition when they marry, that their wives shall never set foot outside the threshold, and that no man or woman shall be admitted to see them for any reason whatever, not even their nearest relations, except their fathers and mothers, who are allowed to pay a visit to their daughters at the Turkish Easter.[1]

On the other hand, if the wife has a father of high rank, or has brought a larger dowry than usual, the husband promises on his part that he will take no concubine, but will keep to her alone. Otherwise, the Turks are not forbidden by any law to have as many concubines as they please in addition to their lawful wives. Between the children of wives and those of concubines there is no distinction, and they are considered to have equal rights. As for concubines they either buy them for themselves or win them in war; when they are tired of them there is nothing to prevent their bringing them to market and selling them; but they are entitled to their freedom if they have borne children to their master. This privilege Roxolana, Suleiman's wife, turned to her own advantage, when she had borne him a son while still a slave. Having thus obtained her freedom, and become her own mistress, she refused to submit any longer to his will, unless, contrary to the custom of the Ottoman Sultans, she was made his lawful wife. The only distinction between the lawful wife and the concubine is, that the former has a dowry, while the slaves have none. A wife who has a portion settled on her is mistress of her husband's house, and all the other women have to obey her orders. The husband, however, may choose which of them shall spend the night with him. He makes known his wishes to the wife, and she sends to him the slave he has selected. . . . Only Friday night, which is their Sabbath,[2] is supposed to belong to the wife; and she grumbles if her husband deprives her of it. On all the other nights he may do so as he pleases.

Divorces are granted among them for many reasons which it is easy for the husbands to invent. The divorced wife receives back her dowry, unless the divorce has been caused by some fault on her part. There is more difficulty in a woman's getting a divorce from her husband.

---

1. Busbecq apparently is referring to the festival of Bairam, which follows Ramadan, the Muslim month of fasting from sunup to sundown. He equated Ramadan with the Christian practice of Lent, so the identification of Bairam with Easter is logical but lacking in theological merit.

2. Like Sundays in Christian lands, Fridays (actually beginning at sunset on Thursday) in the Muslim world were days of rest, given over to religious acts and rituals.

Among the reasons which are considered sufficient for granting a divorce are the deprivation of the necessaries of life by the husband, and certain kinds of ill treatment. In the latter case the woman goes before the judge, and makes a declaration that she is unable to remain any longer with her husband; when the judge asks the reason, she gives no answer, but takes off one of her shoes and turns it upside down. This the judge accepts as sufficient evidence that her husband has treated her improperly.

Sigismund von Herberstein

NOTES UPON RUSSIA

Sigismund von Herberstein (1486–1566) was an Austrian nobleman whose diplomatic missions for the Hapsburg Dynasty of Austria took him to many of the courts of Europe. He is best remembered today for his *Notes upon Russia,* published in 1549, in which he recorded his observations of Russian society during his residence there between 1516 and 1518.

Questions for Analysis

1. Does the Russian practice of arranged marriages seem to limit the freedom of young women or young men?
2. What does the Russian attitude toward adultery say about the status of women?
3. What similarities and differences do you see between the position of women in Russia and in Turkey? In Benin?

*I*t is held to be dishonorable and a disgrace for a young man to address a girl, in order that he may obtain her hand in marriage. It is the part of the father to communicate with the young man upon the subject of his marrying his daughter. It is generally the custom for them to use such words as the following: "As I have a daughter, I should wish to have you for a son-in-law." To which the young man replies: "If you desire to have me for a son-in-law, I will, if you think fit, have a meeting with my parents, and confer with them upon the subject." Then, if his parents and nearest relatives agree, a meeting is held to treat of the sum which the girl's father is willing to give by way of dowry. After the dowry is settled, a day is appointed for the wedding. Meanwhile, the young man is forbidden the house of his betrothed; so strictly indeed, that if he should happen to try to get a sight of her, the parents usually reply: "Learn what she is from others who have known her." Certainly, unless the espousals have been first confirmed with very heavy penalties, so that the young man who is betrothed could not, if he would, repudiate her without a heavy punishment, no access is permitted to him. Horses, dresses, weapons, cattle, servants, and the like, are generally given as dowry. . . .

They do not call it adultery unless one have the wife of another. Love between those that are married is for the most part lukewarm, especially among the nobles and princes, because they marry girls whom they have never seen before; and being engaged in the service of the prince, they are compelled to desert them, and become corrupted with disgraceful connections with others.

The condition of the women is most miserable; for they consider no woman virtuous unless she live shut up at home, and be so closely guarded, that she go out nowhere. They give a woman, I say, little credit for modesty, if she be seen by strangers or people out of doors. But shut up at home they do nothing but spin and sew, and have literally no authority or influence in the house. All the domestic work is done by the servants. Whatever is strangled by the hands of a woman, whether it be a fowl, or any other kind of animal, they abominate as unclean. The wives, however, of the poorer classes do the household work and cook. But if their husbands and the men-servants happen to be away, and they wish to strangle a fowl, they stand at the door holding the fowl, or whatever other animal it may be, and a knife, and generally beg the men that pass by to kill it. They are very seldom admitted into the churches . . . unless they be very old and free from all suspicion. On certain holidays, however, men allow their wives and daughters, as a special gratification, to meet in very pleasant meadows, where they seat themselves on a sort of wheel of fortune, and are moved alternately up and down, or they fasten a rope somewhere, with a seat to it, in which they sit, and are swung backwards and forwards; or they otherwise make merry with clapping their hands and singing songs, but they have no dances whatever.

Peasants in Traditional Societies

Of the estimated 500 million human beings who inhabited the earth around A.D. 1500, the vast majority grew crops or raised animals. They included relatively small numbers of pastoral nomads who inhabited the swath of dry territory extending east to west from the Sahara in Africa, through the Arabian Desert, across the Iranian plateau, and all the way to Mongolia in east Asia. They also included a small number of peoples in Africa, Australia, the Americas, and the Pacific islands who were food gatherers or who practiced "slash-and-burn" agriculture, in which an area was cleared, burned, farmed intensively, and then abandoned once it lost its fertility. For the most part, however, settled areas of intensive cultivation produced the world's foods, hides, and fibers.

The men and women who performed the labor in these areas of intensive agriculture are generally classed as peasants, making them the world's largest socioeconomic group in the pre-industrial world. Dictionary definitions of a peasant — "a worker who farms the land" and a "person tilling the soil as a small land owner or laborer" — are helpful only to a certain point. Peasant existence is further defined by the obligations peasants owed their landlords and/or rulers in return for the land they worked. These obligations almost always included giving the landlord or ruler a certain percentage of their crops and sometimes required peasants to labor on the landlord's estate or on public works projects, such as the maintenance of roads or irrigation systems. Peasant existence was generally characterized by subsistence farming rather than by specialization in raising cash crops for sale in an outside market. The peasants' goal was to raise sufficient crops so that after paying taxes and tribute, they had sufficient food to survive the year. The condition of peasants in the sixteenth and seventeenth centuries varied greatly from society to society, and it would take dozens of selections to illustrate fully the diversity of their situations. The following documents reveal some of the common denominators and some of the differences in the experiences of peasants in the widely separate areas of Mexico, Russia, and Japan.

Gonzalo Fernández de Ovieto y Valdés

A GENERAL AND NATURAL HISTORY OF THE INDIES

Before the arrival of the Spaniards in Mexico in 1519, Aztec society was divided into clans comprised of families who claimed descent from a common ancestor and were governed by chiefs chosen by a council of elders. Each clan controlled a certain amount of land that was divided and assigned either to the *maceguales*, the free peasantry, or to a lower group, the *mayeques*, similar to sharecroppers. As the following document reveals, the free peasants and sharecroppers remained free only as long as they made required payments to their overlords, priests, and emperor.

The author of the following selection, Gonzalo Fernández de Ovieto y Valdés, was born in 1478 into a Spanish aristocratic family. After serving in the Spanish army, he made in 1514 his first trip to the Americas, where he served as overseer of Spanish gold-mining operations in the Indies. Subsequently he held administrative posts in the regions of modern Mexico, Panama, and Colombia. He was acquainted with Cortes and Pizarro and carefully recorded his observations of native American religion and society. In the 1530s he retired to Spain, where King Carlos I (also known as Holy Roman Emperor Charles V) gave him a subsidy to write a history of the Spanish conquest of the Americas. The result was his twenty-volume *Natural and General History of the Indies*, published between 1535 and 1537.

Questions
for Analysis

1. On the basis of this document, what can one infer about the divisions of Aztec society? Where did the peasantry fit into Aztec society?
2. In what ways did the Aztec lords control the lives of the peasant laborers?
3. Aside from the peasants themselves, what segments of Aztec society depended on the peasants for their well-being?

*T*he Indians of New Spain . . . are the poorest of the many nations that live in the Indies at the present time. In their homes they have no furnishings or clothing other than the poor garments which they wear on their persons, one or two stones for grinding maize, some pots in which to cook the maize, and a sleeping mat. Their meals consist chiefly of vegetables cooked with chili, and bread. They eat little — not that they would not eat more if they could get it, for the soil is very fertile and yields bountiful harvests, but the common people and plebeians suffer under the tyranny of their Indian lords, who tax away the greater part of their produce in a manner that I shall describe. Only the lords and their relatives, and some principal men and merchants, have estates and lands of their own; they sell and gamble with their lands as they please, and they sow and harvest them but pay no tribute.[1] Nor is any tribute paid by artisans, such as masons, carpenters, feather-workers, or silversmiths, or by singers and kettle-drummers (for every Indian lord has musicians in his household, each according to his station). But such persons render personal service[2] when it is required, and none of them is paid for his labor.

Each Indian lord assigns to the common folk who come from other parts of the country to settle on his land (and to those who are already settled there) specific fields, that each may know the land that he is to sow. And the majority of them have their homes on their land; and between twenty and thirty, or forty and fifty houses have over them an Indian head

who is called *tiquitlato*, which in the Castilian[3] tongue means "the finder (or seeker) of tribute." At harvest time this *tiquitlato* inspects the cornfield and observes what each one reaps, and when the reaping is done they show him the harvest, and he counts the ears of corn that each has reaped, and the number of wives and children that each of the vassals in his charge possesses. And with the harvest before him he calculates how many ears of corn each person in that household will require till the next harvest, and these he gives to the Indian head of that house; and he does the same with the other produce, namely kidney beans, which are a kind of small beans, and chili, which is their pepper; and *chia*, which is as fine as mustard seed, and which in warm weather they drink, ground and made into a solution in water and use for medicine, roasted and ground; and cocoa, which is a kind of almond that they use as money, and which they grind, make into a solution, and drink; and cotton, in those places where it is raised . . .; and pulque,[4] which is their wine; and all the various products obtained from the maguey[5] plant, from which they obtain food and drink and footwear and clothing. . . . Of all these and other products they leave the vassal only enough to sustain him for a year. And in addition the vassal must earn enough to pay the tribute of mantles, gold, silver, honey, wax, lime, wood, or whatever products it is customary to pay as tribute in that country. They pay this tribute every forty, sixty, seventy, or ninety days, according to the terms of the agreement. This tribute also the

---

1. That is, they make no payments to the king or priesthood.

2. Farm labor, work on maintenance of buildings, roads, and temples.

3. The language of Castile, the largest province in Spain.

4. A fermented drink, made from the juice of the agave, a desert plant.

5. A fiber-yielding plant with fleshy leaves, grown in Mexico and the southwestern United States.

tiquitlato receives and carries to his Indian lord.

Ten days before the close of the sixty or hundred days, or whatever is the period appointed for the payment of tribute, they take to the house of the Indian lord the produce brought by the *tiquitlatos;* and if some poor Indian should prove unable to pay his share of tribute, whether for reasons of health or poverty, or lack of work, the *tiquitlato* tells the lord that such-and-such will not pay the proportion of the tribute that had been assigned to him; then the lord tells the *tiquitlato* to take the recalcitrant vassal to a *tianguez* or market, which they hold every five days in all the towns of the land, and there sell him into slavery, applying the proceeds of the sale to the payment of his tribute. . . .

All the towns have their own lands, long ago assigned for the provision of the . . . temples where they kept their idols; and these lands were and are the best of all. And they have this custom: At seeding time all would go forth at the summons of the town council to sow these fields, and to weed them at the proper time, and to cultivate the grain and harvest it and carry it to a house in which lived the pope and the *teupisques, pioches, exputhles* and *piltoutles* (or, as we would say, the bishops, archbishops, and canons and prebendaries, and even choristers, for each major temple had these five classes of officials).[6] And they supported themselves from this harvest, and the Indians also raised chickens for them to eat.

In all the towns Montezuma[7] had his designated lands, which they sowed for him in the same way as the temple lands; and if no garrison was stationed in their towns, they would carry the crops on their backs to the great city of Tenochtitlan;[8] but in the garrison towns the grain was eaten by Montezuma's soldiers, and if the town did not sow the land, it had to supply the garrison with food, and also give them chickens and all other needful provisions.

RUSSIAN LAW CODE OF 1649

The Russian Law Code of 1649, promulgated by Tsar Alexis I (1645–1676) after consultation with a national assembly (*semskii sobor*), consisted of twenty-five chapters, ranging from edicts on "Blasphemers and Heretics," to "Illegal Taverns." The chapter that affected the greatest number of Russians was "Legal Procedure Concerning the Peasants." The laws listed here finalized the process by which free Russian peasants were reduced to serfdom, in which they lost their freedom of movement and were permanently bound to a lord's estate.

This was the landlords' solution to the long-standing problem of the shortage of farm laborers caused by widespread peasant migration to the vast plains of central

---

6. Fernández is drawing an analogy between the Aztec priesthood and the hierarchy of the Roman Catholic Church.

7. The Aztec emperor.

8. The Aztec capital, the site of modern Mexico City.

Russia and Siberia. Peasant flight, an understandable reaction to increasing rents, indebtedness, taxes, and labor demands from the landowners, became an epidemic in the sixteenth and seventeenth centuries. In response, the tsars decreed a series of laws restricting peasant movement and giving aristocratic landlords more legal jurisdiction over peasant tenants. In 1646 and 1647, the state carried out a census that recorded the names of all peasants; they and their descendants were regarded as attached to the estate on which they were registered. The Law Code of 1649 further clarified the landlords' powers over their farmworkers.

By the end of the seventeenth century, serfs could be bought and sold by their lords, and in this respect their condition approached slavery as practiced in the Americas. They differed from slaves only in that each family of serfs had a plot of land on which it grew crops for its own use, whereas slaves farmed no land that was "theirs" and were fed and housed by their owners.

Questions for Analysis

1. Does the Law Code of 1649 provide the peasants any legal rights in their dealings with their landlords?
2. On the basis of this document, what do you infer about the landlords' role in causing the problem of fugitive serfs?
3. To what extent is the Law Code of 1649 sensitive to the situation of the spouses and children of fugitive serfs?

CHAPTER XI. PROCEDURE CONCERNING THE PEASANTS

1. All peasants who have fled from lands belonging to the Tsar[1] and are now living on lands belonging to church officials, hereditary landowners and service landowners[2] are to be returned to the Tsar's lands according to the land cadastres of 1627–31[3] regardless of the fifteen-year limit.[4] These peasants are to be returned with their wives, children, and all movable property.

2. The same applies to peasants who have fled from hereditary landowners and service landowners to other hereditary landowners and service landowners,

---

1. Villages and agricultural land owned by the tsar, the income from which supported the imperial court and other government activities.

2. As the two terms imply, hereditary landowners held their land as private property and could pass it on to their heirs. Service landowners received their land from the tsar in return for serving in the tsar's administration or army. The land was returned to the tsar when the landowner left government service or died.

3. Books that recorded the general census after the Moscow fire of 1626 destroyed earlier records.

4. In the previous century, the number of years in which a landlord could seek out and force the return of fugitive slaves had been raised to fifteen years. Now the limit was lifted altogether.

or to the towns, to the army, or to lands belonging to the Tsar.

3. Fugitive peasants must be returned with their wives, children, and movable property, plus their standing grain and threshed grain. But the possessions which the fugitive peasants owned in the years prior to this code are not to be claimed. If a fugitive peasant gave his daughter, sister, or niece in marriage to a local peasant, do not break up the marriage. Leave the girl with the local peasant. It was not a crime in the past to receive fugitive peasants — there was only a time limit for recovering them. Therefore the lord of the local peasant should not be deprived of his labor, especially as lands have changed hands frequently so that the present lord may not have been the person who received the fugitives anyway.

4. All hereditary landowners, service landowners, and officials managing the Tsar's lands must have proper documents identifying their peasants in case of dispute. Such documents must be written by public scribes. . . . Illiterate landholders must have their documents signed by impartial, trustworthy persons. . . .

7. A hereditary landowner who buys an estate has a right to all the peasants who were inscribed in the land cadastres of 1627–31. If all such peasants are not on the estate as listed in the purchase documents, the purchaser may take from the seller's other estates replacement peasants with all their movable property, their standing grain, and their threshed grain. . . .

10. Henceforth a person who harbors another's peasants must pay the rightful lord ten rubles[5] per year for each fugitive to compensate the plaintiff[6] for his lost income and the taxes he paid while the peasant was absent and must surrender the fugitive peasants to him. . . .

12. If a girl flees after the promulgation of this code and marries another landholder's peasant, then her husband and children will be returned with her to her former landholder. The movable property of her husband, however, will not be returned with them.

13. When a widower marries a fugitive peasant girl, any children he had by a previous marriage will not be surrendered with him to the lord of his new wife, but will remain with the lord of his first wife. . . .

15. If a widowed peasant remarries in flight, then both she and her husband will be returned to the lord of her first husband, provided her first husband was registered with a landholder.

16. If the peasant widow's first husband was not registered with a landholder, then she must live on the premises belonging to the lord of the peasant she married.

17. If a peasant in flight marries off his daughter, then his son-in-law will be returned to the landholder of his wife. . . .

18. A peasant women in flight who marries will be returned with her husband to her former landholder.

19. Peasant women who are permitted to marry another landholder's peasant

---

5. The ruble is a unit of Russian money; to give some idea of its value at the time, a contract between a landlord and a peasant in 1636 reveals that five rubles would buy a horse, two rubles would buy a cow, and one ruble would buy a hog; a document from 1672 states that fifty rubles were needed to set up a peasant with seed, animals, farm implements, and household goods.

6. A person who brings a grievance against a defendant in a court of law; in this case, a landowner demanding the return of fugitive serfs.

must be given release documents in which they are precisely described.

20. When peasants arrive in a hereditary estate or in a service estate and say that they are free people and wish to live with the landholder as peasants, the landholder must ascertain the truth of their claim. Within a year such people must be brought to Moscow or another large city for certification.

21. The lord who did not check carefully whether such people were free must pay the plaintiff to whom the peasants rightfully belong ten rubles per year per fugitive to compensate the plaintiff for his lost income and the taxes he paid while the peasant was absent.

22. Peasant children who deny their parents must be tortured.

23. Those people of any rank who give loans to another lord's peasant to entice them to their lands will lose the loans when the peasants are returned to their rightful lords. . . .

26. If the defendant[7] admits that he has the fugitive peasants but denies that the peasants came to him with any property; and if the plaintiff lists the property in his suit and then wins the case by an oath, award him five rubles for the movable property of each peasant and return the peasants to him.

27. If someone denies during a trial that he has someone's peasant and takes an oath on this, and later the peasant turns up on his estate, return the peasant to the plaintiff with all the movable property listed in the suit. Beat the false oath taker with the knout[8] for three days in the market place as an example to others and then jail him for a year. Henceforth do not believe him in any matter and do not grant him a trial against anyone for anything.

28. The children of peasants who are taken from a defendant and surrendered to a plaintiff by a court order must be surrendered even though they were not inscribed in the land cadastres of 1627–31 — provided they are living with their parents and not separately. . . .

32. Peasants may voluntarily hire themselves out to work for people of all ranks, but the latter may not hire them on condition of servitude or bondage. When the hirelings finish their work, they must be discharged without any hindrance.

33. Bondmen and peasants who flee abroad and then return to Russia cannot claim that they are free men, but must be returned to their former hereditary landowners and service landowners.

34. When fugitive peasants of different landowners marry abroad, and then return to Russia, the landholders will cast lots for the couple. The winning service landowner gets the couple and must pay five rubles to the landholder who lost because both of the peasants were in flight abroad.

---

7. The landowner accused of harboring fugitive serfs.

8. A leather whip used to flog criminals.

▓ Naoe Kanetsugu

INJUNCTIONS FOR PEASANTS

In their efforts to stabilize seventeenth-century Japan, the Tokugawa shoguns and the major aristocratic families (daimyo) gave a good deal of attention to the situation of Japanese peasants. The shoguns, to preserve sharp class divisions between commoners and aristocrats, decreed that no peasant could bear a sword or fight in war, actions traditionally reserved for members of the nobility. The land-owning daimyo wanted to make sure that their peasants were hard workers, likely to produce enough crops to ensure sufficient tax revenue for them. This was the purpose of the following document, directed in 1619 to the peasants in the domain of the daimyo of Aizu. It was written by Naoe Kanetsugu, an official in the service of the Aizu lords.

Questions
for Analysis

1. On the basis of this document and the previous selection by Fernández, what similarities can you see between the situations of the Aztec peasantry and the Japanese?
2. What does this document reveal about the role of women in rural Japan?
3. To what extent do Naoe's injunctions reflect Confucian values?
4. What kinds of power does the landowner exercise over his peasants?

1. Consider the Lord of your domain, the sun and the moon. Respect your fief holder[1] or magistrate as the patron deity of your place. Treat your village head[2] as if he were your own father.

2. During the first five days of the new year, pay respect to those around you in accordance with your position. Within the first fifteen days, make more than enough ropes needed to perform your major and minor public services (corvée labor[3] for the year). After the first fifteen days, when mountains and fields are covered with snow, accumulate all the firewood needed for the year. Use a sleigh to pull nightsoil on the fields. At night make sandals for horses. Daughters and wives must sew and weave China-grass[4] to make clothing for their menfolk. If there is a housewife who makes an excessive amount of tea to entertain others, visits around in the absence of menfolk and gossips, then she must have a hid-

---

1. Landowner.
2. The head of village government was drawn from local landowning families.

3. Corvée labor refers to unpaid labor required of peasants on the lord's lands or on various public works projects.

4. China-grass and miscanthus grass, mentioned later in the document, were both plants grown for their fiber.

den lover. Even if a man has a child with her, that kind of woman must be sent away. . . .

5. During the fourth month, men must work in the fields from dawn to dusk and make furrows as deep as the hoe can penetrate. Wives and daughters must make meals three times, put on red headbands and take the meals to the fields. Old and young alike must put the meals in front of the men who are soiled from their work. By seeing the wives attired in red, men, old and young alike, can be so encouraged . . . to the extent of forgetting their fatigue. Once men are home after dusk, give them bath water, and let them wash their feet. Sisters-in-law and female cousins must put the chapped feet of the man on the stomach of his wife and massage them. Let him forget the toil of the day.

Near the end of the fourth month, put a harrow on the horse and rake the fields. Cut miscanthus grass from the nearby mountains and put them on the China-grass field. If the field is located near a house, always check how the wind is blowing before burning the miscanthus grass. If time is appropriate, sow millet, barley and wheat seeds.

13. During the twelfth month, if there is a notification from the fief holder or magistrate about a tax overdue, quickly make the payment. For this favor he renders you, send a bowl of loach[5] fish soup accompanied by a dish of fried sardines. Although, according to the regulations, all that is expected of a farmer on such an occasion is a bowl of soup and a dish of vegetables, the ones just suggested are more appropriate. If no tax is paid after the due notice, you can have your precious wife taken away from you as security. Do not forget that in your master's house there are many young minor officials and middlemen who may steal your wife. To make sure that kind of thing never happens to you, pay all your taxes before the end of the eleventh month. Take heed that this advice is adhered to. You are known as a man of lowly origin. But even so, you do not wish to see your precious wife exposed to wild winds (misfortunes), being taken away from you and stolen by younger men. In this fashion you may lose the support of the way of heaven, come to the end of the rope, be scorned by your lowly peer groups, and regret the incident forever. Always remember that such a misfortune can befall you, and be diligent in delivering your annual tax rice and in doing work for the magistrate. Once all the annual taxes are paid, prepare for the coming of the new year. Make the remaining rice into rice cake (*mochi*), brew some *sake*, buy some salted fish, and add another year to your life happily. New Year is the time you must be able to chant along with others: I set sail on this journey of longevity. May the moon also accompany me!

---

5. A species of carp.

PART II

A World of Transformation and Tradition, 1650–1850

Two themes dominate human history from the seventeenth century to the early part of the nineteenth century. The first is the challenge many societies faced to resolve tensions between competing claims of tradition and innovation in religion, politics, and intellectual endeavors. The second is the growing interaction among the world's peoples, a phenomenon caused by migration, commercial expansion, and conquest.

The peoples of Europe experienced the most far-reaching changes during these years. The growth of science caused intellectuals to reassess and ultimately abandon medieval and Renaissance assumptions in philosophy, religion, and science itself. Europe and parts of the Americas experienced changes no less profound in their political outlook and institutions. As a result of revolutions in England, the Americas, and France, divine right monarchy and social privilege gave way to a new political order based on constitutionalism, nationalism, and democracy. On the surface, nothing so spectacular took place in economics, but the appearance of a small number of factories and power-driven machines in England in the late 1700s was a sign that the world was on the brink of a major transformation, the Industrial Revolution.

Although no other society underwent changes that equaled those of western Europe and the Americas, many experienced conflict between tradition and innovation. Rulers such as Peter the Great of Russia (1689–1725) and Selim III of the Ottoman Empire (1789–1807) provoked heated debates when they proposed extensive changes in government, religious practices, and education. Shah Jahan (1628–1657) and Aurangzeb (1658–1707) threw India into turmoil when they initiated a campaign of persecution against India's Hindu majority. In China and Japan, eighteenth-century intellectuals challenged reigning Neo-Confucian orthodoxy.

Contacts among the world's societies also increased in this period. Western Europeans migrated to the Americas in greater numbers. So too did black Africans, although they did so involuntarily as slaves. As European settlers slowly moved from the east coast into the interior of North America, native Americans lost not just territory but much of their ancient way of life. Europeans likewise extended their authority over Asia. By the early 1800s, the Dutch controlled some islands of Indonesia and the British ruled parts of India. Europeans also succeeded in opening China to increased trade.

Europeans changed the lives of the peoples of Africa, Asia, and the Americas in many ways. Conversely, the rest of the world stimulated changes in Europe. New crops, new words, and new customs were just a few of the ways Africa, Asia, and the Americas affected Europe. More profoundly, Europeans' increasing familiarity with the diversity of human experience affected their views of their own society and culture. Eighteenth-century Europe experienced a soul-searching debate about the morality of its involvement in slavery. Intellectuals used examples from both the Old World and the New to criticize European institutions and customs. The French writer Voltaire favorably compared the tolerance of China to the intolerance of Europe. The political philosopher Rousseau looked to the "noble savage" of North America to illustrate man's natural capacity for goodness when not corrupted by civilization.

European migration and commercial expansion were not the only causes of greater interaction. The Russians in the eighteenth century continued their thrust into the vast north Eurasian plain and even moved across the Bering Strait to hunt seals on the Pacific coast of North America. The Manchus, the Mongoloid people who conquered China in the mid-seventeenth century, adopted much of the ancient Chinese system as their own, but they also restructured the Chinese army, slightly modified government administration, and forced Chinese men to braid their hair in "pigtails." Eurasian merchants, Islamic missionaries, and newly arriving Chinese immigrants interacted in Indochina and Indonesia. More so than at any time in previous human history, isolation among the world's societies was melting away.

C H A P T E R

5

New Directions in Thought and Culture

Despite the endless diversity of the world's religions and philosophies, most sixteenth-century intellectuals across the globe shared a number of common beliefs and assumptions. Truth, it was believed, had already been revealed in the writings of ancient and revered authorities, and the intellectual's role was to interpret and understand what had already been discovered. In seeking answers to the fundamental problems of human existence, the Chinese drew on the Confucian Classics, western European Christians on Aristotle and the Bible, and Muslims on the Qur'an and other revered texts. Elsewhere, the writings of the Buddha, sacred Hindu texts, and centuries-old myths and legends provided insight and understanding. Intellectuals within a given culture often differed in their interpretation of ancient authorities, but they generally agreed about who those authorities should be.

Although debate was more pronounced in Europe than elsewhere, intellectuals in several parts of the globe rejected ideas of venerated authorities during the seventeenth and eighteenth centuries. In Europe, overseas exploration, the Reformation, and political and economic changes all contributed to a reorientation of intellectual values. Most important, however, were the new discoveries and insights about nature and the universe that defined Europe's Scientific Revolution, a movement that led directly to the secularism and rationalism of the eighteenth-century Enlightenment.

In other parts of the world, artistic and intellectual change often came about because of cross-cultural influence. Much of the brilliance of Mughal India resulted from a fusion of Persian and Indian traditions and the increasing European influence toward the end of the sixteenth century. In Japan continuing commercial contacts maintained by the Dutch, permitted by the Japanese to send one ship per year to their shores, stimulated an interest in European science. And in China, the Manchu conquest of the mid-seventeenth century forced intellectuals to rethink their values and methods of inquiry. Increasing world contacts and intellectual ferment went hand in hand.

Europe's Scientific Revolution

Of the many controversies among seventeenth-century European intellectuals, none matched the intensity or significance of the debate over the content and method of science. As seen in Chapter 2, Nicholas Copernicus, in his *On the Revolutions of the Heavenly Spheres* (1543), broke with the authority of the ancient Greeks and proposed that the sun, not the earth, was the center of the universe. As Copernicus fully expected, his ideas disturbed many intellectuals and religious leaders. He had, after all, challenged the unquestioned medieval notion that the ancient Greeks provided an accurate and unassailable description of the workings of the universe. In addition, his theory clashed with views of both Catholic and Protestant churches. Heliocentrism, the theory of a sun-centered universe, conflicted with biblical passages stating that the sun moved around the earth and called into question the very basis of medieval Christian cosmology, which placed the earth at the center of God's creation.

During the sixteenth and seventeenth centuries, scientists, or, as they were known then, natural philosophers, challenged many other assumptions and theories of Greek science. They also developed a new approach to the study of nature that came to be labeled the *scientific method*. By the end of the seventeenth century, scholars no longer sought to understand nature by analyzing the works of a handful of revered ancient authorities. Instead, they worked according to rigorous standards of proof based on mathematics, experiment, and the thorough collection of data.

Sir Isaac Newton (1642–1727), with the publication of his *Mathematical Principles of Natural Philosophy* (1687), brought to a climax this first stage of Europe's Scientific Revolution. Drawing on the work of hundreds of preceding astronomers, physicists, and mathematicians and using the powerful tool of calculus, which he invented, Newton ended the century-and-a-half European debate about the universe. He offered a description and interpretation of the universe that explained everything from the ebb and flow of tides to the movements of the most distant stars. The key to his theory was the universal law of gravitation, which stated that every object, no matter how large or small, exerted a force on every other object, directly proportional to the product of the two masses and inversely proportional to the square of the distance between them.

Newton's theories, unlike those of Copernicus, gained rapid acceptance among Europe's intellectuals, and science and the scientific method became an integral part of European thought. As the following documents show, however, earlier in the seventeenth century, disciples of the new science needed to defend their discoveries against theological opponents and their methods against philosophical critics.

▓ Galileo Galilei

LETTER TO THE GRAND DUCHESS CHRISTINA

One of the giants of Europe's Scientific Revolution was the Italian physicist and astronomer Galileo Galilei (1564–1642), whose most important work was in mechanics, where he described the theory of inertia and developed a mathematical explanation for the movement of falling bodies. In astronomy, he pioneered the use of the telescope and strongly defended Copernican heliocentric theory. His defense of Copernicus angered powerful Roman Catholic clergymen and theologians, who believed it threatened the orthodoxy and authority of the Church.

In 1615, Galileo, a devout Catholic, defended his approach to science in a published letter addressed to Christina the Grand Duchess of Tuscany. In the short run, Galileo lost his case. The Church officially condemned Copernicanism in 1616 and forced Galileo to renounce many of his ideas in 1632. His works continued to be read, however, and, in the long run, his writings contributed to the acceptance of not just Copernican theory but the new model of scientific inquiry.

Questions
for Analysis

1. How does Galileo perceive the motives of his enemies? Why, in his view, do they raise religious arguments against him?
2. According to Galileo, why is it dangerous to apply scriptural passages to issues relating to science?
3. To Galileo, how does nature differ from the Bible as a source of truth?
4. How do Galileo's thoughts on the relation of science and religion differ from those of Copernicus in his Preface to *On the Revolutions of the Heavenly Spheres* (see Chapter 2)?

Some years ago, as Your Serene Highness well knows, I discovered in the heavens many things that had not been seen before our own age. The novelty of these things, as well as some consequences which followed from them in contradiction to the physical notions commonly held among academic philosophers, stirred up against me no small number of professors — as if I had placed these things in the sky with my own hands in order to upset nature and overturn the sciences. They seemed to forget that the increase of known truths stimulates the investigation, establishment, and growth of the arts; not their diminution or destruction.

Showing a greater fondness for their own opinions than for truth, they sought to deny and disprove the new things which, if they had cared to look for themselves, their own senses would have demonstrated to them. To this end they hurled various charges and published numerous writings filled with vain arguments, and they made the grave mistake of sprinkling these with passages taken from places in the Bible which they had failed to understand properly, and which were ill suited to their purposes.

Persisting in their original resolve to destroy me and everything mine by any means they can think of, these men are aware of my views in astronomy and philosophy. They know that as to the arrangement of the parts of the universe, I hold the sun to be situated motionless in the center of the revolution of the celestial orbs while the earth rotates on its axis and revolves about the sun. They know also that I support this position not only by refuting the arguments of Ptolemy and Aristotle, but by producing many counter-arguments; in particular, some which relate to physical effects whose causes can perhaps be assigned in no other way. In addition there are astronomical arguments derived from many things in my new celestial discoveries that plainly confute the Ptolemaic system while admirably agreeing with and confirming the contrary hypothesis. Possibly because they are disturbed by the known truth of other propositions of mine which differ from those commonly held, and therefore mistrusting their defense so long as they confine themselves to the field of philosophy, these men have resolved to fabricate a shield for their fallacies out of the mantle of pretended religion and the authority of the Bible. These they apply, with little judgment, to the refutation of arguments that they do not understand and have not even listened to.

First they have endeavored to spread the opinion that such propositions in general are contrary to the Bible and are consequently damnable and heretical. . . . Next, becoming bolder, and hoping (though vainly) that this seed which first took root in their hypocritical minds would send out branches and ascend to heaven, they began scattering rumors among the people that before long this doctrine would be condemned by the supreme authority.[1] They know, too, that official condemnation would not only suppress the two propositions which I have mentioned, but would render damnable all other astronomical and physical statements and observations that have any necessary relation or connection with these. . . .

Now as to the false aspersions which they so unjustly seek to cast upon me, I have thought it necessary to justify myself in the eyes of all men, whose judgment in matters of religion and of reputation I must hold in great esteem. I shall therefore discourse of the particulars which these men produce to make this opinion detested and to have it condemned not merely as false but as heretical. To this end they make a shield of their hypocritical zeal for religion. They go about invoking the Bible, which they would have minister to their deceitful purposes. Contrary to the sense of the Bible and the intention of the holy Fathers, if I am not mistaken, they would extend such authorities until even in purely physical matters — where faith is not involved — they would have us altogether abandon reason and the evidence of our senses in favor of some biblical passage, though under the surface meaning of its words this passage may contain a different sense.

I hope to show that I proceed with much greater piety than they do, when I

---

1. The pope.

argue not against condemning this book, but against condemning it in the way they suggest — that is, without understanding it, weighing it, or so much as reading it. . . .

The reason produced for condemning the opinion that the earth moves and the sun stands still is that in many places in the Bible one may read that the sun moves and the earth stands still. Since the Bible cannot err, it follows as a necessary consequence that anyone takes an erroneous and heretical position who maintains that the sun is inherently motionless and the earth movable.

With regard to this argument, I think in the first place that it is very pious to say and prudent to affirm that the holy Bible can never speak untruth — whenever its true meaning is understood. But I believe nobody will deny that it is often very abstruse, and may say things which are quite different from what its bare words signify. Hence in expounding the Bible if one were always to confine oneself to the unadorned grammatical meaning, one might fall into error. Not only contradictions and propositions far from true might thus be made to appear in the Bible, but even grave heresies and follies. Thus it would be necessary to assign to God feet, hands, and eyes, as well as corporeal and human affections, such as anger, repentance, hatred, and sometimes even the forgetting of things past and ignorance of those to come. These propositions uttered by the Holy Ghost were set down in that manner by the sacred scribes[2] in order to accommodate them to the capacities of the common people, who are rude and unlearned. . . .

This being granted, I think that in discussions of physical problems we ought to begin not from the authority of scriptural passages, but from sense-experiences and necessary demonstrations; for the holy Bible and the phenomena of nature proceed alike from the divine Word, the former as the dictate of the Holy Ghost and the latter as the observant executrix of God's commands. It is necessary for the Bible, in order to be accommodated to the understanding of every man, to speak many things which appear to differ from the absolute truth so far as the bare meaning of the words is concerned. But Nature, on the other hand, is inexorable and immutable; she never transgresses the laws imposed upon her, or cares a whit whether her abstruse reasons and methods of operation are understandable to men. For that reason it appears that nothing physical which sense-experience sets before our eyes, or which necessary demonstrations prove to us, ought to be called in question (much less condemned) upon the testimony of biblical passages which may have some different meaning beneath their words. For the Bible is not chained in every expression to conditions as strict as those which govern all physical effects; nor is God any less excellently revealed in Nature's actions than in the sacred statements of the Bible.

---

2. The Holy Ghost is the third divine person of the Trinity (God the Father, God the Son, God the Holy Ghost), who sanctifies and inspires humankind. Christians believe the Sacred Scribes of the Bible wrote under the sacred and infallible inspiration of God the Holy Ghost.

Francis Bacon

NEW ORGANON

Along with the Frenchman René Descartes (1596–1650), the English philosopher Francis Bacon (1561–1626) was instrumental in formulating the strategies and methods of the new science. Both men rejected the medieval belief that scientific truth was attained through the logical analysis of revered ancient texts. Descartes, a superb mathematician and an advocate of the deductive method, stated in his masterpiece, *Discourse on Method* (1637), that humans could find truth through hypothesis formation, deduction, and mathematical reasoning. Bacon, a disciple of the inductive method, put his faith in experiment, observation, and the collection of data. In his view, only after scientists had studied many individual phenomena could they generalize about the laws of nature.

Bacon's *New Organon* (1620), or "New Method of Inquiry," was meant to replace the "old organon," which refers to the "old method of inquiry" based on the logical writings of Aristotle. Written in Latin, and hence directed to a learned audience, it consists of 130 "aphorisms" — concise statements of principles — that summarize his views on scientific knowledge and its potential for humankind.

Questions for Analysis

1. What does Bacon see as the major impediments to scientific progress? How do his concerns differ from those of Galileo?
2. According to Bacon, what is the role of experiment in scientific generalization?
3. Is there any evidence that Bacon viewed mathematics as an integral part of scientific inquiry?
4. What does Bacon mean when he says that a man of science must be like a "bee" rather than an "ant" or a "spider"?
5. What role in the future of humanity does Bacon see for science?
6. To Bacon, what is the relationship between science and technology?

I

Man, being the servant and interpreter of Nature, can do and understand so much and so much only as he has observed in fact or in thought of the course of nature: beyond this he neither knows anything nor can do anything.

II

Neither the naked hand nor the understanding left to itself can effect much. It is by instruments and helps that the work is done, which are as much wanted for the understanding as for the hand. And as the instruments of the hand either give motion or guide it, so the instruments of the mind supply either suggestions for the understanding or cautions.

III

Human knowledge and human power meet in one; for where the cause is not known the effect cannot be produced. Nature to be commanded must be obeyed; and that which in contemplation is as the cause is in operation as the rule.

VIII

Moreover the works already known are due to chance and experiment rather than to sciences; for the sciences we now possess are merely systems for the nice ordering and setting forth of things already invented; not methods of invention or directions for new works.

IX

The cause and root of nearly all evils in the sciences is this — that while we falsely admire and extol the powers of the human mind we neglect to seek for its true helps.

XIX

There are and can be only two ways of searching into and discovering truth. The one flies from the senses and particulars to the most general axioms, and from these principles, the truth of which it takes for settled and immovable, proceeds to judgment and to the discovery of middle axioms. And this way is now in fashion. The other derives axioms from the senses and particulars, rising by a gradual and unbroken ascent, so that it arrives at the most general axioms last of all. This is the true way, but as yet untried.

XXII

Both ways set out from the senses and particulars, and rest in the highest generalities; but the difference between them is infinite. For the one just glances at experiment and particulars in passing, the other

dwells duly and orderly among them. The one, again, begins at once by establishing certain abstract and useless generalities, the other rises by gradual steps to that which is prior and better known in the order of nature.

XXXI

It is idle to expect any great advancement in science from the superinducing[1] and engrafting of new things upon old. We must begin anew from the very foundations, unless we would revolve for ever in a circle with mean and contemptible progress.

XXXVI

One method of delivery alone remains to us; which is simply this: we must lead men to the particulars themselves, and their series and order; while men on their side must force themselves for awhile to lay their notions by and begin to familiarize themselves with facts.

XCV

Those who have handled sciences have been either men of experiment or men of dogmas. The men of experiment are like the ant; they only collect and use: the reasoners resemble spiders, who make cobwebs out of their own substance. But the bee takes a middle course; it gathers its material from the flowers of the garden and of the field, but transforms and digests it by a power of its own. Not unlike this is the true business of philosophy; for it neither relies solely or chiefly on the powers of the mind, nor does it take the matter which it gathers from natural history and mechanical experiments and lay it up in the memory whole, as it finds it;

---

1. To introduce an additional concept over and above some already existing concept.

but lays it up in the understanding altered and digested. Therefore from a closer and purer league between these two faculties, the experimental and the rational, (such as has never yet been made) much may be hoped.

CVIII

So much then for the removing of despair and the raising of hope through the dismissal or rectification of the errors of past time. We must now see what else there is to ground hope upon. And this consideration occurs at once — that if many useful discoveries have been made by accident or upon occasion, when men were not seeking for them but were busy about other things; no one can doubt but that when they apply themselves to seek and make this their business, and that too by method and in order and not by desultory impulses, they will discover far more.

CIX

Another argument of hope may be drawn from this, — that some of the inventions already known are such as before they were discovered it could hardly have entered any man's head to think of; they would have been simply set aside as impossible. . . .

If, for instance, before the invention of ordnance,[2] a man had described the thing by its effects, and said that there was a new invention, by means of which the strongest towers and walls could be shaken and thrown down at a great distance; men would doubtless have begun to think over all the ways of multiplying the force of catapults and mechanical engines by weights and wheels and such machinery for ramming and projecting; but the notion of a fiery blast suddenly and violently expanding and exploding would hardly have entered into any man's imagination or fancy. . . .

In the same way, if before the discovery of silk, any one had said that there was a kind of thread discovered for the purposes of dress and furniture, which far surpassed the thread of linen or of wool in fineness and at the same time in strength, and also in beauty and softness; men would have begun immediately to think of some silky kind of vegetable, or of the finer hair of some animal, or of the feathers and down of birds; but of a web woven by a tiny worm, and that in such abundance, and renewing itself yearly, they would assuredly never have thought. Nay, if any one had said anything about a worm, he would no doubt have been laughed at as dreaming of a new kind of cobwebs.

So again, if before the discovery of the magnet, any one had said that a certain instrument had been invented by means of which the quarters and points of the heavens could be taken and distinguished with exactness; men would have been carried by their imagination to a variety of conjectures concerning the more exquisite construction of astronomical instruments; but that anything could be discovered agreeing so well in its movements with the heavenly bodies, and yet not a heavenly body itself, but simply a substance of metal or stone, would have been judged altogether incredible. . . .

There is therefore much ground for hoping that there are still laid up in the womb of nature many secrets of excellent use, having no affinity or parallelism with any thing that is now known, but lying entirely out of the beat of the imagination, which have not yet been found out. They too no doubt will some time or other, in the course and revolution of many ages, come to light of themselves, just as the

---

2. Cannon and artillery.

others did; only by the method of which we are now treating they can be speedily and suddenly and simultaneously presented and anticipated.

Europe's Age of Enlightenment

Although secularism had been a growing force in Europe since the Renaissance, only in the eighteenth century — Europe's Age of Enlightenment — did it eclipse religion as the dominant influence on European thought and culture. Organized churches, both Catholic and Protestant, still had millions of followers, and revival movements, such as Methodism in England, were signs of continuing religious vitality. Nonetheless, in the eighteenth century, most intellectuals were indifferent or openly hostile to religion, artists painted few religious scenes, and rulers gave little thought to religion in determining policy.

The Scientific Revolution was the main inspiration for the secularism of the eighteenth century. When Newton, drawing on the work of Copernicus, Brahe, Galileo, and many others, discovered the scientific laws of the universe without relying on ancient authorities or religious revelation, he demonstrated to eighteenth-century intellectuals the full power of human reason. These intellectuals, known as *philosophes* (French for philosophers), were convinced that reason could be applied to social, economic, and political problems with results as spectacular as those achieved by seventeenth-century scientists. Specifically, reason could expose the weaknesses, errors, flaws, and injustices inherited from Europe's "unenlightened" past. The philosophes were, therefore, social and political critics who examined and usually condemned legal codes, religious customs, government policies, slavery, sexual mores, educational practices, class privileges, and much else.

The Enlightenment, however, involved more than negative criticism. The philosophes rejected the traditional belief that humans were fated to accept passively the given order of things, even if that order was deeply flawed. Reason provided an instrument to plot and achieve a better future. The philosophes reached no consensus on what that future might contain or how it could be reached. But none of them doubted that improvement of the human condition was not just possible but inevitable, if only reason were given freedom to inquire, question, inspire, and plan.

Voltaire

TREATISE ON TOLERATION

François-Marie Arouet (1694–1778), known to the world by his pen name Voltaire, combined wit, literary elegance, and a passionate social conscience in a long literary career that best represents the values and spirit of the Enlightenment. Born into a well-to-do Parisian bourgeois family, Voltaire published his first work, a tragic drama, *Oedipus*, in 1717. In the next sixty-one years, he wrote thousands of poems, histories, satires, works of fiction, articles, essays, and reviews. The growing European reading public avidly bought his works, making him one of the first authors who not only survived but prospered through his pen.

Although Voltaire's enormous output and popularity ensured his influence on the Enlightenment at many different levels, one particular contribution stands out: his devotion to the principles of toleration and freedom of thought. Voltaire was convinced that throughout history, the intolerance of organized religions, not just Christianity, had been responsible for much of the world's suffering and cruelty. He was angered that even in the "enlightened" eighteenth century, Protestant-Catholic hatreds still resulted in episodes such as the torture and execution of Jean Calas, a French Protestant convicted unjustly of murdering his son. Voltaire's devotion to toleration is revealed in the two following selections, both taken from his *Treatise on Toleration*, written in 1763 in response to the execution of Calas.

Questions for Analysis

1. Does Voltaire feel that intolerance is a monopoly of Christianity or that it characterizes other organized religions?
2. What is the point of Voltaire's reference to the various dialects of Italy?
3. What does Voltaire suggest as the essence of a truly religious person?
4. What attitude toward God and humankind does Voltaire express in his "Prayer to God"?

OF UNIVERSAL TOLERANCE

No great art or studied eloquence is needed to prove that Christians should tolerate one another. I go even further and declare that we must look upon all men as our brothers. But the Turk, my brother? the Chinese, the Jew, the Siamese? Yes, of course; are we not all the children of one father and creatures of the same God?

But these people despise us; they call us idolators! Then I'll tell them they are quite wrong. I think I could at least shock the proud obstinacy of an imam,[1] if I said to them something like this:

This little globe, nothing more than a point, rolls in space like so many other globes; we are lost in this immensity. Man, some five feet tall, is surely a very small part of the universe. One of these imperceptible beings says to some of his neighbors in Arabia or Africa: "Listen to me, for the God of all these worlds has enlightened me: there are nine hundred million little ants like us on the earth, but only my anthill is beloved of God; He will hold all others in horror through all eter-

---

1. For Sunni Muslims, an imam is a prayer leader at a mosque; for Shiites, he is one of the twelve successors of Muhammad. Voltaire is using the word in the former sense.

nity; only mine will be blessed, the others will be eternally wretched."

At that, they would cut me short and ask what fool made that stupid remark. I would be obliged to reply, "You yourselves." Then I would try to mollify them; but that would not be easy.

I would speak now to the Christians and dare say, for example, to a Dominican Inquisitor: "My brother, you know that every province in Italy has its dialect, and people in Venice and Bergamo speak differently from those in Florence. The Academy della Crusca[2] has standardized the language; its dictionary is an inescapable authority, and Buonmattei's[3] grammar is an absolute and infallible guide; but do you believe that the head of the Academy and in his absence, Buonmattei, would have been able in all good conscience to cut out the tongues of all those from Venice and Bergamo who persisted in using their own dialect?"

The Inquisitor replies: "There is a great difference; here it's a question of your salvation. It's for your own good the Director of the Inquisition orders that you be seized on the testimony of a single person, no matter how infamous or criminal he may be; that you have no lawyer to defend you; that the very name of your accuser be unknown to you; that the Inquisitor promise you grace and then condemn you; that you undergo five different degrees of torture and then be whipped or sent to the galleys, or ceremoniously burned at the stake. . . .

I would take the liberty of replying: "My brother, perhaps you are right: I am convinced that you wish me well, but couldn't I be saved without all that?"

To be sure, these horrible absurdities do not soil the face of the earth everyday, but they are frequent enough, and a whole volume could easily be written about them much longer than the Gospels which condemn them. Not only is it very cruel to persecute in this brief existence of ours those who differ from us in opinion, but I am afraid it is being bold indeed to pronounce their eternal damnation. It hardly seems fitting for us atoms of the moment, for that is all we are, to presume to know in advance the decrees of our own Creator. . . .

Oh, sectarians of a merciful God, if you had a cruel heart, if, while adoring Him whose only law consists in the words: "Love God and thy neighbor as thyself (Luke X, 27)," you had overloaded this pure and holy law with sophisms and incomprehensible disputations; if you had lighted the torch of discord either over a new word or a single letter of the alphabet; if you had made eternal punishment the penalty for the omission of a few words or ceremonies which other nations could not know about, I would say to you, as I wept in compassion for mankind: "Transport yourselves with me to the day when all men will be judged and when God will do unto each man according to his works."

"I see all the dead of all centuries, past and present, appear before His presence. Are you quite sure that our Creator and Father will say to the wise and virtuous Confucius, to Solon the law-giver, to Pythagoras, Zaleucus, Socrates, and Plato, to the divine Antoninus, good Trajan, and Titus, the flowering of mankind, to Epictetus and so many other model men:[4] "Go, you monsters; go and suffer punishment, limitless in time and intensity, eter-

---

2. Florentine Academy of Letters, founded in 1582.

3. Seventeenth-century Italian grammarian.

4. These were all men famous for their writings on ethics and morality who lived before Christianity.

nal as I am eternal. And you, my beloved, Jean Chatel, Ravaillac, Damiens, Cartouche, etc.,[5] who died according to the prescribed formulas, share forever at my right hand my empire and my felicity."

You draw back in horror from these words, and since they escaped me, I have no more to say.

PRAYER TO GOD

I no longer address myself to men, but to thee, God of all beings, all worlds, and all ages. If indeed it is allowable for feeble creatures, lost in immensity and imperceptible to the rest of the universe, to dare ask anything of Thee who hast given all things, whose decrees are as immutable as they are eternal, deign to look with compassion upon the failings inherent in our nature, and grant that these failings lead us not into calamity.

Thou didst not give us hearts that we should hate each other or hands that we should cut each other's throats. Grant that we may help each other bear the burden of our painful and brief lives; that the slight difference in the clothing with which we cover our puny bodies, in our inadequate tongues, in all our ridiculous customs, in all our imperfect laws, in all our insensate opinions, in all our stations in life so disproportionate in our eyes but so equal in Thy sight, that all these little variations that differentiate the atoms called *man*, may not be the signals for hatred and persecution. . . .

May all men remember that they are brothers; may they hold in horror tyranny that is exercised over souls, just as they hold in execration the brigandage that snatches away by force the fruits of labor and peaceful industry. If the scourge of war is inevitable, let us not hate each other, let us not tear each other apart in the lap of peace; but let us use the brief moment of our existence in blessing in a thousand different tongues, from Siam to California, Thy goodness which has bestowed this moment upon us.

Jean-Jacques Rousseau

THE SOCIAL CONTRACT

Of all the philosophes, none was more challenging, original, and controversial than the Geneva-born Jean-Jacques Rousseau (1712–1778). Abandoned by his father at an early age, Rousseau wandered about Europe, became the lover of a Swiss aristocratic lady, and drifted into Paris in 1742. There, despite his rustic manners and somewhat quirky ideas, he was welcomed into the circle of the philosophes, many of whom recognized his brilliance. His first two works presented a pessimistic view of the human condition. His *Discourse on the Arts and Sciences* (1750) and *Discourse on Inequality* (1753) argued that the rise of civilization and the establishment of private property had corrupted humanity by destroying the human's natural inclination toward kindness, sympathy, honesty, and selflessness.

Rousseau never advocated or believed that humans could turn back history's clock

---

5. Four notorious criminals, including murderers and highway robbers.

and return to the state of nature. Instead, in his later works he set forth a program by which men and women could become moral and virtuous even while living in society. In *Émile* (1762) he presented an original, albeit impractical, plan for educational reform, and in *The Social Contract* (1762) he vigorously set forth his ideas on power, freedom, and the relation of politics to morality. These political ideas inspired the leaders of the French Revolution and subsequent democratic movements in every corner of the globe.

Questions for Analysis

1. According to Rousseau, what are the deficiencies of a government based solely on force?
2. According to Rousseau, what motivates human beings to leave society and form governments?
3. What is the "social contract"? How, according to Rousseau, is freedom preserved when an individual becomes part of the "social contract"?
4. In what ways is Rousseau's approach to political theory similar to and different from Machiavelli's (see Chapter 2)?
5. Compare Rousseau's and Bodin's views of "sovereignty."
6. Why does Rousseau argue that "the institution of government is not a contract, but a law"?
7. In what ways do Rousseau's ideas provide a theoretical basis for democracy?

I mean to inquire if, in the civil order, there can be any sure and legitimate rule of administration, men being taken as they are and laws as they might be. In this inquiry I shall endeavor always to unite what right sanctions with what is prescribed by interest, in order that justice and utility may in no case be divided.

. . .

Man is born free; and everywhere he is in chains. One thinks himself the master of others, and still remains a greater slave than they. How did this change come about? I do not know. What can make it legitimate? That question I think I can answer.

If I took into account only force, and the effects derived from it, I should say: "As long as a people is compelled to obey, and obeys, it does well; as soon as it can shake off the yoke, and shakes it off, it does still better; for, regaining its liberty by the same right as took it away, either it is justified in resuming it, or there was no justification for those who took it away." But the social order is a sacred right which is the basis of all rights. Nevertheless, this right does not come from nature, and must therefore be founded on conventions.[1] Before coming to that, I have to prove what I have just asserted.

. . .

---

1. Convention in the sense of agreement about general principles.

The strongest is never strong enough to be always the master, unless he transforms strength into right, and obedience into duty. Hence the right of the strongest, which, though to all seeming meant ironically, is really laid down as a fundamental principle. But are we never to have an explanation of this phrase? Force is a physical power, and I fail to see what moral effect it can have. To yield to force is an act of necessity, not of will — at the most, an act of prudence. In what sense can it be a duty?

Suppose for a moment that this so-called "right" exists. I maintain that the sole result is a mass of inexplicable nonsense. For, if force creates right, the effect changes with the cause: every force that is greater than the first succeeds to its right. As soon as it is possible to disobey with impunity, disobedience is legitimate; and, the strongest being always in the right, the only thing that matters is to act so as to become the strongest. But what kind of right is that which perishes when force fails? If we must obey perforce, there is no need to obey because we ought; and if we are not forced to obey, we are under no obligation to do so. Clearly, the word "right" adds nothing to force: in this connection, it means absolutely nothing. . . .

Let us then admit that force does not create right, and that we are obliged to obey only legitimate powers. In that case, my original question recurs.

. . .

I suppose men to have reached the point at which the obstacles in the way of their preservation in the state of nature show their power of resistance to be greater than the resources at the disposal of each individual for his maintenance in that state. That primitive condition can then subsist no longer; and the human race would perish unless it changed its manner of existence.

But, as men cannot engender new forces, but only unite and direct existing ones, they have no other means of preserving themselves than the formation, by aggregation of a sum of forces great enough to overcome the resistance. These they have to bring into play by means of a single motive power, and cause to act in concert.

This sum of forces can arise only where several persons come together: but, as the force and liberty of each man are the chief instruments of his self-preservation, how can he pledge them without harming his own interests, and neglecting the care he owes to himself? This difficulty, in its bearing on my present subject, may be stated in the following terms:

"The problem is to find a form of association which will defend and protect with the whole common force the person and goods of each associate, and in which each, while uniting himself with all, may still obey himself alone, and remain as free as before." This is the fundamental problem of which the *Social Contract* provides the solution. . . .

These clauses, properly understood, may be reduced to one — the total alienation of each associate, together with all his rights, to the whole community; for, in the first place, as each gives himself absolutely, the conditions are the same for all; and, this being so, no one has any interest in making them burdensome to others. . . .

Finally, each man, in giving himself to all, gives himself to nobody; and as there is no associate over which he does not acquire the same right as he yields others over himself, he gains an equivalent for everything he loses, and an increase of force for the preservation of what he has.

If then we discard from the social compact what is not of its essence, we shall find that it reduces itself to the following terms.

"Each of us puts his person and all his powers in common under the supreme direction of the general will, and, in our corporate capacity, we receive each member as an indivisible part of the whole."

. . .

The first and most important deduction from the principles we have so far laid down is that the general will alone can direct the State according to the object for which it was instituted, i.e. the common good: for if the clashing of particular interests made the establishment of societies necessary, the agreement of these very interests made it possible. The common element in these different interests is what forms the social tie; and, were there no point of agreement between them all, no society could exist. It is solely on the basis of this common interest that every society should be governed. . . .

There is only one contract in the State, and that is the act of association, which in itself excludes the existence of a second. It is impossible to conceive of any public contract that would not be a violation of the first.

. . .

Under what general idea then should the act by which government is instituted be conceived as falling? I will begin by stating that the act is complex, as being composed of two others — the establishment of the law and its execution.

By the former, the Sovereign decrees that there shall be a governing body established in this or that form; this act is clearly a law.

By the latter, the people nominates the rulers who are to be entrusted with the government that has been established. This nomination, being a particular act, is clearly not a second law, but merely a consequence of the first and a function of government.

. . .

What we have just said . . . makes it clear that the institution of government is not a contract, but a law; that the depositaries of the executive power are not the people's masters, but its officers; that it can set them up and pull them down when it likes; that for them there is no question of contract, but of obedience; and that in taking charge of the functions the State imposes on them they are doing no more than fulfilling their duty as citizens, without having the remotest right to argue about the conditions.

When therefore the people sets up an hereditary government, whether it be monarchical or confined to one family, or aristocratic and confined to a class, what it enters into is not an undertaking; the administration is given a provisional form, until the people chooses to order it otherwise.

It is true that such changes are always dangerous, and that the established government should never be touched except when it comes to be incompatible with the public good; but the circumspection this involves is a maxim of policy and not a rule of right, and the State is no more bound to leave civil authority in the hands of its rulers than military authority in the hands of its generals.

▓ Condorcet

SKETCH OF THE PROGRESS OF THE HUMAN MIND

The philosophes were convinced that well-intentioned human beings could employ reason to erase the cruelties, superstitions, and prejudices that diminished the human condition. By the end of the century, some went further and developed a complete theory of human progress, which saw humanity gradually ascending from ignorance and darkness to a perfect "utopian" future. The most famous prophet of progress was the Marquis of Condorcet (1743–1794), a mathematician and philosophe who wrote several treatises on educational reform. He supported the French Revolution but, like many moderates, fell afoul of the radical Jacobins and was forced to go into hiding in July 1793. It was then he wrote his *Sketch of the Progress of the Human Mind,* in which he traced human progress in ten stages from the dawn of history to the French Revolution and beyond. Having completed his work in March 1794, he emerged from hiding, was arrested immediately, and was found dead the next morning of unknown causes.

The following excerpts come from "The Ninth Stage," in which he discusses developments from the mid-seventeenth century to the beginning of the French Revolution, and "The Tenth Stage," in which he describes humanity's future.

Questions
for Analysis

1. According to Condorcet, what factors in humankind's past have prevented progress?
2. Condorcet sees science as the key factor in human progress. Why?
3. According to Condorcet, how will progress spread to the non-European areas of the globe?
4. When it has reached perfection, what will future society be like? How will human beings be different?

THE NINTH STAGE

From Descartes to the Foundation of the French Republic

The progress of philosophy and the sciences has favored and extended the progress of letters, and this in turn has served to make the study of the sciences easier, and that of philosophy more popular. The sciences and the arts have assisted one another despite the efforts of the ignorant and the foolish to separate them and make them enemies. Scholarship, which seemed doomed by its respect for the past and its deference towards authority always to lend its support to harmful superstitions, has nevertheless contributed to their eradication, for it was able to borrow the torch of a sounder criticism from philosophy and the sciences. It already knew how to weigh up authorities and compare them; it now learned how to bring every authority before the bar of Reason. It had already discounted prodigies, fantastic anecdotes, facts contrary to all probability; but after attacking the evidence on which such absurdities relied, it now learned that all extraordinary facts must always be rejected, however impressive the evidence in their favor, unless this can truly turn the scale against the weight of their physical or moral probability.

Thus all the intellectual activities of man, however different they may be in their aims, their methods, or the qualities of mind they exact, have combined to further the progress of human reason. Indeed, the whole system of human labor is like a well-made machine, whose several parts have been systematically distinguished but none the less, being intimately bound together, form a single whole, and work towards a single end. . . .

But although everything tells us that the human race will never relapse into its former state of barbarism, although everything combines to reassure us against that corrupt and cowardly political theory which would condemn it to oscillate forever between truth and error, liberty and servitude, nevertheless we still see the forces of enlightenment in possession of no more than a very small portion of the globe, and the truly enlightened vastly outnumbered by the great mass of men who are still given over to ignorance and prejudice. We still see vast areas in which men groan in slavery, vast areas offering the spectacle of nations either degraded by the vices of a civilization whose progress is impeded by corruption, or still vegetating in the infant condition of early times. We observe that the labors of recent ages have done much for the progress of the human mind, but little for the perfection of the human race; that they have done much for the honor of man, something for his liberty, but so far almost nothing for his happiness. At a few points our eyes are dazzled with a brilliant light; but thick darkness still covers an immense stretch of the horizon. There are a few cir-

cumstances from which the philosopher can take consolation; but he is still afflicted by the spectacle of the stupidity, slavery, barbarism and extravagance of mankind; and the friend of humanity can find unmixed pleasure only in tasting the sweet delights of hope for the future. . . .

THE TENTH STAGE

The Future Progress of the Human Mind

Our hopes for the future condition of the human race can be subsumed under three important heads: the abolition of inequality between nations, the progress of equality within each nation, and the true perfection of mankind. Will all nations one day attain that state of civilization which the most enlightened, the freest and the least burdened by prejudices, such as the French and the Anglo-Americans, have attained already? Will the vast gulf that separates these peoples from the slavery of nations under the rule of monarchs, from the barbarism of African tribes, from the ignorance of savages, little by little disappear?

Is there on the face of the earth a nation whose inhabitants have been debarred by nature herself from the enjoyment of freedom and the exercise of reason?

Are those differences which have hitherto been seen in every civilized country in respect of the enlightenment, the resources, and the wealth enjoyed by the different classes into which it is divided, is that inequality between men which was aggravated or perhaps produced by the earliest progress of society, are these part of civilization itself, or are they due to the present imperfections of the social art? . . .

Is the human race to better itself, either by discoveries in the sciences and the arts, and so in the means to individual welfare and general prosperity; or by progress in the principles of conduct or practical morality; or by a true perfection of the intellectual, moral, or physical faculties of man, an improvement which may result from a perfection either of the instruments used to heighten the intensity of these faculties and to direct their use or of the natural constitution of man?

In answering these three questions we shall find in the experience of the past, in the observation of the progress that the sciences and civilization have already made, in the analysis of the progress of the human mind and of the development of its faculties, the strongest reasons for believing that nature has set no limit to the realization of our hopes.

If we glance at the state of the world today we see first of all that in Europe the principles of the French constitution are already those of all enlightened men. We see them too widely propagated, too seriously professed, for priests and despots to prevent their gradual penetration even into the hovels of their slaves; there they will soon awaken in these slaves the remnants of their common sense and inspire them with that smoldering indignation which not even constant humiliation and fear can smother in the soul of the oppressed.

Can we doubt that either common sense or the senseless discords of European nations will add to the effects of the slow but inexorable progress of their colonies, and will soon bring about the independence of the New World? And then will not the European population in these colonies, spreading rapidly over that enormous land, either civilize or peacefully remove the savage nations who still inhabit vast tracts of its land?

Survey the history of our settlements and commercial undertakings in Africa or in Asia, and you will see how our trade monopolies, our treachery, our murderous contempt for men of another color or creed, the insolence of our usurpations, the intrigues or the exaggerated proselytic zeal of our priests, have destroyed the respect and goodwill that the superiority of our knowledge and the benefits of our commerce at first won for us in the eyes of the inhabitants. But doubtless the moment approaches when, no longer presenting ourselves as always either tyrants or corrupters, we shall become for them the beneficent instruments of their freedom. . . .

The progress of the sciences ensures the progress of the art of education which in turn advances that of the sciences. This reciprocal influence, whose activity is ceaselessly renewed, deserves to be seen as one of the most powerful and active causes working for the perfection of mankind. At the present time a young man on leaving school may know more of the principles of mathematics than Newton ever learned in years of study or discovered by dint of genius, and he may use the calculus with a facility then unknown. The same observation, with certain reservations, applies to all the sciences. As each advances, the methods of expressing a large number of proofs in a more economical fashion and so of making their comprehension an easier matter, advance with it. So, in spite of the progress of science, not only do men of the same ability find themselves at the same age on a level with the existing state of science, but with every generation, that which can be acquired in a certain time with a certain degree of intelligence and a certain amount of concentration will be permanently on the increase, and, as the elementary part of each science to which all men may attain grows and grows, it will more and more include all the knowledge necessary for each man to know for the conduct of the ordinary events of his life, and will support him in the free and independent exercise of his reason.

In the political sciences there are some truths that, with free people (that is to say, with certain generations in all countries) can be of use only if they are widely known and acknowledged. So the influence of these sciences upon the freedom and prosperity of nations must in some degree be measured by the number of truths that, as a result of elementary instruction, are common knowledge; the swelling progress of elementary instruction, connected with the necessary progress of these sciences, promises us an improvement in the destiny of the human race, which may be regarded as indefinite, since it can have no other limits than that of this same progress. . . .

All the causes that contribute to the perfection of the human race, all the means that ensure it, must by their very nature exercise a perpetual influence and always increase their sphere of action. The proofs on this we have given and in the great work they will derive additional force from elaboration. We may conclude then that the perfectibility of man is indefinite. Meanwhile we have considered him as possessing the natural faculties and organization that he has at present. How much greater would be the certainty, how much vaster the scheme of our hopes, if we could believe that these natural faculties themselves and this organization could also be improved? This is the last question that remains for us to ask ourselves.

In truth, this average span of life which we suppose will increase indefinitely as time passes, may grow in conformity either with a law such that it continually approaches a limitless length but without ever reaching it, or with a law such that through the centuries it reaches a length greater than any determinate quantity that we may assign to it as its limit. In the latter case such an increase is truly indefinite in the strictest sense of the word,

since there is no term on this side of which it must of necessity stop. . . .

Finally may we not extend such hopes to the intellectual and moral faculties? May not our parents, who transmit to us the benefits or disadvantages of their constitution, and from whom we receive our shape and features, as well as our tendencies to certain physical affections, hand on to us also that part of the physical organization which determines the intellect, the power of the brain, the ardor of the soul or the moral sensibility? Is it not probable that education, in perfecting these qualities, will at the same time influence, modify and perfect the organization itself? Analogy, investigation of the human faculties and the study of certain facts, all seem to give substance to such conjectures which would further push back the boundaries of our hopes.

These are the questions with which we shall conclude this final stage. How consoling for the philosopher who laments the errors, the crimes, the injustices which still pollute the earth and of which he is often the victim is this view of the human race, emancipated from its shackles, released from the empire of fate and from that of the enemies of its progress, advancing with a firm and sure step along the path of truth, virtue and happiness! It is the contemplation of this prospect that rewards him for all his efforts to assist the progress of reason and the defence of liberty. He dares to regard these strivings as part of the eternal chain of human destiny; and in this persuasion he is filled with the true delight of virtue and the pleasure of having done some lasting good which fate can never destroy by a sinister stroke of revenge, by calling back the reign of slavery and prejudice. Such contemplation is for him an asylum, in which the memory of his persecutors cannot pursue him; there he lives in thought with man restored to his natural rights and dignity, forgets man tormented and corrupted by greed, fear or envy; there he lives with his peers in an Elysium[1] created by reason and graced by the purest pleasures known to the love of mankind.

Cultural and Religious Change in Mughal India

From the founding of the Mughal Empire in India in 1526 until the mid-seventeenth century, a succession of cultivated and cosmopolitan emperors made the Mughal court one of the world's most brilliant centers of art, literature, and scholarship. Babur, the founder of the empire, was an accomplished Persian poet, a master of Turkish prose, and the author of memoirs that reveal a deep sensitivity toward nature. Akbar (1556–1605), Babur's grandson, encouraged religious discussions among Hindus, Muslims, and European Christians; supported the work of thousands of poets, historians, and painters; and sponsored dozens of building projects in and around the imperial city of Agra. Jahangir (1605–1627), Akbar's son and in many ways the most colorful of the Mughal emperors, continued the traditions of his predecessors. He showed a keen interest in Christianity and European art, wrote his own memoirs, and patronized numerous historians, scholars, poets, and painters. During the reign of Shah Jahan (1628–1658), Mughal patronage reached its peak. He moved the court to Delhi, where he built a huge palace in which he sat on the newly crafted Peacock Throne, decorated with gems worth many millions of dollars. He also directed the construction of the Taj Mahal in Agra, a mausoleum and memorial for his wife that is considered among the world's most beautiful buildings.

Other developments during Shah Jahan's reign, however, provided a portent of Mughal political and cultural decline. Unlike Akbar and Jahangir, he began to persecute both European Christians and Hindus. Shah Jahan's son, Aurangzeb (1658–1707), deeply devoted to Islam, made the enforcement of Muslim orthodoxy a major priority of his reign. As the following literary and pictorial evidence illustrates, Aurangzeb's single-minded devotion to Islam had important ramifications for Mughal politics and culture.

Bakhta'war Khan

HISTORY OF THE WORLD

Bakhta'war Khan, who served Aurangzeb faithfully for over thirty years in a variety of important posts, is generally acknowledged as the author of this universal history,

---

1. In ancient mythology, a place of bliss after death for the blessed.

completed in the early 1680s. One of several histories, biographies, law commentaries, and collections of poetry written by the author, it was commissioned by Aurangzeb before he cut off support for such endeavors, concluding toward the end of his life that they encouraged self-love and vanity. In this Persian work, Bakhta'war Khan traces the history of the world from the age of the Old Testament Hebrew patriarchs to the reign of Aurangzeb.

Although the author clearly is biased in his admiration for Aurangzeb's religious fervor, the *History of the World* is nevertheless a valuable source, particularly when describing the emperor himself. The following excerpt sheds light on his personality, religiosity, and views of literature and the arts.

Questions
for Analysis

1. In depicting Aurangzeb as the ideal Muslim prince, what characteristics and qualities does Bakhta'war Khan emphasize?
2. What are some notable differences between Aurangzeb's and Jahangir's personalities as depicted here and in Jahangir's *Memoirs* (see Chapter 3)?
3. What is the basis for Aurangzeb's rejection of music and poetry?
4. What does Aurangzeb's view of poetry reveal about his beliefs concerning the purposes of literature?
5. At the end of this selection Bakhta'war Khan expresses the hope that Aurangzeb will continue to prosper. In truth, at the time of the emperor's death in 1707, the Mughal treasury had been drained by continual war and rebellion. On the basis of this source, what might you infer about the reason for this political instability?

*B*e it known to the readers of this work that this humble slave of the Almighty is going to describe in a correct manner the excellent character, the worthy habits and the refined morals of this most virtuous monarch, Aurangzeb, according as he has witnessed them with his own eyes. The Emperor, a great worshiper of God by natural propensity, is remarkable for his rigid attachment to religion. . . . Having made his ablutions, he always occupies a great part of his time in adoration of the Deity, and says the usual prayers, first in the mosque and then at home, both in congregation and in private, with the most heartfelt devotion. He keeps the appointed fasts on Fridays and other sacred days, and he reads the Friday prayers in *Jami* mosque[1] with the common people of the Muslim faith. He keeps vigils during the whole of the sacred nights, and with the light of the favor of God illumines the lamps of religion and prosperity. From his great piety, he passes whole nights in the mosque which is in his palace, and keeps company with men of

---

1. The *Jami* mosque, usually the largest mosque in a city or village, is the cite of the congregational prayers said by Muslims on Friday.

devotion. In privacy he never sits on a throne. He gave away in alms before his accession a portion of his allowance of lawful food and clothing, and now devotes to the same purpose the income of a few villages in the district of Delhi, and the proceeds of two or three salt-producing tracts, which are appropriated to his private purse. . . . During the whole month of Ramadan he keeps fast, says the prayers appointed for that month, and reads the holy Qur'an in the assembly of religious and learned men, with whom he sits for that purpose during six, and sometimes nine hours of the night. During the last ten days of the month, he performs worship in the mosque, and although, on account of several obstacles, he is unable to proceed on a pilgrimage to Mecca,[2] yet the care which he takes to promote facilities for pilgrims to that holy place may be considered equivalent to the pilgrimage. . . .

Though he has collected at the foot of his throne those who inspire ravishment in joyous assemblies of pleasure, in the shape of singers who possess lovely voices and clever instrumental performers, and in the commencement of his reign sometimes used to hear them sing and play, and though he himself understands music well, yet now for several years past, on account of his great restraint and self-denial . . . he entirely abstains from this amusement. If any of the singers and musicians becomes ashamed of his calling, he makes an allowance for him or grants him land for his maintenance. . . .

In consideration of their rank and merit,

he shows much honor and respect to the saints and learned men, and through his cordial and liberal exertions, the sublime doctrines of our pure religion have obtained such prevalence throughout the wide territories of Hindustan as they never had in the reign of any former king.

Hindu writers have been entirely excluded from holding public offices, and all the worshipping places of the infidels[3] and the great temples of these infamous people have been thrown down and destroyed in a manner which excites astonishment at the successful completion of so difficult a task. . . .

As it is a great object with this Emperor that all Muslims should follow the principles of the religion . . . and as there was no book which embodied them all, and as until many books had been collected and a man had obtained sufficient leisure, means and knowledge of theological subjects, he could not satisfy his inquiries on any disputed point, therefore His Majesty, the protector of the faith, determined that a body of eminently learned and able men of Hindustan should take up the voluminous and most trustworthy works which were collected in the royal library, and having made a digest of them, compose a book which might form a standard canon of the law,[4] and afford to all an easy and available means of ascertaining the proper and authoritative interpretation. The chief conductor of this difficult undertaking was the most learned man of the time, Shaikh Nizam, and all the members of the society were very handsomely and liberally paid, so that up to the

---

2. Along with the creed (by which one affirms belief in God and the prophecy of Muhammad), daily prayer, alms-giving, and fasting during the holy month of Ramadan, making a pilgrimage to Mecca, the city of Muhammad's birth, was considered an act that every Muslim should strive to perform.

3. Hindus; although on Aurangzeb's orders many Hindu temples were destroyed, the author wildly exaggerates when he claims that all Hindu edifices were destroyed.

4. Islamic law.

present time a sum of about two hundred thousand rupees[5] has been expended in this valuable compilation, which contains more than one hundred thousand lines. When the work, with God's pleasure, is completed, it will be for all the world the standard exposition of the law. . . .

The Emperor is perfectly acquainted with the commentaries, traditions and law. . . . One of the greatest excellences of this virtuous monarch is, that he has learned the Qur'an by heart. Though in his early youth he had committed to memory some chapters of that sacred book, yet he learned the whole by heart after ascending the throne. He took great pains and showed much perseverance in impressing it upon his mind. He writes in a very elegant . . . hand, and has acquired perfection in this art. He has written two copies of the holy book with his own hand, and having finished and adorned them with ornaments and marginal lines, at the expense of seven thousand rupees, he sent them to the holy cities of Mecca and Medina. . . . He is a very elegant writer in prose, and has acquired proficiency in versification, but agreeably to the words of God, "Poets deal in falsehoods," he abstains from practicing it. He does not like to hear verses except those which contain a moral. "To please Al-mighty God he never turned his eye towards a flatterer, nor gave his ear to a poet."

The Emperor has given a very liberal education to his fortunate and noble children, who, by virtue of his attention and care, have reached to the summit of perfection, and made great advances in rectitude, devotion, and piety, and in learning the manners and customs of princes and great men. Through his instruction they have learned the Book of God[6] by heart, obtained proficiency in the sciences and polite literature, writing the various hands, and in learning the Turkish and the Persian languages.

In like manner, the ladies of the household also, according to his orders, have learned the fundamental and necessary tenets of religion, and all devote their time to the adoration and worship of the Deity, to reading the sacred Qur'an, and performing virtuous and pious acts. The excellence of character and the purity of morals of this holy monarch are beyond all expression. As long as nature nourishes the tree of existence, and keeps the garden of the world fresh, may the plant of the prosperity of this preserver of the garden of dignity and honor continue fruitful!

THREE PAINTINGS FROM THE IMPERIAL MUGHAL COURT

Just as the Mughal emperors held unquestioned political power over their subjects, so too did they exercise supreme authority over the work of the scholars, poets,

5. A unit of Indian money. By comparison, Shah Jahan is reputed to have spent 40,000,000 rupees on the Taj Mahal.

6. The Qur'an.

architects, and painters they so lavishly supported. Their painters were mainly min-
iaturists, many of them Persians, who specialized in small, colorful, and generally
detailed scenes that were collected in albums or used to illustrate episodes described
in historical or biographical manuscripts, such as Abul Fazl's *Akbarnama*. Mughal
painting, therefore, was private art, the purpose of which was to delight the emperor
and impress courtiers, not to edify, inspire, or even be seen by the masses.

The first painting here comes from a 1605 manuscript version of the *Akbarnama*,
illustrated by Nar Singh, a court painter. It depicts one of the religious discussions
in Akbar's House of Worship, where the deeply religious but open-minded Akbar
sponsored dialogue among representatives of many faiths. In this scene, the two
darkly clad gentlemen on Akbar's right are Jesuit priests, sent to Akbar's court at his
request from the Portuguese-held city of Goa in 1578. Surrounding the emperor are
Muslim scholars and holy men, with their holy books at their feet. Outside the wall,
to add a note of realism, is an emaciated beggar holding the hand of a child, followed
by two Muslims and their horses. The crowded scene and the fine attention to detail
reveal Persian influence on this traditional form of Indian painting.

The second painting, *Jahangir Preferring a Sufi Shaikh to Kings,* was the work of a
Hindu painter, Bichter, and was included in an album of imperial miniatures completed around 1620. The painting illustrates Jahangir's avid interest in European art,
examples of which were brought to the court at the emperor's request by Catholic
priests and English and Portuguese merchants. Unlike the painting depicting Akbar,
this work is allegorical, not realistic. The center of the piece is Jahangir himself, who
offers a holy book to a Muslim mystic while sitting on an hourglass throne from
which the sands have almost run out. The angelic figures at the bottom of the
throne, derived from contemporary European painting, inscribe the rather unlikely
hope, "Oh Shah, may the span of your life be a thousand years." Below the Muslim
mystic is one figure representing an Ottoman sultan and another depicting the king
of England, James I (1603–1625), whose portrait had been brought to the Mughal
court by an English merchant. The figure below King James is dressed as a Hindu
and may very well be the painter himself, Bichter, who is holding up a picture in
which a person (Bichter?) is bowing in reverence before Jahangir. The meaning
of the two angels at the top is obscure. The angel on the right might be flinching
from the splendor surrounding Jahangir or expressing grief over the emperor's mortality; the angel on the left, holding a broken arrow, might symbolize the fleeting-
ness of temporal power.

The last miniature, by an unknown artist of the late seventeenth century, needs
little explication. It depicts the aged Aurangzeb against a stark background, in a
posture of piety, as he reads from his prayer book. Islamic prayer beads lie at his
feet.

Questions
   ## for Analysis

1. Compare the three paintings with Abul Fazl's account of Akbar's dealings with Europeans (Chapter 1), Jahangir's *Memoirs* (Chapter 3), and Bakhta'war Kahn's description of Aurangzeb. What in the three paintings confirms or conflicts with impressions gained from the written evidence?
2. Do the first two paintings offer any clues about the reasons for the cultural vitality of the Mughal court?
3. Review Bakhta'war Khan's comments about Aurangzeb's views of poetry. In what ways does the portrait of Aurangzeb reflect such views?
4. What might one conclude from the relative size of the figures in the painting of Jahangir?

Akbar Presiding over Discussions in the House of Worship

Jahangir Preferring a Sufi Shaikh to Kings

Aurangzeb as an Old Man at Prayer

The Critique of Tradition in China and Japan

As seen in Chapter 2, Neo-Confucianism, the school of Confucian interpretation inspired during the Chinese Sung Dynasty by the scholar Chu Hsi (1130–1200) and others, dominated Chinese and Japanese intellectual life after 1600. In China, as had been the case for centuries, mastery of Neo-Confucian commentaries on the Classics was the prerequisite for success in the imperial civil service examinations, and this fact alone guaranteed the primacy of Neo-Confucianism in Chinese intellectual life. In Japan, the Tokugawa shoguns sponsored Neo-Confucian education and scholarship, convinced that its doctrines, which emphasized reverence for authority and acceptance of one's station in life, would contribute to the stability of Japanese society.

In both societies, however, Neo-Confucianism came under attack during the late 1600s and the 1700s. The conquest of China in the mid-seventeenth century by the Manchus, a Mongoloid people from Manchuria, caused many Chinese intellectuals to reevaluate their values and assumptions. Many concluded that their own failures had led to the foreign invasion. Too much energy, they argued, had been devoted to abstract philosophical principles and too little to ethical problems related to effective government. Proponents of Han Learning rejected metaphysical speculation and urged scholars to concentrate on the ethical and political issues that had been the focus of the original Confucian texts.

Neo-Confucianism in Japan never monopolized intellectual life to the extent it did in China. Even in the seventeenth century, it faced competition from several other schools of Confucian interpretation. In the eighteenth century two intellectual developments added to the diversity of late Tokugawa thought. Proponents of the National Learning, or *kokugaku*, rejected Japanese reliance on the foreign doctrines of Buddhism and Confucianism and directed their energies to the study and glorification of Japan's literary and religious traditions. The eighteenth century also saw increasing interest among the Japanese in European ideas and institutions. Their endeavors were known as Dutch Studies, because the only source of information about Europe came from the Dutch, who even after the closing of Japan in the seventeenth century were permitted to send one ship per year to Japan.

Ku Yen-wu

A LETTER TO A FRIEND DISCUSSING THE PURSUIT OF LEARNING

Ku Yen-wu (1613–1682), who as a young man had shown scholarly promise during the last years of the Ming Dynasty, is recognized as the founder of Han Learning.

He refused to serve under the new Manchu rulers, partly because of a promise to his dying foster mother, who starved herself to death rather than live under foreigners. After her death, he wandered about northern China, observing conditions and writing books on politics, government, and literature. He expressed his thoughts about the defects in contemporary scholarship in the following letter written toward the end of his life.

Questions for Analysis

1. What specific flaws does Ku Yen-wu see in the ideas and methods of contemporary intellectuals?
2. With what kind of matters should intellectuals be concerned?
3. What similarities, if any, do you see between the ideas of Ku Yen-wu and Francis Bacon?

*I*t is a matter of great regret to me that for the past hundred odd years, scholars have devoted so much discussion to the mind and human nature, all of it vague and quite incomprehensible. We know from the *Analects*[1] that "fate and humanity were things which Confucius seldom spoke of" (IX, 1) and that Tzu-kung[2] "had never heard him speak on man's nature and the way of Heaven" (V, 12). Though he mentioned the principle of human nature and fate in the appendices to the *Book of Changes*,[3] he never discussed them with others. When asked about the qualities of a gentleman, Confucius said: "In his conduct he must have a sense of shame" (XIII, 20), while with regard to learning he spoke of a "love of antiquity" and "diligent seeking," discussing and praising Yao and Shun[4] and transmitting their tales to his disciples. But he never said so much as a word about the so-called theory of "the precariousness and the subtlety and of the refined and undivided,"[5] but only said "sincerely hold fast to the Mean — if within the four seas there be distress and poverty, your Heaven-conferred revenues will come to a perpetual end." Ah, this is the reason for the learning of the sage. How simple, how easy to follow! . . . But gentlemen of today are not like this. They gather a hundred or so followers and disciples about them in their studies, and though as individuals they may be as different as grass and trees, they discourse with all of them on mind and nature. They set aside broad knowledge and concentrate upon the search for a single, all-

---

1. One of the Confucian Classics.

2. An early disciple of Confucius who contributed to the *Analects*.

3. The *I Ching*, another of the Classics, was a book of divination, with an appendix that included some philosophical speculation.

4. Yao and Shun were mythical rulers from China's pre-historic past who were models of enlightened rule.

5. Four qualities of mind mentioned in *I Ching*, frequently commented on by Ming Neo-Confucianists.

inclusive method; they say not a word about the distress and poverty of the world within the four seas,[6] but spend all their days lecturing on theories of "the weak and subtle," "the refined and the undivided." . . .

What then do I consider to be the way of the sage? I would say "extensively studying all learning" and "in your conduct having a sense of shame." Everything from your own body up to the whole nation should be a matter of study. In everything from your personal position as a son, a subject, a brother, and a friend to all your comings and goings, your giving and taking, you should have things of which you would be ashamed. This sense of shame before others is a vital matter. It does not mean being ashamed of your clothing or the food you eat, but ashamed that there should be a single humble man or woman who does not enjoy the blessings that are his due. This is why Mencius[7] said that "all things are complete in me" if I "examine myself and find sincerity." Alas, if a scholar does not first define this sense of shame, he will have no basis as a person, and if he does not love antiquity and acquire broad knowledge, his learning will be vain and hollow. These baseless men with their hollow learning day after day pursue the affairs of the sage, and yet I perceive that with each day they only depart further from them.

▨ Kamo Mabuchi

A STUDY OF THE IDEA OF THE NATION

The son of a Shinto priest, Kamo Mabuchi (1697–1769) received training in ancient Japanese literature and in Confucianism. He contributed to the National Learning movement in two important ways. As a poet, he sought to imitate the style of ancient Japanese poetry, and as a scholar, he inspired through his prodigious efforts a new interest in the systematic study of ancient Japanese verse. Kamo's greatest work is his extensive commentary on the "Collection of Ten Thousand Leaves," an anthology of Japanese poetry dating from the eighth century. As the following selection illustrates, his overriding purpose was to reveal the original simplicity and spontaneity of the Japanese people before their corruption by foreign influence.

Questions
for Analysis

1. What arguments are brought forth to "prove" that Confucianism is actually detrimental to good government?

---

6. "Within the four seas" means "anywhere in the world"; to the Chinese, "the world" basically meant China.

7. Mencius, the Latinized form of Meng-tzu, lived from about 372 to 289 B.C. His book, simply known as *Mencius*, was accorded the status of a classic in the eleventh century.

2. How, to Kamo, has Confucianism damaged the Japanese as a people?
3. What does the author propose for Japan's future?
4. Although Ku Yen-wu was a Neo-Confucianist and Kamo Mabuchi was a critic of Confucianism, both shared a number of common concerns. What are they?

Someone remarked to me, "I pay no heed to such petty trifles as Japanese poetry; what interests me is the Chinese Way of governing a nation."

I smiled at this and did not answer. Later, when I met the same man he asked, "You seem to have an opinion on every subject — why did you merely keep smiling when I spoke to you?"

I answered, "You mean when you were talking about the Chinese Confucian teachings or whatever you call them? They are no more than a human invention which reduces the heart of Heaven and Earth to something trivial."

At these words he became enraged. "How dare you call our Great Way trivial?"

I answered, "I would be interested in hearing whether or not the Chinese Confucian learning has actually helped to govern a country successfully." He immediately cited the instances of Yao, Shun, Hsia, Yin, Chou, and so on.[1] I asked if there were no later examples, but he informed me that there were not.

I pursued the matter, asking this time about how far back Chinese traditions went. He answered that thousands of years had passed from Yao's day to the present. I then asked, "Why then did the Way of Yao continue only until the Chou and afterwards cease? I am sure that it is because you restrict yourself to citing events which took place thousands of years ago that the Way seems so good. But those are merely ancient legends. It takes more than such specious ideas to run a country!"

When I said this he grew all the more furious, and ranted on about ancient matters. I said, "You are utterly prejudiced. . . ."

Despite the fact that their country has been torn for centuries by disturbances and has never really been well administered, they think that they can explain with their Way of Confucius the principles governing the whole world. Indeed, when one has heard them through, there is nothing to be said: anyone can quickly grasp their doctrines because they consist of mere quibbling. What they value the most and insist on is the establishment and maintenance of good government. Everybody in China would seem to have been in agreement on this point, but belief in it did not in fact lie very deep. It is obvious that many gave superficial assent who did not assent in their hearts. Yet when these principles were introduced to this country it was stated that China had obtained good government through the adoption of them. This was a complete fabrication. I wish it were possible to send to China anyone who clung to such a belief! . . .

"Japan in ancient days was governed

---

1. On Yao and Shun, see note 4 for preceding source; the Hsai, Yin, and Chou were early Chinese dynasties.

in accordance with the natural laws of Heaven and earth. There was never any indulgence in such petty rationalizing as marked China, but when suddenly these teachings were transmitted here from abroad, they quickly spread, for the men of old in their simplicity took them for the truth. In Japan there had been generation after generation, extending back to the remote past, which had known prosperity, but no sooner were these Confucian teachings propagated here than in the time of Temmu[2] a great rebellion occurred. Later, . . . the palace, dress, and ceremonies were Chinesified, and everything took on a superficial elegance; under the surface, however, contentiousness and dishonesty became more prevalent.

Confucianism made men crafty, and led them to worship the ruler to such an excessive degree that the whole country acquired a servant's mentality. . . .

Just as roads are naturally created when people live in uncultivated woodlands or fields, so the Way of the Age of the Gods spontaneously took hold in Japan. Because it was a Way indigenous to the country it caused our emperors to wax increasingly in prosperity. However, the Confucian teachings had not only repeatedly thrown China into disorder, but they now had the same effect in Japan. Yet there are those unwitting of these facts who reverence Confucianism and think that it is the Way to govern the country! This is a deplorable attitude. . . .

When ruling the country a knowledge of Chinese things is of no help in the face of an emergency. In such a situation some man will spontaneously come forth to propose things which are wise and true. In the same way, doctors often study and master Chinese texts, but very seldom do they cure any sickness. On the other hand, medicines which have been transmitted naturally in this country with no reasons or theoretical knowledge behind them, infallibly cure all maladies. It is good when a man spontaneously devotes himself to these things. It is unwise to become obsessed with them. I would like to show people even once what is good in our Way. The fact that the Confucian scholars know very little about government is obvious from the frequent disorders which arise in China whenever the government is left to them. . . .

People also tell me, "We had no writing in this country and therefore had to use Chinese characters. From this one fact you can know everything about the relative importance of our countries." I answer, "I need not recite again how troublesome, evil, turbulent a country China is. To mention just one instance — there is the matter of their picture-writing. There are about 38,000 characters in common use,[3] as someone has determined. . . . Every place name and plant name has a separate character for it which has no other use but to designate that particular place or plant. Can any man, even one who devotes himself to the task earnestly, learn all these many characters? Sometimes people miswrite characters, sometimes the characters themselves change from one generation to the next. What a nuisance, a waste of effort, and a bother! In India, on the other hand, fifty letters suffice for the writing of the more than 5,000 volumes of the Bud-

---

2. Emperor Temmu (631–686) assumed the throne upon the death of his brother, the Emperor Tenchi, after a factional struggle against Konun, Tenchi's son.

3. This is one of Kamo's several distortions. A more accurate number is 2,500.

dhist scriptures. . . . In Holland, I understand, they use twenty-five letters. In this country there should be fifty. The appearance of letters used in all countries is in general the same, except for China where they invented their bothersome system. . . . The opinion that the characters are precious is not worth discussing further. . . ."

As long as a few teachings were carefully observed and we worked in accordance with the Will of Heaven and earth, the country would be well off without any special instruction. Nevertheless, Chinese doctrines were introduced and corrupted men's hearts. Even though these teachings resembled those of China itself, they were of the kind which heard in the morning are forgotten by evening. Our country in ancient times was not like that. It obeyed the laws of Heaven and earth. The emperor was the sun and moon and the subjects the stars. If the subjects as stars protect the sun and moon, they will not hide it as is now the case. Just as the sun, moon, and stars have always been in Heaven, so our imperial sun and moon, and the stars his vassals, have existed without change from ancient days, and have ruled the world fairly.

Sugita Gempaku

THE BEGINNING OF DUTCH STUDIES IN JAPAN

Sugita Gempaku (1733–1817), a physician, was among the first Japanese to appreciate European science. As he relates in the following selection, in 1771 he witnessed the dissection of an executed female criminal and was amazed to discover that his observations agreed exactly with descriptions he had seen in a recently purchased Dutch translation of the treatise *Tabulae Anatomicae (Anatomical Drawings)*, written by the German anatomist Johann Adam Kulmus in 1722. This experience inspired Sugita and several of his friends to translate the work into Japanese, a daunting task for people unfamiliar with the Latin alphabet. The completion of their undertaking promoted Dutch Studies by encouraging the translation of other European works into Japanese. Toward the end of his life Sugita wrote a memoir, an excerpt from which follows.

Questions
for Analysis

1. On the basis of Sugita's account, what can you infer about Japanese methods of medical education?
2. What does his statement reveal about Japanese views of authority?
3. What did Sugita and his friends hope to accomplish by translating the European treatise?
4. How might the arguments of Kamo and the scientific ideas of Sugita have similarly affected Japan's intellectual development?

*S*omehow, miraculously I obtained a book on anatomy written in that country.[1] . . . It was a strange and even miraculous happening that I was able to obtain that book in that particular spring of 1771. Then at the night of the third day of the third month, I received a letter from a man by the name of Tokuno, who was in the service of the Town Commissioner. Tokuno stated in his letter that "A postmortem examination of the body of a condemned criminal by a resident physician will be held tomorrow at Senjukotsugahara. You are welcome to witness it if you so desire."

The next day, when we arrived at the location . . . Ryotaku[2] reached under his kimono to produce a Dutch book and showed it to us. "This is a Dutch book of anatomy called *Tabulae Anatomicae*. I bought this a few years ago when I went to Nagasaki, and kept it." As I examined it, it was the same book I had and was of the same edition. We held each other's hands and exclaimed: "What a coincidence!" Ryotaku continued by saying: "When I went to Nagasaki, I learned and heard," and opened his book. "These are called *long* in Dutch, they are lungs," he taught us. "This is *hart*, or the heart. When it says *maag* it is the stomach, and when it says *milt* it is the spleen." However, they did not look like the heart given in the Chinese medical books, and none of us were sure until we could actually see the dissection.

Thereafter we went together to the place which was especially set for us to observe the dissection. . . . That day, the old butcher pointed to this and that organ. After the heart, liver, gall bladder, and stomach were identified, he pointed to other parts for which there were no names. "I don't know their names. But I have dissected quite a few bodies from my youthful days. Inside of everyone's abdomen there were these parts and those parts." . . . The old butcher again said, "Every time I had a dissection, I pointed out to those physicians many of these parts, but not a single one of them questioned 'what was this?' or 'what was that?'" We compared the body as dissected against the charts both Ryotaku and I had, and could not find a single variance from the charts. The Chinese *Book of Medicine* says that the lungs are like the eight petals of the lotus flower, with three petals hanging in front, three in back, and two petals forming like two ears and that the liver has three petals to the left and four petals to the right. There were no such divisions, and the positions and shapes of intestines and gastric organs were all different from those taught by the old theories. The official physicians . . . had witnessed dissection seven or eight times. Whenever they witnessed the dissection, they found that the old theories contradicted reality. Each time they were perplexed and could not resolve their doubts. Every time they wrote down what they thought was strange. They wrote in their books, "The more we think of it, there must be fundamental differences in the bodies of Chinese and of the eastern barbarians."[3] I could see why they wrote this way.

That day, after the dissection was over, we decided that we also should examine the shape of the skeletons left exposed on the execution ground. We collected the bones, and examined a number of them. Again, we were struck by the fact that they all differed from the old theories while conforming to the Dutch charts.

---

1. The Netherlands.

2. Ryotaku was a friend invited to the dissection by Sugita.

3. A Chinese term for the Japanese.

The three of us, Ryotaku, Junan,[4] and I went home together. On the way home we spoke to each other and felt the same way. "How marvelous was our actual experience today. It is a shame that we were ignorant of these things until now. As physicians who serve their masters through medicine, we performed our duties in complete ignorance of the true form of the human body. How disgraceful it is. Somehow, through this experience, let us investigate further the truth about the human body. If we practice medicine with this knowledge behind us, we can make contributions for people under heaven and on this earth." Ryotaku spoke to us. "Indeed, I agree with you wholeheartedly." Then I spoke to my companion. "Somehow if we can translate anew this book called *Tabulae Anatomicae*, we can get a clear notion of the human body inside out. It will have great benefit in the treatment of our patients. Let us do our best to read it and understand it without the help of translators." . . .

The next day, we assembled at the house of Ryotaku and recalled the happenings of the previous day. When we faced that *Tabulae Anatomicae*, we felt as if we were setting sail on a great ocean in a ship without oars or a rudder. With the magnitude of the work before us, we were dumbfounded by our own ignorance. However, Ryotaku had been thinking of this for some time, and he had been in Nagasaki. He knew some Dutch through studying and hearing, and knew some sentence patterns and words. He was also ten years older than I, and we decided to make him head of our group and our teacher. At that time I did not know the twenty-five letters of the Dutch alphabet. I decided to study the language with firm determination, but I had to acquaint myself with letters and words gradually.

---

4. Another of Sugita's friends.

CHAPTER

6

The Beginnings of a New Political Order

WE OWE ALLEGIANCE TO NO CROWN.

*A*mong the many political changes that took place between the seventeenth and early nineteenth centuries, the most dramatic occurred in Western Europe and the Americas, where revolutionary movements challenged traditional patterns of authoritarian and elitist government. Seventeenth-century English revolutionaries frustrated the absolutist ambitions of their monarchs and established a government based on the rule of law and the rights of subjects. During the Age of Enlightenment, concepts such as liberty, equality, and popular sovereignty inspired dreams of further political change, and by the end of the century these dreams were realized in revolutions on both sides of the Atlantic.

Despite these political upheavals, old institutions and practices did not disappear, and, in fact, monarchy and aristocracy in Europe proved remarkably resilient. When the era of the French Revolution ended in 1815, kings and nobles regained many of their powers and privileges, and in parts of Europe their position seemed as strong as ever. The masses had shed their political apathy, however, and the principles of equality and democracy burned in the hearts of millions. The future belonged to them.

Significant political changes also occurred in Russia during the reign of Peter the Great (1689–1725). This remarkable tsar, stung by military defeats at the hands of the Swedes and inspired by visits to Germany, the Netherlands, and England, initiated a vigorous campaign to remake Russia and the Russians in the image of Western Europe. This made him the first ruler anywhere who attempted to overcome his society's "backwardness" by emulating the institutions, schools, customs, military practices, and technology of the West. He was also the first ruler to discover that successful Westernization involved more than issuing edicts and proclamations. Numerous Russians bitterly opposed Peter's reforms, and many of his projects and proposals failed. For generations Russians passionately debated whether Russia's future lay with the West or with its own unique traditions and values.

Change came to the great empires of Asia, as well, but in the form of decline, not revolution. Within the Ottoman Empire, as early as the 1630s a concerned official, Koji Bey, wrote a report urging the sultan to revitalize the army and administration, halt corruption, and revamp the tax system. Reformers made little progress, however, and in the eighteenth century the Ottomans faced military defeat and loss of territory. Similar problems were affecting China and Japan: by 1800 the outward political success of the

Ch'ing emperors and the Tokugawa shoguns could not hide problems of military and civil corruption, lax maintenance of roads and waterways, fiscal deficits, and increasing poverty among the masses.

For Mughal India, the eighteenth century brought not just decline, but disaster. Turbulence dating from Aurangzeb's reign continued, setting the stage for military humiliation in 1739, when the Persians defeated the imperial army, took Afghanistan, and carried off the wealth of Delhi, including the legendary Peacock Throne. Later, India became the first among the ancient Asian civilizations to learn that despite its glorious past, political weakness now invited European intrusion. By 1795, not Indian princes but officials of the British East India Company ruled the provinces of Orissa, Bihar, and Bengal.

Russia and the West Under Peter the Great

After the expulsion of the Mongols in the late 1400s, Russia embarked on a period of remarkable expansion in which the tsars consolidated their control of European Russia, then pushed eastward across the Urals into Siberia. By 1637 they had extended their authority all the way to the Pacific. In a conquest unrivaled in human history, Russia became in a century and a half what the Soviet Union continues to be today, the largest nation in the world.

The situation on Russia's western border, however, was not so favorable. The long Livonian War (1558–1582), launched against Poland and Sweden, resulted in territorial losses, not gains, and during the period of political breakdown known as the "Time of Troubles," Poland and Sweden sent armies deep into Russian territory, the Poles taking Moscow for a brief time in 1608. In 1612 the Russians drove out the invaders, and for the next several decades the Thirty Years' War (1618–1648) diverted Western European rulers from Russian adventures. The Turks remained a threat from the south, however, and in the late 1600s the Poles and the Swedes resumed their pressure.

Russia's sense of vulnerability gave rise in the early 1700s to a soul-searching debate among the Russian people that continued into the twentieth century. The issue was a simple one: should the Russians abandon much of their past and strive to emulate the technologically superior and ostensibly more successful nations of Western Europe?

Tsar Peter the Great was famous for his unequivocally positive response to this question. He strove throughout his reign to pull Russia out of its perceived backwardness by mandating the adoption of Western European practices and institutions at many different levels. Many Russians found his goals abhorrent. They treasured Russia's uniqueness and believed that in certain respects their country was superior to the nations of Western Europe. These lovers of Russia's Slavic traditions ("Slavophiles") argued that abandonment of Russia's past was too high a price to pay for Westernization.

Variations of Russia's Westernizer-Slavophile debate later appeared among the peoples of Asia and Africa. As Europeans forced themselves into their lives, these people too had to ask themselves how willing they were, if at all, to abandon their cultural and religious traditions for the lure of Western science, military power, and material gain. They, like the Russians, would find no easy answer to this question.

DECREES OF PETER THE GREAT

Peter the Great stands out as one of the most significant figures in world history during the past 300 years. This remarkable man, who was close to seven feet tall, developed a fascination with Western Europe when as a boy he spent hours smoking and drinking in the "German quarter," the Moscow district where Europeans from various countries resided. His captivation grew during two visits to Western Europe, where Dutch and British commerce and naval technology especially impressed him.

But the urgency of Peter's efforts to transform Russia indicates that he was motivated by more than a personal admiration of things European. In 1700 a decisive military defeat by the Swedes at the Battle of Narva spurred him into action. With characteristic energy and single-mindedness, he embarked on his campaign to transform Russia, issuing in the next twenty-five years no fewer than 3,000 decrees on everything from the basic structure of government to male shaving habits. A few examples are included here.

Questions for Analysis

1. How does Peter justify his various decrees?
2. What evidence suggests that Peter expected resistance to some of his decrees?
3. What do the decrees reveal about the tsar's political powers?
4. Judging from Decrees 4 and 5, how do you think Peter viewed the purpose of education?
5. What do you think motivated Peter to order adoption of Western dress and the shaving of beards?

1. Decree on Western Dress (1701)

Western dress shall be worn by all the boyars, members of our councils and of our court . . . gentry of Moscow, secretaries . . . provincial gentry, gosti, government officials, strel'tsy,[1] members of the guilds purveying for our household, citizens of Moscow of all ranks, and residents of provincial cities . . . excepting the clergy and peasant tillers of the soil. The upper dress shall be of French or Saxon cut, and the lower dress . . . — (in-

cluding) waistcoat, trousers, boots, shoes, and hats — shall be of the German type. They shall also ride German saddles. Likewise the womenfolk of all ranks, including the priests', deacons', and church attendants' wives, the wives of the dragoons, the soldiers, and the strel'tsy, and their children, shall wear Western dresses, hats, jackets, and underwear — undervests and petticoats — and shoes. From now on no one of the above-mentioned is to wear Russian dress or Circassian[2] coats, sheepskin coats, or Russian peasant coats, trousers, boots, and

---

1. Boyars were members of Russia's hereditary nobility; gosti were major Russian merchants who often served the tsar in some capacity; strel'tsy were members of the imperial guard stationed in Moscow.

2. Circassia is a region north of the Caucasus mountains on the shore of the Black Sea.

shoes. It is also forbidden to ride Russian saddles, and the craftsmen shall not manufacture them or sell them at the marketplaces.

2. DECREE ON THE INVITATION OF FOREIGNERS (1702)

It is sufficiently known in all the lands which the Almighty has placed under our rule, that since our accession to the throne all our efforts and intentions have tended to govern this realm in such a way that all of our subjects should, through our care for the general good, become more and more prosperous. For this end we have always tried to maintain internal order, to defend the State against invasion, and in every possible way to improve and to extend trade. With this purpose we have been compelled to make some necessary and salutary changes in the administration, in order that our subjects might more easily gain a knowledge of matters of which they were before ignorant, and become more skillful in their commercial relations. We have therefore given orders, made dispositions, and founded institutions indispensable for increasing our trade with foreigners, and shall do the same in future. Nevertheless we fear that matters are not in such a good condition as we desire, and that our subjects cannot in perfect quietness enjoy the fruits of our labors, and we have therefore considered still other means to protect our frontier from the invasion of the enemy, and to preserve the rights and privileges of our State, and the general peace of all Christians, as is incumbent on a Christian monarch to do. To attain these worthy aims, we have endeavored to improve our military forces, which are the protection of our State, so that our troops may consist of well-drilled men, maintained in perfect order and discipline. In order to obtain greater improvement in this respect, and to encourage foreigners, who are able to assist us in this way, as well as artists and artisans profitable to the State, to come in numbers to our country, we have issued this manifesto, and have ordered printed copies of it to be sent throughout Europe. And as in our residence of Moscow, the free exercise of religion of all other sects, although not agreeing with our church, is already allowed, so shall this be hereby confirmed anew in such wise that we, by the power granted to us by the Almighty, shall exercise no compulsion over the consciences of men, and shall gladly allow every Christian to care for his own salvation at his own risk.

3. DECREE ON SHAVING (1705)

A decree to be published in Moscow and in all the provincial cities: Henceforth, in accordance with this, His Majesty's decree, all court attendants . . . provincial service men, government officials of all ranks, military men, all the gosti, members of the wholesale merchants' guild, and members of the guilds purveying for our household must shave their beards and moustaches. But, if it happens that some of them do not wish to shave their beards and moustaches, let a yearly tax be collected from such persons; from court attendants . . . provincial service men, military men, and government officials of all ranks — 60 rubles per person;[3] from the gosti and members of the wholesale merchants' guild of the first class — 100 rubles per person; from members of the wholesale merchants' guild of the middle and

---

3. These were substantial fines; five rubles were enough to buy a horse, and only two were needed to buy a cow.

the lower class (and) . . . from (other) merchants and townsfolk — 60 rubles per person; . . . from townsfolk (of the lower rank), boyars' servants, stagecoachmen, waggoners, church attendants (with the exception of priests and deacons), and from Moscow residents of all ranks — 30 rubles per person. Special badges shall be issued to them from the Administrator of Land Affairs of Public Order . . . which they must wear. . . . As for the peasants, let a toll of two half-copecks[4] per beard be collected at the town gates each time they enter or leave a town; and do not let the peasants pass the town gates, into or out of town, without paying this toll.

4. DECREE ON COMPULSORY EDUCATION OF THE RUSSIAN NOBILITY (1714)

Send to every administrative district some persons from mathematical schools to teach the children of the nobility — except those of freeholders and government clerks — mathematics and geometry; as a penalty for evasion establish a rule that no one will be allowed to marry unless he learns these subjects. Inform all prelates to issue no marriage certificates to those who are ordered to go to schools. . . .

The Great Sovereign has decreed; in all administrative districts children between the ages of ten and fifteen of the nobility, of government clerks, and of lesser officials, except those of freeholders, must be taught mathematics and some geometry. Toward that end, students should be sent from mathematical schools as teachers, several into each administrative district to prelates and to renowned monasteries to establish schools. During their instruction these teachers should be given food and financial remuneration . . . from district revenues set aside for that purpose by

personal orders of His Imperial Majesty. No fees should be collected from students. When they have mastered the material, they should then be given certificates written in their own handwriting. When the students are released they ought to pay one ruble each for their training. Without these certificates they should not be allowed to marry nor receive marriage certificates.

5. AN INSTRUCTION TO RUSSIAN STUDENTS ABROAD STUDYING NAVIGATION (1714)

1. Learn how to draw plans and charts and how to use the compass and other naval indicators.

2. Learn how to navigate a vessel in battle as well as in a simple maneuver, and learn how to use all appropriate tools and instruments; namely, sails, ropes, and oars, and the like matters, on row boats and other vessels.

3. Discover as much as possible how to put ships to sea during a naval battle. Those who cannot succeed in this effort must diligently ascertain what action should be taken by the vessels that do and those that do not put to sea during such a situation (naval battle). Obtain from foreign naval officers written statements, bearing their signatures and seals, of how adequately you are prepared for naval duties.

4. If, upon his return, anyone wishes to receive from the Tsar greater favors for himself, he should learn, in addition to the above enumerated instructions, how to construct those vessels aboard which he would like to demonstrate his skills.

5. Upon his return to Moscow, every foreign-trained Russian should bring with him at his own expense, for which he will

---

4. One hundred copecks equaled one ruble.

later be reimbursed, at least two experienced masters of naval science. They the returnees will be assigned soldiers, one soldier per returnee, to teach them what they have learned abroad. And if they do not wish to accept soldiers they may teach their acquaintances or their own people. The treasury will pay for transportation and maintenance of soldiers. And if anyone other than soldiers learns the art of navigation the treasury will pay 100 rubles for the maintenance of every such individual.

Revolutions in Early Modern Europe

Revolutions involve more than a change in political leadership or the substitution of one ruling faction with another. Successful revolutions result in fundamental changes in the political order itself, often entailing the transfer of power from one social group to another. Revolutions also affect more than a society's politics. They often redefine and reshape legal systems, educational practices, religious institutions, and economic and social relationships.

Revolutions are always the result of political failure on the part of the regime that is overthrown. Usually this failure involves the regime's persistent inability or unwillingness to accommodate the demands of new or recently politicized social groups that have been excluded from political power or that feel threatened by government policies.

Finally, revolutions are always "illegal" and involve violence. Opponents of a regime become revolutionaries only after they convince themselves that change through legal methods is impossible.

Because revolutions are most likely to occur in societies undergoing intellectual, economic, and social transformations, it is not surprising that during the past 500 years the world's first political revolutions took place in western Europe, where economic and intellectual developments had undermined traditional religious authorities and the feudal-agrarian basis of the political and social order. Nor is it surprising that revolutions have become more frequent throughout the world in recent history, as one society after another has experienced the unsettling effect of new ideologies and economic change.

In the seventeenth century, England experienced two revolutions, the Puritan Revolution of the 1640s and '50s and the Glorious Revolution of 1688–1689. The result was the establishment of a political framework that clearly defined the limits of royal authority; confirmed the fiscal and legislative powers of England's representative assembly, the Parliament; and guaranteed many basic rights of the English people. Thus emerged constitutionalism, the principle that governments should operate not according to the whim of individual rulers but to rules that apply both to rulers and subjects.

The French Revolution of 1789 looms much larger in world history than the seventeenth-century English revolutions. A wider spectrum of society — peasants, urban workers, and women — took part, and it affected and inspired more people around the globe. More important, the French Revolution raised issues beyond liberalism and constitutionalism. It championed the principle of democracy — that every person irrespective of social standing should have a voice in government — and the principle of equality — that before the law all people should be treated identically. It also aroused the first nationalist movements in European history and inspired disaffected groups throughout the world to seek political and social change through revolution.

ENGLISH BILL OF RIGHTS

The acceptance of the English Bill of Rights ended a clash between the Crown and Parliament that had convulsed English politics for almost a century. Ever since the reigns of the first two Stuart kings, James I (1603–1625) and his son, Charles I (1625–1649) the landowners, merchants, and lawyers who dominated the House of Commons fought the king on a wide range of religious, economic, diplomatic, and political issues that all centered on the fundamental question of Parliament's place in England's system of government.

A political impasse over new taxes led to civil war between Parliamentarians and Royalists in 1642. After a triumphant Parliament ordered the execution of Charles I in 1649, power fell into the hands of a faction of Puritans led by Oliver Cromwell who for the next eleven years sought to impose its strict Protestant beliefs on the English people. The Puritans' grip on England loosened after the death of Cromwell in 1658 and was lost altogether when a newly elected Parliament restored the Stuarts in 1660.

Charles II (1660–1685) and his brother, James II (1685–1688), however, also alienated their subjects through pro-French and pro-Catholic policies and their tendency to ignore Parliament. James II was a professed Catholic, and his fathering of a male heir in 1688 raised the possibility of a long line of English Catholic kings. Most of his predominantly Protestant subjects found this unacceptable, and the result was the Glorious Revolution of 1688–1689. In a change that resembled a coup d'état more than a revolution, Parliament offered the crown to James's Protestant daughter, Mary, and her husband, William of Orange of Holland. After James mounted only token resistance and then fled the country, his daughter and son-in-law became King William III and Queen Mary II. As such, they signed the English Bill of Rights, passed by Parliament in 1689. By doing so, they accepted parliamentary limitations on royal authority that became a permanent part of England's constitutional framework.

Questions for Analysis

1. According to the Bill of Rights, what abuses of royal power seem to have most disturbed its authors? Did political, economic, or religious issues seem most important to them?
2. In what specific ways does the Bill of Rights limit royal authority? What powers remain in the hands of the monarch?
3. In what ways, if at all, might the common people benefit from the Bill of Rights?

Whereas the Lords Spiritual and Temporal and Commons[1] assembled at Westminster, lawfully, fully and freely representing all the estates of the people of this realm, did upon the thirteenth day of February . . . present unto their Majesties, then called and known by the names and style of William and Mary, prince and princess of Orange, being present in their proper persons, a certain declaration in writing made by the said Lords and Commons in the words following, viz.:

Whereas the late King James the Second, by the assistance of diverse evil counselors, judges and ministers employed by him, did endeavor to subvert and extirpate the Protestant religion and the laws and liberties of this kingdom;

By assuming and exercising a power of dispensing with and suspending of laws and the execution of laws without consent of Parliament;

By committing and prosecuting diverse worthy prelates for humbly petitioning to be excused from concurring to the said assumed power;

By issuing and causing to be executed a commission under the great seal for erecting a court called the Court of Commissioners for Ecclesiastical Causes;[2]

By levying money for and to the use of the Crown by pretense of prerogative for other time and in other manner than the same was granted by Parliament;

By raising and keeping a standing army within this kingdom in time of peace without consent of Parliament, and quartering soldiers contrary to law;

By causing several good subjects being Protestants to be disarmed at the same time when papists were both armed and employed contrary to law;

By violating the freedom of election of members to serve in Parliament;

By prosecutions in the Court of King's Bench for matters and causes cognizable only in Parliament, and by diverse other arbitrary and illegal courses;

And whereas of late years partial corrupt and unqualified persons have been returned and served on juries in trials, and particularly diverse jurors in trials for high treason which were not freeholders;

And excessive bail hath been required of persons committed in criminal cases to

---

1. The Lords Spiritual were the prelates of the Anglican Church who sat in the House of Lords; the Lords Temporal were titled peers who sat in the House of Lords; Commons refers to the House of Commons, to which nontitled Englishmen were elected.

2. A special royal court established to try religious cases.

elude the benefit of the laws made for the liberty of the subjects;

And excessive fines have been imposed;

And illegal and cruel punishments inflicted;

And several grants and promises made of fines and forfeitures before any conviction or judgment against the persons upon whom the same were to be levied;

All which are utterly and directly contrary to the known laws and statutes and freedom of this realm;

And whereas the said late King James the Second having abdicated the government and the throne being thereby vacant, his Highness the prince of Orange (whom it hath pleased Almighty God to make the glorious instrument of delivering this kingdom from popery and arbitrary power) did . . . cause letters to be written to the Lords Spiritual and Temporal being Protestants, and other letters to the several counties, cities, universities, boroughs and cinque ports,[3] for the choosing of such persons to represent them as were of right to be sent to Parliament, to meet and sit at Westminster upon the two and twentieth day of January in this year one thousand six hundred eighty and eight,[4] in order to make such an establishment as that their religion, laws and liberties might not again be in danger of being subverted, upon which letters elections having been accordingly made;

And thereupon the said Lords Spiritual and Temporal and Commons, pursuant to their respective letters and elections, being now assembled in a full and free representative of this nation, taking into their most serious consideration the best means for attaining the ends aforesaid, do in the first place (as their ancestors in like case have usually done) for the vindicating and asserting their ancient rights and liberties declare

That the pretended power of suspending of laws or the execution of laws by regal authority without consent of Parliament is illegal;

That the pretended power of dispensing with laws or the execution of laws by regal authority, as it hath been assumed and exercised of late, is illegal;

That the commission for erecting the late Court of Commissioners for Ecclesiastical Causes, and all other commissions and courts of like nature, are illegal and pernicious;

That levying money for or to the use of the Crown by pretense of prerogative, without grant of Parliament, for longer time, or in other manner than the same is or shall be granted, is illegal;

That it is the right of the subjects to petition the king, and all commitments and prosecutions for such petitioning are illegal;

That the raising or keeping a standing army within the kingdom in time of peace, unless it be with consent of Parliament, is against law;

That the subjects which are Protestants may have arms for their defense suitable to their conditions and as allowed by law;

That election of members of Parliament ought to be free;

That the freedom of speech and debates or proceedings in Parliament ought not to be impeached or questioned in any court or place out of Parliament;

That excessive bail ought not to be required, nor excessive fines imposed nor cruel and unusual punishments inflicted;

That jurors ought to be duly impaneled and returned, and jurors which pass upon

---

3. Five maritime towns in southeast England that during the Middle Ages gained the right to send representatives to Parliament in return for aiding the naval defense of the realm.

4. Until the eighteenth century, the English New Year began on March 25, not January 1; by modern reckoning the year should be 1689.

men in trials for high treason ought to be freeholders;[5]

That all grants and promises of fines and forfeitures of particular persons before conviction are illegal and void;

And that for redress of all grievances, and for the amending, strengthening and preserving of the laws, Parliaments ought to be held frequently.

And they do claim, demand and insist upon all and singular the premises as their undoubted rights and liberties, and that no declarations, judgments, doings or proceedings to the prejudice of the people in any of the said premises ought in any wise to be drawn hereafter into consequence or example; to which demand of their rights they are particularly encouraged by the declaration of his Highness the prince of Orange as being the only means for obtaining a full redress and remedy therein. Having therefore an entire confidence that his said Highness the prince of Orange will perfect the deliverance so far advanced by him, and will still preserve them from the violation of their rights which they have here asserted, and from all other attempts upon their religion, rights and liberties, the said Lords Spiritual and Temporal and Commons assembled at Westminster do resolve that William and Mary, prince and princess of Orange, be and be declared king and queen of England, France[6] and Ireland and the dominions thereunto belonging.

DECLARATION OF THE RIGHTS OF MAN AND OF THE CITIZEN

The French Revolution began because of a problem that has plagued rulers since the beginning of organized government — King Louis XVI (1774–1792) could not balance his budget. Having exhausted every other solution, he agreed to convene a meeting of the Estates General, France's medieval representative assembly, which had not met since 1613, in the hope that it would solve the government's fiscal plight by voting new taxes. The nobility, having fended off every effort to curtail its tax exemptions and privileges in the eighteenth century, saw the convening of the Estates General as an opportunity to increase its political power at the expense of the monarchy. For both king and nobility, the calling of the Estates General had unexpected results: the nobility lost its privileged status, and the king lost most of his power, and, in 1793, having been judged a traitor to the Revolution, his head.

Neither Louis nor the French nobles had comprehended the pervasive disgust within the French population with royal absolutism and aristocratic privilege. At a time when the leading intellectuals talked approvingly of natural rights, human dignity, popular sovereignty, liberty, and equality, and after the English and Americans had established constitutional regimes, the inconsistencies and failures of the French

---

5. Property holders.

6. An anachronistic reference to the time in the Middle Ages when English kings ruled parts of France as fiefdoms, and, for a time, claimed the French throne.

regime were intolerable. Thus, with the aid of the peasants and urban workers, who in 1789 advanced the cause of revolution through violence, the mostly middle-class representatives to the Estates General proceeded to dismantle the laws and institutions of the Old Regime and replace them with a system of government based on reason and natural law.

The Estates General had its first meeting on May 5, 1789. By June 23, with the king's grudging approval, it had been transformed into a National Assembly, with the self-proclaimed goal of writing a constitution for France. This represented a crucial victory for the assembly's middle-class members, who now had an opportunity to end absolutism and class privilege. In this process, the approval of the Declaration of the Rights of Man and of the Citizen on August 27 was a step of signal importance. Drawing on the political principles of the seventeenth-century English revolutions, the American Revolution, and the Enlightenment, this document (which served as preamble to the Constitution of 1791) summarizes the political and social goals that motivated the French revolutionaries of 1789 and countless others in the decades to follow.

Questions for Analysis

1. According to the Declaration, in what ways are the powers of government limited?
2. Is it possible to detect in the Declaration any signs that the authors were influenced by Rousseau (see Rousseau's *Social Contract* in Chapter 5)?
3. To what extent are the principles of the Declaration compatible with monarchical government?
4. In what respects are the principles of the Declaration similar to those of the English Bill of Rights? To what extent does the Declaration touch on issues not addressed in the Bill of Rights?
5. What does the document say about the origin and purpose of "law"?
6. How might people from the lower classes benefit from the implementation of the principles of the Declaration?

The representatives of the French people, organized as a national assembly, considering that ignorance, neglect, and scorn of the rights of man are the sole causes of public misfortunes and of corruption of governments, have resolved to display in a solemn declaration the natural, inalienable, and sacred rights of man, so that this declaration, constantly in the presence of all members of society, will continually remind them of their rights and their duties; so that the acts of the legislative power and those of the executive power, being subject at any time to comparison with the purpose of any political institution, will be better respected; so that the demands of the citizens, based henceforth on simple and incontestable principles, will always contribute to the maintenance of the constitution and the happiness of all.

Consequently, the National Assembly

recognizes and declares, in the presence and under the auspices of the Supreme Being, the following rights of man and citizen.

Article 1. Men are born and remain free and equal in rights; social distinctions can be established only for the common benefit.

2. The aim of every political association is the conservation of the natural and imprescriptible rights of man; these rights are liberty, property, security, and resistance to oppression.

3. The source of all sovereignty is located in essence in the nation; no body, no individual can exercise authority which does not emanate from it expressly.

4. Liberty consists in being able to do anything that does not harm another person. Thus the exercise of the natural rights of each man has no limits except those which assure to the other members of society the enjoyment of these same rights; these limits can be determined only by law.

5. The law has the right to forbid only those actions harmful to society. All that is not forbidden by the law cannot be hindered, and no one can be forced to do what it does not order.

6. The law is the expression of the general will; all citizens have the right to concur personally or through their representatives in its formation; it must be the same for all, whether it protects or punishes. All citizens being equal in its eyes are equally admissible to all honors, positions, and public employments, according to their capabilities and without other distinctions than those of their virtues and talents.

7. No man can be accused, arrested, or detained except in cases determined by the law, and according to the forms which it has prescribed. Those who solicit, draw up, execute, or have executed arbitrary orders must be punished; but any citizen summoned or seized by virtue of the law must obey instantly; he renders himself culpable by resisting.

8. The law must establish only penalties that are strictly and clearly necessary, and no one can be punished except in virtue of a law established and published prior to the offense and legally applied.

9. Every man being presumed innocent until he has been declared guilty, if it is judged indispensable to arrest him, all severity that is not necessary for making sure of his person must be severely repressed by the law.

10. No one may be disturbed because of his opinions, even religious, provided that their public demonstration does not disturb the public order established by law.

11. The free communication of thoughts and opinions is one of the most precious rights of man: every citizen can therefore freely speak, write, and print: he is answerable for abuses of this liberty in cases determined by the law.

12. The guaranteeing of the rights of man and citizen necessitates a public force; this force is therefore instituted for the advantage of all, and not for the private use of those to whom it is entrusted.

13. For the maintenance of the public force, and for the expenses of administration, a tax supported in common is indispensable; it must be assessed on all citizens in proportion to their capacities to pay.

14. Citizens have the right to determine for themselves or through their representatives the need for taxation of the public, to consent to it freely, to investigate its use, and to determine its rate, basis, collection, and duration.

15. Society has the right to demand an

accounting of his administration from every public agent.

16. Any society in which guarantees of rights are not assured nor the separation of powers determined has no constitution.

17. Property being an inviolable and sacred right, no one may be deprived of it unless public necessity, legally determined, and on condition of a just and prior indemnity.

FRENCH CONSTITUTION OF 1791

After laboring for more than two years, the National Assembly completed its task of writing France's first constitution, and on September 13, 1791, an unenthusiastic Louis XVI officially approved it. The document grew out of long debate and compromise and sought to apply the ideals of the Enlightenment and the model of English and American government to France. From one perspective, the constitution was a failure. It was scrapped in August 1792, the victim of war hysteria, inflation, lower-class discontent, and committed republicans' impatience with its numerous compromises. Nonetheless, the Constitution of 1791 best represents the early, moderate phase of the Revolution and, like the Declaration of the Rights of Man and of the Citizen, served as an inspiration and model for future generations.

Questions
for Analysis

1. In what ways does the French constitution address issues not discussed in the English Bill of Rights?
2. How did the constitution affect the status of the nobility?
3. Radical republicans denounced the Constitution of 1791 as undemocratic for failing to extend the benefits of the Revolution to the lower classes. Do you feel their criticisms were justified? Why or why not?
4. What was to be the king's role in the French state? What powers were accorded to the Legislative Assembly? Who was to control the judiciary?

*T*he National Assembly, wishing to establish the French Constitution on the principles which it has just recognized and declared . . . abolishes irrevocably institutions which offended against liberty and equality of rights.

There no longer exists either nobility, peerage, hereditary distinctions, distinctions of order, feudal system or patrimonial courts, or any titles, denominations or prerogatives deriving from them, or any order of chivalry, or any corporations or decorations requiring proofs of nobility, or presupposing distinctions of birth, or any predominance other than that of public officials in the exercise of their duties.

Neither venality nor inheritance of any public office exists any longer.[1]

Neither privilege nor exception to the law common to all Frenchmen exists any longer for any part of the nation nor for any individual.

Neither craft guilds, nor corporations of professions, arts and crafts exist any longer.

The law no longer recognizes either religious vows or any other pledge contrary to natural rights or to the Constitution.

TITLE I. FUNDAMENTAL PROVISIONS GUARANTEED BY THE CONSTITUTION

The Constitution guarantees as natural and civil rights:

1. That all citizens are admissible to offices and employments without any other distinction than that of virtues and talents;

2. That all taxes shall be borne equally by all citizens in proportion to their resources;

3. That like crimes shall be punished by like penalties without any distinction of persons.

The Constitution guarantees likewise as natural and civil rights:

Freedom to every man to come and go or remain without being arrested or detained except in accordance with the forms determined by the Constitution;

Freedom to every man to speak, write, print, and publish his opinions without his writings being subject to any censorship or inspection before publication, and to practice the religious faith which he accepts;

Freedom to citizens to assemble peacefully and without arms, in accordance with police regulations.

Freedom to address individually signed petitions to constituted authorities.

The legislative power may not make any law which interferes with or hinders the exercise of the natural and civil rights recorded in the present Title and guaranteed by the Constitution. But as liberty consists only in being able to do whatever is not harmful to the rights of others, or to public safety, the law may establish penalties for acts, which, by assailing either public safety or the rights of others, might be harmful to society.

The Constitution guarantees the inviolability of property, or just and prior indemnification for that of which public necessity, legally determined, requires the sacrifice.

Property intended for the expenses of worship, and for all services of public utility, belongs to the nation and is at its disposal at all times.

The Constitution guarantees transfers (of property) which have been or which shall be made according to the forms established by law.

Citizens have the right to elect or choose their ministers of religion.

A general establishment for *public assistance* shall be formed and organized to raise abandoned children, to relieve the infirm poor, and to provide work for the able-bodied poor who have not been able to obtain it themselves.

A system of *Public Instruction*, common to all citizens, free with respect to those aspects of education indispensable for all men, shall be inaugurated and organized and the institutions shall be apportioned gradually in relation to the division of the Kingdom.

---

1. In pre-Revolutionary France many political offices and the income attached to them were viewed as a form of private property that could be bought and sold and passed on to heirs.

National festivals shall be established to preserve the memory of the French Revolution, to maintain fraternity among citizens, and to bind them to the Constitution, the *Patrie*, and the laws.

A code of civil law common to the whole Kingdom shall be instituted. . . .

TITLE III. CONCERNING PUBLIC POWERS

Article 1. Sovereignty is one, indivisible, inalienable, and imprescriptible; it belongs to the nation; no section of the people, nor any individual, may arrogate to itself the exercise thereof.

2. The nation, from which alone all powers emanate, may not exercise them except by delegation.

The French Constitution is representative: the representatives are the legislative body and the King.

3. Legislative power is delegated to a national assembly consisting of temporary representatives, freely elected by the people, to be exercised by it, with the sanction of the King, in the manner laid down hereafter. . . .

5. Judicial power is delegated to judges elected by the people at predetermined intervals.

Chapter One. Concerning the National Legislative Assembly

Article 1. The National Assembly, which constitutes the legislative body, is permanent and is composed of only a single chamber.

2. It shall be constituted every two years by new elections. Each period of two years shall constitute a legislature. . . .

5. The legislative body may not be dissolved by the King.

Section II. Primary Assemblies. Nomination of Electors.

Article 1. To form the National Legislative Assembly, active citizens shall meet every two years in primary assemblies in towns and cantons.

2. To be an active citizen it is necessary:
To be born or have become a Frenchman;
To be fully twenty-five years of age;
To be domiciled in the city or canton for the time determined by law.
To pay, in any part of the Kingdom whatever, direct taxation equal at least to the value of three days' work and to present the receipt for it;
Not to be in a condition of domesticity, that is to say a hired servant;
To be registered in the municipality of domicile on the role of the National Guard;
To have taken the civic oath.[2]

3. Every six years, the legislative body shall determine the *minimum* and *maximum* of the value of a day's labor, and the departmental administrators shall make the local determination for each district.

4. No one may exercise the rights of an active citizen in more than one locality, nor appoint another as his proxy.

5. The following are excluded from the rights of active citizenship:
Those who are under indictment;
Those who, having been declared bankrupt or insolvent on the proof of authentic evidence, do not produce a general discharge from their creditors.

6. Primary Assemblies shall name electors in proportion to the number of active citizens resident in the city or canton.
One elector shall be named for every 100

---

2. An oath to support the Revolution.

active citizens, whether present at the Assembly or not.

Two shall be named for from 151 to 250 and so on.

7. No one may be named an elector if he does not, in addition to the conditions necessary for active citizenship, fulfill the following requirements:

In cities of more than 6,000 inhabitants, that of being the proprietor or usufructuary[3] of property assessed on the taxation rolls at a revenue equal to the local value of 200 days labor, or of being the occupier of a dwelling assessed on the same rolls at a revenue equal to the value of 150 days labor.

In cities of less than 6,000 inhabitants, that of being proprietor or usufructuary of property assessed on the taxation rolls at a revenue equal to the local value of 150 days labor, or of being occupier of a dwelling assessed on the same rolls at a revenue equal to the value of 100 days labor;

And in rural areas, that of being proprietor or usufructuary of property assessed on the taxation rolls at a revenue equal to the local value of 150 days labor, or of being farmer or share-farmer of properties assessed on the same rolls at the value of 400 days labor . . .

Chapter II. Concerning Royalty, Regency, and Ministers

Section I. Concerning Royalty and the King

Article 1. Royalty is indivisible and delegated hereditarily to the reigning family, from male to male, by order of primogeniture, to the perpetual exclusion of women and their offspring. (Nothing is presumed concerning the effect of abdications in the family now reigning.)

2. The person of the King is inviolable and sacred. His only title is *King of the French.*

3. In France there is no authority superior to that of the law. The King only reigns in consequence of it, and it is only in the name of the law that he may exact obedience.

4. On his accession to the throne, or as soon as he shall have reached his majority, the King, in the presence of the legislative body, shall swear to the nation the oath *to be faithful to the nation and the law, to use all the power delegated to him to maintain the Constitution decreed by the National Constituent Assembly in the years 1789, 1790, and 1791, and to have the laws executed.*

LEVÉE EN MASSE

Nationalism, simply defined, is dedication to and identification with the interests, purposes, and well-being of one's nation-state. Such dedication is deeply emotional and often takes precedence over competing loyalties of family, church, locality, and even humanity at large. This powerful ideology emerged only in the 1790s, during the first years of the French Revolution, when the French transformed themselves

---

3. One who has the right to use and enjoy all the advantages and profit from another's property.

from "subjects" into "citizens" by abolishing monarchy and establishing a regime based on equality and popular sovereignty.

When war broke out in 1792 between republican France and avowedly antirevolutionary Austria and Prussia, previously apathetic Frenchmen eagerly volunteered to serve in their army. They successfully halted the Austro-Prussian invaders, but one year later France faced a coalition of Austria, Prussia, Spain, and Great Britain, whose armies drove the French out of the Austrian Netherlands (modern Belgium) and were poised for another strike at Paris. Against the backdrop of inflation and domestic unrest, the Revolution's fortunes looked precarious. At this moment, on August 13, 1793, the National Assembly adopted the *Levée en Masse*, a "total" conscription order that provided for the defense of France and the Revolution.

By 1794 the French republic had an army of 800,000 men, the largest in European history. The army was unique in other ways. The fighting men were citizen-soldiers committed to their cause and country, not indifferent mercenaries or unwilling recruits; officers had won commissions on merit, not through purchase or aristocratic privilege.

This "new" French army not only saved the Revolution but conquered much of Europe in the next decade and a half. By 1811 Napoleon, the Corsican who rose to become emperor of France, controlled an empire that stretched from Spain to Poland. Four years later, his armies had been defeated and Napoleon was in exile on the South Atlantic island of St. Helena, where he died in 1821.

Questions for Analysis

1. As outlined, how would this decree affect the powers of the central government?
2. How did the decree affect French economic life?
3. What specific tasks are assigned the various groups mentioned in the decree?
4. According to the language of the decree, what is the purpose of the war being fought by the French?

*T*he National Convention,[1] having heard the report of the Committee of Public Safety[2] decrees:

1. From this moment, until our enemies have been driven from the soil of the Republic, the whole French people is in permanent requisition for army service.

    Young men shall go into battle; married men shall forge arms and

---

1. The democratically elected legislative assembly that was originally convened in 1792 to write a republican constitution for France. It sat until 1795.

2. The Committee of Public Safety was made up of twelve men, named by the Convention, who were granted wide executive powers. One of the committee's major purposes was to propose legislation to the Convention.

transport supplies; women shall make tents and clothing and serve in hospitals; children shall turn old linen into lint[3] and old men shall have themselves taken to public places to arouse the courage of the warriors and hatred of kings, and to encourage the unity of the Republic.

2. National buildings shall be converted into barracks, public squares into armament workshops; the soil of cellars shall be washed in lye to extract saltpeter.[4]

3. Muskets shall be given only to those who march against the enemy; service in the interior shall be performed with shotguns and side arms.

4. Saddle horses shall be requisitioned to complete the cavalry corps; draught horses, other than those used in agriculture, shall haul artillery and provisions.

5. The Committee of Public Safety is charged with taking all possible steps to establish, without delay, an extraordinary manufacture of arms of all kinds, consonant with the condition and energy of the French people. It is authorized, as a consequence, to create all establishments, manufactories, workshops, and factories considered necessary for the execution of the works, as well as to requisition for this purpose, throughout the whole Republic, artists and workmen who may contribute to their success. For this purpose, a sum of 30,000,000 . . . *assignats*[5] shall be put at the disposal of the Ministry of War. The central establishment of this extraordinary manufacture shall be set up in Paris.

6. The representatives of the people despatched to execute the present law shall have the same authority in their respective *arrondissements*[6] and shall act in concert with the Committee of Public Safety. They are invested with the unlimited powers assigned to the representatives of the people attached to the armies.

7. No one may be replaced by a substitute in the service for which he is requisitioned. Public officials shall remain at their posts.

8. The levy shall be general; unmarried citizens, or widowers without children, between eighteen and twenty-five years, shall go first. They shall report without delay to the chief town of their district, where they shall train in the use of arms each day, while they await the order to depart.

9. The representatives of the people shall so regulate the levies and marches as to ensure that armed citizens arrive at the point of assembly only to the extent that supplies, munitions and all the material requirements of an army are available in sufficient quantities.

10. Assembly points shall be determined by circumstances and designated by the representatives of the people sent to execute the present law, on the advice of the generals, and in collaboration with the Committee of Public Safety and the Provisional Executive Council.

11. The battalion organized in each district shall be united under a banner bearing this inscription: *The French people risen against tyrants.*

---

3. Softened linen, formerly used for bandaging wounds.

4. Potassium nitrate, used for making gunpowder.

5. Paper money issued by the Revolutionary government, backed by land confiscated from the Catholic Church.

6. An administrative district.

12. These battalions shall be organized according to established law, and their pay shall be the same as that of the battalions at the frontiers.

13. To collect supplies in sufficient quantity, farmers and managers of national properties shall take to the chief towns of their districts, the produce of these properties, in the form of grain.

14. Owners, farmers, and all who possess grain, shall be required to pay, in kind, as arrears of taxes, two-thirds of those of 1793, according to the rolls which served to effect the last payment.

Anticolonial Revolts in the Americas

Despite the many differences between the British colonies of eastern North America and the Portuguese-Spanish colonies of Central and South America, between the 1770s and the 1830s almost all of them fought successfully for independence from European domination. In both North and South America many similar grievances and ideals inspired the struggle for independence. The grievances included resentment over economic restrictions, resistance to higher taxes, and an interest in greater self-government; the ideals were provided by the Enlightenment, and, in Latin America, the French Revolution.

Significant differences also characterized the American independence movements. In North America, although a good part of the population was hostile or indifferent to independence, the opponents of British rule coalesced into a centrally directed movement under the Continental Congress and George Washington. Nothing like this took place in Latin America, where the struggle for independence was carried out on a regional basis under the leadership of generals such as Simón Bolívar, Bernardo O'Higgins, and José de San Martín. Furthermore, the societies established in the wake of the independence movements were different in several respects. In North America, the new United States government and the governments of the thirteen original states drew on the traditions of English constitutionalism and the Enlightenment, guaranteeing basic freedoms and extending political rights to the majority of white males. In Latin America, the upper-class leaders of the revolts maintained political control over the newly independent states, excluding the peasant masses from the political process.

Finally, the independence movements in North America and Latin America did not result in any basic changes in inherited social and economic relationships. In the United States, this meant the preservation of black slavery and the continuation of women's second-class status. Property holding was widespread, however, and a fluid class structure and many economic opportunities ensured that not just the elite leadership but the common people would benefit from independence. In Latin America, however, this meant the continuation of a social structure characterized by a vast economic gap between the mass of propertyless peasants and the narrow elite of white property owners. Even more so than in North America, the independence movement in Latin America was a significant reorientation in political relationships but no true revolution.

DECLARATION OF INDEPENDENCE

After more than a decade of growing tension, in April 1775 the American Revolution began with the clash between British and American troops at the Battle of Lexington and Concord. In the following months, Americans vigorously debated whether the colonies should officially declare their independence from Great Britain. Many viewed such a step as catastrophic; others had severe misgivings. Gradually those favoring independence gained the upper hand. Many colonists were angered by British use of German mercenaries and by rumors that the British were inciting slave rebellions and encouraging Indian attacks on frontier regions. Pragmatic politicians argued that as long as the colonies' relationship with Great Britain remained ambiguous, effective government, the direction of the war effort, and the attraction of foreign support would be difficult or impossible. The debate ended in June and early July 1776. On June 7, Richard Henry Lee of Virginia, acting on instructions from the Virginia Convention, proposed an independence resolution to the Second Continental Congress, meeting in Philadelphia. On July 2, the congress voted 12–0 in favor of independence, with only the delegation from New York abstaining. Two days later the congress voted by the same margin to accept the Declaration of Independence, largely the work of the Virginia planter Thomas Jefferson. The Declaration powerfully stated humanity's right to revolution and eloquently justified the colonies' actions. New York did ultimately make the vote for independence unanimous; on July 9, the New York Provincial Congress met and approved Jefferson's Declaration.

Questions
for Analysis

1. On what basis does Jefferson justify the political separation of the American colonies from England?
2. To what extent does the Declaration simply confirm political ideas already enunciated in the English Bill of Rights?
3. In what respects does the Declaration go beyond the basic ideas of the Bill of Rights? What might explain these differences?

When in the Course of human events, it becomes necessary for one people to dissolve the political bands which have connected them with another, and to assume among the Powers of the earth, the separate and equal station to which the Laws of Nature and of Nature's God entitle them, a decent respect to the opinions of mankind requires that they should declare the causes which impel them to the separation.

We hold these truths to be self-evident, that all men are created equal, that they are endowed by their Creator with certain unalienable Rights, that among these are Life, Liberty and the pursuit of Happiness. That to secure these rights, Governments are instituted among Men, deriving their just powers from the consent of the governed, That whenever any Form of Government becomes destructive of these ends, it is the Right of the People to alter or to abolish it, and to institute new Government, laying its foundation on such principles and organizing its powers in such form, as to them shall seem most likely to effect their Safety and Happiness. Prudence, indeed, will dictate that Governments long established should not be changed for light and transient causes; and accordingly all experience hath shown, that mankind are more disposed to suffer, while evils are sufferable, than to right themselves by abolishing the forms to which they are accustomed. But when a long train of abuses and usurpations, pursuing invariably the same Object evinces a design to reduce them, under absolute Despotism, it is their right, it is their duty, to throw off such Government, and to provide new Guards for their future security. — Such has been the patient sufferance of these Colonies; and such is now the necessity which constrains them to alter their former Systems of Government. The history of the present King of Great Britain is a history of repeated injuries and usurpations, all having in direct object the establishment of an absolute Tyranny over these States. . . .

In every stage of these Oppressions We have Petitioned for Redress in the most humble terms: Our repeated Petitions have been answered only by repeated injury. A Prince, whose character is thus marked by every act which may define a Tyrant, is unfit to be the ruler of a free People.

Nor have We been wanting in attention to our British brethren. We have warned them from time to time of attempts by their legislature to extend an unwarrantable jurisdiction over us. We have reminded them of the circumstances of our emigration and settlement here. We have appealed to their native justice and magnanimity, and we have conjured them by the ties of our common kindred to disavow these usurpations, which would inevitably interrupt our connections and correspondence. They too have been deaf to the voice of justice and of consanguinity. We must, therefore, acquiesce in the necessity, which denounces our Separation, and hold them, as we hold the rest of mankind, Enemies in War, in Peace Friends.

We, therefore, the Representatives of the United States of America, in General Congress, Assembled, appealing to the Supreme Judge of the world for the rectitude of our intentions, do, in the Name, and by Authority of the good People of these Colonies, solemnly publish and declare, That these United Colonies are, and of Right ought to be Free and Independent States; that they are Absolved from all Allegiance to the British Crown, and that all political connection between them and the State of Great Britain, is and ought to be totally dissolved; and that as Free and Independent States, they have full Power to levy War, conclude Peace, contract Alliances, establish Commerce, and to do all other Acts and Things which Independent States may of right do. And for the support of this Declaration, with a firm reliance on the Protection of Divine Providence, we mutually pledge to each other our Lives, our Fortunes and our sacred Honor.

■ **Manuel Belgrano**

AUTOBIOGRAPHY

Although not as famous as Simón Bolívar or his fellow Argentine, José de San Martín, Manuel Belgrano (1770–1820) was an important figure in the struggle against Spanish rule in South America. As he relates in his autobiography, he was a lawyer who in the 1790s began a career as secretary of the government-controlled *consulado* in Buenos Aires, an advisory council on economic matters for the colonial administration. Disillusioned with Spanish rule, he joined the Argentine independence movement at the start, playing a variety of military, political, and diplomatic roles. In the following excerpt from his *Autobiography*, he describes his transformation to an active opponent of Spain and some of the events in the struggle itself.

Questions
for Analysis

1. What role did Belgrano's experience in Europe play in shaping his political ideas?
2. When and why did Belgrano become disillusioned with the Spanish colonial administration?
3. What impact did the British occupation of Buenos Aires have on Belgrano?
4. On the basis of Belgrano's account, what conclusions can you draw about popular participation in the anti-Spanish movement?
5. Why did Belgrano feel that the prospects for Latin American independence were so hopeless?

The place of my birth was Buenos Aires; my parents were Don Domingo Belgrano y Peri, known as Pérez, a native of Onella in Spain, and Doña María Josefa González Casero, a native of Buenos Aires. My father was a merchant, and since he lived in the days of monopoly he acquired sufficient wealth to live comfortably and to give his children the best education to be had in those days.

I studied my first letters, Latin grammar, philosophy, and a smattering of theology in Buenos Aires. My father then sent me to Spain to study law, and I began my preparation at Salamanca; I was graduated at Valladolid, continued my training at Madrid, and was admitted to the bar at Valladolid. . . .

Since I was in Spain in 1789, and the French Revolution was then causing a change in ideas, especially among the men of letters with whom I associated, the ideals of liberty, equality, security, and property took a firm hold on me, and I saw only tyrants in those who would restrain a man, wherever he might be, from enjoying the rights with which God and Nature had endowed him. . . .

When I completed by studies in 1793 political economy enjoyed great popularity in Spain; I believe this was why I was appointed secretary of the *consulado* of Buenos Aires, established when Gardoqui was minister. The official of the department in charge of these matters even asked me to suggest some other well-informed persons who could be appointed to similar bodies to be established in the principal American ports.

When I learned that these consulados were to be so many Economic Societies that would discuss the state of agriculture, industry, and commerce in their sessions, my imagination pictured a vast field of activity, for I was ignorant of Spanish colonial policy. I had heard some muffled murmuring among the Americans, but I attributed this to their failure to gain their ends, never to evil designs of the Spaniards that had been systematically pursued since the Conquest.

On receiving my appointment I was infatuated with the brilliant prospects for America. I had visions of myself writing memorials concerning the provinces so that the authorities might be informed and provide for their well-being. It may be that an enlightened minister like Gardoqui, who had resided in the United States, had the best of intentions in all this. . . .

I finally departed from Spain for Buenos Aires; I cannot sufficiently express the surprise I felt when I met the men named by the king to the council which was to deal with agriculture, industry, and commerce and work for the happiness of the provinces composing the vice-royalty of Buenos Aires. All were Spanish merchants. With the exception of one or two they knew nothing but their monopolistic business, namely, to buy at four dollars and sell for eight. . . .

My spirits fell, and I began to understand that the colonies could expect nothing from me who placed their private interests above those of the community. But since my position gave me an opportunity to write and speak about some useful topics, I decided at least to plant a few seeds that some day might bear fruit. . . .

I wrote various memorials about the establishment of schools. The scarcity of pilots and the direct interest of the merchants in the project presented favorable circumstances for the establishment of a school of mathematics, which I obtained on condition of getting the approval of the Court. This, however, was never secured; in fact, the government was not satisfied until the school had been abolished, because although the peninsulars[1] recognized the justice and utility of such establishments, they were opposed to them because of a mistaken view of how the colonies might best be retained.

The same happened to a drawing school which I managed to establish without spending even half a real[2] for the teacher. The fact is that neither these nor other proposals to the government for the development of agriculture, industry, and commerce, the three important concerns of the consulado, won its official approval; the sole concern of the Court was with the revenue that it derived from each of these branches. They said that all the proposed establishments were luxuries, and that Buenos Aires was not yet in a condition to support them.

I promoted various other useful and necessary projects, which had more or less the same fate, but it will be the business of the future historian of the consulado to give an account of them; I shall simply say that from the beginning of 1794 to July, 1806, I passed my time in futile efforts to serve my country. They all foundered on the rock of the opposition of the government of Buenos Aires, or that of Madrid, or that of the merchants who composed the consulado, for whom there was no other reason, justice, utility, or necessity than their commercial interest. Anything that came into conflict with that

---

1. A reference to Spaniards, who came from the Iberian Peninsula.

2. A silver coin equal in value to one-half of a piece of eight.

interest encountered a veto, and there was nothing to be done about it.

It is well known how General Beresford[3] entered Buenos Aires with about four hundred men in 1806. At that time I had been a captain in the militia for ten years, more from whim than from any attachment to the military art. My first experience of war came at that time. The Marqués de Sobremonte, than viceroy of the provinces of La Plata,[4] sent for me several days before Beresford's disastrous entrance and requested me to form a company of cavalry from among the young men engaged in commerce. He said that he would give me veteran officers to train them; I sought them but could not find any, because of the great hostility felt for the militia in Buenos Aires. . . .

The general alarm was sounded. Moved by honor, I flew to the fortress, the point of assembly; I found there neither order nor harmony in anything, as must happen with groups of men who know nothing of discipline and are completely insubordinate. The companies were formed there, and I was attached to one of them. I was ashamed that I had not the slightest notion of military science and had to rely entirely on the orders of a veteran officer — who also joined voluntarily, for he was given no assignment. . . .

Meanwhile the others argued with the viceroy himself that they were obliged only to defend the city and not to go out into the country; consequently they would agree only to defend the heights. The result was that the enemy, meeting with no opposition from veteran troops or disciplined militia, forced all the passes with the greatest ease. There was some stupid firing on the part of my company and some others in an effort to stop the invaders, but all in vain, and when the order came to retreat and we were falling back I heard someone say: "They did well to order us to retreat, for we were not made for this sort of thing."

I must confess that I grew angry, and that I never regretted more deeply my ignorance of even the rudiments of military science. My distress grew when I saw the entrance of the enemy troops, and realized how few of them there were for a town of the size of Buenos Aires. I could not get the idea out of my head, and I almost went out of my mind, it was so painful to me to see my country under an alien yoke, and above all in such a degraded state that it could be conquered by the daring enterprise of the brave and honorable Beresford, whose valor I shall always admire.

———————— ✧ ————————

A resistance movement against the British is organized by Santiago Liniers, a Frenchman in the service of Spain. The British are expelled from Buenos Aires, and Liniers is proclaimed viceroy to replace the discredited Sobremonte. Another British expedition under John Whitelock is defeated, and the entire British force surrenders.

———————— ✧ ————————

General Liniers ordered the quartermaster-general to receive the paroles of the officer prisoners; for this reason Brigadier-General Crawford, together with his aides and other high officers, came to his house. My slight knowledge of French, and perhaps certain civilities that I showed him, caused General Crawford to prefer to converse with me, and we

---

3. General William C. Beresford and Sir Home Popham of the Royal Navy sailed to South America in 1806 with about 1,600 men and the intent of fomenting rebellion and annexing territories of Spain, now a client state of their enemy, Napoleon. In June 1806 Beresford took Buenos Aires with a band of 400 soldiers.

4. The name of the administrative region that included the area of modern Argentina.

entered upon a discussion that helped to pass the time — although he never lost sight of his aim of gaining knowledge of the country and, in particular, of its opinion of the Spanish Government.

So, having convinced himself that I had no French sympathies or connections, he divulged to me his ideas about our independence, perhaps in the hope of forming new links with this country, since the hope of conquest had failed. I described our condition to him, and made it plain that we wanted our old master or none at all; that we were far from possessing the means required for the achievement of independence; that even if it were won under the protection of England, she would abandon us in return for some advantage in Europe, and then we would fall under the Spanish sword; that every nation sought its own interest and did not care about the misfortunes of others. He agreed with me, and when I had shown how we lacked the means for winning independence, he put off its attainment for a century.

How fallible are the calculations of men! One year passed, and behold, without any effort on our part to become independent, God Himself gave us our opportunity as a result of the events of 1808 in Spain and Bayonne.[5] Then it was that the ideals of liberty and independence came to life in America, and the Americans began to speak frankly of their rights.

The Decline of the Mughal and Ottoman Empires

While Russia expanded and slowly moved toward great power status, the once splendid Ottoman and Mughal empires showed clear signs of decline in the seventeenth and eighteenth centuries. In each case, administrative inefficiency, corruption, exorbitant spending by the court, economic stagnation, indifferent or misguided leadership, and a decline in military effectiveness contributed to the empires' deterioration. In each case, too, special circumstances played a role. With the Mughals, the anti-Hindu policies and continual wars of Aurangzeb (1658–1707) provoked rebellion, exhausted the treasury, and opened the country to invasion by the Persians and political control by the British. With the Ottomans, the determined opposition to change on the part of Muslim clerics, entrenched bureaucrats, and certain military factions undermined reformers' every effort to effect meaningful change.

In the following documents, two Europeans analyze some of the problems of the Mughal and Ottoman empires that led to their loss of territory and ultimately their demise.

---

5. Belgrano is referring to Napoleon's decision in 1808 to depose Ferdinand VII, Bourbon king of Spain, and replace him with his brother, Joseph Bonaparte. Although the Spanish monarchy's prestige had plummeted during the corrupt and ineffectual reign of Charles IV (1788–1808), the Spaniards wanted nothing to do with French rule. Their revolt against Napoleon was one of the first signs that the emperor's grip on Europe was loosening.

■ **François Bernier**

LETTER TO JEAN-BAPTISTE COLBERT ON THE MUGHAL EMPIRE

Born in 1620 and orphaned at an early age, Bernier originally hoped to pursue a career in the Church. While a student at the University of Paris, however, he abandoned theology, joined a circle of intellectuals led by the materialist philosopher Pierre Gassendi, and in the late 1640s traveled through much of north central Europe in the service of an aristocratic French diplomat. He then obtained his medical degree from the University of Montpellier and immediately departed for Asia, where he hoped to practice medicine.

Bernier's improbable undertaking had improbable results. In 1658 he became the personal physician of no less a figure than the Mughal emperor Aurangzeb. He left India in 1669, returning to France to write books on Asia and edit Gassendi's philosophical works. Bernier was an astute observer who recognized weaknesses in the Mughal Empire despite its apparent power and riches. In 1670 he communicated his thoughts on India to Colbert, the French Comptroller-General, in a letter.

Questions for Analysis

1. What is Bernier's overall assessment of the Mughal government? What does he see as the major political problems Aurangzeb faces?
2. What seems to impress Bernier most about India? As a European what does he find most deplorable in Indian society?
3. According to Bernier, what problems resulted from the fact that Aurangzeb was a Muslim? How well does Bernier seem to understand the religious conflicts in India under Aurangzeb?
4. According to Bernier, what conditions weakened Mughal military strength?
5. What factors does Bernier mention that hindered Indian economic development?

I think I have shown that the precious metals must abound in Hindustan,[1] although the country be destitute of mines; and that the Great Mughal, lord and master of the greater part, must necessarily be in the receipt of an immense revenue, and possess incalculable wealth.

But there are many circumstances to be considered, as forming a counterpoise to these riches.

First. — Of the vast tracts of country constituting the empire of Hindustan, many are little more than sand, or barren mountains, badly cultivated, and thinly peopled; and even a considerable portion of the good land remains untilled from

---

1. The region of northern India.

want of laborers; many of whom perish in consequence of the bad treatment they experience from the Governors. These poor people, when incapable of discharging the demands of their rapacious lords, are not only often deprived of the means of subsistence, but are bereft of their children, who are carried away as slaves. Thus it happens that many of the peasantry, driven to despair by so execrable a tyranny, abandon the country, and seek a more tolerable mode of existence, either in the towns, or camps; as bearers of burdens, carriers of water, or servants to horsemen. Sometimes they fly to the territories of a Raja,[2] because there they find less oppression, and are allowed a greater degree of comfort.

Second. — The empire of the Great Mughal comprehends several nations, over which he is not absolute master. Most of them still retain their own peculiar chiefs or sovereigns, who obey the Mughal or pay him tribute only by compulsion. In many instances this tribute is of trifling amount; in others none is paid; and I shall adduce instances of nations which, instead of paying, receive tribute.

The petty sovereignties bordering the Persian frontiers, for example, seldom pay tribute either to the Mughal or to the King of Persia. . . .

Third. — It is material to remark that the Great Mughal is a Muslim, of the sect of the Sunnis, who, believing with the Turks that Osman was the true successor of Muhammad, are distinguished by the name of Osmanlys.[3] The majority of his courtiers, however, being Persians, are of the party known by the appellation of Shias,[4] believers in the real succession of Aly. Moreover, the Great Mughal is a foreigner in Hindustan, a descendant of Tamerlane,[5] . . . who, about the year 1401, overran and conquered the Indies. Consequently he finds himself in an hostile country, or nearly so; a country containing hundreds of Gentiles[6] to one Mughal, or even to one Muslim. To maintain himself in such a country, in the midst of domestic and powerful enemies, and to be always prepared against any hostile movement on the side of Persia or Usbec,[7] he is under the necessity of keeping up numerous armies, even in the time of peace. . . .

It is also important to remark the absolute necessity which exists of paying the whole of this army every two months . . . for the King's pay is their only means of sustenance. In France, when the exigencies of the times prevent the government from immediately discharging an arrear of debt, an officer, or even a private soldier, may contrive to live for some time by means of his own private income; but in the Indies, any unusual delay in the payment of the troops is sure to be attended with fatal consequences; after selling whatever trifling articles they may possess, the soldiers disband and die of hunger. Toward the close of the late civil war, I discovered a growing disposition in the troopers to sell their horses, which they would, no doubt, soon have done if the war had been prolonged. And no wonder; for consider, My Lord, that it is

---

2. An Indian prince.

3. Osman I (1299–1326) established the first small Ottoman state in the northwest corner of Asia Minor.

4. The Shi'ites believed that Ali, Muhammad's son-in-law and adopted son, was the true successor to the prophet; they rejected the line

of succession begun when Mu'awiya I (661–680) established the Umayyad dynasty of caliphs.

5. Refers to Timur, or Tamerlane (1336–1405), the great Turkic conqueror.

6. Nonbelievers, that is, Hindus.

7. Usbecs (Uzbeks) were a Turkic people centered in a region east of Persia.

difficult to find in the Mughal's army, a soldier who is not married, who has not wife, children, servants, and slaves, all depending upon him for support. I have known many persons lost in amazement while contemplating the number of persons, amounting to millions, who depend for support solely on the King's pay. Is it possible, they have asked, that any revenue can suffice for such incredible expenditure? seeming to forget the riches of the Great Mughal, and the peculiar manner in which Hindustan is governed.

But I have not enumerated all the expenses incurred by the Great Mughal. He keeps in Delhi and Agra from two to three thousand fine horses, always at hand in case of emergency: eight or nine hundred elephants, and a large number of baggage horses, mules, and porters, intended to carry the numerous and capacious tents, with their fittings, his wives and women, furniture, kitchen apparatus, Ganges'-water,[8] and all the other articles necessary for the camp, which the Mughal has always about him, as in his capital, things which are not considered necessary in our kingdoms in Europe.

Add to this, if you will, the enormous expenses of the Seraglio,[9] where the consumption of fine cloths of gold, and brocades, silks, embroideries, pearls, musk, amber and sweet essences, is greater than can be conceived.

Thus, although the Great Mughal be in receipt of an immense revenue, his expenditure being much in the same proportion, he cannot possess the vast surplus of wealth that most people seem to imagine. I admit that his income exceeds probably the joint revenues of the Grand Seignior[10] and of the King of Persia; but if I were to call him a wealthy monarch, it would be in the sense that a treasurer is to be considered wealthy who pays with one hand the large sums which he receives with the other. . . .

Before I conclude, I wish to explain how it happens that, although this Empire of the Mughal is such an abyss for gold and silver;[11] as I said before, these precious metals are not in greater plenty here than elsewhere; on the contrary, the inhabitants have less the appearance of a moneyed people than those of many other parts of the globe.

In the first place, a large quantity is melted, re-melted, and wasted, in fabricating women's bracelets, both for the hands and feet, chains, ear-rings, nose and finger rings, and a still larger quantity is consumed in manufacturing embroideries; alachas, or striped silken stuffs; touras, or fringes of gold lace, worn on turbans; gold and silver cloths, scarfs, turbans, and brocades. The quantity of these articles made in India is incredible. . . .

In the second place, the King, as proprietor of the land, makes over a certain quantity to military men, as an equivalent for their pay; and this grant is called jah-ghir . . . the word jah-ghir signifying the spot from which to draw, or the place of salary. Similar grants are made to governors, in lieu of their salary, and also for the support of their troops, on condition that they pay a certain sum annually to the King out of any surplus revenue that the land may yield. The lands not so granted are retained by the King as the

---

8. Aurangzeb, like other Mughal rulers, was a connoisseur of pure water; water from the Ganges was his favorite.

9. Harem.

10. The king of France.

11. Bernier refers to the economic fact that India, and most of the rest of Asia, received vast quantities of European gold and silver in return for their products.

peculiar domains of his house, and are seldom, if ever, given in the way of jahghir; and upon these domains he keeps contractors, who are also bound to pay him an annual rent.

The persons thus put in possession of the land, whether as governors or contractors, have an authority almost absolute over the peasantry, and nearly as much over the artisans and merchants of the towns and villages within their district; and nothing can be imagined more cruel and oppressive than the manner in which it is exercised. There is no one before whom the injured peasant, artisan, or tradesman can pour out his just complaints; no great lords, parliaments, or judges of local courts, exist, as in France, to restrain the wickedness of those merciless oppressors, and the Kadis, or judges, are not invested with sufficient power to redress the wrongs of these unhappy people. This sad abuse of the royal authority may not be felt in the same degree near capital cities such as Delhi and Agra, or in

the vicinity of large towns and seaports, because in those places acts of gross injustice cannot easily be concealed from the court.

This debasing state of slavery obstructs the progress of trade and influences the manners and mode of life of every individual. There can be little encouragement to engage in commercial pursuits, when the success with which they may be attended, instead of adding to the enjoyments of life, provokes the cupidity of a neighboring tyrant possessing both power and inclination to deprive any man of the fruits of his industry. When wealth is acquired, as must sometimes be the case, the possessor, so far from living with increased comfort and assuming an air of independence, studies the means by which he may appear indigent: his dress, lodging, and furniture, continue to be mean, and he is careful, above all things, never to indulge in the pleasures of the table. In the meantime, his gold and silver remain buried at a great depth in the ground. . . .

William Eton

A SURVEY OF THE TURKISH EMPIRE

Sir William Eton was a British government official who held diplomatic posts in Russia and Turkey in the late eighteenth century. On his retirement, he wrote several books about his experiences, the most widely read of which was *A Survey of the Turkish Empire*, published in 1799. In it he sought to describe the nature of Turkish government, religion, and society. The following excerpt depicts the condition of the once mighty Ottoman army.

Questions
for Analysis

1. How, according to Eton, does Turkey's military situation in the 1700s differ from that of earlier times?
2. What is his estimate of the fighting qualities of the Turkish troops? How does this compare with the comments of Ogier Ghiselin de Busbecq, who praises the Turkish army in his sixteenth-century *Turkish Letters*?

3. How does the lack of technological expertise weaken the Turkish military?
4. Does Eton believe the reforms initiated by Selim III have much chance to succeed? Why or why not?

*I*t is undeniable that the power of the Turks was once formidable to their neighbors not by their numbers only, but by their military and civil institutions, far surpassing those of their opponents.[1] . . . and they all trembled at the name of the Turks, who with a confidence procured by their constant successes, held the Christians no less in contempt as warriors than they did on account of their religion. Proud and vainglorious, conquest was to them a passion, a gratification, and even a means of salvation, a sure way of immediately attaining a delicious paradise. Hence their zeal for the extension of their empire, or rather a wild enthusiasm, even beyond the pure patriotism of the heroes of antiquity; hence their profound respect for the military profession, and their glory even in being obedient and submissive to discipline. . . .

Formerly, when the whole nation was in some manner inflamed with the warlike genius of the janissaries,[2] when the people were inflated by success, and everyone knew more or less the use of arms, these were often found useful and valiant troops; but at present they consist chiefly of an undisciplined rabble, instigated either by a momentary rashness or a desire of plunder. Some go, because they are ashamed to stay at home, on account of the ridicule of their neighbors; others, to secure the privileges and pecuniary advantage which they derive from being attached to a chamber (or company) of janissaries; another part of these volunteers are robbers, and the outcast of the Turks, who go to plunder on their march, as well going as coming, under the sanction of their military profession. . . .

The mullahs and mu'azzim cry from the minarets of the mosques, in time of war, that all good Muslims must go to fight against the infidels,[3] with a long enumeration of the obligations on all true believers to take the field.

Hence, a young man is often seized with a fit of enthusiasm, he takes a pair of richly furnished pistols, a saber covered with silver, and a carbine, and mounts his horse to conquer the infidels, and make them become Muslims, and to bring back with him young girls for his harem. If he does not repent and turn back before he sees the camp, nor when arrived at the army, he soon learns from others the danger there is, and the difficulty of vanquishing the infidels; but when he has been a witness of it, and seen that there are only hard blows to be gotten, he generally sets spurs to his horse, and rides off. Thus by whole troops, in every war, these volunteers return, plundering the poor

---

1. Eton does not identify the Ottomans' "opponents"; his point is that the Ottomans then had none of the weaknesses he goes on to describe.

2. Janissaries, conscripted from Christian families and converted to Islam, had once been the best disciplined and most feared unit in the Turkish army. By the eighteenth century they had deteriorated into a large, ineffective military organization, concerned mainly with protecting their privileges.

3. Mullahs were interpreters of Muslim law and doctrine; mu'azzim called the people to their daily prayers from minarets, tall towers built next to mosques; infidels were non-Muslims.

peasants, and often murdering them, particularly if they are Christians, to be able to swear, when they return home, how many infidels they have killed. The Asiatic foot soldiers desert in the same manner, and by thousands, though they are most of them janissaries.

Besides that the Turks refuse all reform, they are seditious and mutinous; their armies are incumbered with immense baggage, and their camp has all the conveniences of a town, with shops, etc., for such was their ancient custom when they wandered with their hordes. When their sudden fury is abated, which is at the least obstinate resistance, they are seized with a panic, and have no rallying as formerly. . . . The calvary is as much afraid of their own infantry as of the enemy; for in a defeat they fire at them to get their horses to escape more quickly. In short, it is a mob assembled rather than an army levied. None of those numerous details of a well-organized body, necessary to give quickness, strength, and regularity to its actions, to avoid confusion, to repair damages, to apply every part to some use; . . . no systematic attack, defense, or retreat; no accident foreseen, or provided for. . . .

The Turkish weapons require some notice. The artillery which they have, and which is chiefly brass, comprehends many fine pieces of cannon; but notwithstanding the reiterated instruction of so many French engineers, they are ignorant of its management.

Their musket-barrels are much esteemed but they are too heavy; nor do they possess any quality superior to common iron barrels which have been much hammered, and are very soft Swedish iron. The art of tempering their sabers is now

lost, and all the blades of great value are ancient. . . .

The naval force of the Turks is by no means considerable. Their grand fleet consisted of not more than 17 or 18 sail of the line in the last war,[4] and those not in very good condition; at present their number is lessened. . . . Their ships in general are roomy, and larger, for the number of guns, than ours. In regard to their construction, they are built of good oak wood, but the timbers being too far apart, they are very weak. . . . Such ships do not last long, and are subject to be leaky.

. . .

The present reigning sultan, Selim,[5] has made an attempt to introduce the European discipline into the Turkish army, and to abolish the body of janissaries; an attempt, which, whatever success it may ultimately be attended with, will form a memorable epoch in the history of the empire.

A trifling circumstance gave rise to it. The grand vizir, Yusef Pasha, in the late Russian war, had a prisoner who was by birth a Turk, but being carried early in his youth to Moscow, he had become a Christian, and found in a Russian nobleman a patron who gave him a good education, and placed him in the army. He was a lieutenant when he was taken prisoner, and had the reputation of being a good officer. The vizir[6] took pleasure in conversing with him, for he had not wholly forgotten his mother tongue. He represented the advantages of the European discipline, not only in battle, but in many other points of view, and particularly in securing the army from mutiny. By his persuasion the vizir formed a small corps,

<hr />

4. The war against Russia between 1787 and 1792.

5. Selim III (1789–1807), who attempted to replace the janissaries with his New Regulation Army, trained according to European standards.

6. The sultan's prime minister.

composed of renegades and a few indigent Turks, to whom the prisoner taught the European exercise, which they used to perform before the vizir's tent to divert him.

Peace being concluded, the vizir returned to Constantinople, and conducted this little corps with him. They were left at a village a few leagues from the capital. The sultan hearing of them, went to see how the infidels fought battles, as he would have gone to a puppet-show; but he was so struck with the superiority of their fire, that from that instant he resolved to introduce the European discipline into his army, and to abolish the janissaries; he therefore caused the corps to be recruited, set apart a branch of the revenue for their maintenance, and finally declared his intention of abolishing the institution of janissaries. This step, as might be expected, produced a mutiny, which was only appeased by the sultan's consenting to continue their pay during their lifetimes; but he at the same time ordered that no recruits should be received into their corps.

The new soldiers are taught their exercise with the musket and bayonet, and a few maneuvers. When they are held to be sufficiently disciplined, they are sent to garrison the fortresses on the frontiers. Their officers are all Turks and are chosen out of those who perform their exercise the best.

What they may become in time it is difficult to foretell; at present there is no other knowledge in the army than is possessed by their drill sergeants; nor indeed can more be expected from them, till they have gained experience in actual war; and it must be remembered that they are still Turks, a very different people from those whom Peter the Great taught to conquer the Swedes.[7] Their ignorance of maneuvers, which more than numbers or personal bravery, decide the fate of battles, will make their defeat easy to the Russians, the first time they meet in the field; it will then be seen whether they can make a retreat, or are to be rallied, and whether the new discipline will not all at once be abandoned. . . .

The mere institution of this militia is an important event; and Selim may, perhaps, effect by policy, what several of his ancestors have attempted by force. Could he put himself at the head of a disciplined army, he would conquer the ulema[8] as easily as the janissaries, and the Turkish power, though it would never again be formidable to Europe, might be respectable in Asia. The ulema see their danger, and oppose these changes with all their might. The whole situation is too new, has too many difficulties to encounter, and has made too small a progress for us to form an opinion how far the sultan will ultimately succeed.[9] The man who was the cause of this revolution in the military system, the Russian prisoner, and who had again become a Muslim, was rewarded for his services in the Turkish manner; for some misdemeanor, real or imputed, his head was struck off.

---

7. Eton refers to the success of Peter the Great in strengthening the Russian army during the struggle against Sweden in the Great Northern War (1700–1721).

8. Ulema, or ulama, means "those learned in religion"; it refers to Muslim clergy responsible for interpreting Muslim law in the community.

9. Selim's efforts to reform the army failed; he was deposed in 1807 and murdered in 1808.

The World Impact of European Commercial Expansion

As seen in Chapter 4, during the sixteenth and early seventeenth centuries, Western Europeans reshaped world commerce by initiating trade with the Americas and establishing control over the ancient oceanic trade routes connecting Asia, Africa, and Europe. From the mid-1600s to the early part of the 1800s, Europeans maintained their commercial dominance but with characteristics and implications quite different from the previous era's.

One major difference was the decline in the number of successful European trading nations by the eighteenth century. Spain and Portugal lost their commercial vigor in the early 1600s, and other states — Sweden, Denmark, Venice, and a few German states on the North Sea — now maintained only modest commercial fleets. The Netherlands, Great Britain, and France alone remained commercial powers. The Dutch still dominated the European coastal trade, and their control of the East Indies ensured handsome profits from trade in coffee, spices, and cocoa. Even the Dutch, however, could not keep up with the French and especially the British, whose commercial profits soared in the 1700s.

World trade in this period experienced a huge increase in volume, reflecting the full integration of the Americas into trade with Europe and Africa. As a result of population increases caused by immigration and internal growth, the Americas became an important market for African slaves and European exports and a producer of agricultural goods such as tobacco, indigo, and sugar. French and British commerce quadrupled during the eighteenth century, mainly because of trade with the Americas.

These changes in world commerce had unfortunate results for Africa, China, and India. Even as some Europeans in the eighteenth century began to raise their voices against the slave trade, the number of African blacks enslaved and shipped to the Americas reached an unprecedented level of 75,000 to 90,000 per year. It is estimated that in the whole history of the slave trade, of the 9 or 10 million blacks who survived the grisly trip from Africa to the Americas and were sold into slavery, 6 million or more did so in the 1700s. Anglo-French commercial expansion also led to British political subjugation of parts of India in the eighteenth century. The British were responsible as well for forcing China to open its major ports to European merchants in the 1800s. They flooded the market with opium, and, when the Chinese resisted, answered with force. The disdained "South Sea barbarians," lured as always by commercial profits, were about to bring the proud Middle Kingdom to its knees.

The Foundation for British Commercial Dominance

After the decline of Dutch trade in the late seventeenth century, it was by no means clear whether France or Great Britain would assume primacy in world commerce. France, with three to four times Britain's population, a well-equipped merchant fleet, rich natural resources, productive agriculture, and ample colonies, might well have appeared to have the advantage over its long-standing rival. During the second half of the eighteenth century, however, France slowly fell behind England, and on the eve of the French Revolution the value of British trade was double that of France.

The British pulled away from the French during the eighteenth century for several reasons. They were, first of all, more successful than the French in warfare and diplomacy. In the Treaty of Utrecht, following the War of the Spanish Succession (1701–1713), a member of the French Bourbon dynasty, Philip V, was recognized as king of Spain, but Great Britain gained Nova Scotia and Newfoundland, and, more important, the lucrative privilege of supplying Spanish America with African slaves. Then, in the Treaty of Paris, following the Seven Years' War (1756–1763), France, although it maintained its slave stations in Africa, surrendered its holdings in Canada and North America to the English and Spanish and conceded to England a dominant role in India. The wars of the eighteenth century also confirmed the naval superiority of Britain and its ability to protect its commercial interests on the world's oceans.

In addition, Great Britain had a business climate more favorable to commerce than did France. Despite the growth of French trade, in the eighteenth century most French businessmen and aristocrats still believed that commercial wealth was inferior to wealth derived from landowning or government office. This discouraged investment by aristocrats in commercial enterprises and spurred many successful businessmen to purchase country estates and abandon business for the life of a gentleman. Furthermore, many eighteenth-century Frenchmen avoided investments because of the "Mississippi Bubble," an episode that resulted from a plan devised in 1716 to fund the French national debt through the foundation of a central bank and stock sales in a new commercial enterprise, the Mississippi Company. Frenzied speculation caused stock prices to soar until the "bubble" broke in 1720, leaving thousands of penniless investors and confirming the French belief that investment in land and office was not only more "honorable" but safer than investment in commercial ventures.

England also experienced a stock crash in 1720, one connected with the South Sea Company, and wealthy Englishmen too were lured by the prestige of landowning. But in the wake of this stock collapse, the English government salvaged the Bank of England and other joint stock companies, thereby maintaining a more favorable foundation for finance and commercial investment and growth. In addition, the English, more dependent on trade than France, had always had a more positive view of mercantile activity, and sons of aristocrats who pursued business careers suffered none of the social ostracism their French counterparts experienced.

Great Britain also offered relatively more freedom to the merchant than did France. Although government protection, investment, and regulation had served France well in the seventeenth century, when it was trying to establish itself as a commercial and industrial power, by the late eighteenth century excessive government interference often stifled individual initiative by imposing long lists of regulations.

In England, mercantilist doctrine determined overall policy, but the government allowed individual traders and trading companies greater latitude in economic decision-making. By the end of the century, growing support for the doctrine of free trade promised to liberate further business from government restrictions, allowing individual investors and entrepreneurs to take full advantage of economic opportunities.

R. Campbell

OF THE MERCHANT

The London Tradesman, from which this excerpt is drawn, was described in its complete title as a "Compendious View of all the Trades, Professions and Arts both Liberal and Mechanical now Practiced in the City of London, Calculated for the Instruction of Youth in their Choice of Business." We know that the book was successful because it went through three editions in the decade after its publication in 1747. We know almost nothing, however, about "R. Campbell," the book's author. His rough style and unorthodox spelling suggest a limited formal education, but the title "esquire," which he affixed to his name on the title page, suggests that in his own eyes he had some social standing. In any case, Campbell knew London well and was familiar with its many businesses and trades. His section on merchants not only summarizes Great Britain's role in the world economy but expresses an admiration for commerce shared by many of his countrymen.

Questions
for Analysis

1. In Campbell's view, what distinguishes the career of a merchant from other trades?
2. What does Campbell see as the major social and economic benefits of commerce? How do his ideas about commerce compare with those of Colbert and those of the Chinese officials described in the biographies of Wang Tao-k'un (see Chapter 4)?
3. According to Campbell, how does commerce contribute to the strength of nations?
4. On the basis of Campbell's summation, describe and evaluate the relative impor-

tance of England's trade with (a) Ireland, (b) the Americas, (c) continental Europe, (d) the West Indies, (e) Asia, and (f) Africa.

Having gone through the several arts and trades, and discovered their dependence one upon another, we come now to a larger field, to the life, spring and motion of the trading world. The trades we have been hitherto speaking of, are confined to one place, one city or country; but commerce, the sphere of the merchant, extends itself to all the known world, and gives life and vigor to the whole machine. Some tradesmen we have treated of employ several different branches, some particular crafts dependent on them; but the merchant employs them all, sets the whole society at work, supplies them with materials to fabricate their goods, and vends their manufactures in the most distant corners of the globe. Other arts, crafts and mysteries[1] live upon one another, and never add one sixpence[2] to the aggregate wealth of the kingdom, but the merchant draws his honest gain from the distant poles, and every shilling[3] he returns more than he carried out, adds so much to the national riches and capital stock of the kingdom. Wherever he comes, wherever he lives, wealth and plenty follow him: The poor is set to work, manufactures flourish, poverty is banished, and public credit increases. The advantages of commerce is evident to all mankind; the wisest, the politest nations on earth now court her to their dominions: The Dutch and us are

two pregnant proofs of the power and advantages of traffic. Before we were a trading people, we were, it is true, subsisted by the natural produce of the Island; but we lived in a kind of penury, a stranger to money or affluence, inconsiderable in ourselves, and of no consequence to our neighbors: Our manners were rude, our knowledge of the world trifling; politeness was a stranger at our courts; ignorance and barbarous simplicity spread their empire over the whole Island: But we no sooner became a trading people, than the arts and sciences began to revive, and polished us out of our rustic simplicity and ignorance; the people found out new means of supplying their wants, and the nation in general accumulated riches at home, and commanded respect abroad; a new scene of power started out of commerce, and the wide ocean owned the sovereignty of imperial Britain. . . .

The Dutch is another instance of the mighty power of traffic; they possess a country not much larger than Yorkshire,[4] of a soil naturally barren: The number of people in the United Provinces are not one fifth of the number of the inhabitants of Great Britain; and yet this little state, but a few years ago a petty province of the Crown of Spain, can maintain armies and fleets capable of checking the power of the greatest monarchs on earth; they set themselves upon a level with crowned

---

1. In one of its eighteenth-century meanings, "mysteries" meant the specialized operations peculiar to an occupation.

2. Six English pennies, equaling half a shilling.

3. English coin, equaling 1/20 of a pound.

4. The largest English county, 6,122 square miles.

heads, and many private burgo-masters[5] can raise as much money upon their own credit, as the amount of the revenues of some kingdoms in Europe. We have had but a few days ago a flagrant instance of the vast influence of commerce, when six million sterling [pounds] was subscribed for the use of the government by private merchants in less than four hours. Tho' Spain is possessed of the rich gold and silver mines of Mexico and Peru, and the French King governs a large, populous, and rich kingdom, yet neither the kings of these two potent monarchies, nor all their subjects put together, could raise such a sum on private subscription. An alderman[6] of London can undertake for supplying the state with three or four million sterling, and raise it within the circle of his own acquaintance; a thing unheard-of in former ages, and would have been thought arrogance and folly even in the days of Queen Elizabeth,[7] to have supposed such a thing practicable. . . .

The trade of Britain may be divided into inland and foreign: Inland trade is the transporting of the commodities of one part of the kingdom to another, and especially to the grand mart of trade, the City of London. The chief articles imported to London from other parts of the Island are corn,[8] coal, hops, woolen and linen goods. . . .

The foreign merchant exports the goods of the growth or manufacture of this kingdom to the proper markets, and imports the commodities of other countries in exchange. . . .

We export to Jamaica, and the rest of the sugar colonies, all manner of materials for wearing apparel, household furniture of all sorts, cutlery and haberdashery wares,[9] watches, jewels and toys, East-India goods[10] of all sorts, some French wines, English malt liquor, linen cloths of the growth of Scotland, Ireland, and Germany, and our ships generally touch in Ireland and take in provisions, such as beef, pork, and butter. The returns from thence are rums, sugars, cotton, indigo, some fine woods, such as mahogany. . . .

We export to New England, New York, Pennsylvania, and the rest of our Northern Colonies, the same articles mentioned in the last paragraph; in a word, every article for the use of life, except provisions: We have in return, wood for shipping, corn and other provisions for the Southern Colonies: Some furs and skins, flax, rice and flax-seed from the provinces of Georgia and Pennsylvania, and fish from New England, for the Levant[11] market.

We export to Virginia and Maryland every article mentioned before, and have in return tobacco and pig-iron. From all the colonies we have ready money,[12] besides the goods sent them, which they procure by the illicit trade carried on between our island and the Spanish Main.

We export to Ireland the growth of our plantations, sugar and tobacco, East-India goods of all sorts, silks of the manufacture of England, and raw-silk, the product of Italy; broad-cloths, hats and stockings, gold and silver lace, and many other articles of the product of this country; for which we take nothing from them in return but ready money, except some linen cloth, and provisions for our Southern Colonies: The balance paid by Ireland in

---

5. Dutch municipal officials.

6. A London municipal official.

7. Elizabeth I, Queen of England from 1558 to 1603.

8. All grain crops, not just maize.

9. Needles, threads, buttons, and like goods.

10. Silks, porcelain, tea, coffee, spices.

11. Eastern Mediterranean.

12. Cash.

exchange of goods, and the money spent by their gentry and nobility in England, amount at least to one million sterling per annum. . . .

We export to Holland and Flanders some woolen goods, Birmingham and Sheffield goods,[13] coals, lead, tin, and lead-oar; sometimes corn, butter, cheese, and hides from Ireland; some leather, tobacco, and sugars. From thence we have Holland,[14] cambrick,[15] paper, whale-fin, and whale-oil, delft[16] and earthen-ware, thread and thread-laces, and a monstrous quantity of East-India goods run in upon our coast by the smugglers. The Dutch have scarce any export of commodities peculiar to themselves; the ground of their commerce is East-India goods and fish catched upon the coast of Britain; with these two articles they purchase all the product of the earth, and are more masters of the American wealth than the proud monarch, whose property it is.

We send to Germany, some woolen goods; but fewer of late years than formerly; some lead, leather, and tin: And in return have linen cloths, for our home consumption, and the use of our plantations; and pay a large balance in ready money.

We export to France scarce any thing but lead and tin, some tobacco to Dunkirk, and some salmon from Scotland; but we import wine, brandy, silks of various sorts, cambricks, laces of thread and of gold and silver, paper, cards, and an innumerable quantity of trifling jewels and toys; for all which we pay an annual balance of one million and a half. In reckoning up the imports from France, I should

have mentioned pride, vanity, luxury, and corruption; but as I could make no estimate by the custom-house books of the quantity of these goods entered, I chose to leave them out.

We export to Sweden and Denmark some woolen goods, tobacco, sugar, and a few East-India goods; but this last article is daily decaying: We send them soap and salt, and some fish; but the Dutch monopolize that branch. We receive in return deal, iron, copper, and oaken-planks; and pay them a great balance in ready money.

We send to the East country much the same goods last mentioned, and receive in return naval stores of all sorts, some linen cloth, and some goods of the growth of Persia, brought through Russia by land.

We used to send to Spain woolen goods of various fabrics, and furnished their plantations with the same articles we send to our own; we furnished them with Negroes from the coast of Guinea. For all which we had in return, some wines of the growth of Spain, fruits, oil, and olives, and a large remittance in gold and silver; but this trade has now dwindled to nothing, the French have engrossed it wholly to themselves.

We send to Portugal lead, tin, woolen goods, goods for their plantations in the Brazils, and have our returns in wines, oils, and ready money.

We send to Italy, fish from New England and Newfoundland, lead, tin, some woolen goods, leather, tobacco, sugars, and East-India goods; and have, in return, some rich wines, currants, silks wrought and raw, oils, olives and pickles.

To the East-Indies we send out some

---

13. Knives, scissors, swords, medical instruments.

14. A cotton and linen fabric.

15. A finely woven white cotton or linen fabric.

16. Glazed earthenware, usually blue and white.

woolen goods, lead, watches, clocks, fire-arms, hats; but our chief export is silver bullion: For which we receive in exchange, gold, diamonds, spices, drugs, teas, porcelain or china-ware, silk wrought and raw, cotton-cloths of different kinds, saltpeter,[17] etc. A great part of these goods are consumed at home and in our plantations, and the remainder is exported to other countries of Europe; the return of which makes amends for the bullion exported.

To Guinea[18] we send some woolen and linen goods, cutlery ware, fire-arms, swords, cutlasses, toys of glass and metal, etc. and receive in return Negroes for the use of our plantations, gold dust, and elephant's teeth.

To Turkey we send woolen goods of all sorts, lead, tin, East-India goods, sugars, etc. and receive in return, coffee, silks, mohair, carpets, etc. This is a beneficial branch of trade; the imports and exports being near upon a par.

Adam Smith

THE WEALTH OF NATIONS

Surprisingly little is known about Adam Smith, the leading economic thinker of the eighteenth century, famed for his devastating attack on mercantilism in *The Wealth of Nations.* Born in 1723 in a small Scottish fishing village and educated at Glasgow and Oxford, between 1751 and 1763 he held chairs in logic and moral philosophy at the University of Glasgow. The publication of his *Theory of Moral Sentiments* in 1759 ensured his literary and philosophical reputation. In 1763, he accepted a position as tutor of an English aristocrat's son and lived in France for three years, meeting many of the leading philosophes. From 1767 to 1776, he lived in semiretirement in Scotland and finished *The Wealth of Nations,* published in 1776. In 1778 he became commissioner of customs in Scotland and died in Edinburgh in 1790.

The Wealth of Nations went through five English editions and was published in several European translations in the eighteenth century. Its importance lies in its general approach to economics, which brought systematic analysis to wages, labor, trade, population, rents, and money supply, and in its theoretical assault on mercantilism, the theory and system that had guided government economic policies in Europe for two centuries. The key to economic growth, Smith asserted, was not regulation but free competition, among individuals and among nations.

Many English businessmen and a few politicians embraced Smith's doctrines of economic freedom, but the French Revolution and the Napoleonic wars prevented their implementation. Only in the early 1800s did the British convert a theoretical acceptance of free trade into actual policy.

---

17. Potassium nitrate, an ingredient in gunpowder.

18. West Africa, a center of the slave trade.

Questions
for Analysis

1. Smith denies that a nation's wealth consists in the amount of gold and silver it controls. What is the basis for his argument?
2. The novelty of Smith's ideas can best be understood by comparing them with those of a leading mercantilist such as Colbert (see Chapter 4). How do the two men differ on the following issues: (a) the benefits of government regulation, (b) economic competition among nations, and (c) the meaning of the balance of trade?
3. Smith suggests the paradox that each individual by pursuing his or her own self-interest promotes the general welfare of society. How is this possible?
4. Why, according to Smith, is the government establishment of high tariffs self-defeating?
5. What will be the short-term and long-term effects of free trade, according to Smith?

BOOK IV

Chapter I. Of the Principle of the Commercial or Mercantile System

That wealth consists in money, or in gold and silver, is a popular notion which naturally arises from the double function of money, as the instrument of commerce, and as the measure of value. In consequence of its being the instrument of commerce, when we have money we can more readily obtain whatever else we have occasion for, than by means of any other commodity. The great affair, we always find, is to get money. When that is obtained, there is no difficulty in making any subsequent purchase. In consequence of its being the measure of value, we estimate that of all other commodities by the quantity of money which they will exchange for. We say of a rich man that he is worth a great deal, and of a poor man that he is worth very little money. . . . To grow rich is to get money; and wealth and money, in short, are in common language, considered as in every respect synonymous.

A rich country, in the same manner as a rich man, is supposed to be a country abounding in money; and to heap up gold and silver in any country is supposed to be the readiest way to enrich it. . . .

In consequence of these popular notions, all the different nations of Europe have studied, though to little purpose, every possible means of accumulating gold and silver in their respective countries. Spain and Portugal, the proprietors of the principal mines which supply Europe with those metals, have either prohibited their exportation under the severest penalties, or subjected it to a considerable duty. The like prohibition seems anciently to have made a part of the policy of most other European nations. It is even to be found, where we should least of all expect to find it, in some old Scotch acts of parliament, which forbid, under heavy penalties, the carrying gold or silver *forth of the kingdom*. The like policy anciently took place in the kingdoms of France and England.

When those countries became commercial, the merchants found this prohibition, upon many occasions, extremely inconvenient. They could frequently buy more advantageously with gold and silver than with any other commodity, the foreign goods which they wanted, either to import into their own, or to carry to some other foreign country. They remonstrated, therefore, against this prohibition as hurtful to trade.

They represented, first, that the exportation of gold and silver in order to purchase foreign goods, did not always diminish the quantity of those metals in the kingdom. That, on the contrary, it might frequently increase that quantity; because, if the consumption of foreign goods was not thereby increased in the country, those goods might be re-exported to foreign countries, and, being there sold for a large profit, might bring back much more treasure than was originally sent out to purchase them. . . .

They represented, secondly, that this prohibition could not hinder the exportation of gold and silver, which, on account of the smallness of their bulk in proportion to their value, could easily be smuggled abroad. That this exportation could only be prevented by a proper attention to, what they called, the balance of trade. That when the country exported to a greater value than it imported, a balance became due to it from foreign nations, which was necessarily paid to it in gold and silver, and thereby increased the quantity of those metals in the kingdom. But that when it imported to a greater value than it exported, a contrary balance became due to the foreign nations, which was necessarily paid to them in the same manner, and thereby diminished that quantity. . . .

Those arguments were partly solid and partly sophistical. They were solid so far as they asserted that the exportation of gold and silver in trade might frequently be advantageous to the country. They were solid too, in asserting that no prohibition could prevent their exportation, when private people found any advantage in exporting them. But they were sophistical in supposing, that either to preserve or to augment the quantity of those metals required more the attention of government, than to preserve or to augment the quantity of any other useful commodities, which the freedom of trade, without any such attention, never fails to supply in the proper quantity. . . .

It would be too ridiculous to go about seriously to prove that wealth does not consist in money, or in gold and silver, but in what money purchases, and is valuable only for purchasing. Money, no doubt, makes always a part of the national capital; but it has already been shown that it generally makes but a small part, and always the most unprofitable part of it. . . .

The importation of gold and silver is not the principal, much less the sole, benefit which a nation derives from its foreign trade. Between whatever places foreign trade is carried on, they all of them derive two distinct benefits from it. It carries out that surplus part of the produce of their land and labor for which there is no demand among them, and brings back in return for it something else for which there is a demand. . . . By opening a more extensive market for whatever part of the produce of their labor may exceed the home consumption, it encourages them to improve its productive powers, and to augment its annual produce to the utmost, and thereby to increase the real revenue and wealth of the society. . . .

I thought it necessary, though at the hazard of being tedious, to examine at full length this popular notion that wealth consists in money, or in gold and silver. Money in common language, as I have already observed, frequently signifies wealth; and this ambiguity of expression has rendered this popular notion so familiar to us, that even they who are convinced of its absurdity are very apt to forget their own principles, and in the course of their reasonings to take it for granted as a certain and undeniable truth. Some of the best English writers upon commerce set out with observing that the wealth of a country consists, not in its gold and silver only, but in its lands, houses, and consumable goods of all different kinds. In the course of their reasonings, however, the lands, houses, and consumable goods seem to slip out of their memory, and the strain of their argument frequently supposes that all wealth consists in gold and silver, and that to multiply those metals is the great object of national industry and commerce. . . .

Chapter II. Of Restraints upon the Importation from Foreign Countries of Such Goods as Can Be Produced at Home

By restraining, either by high duties, or by absolute prohibitions, the importation of such goods from foreign countries as can be produced at home, the monopoly of the home market is more or less secured to the domestic industry employed in producing them. . . .

That this monopoly of the home market frequently gives great encouragement to that particular species of industry which enjoys it, and frequently turns towards that employment a greater share of both the labor and stock of the society than would otherwise have gone to it cannot be doubted. But whether it tends either to increase the general industry of the society, or to give it the most advantageous direction, is not, perhaps, altogether so evident. . . .

Every individual is continually exerting himself to find out the most advantageous employment for whatever capital he can command. It is his own advantage, indeed, and not that of the society, which he

has in view. But the study of his own advantage, naturally, or rather necessarily, leads him to prefer that employment which is most advantageous to the society.

First, every individual endeavors to employ his capital as near home as he can, and consequently as much as he can in the support of domestic industry, provided always that he can thereby obtain the ordinary, or not a great deal less than the ordinary, profits of stock.

Secondly, every individual who employs his capital in the support of domestic industry, necessarily endeavors so to direct that industry, that its produce may be of the greatest possible value. . . .

But the annual revenue of every society is always precisely equal to the exchangeable value of the whole annual produce of its industry, or rather is precisely the same thing with that exchangeable value. As every individual, therefore, endeavors as much as he can both to employ his capital in the support of domestic industry, and so to direct that industry that its produce may be of the greatest value, every individual necessarily labors to render the annual revenue of the society as great as he can. He generally, indeed, neither intends to promote the public interest, nor knows how much he is promoting it. By preferring the support of domestic to that of foreign industry, he intends only his own security; and by directing that industry in such a manner as its produce may be of the greatest value, he intends only his own gain, and he is in this, as in many other cases, led by an invisible hand to promote an end which was no part of his intention. Nor is it always the worse for the society that it was no part of it. By pursuing his own interest he frequently promotes that of the society more effectually than when he really intends to promote it. . . .

What is the species of domestic industry which his capital can employ, and of which the produce is likely to be of the greatest value, every individual, it is evident, can, in his local situation, judge much better than any statesman or lawgiver can do for him. The statesman who should attempt to direct private people in what manner they ought to employ their capitals, would not only load himself with a most unnecessary attention, but assume an authority which could safely be trusted, not only to no single person, but to no council or senate whatever, and which would nowhere be so dangerous as in the hands of a man who had folly and presumption enough to fancy himself fit to exercise it.

To give the monopoly of the home market to the produce of domestic industry, in any particular art or manufacture, is in some measure to direct private people in what manner they ought to employ their capitals, and must, in almost all cases, be either a useless or a hurtful regulation. If the produce of domestic can be brought there as cheap as that of foreign industry, the regulation is evidently useless. If it cannot, it must generally be hurtful. It is the maxim of every prudent master of a family, never to attempt to make at home what it will cost him more to make than to buy. The tailor does not attempt to make his own shoes, but buys them of the shoemaker. The shoemaker does not attempt to make his own clothes, but employs a tailor. The farmer attempts to make neither the one nor the other, but employs those different artificers. All of them find it for their interest to employ their whole industry in a way in which they have some advantage over their neighbors, and to purchase with a part of its produce, or, what is the same thing, with the price of a part of it, whatever else they have occasion for.

What is prudence in the conduct of every private family, can scarce be folly in that of a great kingdom. If a foreign country can supply us with a commodity cheaper than we ourselves can make it, better buy it of them with some part of the produce of our own industry, employed in a way in which we have some advantage. . . .

The natural advantages which one country has over another in producing particular commodities are sometimes so great, that it is acknowledged by all the world to be in vain to struggle with them. By means of glasses, hotbeds, and hot-walls, very good grapes can be raised in Scotland, and very good wine too can be made of them at about thirty times the expense for which at least equally good can be brought from foreign countries. Would it be a reasonable law to prohibit the importation of all foreign wines merely to encourage the making of claret and burgundy in Scotland? But if there would be a manifest absurdity in turning towards any employment thirty times more of the capital and industry of the country than would be necessary to purchase from foreign countries an equal quantity of the commodities wanted, there must be an absurdity, though not altogether so glaring, yet exactly of the same kind, in turning towards any such employment a thirtieth, or even a three hundredth part more of either. Whether the advantages which one country has over another be natural or acquired, is in this respect of no consequence. As long as the one country has those advantages, and the other wants them, it will always be more advantageous for the latter rather to buy of the former than to make. It is an acquired advantage only which one artificer has over his neighbor who exercises another trade; and yet they both find it more advantageous to buy of one another than to make what does not belong to their particular trades. . . .

To expect, indeed, that the freedom of trade should ever be entirely restored in Great Britain, is as absurd as to expect that an Oceania or Utopia should ever be established in it. Not only the prejudices of the public, but what is much more unconquerable, the private interests of many individuals, irresistibly oppose it. . . .

The undertaker of a great manufacture, who, by the home markets being suddenly laid open to the competition of foreigners, should be obliged to abandon his trade, would no doubt suffer very considerably. That part of his capital which had usually been employed in purchasing materials and in paying his workmen might, without much difficulty perhaps, find another employment. But that part of it which was fixed in workhouses, and in the instruments of trade, could scarce be disposed of without considerable loss. The equitable regard, therefore, to his interest requires that changes of this kind should never be introduced suddenly, but slowly, gradually, and after a very long warning.

Africa's Curse: The Slave Trade

During the eighteenth century Africa played a central role in the global economy, and the key was slavery. In Africa European merchants purchased slaves while profitably selling goods manufactured in Europe, such as hardware, rum, guns, and textiles; Europeans made further profits when they sold the slaves in the Americas; to complete the triangle, slave labor produced many of the goods sent from the Americas to Europe to be processed and sold in the world market. These included tobacco, indigo, and, most important, sugar and molasses. Thus, the growing prosperity of eighteenth-century Europe, especially Great Britain, depended to a great extent on the enslavement of Africans.

During the 1600s, and even more so in the 1700s, the numbers of slaves shipped to the Americas skyrocketed, largely in response to the demands of the Caribbean sugar growers. In the seventeenth century, more than 1.3 million Africans were enslaved and in the eighteenth more than 6 million. Throughout this period, the purveyors of these human commodities also changed. During the sixteenth century the Portuguese dominated the trade, during the seventeenth it was the Dutch, and during the eighteenth, the English, with the substantial involvement of New England and France.

AN AGREEMENT TO DELIVER TWO THOUSAND OR MORE SLAVES TO CURAÇAO

After the early success of the Dutch East India Company, the leaders of the Netherlands created a similar joint stock company, the West India Company, to carry on trade with the Americas. During its early existence, its most profitable commodity was human beings, especially after the Netherlands and Spain made peace in 1648. When in 1715 the company lost to the English the *asiento*, the contract for slave deliveries to Spanish America, profits plummeted. The following contract, drawn up on September 15, 1662, between the West India Company and a Spanish agent provides some chilling insights into the business of African slavery.

Questions for Analysis

1. What can you infer from this contract about the attitudes of the contracting parties toward blacks?
2. How many Europeans mentioned in the contract benefited financially from this venture?
3. What other Europeans *not* specifically mentioned also stood to benefit economically from the slave trade?
4. According to this document, what is the ideal "mix" of age and sex for a delivery of slaves?

*T*his day, September 15, 1662, there appeared before me, Pieter Padthuysen, notary public admitted to practice before the Court of Holland and resident in Amsterdam, in the presence of witnesses . . . , administrators of the chamber of the chartered West India Company in this city, with special commissions, on the one side, and Mr. Alexandro Bosco, having powers of attorney and instructions from Messrs. Domingo Grillo and Ambrosio Lomelino, resident in Madrid, Spain . . . on the other side, and declared that they had reached a mutual agreement and promise, which they, the parties in presence, do hereby agree and promise as follows.

The aforesaid administrators will without delay fit out one, two, or more ships, as they shall decide, and must have them ready in the Texel[1] one month after the signing of these presents, provided with cargoes, all necessary stores, and orders which shall be required for the voyage to be undertaken, so that they can sail with the first good wind.

Secondly, eight months after the sailing of the said ships, the above-named administrators shall deliver to the above-named Alexandro Bosco in his aforesaid quality or upon his orders, at the island of Curaçao,[2] 1,000 Negroes, under the conditions stipulated hereafter, but with the proviso that if the administrators are unable to purchase 1,000 Negroes and therefore bring a smaller number to Curaçao, but at least 700, that this number shall suffice, and likewise that they may deliver as many as 1,400 slaves to the aforesaid Alexandro Bosco if they possess them, and these may not be sold by the aforesaid administrators to others; with the further

---

1. The southernmost of the West Frisian Islands, at the entrance of the North Sea.

2. An island some sixty miles north of Venezuela, originally discovered by the Spaniards but taken over by the Dutch West India Company in 1634. Its major city, Willemstad, was an important port of exchange in the slave trade of the seventeenth and eighteenth centuries.

proviso, however, that if the aforesaid administrators deliver to the above-named Bosco 1,000 slaves of the stated quality, they may keep 100 of any remainder for their own use to be sent to their colonies in New Netherlands, Cayenne, etc.

On the other hand, the above-named Alexandro Bosco must be ready upon the expiration of the aforesaid eight months . . . to receive and to disembark upon the said island not only the aforesaid 1,000 Negroes but also such number as the aforesaid administrators may bring, to a total of 1,400, at the price established hereinafter, without any exceptions; but if the aforesaid administrators, upon the expiration of the aforesaid eight months . . . bring and deliver to Curaçao a total of less than 700 slaves, then the above-named Bosco shall also be obligated to receive the number brought in, but he may subtract from the monies to be paid for the Negroes delivered the sum of 20 pieces of eight[3] for each slave less than the figure of 700. . . .

All the aforesaid slaves shall be aged from 15 to 36 years, in good health, not blind or crippled, but able to board ship without help, and each shall be calculated as one piece fit for delivery; but all who are older than 36 and less than 45 years of age, or less than 15 years and more than 8 years, shall be counted at the rate of 3 to 2; those between 8 and 4 years, 2 for 1; and those below 4 years of age shall follow the mother; provided, however, that the second party to this contract shall not be held to accept Negroes older than 45 years of age except at his own discretion and after agreement on price with the clerk of the aforesaid administrators. With regard to their sex, two-thirds of the slaves must be men and one-third women, but in the

event that the discrepancy amounts to ten to twelve percent, then the respective contractors shall make a mutual settlement.

All these slaves being delivered in this condition, the second party to this contract must pay in his aforesaid quality at Curaçao 107½ pieces of eight of full value for each slave fit for delivery who is actually delivered to him there. Furthermore, the aforesaid Alexandro Bosco shall be obliged to pay a sum of 50,000 guilders (at the rate of 50 stivers to each piece of eight) as security as soon as the said ships to be fitted out in the Texel shall be ready to sail, so that the aforesaid second party may subtract for these 50,000 guilders the sum of 20,000 pieces of eight in Curaçao from the purchase price of the slaves who will be delivered in Curaçao.

If any ships of the aforesaid administrators should happen to meet any accident on their voyage to the Guinea coast or from there to Curaçao (which God forbid), or be taken by enemies or pirates, then a third shall be subtracted from the figure of 700 slaves if one ships fails to arrive and two-thirds if two ships out of three; and if all the slaves to be delivered are carried in two ships, then, if one ship fails to appear, the aforesaid administrators may complete their contract with half of the said 700, without any penalty for delivery of a lesser number or longer wait as stated above. But if (God forbid) all the ships should fail to arrive, or the ships of the party of the second part meet the same difficulties, both parties to this contract shall be released from the performance thereof for this period but shall also be held to repeat the voyage upon the same conditions as before.

The aforesaid Alexandro Bosco shall in the aforesaid quality name and maintain

---

3. One piece of eight, or *real*, equaled approximately fifty stivers; twenty stivers equaled one guilder.

in Curaçao a clerk to correspond with the director (of the West India Company) there and to receive the aforesaid slaves, and the director of that place shall provide him with every help and assistance without payment, and furnish him with wagons or ships to go any place he wishes to, provided that they reach agreement beforehand.

Finally, the aforesaid administrators shall fit out other ships six months after the departure of the first ships mentioned above, to deliver a number of slaves as above to Curaçao, except that the aforesaid administrators agree to deliver half of the aforesaid 700 slaves five months after the delivery of the first number and the other half three months later. . . .

To assure the performance of this contract, the above-mentioned administrators first obligate themselves in their aforesaid character to make available all the property, real and otherwise, of the Company, and especially all the slaves which the aforesaid administrators shall have brought to Curaçao as security for nondelivery at the prices established above, and also as security for the 50,000 guilders to be paid in cash, but not further, do pledge their own persons and property real and personal, present and future; and the said Alexandro Bosco in the said quality, places at the disposal of all courts the said sum of 50,000 guilders in particular and in addition the persons and property, real and personal without exception. Done in good faith in this city of Amsterdam in the presence of Mr. Jeuriaen Baechaet and the Honorable Jeuriaen Baeck, castellan of the Company's lodgings here, as witnesses thereto.

Olaudah Equiano

THE INTERESTING NARRATIVE OF THE LIFE OF OLAUDAH EQUIANO WRITTEN BY HIMSELF

Olaudah Equiano (1745?–1797) was born in Benin, an area that today is part of Nigeria. Captured and sold into slavery when he was about eleven, during his teens he served several masters, including Michael Henry Pascal, a lieutenant in the Royal Navy, and Robert King, a Quaker merchant from Philadelphia. Equiano accompanied Pascal on several naval campaigns during the Seven Years' War, and, after having been sold to King, made a dozen voyages from London to the West Indies. He learned English, enabling him to pursue a career as a shipping clerk and navigator in England after King granted his freedom in the late 1760s. Beginning in the 1770s he joined the English abolitionist movement, speaking out against slavery in a lecture tour that took him to dozens of cities in England, Scotland, and Ireland.

English abolitionists encouraged and supported his autobiography, which went through eight editions after it was published in 1789. Although part of a general strategy to turn the English public against the slave trade, Equiano's account of his experiences seems generally accurate and balanced. He describes the cruelties of the white slave traders as well as the kindness of his white masters and the English who befriended him. He shows great pride in his African ancestry but denounces the

Africans who bought and sold slaves. In the following excerpt, he describes his harsh introduction to slavery.

Questions
for Analysis

1. On the basis of Equiano's account, describe the role of Africans in the slave trade.
2. What does Equiano's account reveal about the impact of slaving on African society?
3. What were the characteristics of slavery in Africa itself?
4. Once aboard the slave ship, what in the slaves' experiences contributed to their despair and demoralization?
5. What explains the brutality of the crew members on the slave ship? To what extent was their treatment of slaves dictated by economic considerations?

KIDNAPPED

Generally when the grown people in the neighborhood were gone far in the fields to labor, the children assembled together in some of the neighbors' premises to play, and commonly some of us used to get up a tree to look out for any assailant or kidnapper that might come upon us, for they sometimes took those opportunities of our parents' absence to attack and carry off as many as they could seize. . . . One day, when all our people were gone out to their works as usual and only I and my dear sister were left to mind the house, two men and a woman got over our walls, and in a moment seized us both, and without giving us time to cry out or make resistance they stopped our mouths and ran off with us into the nearest wood. . . .

For a long time we had kept to the woods, but at last we came into a road which I believed I knew. I had now some hopes of being delivered, for we had advanced but a little way before I discovered some people at a distance, on which I began to cry out for their assistance: but my cries had no other effect than to make them tie me faster and stop my mouth, and then they put me into a large sack.

They also stopped my sister's mouth and tied her hands, and in this manner we proceeded till we were out of the sight of these people. When we went to rest the following night they offered us some victuals, but we refused it, and the only comfort we had was in being in one another's arms all that night and bathing each other with our tears. But alas! we were soon deprived of even the small comfort of weeping together. The next day proved a day of greater sorrow than I had yet experienced, for my sister and I were then separated while we lay clasped in each other's arms. It was in vain that we besought them not to part us; she was torn from me and immediately carried away, while I was left in a state of distraction not to be described. I cried and grieved continually, and for several days I did not eat anything but what they forced into my mouth. At length, after many days' traveling, during which I had often changed masters, I got into the hands of a chieftain in a very pleasant country. This man had two wives and some children, and they all used me extremely well and did all they could to comfort me, particularly the first wife, who was something like my mother. . . . This first master of mine, as I may call him, was a smith, and my principal employment was working his bellows, which were the same kind as I had seen in my vicinity. . . . I believe it was gold he worked, for it was of a lovely bright yellow color and was worn by the women on their wrists and ankles. I was there I suppose about a month, and they at last used to trust me some little distance from the house. This liberty I used in embracing every opportunity to inquire the way to my own home: and I also sometimes, for the same purpose, went with the maidens in the cool of the evenings to bring pitchers of water from the springs for the use of the house.

_____ ✧ _____

Equiano escapes but, terrified of being alone in the forest at night, returns to his household.

_____ ✧ _____

Soon after this my master's only daughter and child by his first wife sickened and died, which affected him so much that for some time he was almost frantic, and really would have killed himself had he not been watched and prevented. However, in a small time afterwards he recovered and I was again sold. I was now carried to the left of the sun's rising, through many different countries and a number of large woods. The people I was sold to used to carry me very often when I was tired either on their shoulders or on their backs. I saw many convenient well-built sheds along the roads at proper distances, to accommodate the merchants and travelers who lay in those buildings along with their wives, who often accompany them; and they always go well armed.

_____ ✧ _____

Equiano encounters his sister, but they are again quickly separated.

_____ ✧ _____

I was now more miserable, if possible, than before. The small relief which her presence gave me from pain was gone, and the wretchedness of my situation was redoubled by my anxiety after her fate and my apprehensions lest her sufferings should be greater than mine, when I could not be with her to alleviate them. Yes, thou dear partner of all my childish sports! thou sharer of my joys and sorrows! happy should I have ever esteemed myself to encounter every misery for you, and to procure your freedom by the sacrifice of my own. . . .

I did not long remain after my sister [departed]. I was again sold and carried through a number of places till, after traveling a considerable time, I came to a town called Tinmah in the most beautiful country I had yet seen in Africa. . . . I was sold here . . . by a merchant who lived and brought me there. I had been about two or three days at his house when a wealthy widow, a neighbor of his, came there one evening, and brought with her an only son, a young gentleman about my own age and size. Here they saw me; and, having taken a fancy to me, I was bought of the merchant, and went home with them. . . . The next day I was washed and perfumed, and when meal-time came I was led into the presence of my mistress, and ate and drank before her with her son. This filled me with astonishment; and I could scarce help expressing my surprise that the young gentleman should suffer me, who was bound, to eat with him who was free; and not only so, but that he would not at any time either eat or drink till I had taken first, because I was the eldest, which was agreeable to our custom. Indeed everything here, and all their treatment of me, made me forget that I was a slave. . . . There were likewise slaves daily to attend us, while my young master and I with other boys sported with our darts and bows and arrows, as I had been used to do at home.

In this resemblance to my former happy state I passed about two months; and I now began to think I was to be adopted into the family, and was beginning to be reconciled to my situation, and to forget by degrees my misfortunes, when all at once the delusion vanished; for without the least previous knowledge, one morning early, while my dear master and companion was still asleep, I was wakened out of my reverie to fresh sorrow, and hurried away. . . .

At last I came to the banks of a large river, which was covered with canoes in which the people appeared to live with their household utensils and provisions of all kinds. I was beyond measure astonished at this, as I had never before seen any water larger than a pond or a rivulet: and my surprise was mingled with no small fear when I was put into one of these canoes and we began to paddle and move along the river. We continued going on thus till night, and when we came to land and made fires on the banks, each family by themselves, some dragged their canoes on shore, others stayed and cooked in theirs and laid in them all night. . . . Thus I continued to travel, sometimes by land, sometimes by water, through different countries and various nations, till at the end of six or seven months after I had been kidnapped I arrived at the sea coast.

THE SLAVE SHIP

The first object which saluted my eyes when I arrived on the coast was the sea, and a slave ship which was then riding at anchor and waiting for its cargo. These filled me with astonishment, which was soon converted into terror when I was carried on board. I was immediately handled and tossed up to see if I were sound by some of the crew, and I was now persuaded that I had gotten into a world of bad spirits and that they were going to kill me. Their complexions too differing so much from ours, their long hair and the language they spoke (which was very different from any I had ever heard) united to confirm me in this belief. Indeed such were the horrors of my views and fears at the moment that, if ten thousand worlds had been my own, I would have freely parted with them all to have exchanged my condition with that of the meanest slave in my own country. When I looked round the ship too and saw a large furnace or copper boiling and a multitude of black people of every description chained together, every one of their countenances expressing dejection and sorrow, I no longer doubted of my fate; and quite overpowered with horror and anguish, I fell motionless on the deck and fainted. When I recovered a little I found some black people about me, who I believed were some of those who had brought me on board and had been receiving their pay; they talked to me in order to cheer me, but all in vain. . . .

I was soon put down under the decks, and there I received such a salutation in my nostrils as I had never experienced in my life: so that with the loathsomeness of the stench and crying together, I became so sick and low that I was not able to eat, nor had I the least desire to taste anything. I now wished for the last friend, death, to relieve me; but soon, to my grief, two of the white men offered me eatables, and on my refusing to eat, one of them held me fast by the hands and laid me across I think the windlass, and tied my feet while the other flogged me severely. I had never experienced anything of this kind before, and although, not being used to the water, I naturally feared that element the first time I saw it, yet nevertheless could I have got over the nettings I would have jumped over the side, but I could not; and besides, the crew used to watch us very closely who were not chained down to the decks, lest we should leap into the water: and I have seen some of these poor African prisoners most severely cut for attempting to do so, and hourly whipped for not eating. This indeed was often the case with myself. In a little time after, amongst the poor chained men I found some of my own nation, which in a small degree gave ease to my mind. I inquired of these what was to be done with us; they gave me to understand we were to be carried to these white people's country to work for them. I then was a little revived, and thought if it were no worse than working, my situation was not so desperate: but still I feared I should be put to death, the white people looked and acted, as I thought, in so savage a manner; for I had never seen among my people such instances of brutal cruelty, and this not only shown towards us blacks but also to some of the whites themselves. One white man in particular I saw, when we were permitted to be on deck, flogged so unmercifully with a large rope near the foremast that he died in consequence of it; and they tossed him over the side as they would have done a brute. This made me fear these people the more, and I expected nothing less than to be treated in the same manner. . . .

At last, when the ship we were in had got in all her cargo, they made ready with many fearful noises, and we were all put under deck so that we could not see how they managed the vessel. But this disappointment was the last of my sorrow. The stench of the hold while we were on the coast was so intolerably loathsome that it was dangerous to remain there for any time, and some of us had been permitted to stay on the deck for the fresh air; but now that the whole ship's cargo were confined together it became absolutely pestilential. The closeness of the place and the heat of the climate, added to the number in the ship, which was so crowded that

each had scarcely room to turn himself, almost suffocated us. This produced copious perspirations, so that the air soon became unfit for respiration from a variety of loathsome smells, and brought on a sickness among the slaves, of which many died, thus falling victims to the improvident avarice, as I may call it, of their purchasers. This wretched situation was again aggravated by the galling of the chains, now become insupportable, and the filth of the necessary tubs, into which the children often fell and were almost suffocated. The shrieks of the women and the groans of the dying rendered the whole a scene of horror almost inconceivable. Happily perhaps for myself I was soon reduced so low here that it was thought necessary to keep me almost always on deck, and from my extreme youth I was not put in fetters. . . .

One day, when we had a smooth sea and moderate wind, two of my wearied countrymen who were chained together (I was near them at the time), preferring death to such a life of misery, somehow made through the nettings and jumped into the sea: immediately another quite dejected fellow, who on account of his illness was suffered to be out of irons, also followed their example; and I believe many more would very soon have done the same if they had not been prevented by the ship's crew, who were instantly alarmed. Those of us that were the most active were in a moment put down under the deck, and there was such a noise and confusion amongst the people of the ship as I never heard before, to stop her and get the boat out to go after the slaves. However two of the wretches were drowned, but they got the other and afterwards flogged him unmercifully for thus attempting to prefer death to slavery. In this manner we continued to undergo more hardships than I can now relate, hardships which are inseparable from this accursed trade. Many a time we were near suffocation from the want of fresh air, which we were often without for whole days together. This and the stench of the necessary tubs carried off many. . . .

At last we came in sight of the island of Barbados, at which the whites on board gave a great shout and made many signs of joy to us. We did not know what to think of this, but as the vessel drew nearer we plainly saw the harbor and other ships of different kinds and sizes, and we soon anchored amongst them off Bridgetown. Many merchants and planters now came on board, though it was in the evening. They put us in separate parcels and examined us attentively. They also made us jump, and pointed to the land, signifying we were to go there. . . .

We were not many days in the merchant's custody before we were sold after their usual manner, which is this: On a signal given, (as the beat of a drum) the buyers rush at once into the yard where the slaves are confined, and make choice of that parcel they like best. The noise and clamor with which this is attended and the eagerness visible in the countenances of the buyers serve not a little to increase the apprehensions of the terrified Africans, who may well be supposed to consider them as the ministers of that destruction to which they think themselves devoted. In this manner, without scruple, are relations and friends separated, most of them never to see each other again. I remember in the vessel in which I was brought over, in the men's apartment there were several brothers who, in the sale, were sold in different lots; and it was very moving on this occasion to see and hear their cries at parting. O, ye nominal Christians! might not an African ask you, Learned you this from your God who says unto you, Do unto all men as you would men shall do unto you?

Indian Politics and European Trade

The relationship between India and Europe changed dramatically during the eighteenth century. Until then European merchants, content to remain in coastal cities to buy and sell their goods, had avoided Indian politics. In the early 1700s, however, the disintegration of the Mughal Empire forced the English East India Company, founded in 1600, and the French East India Company, founded in 1664, to intervene in Indian politics, preparing the way for British domination of the subcontinent.

During the War of the Austrian Succession (1740–1748) and the Seven Years' War (1756–1763), England and France were enemies, fighting not just in Europe but in the Americas and India. The Indian issue was decided in 1757 at the Battle of Plassey, when Robert Clive, the agent of the English East India Company, defeated his French rival, François Dupleix, and his ally, Siraj-ud-Daula, the native governor, or nawab, of the large east Indian state of Bengal. The British placed Mir Ja'far, their own puppet nawab, in power, an action that marks the beginning of British rule in India, even though their power barely extended beyond Bengal for the next fifty years.

These events mark a watershed in world history. Previously Europeans had subjugated only the poorly armed and disorganized peoples of the Americas. British rule in India was the first example of a European nation achieving political dominance over one of the ancient civilizations of Asia. That it was accomplished by a small number of traders and adventurers thousands of miles from home showed how large a gap had opened between the profit-seeking, politically unified, and technologically sophisticated Europeans and the peoples of the world's traditional societies.

François Dupleix

MEMOIR OF 1753

The son of a merchant, François Dupleix (1697–1763) arrived in India in 1721, and, after amassing a huge fortune, in 1742 became governor general of the French East India Company, with authority to oversee all French interests in India. Dupleix believed that France should conquer Indian territories and use local tax revenues to pay for the military costs of fighting the British. He took this step in 1749, when, in return for intervening in a local struggle, France gained control of territories in Pondicherry, an area in southeast India. The cautious directors of the French East India Company opposed such adventures and in 1754 recalled Dupleix in disgrace when he defied their orders to end his meddling in local politics. Before his dismissal, he prepared the following *Memoir*, or memorandum, for the company directors in defense of his policies.

Questions for Analysis

1. Why does Dupleix feel that the prospects of French trade in India are bleak?
2. What is Dupleix's solution to the problem of the outflow of gold and silver from France to India?
3. To what extent do Dupleix's arguments reflect Colbert's mercantilistic philosophy (see Chapter 4)?

*T*hese two points form the subject matter of this *mémoire*. . . .

All the Company's commerce in India is shared with the English, the Dutch, the Portuguese and the Danes. . . . This division of trade, or rather this rivalry, has served to raise considerably the price of merchandise here and has contributed quite a little toward cheapening the qual-ity — two unfortunate circumstances which, of course, further reduce the price and profits in Europe. . . . Our Company can hope for no monopoly in the Indian trade. We shall always share whatever we deal in with other countries. We can, therefore, hope for no other profits than those being made at present. We should even anticipate that instead of increasing, they are likely to decline and that very soon, if we force the trade beyond a certain point. . . . The only possible way of making profits on inferior merchandise would be to have a large and regular revenue; then the losses could be offset by our income. Those of our rivals who did not have such a resource would be obliged to give up this branch of commerce, or else restrict themselves to their national market. . . .

I think that I have shown the truth of the first point of this memorandum, and the complete proof can be found in the Company's books. I pass now to the second truth, which is that every commercial company should avoid the exportation of bullion from the kingdom. It is a maxim long established that the more the specie[1] circulates in a state, the more flourishing is the state's condition, and the more the state can be helped and sustained by it. It is, then, good policy to seek every means of preventing its exportation. But it is very hard, not to say impossible, to trade in China and India without exporting a specie. . . . Since it is obviously impossible to keep all our specie in France, we should neglect nothing to reduce to a minimum its exportation to India, whence it will never flow back to Europe. Our manufactures in wool, gilt, etc., can diminish such exportation, but not to the extent we desire; we need something else, and this can only be found in a fixed, constant, and abundant local revenue. Permit me, kindly, to give you[2] a brief illustration.

Let us suppose that the Company is obliged yearly to send twelve millions to India. Wool, cloth, and other exported manufactures amount to two millions, so there remains ten millions to be sent in specie, a large sum and one exported only too frequently. It could be reduced by at least half, and might even entirely cease, if the local revenue amounted to ten millions. . . .

These are the motives which have led me to sacrifice everything to attain this end. I have been deprived myself of the rest to which my long years of work have entitled me. . . . This work . . . would have been already accomplished, if I had been better supported, not only here but in my native land, which has looked upon the benefits I have acquired for it with too great indifference. . . . I shall content myself by saying that, in spite of all the obstacles, I have succeeded in procuring for my nation a revenue of at least five millions. My intention was to raise it to ten millions, and I would have succeeded. . . . Yes, I can truly say that if what has arrived this year had been drawn from France's regular troops, all the fighting would now be over and the Company would be enjoying more than ten millions in revenue.

▨ Robert Clive

LETTER TO WILLIAM PITT ON INDIA

Robert Clive (1725–1774) was the son of an English landowner and politician, who, after an unspectacular career as a student, at the age of eighteen entered the service of the East India Company and sailed to India. Commissioned in the company's

---

1. Gold and silver.

2. The directors of the French West India Company.

army four years later, he distinguished himself by helping to defeat the French and their Indian supporters at the Battle of Arcot in 1751. Six years later he led British forces in their decisive victory at Plassey. Subsequently, he became governor of Bengal and established the practice by which the British gained the right of collecting taxes in return for making annual payments to the Mughal emperor.

The following letter, written on January 7, 1759, is directed to William Pitt the Elder, later Earl of Chatham (1708–1778), who since 1757 was the minister responsible for directing the British effort against France in the Seven Years' War. In it Clive describes the situation in India two years after the Battle of Plassey.

Questions
for Analysis

1. What is Clive's vision of Great Britain's role in India?
2. Why does Clive feel the British will encounter little difficulty in establishing their political authority in India?
3. According to Clive, what benefits will accrue to Great Britain if it is able to gain control over India?
4. What does Clive's letter reveal about the state of the Mughal Empire in the mid-eighteenth century?
5. What seems to be Clive's attitude toward the Indians and their rulers?
6. What similarities and differences are there between Dupleix's and Clive's arguments in favor of more government support for their Indian enterprises?

The close attention you bestow on the affairs of the British nation in general has induced me to trouble you with a few particulars relative to India, and to lay before you an exact account of the revenues of this country, the genuineness whereof you may depend upon, as it has been faithfully extracted from the Minister's books.

The great revolution that has been effected here by the success of the English arms, and the vast advantages gained to the Company[1] by a treaty concluded in consequence thereof, have, I observe, in some measure, engaged the public attention; but much more may yet in time be done, if the Company will exert themselves in the manner the importance of their present possessions and future prospects deserves. I have represented to them in the strongest terms the expediency of sending out and keeping up constantly such a force as will enable them to embrace the first opportunity of further aggrandizing themselves; and I dare pronounce, from a thorough knowledge of this country's government, and of the genius of the people, acquired by two years' application and experience, that such an opportunity will soon offer. The reigning Subah,[2] whom the victory at Plassey invested with the sovereignty of

---

1. The British East India Company.

2. Subah is synonymous with nawab; both terms refer to provincial governors within the

Mughal Empire. The individual to whom Clive refers is Mir Ja'far, the British puppet named nawab of Bengal after the Battle of Plassey.

these provinces, still, it is true, retains his attachment to us, and probably, while he has no other support, will continue to do so; but Muslims are so little influenced by gratitude, that should he ever think it his interest to break with us, the obligations he owes us would prove no restraint: and this is very evident from his having lately removed his Prime Minister, and cut off two or three principal officers, all attached to our interest, and who had a share in his elevation. Moreover, he is advanced in years; and his son is so cruel, worthless a young fellow, and so apparently an enemy to the English, that it will be almost unsafe trusting him with the succession. So small a body as two thousand Europeans will secure us against any apprehensions from either the one or the other; and, in case of their daring to be troublesome, enable the Company to take the sovereignty upon themselves.

There will be the less difficulty in bringing about such an event, as the natives themselves have no attachment whatever to particular princes; and as, under the present Government, they have no security for their lives or properties, they would rejoice in so happy an exchange as that of a mild for a despotic Government: and there is little room to doubt our easily obtaining the Mughal's grant in confirmation thereof, provided we agreed to pay him the stipulated allotment out of the revenues, viz. fifty lacs[3] annually. This has, of late years, been very ill-paid, owing to the distractions in the heart of the Mughal Empire, which have disabled that court from attending to their concerns in the distant provinces: and the Vizier[4] has actually wrote to me, desiring I would engage the Nawab to make the payments agreeable to the former usage. . . . That

this would be agreeable to the Mughal can hardly be questioned, as it would be so much to his interest to have these countries under the dominion of a nation famed for their good faith, rather than in the hands of people who, a long experience has convinced him, never will pay him his proportion of the revenues, unless awed into it by the fear of the Imperial army marching to force them thereto.

But so large a sovereignty may possibly be an object too extensive for a mercantile Company; and it is to be feared they are not of themselves able, without the nation's assistance, to maintain so wide a dominion. I have therefore presumed, Sir, to represent this matter to you, and submit it to your consideration, whether the execution of a design, that may hereafter be still carried to greater lengths, be worthy of the Government's taking it into hand. I flatter myself I have made it pretty clear to you, that there will be little or no difficulty in obtaining the absolute possession of these rich kingdoms; and that with the Mughal's own consent, on condition of paying him less than a fifth of the revenues thereof. Now I leave you to judge, whether an income yearly of upwards of two millions sterling, with the possession of three provinces abounding in the most valuable productions of nature and of art, be an object deserving the public attention; and whether it be worth the nation's while to take the proper measures to secure such an acquisition — an acquisition which, under the management of so able and disinterested a minister, would prove a source of immense wealth to the kingdom, and might in time be appropriated in part as a fund towards diminishing the heavy load of debt under which we at present labor. Add to these advantages

---

3. Synonymous with lakh, meaning 100,000. Clive states the British will pay 5 million rupees, a unit of Indian money, to the emperor.

4. A high official in the imperial administration.

the influence we shall thereby acquire over the several European nations engaged in the commerce here, which these could no longer carry on but through our indulgence, and under such limitations as we should think fit to prescribe. It is well worthy of consideration, that this project may be brought about without draining the mother country, as has been too much the case with our possessions in America. A small force from home will be sufficient, as we always make sure of any number we please of black[5] troops, who, being both much better paid and treated by us than by the country powers, will very readily enter into our service. . . .

The greatest part of the troops belonging to this establishment are now employed in an expedition against the French in Deccan; and, by the accounts lately received from thence, I have great hopes we shall succeed in extirpating them from the province of Golconda,[6] where they have reigned lords paramount so long, and from whence they have drawn their principal resources during the troubles upon the coast. . . .

May the zeal and the vigorous measures, projected from the service of the nation, which have so eminently distinguished your ministry, be crowned with all the success they deserve, is the most fervent wish of him who is, with the greatest respect,

Sir,
Your most devoted humble servant,
(Signed)   Robert Clive

Calcutta,
7th January, 1759

The Opening of China to Western Trade

As discussed in Chapter 4, in 1513, only fifteen years after reaching India, the Portuguese sailed into Canton in southern China, dreaming of lucrative profits. Subsequently, merchants from every major European trading nation sailed to China, with similar dreams. They all were disappointed.

In comparison to European trade with India, the East Indies, the Americas, and Africa, commerce with China was minimal. The emperor and his officials were not averse to the gold and silver European merchants brought to China in exchange for silk, tea, and porcelain, but they nonetheless limited and closely regulated commercial contacts with the "South Sea barbarians." These actions stemmed partly from their traditional Confucian disdain for commercial activity and partly from their conviction that contact with outsiders, especially aggressive Europeans, endangered the stability and conservative values of China. They thus limited Chinese-European trade to Macao, a Portuguese enclave, and Canton, where Europeans were required to deal only with government-appointed merchants and to depart as soon as their business was finished.

In the nineteenth century, however, the Chinese had no choice but to abandon

---

5. Clive's term for native Indians.   6. An area of central India.

their self-imposed isolation. Europeans forced them to accept a series of humiliating treaties, which not only opened their country to Western trade but also to heightened Western missionary activity, economic control, and political interference. The West's intrusion forced the Chinese into an agonizing reappraisal of their values and sped the demise of the ancient imperial system.

Ch'ien Lung

LETTER TO GEORGE III

During the eighteenth century, the British, the leading traders with China, became increasingly dissatisfied with the inconveniences and limitations of their trade agreement. The East India Company petitioned the emperor several times for a liberalization of China's policy, but, after repeated failures, the government sent an official envoy from King George III himself to the imperial court. Thus, in 1792 Lord George Macartney arrived in Peking (modern Beijing) with a letter from the king to Emperor Ch'ien Lung (1735–1795), requesting British diplomatic representation at the imperial court, an easing of trade regulations, and the opening of more Chinese ports to trade. The emperor rejected all the British requests for reasons stated in the following letter.

Questions
for Analysis

1. What reasons does the emperor state for his rejection of the British proposals?
2. How does the emperor view the British? What is his sense of his and China's position in the world?
3. According to the emperor, what harm would result if he granted the British requests?
4. How does he view China's economic position?

You, O King, from afar have yearned after the blessings of our civilization, and in your eagerness to come into touch with our converting influence have sent an Embassy across the sea bearing a memorial.[1] I have already taken note of your respectful spirit of submission, have treated your mission with extreme favor and loaded it with gifts, besides issuing a mandate to you, O King, and honoring you with the bestowal of valuable presents. Thus has my indulgence been manifested.

Yesterday your Ambassador petitioned my Ministers to memorialize me regard-

---

1. Memorandum.

ing your trade with China, but his proposal is not consistent with our dynastic usage and cannot be entertained. Hitherto, all European nations, including your own country's barbarian merchants, have carried on their trade with our Celestial Empire at Canton. Such has been the procedure for many years, although our Celestial Empire possesses all things in prolific abundance and lacks no product within its own borders. There was therefore no need to import the manufactures of outside barbarians in exchange for our own produce. But as the tea, silk and porcelain which the Celestial Empire produces, are absolute necessities to European nations and to yourselves, we have permitted, as a signal mark of favor, that foreign *hongs*[2] should be established at Canton, so that your wants might be supplied and your country thus participate in our beneficence. But your Ambassador has now put forward new requests which completely fail to recognize the Throne's principle to "treat strangers from afar with indulgence," and to exercise a pacifying control over barbarian tribes, the world over. Moreover, our dynasty, swaying the myriad races of the globe, extends the same benevolence towards all. Your England is not the only nation trading at Canton. If other nations, following your bad example, wrongfully importune my ear with further impossible requests, how will it be possible for me to treat them with easy indulgence? Nevertheless, I do not forget the lonely remoteness of your island, cut off from the world by intervening wastes of sea, nor do I overlook your excusable ignorance of the usages of our Celestial Empire. I have consequently commanded my Ministers to enlighten

your Ambassador on the subject, and have ordered the departure of the mission. But I have doubts that, after your Envoy's return he may fail to acquaint you with my view in detail or that he may be lacking in lucidity, so that I shall now proceed . . . to issue my mandate on each question separately. In this way you will, I trust, comprehend my meaning. . . .

Your request for a small island near Chusan,[3] where your merchants may reside and goods be warehoused, arises from your desire to develop trade. As there are neither foreign *hongs* nor interpreters in or near Chusan, where none of your ships have ever called, such an island would be utterly useless for your purposes. Every inch of the territory of our Empire is marked on the map and the strictest vigilance is exercised over it all: even tiny islets and far-lying sand-banks are clearly defined as part of the provinces to which they belong. Consider, moreover, that England is not the only barbarian land which wishes to establish . . . trade with our Empire: supposing that other nations were all to imitate your evil example and beseech me to present them each and all with a site for trading purposes, how could I possibly comply? This also is a flagrant infringement of the usage of my Empire and cannot possibly be entertained.

The next request, for a small site in the vicinity of Canton city, where your barbarian merchants may lodge or, alternatively, that there be no longer any restrictions over their movements at Aomen,[4] has arisen from the following causes. Hitherto, the barbarian merchants of Europe have had a definite locality assigned to them at Aomen for residence and trade,

2. Groups of merchants.

3. A group of islands in the East China Sea at the entrance to Hangchow Bay.

4. A city some 45 miles to the south of Canton, at the lower end of the Pearl (Zhu) River delta.

and have been forbidden to encroach an inch beyond the limits assigned to that locality. . . . If these restrictions were withdrawn, friction would inevitably occur between the Chinese and your barbarian subjects, and the results would militate against the benevolent regard that I feel towards you. From every point of view, therefore, it is best that the regulations now in force should continue unchanged. . . .

Regarding your nation's worship of the Lord of Heaven, it is the same religion as that of other European nations. Ever since the beginning of history, sage Emperors and wise rulers have bestowed on China a moral system and inculcated a code, which from time immemorial has been religiously observed by the myriads of my subjects.[5] There has been no hankering after heterodox doctrines. Even the European (missionary) officials in my capital are forbidden to hold intercourse with Chinese subjects; they are restricted within the limits of their appointed residences, and may not go about propagating their religion. The distinction between Chinese and barbarian is most strict, and your Ambassador's request that barbari-

ans shall be given full liberty to disseminate their religion is utterly unreasonable.

It may be, O King, that the above proposals have been wantonly made by your Ambassador on his own responsibility, or peradventure you yourself are ignorant of our dynastic regulations and had no intention of transgressing them when you expressed these wild ideas and hopes. . . . If, after the receipt of this explicit decree, you lightly give ear to the representations of your subordinates and allow your barbarian merchants to proceed to Chêkiang and Tientsin,[6] with the object of landing and trading there, the ordinances of my Celestial Empire are strict in the extreme, and the local officials, both civil and military, are bound reverently to obey the law of the land. Should your vessels touch the shore, your merchants will assuredly never be permitted to land or to reside there, but will be subject to instant expulsion. In that event your barbarian merchants will have had a long journey for nothing. Do not say that you were not warned in due time! Tremblingly obey and show no negligence! A special mandate!

▓ Lin Tse-hsu

LETTER TO QUEEN VICTORIA

Emperor Ch'ien Lung was correct when he stated in his letter to King George III that the Chinese had "no need to import the manufactures of outside barbarians." In China, more so than any other part of Asia, demand for European goods was minimal. For centuries Europeans had no choice but to leave large amounts of gold and silver in China to pay for the goods they prized.

In the late eighteenth century, however, European merchants, mainly British, discovered a product that millions of Chinese could not resist: opium. Although the Chinese had used opium as a medicine for centuries, smoking it as a narcotic dates

---

5. The reference is to Confucianism.   6. Two Chinese port cities.

from the seventeenth century, when the Spaniards and Portuguese introduced it. By the early 1800s, opium addiction affected millions of Chinese at every social and economic level. In the 1830s, almost 2 million pounds of opium were being sold in China every year, mostly by the British, who in India now had access to the world's major poppy-growing areas.

Among Chinese officials, alarm over the opium trade was evident in the eighteenth century, partly because of the ruination that opium addiction caused to millions of Chinese but largely because of the outflow of bullion resulting from the enormous Chinese demand. Until 1838, however, efforts to restrict the opium trade were halfhearted and ineffectual. In that year, Emperor Tao-kuang (1821–1851) decided to ban the importation of opium altogether and sent one of his most capable officials, Lin Tse-hsu (1785–1850), to Canton to implement his decree. Lin arrived in 1839, confiscated several thousand tons of opium owned by foreign merchants, and had it burned. He also demanded that all merchants pledge to refrain from further sales of opium in China. When some refused, he took two actions: he had many Britishers jailed, and, on August 27, 1839, he wrote to their sovereign, Queen Victoria, imploring her to halt the trade in opium. Thus he combined the use of force with the traditional Confucian approach of winning over one's political opponents through moral persuasion.

Questions for Analysis

1. What differences does Lin Tse-hsu see in the motives of the Chinese and Europeans in regard to trade?
2. By what moral arguments does Lin Tse-hsu hope to persuade Queen Victoria to order the end of opium trading?
3. What seems to be Lin Tse-hsu's sense of Victoria's powers as queen of England?
4. Are there differences between Lin's view of the outside world and that of Emperor Ch'ien Lung?

His Majesty the Emperor comforts and cherishes foreigners as well as Chinese: he loves all the people in the world without discrimination. Whenever profit is found, he wishes to share it with all men; whenever harm appears, he likewise will eliminate it on behalf of all of mankind. His heart is in fact the heart of the whole universe.

Generally speaking, the succeeding rulers of your honorable country have been respectful and obedient. Time and again they have sent petitions to China, saying: "We are grateful to His Majesty the Emperor for the impartial and favorable treatment he has granted to the citizens of my country who have come to China to trade," etc. I am pleased to learn that you, as the ruler of your honorable country, are thoroughly familiar with the principle of righteousness and are grateful for the favor that His Majesty the Emperor has bestowed upon your subjects. Because of this fact, the Celestial Empire, following its traditional policy of treating foreigners with kindness, has been doubly considerate towards the people from England. You have traded in China for almost 200 years, and as a result, your country has become wealthy and prosperous.

As this trade has lasted for a long time, there are bound to be unscrupulous as well as honest traders. Among the unscrupulous are those who bring opium to China to harm the Chinese; they succeed so well that this poison has spread far and wide in all the provinces. You, I hope, will certainly agree that people who pursue material gains to the great detriment of the welfare of others can be neither tolerated by Heaven nor endured by men. . . .

Your country is more than 60,000 *li*[1] from China. The purpose of your ships in coming to China is to realize a large profit. Since this profit is realized in China and is in fact taken away from the Chinese people, how can foreigners return injury for the benefit they have received by sending this poison to harm their benefactors? They may not intend to harm others on purpose, but the fact remains that they are so obsessed with material gain that they have no concern whatever for the harm they can cause to others. Have they no conscience? I have heard that you strictly prohibit opium in your own country, indicating unmistakably that you know how harmful opium is. You do not wish opium to harm your own country, but you choose to bring that harm to other countries such as China. Why?

The products that originate from China are all useful items. They are good for food and other purposes and are easy to sell. Has China produced one item that is harmful to foreign countries? For instance, tea and rhubarb are so important to foreigners' livelihood that they have to consume them every day. Were China to concern herself only with her own advantage without showing any regard for other people's welfare, how could foreigners continue to live? Foreign products like woolen cloth and beiges[2] rely on Chinese raw materials such as silk for their manufacturing. Had China sought only her own advantage, where would the foreigners' profit come from? The products that foreign countries need and have to import from China are too numerous to enumerate: from food products such as molasses, ginger, and cassia[3] to useful necessities such as silk and porcelain. The imported goods from foreign countries, on the other hand, are merely playthings which can be easily dispensed with without causing any ill effect. Since we do not need these things really, what harm would come if we should decide to stop foreign trade altogether? The reason why we unhesitantly allow foreigners to ship out such Chinese products as tea and silk is that we feel that wherever there is an advantage, it should be shared by all the people in the world. . . .

I have heard that you are a kind, compassionate monarch. I am sure that you will not do to others what you yourself do not desire. I have also heard that you have instructed every British ship that sails for Canton not to bring any prohibited goods to China. It seems that your policy is as enlightened as it is proper. The fact that British ships have continued to bring opium to China results perhaps from the impossibility of making a thorough in-

---

1. A Chinese measurement of distance, approximately equal to one-third of a mile.

2. A soft wool fabric, unbleached and undyed, thus having a tan color.

3. A spice similar to cinnamon.

spection of all of them owing to their large numbers. I am sending you this letter to reiterate the seriousness with which we enforce the law of the Celestial Empire and to make sure that merchants from your honorable country will not attempt to violate it again.

I have heard that the areas under your direct jurisdiction such as London, Scotland, and Ireland do not produce opium; it is produced instead in your Indian possessions such as Bengal, Madras, Bombay, Patna, and Malwa. In these possessions the English people not only plant opium poppies that stretch from one mountain to another but also open factories to manufacture this terrible drug. As months accumulate and years pass by, the poison they have produced increases in its wicked intensity, and its repugnant odor reaches as high as the sky. Heaven is furious with anger, and all the gods are moaning with pain! It is hereby suggested that you destroy and plow under all of these opium plants and grow food crops instead, while issuing an order to punish severely anyone who dares to plant opium poppies again. If you adopt this policy of love so as to produce good and exterminate evil, Heaven will protect you, and gods will bring you good fortune. Moreover, you will enjoy a long life and be rewarded with a multitude of children and grandchildren! In short, by taking this one measure, you can bring great happiness to others as well as yourself. Why do you not do it?

The right of foreigners to reside in China is a special favor granted by the Celestial Empire, and the profits they have made are those realized in China. As time passes by, some of them stay in China for a longer period than they do in their own country. For every government, past or present, one of its primary functions is to educate all the people living within its jurisdiction, foreigners as well as its own cit-

izens, about the law and to punish them if they choose to violate it. Since a foreigner who goes to England to trade has to obey the English law, how can an Englishman not obey the Chinese law when he is physically within China? The present law calls for the imposition of the death sentence on any Chinese who has peddled or smoked opium. Since a Chinese could not peddle or smoke opium if foreigners had not brought it to China, it is clear that the true culprits of a Chinese's death as a result of an opium conviction are the opium traders from foreign countries. Being the cause of other people's death, why should they themselves be spared from capital punishment? A murderer of one person is subject to the death sentence; just imagine how many people opium has killed! This is the rationale behind the new law which says that any foreigner who brings opium to China will be sentenced to death by hanging or beheading. Our purpose is to eliminate this poison once and for all and to the benefit of all mankind. . . .

Our Celestial Empire towers over all other countries in virtue and possesses a power great and awesome enough to carry out its wishes. But we will not prosecute a person without warning him in advance; that is why we have made our law explicit and clear. If the merchants of your honorable country wish to enjoy trade with us on a permanent basis, they must fearfully observe our law by cutting off, once and for all, the supply of opium. Under no circumstance should they test our intention to enforce the law by deliberately violating it. You, as the ruler of your honorable country, should do your part to uncover the hidden and unmask the wicked. It is hoped that you will continue to enjoy your country and become more and more respectful and obeisant. How wonderful it is that we can all enjoy the blessing of peace!

■

TREATIES OF NANKING, THE BOGUE, AND TIENTSIN

No one knows how Queen Victoria reacted to Lin Tse-hsu's letter. We are better informed about the response of her flamboyant Secretary of State for Foreign Affairs, Lord Palmerston (1784–1865), who was never one to suffer insults to the dignity of Great Britain. He fired off a series of demands to the Chinese, including complete payment by the imperial government for the destroyed opium, and dispatched British ships and soldiers to China in order to convince the Chinese of his "seriousness." The result was the Opium War (1839–1842), in which the poorly trained and technologically inferior Chinese troops were overwhelmed by the outnumbered British. Sixteen years later, a combined English and French force defeated the Chinese again in the Anglo-French War. After these defeats, the Chinese had no choice but to accept the Treaties of Nanking (1842), the Bogue (1843), and Tientsin (1858), all of which mocked the bold words of Emperor Ch'ien Lung and Lin Tse-hsu, and set the pattern of relations between China and the West for the rest of the nineteenth century.

Questions for Analysis

1. How did the British trading position in China change as a result of the Treaty of Nanking?
2. How does the Treaty of Nanking limit the authority and powers of the Chinese government?
3. How does the Treaty of the Bogue protect the British against potential foreign competition?
4. Taken together, in what specific ways do the three treaties undermine the sovereign authority of the Chinese government?
5. Of the three treaties, Chinese officials resisted most bitterly the Treaty of Tientsin. What in this treaty may explain this?

TREATY OF NANKING (1842)

Article I. There shall henceforward be Peace and Friendship between. . . . (England and China) and between their respective Subjects, who shall enjoy full security and protection for their persons and property within the Dominions of the other.

Article II. His Majesty the Emperor of China agrees that British Subjects, with

their families and establishments, shall be allowed to reside, for the purpose of carrying on their Mercantile pursuits, without molestation or restraint at the Cities and Towns of Canton, Amoy, Foochowfu, Ningpo, and Shanghai, and Her Majesty the Queen of Great Britain, etc., will appoint Superintendents or Consular Officers, to reside at each of the above-named Cities or Towns, to be the medium of communication between the

Chinese Authorities and the said Merchants, and to see that the just Duties and other Dues of the Chinese Government as hereafter provided for, are duly discharged by Her Britannic Majesty's Subjects.

Article III. It being obviously necessary and desirable, that British Subjects should have some Port whereat they may careen[1] and refit their Ships, when required, and keep Stores for that purpose, His Majesty the Emperor of China cedes to Her Majesty the Queen of Great Britain, etc., the Island of Hongkong, to be possessed in perpetuity by Her Britannic Majesty, Her Heirs and Successors, and to be governed by such Laws and Regulations as Her Majesty the Queen of Great Britain, etc., shall see fit to direct.

Article IV. The Emperor of China agrees to pay the sum of Six Millions of Dollars[2] as the value of Opium which was delivered up at Canton in the month of March, 1839, as a Ransom for the lives of Her Britannic Majesty's Superintendent and Subjects, who had been imprisoned and threatened with death by the Chinese High Officers.

Article V. The Government of China having compelled the British Merchants trading at Canton to deal exclusively with certain Chinese Merchants called Hong Merchants (or Cohong) who had been licensed by the Chinese Government for that purpose, the Emperor of China agrees to abolish that practice in future at all Ports where British Merchants may reside, and to permit them to carry on their mercantile transactions with whatever persons they please, and His Imperial Majesty further agrees to pay to the British Government the sum of Three Millions of Dollars, on account of Debts due to British Subjects by some of the said Hong Merchants (or Cohong), who have become insolvent, and who owe very large sums of money to Subjects of Her Britannic Majesty.

Article VI. The Government of Her Britannic Majesty having been obliged to send out an Expedition to demand and obtain redress for the violent and unjust Proceedings of the Chinese High Authorities towards Her Britannic Majesty's Officer and Subjects, the Emperor of China agrees to pay the sum of Twelve Millions of Dollars on account of the Expenses incurred. . . .

Article VIII. The Emperor of China agrees to release unconditionally all Subjects of Her Britannic Majesty (whether Natives of Europe or India) who may be in confinement at this moment, in any part of the Chinese Empire.

Article IX. The Emperor of China agrees to publish and promulgate, under His Imperial Sign Manual and Seal, a full and entire amnesty and act of indemnity, to all Subjects of China on account of their having resided under, or having had dealings and intercourse with, or having entered the Service of Her Britannic Majesty, or of Her Majesty's Officers, and His Imperial Majesty further engages to release all Chinese Subjects who may be at this moment in confinement for similar reasons.

Article X. His Majesty the Emperor of China agrees to establish at all the Ports which are by the 2nd Article of this Treaty

---

1. To clean, caulk, and repair ships.
2. These are not United States but Mexican dollars, silver coins that had been used mainly in the Spanish Philippines for many years to purchase Chinese goods.

to be thrown open for the resort of British Merchants, a fair and regular Tariff of Export and Import Customs and other Dues, which Tariff shall be publicly notified and promulgated for general information, and the Emperor further engages, that when British Merchandise shall have once paid at any of the said Ports the regulated Customs and Dues agreeable to the Tariff, to be hereafter fixed, such Merchandise may be conveyed by Chinese Merchants, to any Province or City in the interior of the Empire of China on paying a further amount as Transit Duties.

TREATY OF THE BOGUE (1843)

Article VIII. The Emperor of China having been graciously pleased to grant to all foreign Countries whose Subjects, or Citizens, have hitherto traded at Canton the privilege of resorting for purposes of Trade to the other four Ports of Fuchow, Amoy, Ningpo and Shanghai, on the same terms as the English,[3] it is further agreed, that should the Emperor hereafter, from any cause whatever, be pleased to grant additional privileges or immunities to any of the subjects or Citizens of such Foreign Countries, the same privileges and immunities will be extended to and enjoyed by British Subjects; but it is to be understood that demands or requests are not, on this plea, to be unnecessarily brought forward.[4]

TREATY OF TIENTSIN (1858)[5]

Article V. His Majesty the Emperor of China agrees to nominate one of the Secretaries of State, or a President of one of the Boards, as the High Officer with whom the Ambassador, Minister, or other Diplomatic Agent of Her Majesty the Queen shall transact business, either personally or in writing, on a footing of perfect equality.

Article VII. Her Majesty the Queen may appoint one or more Consuls in the dominions of the Emperor of China, and such Consul or Consuls shall be at liberty to reside in any of the Open Ports. . . . They shall be treated with due respect by the Chinese authorities, and enjoy the same privileges and immunities as the Consular Officers of the most favored nation. . . .

Article VIII. The Christian religion as professed by Protestants or Roman Catholics, inculcates the practice of virtue and teaches man to do as he would be done by. Persons teaching it, or professing it, therefore, shall alike be entitled to the protection of the Chinese authorities, nor shall any such, peaceably pursuing their calling, and not offending against the laws, be persecuted or interfered with.

Article IX. British subjects are hereby authorized to travel for their pleasure or for purposes of trade, to all parts of the Interior, under Passports, which will be issued by their Consuls and countersigned by the Local Authorities. . . .

Article X. British merchant ships shall have authority to trade upon the Great River (Yangtze). The Upper and Lower Valley being, however, disturbed by outlaws, no Port shall be for the present opened to trade, with the exception of Chinkiang, which shall be opened in a year from the date of the signing of this Treaty. . . .

---

3. These concessions were granted soon after the acceptance of the Treaty of Nanking.

4. Great Britain now had what was referred to as "most favored nation status."

5. A separate treaty dealt with France.

Article XI. In addition to the Cities and Towns of Canton, Amoy, Foochow, Ningpo and Shanghai, opened by the Treaty of Nanking, it is agreed that British subjects may frequent the Cities and Ports of Newchwang, Tangchow, Taiwan (Formosa), Chawchow (Swatow) and Kiungchow (Hainan). . . .

Article XV. All questions in regard to rights, whether of property or person, arising between British subjects, shall be subject to the jurisdiction of the British authorities.

Article XVI. Chinese subjects who may be guilty of any criminal act towards British subjects shall be arrested and punished by the Chinese authorities according to the Laws of China.

British subjects who may commit any crime in China shall be tried and punished by the Consul or other Public Functionary authorized thereto according to the Laws of Great Britain.

PART III

The World in the Age of Western Dominance, 1800–1914

The direction of world history during the nineteenth century is perhaps best symbolized by Africa's experience. In 1800, except for the far north, the far south, and the regions affected by the slave trade, Africa was untouched by Europeans. A century later, except for Ethiopia and Liberia, the whole continent had succumbed to the control of the major European powers, who accomplished their takeover with scant regard for the interests and wishes of the Africans themselves. In 1885 rules for dividing Africa were established, but the rule makers were not Africans but Europeans. Meeting at the Congress of Berlin, they decided that each power had to give the others proper notice if it intended to annex African lands and, on doing so, could not simply ink its name on a map: it had to place real troops or officials on the scene. During World War I, thousands of Africans were conscripted and dispatched to Europe, where they fought and gave their lives for their colonial masters.

The changes in Africa were striking in terms of their suddenness and magnitude, but they were not unique. During the nineteenth century, Burma, India, Southeast Asia, and many Pacific islands also came under direct European or United States rule. Other states, such as Cuba, Nicaragua, Haiti, the Dominican Republic, Egypt, and China, maintained their theoretical independence but were forced to accept extensive Western control of their finances and foreign policy. Still others, such as Australia, New Zealand, Canada, South Africa, the Philippines, and the East and West Indies remained part of pre–nineteenth-century empires, although Canada in 1867, Australia in 1901, New Zealand in 1907, and South Africa in 1910 were granted extensive powers of self-government and the Philippines in 1898 changed masters from Spain to the United States. Another group of states, including the Ottoman Empire, Mexico, and the nations of South America, maintained their full political sovereignty but saw their banks, railroads, industries, and even much of their agriculture fall into the hands of foreign investors. Only Japan, by successfully adopting Western science, technology, and industry, avoided subservience to the West.

Millions of people around the globe faced the same reality: the need to respond to the military might, political aggressiveness, and economic drive of the United States and a handful of Western European nations. During the nineteenth century, the gap between the West and the rest of the world, already large, widened even further. Strengthened by the Industrial Revolution, advances in science and technology, and the growth in state power, Western nations faced little effective resistance when they sought new commercial privileges and established new colonies throughout the world.

Ignoring the Western nations was no longer an option. The peoples of India, Turkey, China, Japan, and Latin America had to confront the issues first addressed by the Russians during and after the reign of Peter the Great. Do we want to westernize? If so, how thoroughly? At what human cost? How quickly? No people answered these questions identically, and their response to the West varied from stunning success to dismal failure. This is the central theme of nineteenth-century world history.

C H A P T E R

8

The West in the Age of Industrialization

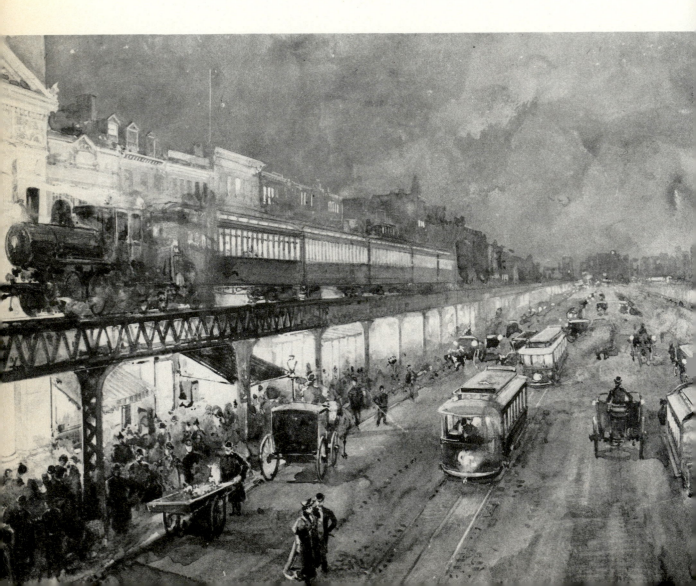

As far-reaching as the transformation of Western civilization since the Renaissance had been, no one could have predicted the even more profound changes that occurred in the nineteenth century. When Napoleon was defeated at Waterloo in 1815, Europe's population was 200 million, with as many as 25 million people of European descent living in the rest of the world. In 1914, when World War I began, these numbers stood at 450 million and 150 million respectively. In 1815 most Europeans and Americans lived in rural villages and worked the land; in 1914 most lived in cities and worked in factories, businesses, government offices, schools, hospitals, and stores. In 1815, despite two decades of revolution, most governments were aristocratic and monarchical, with few visible concessions to the principles of democracy and freedom; in 1914 representative assemblies and universal manhood suffrage were the norm in most of Europe, the United States, and the British dominions of Canada, Australia, and New Zealand. In 1815 most governments limited their activities to defense, the preservation of law and order, and some economic regulation; in 1914 governments in industrialized states subsidized education, sponsored scientific research, monitored industry, provided social welfare care, and supported gargantuan military establishments.

To a certain extent, these and other changes reflected the acceleration of trends rooted in Europe's past. The scientific and technological progress of the age, though impressive, was built on a foundation of consistent achievement in these areas dating back to the Middle Ages. Nor was the profusion of new literary, philosophical, and artistic movements unique; intellectual ferment had characterized Europe since the twelfth century. Late–nineteenth-century imperialism was but a final chapter in a long story of Western expansionism, and the struggle of disenfranchised groups such as factory workers and women for political rights was the logical extension of the doctrine of equality and natural rights enunciated in the Enlightenment and the French Revolution.

The most important single cause of the West's transformation during the nineteenth century was the Industrial Revolution, a wide-ranging economic movement involving the application of technology to industrial production, communication, and transportation. These changes began in England in the late eighteenth century, when power-driven machines began to produce cotton textiles. By 1914 industrialization had taken root in Europe, Japan, and the United States and was spreading to Canada, Russia, and parts of Latin America. As much as the discovery of agriculture many centuries earlier, industrialization profoundly altered the human condition.

The Industrial Revolution in Europe

The English were the first, and for many decades, the only people in the world to experience the material benefits and social costs of industrialization. Factories began to appear in England in the 1760s, and, by the early 1800s, power-driven machines were producing textiles and a wide variety of other goods. Economic historians have suggested many reasons for England's early industrial lead: population growth, an abundant labor supply, strong domestic and overseas markets, the availability of capital, a sophisticated banking system, good transportation, a stable government, a climate of opinion favorable to business, and, finally, a series of remarkable inventions that first transformed the cotton industry and subsequently a host of others.

During the nineteenth century industrialization spread from England to western Europe, the United States, and Japan. In the process it changed considerably. The late nineteenth century saw the appearance of larger forms of business organizations such as corporations, monopolies, and cartels; the growing importance of finance capital; the development of new energy sources based on petroleum and electricity; and, most important, the increasing application of new technologies to thousands of industrial processes.

The industrialization of Europe and the United States guaranteed continuation of the West's economic ascendancy. As Western businessmen marketed their products throughout the world and as Western investors established control of much of the world's trade, mines, oil reserves, and manufacturing, Westerners gained unprecedented dominion over the earth's wealth and resources. Industrialization had its ugly side, however. Social dislocation, overcrowded cities, inadequate housing, exploitation of workers, child labor, extremes of wealth and poverty, political conflict, and polluted air and water were some of the costs that accompanied the transition from an agrarian to an industrial order.

Arthur Young

TOURS IN ENGLAND AND WALES

Having failed as a businessman, journalist, and farmer, Arthur Young (1741–1820) began a successful career in the 1770s as the author of tour books that recorded his observations of social and economic conditions in Great Britain and France. Although primarily interested in agriculture, he also described conditions in England's new industrial cities and commented on political developments. In the following excerpt from *Tours in England and Wales*, published in 1791, he characterizes the impact of industrialization on Birmingham, a city of England's Midlands, some 110 miles north of London. In 1700 it had but 15,000 inhabitants and only local economic significance. But its proximity to England's coal mines and the technological genius of its citizens, most notably James Watt, the inventor of the first practical steam engine, made it a center of England's early Industrial Revolution. The changes Young describes were not unique to Birmingham; the new factory economy also transformed Leeds, Manchester, Glasgow, and dozens of other new industrial centers.

Questions for Analysis

1. What are the most notable signs of change Young observes in Birmingham?
2. On the basis of his description, how important to Birmingham's growth was the (1) opening up of the canal system and (2) the availability of capital for investment?
3. What is Young's view of the impact of the new factory economy on working-class families?

*T*he capital improvement wrought since I was here before is the canal to Oxford, Coventry, Wolverhampton, etc.; the port, as it may be called, or double canal head in the town crowded with coal barges is a noble spectacle, with that prodigious animation, which the immense trade of this place could alone give. I looked around me with amazement at the change effected in twelve years; so great that this place may now probably be reckoned, with justice, the first manufacturing town in the world. From this port and these quays[1] you may now go by water to Hull, Liverpool, Bristol, Oxford (130 miles) and London. The cut was opened through the coal mines to Wolverhampton in 1769. In 1783, into the new mines of Wednesbury, and to the junction with the Coventry canal, at Faseley, near Tamworth. From Birmingham to the Staffordshire canal is 22 miles, and to Faseley 15. In the 22 miles from hence to Wolverhampton only three locks; but down to Faseley there are 44 locks; not one rivulet to supply water, and only 30 acres of reservoirs, the water coming out of the earth. At Ocher hills they have a powerful steam engine for throwing back the waste water: and in the whole extent one that cost £4,000,[2] another of £3,000; another of £2,500, another of £1,200; and yet another building that will cost £3,500. The first-mentioned works at the charge of £200 for six months. The old and new cuts were executed at the expense of about £250,000; one mile where it is open to the depth of 44 feet £30,000 for sinking only 18 feet lower than the original level. There are 13 locks between the port and Deritan, 8 feet 2 inches wide, and the boats 7 feet; to pass the 13 takes only two hours. Coals, before

---

1. Wharfs for loading and unloading goods.
2. £ is the symbol of the pound, the basic unit of British currency. Decimalized into 100 new pence in 1971, it previously was divided into 20 shillings (s.), which in turn were divided into 12 pence (d.).

these canals were made, were 6d per cwt.[3] at Birmingham, now 4 1/2d. The consumption is about 200,000 tons a year, which exhausts about 20 or 22 acres; it employs 40 boats, each 20 tons a day for the six summer months, besides 15 to 20 boats to Oxford, a new supply since the new cut. In the Wednesbury mines the coal is 10 yards thick, and in some even to 12 and 14, a thing elsewhere almost unheard of: a cubical yard they reckon a ton. Shares in the navigation, which were at first done at 140 per cent are now at 1040. I was assured that shares in the Aire and Calder navigation are yet higher, even 100 per cent per annum.

These immense works, which wear so animated a face of business, correspond well with the prodigious increase of the town, which I viewed to good advantage from the top of the new church of St. Paul: it is now a very great city indeed; and it was abundantly curious to have it pointed out to me the parts added since I was here. They form the greatest part of the town, and carry in their countenance undoubted marks of their modern date. In 1768 the population was under 30,000; now the common calculation is 70,000, but more accurate calculation extend it to 80,000, which I am told is the number assigned by Dr. Priestley.[4] In the last 10 years above 4,000 new houses have been built: and the increase is at present going on much more rapidly, for I was told that the number this year is not less than 700.

The earnings of the workmen in the manufacture are various, but in general very high: a boy of 10 or 12 years, 2s. 6d. to 3s. a week; a woman from 4s. to 10s. a week, average about 6s.; men from 10s. to 25s. a week, and some much higher; colliers earn yet more. These are immense wages, when it is considered that the whole family is sure of constant steady employment; indeed they are so great that I am inclined to think labor higher at Birmingham than in any other place in Europe: a most curious circumstance for the politician to reflect on, and which shows of how little effect to manufactures is cheap labor, for here is the most flourishing fabric that was perhaps ever known, paying the highest rates of labor. Such an instance ought to correct those common notions that have been retailed from hand to hand a thousand times, that cheap provisions[5] are necessary for the good of manufactures, because cheap provisions suppose cheap labor, which is a combination founded in ignorance and error. Provisions at Birmingham are at the same rate as everywhere else in England, for it is remarkable that the level of price at present is very general, except the division of the east and west of the kingdom for corn,[6] but while Birmingham and Norwich eat their provisions at nearly the same price (with allowance that the former is much the more quick, ready and active market) the price of labor is at least 150 per cent higher in one of those places than the other.

---

3. A hundredweight, equal to 100 pounds.

4. Joseph Priestley (1733–1804), an English clergyman best known for his discoveries concerning the nature of gases. He served a church in Birmingham during the 1780s.

5. Food supply.

6. In England, this refers to all grain crops.

TESTIMONY BEFORE BRITISH PARLIAMENTARY COMMITTEES ON WORKING CONDITIONS IN ENGLAND

A major factor in England's early industrial growth was the availability of a large pool of workers willing to accept low wages for long hours of labor in factories and mines. Many of these workers were displaced farmers or farm workers, forced from rural areas because of land shortages caused by population growth and the consolidation of small farms into large agricultural estates by wealthy aristocrats. Many rural families moved to the new industrial cities, where parents and children, some as young as five years old, took jobs in the factories. Even with whole families working, they experienced poverty, overcrowding, poor health, illiteracy, and few prospects for improvement.

Eventually the English government abandoned its commitment to unlimited free enterprise and passed laws in the 1800s to protect workers, especially children, from exploitation. When considering legislation, parliamentary committees took testimony from workers, employers, physicians, clergy, and local officials. Their statements present a vivid picture of working-class conditions in the first half of the nineteenth century.

Section 1 includes testimony taken by the Sadler Committee, chaired by Michael Thomas Sadler in 1831 and charged with investigating conditions of child labor in cotton and linen factories; section 2 includes testimony recorded by a parliamentary commission appointed in 1833 to investigate working conditions, especially for children, in other textile industries; and section 3 includes evidence taken by the committee chaired by Lord Ashley in 1842 to investigate conditions in coal mines.

Questions for Analysis

1. How young were children when they first began working in the textile factories? In the coal mines? How many hours did they work?
2. Young, who wrote much more about the condition of rural workers than that of factory workers, considered factory workers' wages in Birmingham in 1791 "immense." Yet much of the testimony in the parliamentary hearings paints a picture of workers' poverty. What might Young's assertion imply about economic conditions in the English countryside? What might he have failed to consider when he assessed factory workers' well-being simply on the basis of their wages?
3. Consider the testimony of the workers themselves. Do they express anger? Do they demand changes?

4. What does the testimony of Hannah Richardson and George Armitage reveal about (1) the economic circumstances of working-class families and (2) the attitudes of working-class families toward their children?
5. Why do William Harter and Thomas Wilson oppose factory laws? How do their views reflect the economic philosophy of Adam Smith in *The Wealth of Nations* (Chapter 7)?
6. Injury rates among factory workers were high. What in the testimony explains this phenomenon?

[*1. Testimony Before the Sadler Committee, 1831*]

Elizabeth Bentley, Called in; and Examined

What age are you? — Twenty-three. . . .

What time did you begin to work at a factory? — When I was six years old. . . .

What kind of mill is it? — Flax-mill. . . .

What was your business in that mill? — I was a little doffer.[1]

What were your hours of labor in that mill? — From 5 in the morning till 9 at night, when they were thronged.

For how long a time together have you worked that excessive length of time? — For about half a year.

What were your usual hours of labor when you were not so thronged?[2] — From 6 in the morning till 7 at night.

What time was allowed for your meals? — Forty minutes at noon.

Had you any time to get your breakfast or drinking? — No, we got it as we could.

And when your work was bad, you had hardly any time to eat it at all? — No; we were obliged to leave it or take it home, and when we did not take it, the overlooker took it, and gave it to his pigs.

Do you consider doffing a laborious employment? — Yes.

Explain what it is you had to do? — When the frames are full, they have to stop the frames, and take the flyers off, and take the full bobbins off, and carry them to the roller; and then put empty ones on, and set the frames on again.

Does that keep you constantly on your feet? — Yes, there are so many frames and they run so quick.

Your labor is very excessive? — Yes; you have not time for any thing.

Suppose you flagged a little, or were too late, what would they do? — Strap us.

Are they in the habit of strapping those who are last in doffing? — Yes.

Constantly? — Yes.

Girls as well as boys? — Yes.

Have you ever been strapped? — Yes.

Severely? — Yes.

Could you eat your food well in that factory? — No, indeed, I had not much to eat, and the little I had I could not eat it, my appetite was so poor, and being covered with dust; and it was no use to take it home, I could not eat it, and the overlooker took it, and gave it to the pigs. . . .

Did you live far from the mill? — Yes, two miles.

Had you a clock? — No, we had not.

Supposing you had not been in time enough in the morning at the mills, what would have been the consequence? — We should have been quartered.

---

1. A worker, usually a young child, whose job was to clean the machines used in textile manufacturing.

2. Busy.

What do you mean by that? — If we were a quarter of an hour too late, they would take off half an hour; we only got a penny an hour, and they would take a halfpenny more. . . .

Were you generally there in time? — Yes, my mother has been up at 4 o'clock in the morning, and at 2 o'clock in the morning; the colliers used to go to their work about 3 or 4 o'clock, and when she heard them stirring she has got up out of her warm bed, and gone out and asked them the time, and I have sometimes been at Hunslet Car at 2 o'clock in the morning, when it was streaming down with rain, and we have had to stay till the mill was opened. . . .

[2. *Commission for Inquiry into the Employment of Children in Factories*, Second Report, 1833]

TESTIMONY OF JOHN WRIGHT[3]

Are silk-mills clean in general? — They are; they are swept every day, and white-washed once a year.

What is the temperature of silk-mills? — I don't know exactly the temperature, but it is very agreeable.

Is any artificial heat required? — In the winter it is heated by steam.

To what degree? — I cannot speak positively; but it is not for the work, only to keep the hands warm and comfortable.

Why, then, are those employed in them said to be in such a wretched condition? — In the first place, the great number of hands congregated together, in some rooms forty, in some fifty, in some sixty, and I have known some as many as 100, which must be injurious to both health and growing. In the second place, the privy is in the factory, which fre-

quently emits an unwholesome smell; and it would be worth while to notice in the future erection of mills, that there be betwixt the privy door and the factory wall a kind of a lobby of cage-work. 3dly, The tediousness and the everlasting sameness in the first process preys much on the spirits, and makes the hands spiritless. 4thly, the extravagant number of hours a child is compelled to labor and confinement, which for one week is seventy-six hours, which makes 3,952 hours for one year, we deduct 208 hours for meals within the factory which makes the net labor for one year 3,744; but the labor and confinement together of a child between ten years of age and twenty is 39,520 hours, enough to fritter away the best constitution. 5thly, About six months in the year we are obliged to use either gas, candles, or lamps, for the longest portion of that time, nearly six hours a day, being obliged to work amid the smoke and soot of the same; and also a large portion of oil and grease is used in the mills.

What are the effects of the present system of labor? — From my earliest recollections, I have found the effects to be awfully detrimental to the well-being of the operative; I have observed frequently children carried to factories, unable to walk, and that entirely owing to excessive labor and confinement. The degradation of the workpeople baffles all description: frequently have two of my sisters been obliged to be assisted to the factory and home again, until by-and-by they could go no longer, being totally crippled in their legs. . . .

TESTIMONY OF WILLIAM HARTER[4]

What effect would it have on your manufacture to reduce the hours of labor to ten?

3. A silk factory worker in his mid-30s.

4. The owner of a silk mill in Manchester.

— It would instantly much reduce the value of my mill and machinery, and consequently of far prejudice my manufacture.

How so? — They are calculated to produce a certain quantity of work in a given time. Every machine is valuable in proportion to the quantity of work which it will turn off in a given time. It is impossible that the machinery could produce as much work in ten hours as in twelve. If the tending of the machines were a laborious occupation, the difference in the quantity of work might not always be in exact proportion to the difference of working time; but in my mill, and silk-mills in general, the work requires the least imaginable labor; therefore it is perfectly impossible that the machines could produce as much work in ten hours as in twelve. The produce would vary in about the same ratio as the working time.

What may be said about the sum invested in your mill and machinery? — It is not yet near complete, and the investment is a little short of 20,000 pounds.

Then to what extent do you consider your property would be prejudiced by a bill limiting the working hours to ten? — All other circumstances remaining the same, it is obvious that any property in the mill and machinery would be prejudiced to the extent of one-sixth its value, or upwards of 3,000 pounds.

How would the reduction in the hours of labor affect the cost of your manufactures? — The cost of our manufactures consists in the price of the raw materials and of the expense of putting that said material into goods. Now the mere interest of the investment in buildings and machinery, and the expense of keeping the same in repair, forms a large item in the cost of manufacturing. Of course it follows, that the *gross* charge under this head would be the same upon a production of 10,000 pounds and 12,000 pounds, and this portion of the cost of manufacturing would consequently be increased by about 16%.

Do you mean to say, that to produce the same quantity of work which your present mill and machinery is capable of, it requires an additional outlay of upwards of 3,000 pounds? — I say distinctly, that to produce the same quantity of work under a ten-hours bill will require an additional outlay of 3,000 or 4,000 pounds; therefore a ten-hours bill would impose upon me the necessity of this additional outlay in such perishable property as buildings and machinery, or I must be content to relinquish one-sixth portion of my business.

[3. *Testimony Before the Ashley Committee on the Conditions in Mines, 1842*]

Edward Potter

I am a coal viewer, and the manager of the South Hetton colliery. We have about 400 bound people (contract laborers), and in addition our bank people (foremen), men and boys about 700. In the pits 427 men and boys; of these, 290 men. . . .

Of the children in the pits we have none under eight, and only three so young. We are constantly beset by parents coming making application to take children under the age, and they are very anxious and very dissatisfied if we do not take the children; and there have been cases in times of brisk trade, when the parents have threatened to leave the colliery, and go elsewhere if we did not comply. At every successive binding, which takes place yearly, constant attempts are made to get the boys engaged to work to which they are not competent from their years. In point of fact, we would rather not have boys until nine years of age complete. If younger than that, they are apt to fall asleep and get hurt: some get killed. It is no interest to the company to take any boys under nine. . . .

HANNAH RICHARDSON

I've one child that works in the pit; he's going on ten. He is down from 6 to 8. . . . he's not much tired with the work, it's only the confinement that tires him. He likes it pretty well, for he'd rather be in the pit than go to school. There is not much difference in his health since he went into the pit. He was at school before, and can read pretty well, but can't write. He is used pretty well; I never hear him complain. I've another son in the pit, 17 years old. . . . He went into the pit at eight years old. It's not hurt his health nor his appetite, for he's a good size. It would hurt us if children were prevented from working till 11 or 12 years old, because we've not jobs enough to live now as it is. . . .

MR. GEORGE ARMITAGE

I am now a teacher at Hoyland school; I was a collier at Silkstone until I was 22 years old and worked in the pit above 10 years. . . . I hardly know how to reprobate the practice sufficiently of girls working in pits; nothing can be worse. I have no doubt that debauchery is carried on, for which there is every opportunity; for the girls go constantly, when hurrying, to the men, who work often alone in the bank-faces apart from every one. I think it scarcely possible for girls to remain modest who are in pits, regularly mixing with such company and hearing such language as they do — it is next to impossible. I dare venture to say that many of the wives who come from pits know nothing of sewing or any household duty, such as women ought to know — they lose all disposition to learn such things; they are rendered unfit for learning them also by

being overworked and not being trained to the habit of it. I have worked in pits for above 10 years, where girls were constantly employed, and I can safely say it is an abominable system; indecent language is quite common. I think, if girls were trained properly, as girls ought to be, that there would be no more difficulty in finding suitable employment for them than in other places. Many a collier spends in drink what he has shut up a young child the whole week to earn in a dark cold corner as a trapper. The education of the children is universally bad. They are generally ignorant of common facts in Christian history and principles, and, indeed, in almost everything else. Little can be learned merely on Sundays, and they are too tired as well as indisposed to go to night schools. . . .

THE REV. ROBERT WILLAN, CURATE OF ST. MARY'S, BARNSLEY

I have been resident here as chief minister for 22 years. I think the morals of the working classes here are in an appalling state. . . . The ill manners and conduct of the weavers are daily presented to view in the streets, but the colliers work under ground and are less seen, and we have less means of knowing. . . . The master-sin among the youths is that of gambling; the boys may be seen playing at pitch-and-toss on the Sabbath and on week-days; they are seen doing this in all directions. The next besetting sin is promiscuous sexual intercourse; this may be much induced by the manner in which they sleep — men, women, and children often sleeping in one bed-room. I have known a family of father and mother and 12 children, some of them up-grown, sleeping on a kind of sacking and straw bed, reaching from one side of the room to the other, along the floor; they were an English family. Sexual intercourse begins very young. This and gambling pave the way; then drinking ensues, and this is the vortex which draws in every other sin.

THOMAS WILSON, ESQ., OWNER OF THREE COLLIERIES

I object on general principles to government interference in the conduct of any trade, and I am satisfied that in the mines it would be productive of the greatest injury and injustice. The art of mining is not so perfectly understood as to admit of the way in which a colliery shall be conducted being dictated by any person, however experienced, with such certainty as would warrant an interference with the management of private business. I should also most decidedly object to placing collieries under the present provisions of the Factory Act[5] with respect to the education of children employed therein. First, because, if it is contended that coal-owners, as employers of children, are bound to attend to their education, this obligation extends equally to all other employers, and therefore it is unjust to single out one class only; secondly, because, if the legislature asserts a right to interfere to secure education, it is bound to make that interference general; and thirdly, because the mining population is in this neighborhood so intermixed with other classes, and is in such small bodies in any one place, that it would be impossible to provide separate schools for them.

◼ Otto von Leixner

LETTERS FROM BERLIN WITH SPECIAL REFERENCE TO SOCIAL-DEMOCRATIC MOVEMENTS

One should not assume that the horrid working conditions described in early English sources were the norm for all nineteenth-century factory workers. In countries such as Germany, where the Industrial Revolution started later, workers benefited from trade unions, prolabor political parties, and the right to vote. Nevertheless, even relatively well-paid workers in the late 1800s needed regular employment to avert economic disaster.

The following description of a Berlin working-class family in 1890 is provided in a book published in 1891 by Otto von Leixner (1847–1907), a prolific German writer of poetry, short fiction, literary history, and political comment. In his *Letters from Berlin*, based largely on personal interviews, he describes living and working conditions of Berlin factory workers for the general reading public.

---

5. The Factory Act of 1833, which regulated employment of children and women, applied to textile factories.

Questions for Analysis

1. Based on von Leixner's description, how does the situation of this late–nineteenth-century Berlin working-class family differ from family conditions described in the parliamentary hearings?
2. What circumstances may explain these differences?
3. How does this document shed light on the status of women in late–nineteenth-century German working-class families?

The head of the first household is a member of the better paid class. He is a molder in a bronze casting shop, a hardworking, estimable man, a good husband and father. . . . He hardly ever goes to political meetings; very rarely to the public house.[1] His wife, a former servant girl, is industrious and economical, despite suffering from ill health. The flat consists of a fairly large room and an adjoining kitchen. Although husband, wife and two children live and sleep there, it is all beautifully clean. There are cotton curtains in flowery patterns over the windows; modest flower pots on the window sills. One length of wall is occupied by the two beds and a sofa on which the children sleep; the other, by a cupboard, a wardrobe and a wash stand. A table and chairs complete the furniture.

The average income is 1,700 marks.[2] There have been years when it has been more, but also some in which it has been less. The work is very hard, and if the firm is very busy, the head of the household suffers from exhaustion and has to take to his bed for a week at a time.

Rent for the flat is 259 marks. . . .

When the molder gets his wage on the Saturday, he puts the share of the rent, which is payable monthly in advance, to one side. His wife gets 18 marks a week for housekeeping, i.e., 2.57 marks a day, 64 pfennigs a head; lighting has also to be paid out of that. The husband pays for heating. . . . If need be, they sit in the evenings by the cooker in the kitchen. Fuel . . . comes annually to 40–50 marks.

The daily consumption of food is interesting. The following is an average, since the menu is not always the same. There is a large consumption of lentils, potatoes, flour, bread and milk. As far as meat is concerned, consumption is mostly limited to cheap sausage (spread on the bread, not put on in slices) or chopped beef and lung, in the form of meat balls (chopped meat mixed with breadcrumbs and baked in a little fat). Food is always sparse on weekdays in order to have more on Sundays and holidays. . . .

Nothing whatever is bought on credit; this is absolutely essential if the household is to remain in order. If larger expenses become necessary a carefully calculated sum is put by every week in order to pay cash when the time comes.

The husband takes coffee with him in the morning, in a tin can, at midday and in the evening he drinks at most 3 glasses of beer, at 10 pfennigs (he never touches Schnapps), he smokes 2 cigars a day on weekdays, 3 on Sundays at 3 pfennigs each, he goes to the public house perhaps

---

1. Tavern.

2. The basic unit of German currency.

once a week, but returns home by 10.30 P.M. at the latest.

I now put together all the figures I could obtain:

(Earnings: 1,700 marks)

Expenditure	Marks
Rent	259
Household	924
Taxes	30
Health insurance, etc.	13
Heating, average	45
Overcoat, for husband	30
Hat	2.50
Footwear for husband	16
Footwear for wife	11
Footwear for children	10
Clothes for wife and children	23
Doctor and medicaments for wife	20
Newspaper, shared with another, at 6 marks, i.e.	3
Miscellaneous (mending, washing, entertainment)	64
Husband (drinking, smoking, club collections, etc.)	162
	1,612.50

In 1889 savings amounted to 82 marks. A glance at the expenditure will make clear what strict economy is required to save anything at all at that rate of income. Husband and wife must use all their moral strength to make their way decently, and must know how to keep their expenditure firmly within the frame of their circumstances. Entertainment costing money is very rare, they may just afford excursions to the Zoo on "cheap Sundays," taking a picnic lunch, or to the heath out of town; once in a blue moon, i.e. once in years, they visit the music hall. This is the total of outside entertainment. The husband gets by: he borrows books from the Free Library and reads in the evenings when he is not too tired; the wife makes do with reading the serial story in the paper and the local news or she chats with the neighbors after the children have been put to bed.

As long as conditions do not change, the better-paid worker who lives decently can make ends meet, and may even put something by for emergencies. But even that requires a moral character above the average. How many of us, possessing more education and higher incomes, can say as much about ourselves?

But if the husband or the wife are irresponsible, or even not wholly dutiful, the rot sets in. Once there is disorder or dirt in the house, one can bet a hundred to one that the husband will begin to frequent the public house. Or if it is he who starts to drink and uses up more for himself, the best housewife will not be able to prop up the shaking building.

The Socialist Challenge to Capitalism

Socialism was a powerful ideology originating in nineteenth-century Europe that took the goal of human equality, raised as a political ideal during the French Revolution, and extended it to social and economic relationships. Mere political equality was a hoax, claimed socialists, as long as extremes of wealth and poverty divided society. They asserted that capitalist principles of private property, individualism, and free competition should be replaced by a new value system based on harmony, cooperation, sharing, and social equality.

The socialists' disillusionment with conditions resulted only in part from the social upheavals caused by the Industrial Revolution. Industrialization did create a highly visible new class of factory workers, who, as the previous readings have shown, suffered subsistence wages, long hours, dangerous working conditions, substandard housing, and frequent unemployment. To the socialists, such conditions were particularly odious because of the large fortunes many capitalists accrued from the new factories. But industrialization by itself did not give rise to socialism. Socialism also drew on the democratic heritage of the French Revolution, the first major political movement to take seriously the welfare and importance of common men and women. Socialism was further inspired by the Age of Enlightenment's humanitarianism and its faith that social defects need not be passively accepted but could be eliminated by the application of human reason.

The first socialists in Europe were idealists and visionaries, subsequently dubbed "utopian," who proposed schemes for society's improvement but gave little thought to the practical problems of achieving their goals. In the 1840s, a number of French thinkers, most notably Louis Blanc (1811–1882) and Pierre Joseph Proudhon (1809–1865), linked socialist programs with political strategies for their realization. From the 1850s onward, the towering figure of Karl Marx (1818–1883), who gave socialism a "scientific" philosophical basis and who worked indefatigably to organize the first socialist political parties, came to dominate the socialist movement. By the end of the century, socialist parties existed, legally or illegally, in the United States and every major European state, and socialism was an important political force.

Like other European ideologies, socialism spread throughout the world during the twentieth century. In the late twentieth century, dozens of states are officially "socialist," and, among the rest, all have been affected by the socialist vision.

Karl Marx and Friedrich Engels

THE COMMUNIST MANIFESTO

No document in the history of socialism rivals the importance of *The Communist Manifesto*, begun by Karl Marx and Friedrich Engels (1820–1895) in 1847 and published in 1848. The son of a German lawyer, Marx, after studying philosophy at the University of Berlin, in the 1840s became a journalist and radical politician. Engels, the son of a prosperous German textile manufacturer, was an ardent critic of capitalism despite the fortune he built from managing a textile mill in Manchester, England. The two men first met in Paris in 1844, and three years later they joined the Communist League, a revolutionary society dominated by German radicals living in exile in France and England. They wrote *The Manifesto* to publicize the purposes of the League.

After 1848, although both men continued to write on behalf of socialism, Marx's works, especially his masterpiece *Das Kapital* (*Capitalism*), assumed the greater role in shaping modern socialist thought. Furthermore, Marx's views of history, human behavior, and social conflict have influenced far more than politics, leaving their mark on philosophy, religion, literature, and all the social sciences.

Questions
for Analysis

1. How do Marx and Engels define "class," and what do they mean by the "class struggle"? How has the class struggle changed in recent history?
2. According to Marx and Engels, what caused the emergence of the bourgeoisie as Europe's dominant class? In their view, what characterizes the bourgeoisie?
3. Marx and Engels argue that the overthrow of bourgeois society is inevitable and that the bourgeoisie will be the cause of their own destruction. Why?
4. Marx and Engels dismiss the importance of ideas as a force in human affairs. Why? Ultimately, what is the cause of historical change in their view?
5. What might explain the enormous popularity and influence of *The Communist Manifesto* among the working class?
6. In what respects is Marx's and Engels's vision of the past and future similar to Condorcet's in *Sketch of the Progress of the Human Mind* (Chapter 5)?

I. THE BOURGEOISIE AND PROLETARIAT

The history of all hitherto existing society is the history of class struggles.

Freeman and slave, patrician and plebeian, lord and serf, guild-master and journeyman, in a word, oppressor and oppressed, stood in constant opposition to one another, carried on an uninterrupted, now hidden, now open fight, a fight that each time ended, either in a revolutionary reconstitution of society at large, or in the common ruin of the contending classes. . . .

The modern bourgeois society that has sprouted from the ruins of feudal society has not done away with class antagonisms. It has but established new classes, new conditions of oppression, new forms of struggle in place of the old ones.

Our epoch, the epoch of the bourgeoisie, possesses, however, this distinctive feature: It has simplified the class antagonisms. Society as a whole is more and more splitting up into two great hostile camps, into two great classes directly facing each other — bourgeoisie and proletariat.

From the serfs of the Middle Ages sprang the chartered burghers of the earliest towns. From these burgesses the first elements of the bourgeoisie were developed.

The discovery of America, the rounding of the Cape, opened up fresh ground for the rising bourgeoisie. The East-Indian and Chinese markets, the colonization of America, trade with the colonies, the increase in the means of exchange and in commodities generally, gave to commerce, to navigation, to industry, an impulse never before known, and thereby, to the revolutionary element in the tottering feudal society, a rapid development.

The feudal system of industry, in which industrial production was monopolized by closed guilds, now no longer sufficed for the growing wants of the new markets. The manufacturing system took its place. The guild-masters were pushed aside by the manufacturing middle class; division of labor between the different corporate guilds vanished in the face of division of labor in each single workshop.

Meantime the markets kept ever growing, the demand ever rising. Even manufacture no longer sufficed. Thereupon, steam and machinery revolutionized industrial production. The place of manufacture was taken by the giant, modern industry, the place of the industrial middle class by industrial millionaires, the leaders of whole industrial armies, the modern bourgeois. . . .

We see, therefore, how the modern bourgeoisie is itself the product of a long course of development, of a series of revolutions in the modes of production and of exchange. . . .

The bourgeoisie, historically, has played a most revolutionary part.

The bourgeoisie, wherever it has got the upper hand, has put an end to all feudal, patriarchal, idyllic relations. It has pitilessly torn asunder the motley feudal ties that bound man to his "natural superiors," and has left no other nexus between man and man than naked self-interest, than callous "cash payment." . . . It has resolved personal worth into exchange value, and in place of the numberless indefeasible chartered freedoms, has set up that single, unconscionable freedom — Free Trade. In one word, for exploitation, veiled by religious and political illusions, it has substituted naked, shameless, direct, brutal exploitation. . . .

We see then: the means of production and of exchange, on whose foundation the bourgeoisie built itself up, were generated in feudal society. At a certain stage in the development of these means of production and of exchange, the conditions under which feudal society produced and exchanged, the feudal organization of agriculture and manufacturing industry, in one word, the feudal relations of property became no longer compatible with the already developed productive forces; they became so many fetters. They had to be burst asunder; they were burst asunder.

Into their place stepped free competition, accompanied by a social and political constitution adapted to it, and by the economic and political sway of the bourgeois class.

A similar movement is going on before our own eyes. Modern bourgeois society with its relations of production, of exchange and of property, a society that has conjured up such gigantic means of production and of exchange, is like the sorcerer who is no longer able to control the powers of the nether world whom he has called up by his spells. For many a decade past the history of industry and commerce is but the history of the revolt of modern productive forces against modern conditions of production, against the property relations that are the conditions for the existence of the bourgeoisie and of its rule. It is enough to mention the commercial crises that by their periodical return put the existence of the entire bourgeois society on its trial, each time more threateningly. In these crises a great part not only of the existing products, but also of the previously created productive forces, are periodically destroyed. In these crises there breaks out an epidemic that, in all earlier epochs, would have seemed an absurdity — the epidemic of overproduction. . . .

And how does the bourgeoisie get over these crises? On the one hand, by enforced destruction of a mass of productive forces; on the other, by the conquest of new markets, and by the more thorough exploitation of the old ones. That is to say, by paving the way for more extensive and more destructive crises, and by diminishing the means whereby crises are prevented.

The weapons with which the bourgeoisie felled feudalism to the ground are now turned against the bourgeoisie itself.

But not only has the bourgeoisie forged the weapons that bring death to itself; it has also called into existence the men who are to wield those weapons — the modern working class — the proletarians. . . .

Modern industry has converted the little workshop of the patriarchal master into the great factory of the industrial capitalist. Masses of laborers, crowded into the factory, are organized like soldiers. As privates of the industrial army they are placed under the command of a perfect hierarchy of officers and sergeants. Not only are they slaves of the bourgeois class, and of the bourgeois state; they are daily and hourly enslaved by the machine, by the overseer, and, above all, by the individual bourgeois manufacturer himself. The more openly this despotism proclaims gain to be its end and aim, the more petty, the more hateful and the more embittering it is. . . .

The lower strata of the middle class — the small tradespeople, shopkeepers, and retired tradesmen generally, the handicraftsmen and peasants — all these sink gradually into the proletariat, partly because their diminutive capital does not suffice for the scale on which modern industry is carried on, and is swamped in the competition with the large capitalists, partly because their specialized skill is rendered worthless by new methods of production. Thus the proletariat is recruited from all classes of the population.

But with the development of industry the proletariat not only increases in number; it becomes concentrated in greater masses, its strength grows, and it feels that strength more. The various interests and conditions of life within the ranks of the proletariat are more and more equalized, in proportion as machinery obliterates all distinctions of labor, and nearly everywhere reduces wages to the same low level. The growing competition among the bourgeois, and the resulting commercial crises, make the wages of the workers ever more fluctuating. The unceasing improvement of machinery, ever more rapidly developing, makes their livelihood more and more precarious; the collisions between individual workmen and individual bourgeois take more and more the character of collisions between two classes. Thereupon the workers begin to form combinations (trade unions) against the bourgeois; they club together in order to keep up the rate of wages; they found permanent associations in order to make provision beforehand for these occasional revolts. Here and there the contest breaks out into riots.

Now and then the workers are victorious, but only for a time. The real fruit of their battle lies, not in the immediate result, but in the ever expanding union of the workers. This union is helped on by the improved means of communication that are created by modern industry, and that place the workers of different localities in contact with one another. It was just this contact that was needed to centralize the numerous local struggles, all of the same character, into one national struggle between classes. . . .

This organization of the proletarians into a class, and consequently into a political party, is continually being upset again by the competition between the workers themselves. But it ever rises up again, stronger, firmer, mightier. . . .

Further, as we have already seen, entire sections of the ruling classes are, by the advance of industry, precipitated into the proletariat, or are at least threatened in their conditions of existence. These also supply the proletariat with fresh elements of enlightenment and progress.

Finally, in times when the class struggle nears the decisive hour, the process of dissolution going on within the ruling class, in fact within the whole range of old society, assumes such a violent, glaring character, that a small section of the ruling class cuts itself adrift, and joins the revolutionary class, the class that holds the future in its hands. Just as, therefore, at an earlier period, a section of the nobility went over to the bourgeoisie, so now a portion of the bourgeoisie goes over to the proletariat, and in particular, a portion of the bourgeois ideologists, who have raised themselves to the level of comprehending theoretically the historical movement as a whole.

II. PROLETARIANS AND COMMUNISTS

The distinguishing feature of communism is not the abolition of property generally, but the abolition of bourgeois property. But modern bourgeois private property is the final and most complete expression of the system of producing and appropriating products that is based on class antagonisms, on the exploitation of the many by the few.

In this sense, the theory of the Communists may be summed up in the single sentence: Abolition of private property. . . .

You are horrified at our intending to do away with private property. But in your existing society, private property is already done away with for nine-tenths of its population; its existence for the few is solely due to its non-existence in the hands of those nine-tenths. You reproach us, therefore, with intending to do away with a form of property, the necessary condition for whose existence is the non-existence of any property for the immense majority of society.

In one word, you reproach us with intending to do away with your property. Precisely so; that is just what we intend. . . .

The Communists are further reproached with desiring to abolish countries and nationality.

The working men have no country. We cannot take from them what they have not got. . . .

National differences and antagonism between peoples are daily more and more vanishing, owing to the development of the bourgeoisie, to freedom of commerce, to the world market, to uniformity in the mode of production and in the conditions of life corresponding thereto.

The supremacy of the proletariat will cause them to vanish still faster. United action of the leading civilized countries at least, is one of the first conditions for the emancipation of the proletariat.

In proportion as the exploitation of one individual by another is put an end to, the exploitation of one nation by another will also be put an end to. In proportion as the antagonism between classes within the nation vanishes, the hostility of one nation to another will come to an end.

The charges against communism made from a religious, a philosophical and, generally, from an ideological standpoint, are not deserving of serious examination.

Does it require deep intuition to comprehend that man's ideas, views, and conceptions, in one word, man's consciousness, change with every change in the conditions of his material existence, in his social relations and in his social life?

What else does the history of ideas prove, than that intellectual production changes its character in proportion as material production is changed? The ruling ideas of each age have ever been the ideas of its ruling class. . . .

IV. Position of the Communists in Relation to the Various Existing Opposition Parties

The Communists turn their attention chiefly to Germany, because that country is on the eve of a bourgeois revolution that is bound to be carried out under more advanced conditions of European civilization[1] and with a much more developed proletariat than that of England was in the seventeenth, and of France in the eighteenth century, and because the bourgeois revolution in Germany will be but the pre-lude to an immediately following proletarian revolution.

In short, the Communists everywhere support every revolutionary movement against the existing social and political order of things.

In all these movements they bring to the front, as the leading question in each, the property question, no matter what its degree of development at the time. . . .

The Communists disdain to conceal their views and aims. They openly declare that their ends can be attained only by the forcible overthrow of all existing social conditions. Let the ruling classes tremble at a communist revolution. The proletarians have nothing to lose but their chains. They have a world to win.

Working men of all countries, unite!

ERFURT PROGRAM OF THE GERMAN SOCIAL DEMOCRATIC PARTY

Marx envisioned an ever-growing working class, sinking into greater and greater misery, and then a massive proletarian revolution that would destroy capitalism and introduce a classless society. Actual developments in Europe were quite different. Many workers and socialist intellectuals spurned revolution and instead formed political parties to achieve socialist goals through the ballot box rather than insurrection. Among Marxist political parties, the most powerful was the German Social Democratic party, founded in 1875. Despite efforts by the German chancellor, Otto von Bismarck, to scuttle socialism by outlawing socialist newspapers and meetings and by sponsoring social legislation to improve the worker's lot, the Social Democrats became Germany's largest political party in the 1890s and early twentieth century. They adopted the following statement of their goals at a party congress in Erfurt in 1891.

---

1. Marx and Engels predicted correctly that Germany was poised for rapid industrialization. It would, in their view, take place "under more advanced conditions," i.e., the presence of so-phisticated technology and the ideals of democracy and human equality popularized during the Enlightenment and the French Revolution.

Questions for Analysis

1. What are the similarities and differences between the demands of the Erfurt Program and the future Marx envisions in *The Communist Manifesto*?
2. According to this document, how are socialists to attain their goals?
3. If adopted, how would the demands of the socialists affect the German state?
4. What are the Social Democrats' views of the army? Of organized religion? Of women's position in society?
5. To what extent does the Erfurt Program reflect the ideals of the French Revolution as enunciated in the Declaration of the Rights of Man and of the Citizen (Chapter 6)?

*T*he struggle of the working class against capitalistic exploitation is of necessity a political struggle. The working class cannot carry on its economic contests, and cannot develop its economic organization, without political rights. It cannot bring about the transference of the means of production into the possession of the community without acquiring political power.

To give to this fight of the working class a conscious and unified form, and to show it its necessary goal — that is the task of the Social Democratic Party.

The interests of the working class are the same in all countries with a capitalist mode of production. With the extension of the world's commerce and of production for the world market, the position of the worker in every country grows ever more dependent on the position of the worker in other countries. . . .

The Social Democratic Party of Germany does not fight, accordingly, for new class privileges and class rights, but for the abolition of class rule and of classes themselves, for equal rights and equal duties of all, without distinction of sex or descent. Starting from these views, it combats, within existing society, not only the exploitation and oppression of wage earners, but every kind of exploitation and oppression, whether directed against a class, a party, a sex, or a race.

Proceeding from these principles, the Social Democratic Party of Germany demands, to begin with:

1. Universal, equal, and direct suffrage, with secret ballot, for all elections, of all citizens of the Empire over 20 years of age, without distinction of sex. Proportional representation and, until this is introduced, legal redistribution of electoral districts after every census. Biennial legislative periods. Holding of the elections on a legal holiday. Compensation for the elected representatives. Abolition of every limitation of political rights, except in the case of legal incapacity.

2. Direct legislation through the people, by means of the rights of proposal and rejection. Self-determination and self-government of the people in realm, state, province, and parish. Election of magistrates by the people, with responsibility to the people. Annual voting of taxes.

3. Education of all to bear arms. Militia in the place of the standing army. Decision by the popular representatives on questions of war and peace. Settlement of all international disputes by arbitration.

4. Abolition of all laws which limit or suppress the right of meeting and association.[1]

5. Abolition of all laws which place women, whether in a public or a private capacity, at a disadvantage as compared with men.

6. Declaration that religion is a private matter. Abolition of all expenditure of public funds upon ecclesiastical and religious objects. Ecclesiastical and religious bodies are to be regarded as private associations, which regulate their affairs entirely independently.

7. Secularization of schools. Compulsory attendance at the public national schools. Free education, free supply of educational materials, and free maintenance in the public schools, as well as in the higher educational institutions, for those boys and girls who, on account of their capacities, are considered fit for further education.

8. Free administration of justice and free legal assistance. Administration of the law through judges elected by the people. Appeal in criminal cases. Compensation of persons unjustly accused, imprisoned, or condemned. Abolition of capital punishment.

9. Free medical attendance, including midwifery, and free supply of medicines. Free burial.

10. Graduated income and property tax for defraying all public expenses, so far as these are to be covered by taxation. . . . Abolition of all indirect taxes, customs, and other economic measures, which sacrifice the interests of the community to those of a privileged minority.

For the protection of the working classes, the Social Democratic Party of Germany demands immediately:

1. An effective national and international legislation for the protection of labor on the following principles:
   a. Fixing of a normal working day, which shall not exceed 8 hours.
   b. Prohibition of the employment of children under 14.
   c. Prohibition of night work, except in those industries which, by their nature, require night work, from technical reasons or for the public welfare.
   d. An unbroken rest of at least 36 hours in every week for every worker. . . .

2. Inspection of all industrial establishments, investigation and regulation of conditions of labor in town and country by a central labor department, district labor councils and chambers of labor.

3. Legal equality of agricultural laborers and domestic servants with industrial workers. Abolition of the special regulations concerning servants.

4. Guarantee of the right of combination.

5. Taking over by the Imperial Government of the whole system of working people's insurance, though giving the working people a controlling share in the administration.

6. Separation of the Churches and the State.
   a. Suppression of the grant for public worship.
   b. Philosophic or religious associations to be civil persons at law.

7. Revision of selections in the Civil Code concerning marriage and the paternal authority.
   a. Civil equality of the sexes, and of children, whether natural or legitimate.

---

1. Refers to the establishment of labor unions.

b. Revision of the divorce laws, maintaining the husband's liability to support the wife or the children.

c. Inquiry into paternity to be legalized.

d. Protective measures in favor of children materially or morally abandoned.

The Struggle for Women's Political Rights

The Enlightenment and the French Revolution each proclaimed the ideals of liberty, equality, and the rights of man, but it was never clear whether "man" meant "humanity" or "only males." Even though the leaders of the French Revolution and Napoleon approved laws allowing civil divorce and guaranteeing the inheritance rights of women, their response to women's demands for the political rights to vote and hold public office was "only males."

During the nineteenth century, the heritage of the French Revolution, social changes accompanying industrialization, the emergence of socialism, and the growth of literacy kept alive the issue of women's political rights, especially in England, France, and the United States. A small but growing number of feminists demanded educational opportunities, political rights, equal pay with men, expanded vocational possibilities, and legal protection on matters of inheritance, divorce, child custody, and physical abuse. Some progress was made. Most Western states made some efforts to provide for women's education and to improve their legal status. Certain professions such as nursing, teaching, and government service provided new vocational opportunities for many middle-class women, and a few women established careers in medicine and law. Only a handful of states, among them Australia, New Zealand, Finland, and Norway, granted women full voting privileges. Elsewhere they were permitted to vote in municipal elections or, more frequently, not at all. Yet the efforts of nineteenth-century feminists were not in vain. After World War I most democratic governments granted women full political rights.

"RESOLUTIONS," OHIO WOMEN'S CONVENTION

Two years after the first United States women's rights convention, held in Seneca Falls, New York, in 1848, a group of Ohio women gathered in Salem to make recommendations about the status of women to a forthcoming convention to amend the state constitution. The Salem meeting has a special place in the history of the feminist movement because it was the first women's rights convention held in the

United States that excluded men. The "resolutions," sent to the constitutional convention on April 19 and 20, 1850, are included in the following selection.

Questions for Analysis

1. On what principles does the petition base its arguments for the improvement in the condition of women?
2. What does the document say or imply about the reasons for the subjugation of women?
3. What are the demands in the area of education? The family? Politics?

Whereas, all men are created equal and endowed with certain God-given rights, and all just government is derived from the consent of the governed; and whereas, the doctrine that "man shall pursue his own substantial happiness" is acknowledged by the highest authority to be the great precept of Nature; and whereas, this doctrine is not local, but universal, being dictated by God himself; therefore,

Resolved, That the prohibition of Woman from participating in the enactment of the laws by which she is governed is a direct violation of this precept of Nature, as she is thereby prevented from occupying that position which duty points out, and from pursuing her own substantial happiness by acting up to her conscientious convictions; and that all statutes and constitutional provisions which sanction this prohibition are null and void.

Resolved, That all rights are *human* rights, and pertain to human beings, without distinction of sex; therefore justice demands that all laws shall be made, not for man, or for woman, but for mankind, and that the same legal protection be afforded to the one sex as to the other.

Resolved, That the servile submission and quiet indifference of the Women of this country in relation to the unequal and oppressive laws by which they are governed, are the fruit either of ignorance or degradation, both resulting legitimately from the action of those laws.

Resolved, That the evils arising from the present social, civil and religious condition of women proclaim to them in language not to be misunderstood, that not only their *own* welfare, but the highest good of the race demands of them, as an imperative duty, that they should secure to themselves the elective franchise.

Resolved, That in those laws which confer on man the power to control the property and person of woman, and to remove from her at will the children of her affection, we recognize only the modified code of the slave plantation; and that thus we are brought more nearly in sympathy with the suffering slave, who is despoiled of all his rights.

Resolved, That we, as human beings, are entitled to claim and exercise all the rights that belong by nature to any members of the human family.

Resolved, That all distinctions between men and women in regard to social, literary, pecuniary, religious or political customs and institutions, based on a distinction of sex, are contrary to the laws of Nature, are unjust, and destructive to the purity, elevation and progress in knowledge and goodness of the great human family, and ought to be at once and forever abolished.

Resolved, That the practice of holding women amenable to a different standard of propriety and morality from that to which men are held amenable, is unjust and unnatural, and highly detrimental to domestic and social virtue and happiness.

Resolved, That the political history of Woman demonstrates that tyranny, the most degrading, cruel and arbitrary, can be exercised and produced the same in effect under a mild and republican form of government as by an hereditary despotism.

Resolved, That while we deprecate thus earnestly the political oppression of Woman, we see in her social condition, the regard in which she is held as a moral and intellectual being, the fundamental cause of that oppression.

Resolved, That amongst the principal causes of such social condition we regard the public sentiment which withholds from her all, or almost all, lucrative employment, and enlarged spheres of labor.

Resolved, That in the difficulties thus cast in the way of her self-support, and in her consequent *dependence* upon man, we see the greatest influence at work in imparting to her that tone of character which makes her to be regarded as the "weaker vessel." . . .

Resolved, That we regard those women who content themselves with an idle, aimless life, as involved in the guilt as well as the suffering of their own oppression; and that we hold those who go forth into the world, in the face of the frowns and the sneers of the public, to fill larger spheres of labor, as the truest preachers of the cause of Woman's Rights.

Whereas, one class of society dooms woman to a life of drudgery, another to one of dependence and frivolity; and whereas, the education she generally receives is calculated to cultivate vanity and dependence, therefore,

Resolved, That the education of woman should be in accordance with responsibility in life, that she may acquire the self-reliance and true dignity so essential to the proper fulfillment of the important duties devolving on her.

Resolved, That as woman is not permitted to hold office, nor have any voice in the government, she should not be compelled to pay taxes out of her scanty wages to support men who get eight dollars a-day for *taking* the right to *themselves* to enact laws *for* her.

Resolved, That we, the Women of Ohio, will hereafter meet annually in Convention to consult upon and adopt measures for the removal of various disabilities — political, social, religious, legal and pecuniary — to which women as a class are subjected, and from which results so much misery, degradation and crime.

E. Sylvia Pankhurst

THE SUFFRAGETTE

During the nineteenth century, women sought to advance their cause by making resolutions, publicizing their views, and performing peaceful symbolic acts such as appearing at polling places and requesting to vote, even while knowing they would be turned down. In the years before World War I, however, militancy and confrontation characterized the feminist movement in England. By 1900 Englishwomen could vote in local elections and win election to school boards and other municipal offices, including that of mayor. This was not enough for the remarkable Emmeline Pankhurst (1858–1928), the widow of a Manchester lawyer, who in 1903 founded the Women's Social and Political Union (WSPU). Under the leadership of Pankhurst and her two daughters, Christabel (1880–1958) and Sylvia (1882–1960), the WSPU tried at first to advance its cause by organizing the heckling of politicians and then moved on to smashing windows, slashing paintings in museums, burning letters in mailboxes, bombings, arson, and finally martyrdom, when in May 1913 a young woman threw herself under the hooves of the king's racehorse and was killed before thousands of shocked spectators. When arrested, many Suffragettes, as they were called, went on hunger strikes. The government responded by approving the force feeding of prisoners and the "Cat and Mouse Bill," by which fasting women were released from prison until they had eaten and then rearrested.

The following selection is drawn from Sylvia Pankhurst's work, *The Suffragette*, a history of the suffragette movement between 1905 and 1910. It describes events of December 1909 and January 1910 in which key figures are Selina Martin and Leslie Hall, two commoners, and Lady Constance Lytton, one of the few aristocrats devoted to the cause of women's right to vote.

Questions
for Analysis

1. Because this is an account by one of the founders of the WSPU, the reader must be sensitive to possible biases. Do you see any signs of bias in this account?
2. What does this account tell us about the motivation of Lady Lytton?
3. How would you characterize the actions and attitudes of the prison doctors?
4. What does the selection reveal about class attitudes in England?

On December 20th, Mr. Asquith[1] had arranged to speak both at Liverpool and Birkenhead, and owing to his desire to avoid the Suffragettes, detectives smuggled him across the river, amongst the luggage. Nevertheless outside the Liberal Club Miss Selina Martin and Miss Leslie Hall, who stood in the gutter, the one disguised as a match girl, and the other as an orange seller, spoke to him as he stepped from his motor car, and urged upon him the necessity for granting the franchise to women. He dashed away without answering, and in protest, and by way of warning, Miss Selina Martin tossed a ginger beer bottle into the empty car which he had left.

Both women were at once arrested, and

---

1. Herbert Henry Asquith (1852–1928) a leading member of the Liberal party and prime minister from 1908 to 1916.

were afterwards remanded in custody for six days. . . . The women were removed to Walton Gaol, and were there treated as though they had been ordinary convicted criminals. They protested by refusing to eat just as so many of their comrades had done before them. Miss Martin also barricaded her cell, but the officials forced their way in, pulled her off the bed and flung her on the floor, shaking and striking her unmercifully. Shortly afterwards her cell was visited by the deputy medical officer, who ordered that she should get up and dress. She explained that she had been wet through by the snowstorm on the previous day and that her clothes were still saturated, for no attempt had been made to get them dry, but she was forcibly dressed and, with her hands handcuffed behind her, was dragged to a cold, dark punishment cell and flung on the stone floor. She lay there in an exhausted state for some hours, being unable to rise without the aid of her hands and arms, which were still fastened behind her back, until, at last, a wardress came in and lifted her onto the bed board. . . .

Meanwhile, Miss Leslie Hall had also broken her windows and had been placed in a punishment cell and kept in handcuffs continuously for three days. After two and a half days' fasting she was fed by the stomach tube. The doctor had taunted her meanwhile, and jokingly told the wardress that she was "mentally sick," and that it was "like stuffing a turkey for Christmas." . . .

Now Lady Constance Lytton, in spite of her fragile constitution and the disease from which she suffered, again determined to place herself beside the women in the fighting ranks who were enduring the greatest hardship. Believing that she had been released from Newcastle prison on account of her rank, and family influence, she determined that this time she would go disguised. She knew that, not only her family, but the leaders of the militant movement would try to dissuade her on account of her health. She, therefore, decided to speak of her intention to no one except Mrs. Baines and a few local workers whom she pledged to secrecy. On January 14th, she and Mrs. Baines organized a procession to Walton Gaol. A halt was called opposite the prison, and, having told the story of what was happening inside Lady Constance called the people to follow her to its gates, and demand the release of the tortured women. Then she moved forward and, as she had foreseen, she was immediately placed under arrest. . . . Lady Constance had disguised herself by cutting her hair, wearing spectacles, and dressing herself in poor and plain garments, and now she gave Jane Warton, seamstress, as her name and occupation. Next morning she was sentenced to fourteen days' hard labor without the option of a fine. . . . On arriving at the prison, on Saturday, January 15th, they[2] made the usual claim to be treated as political prisoners, and, on this being refused, signified their intention of refusing to conform to any of the prison rules. Thereupon they were forcibly stripped by the wardresses and dressed in the prison clothes. At five o'clock, on Tuesday, the doctor entered Lady Constance Lytton's cell with four wardresses and the forcible feeding apparatus. Then, without testing her heart or feeling her pulse, though she had not been medically examined since entering the prison, he ordered that she should be placed in position. She did not resist, but lay down on the bed board voluntarily, well knowing that she would need all her strength for the ordeal that was to come. Her poor heart was palpitating wildly, but she set

---

2. Lady Lytton and others arrested with her.

her teeth and tried to calm herself. The doctor then produced a wooden and a steel gag and told her that he would not use the latter, which would hurt, unless she resisted him; but, as she would not unlock her teeth, he threw the milder wooden instrument aside and pried her mouth open with the steel one. Then the stomach tube was forced down and the whole hateful feeding business was gone through. "The reality surpassed all that I had anticipated," she said. "It was a living nightmare of pain, horror and revolting degradation. The sense is of being strangled, suffocated by the thrust down of the large rubber tube, which arouses great irritation in the throat and nausea in the stomach. The anguish and effort of retching whilst the tube is forcibly pressed back into the stomach and the natural writhing of the body restrained, defy description. I forgot what I was in there for, I forgot women, I forgot everything, except my own sufferings, and I was completely overcome by them." The doctor, annoyed by her one effort to resist, affected to consider her distress assumed, and struck her contemptuously on the cheek as he rose to leave, but the wardresses showed pity for her weakness, and they helped her to wipe her clothes, over which she had been sick. . . . When she was fed the second time the vomiting was more excessive and the doctor's clothes suffered. He was angry and left her cell hastily, saying, "You did that on purpose. If you do it again tomorrow I shall feed you twice." . . .

The third time she was fed she vomited continuously, but the doctor kept pouring in more food until she was seized with a violent fit of shivering. Then he became

alarmed. He hastily told the wardresses to lay her on the floor and called in his assistant to test her heart, but, after a brief and superficial investigation, it was pronounced "quite sound" and the pulse "steady." Next time he appeared he pleaded with her, saying, "I do beg of you, I appeal to you, not as a prison doctor, but as a man, to give over. You are a delicate woman, you are not fit for this sort of thing." "Is anybody fit for it?" she answered. "I beg of you, I appeal to you, not as a prisoner, but as a woman, to refuse to continue this inhuman treatment."

From Wednesday, January 19th, and onwards, she began to find that not only did she receive greater consideration from the doctor, but that there was a marked change in her treatment generally. This led her to conclude that her identity had been discovered or at least suspected, and she therefore tried to take advantage of whatever privileges might be made to her in order to secure concessions for her comrades and to induce the officials to act with more humanity. . . . On Friday the authorities made up their minds that she was not Jane Warton, and on Sunday morning both the governor and doctor appeared and told her that she was to be released and that her sister had come to fetch her.

Lady Constance Lytton now sent a careful statement to Mr. Gladstone[3] asserting that the forcible feeding was performed with unnecessary cruelty and without proper care. He declared that all her charges were unfounded, and the visiting magistrates, having held a one-sided enquiry into the matter, announced that the regulations had been carried out with the greatest care and consideration.

---

3. The son of the famous Liberal politician and prime minister, William Ewart Gladstone, Herbert John Gladstone (1854–1930) was secretary of state for home affairs at the time of these events.

New Perspectives on Humanity

Intellectual developments during the nineteenth century were, if anything, just as revolutionary as those in politics and economics. Never before in so short a time were discoveries and provocative ideas produced in such abundance. Many of these discoveries, especially in science, medicine, and technology, confirmed the Enlightenment's faith in human reason as an instrument for progress. Railroads, steamships, automobiles, dirigibles, airplanes, submarines, telegraph systems, telephones, radios, electric lights, anesthetics, x-ray machines, antiseptics, coal-tar dyes, and countless new drugs were only the most notable of the scientific and technological wonders of the nineteenth and early twentieth centuries.

New scientific theories, however, could also be troubling. This was true of the work of Charles Darwin (1809–1882), the English naturalist who proposed that all species of plants and animals, including human beings, evolved from more primitive forms and, furthermore, that evolution resulted not from a divine plan but from a process he called "natural selection." Darwin's ideas clashed with the creation story set forth in the Old Testament's Book of Genesis, in which God creates the whole universe, including the first humans, Adam and Eve, in seven days. Darwin's ideas outraged members of religious groups who believed in the literal truth of the Bible, and ever since Darwinism has symbolized the clash between science and religion.

The nineteenth century also saw developments in what are now known as the social sciences. New disciplines emerged, including sociology (the study of society and social relationships), anthropology (the study of the origin, development, and culture of humankind), and psychology (the study of the mind and behavior). Older intellectual endeavors such as the study of history, politics, and economics formulated new methodologies consistent with the standards of the scientific method.

Among the social scientists of the late nineteenth century, no one disturbed established ways of thinking as deeply as Sigmund Freud (1856–1939). A Viennese physician, Freud suggested that much in human behavior was controlled not by rational thought, as the *philosophes* of the Enlightenment had supposed, but by unconscious sexual and aggressive drives that were largely unknown and uncontrollable. In his view, mental and emotional diseases resulted from the strain of attempting to repress these drives or channel them into what the individual sensed to be socially accepted behavior. Such diseases could be cured when an individual, through sessions with a therapist, came to understand what unconscious drives were being repressed.

Freud's theory that patients could be cured through knowledge confirmed the Enlightenment's faith in the power of rational analysis, yet many contemporaries saw his theories differently. His assertion that powerful sexual instincts drove human behavior seemed to demolish the idea of humans as rational creatures, capable of moral improvement. Like Darwin, Freud appeared to erase the distinction between animals and human beings.

Charles Darwin

ON THE ORIGIN OF SPECIES
AND
THE DESCENT OF MAN

After studying at the universities of Edinburgh and Cambridge, Darwin spent five years on the H.M.S. *Beagle* as the chief naturalist on a scientific expedition that explored the South Pacific and the western coast of South America. Darwin observed the bewildering variety of nature and began to speculate about how millions of species of plants and animals had come into existence. On his return to England, he developed his theory of evolution, basing his hypothesis on his own formidable biological knowledge, recent discoveries in geology, work on the selective breeding of plants and animals, and the suggestion of several authors that competition was the norm for all living things. In 1859, he published his theories in *On the Origin of Species by Means of Natural Selection*, followed in 1871 by *The Descent of Man*.

Questions
for Analysis

1. What does Darwin mean by the terms *struggle for existence* and *natural selection?*
2. What is the cause of the "struggle for existence"?
3. What were some implications of Darwin's work for nineteenth-century views of progress? Of nature? Of human nature?
4. How does Darwin defend himself from the attacks on his work motivated by religion? How do his views compare with those of Galileo in "Letter to the Grand Duchess Christina" (Chapter 5)?
5. Advocates of laissez-faire capitalism sometimes invoked Darwinian concepts in their arguments against socialism. Which concepts might they have used?
6. Defenders of militarism and late–nineteenth-century Western imperialism also drew on Darwin's ideas. Which of his theories might they have invoked?

ON THE ORIGIN OF SPECIES

Chapter III   Struggle for Existence

Before entering on the subject of this chapter, I must make a few preliminary remarks, to show how the struggle for existence bears on Natural Selection. It has been seen in the last chapter that amongst organic beings in a state of nature there is some individual variability: indeed I am not aware that this has ever been disputed. . . . But the mere existence of individual variability and of some few well-marked varieties, though necessary as the foundation for the work, helps us but little in understanding how species arise in nature. How have all those exquisite adaptations of one part of the organization to another part, and to the conditions of life, and of one organic being to another being, been perfected? We see these beautiful co-adaptations most plainly in the woodpecker and the mistletoe;[1] and only a little less plainly in the humblest parasite which clings to the hairs of a quadruped or feathers of a bird; in the structure of the beetle which dives through the water: in the plumed seed which is wafted by the gentlest breeze; in short, we see beautiful adaptations everywhere and in every part of the organic world.

Again, it may be asked, how is it that varieties, which I have called incipient species, become ultimately converted into good and distinct species, which in most cases obviously differ from each other far more than do the varieties of the same species? . . . All these results, as we shall more fully see in the next chapter, follow from the struggle for life. Owing to this struggle, variations, however slight and from whatever cause proceeding, if they be in any degree profitable to the individuals of a species, in their infinitely complex relations to other organic beings and to their physical conditions of life, will tend to the preservation of such individuals, and will generally be inherited by the offspring. The offspring, also, will thus have a better chance of surviving, for, of the many individuals of any species which are periodically born, but a small number can survive. I have called this principle, by which each slight variation, if useful, is preserved, by the term Natural Selection, in order to mark its relation to man's power of selection. But the expression often used by Mr. Herbert Spencer[2] of the Survival of the Fittest is more accurate, and is sometimes equally convenient. . . .

[The Term, Struggle for Existence, Used in a Large Sense]

I should premise that I use this term in a large and metaphorical sense including dependence of one being on another, and including (which is more important) not only the life of the individual, but success in leaving progeny. Two canine animals, in a time of dearth, may be truly said to struggle with each other which shall get food and live. But a plant on the edge of a desert is said to struggle for life against the drought, though more properly it should be said to be dependent on the moisture. A plant which annually produces a thousand seeds, of which only one of an average comes to maturity, may be more truly said to struggle with the plants of the same and other kinds which already clothe the ground. The mistletoe is dependent on the apple and a few other trees, but can only in a far-fetched sense be said to struggle with these trees, for, if too many of these parasites grow on the same tree, it languishes and dies. But several seedling mistletoes, growing close together on the same branch, may more truly be said to struggle with each other. . . . In these several senses, which pass into each other, I use for convenience's sake the general term of Struggle for Existence.

[Geometrical Ratio of Increase]

A struggle for existence inevitably follows from the high rate at which all organic beings tend to increase. Every being, which during its natural lifetime produces several eggs or seeds, must suffer destruc-

---

1. In a previous chapter, Darwin had discussed at length how perfectly the structure of the woodpecker and mistletoe suited them for survival as a bird that pecked insects out of trees and as a parasitic plant.

2. An English philosopher (1820–1903) influenced by Darwin's work.

tion during some period of its life, and during some season or occasional year, otherwise . . . its numbers would quickly become so inordinately great that no country could support the product. Hence, as more individuals are produced than can possibly survive, there must in every case be a struggle for existence, either one individual with another of the same species, or with the individuals of distinct species, or with the physical conditions of life. It is the doctrine of Malthus[3] applied with manifold force to the whole animal and vegetable kingdoms; for in this case there can be no artificial increase of food, and no prudential restraint from marriage. Although some species may be now increasing, more or less rapidly, in numbers, all cannot do so, for the world would not hold them. . . .

THE DESCENT OF MAN

Chapter II   On the Manner of Development of Man from Some Lower Form

In this chapter we have seen that as man at the present day is liable, like every other animal, to multiform individual differences or slight variations, so no doubt were the early progenitors of man; the variations being formerly induced by the same general causes, and governed by the same general and complex laws as at present. As all animals tend to multiply beyond their means of subsistence, so it must have been with the progenitors of man; and this would inevitably lead to a struggle for existence and to natural selection. The latter process would be greatly aided by the inherited effects of the increased use of parts, and these two proc-

esses would incessantly react on each other. It appears, also, as we shall hereafter see, that various unimportant characters have been acquired by man through sexual selection. An unexplained residuum of change must be left to the assumed uniform action of those unknown agencies, which occasionally induce strongly marked and abrupt deviations of structure in our domestic productions.

Chapter VI   On the Affinities and Genealogy of Man

Now as organisms have become slowly adapted to diversified lines of life by means of natural selection, their parts will have become more and more differentiated and specialized for various functions, from the advantage gained by the division of physiological labor. The same part appears often to have been modified first for one purpose, and then long afterwards for some other and quite distinct purpose; and thus all the parts are rendered more and more complex. But each organism still retains the general type of structure of the progenitor from which it was aboriginally derived. In accordance with this view it seems, if we turn to geological evidence, that organization on the whole has advanced throughout the world by slow and interrupted steps. In the great kingdom of the Vertebrata it has culminated in man. . . .

The most ancient progenitors in the kingdom of the Vertebrata, at which we are able to obtain an obscure glance, apparently consisted of a group of marine animals, resembling the larvae of existing Ascidians.[4] These animals probably gave rise to a group of fishes, as lowly organ-

---

3. The English economist Thomas Robert Malthus (1766–1834), whose *An Essay on the Principle of Population* (1798) warned that human population growth, if unchecked, would lead to catastrophic famine.

4. Saclike marine animals.

ized as the lancelet;[5] and from these the Ganoids,[6] and other fishes must have developed. From such fish a very small advance would carry us on to the Amphibians. We have seen that birds and reptiles were once intimately connected together; and the Monotremata[7] now connect mammals with reptiles in a slight degree. But no one can at present say by what line of descent the three higher and related classes, namely, mammals, birds, and reptiles, were derived from the two lower vertebrate classes, namely, amphibians and fishes. In the class of mammals the steps are not difficult to conceive which led from the ancient Monotremata to the ancient Marsupials,[8] and from these to the early progenitors of the placental mammals. We may thus ascend to the Lemuridae,[9] and the interval is not very wide from these to the Simiadae.[10] The Simiadae then branched off into two great stems, the New World and Old World monkeys; and from the latter, at a remote period, Man, the wonder and glory of the Universe, proceeded.

Chapter XXI   General Summary and Conclusion

I am aware that the conclusions arrived at in this work will be denounced by some as highly irreligious; but he who denounces them is bound to show why it is more irreligious to explain the origin of man as a distinct species by descent from some lower form, through the laws of variation and natural selection, than to explain the birth of the individual through the laws of ordinary reproduction. The birth both of the species and of the individual are equally parts of that grand sequence of events, which our minds refuse to accept as the result of blind chance. The understanding revolts at such a conclusion, whether or not we are able to believe that every slight variation of structure, — the union of each pair in marriage, — the dissemination of each seed, — and other such events, have all been ordained for some special purpose. . . .

The main conclusion arrived at in this work, namely that man is descended from some lowly organized form, will, I regret to think, be highly distasteful to many. But there can hardly be a doubt that we are descended from barbarians. The astonishment which I felt on first seeing a party of Fuegians[11] on a wild and broken shore will never be forgotten by me, for the reflection at once rushed into my mind — such were our ancestors. These men were absolutely naked and bedaubed with paint, their long hair was tangled, their mouths frothed with excitement, and their expression was wild, startled, and distrustful. They possessed hardly any arts, and like wild animals lived on what they could catch; they had no government, and were merciless to every one not of their own small tribe. He who has seen a savage in his native land will not feel much shame, if forced to acknowledge that the blood of some more humble

---

5. Marine animals with a rodlike primitive backbone.

6. Bony fish such as the sturgeon and gar, covered with large armorlike scales.

7. Order of egg-laying mammals such as the platypus.

8. Mammals such as the kangaroo, whose females lack placentas and carry their young in an abdominal pouch.

9. Largely nocturnal, tree-dwelling mammals related to monkeys but a distinct superfamily.

10. Apes and monkeys.

11. Inhabitants of Tierra del Fuego, an island at the southernmost tip of South America.

creature flows in his veins. For my own part I would as soon be descended from that heroic little monkey, who braved his dreaded enemy in order to save the life of his keeper, or from that old baboon, who descending from the mountains, carried away in triumph his young comrade from a crowd of astonished dogs — as from a savage who delights to torture his enemies, offers up bloody sacrifices, practices infanticide without remorse, treats his wives like slaves, knows no decency, and is haunted by the grossest superstitions.

Man may be excused for feeling some pride at having risen, though not through his own exertions, to the very summit of the organic scale; and the fact of his having thus risen, instead of having been ab-originally placed there, may give him hope for a still higher destiny in the distant future. But we are not here concerned with hopes or fears, only with the truth as far as our reason permits us to discover it; and I have given the evidence to the best of my ability. We must, however, acknowledge, as it seems to me, that man with all his noble qualities, with sympathy which feels for the most debased, with benevolence which extends not only to other men but to the humblest living creature, with his god-like intellect which has penetrated into the movements and constitution of the solar system — with all these exalted powers — Man still bears in his bodily frame the indelible stamp of his lowly origin.

Imperialism: The European Justification

Western expansionism continued in the first half of the nineteenth century. The British added piecemeal to their territories in India; the French strengthened their hold on Algeria; and the Western powers combined to "open" China and Japan to trade. Then, in the closing decades of the 1800s, the long history of Western expansionism culminated in the Era of Imperialism — one final orgiastic land grab unprecedented in human history. The following figures show how much land and how many people the major powers added to their empires between 1871 and 1900: Great Britain: 4.25 million square miles and 66 million people, France: 3.5 million square miles and 26 million people, Germany: 1 million square miles and 13 million people, Belgium: 900,000 square miles and 13 million people.[1] Acquisitions by Italy, the United States, and the Netherlands increased these totals even more.

The phenomenon of late-nineteenth-century imperialism resulted in part from the West's continuing technological progress. The abandonment of sailing vessels for metal-hulled steamships reduced two-month oceanic voyages to two weeks; undersea telegraph lines enabled governments and businessmen to communicate in seconds, not weeks or months; new drugs such as quinine protected Europeans from tropical diseases like malaria; improved firearms increased the West's ability to subdue and control native populations.

But technology alone cannot explain the expansionist fever that swept the Western

---

[1]L. S. Stavrianos, *The World Since 1500*, 4th ed. (Englewood Cliffs, N.J.: Prentice-Hall, 1982), p. 187.

nations in the late 1800s. As the following documents reveal, political rivalries, anticipated economic gains, and even altruism all contributed to the psychological atmosphere that led to this final chapter of Western expansion.

Jules Ferry

SPEECH BEFORE THE FRENCH NATIONAL ASSEMBLY

Jules Ferry (1832–1893) was a French politician who twice served as premier during the Third Republic, the name of the French government from 1871 until 1940. Ferry was an enthusiastic imperialist, and during his premierships France annexed Tunisia and parts of Indochina and began exploring Africa's Congo River region. In debates in the French National Assembly he frequently defended his policies against both socialist and conservative critics who, for different reasons, opposed French imperialism. The following selection from his speech on July 28, 1883, summarizes Ferry's reasons for supporting French expansionism and also sheds light on his opponents' views.

Questions for Analysis

1. What economic forces, according to Ferry, make imperialism a necessity for France? What economic benefits will result?
2. What other arguments does Ferry present in favor of imperialism?
3. What are the antiimperialist arguments of his opponents? How does he counter them?

M. Jules Ferry. Gentlemen, it embarrasses me to make such a prolonged demand upon the gracious attention of the Chamber, but I believe that the duty I am fulfilling upon this platform is not a useless one: It is as strenuous for me as for you, but I believe that there is some benefit in summarizing and condensing, in the form of arguments, the principles, the motives, and the various interests by which a policy of colonial expansion may be justified; it goes without saying that I will try to remain reasonable, moderate, and never lose sight of the major continental interests which are the primary concern of this country. What I wish to say, to support this proposition, is that in fact, just as in word, the policy of colonial expansion is a political and economic system; I wish to say that one can relate this system to three orders of ideas: economic ideas, ideas of civilization in its highest sense, and ideas of politics and patriotism.

In the area of economics, I will allow myself to place before you, with the support of some figures, the considerations which justify a policy of colonial expansion from the point of view of that need, felt more and more strongly by the industrial populations of Europe and particularly those of our own rich and hard working country: the need for export markets. Is this some kind of chimera? Is this a view of the future or is it not rather a pressing need, and, we could say, the cry of our industrial population? I will formulate only in a general way what each of you, in the different parts of France, is in a position to confirm. Yes, what is lacking for our great industry, drawn irrevocably on to the path of exportation by the (free trade) treaties of 1860,[1] what it lacks more and more is export markets. Why? Because next door to us Germany is surrounded by barriers, because beyond the ocean, the United States of America has become protectionist, protectionist in the most extreme sense, because not only have these great markets, I will not say closed but shrunk, and thus become more difficult of access for our industrial products, but also these great states are beginning to pour products not seen heretofore onto our own markets. . . . It is not necessary to pursue this demonstration any farther. . . .

. . . Gentlemen, there is a second point, a second order of ideas to which I have to give equal attention, but as quickly as possible, believe me; it is the humanitarian and civilizing side of the question. On this point the honorable M. Camille Pelletan[2] has jeered in his own refined and clever manner; he jeers, he condemns, and he says "What is this civilization which you impose with cannon-balls? What is it but another form of barbarism? Don't these populations, these inferior races, have the same rights as you? Aren't they masters of their own houses? Have they called upon you? You come to them against their will, you offer them violence, but not civilization." There, gentlemen, is the thesis; I do not hesitate to say that this is not politics, nor is it history: it is political metaphysics. ("Ah, Ah" on far left.)[3]

. . . Gentlemen, I must speak from a higher and more truthful plane. It must be stated openly that, in effect, superior races have rights over inferior races. (*Movement on many benches on the far left.*)

M. Jules Maigne. Oh! You dare to say this in the country which has proclaimed the rights of man!

M. de Guilloutet. This is a justification of slavery and the slave trade!

M. Jules Ferry. If M. Maigne is right, if the declaration of the rights of man was written for the blacks of equatorial Africa, then by what right do you impose regular commerce upon them? They have not called upon you.

M. Raoul Duval. We do not want to impose anything upon them. It is you who wish to do so!

M. Jules Maigne. To propose and to impose are two different things!

M. Georges Perin.[4] In any case, you cannot bring about commerce by force.

M. Jules Ferry. I repeat that superior races have a right, because they have a duty. They have the duty to civilize inferior races. . . . (*Approbation from the left. New interruptions from the extreme left and from the right.*) . . .

---

1. The reference is to a trade treaty between Great Britain and France that lowered tariffs between the two nations.

2. Pelletan (1846–1815) was a patriotic, radical republican politician.

3. Adhering to a tradition begun in the legislative assemblies of the French Revolution, democrats and republicans sat on the far left, moderates in the center, and conservatives on the right. By the 1880s, the "left" also included socialists.

4. Maigne, Guilloutet, Duval, and Perin were all members of the National Assembly.

That is what I have to answer M. Pelletan in regard to the second point upon which he touched.

He then touched upon a third, more delicate, more serious, and upon which I ask your permission to express myself quite frankly. It is the political side of the question. The honorable M. Pelletan, who is a distinguished writer, always comes up with remarkably precise formulations. I will borrow from him the one which he applied the other day to this aspect of colonial policy.

"It is a system," he says, "which consists of seeking out compensations in the Orient with a circumspect and peaceful seclusion which is actually imposed upon us in Europe."

I would like to explain myself in regard to this. I do not like this word "compensation," and, in effect, not here but elsewhere it has often been used in a treacherous way. If what is being said or insinuated is that a republican minister could possibly believe that there are in any part of the world compensations for the disasters which we have experienced,[5] an injury is being inflicted . . . and an injury undeserved by that government. (*Applause at the center and left.*) I will ward off this injury with all the force of my patriotism! (*New applause and bravos from the same benches.*)

Gentlemen, there are certain considerations which merit the attention of all patriots. The conditions of naval warfare have been profoundly altered. ("Very true! Very true!")

At this time, as you know, a warship cannot carry more than fourteen days' worth of coal, no matter how perfectly it is organized, and a ship which is out of coal is a derelict on the surface of the sea,

abandoned to the first person who comes along. Thence the necessity of having on the oceans provision stations, shelters, ports for defense and revictualling. (*Applause at the center and left. Various interruptions.*) And it is for this that we needed Tunisia, for this that we needed Saigon and the Mekong Delta, for this that we need Madagascar, that we are at Diégo-Suarez and Vohemar[6] and will never leave them! (*Applause from a great number of benches.*) Gentlemen, in Europe as it is today, in this competition of so many rivals which we see growing around us, some by perfecting their military or maritime forces, others by the prodigious development of an ever growing population; in a Europe, or rather in a universe of this sort, a policy of peaceful seclusion or abstention is simply the highway to decadence! Nations are great in our times only by means of the activities which they develop; it is not simply "by the peaceful shining forth of institutions" (*Interruptions on the extreme left and right*) that they are great at this hour. . . .

As for me, I am astounded to find the monarchist parties becoming indignant over the fact that the Republic of France is following a policy which does not confine itself to that ideal of modesty, of reserve, and, if you will allow me the expression, of bread and butter (*Interruptions and laughter on the left*) which the representatives of fallen monarchies wish to impose upon France. (*Applause at the center.*) . . .

(The Republican Party) has shown that it is quite aware that one cannot impose upon France a political ideal conforming to that of nations like independent Belgium and the Swiss Republic; that something else is needed for France: that she cannot be merely a free country, that she

---

5. The reference is to France's defeat by Prussia and the German states in the Franco-Prussian War of 1870–1871.

6. Madagascar port cities.

must also be a great country, exercising all of her rightful influence over the destiny of Europe, that she ought to propagate this influence throughout the world and carry everywhere that she can her language, her customs, her flag, her arms, and her genius. (*Applause at center and left.*)

Rudyard Kipling

THE WHITE MAN'S BURDEN

Rudyard Kipling (1865–1936) was one of the most popular British writers of the late nineteenth and early twentieth centuries. Born in Bombay, India, he was educated in England, and on his return to India in 1882 he established a career as a journalist, poet, and story-writer. He is best remembered today for his glorification of the British Empire and the heroism of the British soldier in India and Burma. He wrote "The White Man's Burden" in 1898, dedicating it to the United States in 1899, shortly after its annexation of the Philippines.

Questions
for Analysis

1. What is the "white man's burden"?
2. What does the poem imply about Kipling's attitude toward non-Western peoples?
3. What does Kipling's poem describe as imperialism's major purpose?
4. What do you think accounts for the poem's wide appeal?
5. To what extent do Kipling's ideas agree with Jules Ferry's arguments?

Take up the White Man's burden —
   Send forth the best ye breed —
Go bind your sons to exile
   To serve your captives' need;
To wait in heavy harness,
   On fluttered folk and wild —
Your new-caught, sullen peoples,
   Half-devil and half-child.

Take up the White Man's burden —
   In patience to abide,
To veil the threat of terror
   And check the show of pride;
By open speech and simple,
   An hundred times made plain,

To seek another's profit,
   And work another's gain.

Take up the White Man's burden —
   The savage wars of peace —
Fill full the mouth of Famine
   And bid the sickness cease;
And when your goal is nearest
   The end for others sought,
Watch Sloth and heathen Folly
   Bring all your hope to nought.

Take up the White Man's burden —
   No tawdry rule of kings,
But toil of serf and sweeper —

The tale of common things.
The ports ye shall not enter,
   The roads ye shall not tread,
Go make them with your living,
   And mark them with your dead.

Take up the White Man's burden —
   And reap his old reward:
The blame of those ye better,
   The hate of those ye guard —
The cry of hosts ye humor
   (Ah, slowly!) toward the light: —
"Why brought ye us from bondage,
   "Our loved Egyptian night?"

Take up the White Man's burden —
   Ye dare not stoop to less —

Nor call too loud on Freedom
   To cloak your weariness;
By all ye cry or whisper,
   By all ye leave or do,
The silent, sullen peoples
   Shall weigh your Gods and you.

Take up the White Man's burden —
   Have done with childish days —
The lightly proffered laurel,
   The easy, ungrudged praise.
Comes now, to search your manhood
   Through all the thankless years,
Cold, edged with dear-bought wisdom,
   The judgment of your peers!

C H A P T E R

9

Colonialism and Nationalism in Africa, the Middle East, and India

When the nineteenth century began, Africa, the Middle East, and India had little in common. Africa, as had been true for centuries, consisted of hundreds of independent kingdoms, cities, and tribes. The Middle East was dominated by two large empires, the Persian Qajar (1794–1925) in the east, and the Ottoman in the west. Although each had lost territory in the previous century and a half, the empires were independent and fiercely anti-Western. Conversely, parts of India were already under British control, and, given the aggressiveness of the British and the continuing breakdown of the Mughal political order, it seemed inevitable that British authority would increase.

A century later, however, these three regions shared much in common. As a result of Western encroachment and interference, all were colonies or semi-colonies of European nations. The British in the nineteenth century did indeed extend their empire until it virtually encompassed the whole Indian subcontinent. Meanwhile, previously independent Africa became another India; that is, it too fell victim to European imperialism. The main difference was that India had but one colonial master, whereas Africa had half a dozen. In the Middle East, Persia's Qajar dynasty faced growing British and Russian interference, culminating in the Anglo-Russian Agreement of 1907, which divided the country into a Russian-dominated north, a British-dominated south, and a supposedly independent center. The Ottoman Empire maintained its political independence but lost thousands of square miles of territory in North Africa and Europe. Continuing internal problems and military decline largely explain these losses, but European pressure and meddling also played a role. European nations supported the nineteenth-century insurrections by which Greece, Serbia, Rumania, and Bulgaria won their independence, and Great Britain established economic and political control over Egypt, although in theory, the north African country remained part of the Ottoman Empire. Furthermore, Europeans reduced the Ottoman government itself to semicolonial status. Foreigners controlled state revenues through the Ottoman Public Debt Administration, an agency established to guarantee payment of the government's huge debts. Foreign businessmen, who controlled most of Turkey's banks, railroads, and mines, influenced Turkish tariff policy and were exempt from many Turkish laws, taxes, and courts.

European colonialism in Africa, the Middle East, and India varied, and so too did the response that the European presence evoked. In all three areas, however, European domination had a similar impact. It weakened or destroyed existing political structures and introduced new economic practices. It challenged traditional beliefs and forced the colonial peoples to reconsider their religious and social customs. The nineteenth-century European intrusion forced the people of Africa, the Middle East, and India to abandon much of their past and face an uncertain future.

The European Assault on Africa

Paradoxically, the century that saw the near total submission of Africa to European rule began with an apparent European withdrawal from African involvement. Responding to religious and humanitarian arguments, around 1800 several Western states, including Denmark, France, the United States, and, most important, Great Britain, outlawed the slave trade. Unexpectedly, however, for Great Britain the end of the slave trade meant more, not less, involvement in African affairs. Realizing the importance of the slave trade to the African economy, the British government now felt responsible for encouraging farming, mining, and commerce in nonhuman commodities. These efforts often meant that British officials left their coastal bases and traveled to the interior to deal with tribal chiefs. In addition, the British sent large numbers of naval vessels to African coastal waters to prevent illegal slaving. This increased involvement in African affairs, combined with the excitement generated by the exploits of early explorers, sparked an interest in Africa that paved the way for its subsequent takeover.

This takeover took only two decades. In 1878 King Leopold II of Belgium (1865–1909) commissioned the Welsh-born newspaperman and explorer H. M. Stanley (1841–1904) to negotiate "treaties" with Bantu chieftains in the Congo basin in which they effectively surrendered their territories to Leopold and his business associates. Shortly thereafter, the French explorer Pierre de Brazza (1852–1905) was dispatched by the French government to sign hundreds of similar treaties that ceded African tribal lands to France and served as the foundation for the colony of French Equatorial Africa. When France established a protectorate over Tunisia in 1881 and Great Britain occupied Egypt in 1882, the scramble for Africa began in earnest. In 1885 fourteen nations, including the United States, attended the Congress of Berlin, which established guidelines for the European conquest of Africa.

All Africans did not passively accept their new subservience. Especially in Muslim areas, they offered military resistance that Europe's artillery, high explosive shells, and machine guns doomed to failure. In 1898 the Battle of Omdurman in modern Sudan resulted in some 11,000 casualties for the Muslim tribesmen and 40 for the British and their Egyptian allies. When World War I began in 1914, only Ethiopia and tiny Liberia were independent.

Captain Robert Craigie

REPORT ON A DISCUSSION WITH KING PEPPLE OF BONNY ON BOARD HER MAJESTY'S SHIP, *BONETTA*

After abolishing the slave trade in 1805, British officials soon realized that antislavery laws by themselves would not end the African slave traffic. To the contrary, the

Industrial Revolution's demand for cotton fiber strengthened the market for slaves to work on the cotton plantations of the American South. With large profits still to be made, African chiefs were disinclined to end slaving, and Spanish and Portuguese merchants replaced the British and French in many coastal slave markets.

The following report illustrates British efforts to discourage the slave trade. Robert Craigie, a naval officer, submitted it to the British government on March 11, 1839, after it sent him to negotiate the end of slaving by King Pepple of Bonny, a town on the Niger delta in modern Nigeria. Before his visit, the British had freed no less than 3,222 slaves from ships off Bonny's coast. Captain Craigie's negotiations proved a failure. Ten years later another British naval officer reported to Parliament that King Pepple, while collecting British money for not selling slaves, was still selling 1,000 humans a year to the Spanish and Portuguese.

Questions
for Analysis

1. What kind of impression does Captain Craigie hope to make on King Pepple and his entourage?
2. What do the British offer King Pepple to encourage his abandonment of the slave trade? What threats do they use?
3. King Pepple ignored the agreements made with Captain Craigie in 1839. What do you think were his reasons?

King Pepple, of Bonny, accompanied by Anna Pepple,[1] by his Juju man or high priest, and Hee Chee, Anna Pepple's secretary, for the first time went on board a man-of-war, for the purpose of paying a visit to Captain Craigie, where he was received with the usual salutes.

The King, in going round the decks, expressed his surprise and delight at everything he saw; but the astonishment of the whole party knew no bounds when the great guns were exercised in firing at the target. . . .

When the King and suite had finished breakfast, Captain Craigie presented to His Majesty a box containing presents from the English Government, which the King desired might be opened. As the bales of scarlet and green broad cloth were being lifted out of the case, the King and Anna Pepple especially were struck with the magnificence of the gifts, and Captain Craigie, anxious to show Anna Pepple how much he approved of his late conduct towards the English, and proper respect for the King, made a request of His

---

1. A male relative of the king who held some sort of position in directing the family's slaving operations.

Majesty to allow Anna Pepple to have one piece of the cloth and a shawl, which the King at once complied with.

Captain Craigie then proceeded to read to King Pepple and suite the despatch of Lord Palmerston[2] dated 14th April, 1838, relative to Slave abolition, and strongly impressed upon His Majesty that part which states that treaties had already been made between England and other African Princes for the purpose of putting an end to the Slave Trade, and that in those cases the Articles of Treaty had been faithfully maintained.

Captain Craigie assured the King that England ever dispensed justice, and would encourage the lawful commerce of the Bonny in every way; that she would send out ships in abundance for their palm-oil and other products; and if the Bonny men directed their attention properly to these, he was certain they could easily get rich without exporting slaves.

Captain Craigie further told His Majesty that the Queen of England[3] wished to make a friendly agreement with the King of Bonny to put an end to Slave exportation; and moreover added that his mistress was determined to put a stop to it at all hazards.

The King, Anna Pepple, and the Juju man for some time remained silent; their countenances, however, were indicative of their consternation; the idea of making such a proposal seemed to them to be incomprehensible. At length Anna Pepple said —

"If we cease to sell slaves to foreign ships, our principal source of wealth will be gone; the English were our first cus-tomers, and the trade has since been our chief means of support."

Captain Craigie. "How much would you lose if you gave up selling slaves for exportation?"

Anna Pepple. "Too much — very much — we gain more by one slave-ship than by five palm-oil ships."

Hee Chee, Anna Pepple's Secretary. "We depend entirely on selling slaves and palm-oil for our subsistence; suppose then the Slave Trade done away with, the consumption of palm-oil in England to stop, the crop to fail, or that the English ships did not come to the Bonny, what are we to do? We must starve, as it is contrary to our religion to cultivate the ground."

Captain Craigie. "There need be no apprehension of the demand for palm-oil in England ceasing, or of English ships not coming out to the Bonny to take from you your products in exchange for British merchandise; but if you can show clearly that your losses will be so great by giving up slave exportation, I think it possible that the Queen of England may in some measure remunerate you for such loss. I have no authority whatever to make any agreement with you with regard to such compensation, I only wish to know if you are disposed to treat[4] for the abolition of the Slave Trade, to enable me to represent your views and demands thereon to my own Government."

Juju Man. "Suppose a Spanish ship's coming to Bonny with goods to exchange

---

2. Palmerston (1789–1865) was British foreign secretary at the time; he held several government positions in his long career, including prime minister.

3. Queen Victoria reigned from 1837 to 1901; referred to later in the paragraph as Craigie's "mistress."

4. Negotiate.

for slaves; are we to send her away? This morning you made a breakfast for me, and as I was hungry it would have been foolish not to have eaten; in like manner, if the Spanish ship had things which we stood in need of, it would be equally foolish not to take them."

Captain Craigie. "How would the abolition of the slave exportation so materially affect you?"

King Pepple. "It would affect myself and chiefs thus —

"First, by stopping the revenues arising from slaves being exported.

"Secondly, our own profit on slaves, and that arising from piloting slave-ships up and out of Bonny would be lost."

Captain Craigie. "I again assure you that the Slave Trade must be stopped. Not one vessel can escape from the Bonny, as you will know from 'Scout's' blockade[5] of the river in 1836 and 1839. If it becomes necessary, I shall anchor a vessel off Juju Point, and to pass her you are aware will be impossible; but as the English Government always adopt the principle of putting an end to evils by friendly agreements than by compulsion, and as it is that they may be disposed, if your requests are within reasonable limits, to make you an annual 'dash,' or remuneration, for a term of years (perhaps five years), how much would you consider to be sufficient?"

After some consultation among themselves, Hee Chee, Anna Pepple's Secretary, said "The King will take 4,000 dollars yearly."

Captain Craigie. "As I said before, I am not authorized to treat for any sum, but I am certain 4,000 would be considered too much; indeed I would not venture to propose more than 2,000 dollars. If you will say that this sum (for the time above specified) will be sufficient, I shall lay the matter before the English Government."

The King, Anna Pepple, the Juju man, and Hee Chee, had a discussion for some time. They for a long while insisted on not naming less than 3,000 dollars, till they at last came down to 2,000; and when Captain Craigie proposed that it should be named to the other chiefs on shore, they said that it was not necessary, as the King's party could carry any measure they thought proper.

Captain Craigie then read to them distinctly the Articles he proposed to be added to the Treaty of the 9th April, 1837, and gave them to understand that in the event of the English Government determining to grant the King of Bonny any compensation for his alleged losses consequent on the abolition of slave exportation from his kingdom and dependencies, that the amount of such compensation would most likely be paid in such articles of British merchandise as he (the King of Bonny) should point out as most useful to himself; moreover, that the British Government would require annually a document in the form of a certificate from the captains of British merchantships in the Bonny, declaring that no slaves had to their knowledge been exported from that river, or from the dominions of King Pepple of Bonny; and further, that the slightest infringement of the Treaty would be followed, not only by the immediate stoppage of the compensation, but by a severe example of the displeasure of the Government of Great Britain.

King Pepple and suite then returned to the shore under the same salute as that with which they were received.

---

5. The "Scout" was a British naval vessel.

▨ Royal Niger Company

STANDARD TREATY

The following document illustrates the almost mechanical process by which large parts of Africa succumbed to European rule. In 1886 the British government commissioned the Royal Niger Company to administer and direct the economic development of the potentially valuable region of the Niger River delta and its hinterland. With hundreds of tribes and with other European states as possible competitors, the company's representatives had to move quickly, so they drew up a standard treaty to use with the African chieftains during the late 1880s. One needed only to fill in the blanks.

Questions
for Analysis

1. By accepting this treaty what are the tribal chieftains giving up?
2. What benefits are the tribes to receive?
3. What does use of the "standard treaty" imply about English attitudes toward the Africans?

We, the undersigned Chiefs of ____, with the view to the bettering of the condition of our country and people, do this day cede to the Royal Niger Company, for ever, the whole of our territory extending from ____.

We also give to the said Royal Niger Company full power to settle all native disputes arising from any cause whatever, and we pledge ourselves not to enter into any war with other tribes without the sanction of the said Royal Niger Company.

We understand that the said Royal Niger Company have full power to mine, farm, and build in any portion of our country.

We bind ourselves not to have any intercourse with any strangers or foreigners except through the said Royal Niger Company.

In consideration of the foregoing, the said Royal Niger Company (Chartered and Limited) bind themselves not to interfere with any of the native laws or customs of the country, consistently with the maintenance of order and good government.

The said Royal Niger Company agree to pay native owners of land a reasonable amount for any portion they may require.

The said Royal Niger Company bind themselves to protect the said Chiefs from the attacks of any neighboring aggressive tribes.

The said Royal Niger Company also agree to pay the said Chiefs ____ measures native value.

We, the undersigned witnesses, do hereby solemnly declare that the ____ Chiefs whose names are placed opposite their respective crosses have in our presence affixed their crosses of their own free will and consent, and that the said ____ has in our presence affixed his signature.

Done in triplicate at ____, this ____ day of ____, 188____.

Declaration by Interpreter

I, ____, of ____, do hereby solemnly declare that I am well acquainted with the language of the ____ country, and that on the ____ day of ____, 188____, I truly and faithfully explained the above Agreement to all the Chiefs present, and that they understood its meaning.

■ A. E. Scrivener

JOURNAL

The experience of the peoples of the Congo basin shows how quickly the Europeans' professed altruism and scientific curiosity could be transformed into crass exploitation. In 1876 King Leopold II of Belgium convened a meeting of seven European nations that formed, ostensibly for humanitarian reasons, the International Association for the Exploration and Civilization of Africa. Within three years, however, he dispatched his agents to the Congo basin, where they obtained treaties from the region's tribes that gave him and his business associates effective control of 900,000 square miles of territory. In 1882 he founded and placed under his personal control the International Association of the Congo, an organization designed to enrich him and his associates. The association sold monopolies to private investors, and it exploited directly the region's rich rubber and mineral resources.

The collection of rubber became a gruesome business, in which company agents killed or maimed African workers if they failed to reach their quotas for collecting raw rubber. Leopold tried to keep his forced-labor system a secret, but missionaries' reports and journalists' investigations soon revealed its horror. In 1908, after a long investigation, the Belgian Parliament took the Congo Free State away from its king and placed it under state control.

A. E. Scrivener, an American Baptist missionary, was one of the first non-Belgians to observe conditions in Leopold's Congo, when a guilt-ridden Belgian official who wanted the world to know what was happening gave him permission to enter the area. In 1904 the bitter English opponent of African imperialism, Edmund D. Morel, published excerpts form Scrivener's diary. The following excerpt begins with the missionary's description of practices at a rubber plantation.

*Q*uestions
for Analysis

1. How do the Africans describe their first reactions to the Belgians?
2. In what ways did Belgian activities in the Congo affect native life and customs?

3. Compare Scrivener's account of the Belgians' brutalities with Equiano's description of the slave ships in his autobiography (Chapter 7). How do the attitudes and practices of the slavers compare with those of the Belgians? What seems to have motivated them?

4. Elsewhere in his diary Scrivener expresses amazement that the natives do not resist their poor treatment. From his account, what explains this phenomenon?

*E*verything was on a military basis, but so far as I could see, the one and only reason for it all was rubber. It was the theme of every conversation, and it was evident that the only way to please one's superiors was to increase the output somehow. I saw a few men come in, and the frightened look even now on their faces tells only too eloquently of the awful time they have passed through. As I saw it brought in, each man had a little basket, containing say, four or five pounds of rubber. This was emptied into a larger basket and weighed, and being found sufficient, each man was given a cupful of coarse salt, and to some of the headmen a fathom of calico. . . . I heard from the white men and some of the soldiers some most gruesome stories. The former white man[1] (I feel ashamed of my color every time I think of him) would stand at the door of the store to receive the rubber from the poor trembling wretches, who after, in some cases, weeks of privation in the forests, had ventured in with what they had been able to collect. A man bringing rather under the proper amount, the white man flies into a rage, and seizing a rifle from one of the guards, shoots him dead on the spot. Very rarely did rubber come in, but one or more were shot in that way at the door of the store "to make the survivors bring more next time." Men who had tried to run from the country and had been caught, were brought to the station and made to stand one behind the other, and a bullet sent through them. . . . On ____ removing from the station, his successor[2] almost fainted on attempting to enter the station prison, in which were numbers of poor wretches so reduced by starvation and the awful stench from weeks of accumulation of filth, that they were not able to stand. Some of the stories are unprintable. . . . Under the present régime a list is kept of all the people. Every town is known and visited at stated intervals. Those stationed near the posts are required to do the various tasks, such as the bringing in of timber and other material. A little payment is made, but that it is in any respect an equivalent it would be absurd to suppose. The people are regarded as the property of the State for any purpose for which they may be needed. That they have any desires of their own, or any plans worth carrying out in connection with their own lives, would create a smile among the officials. It is one continual grind, and the native intercourse between one district and another in the old style is practically non-existent. Only the roads to and fro from the various posts are kept open, and large tracts of country are abandoned to the wild beasts. The white man himself told me that you could walk on for five days in one direction and not see a single village or a single human being. And this where formerly there was a big tribe!

---

1. A term used by Scrivener for the Belgian official in charge of a plantation.

2. The successor to the "former white man" mentioned earlier in the paragraph.

Scrivener continues his journey and joins a group of refugees who have fled from a plantation; his party has recently arrived in the town of Ngongo.

As one by one the surviving relatives of my men arrived, some affecting scenes were enacted. There was no falling on necks and weeping, but very genuine joy was shown and tears were shed as the losses death had made were told. How they shook hands and snapped their fingers! What expressions of surprise — the wide-opened mouth covered with the open hand to make its evidence of wonder the more apparent. . . . So far as the State post was concerned, it was in a very dilapidated condition. . . . On three sides of the usual huge quadrangle there were abundant signs of a former population, but we only found three villages — bigger indeed than any we had seen before, but sadly diminished from what had been but recently the condition of the place. . . . Soon we began talking, and, without any encouragement on my part, they began the tales I had become so accustomed to. They were living in peace and quietness when the white men came in . . . with all sorts of requests to do this and to do that, and they thought it meant slavery. So they attempted to keep the white men out of their country, but without avail. The rifles were too much for them. So they submitted, and made up their minds to do the best they could under the altered circumstances. First came the command to build houses for the soldiers, and this was done without a murmur. Then they had to feed the soldiers, and all the men and women — hangers-on who accompanied them. Then they were told to bring in rubber. This was quite a new thing for them to do. There was rubber in the forest several days away from their home, but that it was worth anything was news to them. A small reward was offered, and a rush was made for the rubber; "What strange white men to give us cloth and beads for the sap of a wild vine." They rejoiced in what they thought was their good fortune. But soon the reward was reduced until they were told to bring in the rubber for nothing. To this they tried to demur, but to their great surprise several were shot by the soldiers, and the rest were told, with many curses and blows, to go at once or more would be killed. Terrified, they began to prepare their food for the fortnight's absence from the village, which the collection of the rubber entailed. The soldiers discovered them sitting about. "What, not gone yet!" Bang! bang! bang! And down fell one and another dead, in the midst of wives and companions. There is a terrible wail, and an attempt made to prepare the dead for burial, but this is not allowed. All must go at once to the forest. And off the poor wretches had to go without even their tinder-boxes to make fires. Many died in the forests from exposure and hunger, and still more from the rifles of the ferocious soldiers in charge of the post. In spite of all their efforts, the amount fell off, and more and more were killed. . . . I was shown round the place, and the sites of former big chiefs' settlements were pointed out. A careful estimate made the population of, say, seven years ago, to be 2000 people in and about the post, within the radius of, say, a quarter of a mile. All told they would not muster 200 now, and there is so much sadness and gloom that they are fast decreasing. . . . Lying about in the grass, within a few yards of the house I was occupying, were numbers of human bones, in some cases complete skeletons. I counted thirty-six skulls, and saw many sets of bones from which the skulls were missing. I called one of the men, and asked the meaning of it. "When the rubber palaver[3] began," said he, "the soldiers shot so many we grew tired of burying, and very often we were not allowed to bury, and so just dragged the bodies out into the grass and left them. There are hundreds all round if you would like to see them." But I had seen more than enough, and was sickened by the stories that came from men and women alike of the awful time they had passed through. The Bulgarian atrocities[4] might be considered as mildness itself when compared with what has been done here. . . . In due course we reached Ibali. There was hardly a sound building in the place. . . . Why such dilapidation? The Comman-

dant away for a trip likely to extend into three months, the sub-lieutenant away in another direction on a punitive expedition. In other words, station must be neglected and rubber-hunting carried out with all vigor. I stayed here two days, and the one thing that impressed itself upon me was the collection of rubber. I saw long files of men come as at Mbongo with their little baskets under their arms, saw them paid their milk-tin-full of salt, and the two yards of calico flung to the head men; saw their trembling timidity, and in fact a great deal more, to prove the state of terrorism that exists, and the virtual slavery in which the people are held.

Reform in Turkey and Persia

During the nineteenth century, internal weakness and military decline continued to take their toll on the Persian and Turkish empires. The Ottomans acquiesced to what amounted to British suzerainty in Egypt and, in the face of growing nationalism among the Balkan peoples, lost most of their European empire. The Persians, now ruled by the Qajar dynasty, surrendered Afghanistan to the British and territory on both sides of the Caspian Sea to the Russians. In addition, both Turks and Persians lost control of much of their economic affairs. Ottoman sultans and Persian shahs granted dozens of concessions or monopolies to European businessmen, usually in return for lump-sum payments and an annual return on profits. These one-sided agreements gave foreigners control of railroads, banks, mines, major construction projects, and the sale of widely used commodities like tobacco. An example of such an arrangement was the Persian Tobacco Concession of 1890, in which a group of Englishmen received a monopoly over all tobacco sales in Persia in return for paying the shah £15,000 and 25 percent of the annual profits. The English expected profits of approximately £500,000 per year, and the Persians would pay inflated prices to foreign businessmen for a product they grew themselves.

The Turkish and Persian response to the European intrusion was similar. In each

---

3. Slang for "business."

4. A reference to the slaughter of some 15,000 Bulgarians by the Ottoman Turks during an abortive Bulgarian revolt in 1876. For Europeans, the event was the epitome of senseless cruelty.

country one group of reformers sought to reorganize the army, root out corruption, and tighten administration while leaving intact the autocracy of the sultan or shah. Other groups, many of whom had visited Europe or had studied in European or American-founded schools, accepted the need for military and administrative reform and also demanded constitutional changes that would establish representative government and guarantee individual freedoms.

In each country, too, the Muslim clergy complicated efforts to bring about meaningful changes. Although they detested the Western intruders, the clergy also opposed many of the internal reforms aimed at resisting them. For example, in 1851 the clergy in Persia cooperated in the dismissal of Mizra Taqi Khan, a reforming minister who since 1848 had worked to reorganize the government and army, facilitate trade with Europeans, and establish schools that would teach Western science and history. Later, in the Persian revolution of 1906, the clergy joined merchants, Western-educated intellectuals, and reformers to force Shah Mozaffar al-Din to grant a constitution and a representative assembly, known as the Majlis. The revolutionary front soon disintegrated, however, when the clergy demanded rule by the Shari'a, Islam's religious law, and the nationalists called for a Western-style legal system based on approval by the Majlis. These divisions enabled conservative cabinet ministers in 1911 to dismiss the Majlis and reestablish authoritarian government.

As the following selections illustrate, despite their commitment and the intrinsic merit of their ideas, reformers in Turkey and Persia were unable to stave off collapse and further foreign encroachment. In 1907 Russia and England divided Persia between them, leaving only the central part of the country under direct Persian control. The Ottoman Empire lost its Arab empire after its defeat in World War I and disappeared altogether when it was overthrown by Turkish nationalists in 1920.

Sultan Abdul Mejid

IMPERIAL RESCRIPT

The first serious effort to revitalize the Ottoman army took place during the reign of Selim III (1789–1807), who introduced foreign advisers and established higher standards for recruits and officers. Bitterly opposed by entrenched military and religious establishments, Selim was deposed in 1807 and murdered in 1808. After his death a second period of reform, known as Tanzimat or "Regulations," began in 1839, at the end of the reign of Mahmud II. This movement, which aimed to save the empire through administrative reform, the encouragement of education, and the adoption of certain legal and judicial practices from the West, had many supporters within and outside the government.

Two of the most important documents in the Tanzimat movement were proclamations issued by Sultan Abdul Mejid (1839–1861). Shortly after he became sultan,

Abdul Mejid gathered the notables of the empire in Constantinople and had an official read them a statement known as the "Noble Rescript." In it the sultan committed himself to ending government corruption, confirming the rights of non-Muslims, and protecting all subjects from arbitrary arrest. Seventeen years later, on February 18, 1856, Abdul Mejid issued another, more encompassing statement known as the "Imperial Rescript." This represented the high point of efforts to reform the Ottoman Empire while maintaining its authoritarian government and its traditional mix of Islamic, Christian, and Jewish subjects.

Questions for Analysis

1. What benefits are the sultan's non-Muslim subjects to receive as a result of this proclamation?
2. What efforts are to be made to improve the empire's system of justice?
3. What do the decrees on the economy suggest about the state of the empire's economic situation?
4. In what respects does this document reflect Western liberal ideals, as expressed in the Declaration of the Rights of Man and of the Citizen (Chapter 6)?
5. To what extent does this document extend political rights to the sultan's subjects?

*L*et it be done as herein set forth. . . .

It being now my desire to renew and enlarge still more the new Institutions ordained with the view of establishing a state of things conformable with the dignity of my Empire and — . . . by the kind and friendly assistance of the Great Powers, my noble Allies,[1] . . . The guarantees promised on our part by the Hatti-Humaïoun of Gülhané,[2] and in conformity with the Tanzimat, . . . are today confirmed and consolidated, and efficacious measures shall be taken in order that they may have their full and entire effect.

All the Privileges and Spiritual Immunities granted by my ancestors *ab antiquo*,[3] and at subsequent dates, to all Christian communities or other non-Mussulman[4] persuasions established in my Empire under my protection, shall be confirmed and maintained.

Every Christian or other non-Mussulman community shall be bound within a fixed period, and with the concurrence of a

---

1. During the Crimean War (1853–1856), Turkey was allied with Great Britain, France, and Sardinia against Russia. France and Great Britain at the time were encouraging Turkish military reform to offset Russia's power in the region.

2. This refers to the Noble Rescript of 1839.
3. Latin for "from the distant past."
4. Non-Muslim.

Commission composed *ad hoc* of members of its own body, to proceed with my high approbation and under the inspection of my Sublime Porte,[5] to examine into its actual Immunities and Privileges, and to discuss and submit to my Sublime Porte the Reforms required by the progress of civilization and of the age. The powers conceded to the Christian Patriarchs and Bishops[6] by the Sultan Mahomet II[7] and his successors, shall be made to harmonize with the new position which my generous and beneficent intentions ensure to these communities. . . . The principles of nominating the Patriarchs for life, after the revision of the rules of election now in force, shall be exactly carried out, conformably to the tenor of the Firmans of Investiture. . . . The ecclesiastical dues, of whatever sort or nature they be, shall be abolished and replaced by fixed revenues of the Patriarchs and heads of communities. . . . In the towns, small boroughs, and villages, where the whole population is of the same Religion, no obstacle shall be offered to the repair, according to their original plan, of buildings set apart for Religious Worship, for Schools, for Hospitals, and for Cemeteries. . . .

Every distinction or designation tending to make any class whatever of the subjects of my Empire inferior to another class, on account of their Religion, Language, or Race, shall be for ever effaced from the Administrative Protocol. The laws shall be put in force against the use of any injurious or offensive term, either among private individuals or on the part of the authorities.

As all forms of Religion are and shall be freely professed in my dominions, no subject of my Empire shall be hindered in the exercise of the Religion that he professes. . . . No one shall be compelled to change their Religion . . . and . . . all the subjects of my Empire, without distinction of nationality, shall be admissible to public employments. . . . All the subjects of my Empire, without distinction, shall be received into the Civil and Military Schools of the Government. . . . Moreover, every community is authorized to establish Public Schools of Science, Art, and Industry. . . .

All Commercial, Correctional, and Criminal Suits between Mussulmans and Christian or other non-Mussulman subjects, or between Christians or other non-Mussulmans of different sects, shall be referred to Mixed Tribunals. The proceedings of these Tribunals shall be public: the parties shall be confronted, and shall produce their witnesses, whose testimony shall be received, without distinction, upon oath taken according to the religious law of each sect. . . .

Penal, Correctional, and Commercial Laws, and Rules of Procedure for the Mixed Tribunals, shall be drawn up as soon as possible, and formed into a code. . . . Proceedings shall be taken, for the reform of the Penitentiary System. . . .

The organization of the Police . . . shall be revised in such a manner as to give to all the peaceable subjects of my Empire the strongest guarantees for the safety both of their persons and property. . . .

---

5. "Sublime Porte" refers to the building that housed the grand vizier and other high officials of the Ottoman state. It is a translation of the Turkish words *Bab-i-Ali,* or "high gate." The term is used in much the same way that the "White House" refers to the American presidency and the "Kremlin" refers to the government of Soviet Russia.

6. The reference is to high officials in the Greek Orthodox Church, the predominant form of Christianity in the Ottoman Empire.

7. Ottoman ruler from 1451 to 1481; also known as Mehmed II.

Christian subjects, and those of other non-Mussulman sects, . . . shall, as well as Mussulmans, be subject to the obligations of the Law of Recruitment. The principle of obtaining substitutes, or of purchasing exemption, shall be admitted.

Proceedings shall be taken for a Reform in the Constitution of the Provincial and Communal Councils, in order to ensure fairness in the choice of the Deputies of the Mussulman, Christian, and other communities, and freedom of voting in the Councils. . . .

As the Laws regulating the purchase, sale, and disposal of Real Property are common to all the subjects of my Empire, it shall be lawful for Foreigners to possess Landed Property in my dominions. . . .

The Taxes are to be levied under the same denomination from all the subjects of my Empire, without distinction of class or of Religion. The most prompt and energetic means for remedying the abuses in collecting the Taxes, and especially the Tithes, shall be considered. The system of direct collection shall gradually, and as soon as possible, be substituted for the plan of Farming, in all the branches of the Revenues of the State.

A special Law having been already passed, which declared that the Budget of the Revenue and Expenditure of the State shall be drawn up and made known every year, the said law shall be most scrupulously observed. . . .

The heads of each Community and a Delegate, designated by my Sublime Porte, shall be summoned to take part in the deliberations of the Supreme Council of Justice on all occasions which might interest the generality of the subjects of my Empire. . . .

Steps shall be taken for the formation of Banks and other similar institutions, so as to effect a reform in the monetary and financial system, as well as to create Funds to be employed in augmenting the sources of the material wealth of my Empire.

PROCLAMATION OF THE YOUNG TURKS

During the 1870s a group of reformers known as the Young Ottomans began to seek changes that went beyond the Tanzimat reforms. They believed that only the establishment of a constitutional regime would save their country from destruction. Led by Grand Vizier Midhat Pasha (1872, 1876–1877), a committee of ministers produced the Constitution of 1876, which the new sultan, Abdul Hamid II (1876–1909), accepted with seeming enthusiasm. He showed his true colors in 1877, however, when he abolished the first elected parliament and successfully re-established an autocratic regime stubbornly opposed to reform.

Opposition to the sultan was centered in a secret revolutionary society founded in 1889, officially named the Committee of Union and Progress but commonly known as the Young Turks. Fierce nationalists, they called for the resignation of Abdul Hamid and the restoration of the 1876 constitution. Many members were imprisoned or went into exile, and those who remained in Turkey lived in dread of the secret police. The Young Turks' opportunity came in 1908, when a widespread army mutiny allowed them to come into the open and demand the restoration of the constitution. The sultan had no choice but to acquiesce, and a parliamentary regime was re-established. Shortly after the constitution was reinstated, the Young Turks outlined their plans for a "new Turkey" in the following proclamation.

Questions for Analysis

1. How does the proclamation differ from the Imperial Rescript of 1856 regarding the status of religious minorities within the empire?
2. To what extent does this document reflect a commitment to the Western principles of liberalism and democracy?
3. How would the proposals in the proclamation affect the empire's ethnic minorities?
4. To what extent does this document express the Young Turks' nationalism?
5. What is the position of the Young Turks on the relationship between the Turkish state and Islam?

*A*ll the general rights accorded by the Constitution of 1293 (1876) and confirmed by the Imperial decree communicated to the Sublime Porte[1] the 4th of *redjeb* 1326[2] (1908), as well as the parts of those rights which are not in opposition to the foresaid Constitution, will be respected and preserved intact, as long as they are not abolished by the Parliament.

1. The basis for the Constitution will be respect for the predominance of the national will. One of the consequences of this principle will be to require without delay the responsibility of the minister before the Chamber, and, consequently, to consider the minister as having resigned, when he does not have a majority of the votes of the Chamber.

2. Provided that the number of senators does not exceed one third the number of deputies, the Senate will be named (which is not provided for in article 62 of the Constitution) as follows: one third by the Sultan and two thirds by the nation, and the term of senators will be of limited duration;

3. It will be demanded that all Ottoman subjects having completed their twentieth year, regardless of whether they possess property or fortune, shall have the right to vote. Those who have lost their civil rights will naturally be deprived of this right.

4. It will be demanded that the right freely to constitute political groups be inserted in a precise fashion in the constitutional charter, in order that article 1 of the Constitution of 1293 (1876) be respected. . . .

7. The Turkish tongue will remain the official state language. Official correspondence and discussion will take place in Turk. . . .

---

1. See note 5 of Sultan Abdul Mejid's "Imperial Rescript."

2. July 24 on the Western calendar.

9. Every citizen will enjoy complete liberty and equality, regardless of nationality or religion, and be submitted to the same obligations. All Ottomans, being equal before the law as regards rights and duties relative to the State, are eligible for government posts, according to their individual capacity and their education. Non-Muslims will be equally liable to the military law.

10. The free exercise of the religious privileges which have been accorded to different nationalities will remain intact.

11. The reorganization and distribution of the State forces, on land as well as on sea, will be undertaken in accordance with the political and geographical situation of the country, taking into account the integrity of the other European powers. . . .

14. Provided that the property rights of landholders are not infringed upon (for such rights must be respected and must remain intact, according to the law), it will be proposed that peasants be permitted to acquire land, and they will be accorded means to borrow money at a moderate rate. . . .

16. Education will be free. Every Ottoman citizen, within the limits of the prescriptions of the Constitution, may operate a private school in accordance with the special laws.

17. All schools will operate under the surveillance of the state. In order to obtain for Ottoman citizens an education of a homogenous and uniform character, the official schools will be open, their instruction will be free, and all nationalities will be admitted. Instruction in Turk will be obligatory in public schools. In official schools, public instruction will be free.

Secondary and higher education will be given in the public and official schools indicated above; it will use the Turkish tongue as a basis. . . . Schools of commerce, agriculture and industry will be opened with the goal of developing the resources of the country. . . .

Steps shall also be taken for the formation of Roads and Canals to increase the facilities of communication and increase the sources of the wealth of the country. Everything that can impede commerce or agriculture shall be abolished.

ANGLO-RUSSIAN AGREEMENT CONCERNING PERSIA

The 1907 diplomatic agreement on Persia between Russia and Great Britain ended a century-old rivalry between the two European powers over which would dominate the region. The Russians had for centuries coveted Persian territory around the Caspian Sea and valued influence in the region as a step toward gaining a warmwater port that would give them access to the Mediterranean. British interest dated from the late eighteenth century, when they sought to establish themselves in Persia to carry on business and to protect their Indian empire from Russia.

In the course of the nineteenth century, Russia and Great Britain succeeded in taking Persian territory and winning control of much of the country's wealth and industry. Their competition ended in the early 1900s, when they entered into an alliance against newly powerful and belligerent Germany. As part of their diplomatic understanding, in 1907 they signed the Anglo-Russian Agreement, by which they settled outstanding differences in Persia, Afghanistan, and Tibet. This excerpt summarizes the major points of the agreement regarding Persia. The map on page 331 shows the location of the places mentioned in the document.

Questions for Analysis

1. What is the stated purpose of the Anglo-Russian Agreement?
2. What do the various agreements about economic issues reveal about recent Persian economic development?
3. What reasons might have discouraged the English and Russians from dividing the whole country between them?
4. What does the map on page 331 suggest about noneconomic motives on the part of the English?
5. Are there any signs in the agreement that Russia and England consulted the Persian government about its contents?

The Governments of Great Britain and Russia having mutually engaged to respect the integrity and independence of Persia, and sincerely desiring the preservation of order throughout that country and its peaceful development, as well as the permanent establishment of equal advantages for the trade and industry of all other nations;

Considering that each of them has, for geographical and economic reasons, a special interest in the maintenance of peace and order in certain provinces of Persia adjoining, or in the neighborhood of, the Russian frontier on the one hand, and the frontiers of Afghanistan and Baluchistan[1] on the other hand; and being desirous of avoiding all cause of conflict between their respective interests in the above-mentioned provinces of Persia;

Have agreed on the following terms: —

I. Great Britain engages not to seek for herself, and not to support in favor of British subjects, or in favor of the subjects of third Powers, any Concessions of a political or commercial nature — such as Concessions for railways, banks, telegraphs, roads, transport, insurance, etc. — beyond a line starting from Kasr-i-Shirin, passing through Isfahan, Yezd, Kakhk, and ending at a point on the Persian frontier at the intersection of the Russian and Afghan frontiers, and not to oppose, directly or indirectly, demands for similar Concessions in this region

---

1. A region then south of Afghanistan, presently part of Pakistan.

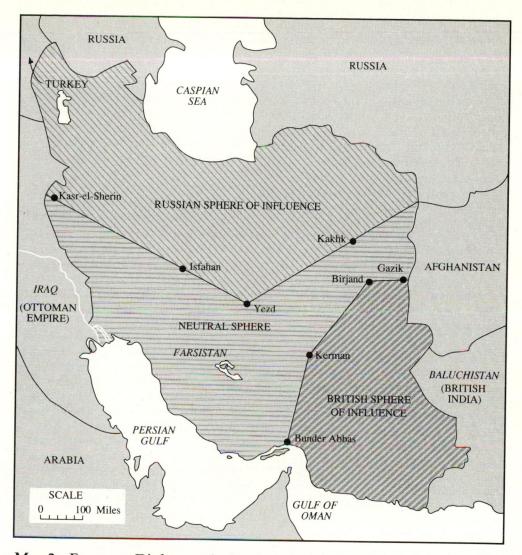

Map 2   European Diplomacy in Southwest Asia, 1907–1917

which are supported by the Russian Government. It is understood that the above-mentioned places are included in the region in which Great Britain engages not to seek the Concessions referred to.

II. Russia, on her part, engages not to seek for herself and not to support, in favor of Russian subjects, or in favor of the subjects of third Powers, any Concessions of a political or commercial nature — such as Concessions for railways, banks, telegraphs, roads, transport, insurance, etc. — beyond a line going from the Afghan frontier by way of Gazik, Birjand, Kerman, and ending at Bunder Abbas, and not to oppose, directly or indirectly, demands for similar Concessions in this region which are supported by the British Government. It is understood that the above-mentioned places are included in the region in which Russia engages not to seek the Concessions referred to.

III. Russia, on her part, engages not to oppose, without previous arrangement with Great Britain, the grant of any Concessions whatever to British subjects in the regions of Persia situated between the lines mentioned in Articles I and II.

Great Britain undertakes a similar engagement as regards the grant of Concessions to Russian subjects in the same regions of Persia.

All Concessions existing at present in the regions indicated in Articles I and II are maintained.

IV. It is understood that the revenues of all the Persian customs, with the exception of those of Farsistan and of the Persian Gulf, revenues guaranteeing the amortization and the interest of the loans concluded by the Government of the Shah with the "Banque d'Escompte et des Prêts de Perse"[2] up to the date of the signature of the present Agreement, shall be devoted to the same purpose as in the past.

It is equally understood that the revenues of the Persian customs of Farsistan and of the Persian Gulf, as well as those of the fisheries on the Persian shore of the Caspian Sea and those of the Posts and Telegraphs, shall be devoted, as in the past, to the service of the loans concluded by the Government of the Shah with the Imperial Bank of Persia up to the date of the signature of the present Agreement.

V. In the event of irregularities occurring in the amortization or the payment of the interest of the Persian loans concluded with the "Banque d'Escompte et des Prêts de Perse" and with the Imperial Bank of Persia up to the date of the signature of the present Agreement, and in the event of the necessity arising for Russia to establish control over the sources of revenue guaranteeing the regular service of the loans concluded with the first-named bank, and situated in the region mentioned in Article II of the present Agreement, or for Great Britain to establish control over the sources of revenue guaranteeing the regular service of the loans concluded with the second-named bank, and situated in the region mentioned in Article I of the present Agreement, the British and Russian Governments undertake to enter beforehand into a friendly exchange of ideas with a view to determine, in agreement with each other, the measures of control in question and to avoid all interference which would not be in conformity with the principles governing the present Agreement.

---

2. "Persian Discount and Loan Bank," founded by Russia in 1890.

India Under British Domination

As Great Britain extended its hold on India during the nineteenth century, administrators, policymakers, and the British public generally accepted the traditional mercantilist doctrine that this new colony should serve the economic interests of the mother country. It would be a source of raw materials, an area for investment, and a market for British manufactured goods. Other issues, however, sparked lively debate. Most of the British agreed that at some point in the future they would end their rule and India would become a self-governing, independent state. They had no timetable for leaving, however, and they disagreed about how to prepare the Indians for that day of independence. They would bring some Indians into the colonial administration, but how many and at what levels? They would provide India with schools and colleges, but would they offer Western curricula or traditional Indian learning? They would attempt to "civilize" the Indians, but, in doing so, how much damage were they willing to inflict on traditional Hindu customs such as child marriage and sati?

The debate among the British was complicated by the sharp disagreements among the Indians about their relationship to their colonial masters. Many at first believed that British rule was a blessing and that it would enable them to attain the benefits of Western science, constitutional government, and prosperity. Although such views persisted into the twentieth century, by the end of the 1800s only a minority embraced them. Many Indians resented the British assumption that Western ways were necessarily superior to centuries-old Indian beliefs and practices. They were also offended by Britain's one-sided economic policies, which drained off India's resources, stifled development, and ruined traditional industries. Finally, Great Britain's reluctance to consider seriously Indian self- or even partial rule angered many.

As the following documents reveal, an evaluation of the benefits and harm of British rule in India is no simple matter. Historians continue to debate the issue in the late twentieth century.

Rammohun Roy

LETTER TO LORD AMHERST ON EDUCATION

Rammohun Roy, the "father of modern India," was born into a devout high-caste Hindu family in 1772. He showed an early genius for languages and a keen interest in religions. By the age of twenty he had learned Arabic, Persian, Greek, and Sanskrit (the ancient language of India) and had spent five years wandering through India seeking religious enlightenment. He then learned English and entered the service of the English East India Company, ultimately attaining the highest administrative rank possible for an Indian. In 1814, at the age of forty-two, he retired to Calcutta, where he established several newspapers, founded a number of schools, and campaigned to abolish sati. He also established the Society of God, a religion that sought to combine Christian ethical teaching with certain Hindu beliefs. He spent his final years in England, where he died in 1833.

Roy wrote the following letter in 1823 to the British governor general of India, Lord Amherst (1773–1857), to oppose a British plan to sponsor a school in Calcutta that would teach Sanskrit and Indian literature and religion. Roy believed that Indian students should study English and receive a Western education.

In 1835 the debate over Indian education was settled, when the committee appointed by the British government decided that Indian schools should offer an English-style education. In the words of the committee's chair, Thomas B. Macaulay (1800–1859), the goal was to produce young men who were "Indian in blood and color, but English in taste, in opinions, in morals, and in intellect."

Questions
for Analysis

1. How would you characterize Roy's attitude toward the British? Does he seem comfortable offering the British advice?
2. What does he especially admire in Western civilization?
3. What does he consider to be the weaknesses of an education based on traditional Indian learning?
4. In Roy's view, what is the ultimate purpose of learning?

To His Excellency the Right Honorable Lord Amherst, Governor-General in Council

My Lord,

Humbly reluctant as the natives of India are to obtrude upon the notice of government the sentiments they entertain on any public measure, there are circumstances when silence would be carrying this respectful feeling to culpable excess. The present rulers of India, coming from a distance of many thousand miles to govern a people whose language, literature, manners, customs, and ideas, are almost entirely new and strange to them, cannot easily become so intimately acquainted with their real circumstances as the natives of the country are themselves. We should therefore be guilty of a gross dereliction of duty to ourselves and afford our rulers just grounds of complaint at our apathy did we omit, on occasions of importance like the present, to supply them with such accurate information as might enable them to devise and adopt measures calculated to be beneficial to the country, and thus second by our local knowledge and experience their declared benevolent intentions for its improvement.

The establishment of a new Sanskrit School in Calcutta evinces the laudable desire of government to improve the natives of India by education — a blessing for which they must ever be grateful, and every well-wisher of the human race must be desirous that the efforts made to promote it should be guided by the most enlightened principles, so that the stream of intelligence may flow in the most useful channels.

When this seminary of learning was proposed, we understood that the government in England had ordered a considerable sum of money to be annually devoted to the instruction of its Indian subjects. We were filled with sanguine hopes that this sum would be laid out in employing European gentlemen of talent and education to instruct the natives of India in mathematics, natural philosophy, chemistry, anatomy, and other useful sciences, which the natives of Europe have carried to a degree of perfection that has raised them above the inhabitants of other parts of the world.

While we looked forward with pleasing hope to the dawn of knowledge thus promised to the rising generation, our hearts were filled with mingled feelings of delight and gratitude, we already offered up thanks to Providence for inspiring the most generous and enlightened nations of the West with the glorious ambition of planting in Asia the arts and sciences of modern Europe.

We find that the government are establishing a Sanskrit school under Hindu pandits[1] to impart such knowledge as is already current in India. This seminary (similar in character to those which existed in Europe before the time of Lord Bacon)[2] can only be expected to load the minds of youth with grammatical niceties and metaphysical distinctions of little or no practical use to the possessors or to society. The pupils will there acquire what was known two thousand years ago with the addition of vain and empty subtleties since then produced by speculative men such as is already commonly taught in all parts of India.

The Sanskrit language, so difficult that almost a lifetime is necessary for its acquisition, is well known to have been for ages a lamentable check to the diffusion of knowledge, and the learning concealed under this almost impervious veil is far from sufficient to reward the labor of acquiring it. But if it were thought necessary to perpetuate this language for the sake of the portion of valuable information it contains, this might be much more easily accomplished by other means than the establishment of a new Sanskrit College; for there have been always and are now numerous professors of Sanskrit in the different parts of the country engaged in teaching this language, as well as the other branches of literature which are to be the object of the new seminary. Therefore their more diligent cultivation, if desirable, would be effectually promoted, by holding out premiums and granting certain allowances to their most eminent professors, who have already undertaken on their own account to teach them, and would by such rewards be stimulated to still greater exertion. . . .

Neither can much improvement arise from such speculations as the following which are the themes suggested by the

---

1. Wise and learned men of India.

2. The reference is to the English philosopher and prophet of science, Francis Bacon (1561–1626). Excerpts from his *New Organon* are included in Chapter 5.

Vedanta:[3] In what manner is the soul absorbed in the Deity? What relation does it bear to the Divine Essence? Nor will youths be fitted to be better members of society by the Vedantic doctrines which teach them to believe that all visible things have no real existence, that as father, brother, etc. have no real entity, they consequently deserve no real affection, and therefore the sooner we escape from them and leave the world the better. . . .

If it had been intended to keep the British nation in ignorance of real knowledge, the Baconian philosophy would not have been allowed to displace the system of the schoolmen which was the best calculated to perpetuate ignorance. In the same manner the Sanskrit system of education would be the best calculated to keep this country in darkness, if such had been the policy of the British legislature. But as the improvement of the native population is the object of the government, it will consequently promote a more liberal and enlightened system of instruction, embracing mathematics, natural philosophy, chemistry, anatomy, with other useful sciences, which may be accomplished with the sums proposed by employing a few gentlemen of talent and learning educated in Europe and providing a college furnished with necessary books, instruments, and other apparatus.

In presenting this subject to your Lordship, I conceive myself discharging a solemn duty which I owe to my countrymen, and also to that enlightened sovereign and legislature which have extended their benevolent care to this distant land, actuated by a desire to improve the inhabitants, and therefore humbly trust you will excuse the liberty I have taken in thus expressing my sentiments to your Lordship.

I have the honor, etc.,

Rammohun Roy

Edward Baines

HISTORY OF THE COTTON MANUFACTURE IN GREAT BRITAIN

England's takeover of India occurred simultaneously with the onset of the British Industrial Revolution, and this spelled disaster for India's economy. For centuries millions of Indian artisans supported themselves by weaving cotton textiles for domestic markets and for export to the Americas, Africa, and other parts of Eurasia. As the following document explains, when inexpensive, machine-made cotton fabrics began to flood the Indian and world markets, the Indian cotton industry was ruined.

The selection comes from a book published in 1835 by Sir Edward Baines (1800–

---

3. A major school of Hindu philosophy based on the study and analysis of three ancient texts, the *Upanishads,* the *Vedanta-sutras,* and the *Bhagavad Gita.* The various schools of Vedanta present different views concerning the nature of Brahman, the relationship of the individual to Brahman, and the nature and means of liberation from the cycle of reincarnation.

1890), the owner and editor of a newspaper in the industrial city of Leeds. Inaccurately titled, *History of the Cotton Manufacture in Great Britain* also deals at length with the cotton industry outside of Britain.

Questions for Analysis

1. How does Baines describe the role the cotton industry played in traditional India?
2. How does Baines explain the high quality of Indian cotton fabrics? To what extent is his explanation colored by European prejudices?
3. On the basis of Baines's account, how did the industry's relatively unsophisticated technology guarantee the involvement of large numbers of Indians in cotton manufacture?
4. What seems to have been the impact of the British law designed to limit the import of Indian cottons?
5. According to the petition of the Calcutta merchants, what caused their economic ruin? What do they feel will help them?

*T*he antiquity of the cotton manufacture in India has already been noticed, and all that is known of it in classical times has been stated in the brief quotations from Herodotus, Arrian, Strabo, Pliny, and the Periplus.[1] The present chapter will give some account of the remarkable excellence of the Indian fabrics, — the processes and machines by which they are wrought, — the condition of the population engaged in this department of industry, — the extensive commerce formerly carried on in these productions to every quarter of the globe, — and the decisive check given to that commerce by the manufacturers of England.

The cotton manufacture in India is not carried on in a few large towns, or in one or two districts; it is universal. The growth of cotton is nearly as general as the growth of food; everywhere the women spend a portion of their time in spinning; and almost every village contains its weavers, and supplies its own inhabitants with the scanty clothing they require. Being a domestic manufacture, and carried on with the rudest and cheapest apparatus, it requires neither capital, nor mills, nor an assemblage of various trades. The cotton is separated from the seeds by a small rude hand-mill, or gin. . . .

The mill consists of two rollers of teak wood, fluted longitudinally with five or six grooves, and revolving nearly in contact. The upper roller is turned by a han-

---

1. Herodotus was a Greek historian of the fifth century B.C.; Arrian was a Greek historian of the second century A.D.; Strabo was a Greek geographer, 63 B.C.–A.D. 24; Pliny was a Roman naturalist and writer, A.D. 23–79; the Periplus probably refers to the *Periplus of the Erythraen Sea* (a first-century A.D. manual that describes coastal routes from Egypt to India and along East Africa).

dle, and the lower is carried along with it by a perpetual screw at the axis. The cotton is put in at one side, and drawn through by the revolving rollers; but the seeds, being too large to pass through the opening, are torn off, and fall down on the opposite side from the cotton.

The next operation is that of bowing the cotton, to clear it from dirt and knots. A large bow, made elastic by a complication of strings, is used; this being put in contact with a heap of cotton, the workman strikes the string with a heavy wooden mallet, and its vibrations open the knots of the cotton, shake from it the dust and dirt, and raise it to a downy fleece. . . .

The cotton being thus prepared, without any carding, it is spun by the women; the coarse yarn is spun on a heavy one-thread wheel, of teak wood, and of the rudest carpentry — . . .

The finer yarn is spun with a metallic spindle, sometimes with and sometimes without a distaff;[2] a bit of clay is attached as a weight to one end of the spindle, which is turned round with the left hand, whilst the cotton is supplied with the right; the thread is wound up on a small piece of wood. The spinster keeps her fingers dry by the use of a chalky powder. In this simple way the Indian women, whose sense of touch is most acute and delicate, produce yarns which are finer and far more tenacious than any of the machine-spun yarns of Europe.

The yarn, having been reeled and warped in the simplest possible manner, is given to the weaver, whose loom is as rude a piece of apparatus as can be imagined. . . .

It cannot but seem astonishing, that in a department of industry, where the raw material has been so grossly neglected, where the machinery is so rude, and where there is so little division of labor,

the results should be fabrics of the most exquisite delicacy and beauty, unrivaled by the products of any other nation, even those best skilled in the mechanic arts. This anomaly is explained by the remarkably fine sense of touch possessed by that effeminate people, by their patience and gentleness, and by the hereditary continuance of a particular species of manufacture in families through many generations, which leads to the training of children from their very infancy in the processes of the art. . . .

Owing to the beauty and cheapness of Indian muslins, chintzes, and calicoes, there was a period when the manufacturers of all the countries of Europe were apprehensive of being ruined by their competition. In the seventeenth century, the Dutch and English East India Companies imported these goods in large quantities; they became highly fashionable for ladies' and children's dresses, as well as for drapery and furniture, and the coarse calicoes were used to line garments. To such an extent did this proceed, that as early as 1678 a loud outcry was made in England against the admission of Indian goods, which, it was maintained, were ruining our ancient woolen manufacture. . . .

This prohibition took place by the Act 11 and 12 William III. cap. 10., (1700,) which forbad the introduction of Indian silks and printed calicoes for domestic use, either as apparel or furniture, under a penalty of £200 on the wearer or seller: and as this Act did not prevent the continued use of the goods, which were probably smuggled from the continent of Europe, other Acts for the same purpose were passed at a later date. . . .

It appears, then, that not more than a century ago, the cotton fabrics of India were so beautiful and cheap, that nearly

---

2. A staff on which cotton (and also wool and linen) is wound for use in spinning.

all the governments of Europe thought it necessary to prohibit them, or to load them with heavy duties, in order to protect their own manufactures. How surprising a revolution has since taken place! The Indians have not lost their former skill; but a power has arisen in England, which has robbed them of their ancient ascendancy, turned back the tide of commerce, and made it run more rapidly against the Oriental than it ever ran against the English. Not to dwell upon a point which will afterwards be illustrated, the following document furnishes superabundant proof how a manufacturer which has existed without a rival for thousands of years, is withering under the competition of a power which is but of yesterday: it would be well if it did not also illustrate the very different measure of protection and justice which governments usually afford to their subjects at home, and to those of their remote dependencies: —

"PETITION OF NATIVES OF BENGAL, RELATIVE TO DUTIES ON COTTON AND SILK

"Calcutta, 1*st. Sept.* 1831.

"To the Right Honorable the Lords of His Majesty's Privy Council for Trade, &c.

"The humble Petition of the undersigned Manufacturers and Dealers in Cotton and Silk Piece Goods, the fabrics of Bengal;

"SHOWETH — That of late years your Petitioners have found their business nearly superseded by the introduction of the fabrics of Great Britain into Bengal, the importation of which augments every year, to the great prejudice of the native manufactures.

"That the fabrics of Great Britain are consumed in Bengal, without any duties being levied thereon to protect the native fabrics.

"That the fabrics of Bengal are charged with the following duties when they are used in Great Britain —

"On manufactured cottons, 10 percent.
"On manufactured silks, 24 percent.

"Your Petitioners most humbly implore your Lordships' consideration of these circumstances, and they feel confident that no disposition exists in England to shut the door against the industry of any part of the inhabitants of this great empire.

"They therefore pray to be admitted to the privilege of British subjects, and humbly entreat your Lordships to allow the cotton and silk fabrics of Bengal to be used in Great Britain 'free of duty,' or at the same rate which may be charged on British fabrics consumed in Bengal.

"Your Lordships must be aware of the immense advantages the British manufacturers derive from their skill in constructing and using machinery, which enables them to undersell the unscientific manufacturers of Bengal in their own country: and, although your Petitioners are not sanguine in expecting to derive any great advantage from having their prayer granted, their minds would feel gratified by such a manifestation of your Lordships' good will towards them; and such an instance of justice to the natives of India would not fail to endear the British government to them.

"They therefore confidently trust, that your Lordships' righteous consideration will be extended to them as British subjects, without exception of sect, country, or color.

"And your Petitioners, as in duty bound, will ever pray."

(Signed by 117 natives of high respectability.)

▨ **Dadabhai Naoroji**

THE PROS AND CONS OF BRITISH RULE

The man who best symbolized India's growing ambivalence about British rule was Dadabhai Naoroji (1825–1917). Born into a prosperous Bombay family, he abandoned a promising career as a mathematician at the age of thirty and moved to London, where he believed he could work effectively for improved conditions in India. In 1892, running as a member of the Liberal party, he became the first Indian elected to the British Parliament. During his many return visits to India he was instrumental in founding, in 1885, the Indian National Congress, an organization of moderate and middle-class Indians who appreciated the English but still set independence as their goal.

Naoroji set forth the following evaluation of Great Britain's impact on India in response to a question following a speech he delivered to a learned society in London in 1871. It later was published in a collection of his works that appeared in 1887. He begins by discussing the "credit," or benefit, of British rule.

Questions
for Analysis

1. What does Naoroji see as the benefits of British rule? What does he seem to regard as Britain's most valuable contribution?
2. According to Naoroji, what harm have the British done to India?
3. In Naoroji's view, to what extent can India's problems be solved, short of independence?

Credit — *In the Cause of Humanity:* Abolition of sati and infanticide.

Destruction of Dacoits, Thugs, Pindarees,[1] and other such pests of Indian society.

Remarriage of Hindu widows,[2] and charitable aid in time of famine.

Glorious work all this, of which any nation may well be proud, and such as has not fallen to the lot of any people in the history of mankind.

In the Cause of Civilization: Education, both male and female. Though yet only partial, an inestimable blessing as far as it has gone, and leading gradually to the destruction of superstition, and many moral and social evils. Resuscitation of India's own noble literature, modified and refined by the enlightenment of the West.

Politically: Peace and order. Freedom of speech and liberty of the press. Higher political knowledge and aspirations. Im-

---

1. Indian word for thieves, highway murderers, and robber bands.

2. According to Hindu practice, many castes did not permit women to remarry after their husbands' deaths.

provement of government in the native States. Security of life and property. Freedom from oppression caused by the caprice or avarice of despotic rulers, and from devastation by war. Equal justice between man and man (sometimes vitiated by partiality to Europeans). Services of highly educated administrators, who have achieved the above-mentioned good results.

Materially: Loans for railways and irrigation. . . . The development of a few valuable products, such as indigo, tea, coffee, silk, etc. Increase of exports. Telegraphs.

Generally: A slowly growing desire of late to treat India equitably, and as a country held in trust. Good intentions.

No nation on the face of the earth has ever had the opportunity of achieving such a glorious work as this. I hope in this credit side of the account I have done no injustice, and if I have omitted any item which anyone may think of importance, I shall have the greatest pleasure in inserting it. I appreciate, and so do my countrymen, what England has done for India, and I know that it is only in British hands that her regeneration can be accomplished. Now for the debit side.

Debit — *In the Cause of Humanity:* Nothing. Everything, therefore, is in your favor under this head.

In the Cause of Civilization: As I have said already, there has been a failure to do as much as might have been done, but I put nothing to the debit. Much has been done, or I should not be standing here this evening.

Politically: Repeated breach of pledges to give the natives a fair and reasonable share in the higher administration of their own country, which has much shaken confidence in the good faith of the British word. Political aspirations and the legitimate claim to have a reasonable voice in the legislation and the imposition and disbursement of taxes, met to a very slight degree, thus treating the natives of India not as British subjects, in whom representation is a birthright. . . .

Consequent on the above, an utter disregard of the feelings and views of the natives. The great moral evil of the drain of wisdom and practical administration and statesmanship, leaving none to guide the rising generation.

Financially: All attention is engrossed in devising new modes of taxation, without any adequate effort to increase the means of the people to pay; and the consequent vexation and oppressiveness of the taxes imposed, imperial and local. Inequitable financial relations between England and India, i.e. the political debt of £100,000,000 clapped on India's shoulders, and all home charges also, though the British exchequer contributes nearly £3,000,000 to the expenses of the colonies. . . .

Materially: The political drain,[3] up to this time, from India to England, of above £500,000,000, at the lowest computation, in principal alone, which with interest would be some thousands of millions. The further continuation of this drain at the rate, at present, of above £12,000,000, with a tendency to increase. . . .

The consequent continuous impoverishment and exhaustion of the country, except so far as it has been very partially relieved and replenished by the railway and irrigation loans, and the windfall of the consequences of the American war,[4] since 1850. Even with this relief, the ma-

---

3. Naoroji is referring to the taxes Indians pay to support the British administration in India.

4. Indian cotton exports briefly increased owing to the disruption of American exports during the Civil War.

terial condition of India is such that the great mass of the poor people have hardly $2d^5$ a day and a few rags, or a scanty subsistence.[6]

The famines that were in their power to prevent, if they had done their duty, as a good and intelligent government. The policy adopted during the last fifteen years of building railways, irrigation works, etc., is hopeful, has already resulted in much good to your credit, and if persevered in, gratitude and contentment will follow.

An increase of exports without adequate compensation; loss of manufacturing industry and skill. Here I end the debit side. . . .

To sum up the whole, the British rule has been — morally, a great blessing; politically peace and order on one hand, blunders on the other, materially, impoverishment (relieved as far as the railway and other loans go). The natives call the British system "Sakar ki Churi," the knife of sugar. That is to say there is no oppression, it is all smooth and sweet, but it is the knife, notwithstanding. I mention this that you should know these feelings. Our great misfortune is that you do not know our wants. When you will know our real wishes, I have not the least doubt that you would do justice. The genius and spirit of the British people is fair play and justice.

---

5. *d* is the abbreviation for pence, a British bronze coin equal to one-twelfth of a shilling; a paltry sum.

6. As a result of its growing population, India experienced several famines in the nineteenth century. Many Indians shared Naoroji's opinion that the British did too little to alleviate their impact.

East Asia Confronts the West

*D*uring the nineteenth century the peoples of East Asia, like those of India, the Middle East, and Africa, faced unprecedented challenges and upheavals as a result of new pressures and demands from the West. Until then, despite commercial contacts with Europeans dating from the 1500s, Western impact on this part of the world was limited. Because of their naval superiority, the Portuguese, Dutch, English, and Spanish had captured much of the trade in the Philippines, Indonesia, and some coastal regions of Southeast Asia. Furthermore, the Dutch in parts of Indonesia and the Spanish in the Philippines had established their political authority and some measure of direct control over farming, mining, and industry. Elsewhere, however, rulers of China, Japan, and the many small kingdoms, empires, and sultanates of Southeast Asia, still convinced of their superiority over the Western "barbarians," limited European trade and remained politically independent.

By the early twentieth century, changes, many of which may be called astounding, had affected every area of the region. Southeast Asia went the way of Africa. When World War I began in 1914, Burma, Laos, Cambodia, Vietnam, Singapore, the states of Malaysia, and previously independent Indonesian islands were part of European empires. Thailand alone remained independent but only because France and England, after slicing off some of its territory, could not agree on how to carve up the rest.

Meanwhile, in China, incessant pressure from Europe, the United States, and Japan, combined with overwhelming internal problems, brought not just foreign domination but disintegration and ultimate collapse. Two thousand years of Chinese imperial history ended in 1911, when revolutionaries overthrew the Manchu, or Ch'ing, regime, forcing China to face the daunting prospect of organizing its society without the authority of the emperor, the rule of scholar-officials, and the guidance of Confucianism. No East Asian people had greater difficulty responding to the West than the Chinese.

Conversely, no one had more success than the Japanese. After an intense debate over Japan's future in the mid-nineteenth century, powerful members of the aristocracy brought about the downfall of the Tokugawa shogunate and made a conscious decision to break from the nation's past and remodel Japan in imitation of the West. By the 1890s, Japan had not only avoided an imperialist takeover but had become an imperialist power itself.

The Disintegration of Imperial China

Although deeply humiliating, China's defeat by the British in the Opium War (Chapter 7) was only a foretaste of the galling indignities the country experienced during the rest of the nineteenth century. China's emperors were forced to open dozens of coastal cities to foreign trade, lost control of Korea and influence in Indochina, ceded Hong Kong to the British, granted foreigners the right to collect customs duties, lost legal authority over resident foreigners, promised to protect the lives and property of Christian missionaries, and acquiesced to extensive outside control of its economy. When the Chinese fought back, the result was defeat and further humiliation.

Even without the foreign onslaught, nineteenth-century China faced enormous problems, many of them resulting from its spiraling population. By the middle of the nineteenth century, China's population had reached 450,000,000, more than three times the level of 1500. The inevitable result was land shortages, food scarcity, and an increasingly impoverished peasantry. The iniquitous tax structure, inflation, and the greed of local officials compounded the peasants' woes. Meanwhile, the government neglected public works projects and the military, and, as bureaucratic efficiency declined, landowners, secret societies, and military strong men took over local affairs by default. Some officials, sensing China's crisis, proposed reforms, but the paralyzed imperial government either rejected them or executed them poorly. Rebellion, lawlessness, and foreign exploitation continued to plague the Ch'ing regime until the revolution of 1911 caused it, and China's 2,000-year imperial tradition, to pass into history.

Tseng Kuo-fan

MEMORIAL TO EMPEROR HSIEN-FENG

Tseng Kuo-fan (1811–1872) was one of the few truly impressive statesmen of late Manchu China. Born into a farm family in the province of Hunan, Tseng received a traditional Confucian education and passed the highest civil service examination at age twenty-eight. During his career of scholarship and service to the emperor, his best-known achievement was organizing the Manchu military in its efforts to suppress the Taiping Rebellion (1851–1864). Knowing well the problems of the regime and the unrest among the people, Tseng drew up the following memorandum on February 7, 1852, for Emperor Hsien-feng (1851–1861) shortly after he ascended the throne. It provides a clear and balanced assessment of China's problems at mid-century.

Questions
for Analysis

1. According to Tseng, what is the basis of the security and peace of the regime?
2. What characteristics of the government's tax policies does Tseng deplore? He states at the end of his memorandum that he will draft a plan to deal with these problems. What do you think he included in his proposals for tax reform?
3. How did the tax policies affect groups other than the peasantry?
4. Consider the behavior of the local officials, soldiers, and magistrates. How did their "corruption" affect the lives of the Chinese people?
5. What remedy does Tseng propose for the problem of corruption? Does his solution have a reasonable chance of success? Why or why not?

To comply with Your Majesty's instruction to show compassion and love for all the people in the empire, your humble servant wishes to take this opportunity to describe their plight as follows.

The danger to a nation is not so much the paucity of material wealth as the lack of coherence among its people. In the course of our history rarely was a time so prosperous as the Sui Dynasty during Wen-ti's reign.[1] Yet the country was soon plunged into chaos, and the Sui regime eventually came to an end. Why? Because the people had lost faith in their government despite the country's material wealth. Conversely, seldom was the nation so poor as she was during the reign of Han Chao-ti.[2] Yet the country was peaceful and her people secure. Why? Because the people had faith and confidence in their own government. For a period of fifteen years, from the first to the sixteenth year of K'ang-hsi[3] during the present dynasty, the Yellow River broke its dikes every year with the exception of one, and flood damage was extremely

heavy over a large region. . . . As if this were not enough, the Three Viceroys' Rebellion erupted[4] and ravaged nine provinces; it took the government seven years to suppress it. By then the treasury was almost empty, emptier than it is today. Yet the dynasty remained secure and the country undisturbed. Why? Because the Saintly Progenitor[5] loved the people more than he did himself, and the people, in response, continued to pledge to him their unswerving allegiance and rallied for his support. Though Your Majesty undeniably loves your subjects to the same extent as the Saintly Progenitor loved his, local officials, being indifferent to the plight of their charges, have failed in conveying your compassionate sentiments to the people and bringing to your attention their grievances. Because of this lack of communication, your humble servant wishes to take this opportunity to describe in some detail the ills from which our people suffer most.

The first ill concerns the high price of silver which affects adversely the peas-

---

1. Wen Ti, the founder of the Sui Dynasty, reigned from A.D. 589 to 604.

2. Han Chao-ti reigned from 86 to 74 B.C.

3. 1662–1677.

4. Also known as the Revolt of the Three Feudatories, 1673–1681.

5. Emperor K'ang-hsi, who ruled from 1662 to 1722. (See Chapter 4.)

ants' ability to fulfill their tax obligations. The tax load in Soochow, Sungkiang, Changchow, and Chinkiang[6] is the heaviest in the nation, and the people in these districts also suffer most. The yield for each *mou*[7] of land is anywhere from 15 to 20 pecks[8] of polished rice, and the landowner, after dividing it with his tenant on a fifty-fifty basis, receives approximately 8 pecks as his rent. Though his regular tax is only 2 pecks per *mou*, he has to pay another 2 pecks as rice tribute and 2 pecks more for miscellaneous requisitions, totaling 6 pecks altogether. Thus, for each *mou* of land he owns, his net income is only 2 pecks of polished rice per year. If all these taxes could be paid in rice, the situation would not be so serious. But most of them have to be paid in silver. Rice tribute is sometimes paid in rice, but the regular tax and the miscellaneous requisitions have to be paid in silver. Since a farmer reaps only rice, he has to sell his harvest for standard coins[9] in order to obtain the necessary cash; since the price of standard coins is high in terms of rice, he has understandable grievances. Moreover, in order to pay his taxes, he has to convert his standard coins into silver. . . . Formerly, selling 3 pecks of rice would bring enough silver to pay taxes for one *mou* of land; now, selling 6 pecks will not be enough to achieve the same purpose. While the return to the government remains the same, the burden to the people has been doubled. Besides, there are additional taxes on houses and family cemeteries, all of which have been doubled in terms of rice because they, like most of other taxes, have also to be paid in silver.

Under the circumstances it is not surprising that a large number of taxpayers have become delinquent, despite local governments' effort to enforce payment. Often special officials are assigned to help tax collections, and day and night soldiers are sent out to harass taxpayers. Sometimes corporal punishments are imposed upon tax delinquents; some of them are so badly beaten to exact the last penny that blood and flesh fly in all directions. Cruel though it is, this practice does not necessarily reflect the evil nature of local officials who, more often than not, do not believe that they have a better choice. If they fail to collect 70 percent of the amount due, not only will they be impeached and punished as a matter of routine, they may also have to pay the balance with their own money, that sometimes amounts to thousands of taels,[10] and ruin their families in the process. In short, they are forced to do what they loathe. . . .

Under the circumstances it is not surprising that the people are complaining and angry, and often the resistance to tax payment bursts forth and mushrooms into full-fledged riot. . . .

The second ill of our nation is the great number of bandits[11] which threaten the security of our law-abiding citizens. . . . Lately your humble servant has heard that the bandits have become bolder and more numerous, robbed and raped in broad daylight, and kidnaped people for ransom. Whenever an act of banditry is reported to the government, the local official announces in advance his intention to send troops against the bandits and ad-

---

6. All are located in the Lower Yangtze Valley, Kiangsu Province.

7. One sixth of an acre.

8. One quarter of a bushel.

9. Coins made of copper.

10. Chinese silver coins, each weighing approximately 1⅓ ounces.

11. Chinese officials often blamed "bandits" for disorders they did not understand.

vertises it in public proclamations, so as to make sure that the bandits know the soldiers are coming. Upon arriving at the village where the banditry took place, the official-in-charge expects to learn from the village chiefs, who are afraid of the bandits, that the offenders have already fled. Without anything worthwhile to do, he orders the burning of some of the houses in the village before his departure, so as to impress the villagers with the power of his office. Meanwhile his soldiers use a variety of excuses to exact payment from the bandits' victim, who by then is only too regretful that he reported the banditry to the government in the first place. While the soldiers are busy taking away from his house whatever they can carry, the bandits are still at large, hiding somewhere in the village. Sometimes the official announces that the responsible bandit has in fact been killed and that the case is therefore closed; then he proceeds to show off the bandit's body, after killing some prisoner in his jail who has nothing to do with this particular crime. Not only does the bandits' victim fail to get his grievances redressed and his stolen properties restored; he may also lose everything he has and go bankrupt. After all this, he will probably swallow his tears in silence and make no more complaint, since by then he is no longer financially able to make any appeals.

Suppose he does appeal and that the government responds by mobilizing a large force in its attempt to arrest the bandits. Since these soldiers have always been in collusion with the bandits, they will release the offenders soon after their capture, in return for a handsome bribe, and the offenders will quickly disappear without leaving a trace. Sometimes the soldiers use the reported presence of bandits as an excuse to blackmail the villagers; if the latter refuse to pay the bribes they demand, they will accuse them as the bandits' accomplices, burn their houses, and bring them to the city in chains. . . .

The third ill which your humble servant wishes to stress is the great number of cases in which innocent men are condemned and the inability on the part of the people to have a wrong redressed. Since his appointment at the Ministry of Justice, your humble servant has reviewed several hundred cases of appeal. . . . In most . . . cases, . . . it was the plaintiffs who received punishment in the end, on the ground that they had made false accusations, while the defendants went through the whole litigation unscathed and free. Generally speaking, the officials-in-charge invoke the following rules in the law as legitimate ground to impose heavy penalties upon the plaintiffs. First, the plaintiff has failed to present the truth in his petition, and for such failure he is to receive one hundred blows by a striking rod. Second, the case he presents is not serious enough for him to bypass the local courts and to go straight to the nation's capital, and for such offense he is to be punished by banishment to the frontier as a soldier. Third, he intimidates the government under the pretense of offering constructive suggestions, and for such offense he is to be punished by banishment to a nearby area as a soldier. Fourth, he harbors personal grudges against the official under whose jurisdiction he lives and falsely accuses him of wrongdoing before the latter's superior. For this offense he is to be punished by banishment to the malarious regions as a soldier. . . .

Who can believe that when an ordinary citizen is a plaintiff and a government official a defendant, the defendant is always right and the plaintiff always wrong? The answer to both questions would have to be a clear "No one" if we had conscientious, enlightened officials sitting on the bench as judges. . . .

These three ills are the most serious the nation faces today, and the search for their cure is our most urgent task. Insofar as the second and the third ills — the widespread banditry and the condemnation of innocent men — are concerned, Your Majesty is hereby requested to issue a strict order to all the governors-general and governors to think carefully about them and to devise ways for their cure. As for the first ill or the increasingly higher price of silver, we should find remedies in terms of stabilizing the existing price.

Your humble servant is at present drafting a proposal aimed at the attainment of this goal, which, when completed, will be presented to Your Majesty for reference purposes.

The people are the very foundation of a nation, and it is certainly the fault of us ministers that their sufferings, however small, are not made known to Your Majesty. Insignificant though his opinion is, your humble servant begs for Your Majesty's indulgence to let it be submitted.

THE LAND SYSTEM OF THE HEAVENLY DYNASTY

Given the conditions described by Tseng Kuo-fan, it is not surprising that hundreds of peasant revolts rocked nineteenth-century China. One of them, the Taiping Rebellion, lasted thirteen years and almost caused the collapse of the imperial government. The leader of the rebellion was Hung Hsiu-ch'üan (1814–1864), a native of the Canton (Guangzhou) region who, after failing the civil service examinations three times, developed an intense hatred for the Manchu regime. He also had a powerful vision of a peaceful and egalitarian China, a product in part of his interpretation of Christian principles learned when he was a student at a Baptist mission school in Canton. Calling himself "Heavenly King and Younger Brother of Jesus," he urged China's peasants to smash the power of the landlords and institute a "Heavenly Kingdom of Great Peace."

The despairing Chinese peasants joined Hung's movement by the millions after he raised the banner of revolt in 1851. From their base in south China, Taiping armies marched north and in 1853 captured Nanking (modern Nanjing), which became their capital. There, the movement bogged down, but it took eleven more years of fighting before the rebellion was suppressed. The costs were staggering. Much of China was devastated, and as many as 20 million people died due to famine, battles, and atrocities.

Shortly after taking Nanking, the Taiping leaders issued a series of statements about their aims and beliefs. The most widely distributed document was "The Land System of the Heavenly Dynasty." The author is unknown, but the philosophy undoubtedly reflects that of Hung Hsiu-ch'üan. Taiping leadership was too distracted militarily to implement the document's blueprint, but its vision of a new China fired the imaginations of millions of Taiping followers.

Questions
for Analysis

1. To what extent would the proposals in this document solve the peasants' problems described by Tseng Kuo-fan?
2. How does the social philosophy underlying this document resemble the ideas of Marx and Engels in *The Communist Manifesto* (Chapter 8)?
3. To what extent does the Taipings' religious philosophy underlie their social and economic theories?
4. What does this document reveal about the Taipings' attitude toward women? Toward farmers?
5. In what ways would the individual's life have been regimented if this plan had been implemented?

*T*he division of land must be according to the number of individuals, whether male or female; calculating upon the number of individuals in a household, if they be numerous, then the amount of land will be larger, and if few, smaller; and it shall be a mixture of the nine classes.[1] If there are six persons in a family, then for three there shall be good land and for three poorer land, and of good and poor each shall have half. All the fields in the empire are to be cultivated by all the people alike. If the land is deficient in one place, then the people must be removed to another, and if the land is deficient in another, then the people must be removed to this place. All the fields throughout the empire, whether of abundant or deficient harvest, shall be taken as a whole: if this place is deficient, then the harvest of that abundant place must be removed to relieve it, and if that place is deficient, then the harvest of this abundant place must be removed in order to relieve the deficient place; thus, all the people in the empire may together enjoy the abundant happiness of the Heavenly Father, Supreme Lord and Great God.[2] There being fields, let all cultivate them; there being food, let all eat; there being clothes, let all be dressed; there being money, let all use it, so that nowhere does inequality exist, and no man is not well fed and clothed. . . .

Among all officials and subjects throughout the empire, those who universally keep and obey the Ten Commandments of Heaven and who obey orders and faithfully serve the state shall thus be considered loyal subjects, and shall be raised from a low to a high station, their descendants inheriting their official title. Those officials who break the Ten Commandments of Heaven, disobey orders, receive bribes, or engage in corrupt practices shall thus be considered traitors, and shall be degraded from a high to a low station and reduced to mere husbandry. Those subjects who obey the Commandments and orders and exert themselves in husbandry shall be considered honest and faithful, and either elevated or rewarded; but those subjects who disobey the Commandments and orders and neglect the duties

1. All land was to be classified into nine categories according to productivity.

2. The "Heavenly Father" means the Christian God, although in some Taiping literature the term refers to a supreme deity believed to have been worshiped in ancient China.

of husbandry shall be considered as evil and vicious, to be either put to death or punished. . . .

Within (the court) and without, all the various officials and people must go every Sabbath to hear the expounding of the Holy Bible, reverently offer their sacrifices, and worship and praise the Heavenly Father, the Supreme Lord and Great God. On . . . the forty-ninth day, the Sabbath, the colonel, captains, and lieutenants shall go in turn to the churches in which reside the sergeants under their command and expound the Holy books, instruct the people, examine whether they obey the Commandments and orders or disobey the Commandments and orders, and whether they are diligent or slothful. . . .

Throughout the empire all officials must every Sabbath, according to rank and position, reverently present sacrificial animals and offerings, sacrifice and worship, and praise the Heavenly Father, the Supreme Lord and Great God. They must also expound the Holy books; should any dare to neglect this duty, they shall be reduced to husbandmen. Respect this.

Throughout the empire the mulberry tree is to be planted close to every wall, so that all women may engage in rearing silkworms, spinning the silk, and making garments. Throughout the empire every family should keep five hens and two sows, which must not be allowed to miss their proper season. At the time of harvest, every sergeant[3] shall direct the corporals to see to it that of the twenty-five families under his charge each individual has a sufficient supply of food, and aside from the new grain each may receive, the remainder must be deposited in the public granary. Of wheat, pulse, hemp, flax, cloth, silk, fowls, dogs, etc., and money,

the same is true; for the whole empire is the universal family of our Heavenly Father, the Supreme Lord and Great God. When all the people in the empire will not take anything as their own but submit all things to the Supreme Lord, then the Lord will make use of them, and in the universal family of the empire, every place will be equal and every individual well fed and clothed. . . .

However, the sergeant must keep an account of money and grain figures in a record book, which he must present to those in charge of money and grain, and those in charge of receipts and disbursements. For every twenty-five families there must be established one public granary, and one church where the sergeant must reside. Whenever there are marriages, or births, or funerals, all may go to the public granary; but a limit must be observed, and not a cash be used beyond what is necessary. Thus, every family which celebrates a marriage or a birth will be given one thousand cash and a hundred catties of grain. This one rule is applicable throughout the empire. In the use of all things let there be economy, to provide against war and famine. As for marriages in the empire, wealth should not be a consideration.

In every circle of twenty-five families, the work of the potter, the blacksmith, the carpenter, the mason, and other artisans must all be performed by the corporal and privates; when free from husbandry they are to attend to these matters. Every sergeant, in superintending marriages and funeral events in the twenty-five families, should in every case offer a eucharistic sacrifice to our Heavenly Father, the Supreme Lord and Great God; all corrupt ceremonies of former times are abolished.

In every circle of twenty-five families,

---

3. A Taiping official of middling rank; all Taiping officials received military titles.

all young boys must go to church every day, where the sergeant is to teach them to read the Old Testament and the New Testament, as well as the book of proclamations of the true ordained Sovereign. Every Sabbath the corporals must lead the men and women to the church, where the males and females are to sit in separate rows. There they will listen to sermons, sing praises, and offer sacrifices to our Heavenly Father, the Supreme Lord and Great God.

TWO PROCLAMATIONS FROM THE BOXER REBELLION

The Boxer Rebellion of 1900 was the tragic expression of growing Chinese rage over decades of foreign exploitation and, at the same time, the culmination of a struggle within the Manchu regime between reformers and conservatives. The Taiping Rebellion and continuing military setbacks convinced reformers that only rapid and fundamental changes could ensure China's survival. They called for the introduction of Western-style military training, industry, mining, and transportation while at the same time maintaining Confucian values. Their conservative opponents sought to preserve the time-honored Chinese ways, sometimes because they were sincerely committed to them but often because they benefited financially from the status quo.

The deadlock ended in 1898 when the desperate Emperor Kuang-hsü (1875–1908), fearing further foreign annexations, initiated the One Hundred Days' Reform. He issued hundreds of edicts designed to weed out corrupt officials, streamline the government, stimulate education, reform the military, undermine the power of provincial governors, and introduce Chinese-owned banks, railroads, and newspapers. Opposition coalesced around the emperor's mother, the Empress Dowager Tz'u-hsi, who, with the support of powerful generals, in September 1898 stripped the emperor of his power and threw him in jail. Tz'u-hsi and her entourage quickly repudiated all important reforms, restored abolished offices, and in 1900 lent their support to the Boxer Rebellion, another sad chapter in the story of Chinese-Western relations.

The "Society of Righteous Harmony," known to Westerners as "Boxers" because their formal exercises resembled boxing, was one of hundreds of secret societies that flourished in late Ch'ing China. Centered in the north, the Boxers believed that foreigners, especially Christian missionaries, were at the root of China's problems. In 1899 they launched a campaign of murder against foreign missionaries and businessmen, many of whom fled to Peking (modern Beijing) for protection in the foreign legation quarter. The Boxers followed them and, encouraged by Ch'ing officials and Tz'u-hsi, placed the legation under siege. Despite the Boxers' claim that their magic spells made them impervious to Western bullets, a multinational armed force easily lifted the siege. Thus, the Chinese flirtation with reform in 1898 led to the imposition on China of yet another humiliating treaty, one that included payment of a staggering indemnity of $333,900,000.

As their movement gathered momentum in the summer of 1900, the Boxers sought followers by distributing and posting thousands of proclamations that revealed their views. The two selections that follow are representative examples.

Questions
for Analysis

1. According to these proclamations, what is the Boxers' vision of China's future?
2. How do the Boxers view Western technology?
3. According to the Boxers, what evils have foreigners caused in China?
4. Why were the Boxers so confident of their ultimate victory?

*T*he Gods assist the Boxers,
The Patriotic Harmonious corps,
It is because the "Foreign Devils" disturb
   the "Middle Kingdom."
Urging the people to join their religion,
To turn their backs on Heaven,
Venerate not the Gods and forget the
   ancestors.

Men violate the human obligations,
Women commit adultery,
"Foreign Devils" are not produced by
   mankind,
If you do not believe,
Look at them carefully.

The eyes of all the "Foreign Devils" are
   bluish,
No rain falls,
The earth is getting dry,
This is because the churches stop
   Heaven,
The Gods are angry;
The Genii[1] are vexed;
Both come down from the mountain to
   deliver the doctrine.

This is no hearsay,

The practices of boxing will not be in
   vain;
Reciting incantations and pronouncing
   magic words,
Burn up yellow written prayers,
Light incense sticks
To invite the Gods and Genii of all the
   grottoes.

The Gods come out from grottoes,
The Genii come down from mountains,
Support the human bodies to practice the
   boxing.

When all the military accomplishments or
   tactics
Are fully learned,
It will not be difficult to exterminate the
   "Foreign Devils" then.

Push aside the railway tracks,
Pull out the telegraph poles,
Immediately after this destroy the
   steamers.

The great France
Will grow cold and downhearted.
The English and Russians will certainly
   disperse.

---

1. The Boxers drew on both Buddhism and Taoism, so their references to specific gods and "genii" (minor spirits) are unclear.

Let the various "Foreign Devils" all be killed.

May the whole Elegant Empire of the Great Ching Dynasty be ever prosperous!

*A*ttention: all people in markets and villages of all provinces in China — now, owing to the fact that Catholics and Protestants have vilified our gods and sages, have deceived our emperors and ministers above, and oppressed the Chinese people below, both our gods and our people are angry at them, yet we have to keep silent. This forces us to practise the I-ho[2] magic boxing so as to protect our country, expel the foreign bandits and kill Christian converts, in order to save our people from miserable suffering. After this notice is issued to instruct you villagers, no matter which village you are living in, if there are Christian converts, you ought to get rid of them quickly. The churches which belong to them should be unreservedly burned down. Everyone who intends to spare someone, or to disobey our order by concealing Christian converts, will be punished according to the regulation when we come to his place, and he will be burned to death to prevent his impeding our program. We especially do not want to punish anyone by death without warning him first. We cannot bear to see you suffer innocently. Don't disobey this special notice!

▨   Sun Yat-sen

HISTORY OF THE CHINESE REVOLUTION

After the defeat of the Boxers in 1901, only a decade remained before the 1911 revolution overthrew the Manchu Dynasty and ended China's ancient imperial government. In those ten years, despite one final effort to implement reforms, the Manchus faced growing peasant unrest, continuing foreign interference, and a power vacuum after the death of T'zu-hsi in 1908. The government's prestige fell even further, and many intellectuals, students (many of whom were now studying in Japan), secret societies, Chinese communities around the globe, and even some generals either plotted or yearned for the end of Manchu rule.

The leading revolutionary and the individual mainly responsible for the success of the 1911 revolution was Sun Yat-sen (1866–1925), a man far different from previous Chinese reformers. The son of a peasant from the Macao region, Sun was educated in Hawaii and Chinese missionary schools and had a world-view more Western than Confucian. Galled by Chinese military impotence and Manchu ineptitude, he became an active revolutionary in 1894, when he founded the secret Revive China Society, which in 1895 sought to overthrow the Canton (modern Guangzhou) provincial government. The plot was discovered, and Sun was forced into exile. After sixteen years of traveling, planning, writing, and organizing, his dreams were fulfilled when the Manchu Dynasty was overthrown.

---

2. In Chinese the Boxer organization was known as I-ho ch'üan.

On his return to China from the United States (where he heard about the 1911 revolution while on a speaking tour in Denver), he was elected the first president of the United Provinces of China on December 30, 1911, and in the following year founded the Nationalist, or Kuomintang, party. Sun's moment of glory was short-lived. In 1913 the military strong man Yüan Shi-k'ai (1859–1916) sent him into exile, and after the general's death, national unity and orderly government gave way to the rule of local warlords. Sun never regained power, except briefly in the Canton region.

The following selection summarizes Sun's "three principles of revolution," which served as the ideology of the United League, an organization founded in 1905 by Sun in Tokyo that combined secret societies from China, various overseas Chinese groups, and Chinese students in Japan. It subsequently provided the platform for the Nationalist party. In his *History of the Chinese Revolution*, published in 1923, Sun describes these principles and explains why they were best for China.

Questions
for Analysis

1. What is meant by Sun's principles of (a) nationalism, (b) democracy, and (c) livelihood?
2. What examples from China's past does Sun use to defend his ideas?
3. To what extent do Sun's ideas reflect Western influence?

I. PRINCIPLES OF REVOLUTION

The term *Kemin,* or revolution, was first used by Confucius. Incidents of a revolutionary nature repeatedly happened in Chinese history after Tang and Wu.[1] In Europe revolutionary tides surged in the seventeenth and eighteenth centuries and they have since spread over the whole world. In due course they created republics; they conferred constitutions on monarchies. The principles which I have held in promoting the Chinese revolution were in some cases copied from our traditional ideals, in other cases modeled on European theory and experience and in still others formulated according to original and self-developed theories. They are described as follows:

1. *Principle of Nationalism.* Revelations of Chinese history prove that the Chinese as a people are independent in spirit and in conduct. Coerced into touch with other peoples, they could at times live in peace with them by maintaining friendly relations and at others assimilate them as the result of propinquity. During the periods when their political and military prowess declined, they could not escape for the time from the fate of a conquered nation, but they could eventually vigorously reassert themselves. Thus the Mongol rule of China,[2] lasting for nearly a hundred

1. Tang, or T'ang, led a revolt that replaced the Hsia Dynasty with the Shang in approximately 1766 B.C.; Wu led a revolt against the Shang, which led to the founding of the Chou Dynasty, probably in 1122 B.C.

2. The Mongols ruled China under the Yüan Dynasty from 1279 to 1368.

years, was finally overthrown by Tai Tsu[3] of the Ming Dynasty and his loyal followers. So in our own time was the Manchu yoke thrown off by the Chinese. Nationalistic ideas in China did not come from a foreign source; they were inherited from our remote forefathers. Upon this legacy is based my principle of nationalism, and where necessary, I have developed it, amplified it and improved upon it. No vengeance has been inflicted on the Manchus and we have endeavored to live side by side with them on an equal footing. This is the nationalistic policy toward the races within our national boundaries. Externally, we should strive to maintain independence in the family of nations, and to spread our indigenous civilization as well as to enrich it by absorbing what is best in world civilization, with the hope that we may forge ahead with other nations toward the goal of ideal brotherhood.

2. *Principle of Democracy.* In ancient China we had Emperor Yao and Emperor Shun[4] who departed from the hereditary system and chose their successors. We also had Tang and Wu who overthrew kingdoms by revolution. Preserved in our books are such sayings as "Heaven sees as the people see; Heaven hears as the people hear." "We have heard of a person named Chou having been slain, we have not heard of a monarch having been murdered."[5] "The people are most important, while the king is of the least importance." All these sayings ring with democratic sentiments. Since we have had only ideas about popular rights, and no democratic

system has been evolved, we have to go to Europe and America for a republican form of government. There some countries have become republics and others have adopted constitutional monarchism, under which royal power has shrunk in the face of the rising demand for popular rights. Though hereditary monarchs have not yet disappeared, they are but vestiges and shadows of their former selves.

All through my revolutionary career I have held the view that China must be made a republic. There are three reasons. First, from a theoretical point of view, there is no ground for preserving a monarchical form of government, since it is widely recognized that the people constitute the foundation of a nation and they are all equal in their own country. In the second place, under Manchu occupation the Chinese people were forced into the position of the vanquished, and suffered oppression for more than two hundred and sixty years. While a constitutional monarchy may not arouse deep resentment in other countries and can maintain itself for the time being, it will be an impossibility in China. This is from a historical point of view. A third reason may be advanced with an eye on the future of the nation. That in China a prolonged period of disorder usually followed a revolution was due to the desire of every insurgent to be a king and to his subsequent contention for the throne. If a republican government is adopted, there will be no contention. . . .

My second decision is that a constitu-

---

3. T'ai tsu is the posthumous title meaning "Grand Progenitor," given to the founder of the Ming Dynasty, Chu Yüan-chang (1328–1398).

4. Mythical early Chinese rulers, famous for their wisdom and virtue.

5. This is a quotation from the works of Mencius (Meng-tzu), the follower of Confucius who

lived from about 372 to about 269 B.C. It reflects his theory that the basic justification of an emperor's rule rests in the support of the people. Thus, if an emperor of the Chou Dynasty is murdered through popular insurrection, he has already lost his popular mandate. This means that only a "man named Chou" has been murdered, not a true monarch.

tion must be adopted to ensure good government. The true meaning of constitutionalism was discovered by Montesquieu.[6] The threefold separation of the legislative, judicial, and executive powers as advocated by him was accepted in every constitutional country in Europe. On a tour of Europe and America I made a close study of their governments and laws and took note of their shortcomings as well as their advantages. The shortcomings of election, for instance, are not incurable. In the past China had two significant systems of examination and censoring and they can be of avail where the Western system of government and law falls short. I therefore advocate that the examinative and censorial powers[7] should be placed on the same level with legislative, judicial and executive, thereby resulting in the fivefold separation of powers. On top of that, the system of the people's direct political powers should be adopted in order that the provision that the sovereign power is vested in the people may become a reality. In this way my principle of democracy may be carried out satisfactorily.

3. *Principle of Livelihood*. With the invention of modern machines, the phenomenon of uneven distribution of wealth in the West has become all the more marked. Intensified by cross-currents, economic revolution was flaring up more ferociously than political revolution. This situation was scarcely noticed by our fellow-countrymen thirty years ago. On my tour of Europe and America, I saw with my own eyes the instability of their economic structure and the deep concern of their leaders in groping for a solution. I felt that, although the disparity of wealth under our economic organization is not so great as in the West, the difference is only in degree, not in character. The situation will become more acute when the West extends its economic influence to China. We must form plans beforehand in order to cope with the situation. After comparing various schools of economic thought, I have come to the realization that the principle of state ownership is most profound, reliable and practical. Moreover, it will forestall in China difficulties which have already caused much anxiety in the West. I have therefore decided to enforce the principle of the people's livelihood simultaneously with the principles of nationalism and democracy, with the hope to achieve our political objective and nip economic unrest in the bud.

The Emergence of Modern Japan

In the late nineteenth century, the Japanese accomplished what no other non-Western people had been or has been able to do. Within only three decades Japan

---

6. French political philosopher (1689–1755), best known for *The Spirit of the Laws* (1748).

7. The "examinative power" was to have control over government appointments, a throwback in some respects to the old system of civil service examinations; the "censorial power" was a revival of the old Chinese Board of Censors, which had the capacity to criticize the government.

changed from a secluded, preindustrial society, vulnerable to foreign interference, into a powerful industrialized nation that shocked the world by winning wars against China in 1895 and Russia in 1905. What made this transformation especially remarkable was that little social upheaval accompanied it: despite the magnitude of the changes, the Japanese retained many of their most cherished ideals and beliefs.

Japan's successful metamorphosis began in 1868, when a faction of powerful Japanese aristocrats abolished the Tokugawa shogunate and the previously secluded and ceremonial emperor moved from Kyoto to Edo to become head of the government. This event is known as the Meiji Restoration (1868–1912), based on the Japanese word *meiji*, or "enlightenment," chosen by the emperor, Mutsuhito, as the official name of his reign.

The demise of the shogunate was not surprising. Ever since the late eighteenth century, the descendants of Tokugawa Ieyasu found it increasingly difficult to prevent the undermining of Tokugawa society by population growth, urbanization, the rise of a large and wealthy merchant class, and the decline of the samurai. Nor were they able to control their disgruntled subjects, many of whom forgot the Confucian injunction to revere higher authority. Peasant revolts, urban riots, intellectual ferment such as Dutch Studies and the National Learning Movement (see Chapter 5), and, most ominously, restive aristocrats' increasingly bold criticisms of the shogunate were all signs of a troubled regime. Attempts at "reform," such as the Tempo Reforms of 1841–1843, were actually efforts to turn back the clock by limiting peasant mobility, controlling commerce, and reviving the military traditions of the samurai.

The humiliation of foreign intrusion was the fatal blow to the shogunate. In July 1853, an event that many Japanese had feared for decades finally took place. Four naval vessels, flying United States colors and under the command of the forceful and flamboyant Admiral Matthew Perry, appeared in Edo (Tokyo) Bay. Perry demanded that the Japanese agree to negotiations leading to the opening of Japanese ports to United States trade. Within a decade, Japan granted trading privileges not only to the United States but also to the Netherlands, Russia, Great Britain, and France.

Patriotic Japanese bitterly turned against a government lacking the resources, military strength, and popular support to protect them from such indignities. Opponents of the shogunate raised the cry, "Honor the Emperor, Expel the Barbarian!" They were convinced that only the semidivine emperor, whose ancient powers derived from the Sun Goddess herself, could rally the Japanese to the national effort needed to overcome the foreigners. On January 3, 1868 (by the Japanese calendar, the ninth day of the twelfth month of 1867), under the leadership of the Satsuma and Chosu clans, pro-imperial forces seized the shogun's palace and declared the restoration of the emperor. The young emperor Mutsuhito accepted, and when the new powers crushed the shogun's resistance, more than 250 years of Tokugawa rule ended. Japan now entered the era of the Meiji Restoration, a period of rapid and thoroughgoing change unparalleled in recent world history.

Oshio Heihachiro

MANIFESTO OF 1837

Although little is known about the background of Oshio Heihachiro (1793–1837), he seems to have come from a lower samurai family and been adopted by a member of the Oshio clan, the dominant daimyo family in the area of the large western city of Osaka. After a Confucian education, he accepted an administrative post in the Oshia prefect in Osaka. During his tenure, he gained a reputation for vigorous action against crime and corruption. His retirement in 1830 to pursue a career of scholarship and teaching gave Oshio an opportunity to develop his unique interpretation of Confucius, which called for the end of social injustice and taught that goodness was something to be cultivated equally among all classes. Already critical of the Tokugawa regime, he became deeply angered at the government because of its indifference to the suffering caused by a protracted famine between 1833 and 1837. After selling his precious books to buy food for the starving, Oshio organized an attack on Osaka in 1837 in the hope that this would spark a general insurrection. His supporters laid siege to the shogun's administrative offices and started a fire that burned one quarter of the city. When Oshio and his son realized the rebellion would fail, they committed suicide.

Oshio addressed the following manifesto to the inhabitants of nearby provinces, urging them to join the Osaka insurrection. It explains why he and many other Japanese had lost faith in their Tokugawa rulers.

Questions for Analysis

1. Consider Oshio's criticism of Tokugawa government officials. How do they resemble Tseng Kuo-fan's criticism of Chinese officials?
2. On the basis of Oshio's manifesto and Tseng Kuo-fan's memorandum, what similarities and differences can you see in the plight of Japanese and Chinese peasants?
3. What is Oshio's attitude toward Osaka merchants? How do his views of Japanese society support the theory that he came from a samurai family?
4. Can you infer any reasons from this document why the revolt failed?

*I*f the four seas[1] suffer destitution, the beneficence of heaven cannot long survive. If a man of small stature governs the country, calamities become inevitable. These are the teachings bequeathed by the sage of old[2] to the later generations of rul-

---

1. Here used in the sense of "the world."

2. Confucius.

ers and subjects. The Deity enshrined in Toshogu[3] decreed that to show compassion for the widows, widowers and the lonely is the foundation of benevolent government. However, during the past 240 to 250 years of peace, gradually those who were above became accustomed to luxury and they now live in sheer extravagance. Those officials who are entrusted with important political affairs openly give and receive bribes. Some of them who lack virtue and righteousness still attain high positions as a result of connections they have through the ladies in waiting in the inner palace. They devote their efforts and intelligence to enrich their private coffers. They levy an excessive amount of money from common people and farmers in their own domains or administrative districts. These are the people who have suffered over the years the severe exactions of annual taxes and various types of corvée[4] labor. Now they propose such nonsensical demands. As the needs of those officials increase, the poverty of the four seas is compounded. . . .

The excessive rise in the price of rice today does not deter the commissioner in Osaka and his officials from engaging in their arbitrary handling of policies, forgetting that everything under the sun is one in the way of human heartedness. They transport rice to Edo,[5] but fail to make any provision for delivery of rice to Kyoto where the Emperor resides. Instead they even arrest those people from Kyoto who come to buy rice in the amount of five to ten quarts. . . .

The rich in Osaka have over the years made profitable loans to the daimyo and seized a large sum of gold, silver and stipend rice in interest. They now enjoy unprecedented riches, and even though they are chonin[6] they are treated and appointed to positions comparable to elders in the households of the daimyo. They own numerous fields and gardens and newly cultivated fields and live in plenteous comfort. They observe the natural calamities and punishments of heaven occurring now, but are not afraid. They see the poor and beggars starve to death, but do not lift their fingers to help them. . . . Meanwhile they continue to indulge in their pastime, and act as if nothing has ever happened. This is not different from King Chou's[7] long night's feast. The commissioner and his officials have the power to control the actions of the above mentioned people and help the lowly. But they do not do this, and day after day deal in commodities. They are bandits stealing the beneficence of heaven, whose actions cannot be condoned by the Way of Heaven or by the will of the sage.

We who are confined to our homes find it is no longer possible to tolerate the existing conditions. We lack the power of King T'ang and King Wu.[8] We do not have the virtue of Confucius or Mencius.[9] For the

---

3. The reference is to a Shinto shrine in the city of Nikko dedicated to the spirit of Tokugawa Ieyasu (1542–1616), the founder of the Tokugawa shogunate. He was elevated to the status of a god shortly after his death.

4. Unpaid labor required in addition to or in lieu of taxes.

5. Modern Tokyo; the residence of the Tokugawa shoguns.

6. Townsmen other than nobles and priests.

7. Chou Hsin, the last emperor of the Chinese Shang Dynasty, noted for his debauchery and evil; he was overthrown in 1122 or, as some records suggest, 1027 B.C.

8. The founders of the ancient Shang and Chou dynasties, respectively, famous for their virtue.

9. Mencius, the Latinized name of Meng-tzu (ca 372–289 B.C.), was an important disciple of Confucius whose book of sayings, collected in The Book of Mencius, was elevated to the status of one of the Classics in the twelfth century.

sake of all under heaven, knowing that we have no one to depend on and that we may impute the punishments to our families, those of us who are of like mind are resolved to do the following: First we shall execute those officials who torment and harass those who are lowly. Next we shall execute those rich merchants in the city of Osaka who are accustomed to the life of luxury. Then we shall uncover gold and silver coins and other valuables they hoard as well as bags of rice kept hidden in their storage houses. They will be distributed to those who do not own fields or gardens in the domains of Settsu, Kawachi, Izumi and Harima, and to those who may own lands, but have a hard time supporting fathers, mothers, wives and other members of the family. The above money and rice will be distributed. Thereafter as soon as you hear that there is a disturbance in the city of Osaka, mind not the distance you must travel, come immediately to Osaka.

What we do is to follow the command of heaven to render the punishments of heaven.

Sakuma Shozan

REFLECTIONS ON MY ERRORS

After Admiral Perry left Tokyo in July 1853, promising to return within a year to receive answers to his demands, the Japanese began an uproarious debate involving the shogun's officials, daimyo, samurai, intellectuals, merchants, and the imperial court. Although the first reaction was to reject all things Western and "Expel the Barbarians," many realized that xenophobic pronouncements were no match for superior ships and firepower. Thus, as the debate went on, more Japanese were willing to consider the arguments of Sakuma Shozan, whose philosophy is summarized by the motto he made famous, "Eastern ethics and Western science."

Born of a samurai family in 1811, Sakuma had a Confucian education before entering the service of one of Japan's most powerful aristocrats, Sanada Yukitsura. When the shogun put Sanada in charge of Japan's coastal fortifications in 1841, Sakuma, the scholar, was pushed into the world of artillery, naval strategy, and shipbuilding. He learned Dutch, read all he could of Western science, and became an advocate of adopting Western military technology. In the 1840s, such views were unpopular in the shogun's circles, and, as a result, he and his lord were dismissed. He experienced further problems in 1854 when, at his urging, a student of his attempted to stow away on one of Perry's ships as it left Japan. According to the Seclusion Laws (see Chapter 1), this was a capital offense, but through his aristocratic connections, Sakuma and his student received a jail sentence of only several months.

Sakuma wrote his deceptively titled *Reflections on My Errors* on his release from prison. Far from being an apology for his "errors," it was a vigorous self-defense, made up of fifty-two brief commentaries on various issues. Although he stated that this document was to be "locked up in a box and bequeathed to his descendants," it was widely circulated among Japan's military and political leaders.

After completing *Reflections*, Sakuma continued to advocate the opening of Japan and cooperation between shogun and emperor. His position angered those who sought to abolish the shogunate completely. They arranged his assassination in 1864.

Questions for Analysis

1. What is the meaning of the parable about the "man who is grieved by the illness of his lord or his father"?
2. What does Sakuma mean by "the ethics of the East"? Does he see any difficulty in reconciling them with "the scientific technique of the West"?
3. What does Sakuma see as the major weakness of Japan's military leaders? What is his solution to this problem?
4. According to Sakuma, what are the major flaws of Japan's Confucian scholars? How do his criticisms differ from those of Oshio and Tseng Kuo-fan?
5. What does Sakuma see as the main reason for studying mathematics and science?
6. Apart from his admiration for Western science, how would you characterize Sakuma's attitude toward the West?

*I*n the summer of Kaei 7, the fourth month (May, 1854), I, because of an incident, went down into prison. During my seven months of imprisonment, I pondered over my errors, and, as a result, there were things that I should have liked to say concerning them. However, brush and ink-stone were forbidden in the prison, and I was therefore unable to keep a manuscript. Over that long period, then, I forgot much. Now that I have come out, I shall record what I remember, deposit the record in a cloth box, and bequeath it to my descendants. As for publicizing what I have to say, I dare do no such thing. . . .

2. Take, for example, a man who is grieved by the illness of his lord or his father, and who is seeking medicine to cure it. If he is fortunate enough to secure the medicine, and is certain that it will be efficacious, then, certainly, without questioning either its cost or the quality of its

name, he will beg his lord or father to take it. Should the latter refuse on the grounds that he dislikes the name, does the younger man make various schemes to give the medicine secretly, or does he simply sit by and wait for his master to die? There is no question about it: the feeling of genuine sincerity and heartfelt grief on the part of the subject or son makes it absolutely impossible for him to sit idly and watch his master's anguish; consequently, even if he knows that he will later have to face his master's anger, he cannot but give the medicine secretly. . . .

20. The gentleman has five pleasures, but wealth and rank are not among them. That his house understands decorum and righteousness and remains free from family rifts — this is one pleasure. That exercising care in giving to and taking from others, he provides for himself honestly, free, internally, from shame before his wife and children, and externally, from disgrace before the public — this is the second pleasure. That he expounds and glorifies the learning of the sages, knows in his heart the great Way, and in all situations contents himself with his duty, in adversity as well as in prosperity — this is the third pleasure. That he is born after the opening of the vistas of science by the Westerners, and can therefore understand principles not known to the sages and wise men of old — this is the fourth pleasure. That he employs the ethics of the East and the scientific technique of the West, neglecting neither the spiritual nor material aspects of life, combining subjective and objective, and thus bringing benefit to the people and serving the nation — this is the fifth pleasure. . . .

28. The principal requisite of national defense is that it prevents the foreign barbarians from holding us in contempt. The existing coastal defense installations all lack method; the pieces of artillery that have been set up in array are improperly made; and the officials who negotiate with the foreigners are mediocrities who have no understanding of warfare. The situation being such, even though we wish to avoid incurring the scorn of the barbarians, how, in fact, can we do so? . . .

30. Of the men who now hold posts as commanders of the army, those who are not dukes or princes or men of noble rank, are members of wealthy families. As such, they find their daily pleasure in drinking wine, singing, and dancing; and they are ignorant of military strategy and discipline. Should a national emergency arise, there is no one who could command the respect of the warriors and halt

the enemy's attack. This is the great sorrow of our times. For this reason, I have wished to follow in substance the Western principles of armament, and, by banding together loyal, valorous, strong men of old, established families not in the military class — men of whom one would be equal to ten ordinary men — to form a voluntary group which would be made to have as its sole aim that of guarding the nation and protecting the people. Anyone wishing to join the society would be tested and his merits examined; and, if he did not shirk hardship, he would then be permitted to join. Men of talent in military strategy, planning, and administration would be advanced to positions of leadership, and then, if the day should come when the country must be defended, this group could be gathered together and organized into an army to await official commands. It is to be hoped that they would drive the enemy away and perform greater service than those who now form the military class. . . .

35. Mathematics is the basis for all learning. In the Western world after this science was discovered military tactics advanced greatly, far outstripping that of former times. This development accords with the statement that "one advanced from basic studies to higher learning." In the *Art of War* of Sun Tzu,[1] the statement about "estimation, determination of quantity, calculation, judgment, and victory" has reference to mathematics. However, since Sun Tzu's time neither we nor the Chinese have ceased to read, study, and memorize his teachings, and our art of war remains exactly as it was then. It consequently cannot be compared with that of the West. There is no reason for this other than that we have not devoted

---

1. A classic work on military strategy written during the early fourth century B.C.

ourselves to basic studies. At the present time, if we wish really to complete our military preparations, we must develop this branch of study. . . .

40. What do the so-called scholars of today actually do? Do they clearly and tacitly understand the way in which the gods and sages established this nation, or the way in which Yuao, Shun, and the divine emperors of the three dynasties governed?[2] Do they, after having learned the rites and music, punishment and administration, the classics and governmental system, go on to discuss and learn the elements of the art of war, of military discipline, of the principles of machinery? Do they make exhaustive studies of conditions in foreign countries? Of effective defense methods? Of strategy in setting up strongholds, defense barriers, and reinforcements? Of the knowledge of computation, gravitation, geometry, and mathematics? If they do, I have not heard of it! Therefore I ask what the so-called scholars of today actually do. . . .

47. In order to master the barbarians there is nothing so effective as to ascertain in the beginning conditions among them. To do this, there is no better first step than to be familiar with barbarian tongues. Thus, learning a barbarian language is not only a step toward knowing the barbarians, but also the groundwork for mastering them. . . .

49. Last summer the American barbarians arrived in the Bay of Uraga[3] with four warships, bearing their president's message. Their deportment and manner of expression were exceedingly arrogant, and the resulting insult to our national dignity was not small. Those who heard could but gnash their teeth. A certain person on guard in Uraga suffered this insult in silence, and, having been ultimately unable to do anything about it, after the barbarians had retired, he drew his knife and slashed to bits a portrait of their leader, which they had left as a gift. Thus he gave vent to his rage. In former times Ts'ao Wei of Sung,[4] having been demoted, was serving as an official in Shensi, and when he heard of the character of Chao Yüan-hao, he had a person skillful in drawing paint Chao's image. Ts'ao looked at this portrait and knew from its manly appearance that Chao would doubtless make trouble on the border in the future. Therefore Wei wished to take steps toward preparing the border in advance, and toward collecting together and examining men of ability. Afterwards, everything turned out as he had predicted. Thus, by looking at the portrait of his enemy, he could see his enemy's abilities and thereby aid himself with his own preparations. It can only be regretted that the Japanese guard did not think of this. Instead of using the portrait, he tore it up. In both cases there was a barbarian; in both cases there was a portrait. But one man, lacking the portrait, sought to obtain it, while the other, having it, destroyed it. Their depth of knowledge and farsightedness in planning were vastly different.

---

2. According to the most popular version of earliest Chinese history, China was governed by three early rulers (*huang*), followed by five emperors and then three dynasties, the Hsia, Shang, and Chou. Yuao and Shun, the last two of the "five emperors," were revered for their wisdom and virtue.

3. A small bay at the mouth of Tokyo Bay.

4. The Chinese Sung Dynasty ruled from A.D. 960 to 1279.

Yamagata Aritomo

OPINION ON MILITARY AFFAIRS AND CONSCRIPTION

Few individuals played a more important role in the history of Meiji Japan than Yamagata Aritomo (1838–1922), best known as the architect of the Japanese army but also as a statesman who influenced domestic policy, education, and the writing of Japan's constitution. Born into a low-ranking samurai family, he committed himself to the antiforeign, antishogun movements of the 1860s and was a strong supporter of the imperial restoration. The new regime immediately assigned him its most pressing task, the modernization of Japan's military. After an eighteen-month trip to Europe to observe military practices, Yamagata submitted the following memorandum on the nation's military needs to his country's leaders. One year later, in 1873, he framed the imperial decree that established a conscript army. This had revolutionary social implications for Japan, because it ended once and for all the samurai's monopoly on fighting and made military service the responsibility of every Japanese male, no matter what his social standing.

Questions
for Analysis

1. According to Yamagata, why is it necessary for Japan to strengthen its army and navy?
2. What are some of the lessons Yamagata learned from his observation of Western military practices? In his view, why did Belgium and the Netherlands maintain large armies?
3. What similarities can you see between Yamagata's memorandum and Sakuma's *Reflections on My Errors*?
4. What can you infer about the arguments against a military buildup from this document?
5. What might be some of the ways in which the proposed military buildup would affect Japanese society as a whole?

A military force is required to defend the country and protect its people. Previous laws of this country inculcated in the minds of the samurai these basic functions, and there was no separation between the civilian and military affairs.[1] Nowadays civilian officials and military officials have separate functions, and the practice of having the samurai serve both functions has been abandoned. It is now

---

1. By this Yamagata means that the samurai were the ruling class as well as the class responsible for fighting.

necessary to select and train those who can serve the military functions, and herein lies the change in our military system. . . .

The status of our armed forces today is as follows: We have the so-called Imperial Guards whose functions are nothing more than to protect the sacred person of His Majesty and to guard the Imperial Palace. We have altogether more than twenty battalions manning the four military garrisons who are deployed to maintain domestic tranquility, and are not equipped to fight against any foreign threat. As to our navy, we have a few battleships yet to be completed. How can they be sufficient to counteract foreign threats? . . .

The first concern of the Ministry of Military Affairs is to set up a system to defend our homeland. For this purpose two categories of soldiers are required: a standing army and those on the reserve list. The number of troops differ from country to country. Of the major countries, Russia maintains the largest number of troops and the United States the smallest. The reason for this discrepancy comes from the fact that the governmental system differs from one country to another. Consequently the regulations governing each of the countries also differ. The Netherlands and Belgium are among the smallest countries, but they are located between large countries, and in order to avoid contempt and scorn from their neighbors, they diligently go about the business of defending their countries. Even though one of these countries has a total area not exceeding one-third of the area of our country, it maintains a standing army numbering not less than forty to fifty thousand. If we apply the existing standards prevailing in our country to judge

these two countries, they may appear to be concerned only with military affairs to the neglect of other matters. However, they do attend to hundreds of other affairs of state and do not abandon them. This is possible because their national goals are already set, and they can act accordingly to implement them.

Therefore the creation of a standing army for our country is a task which cannot be delayed. It is recommended that a certain number of strong and courageous young men be selected from each of the prefectures in accordance with the size of the prefectures, and that such young men be trained in the Western-type military science and placed under rigorous drills, so that they may be deployed as occasion demands.

The so-called reservists do not normally remain within the military barracks. During peacetime they remain in their homes, and in an emergency they are called to service. All of the countries in Europe have reservists, and amongst them Prussia has most of them. There is not a single able-bodied man in Prussia who is not trained in military affairs. Recently Prussia and France fought each other and the former won handily. This is due in large measure to the strength of its reservists.[2]

It is recommended that our country adopt a system under which any able-bodied man twenty years of age be drafted into military service, unless his absence from home will create undue hardship for his family. There shall be no distinction made between the common man and those who are of the samurai class. They shall all be formed into ranks, and after completion of a period of service, they shall be returned to their homes.[3] In this way every man will be-

---

2. The reference is to the Franco-Prussian War (1870–1871), in which the Prussians soundly defeated the French.

3. This means they will become reservists.

come a soldier, and not a single region in the country will be without defense. Thus our defense will become complete.

The second concern of the Ministry is coastal defense. This includes building of warships and constructing coastal batteries. Actually, battleships are movable batteries. Our country has thousands of miles of coastline, and any mobile corner of our country can become the advance post of our enemy. However, since it is not possible to construct batteries along the coastline everywhere, it is imperative to expand our navy and construct the largest warships. . . .

The third concern of the Military is to create resources for the navy and the army. There are three items under consideration, namely military academies, a bureau of military supplies, and a bureau of munitions depots. It is not difficult to have one million soldiers in a short time, but it is difficult to gain one good officer during the same span of time. Military academies are intended to train officers for these two services. If we pay little attention to this need today, we shall not be able to have the services of capable officers for another day. Therefore, without delay military academies must be created and be allowed to prosper. Students shall be adequately trained by the faculty consisting of experts from several countries. . . . The bureau of military supplies shall be in charge of procuring military provisions and manufacturing weapons of war for the two services. The bureau of munitions depots shall store such provisions and munitions. If we lack military provisions and weapons and our munitions depots are empty, what good will the million

soldiers in the army or thousands of warships do? Therefore, well-qualified craftsmen from various countries must be hired to make necessary machines and build strong storage houses. We must make our own weapons and store them, and must become self-sufficient without relying on foreign countries. The goal is to create a sufficient amount and if there is any surplus it may be sold to other countries.

Some people may argue that while they are aware of the urgency in the need for the Ministry of Military Affairs, they cannot permit the entire national resources to be committed to the need of one ministry alone. They further aver that from the larger perspective of the imperial government, there are so many other projects covering a wide range of things which require governmental attention. . . . This argument fails to discern the fundamental issues. The recommendations herein presented by the Ministry of Military Affairs in no way asks for the stoppage of all governmental activities or for the monopolization of all government revenues. But in a national emergency, a new set of priorities must be established. Those of us who are given the task of governing must learn from the past, discern the present, and weigh all matters carefully.

In the past there was Emperor Peter[4] who was determined to make his country a great nation. He went overseas and studied naval sciences. After his return he built many battleships and constructed St. Petersburg. He created a standing army numbering several million, and was able to engage in the art of international politics against five or six of the strongest

---

4. The reference is to the famous tsar Peter the Great (Chapter 6), who reigned from 1689 to 1725. Much of what Yamagata says about Peter in this paragraph is inaccurate, either because he received false information or because he distorted the facts to prove his point. His state-

ments that Peter constructed "many battleships," recruited an army of "several million," fought "five or six" strong nations and left domestic politics "to a woman" are simply incorrect.

nations. As to domestic politics, he was satisfied to leave them to a woman. There were one or two internal quarrels, but they were eradicated almost immediately. It is to him that the credit is due for making Russia a great nation.

Those of us who govern must first of all discern the conditions prevailing in the world, set up priorities and take appropriate measures. In our opinion Russia has been acting very arrogantly. Previously, contrary to the provisions of the Treaty of Sevastopol,[5] she placed her warships in the Black Sea. Southward, she has shown her aggressive intent toward Moslem countries and toward India. Westward, she has crossed the borders of Manchuria and has been navigating the Amur River. Her intents being thus, it is inevitable that she will move eastward sooner or later by sending troops to Hokkaido,[6] and then taking advantage of the seasonal wind move to the warmer areas.

At a time like this it is very clear where the priority of this country must lie. We must now have a well-trained standing army supplemented by a large number of reservists. We must build warships and construct batteries. We must train officers and soldiers. We must manufacture and store weapons and ammunitions. The nation may consider that it cannot bear the expenses. However, even if we wish to ignore it, this important matter cannot disappear from us. Even if we prefer to enter into this type of defense undertaking, we cannot do without our defense for a single day.

Iwasaki Yataro

LETTER TO MITSUBISHI EMPLOYEES

After military modernization, the next priority for the Meiji reformers was to establish a strong industrial economy, both to support the army and navy and to protect the country from foreign exploitation. After a rocky start in the 1870s, Japanese industrialization proceeded rapidly, and by 1900 the nation had become one of the world's major economic powers through a combination of government subsidies and individual entrepreneurship — and, significantly, without foreign investment.

The greatest success story in Japan's industrialization was Iwasaki Yataro (1835–1885), the founder of one of the nation's greatest business conglomerates, Mitsubishi. The son of a poor farmer, Iwasaki gained a rudimentary education and held several low-level business jobs before he found employment as an administrator in the domain of the aristocratic Tosa family in the mid-1860s. He was given the daunting task of managing and paying off the domain's huge debt, the result of its recent massive purchases of guns and artillery. His policies, which included paying some debtors with counterfeit currency, quickly eliminated the domain's deficit. In 1871, when the domain abandoned its direct ownership of business enterprises, it gave

5. Yamagata seems to have in mind the 1856 Treaty of Paris, which ended the Crimean War; it stipulated that the defeated Russians could send no warships into the Black Sea. Sevastopol is a city on the Black Sea.

6. One of the islands of Japan north of Honshu.

Iwasaki eleven steamships and all the assets and privileges connected with its business in silk, coal-mining, tea, and lumber. In return, Iwasaki was expected to make payments to reduce some new Tosa debts and provide employment for former samurai. From this start, he systematically wiped out foreign and domestic competition and, through a series of successful (and frequently cutthroat) business moves, turned Mitsubishi into Japan's second largest conglomerate, with interests in shipbuilding, mining, banking, insurance, and manufacturing.

Iwasaki wrote the following letter to his employees in 1876 during Mitsubishi's battle with the British Peninsula and Oriental Steam Navigation Company over control of Japanese coastal trade. He had just cut fares in half but had also reduced wages by a third.

Questions
for Analysis

1. Why does Iwasaki feel the Japanese cannot let foreigners be involved in the coastal trade?
2. Why, according to Iwasaki, are some Japanese willing to accept foreign involvement in the coastal trade?
3. What must Iwasaki do if his company is to compete effectively with foreigners?
4. To what extent is Iwasaki's letter similar in spirit to Yamagata's "Opinion on Military Affairs and Conscription"?

Many people have expressed differing opinions concerning the principles and advantages of engaging foreigners or Japanese in the task of coastal trade. Granted, we may permit a dissenting opinion which suggests that in principle both foreigners and Japanese must be permitted to engage in coastal trade, but once we look into the question of advantages, we know that coastal trade is too important a matter to be given over to the control of foreigners. If we allow the right of coastal navigation to fall into the hands of foreigners in peacetime it means loss of business opportunities and employment for our own people, and in wartime it means yielding the vital right of information to foreigners. In fact, this is not too different from abandoning the rights of our country as an independent nation.

Looking back into the past, in Japan at the time when we abandoned the policy of seclusion and entered into an era of friendly intercourse and commerce with foreign nations, we should have been prepared for this very task. However, due to the fact that our people lack knowledge and wealth, we have yet to assemble a fleet sufficient to engage in coastal navigation. Furthermore, we have neither the necessary skills for navigation nor a plan for developing maritime transportation industry. This condition is the cause of attracting foreign shipping companies to occupy our major maritime transport lines. Yet our people show not a sense of surprise at it. Some people say that our treaties with foreign powers contain an express provision allowing foreign ships to proceed from Harbor A to Harbor B, and others claim that such a provision must not be regarded as granting foreign ships the right to coastal navigation inasmuch as it is intended not to impose unduly heavy taxes on them. While I am not qualified to discuss it, the issue remains an important one.

I now propose to do my utmost, and along with my 35 million compatriots, perform my duty as a citizen of this country. That is to recover the right of coastal trade in our hands, and not to delegate that task to foreigners. Unless we propose to do so, it is useless for our government to revise the unequal treaties[1] or to change our entrenched customs. We need people who can respond, otherwise all the endeavors of the government will come to naught. This is the reason why the government protects our company, and I know that our responsibilities are even greater than the full weight of Mt. Fuji[2] thrust upon our shoulders. There have been many who wish to hinder our progress in fulfilling our obligations. However, we have been able to eliminate one of our worst enemies, the Pacific Mail Company of the United States, from contention by application of appropriate means.[3] Now, another rival has emerged. It is the Peninsula & Oriental Steam Navigation Company of Great Britain which is setting up a new line between Yokohama and Shanghai, and is attempting to claim its right over the ports of Nagasaki, Kobe and Yokohama. The P & O Company comes to compete for the right of coastal navigation with us. How can we decline the challenge? Heretofore, our company has received protection from the government, support from the nation, and hard work

from its employees through which it has done its duty. However, our company is young and not every phase of its operation is well conducted. In contrast, the P & O Company is backed by its massive capital, its large fleet of ships, and by its experiences of operations in Oriental countries. In competing against this giant, what methods can we employ?

I have thought about this problem very carefully and have come to one conclusion. There is no other alternative but to eliminate unnecessary positions and unnecessary expenditures. This is a time-worn solution and no new wisdom is involved. Even though it is a familiar saying, it is much easier said than done, and this indeed has been the root cause of difficulties in the past and present times. Therefore, starting immediately I propose that we engage in this task. By eliminating unnecessary personnel from the payroll, eliminating unnecessary expenditures, and engaging in hard and arduous work, we shall be able to solidify the foundation of our company. If there is a will there is a way. Through our own effort, we shall be able to repay the government for its protection and answer our nation for its confidence shown in us. Let us work together in discharging our responsibilities and not be ashamed of ourselves. Whether we succeed or fail, whether we can gain profit or sustain loss, we cannot anticipate at this time. Hopefully, all of you will join me in a singleness of heart to attain this cherished goal, forebearing and undaunted by setbacks to restore to our own hands the right to our own coastal trade. If we succeed it will not only be an accomplishment for our company alone but also a

---

1. The various commercial treaties the shogunate signed after Admiral Perry's mission.

2. The highest mountain in Japan, near Tokyo.

3. The American firm abandoned its effort to

crack the Japanese market when it found it could not compete with Mitsubishi's price slashing, largely made possible by hefty government subsidies.

glorious event for our Japanese Empire, which shall let its light shine to all four corners of earth. We can succeed or fail, and it depends on your effort or lack of effort. Do your utmost in this endeavor!

Southeast Asia in the Era of Western Imperialism

During the nineteenth century, Southeast Asia, like Africa, felt the full brunt of European imperialism. Inspired by nationalism, still hopeful of making converts to Christianity, and lured by the region's markets, minerals, and agricultural products, Western nations extended their political authority over the whole region except for the Kingdom of Thailand. Although Western colonialism in most of Southeast Asia was relatively brief, lasting on average only a century, it nevertheless had significant impact. In politics it brought government cohesion to diverse island groupings such as the Philippines and Indonesia, and throughout the region it weakened the authority of traditional leaders and local governments. In economics, it stimulated new enterprises such as tin mining and the rubber industry, introduced new crops such as the oil palm, corn, and cassava, and led to the building of new harbors, the introduction of railroads, and improved communications. It also caused substantial demographic changes. As a consequence of improved health care and greater political stability, the region's population swelled from approximately 26 million in 1830 to 123 million in the 1940s. Furthermore, the make-up of Southeast Asia's population changed when millions of Chinese and Indians immigrated to the region to take advantage of expanding economic opportunities.

Western colonialism also brought new educational opportunities for the region's inhabitants and acquainted them with Western concepts of nationalism, constitutionalism, and democracy. Inevitably, these developments stimulated anticolonial movements, and after World War II the establishment of independent states throughout the region began.

LETTER TO THE GOVERNOR GENERAL OF INDIA FROM THE CHIEF MINISTERS OF THE COURT OF AVA

Like the Ottoman sultans and Chinese emperors, many rulers in Southeast Asia underestimated the peril they faced from the West and by doing so fell victim to Western expansionism. The following letter, which the ministers of King Bodawpaya of Burma sent to the British governor general of India in 1802, exemplifies such an attitude.

Burmese-English relations deteriorated in the 1790s because of border problems growing out of the 1784 Burmese conquest of Arakan, a territory on the east coast of the Bay of Bengal. After the conquest and several anti-Burmese revolts, thousands of Arakanese fled into the English-controlled province of Bengal. The Burmese grew angry at the British for allowing the Arakanese to enter Bengal, and the British grew angry at the Burmese for sending troops into Bengal to pursue the refugees. In 1795 the British sent an envoy, Michael Symes, to the Burmese court to settle the border dispute, explore possibilities of British trade in Rangoon, and head off any French effort to establish influence in the area. Symes's mission was successful, but shortly thereafter the new British agent in Rangoon, Hiram Cox, clashed with Burmese officials over renewed border disputes and the sale of muskets to the Burmese government. British officials subsequently sent Symes in 1802 on another mission to the Burmese court, where, after some delay, he convinced the Burmese to adopt the moderate stance expressed in this letter. Tensions between the two countries continued, however, resulting in two wars (1824–1826, 1852) and, eventually, Britain's conquest of Burma.

Questions for Analysis

1. What does this letter reveal about Burmese views of kingship?
2. As described in this document, what is the relationship between the Burmese king and the rulers of China, Ceylon, and Assam?
3. Do the Burmese ministers seem to think that the British threaten Burma?
4. How do the attitudes of the Burmese king compare with those of Emperor Ch'ien-lung in his Letter to King George III (Chapter 7)?

We, chief ministers of the Sovereign Prince of the golden city of Amarapura,[1] to whom the sovereigns of all states and countries owe homage and respect, of him who is lord of the mines of gold, silver, rubies, and the other seven sorts of precious things; Lord of the White Elephants and of the Sikkia Arms,[2] Lord of the present life; We, the said chief ministers of the great God observer of the law, who, ever placing our heads under the golden soles of the royal feet, . . . govern and decide all affairs of state, address this to you, Governor General of Calcutta. As the great princely angel resides in the delightful city of Amarapura, thus our Sovereign Prince, residing in the said great golden city, to which no Sovereign can boast a place equal in magnificence, beauty and delights, and willing to in-

---

1. Capital of Burma in the eighteenth and early nineteenth centuries; located some 350 miles up the Irrawaddy River.

2. Weapons that on the king's command were able to immediately destroy his enemies.

crease the welfare and advantage of all his subjects, great and little, of whatever rank and condition, having received the consecration of the pearl[3] which all Princes through respect dread to receive, and being graced with all the virtues becoming a King . . . following the traces and laudable example of all ancient renowned princes from the time of King Sanandix,[4] he exalts those who deserve to be exalted and humbles those who deserve to be humbled. To this our Sovereign Lord residing in Amarapura, from the Country of the Gandalarit[5] the King of China, from the Country of middle Lazaoi[6] the King of Dezali,[7] and from the Country of Anurada[8] in the island of Cio (Ceylon) the King of Cio having, voluntarily, sent their sons, daughters, and every species of precious stuffs of immense value, they have supplicated to be allowed to maintain, by sea and land, an uninterrupted communication with this kingdom. The King our Sovereign foreseeing in his divine wisdom the advantages that would result from his intercourse to the future generations of his sons and grandsons, graciously granted their petition, and having condescended to allow their presents and arms to be offered to him, he bestowed on them the golden cap and the five other insignia of royalty, and magnificently exalted them. Thus the four kingdoms, as if forming but one state, enjoy the happiness of peace and tranquility. The fame of these great events spreading daily wider, the Sover-

eign of the great country of Kio Cassi,[9] in the region of Pyinslarit,[10] sent Ambassadors from the eastward, with letters and suitable presents, to be assistance towards quelling the disturbances arisen in that country. The King, on the arrival of this Embassy, having consulted his four great ministers of state and the generals of his armies, has issued a sovereign order in which he declares that he receives under his royal protection the King of Kio Cassi, and promises to assist and protect him in the same manner as he assists and protects the Kingdoms of China, Assam and Ceylon.

At this juncture one morning, at the time of public audience, the whole body of ministers represented to the King that Colonel Michael Symes, sent by the Governor General of Bengal, had arrived at the Port of Rangoon with letters and presents. His Majesty had already been informed that the Governor General after having, some years ago, paid homage under the golden soles of his royal feet, and requested to be received into his royal protection, had not only welcomed and refused to deliver up his Arracan subjects, who had taken refuge in the province of Bengal, but that he had even opposed an armed force to those sent to compel them to return. His Majesty had further received information that the Agents sent by him to purchase muskets had met with opposition from the Governor General, for which reason a Royal decision, dreadful as the fulminating arms of the Spirits

---

3. A ceremony involving the king, after which he was doomed to death if he neglected the welfare of his people.

4. According to the Burmese, a legendary world monarch.

5. Burmese term for an area of southern China, part of Szechuan and Yunnan provinces.

6. The reference is probably to Assam, an Indian territory on the border of Burma and Tibet.

7. A corruption of Vesali, the capital of Assam.

8. A reference to Anuradhapura, the ancient capital of Ceylon (modern Sri Lanka) referred to in the document as Cio.

9. The region of northern Vietnam.

10. A region northwest of Delhi, in India.

above, thundered from his golden mouth that considering the conduct of the Governor General's, there was just reason to believe him a man of little faith, and that it was therefore, not expedient to receive his presents.

Colonel Michael Symes, on his arrival from Rangoon, having heard this Royal decision, represented that what he should say might be deemed the express words of the Governor General, Marquis Wellesley.[11] That, as to the affair of the muskets and the subjects of complaint, be entreated that, forgiving the rusticity and ill humor of Captain Hiram Cox, to whom the whole was to be imputed, his Majesty would allow British subjects to trade in Rangoon and the other ports of his dominions according to the ancient custom, and that he would deign to accept the presents he had brought. Colonel Michael Symes having frequently made these representations and entreaties, his Majesty gave the following answer: "What other Princes would with difficulty suffer, I, being a sovereign who performs the ten good works and aspires to become God, will submit to and patiently bear. Whatever has passed I regard as the sole act of Hiram Cox and not of the Governor General, who now sends to make this repre-

sentation, nor of Colonel Symes: Be it allowed him to offer his presents, and to all the inhabitants of Bengal to come to the ports of this Kingdom to sell, purchase and trade according to the ancient practice; let this order be communicated to Colonel Michael Symes." Previous to the execution of this sovereign mandate, and to the offering of the presents, two persons . . . sent by the Governor of the Isle of France with a letter and presents, arrived under the golden soles of the royal feet. His Majesty has granted to the deputies of both countries on different days to offer their presents, and contemplate his royal face, and he has taken into his royal protection the English Nation both of Bengal and Europe in the same manner as he extends it to the countries of Assam, China, Ceylon and Kio Cassi; and letters having just now been received from the chief ministers of the great country of Kio Cassi, His Majesty has ordered that a copy of them be given to Colonel Symes. He therefore informs you that on the arrival of Colonel Symes in Bengal, with a peaceful heart and reciprocal friendly dispositions, and for the mutual advantage of both nations, he allows a free and open trade in all the ports of this Kingdom.

■ Phan Thanh Gian

"LETTER TO EMPEROR TU DUC" AND "LAST MESSAGE TO HIS ADMINISTRATORS"

Phan Thanh Gian (1796–1867) poignantly represents the defeat of traditional Confucian values in Vietnam in the face of superior European armaments. The Nguyen Dynasty, having unified the country and moved its capital from Hanoi to Hué in 1802, attempted to model the new regime strictly on the principles of Confucianism,

---

11. Richard Colley (1760–1842), 1st Marquis Wellesley, was governor general of India from 1797 to 1805; British power in India greatly increased during his term.

which, in contrast to the predominant Hindu-Buddhist influence throughout the rest of the region, had largely shaped Vietnamese scholarship, politics, and values. The Nguyen emperors' efforts to turn Vietnam into a model Confucian society led directly to the persecution of Vietnamese Christians, who, as a result of long-standing efforts by French, Spanish, and Portuguese missionaries, numbered 300,000 by the nineteenth century. When Vietnamese Catholics were implicated in a rebellion in 1833, the emperor ordered the imprisonment and execution of converts and European missionaries. The intensified persecution caused the French, who sixty years earlier had helped the Nguyen Dynasty gain power, to send in 1858 an armed force to Vietnam, ostensibly to protect Christianity but also to advance French imperialism. Although the Vietnamese offered staunch resistance, Emperor Tu Doc in 1862 accepted a settlement by which he ceded to the French three southern provinces around Saigon.

Four years later, an anti-French rebellion broke out in three provinces west of Saigon, then under the governorship of Phan Thanh Gian, one of Vietnam's leading Confucian statesmen and the head of a delegation sent to Paris in 1863 to negotiate with the French government. When he failed to suppress the revolts, the French sent in troops and demanded control of the provinces. Phan Thanh Gian acceded and then committed suicide, but not before he wrote the following two letters, one to Emperor Tu Duc and the other to administrators in his district.

Questions
for Analysis

1. On what basis does Phan Thanh Gian hope the emperor can save Vietnam from further humiliation?
2. What is Phan Thanh Gian's view of the French?
3. What Confucian principles led to his decision to acquiesce to the French?

8, July 1867

I, Phan Thanh Gian, make the (following) report, in expressing frankly, with my head bowed, my humble sentiments, and in soliciting, with my head raised, your discerning scrutiny.

During the period of difficulties and misfortunes that we are presently undergoing, rebellion is rising around the capital, the pernicious influence[1] is expanding on our frontiers. The territorial question is rapidly leading to a situation that it is impossible to end.

My duty compels me to die. I would not dare live thoughtlessly, leaving a heritage of shame to my Sovereign and my Father. Happily, I have confidence in my Emperor, who has extensive knowledge of ancient times and the present and who has studied profoundly the causes of peace and of dissention: . . . In respect-

---

1. The French intervention.

fully observing the warnings of Heaven and in having pity on the misery of man . . . in changing the string (of the guitar), in modifying the track (of the governmental chariot), it is still possible for you to act in accordance with your authority and means.

At the last moment of life, the throat constricted, I do not know what to say, but, in wiping my tears and in raising my eyes toward you affectionately, I can only ardently hope (that this wish will be realized). With respect, I make this report, Tu Duc, twentieth year, sixth moon, seventh day, Phan Thanh Gian.

. . .

Mandarins and people,

It is written: He who lives in accordance with the will of Heaven lives in virtue; he who does not live according to the will of Heaven lives in evil. To work according to the will of Heaven is to listen to natural reason. . . . Man is an intelligent animal created by Heaven. Every animal lives according to his nature, as water flows to low ground, as fire goes out on dry ground. . . . Men, to whom Heaven has given reason, must apply themselves to live in obedience to this reason which Heaven has given them.

The empire of our king is ancient. Our gratitude toward our kings is complete and always ardent; we cannot forget them. Now, the French are come, with their powerful weapons of war to cause dissension among us. We are weak against them; our commanders and our soldiers have been vanquished. Each battle adds to our misery. . . . The French have immense warships, filled with soldiers and armed with huge cannons. No one can resist them. They go where they want, the strongest ramparts fall before them.

I have raised my spirit toward Heaven and I have listened to the voice of reason. And I have said: "It would be as senseless for you to wish to defeat your enemies by force of arms as for a young fawn to attack a tiger. You attract uselessly great misfortunes upon the people whom Heaven has confided to you. I have thus written to all the mandarins and to all the war commanders to break their lances and surrender the forts without fighting.

But, if I have followed the Will of Heaven by averting great evils from the head of the people, I am a traitor to our king in delivering without resistance the provinces which belong to him. . . . I deserve death. Mandarins and people, you can live under the command of the French, who are only terrible during the battle, but their flag must never fly above a fortress where Phan Thanh Gian still lives."

José Rizal

NOLI ME TANGERE

It is no surprise that the first strong anticolonial movement in Southeast Asia took place in the Philippines. Under Spanish domination since the 1500s, the Philippines had a sizable class of educated and socially prominent Filipinos angered by the Spanish refusal to grant them political rights. By the nineteenth century many Filipinos also had come to resent the power and authority of the Catholic religious orders, which monopolized education, censored thought, and owned much of the islands' best agricultural lands.

José Rizal (1861–1896), a Filipino doctor turned novelist, became the arch-symbol of anticolonialism in the Philippines during the late nineteenth century. The son of a moderately well-to-do farmer who clashed frequently with Catholic clergy and Spanish officials, Rizal left the Philippines at the age of 22 to study in Madrid. Finding Spanish authorities indifferent to his country's plight, Rizal began to write a novel, which he completed in 1886 and titled *Noli Me Tangere* (Latin for "Don't touch me"). Filipinos quickly purchased the first 2,000 copies, but soon Spanish authorities banned the book's sale. Nevertheless, Rizal became a national hero and wrote a second novel as well as various nationalist pieces. He returned to the Philippines in the 1890s, but Spanish authorities soon banished him to an obscure island, where he remained until granted permission to serve Spanish troops fighting rebels in Cuba. While on his way, anti-Spanish uprisings broke out in the Philippines, and Rizal was brought back to Manila. Hoping to send a tough message to the rebels, the government found Rizal guilty of treason and executed him by firing squad on December 30, 1896. The execution enraged Philippine nationalists, who continued their struggle and briefly established a republic in 1898.

The hero of *Noli Me Tangere* is Juan Ibarra, an idealistic young Filipino, who, after studying abroad, returns home to work for the betterment of his people and is engaged to the beautiful María Clara. The novel's villains are Spanish officials and members of the Catholic religious orders, who block Ibarra's efforts to establish a school and ruin his plans to marry María Clara. After many twists and turns, the book ends unhappily, with María Clara entering a convent after hearing false reports of Ibarra's death. The following excerpt involves a conversation between Ibarra and Elias, an outlaw who befriended Ibarra in his many adventures and who expresses Rizal's views.

Questions
for Analysis

1. According to Elias, what is the Constabulary's impact on the Philippine villages?
2. Compare Elias's complaints with Tseng Kuo-fan's comments on China's system of justice. In what respects are the abuses the two men describe similar?
3. At this point in the novel Ibarra represents the conservative point of view on the Spanish presence in the Philippines. What arguments does he offer against Elias?
4. What is the basis of Elias's bitterness against the religious orders in the Philippines?
5. Elias is an uneducated Filipino speaking to a member of the Philippines' upper class who was educated in Europe. What are his views of Ibarra and others in his social group?

*E*lias told him in a few words the conversation he had had with the commander of the outlaws, omitting the doubts and threats expressed by the latter. Ibarra heard him attentively. When Elias had finished, a long silence fell which Ibarra was the first to break.

"So they ask for . . ."

"Radical reforms in the armed forces, in the clergy, in the administration of justice, that is to say, a more paternal approach from the Government."

"Reforms? In what sense?"

"For example, more respect for human dignity, greater security for the individual, less strength in the armed forces, less privileges for an organization which so easily abuses them."

"Elias," replied the young man, "I do not know who you are, but I have the feeling that you are not an ordinary man. You do not think and act like the others. You will understand me if I tell you that, although the present state of things has its defects, it would have even more should it be changed. . . . I know very well that, while these institutions have their defects, they are necessary now; they are what is called a necessary evil."

Elias, astonished, raised his head and stared at Ibarra aghast.

"You too believe in necessary evils? You believe that to do good it is necessary to do evil?"

"No, I believe in the necessary evil as I believe in those drastic treatments we use when we want to cure a disease. Now then, the country is an organism which suffers from a chronic sickness, and to cure it the Government feels compelled to use means which, if you wish, are harsh and violent but useful and necessary.". . .

"To weaken the Constabulary would be to endanger the security of the towns."

"The security of the towns!" cried Elias bitterly. "It will soon be fifteen years that those towns have had the protection of the Constabulary, and look: we still have outlaws, we still hear that they sack towns and hold people up on the highways; robberies still take place and the robbers are not discovered; crime exists, and the real criminal goes about freely, but not the peaceful inhabitants of the town. Ask any honest citizen if he looks upon the Constabulary as a good thing, as a means of protection furnished by the Government and not as an imposition, a despotism whose excesses are more harmful than the depredations of the outlaws. True, these depredations are usually on a great scale, but they do not happen often, and a man is allowed to defend himself against them. But one cannot even protest against the impositions of the forces of law and order, and if these impositions are sometimes not so great in extent, they are on the other hand continuous and sanctioned by society. What is the effect of this organization on the life of our towns? It paralyzes communications because everybody is afraid of being harassed for petty causes. It is concerned with appearances rather than with fundamentals — one of the first symptoms of incapacity. A man is tied and beaten up because he has forgotten his identity card, no matter if he is a decent person with a good reputation. The officers think it is their first duty to exact a salute, willing or unwilling, even at night, and they are imitated in this by their subordinates, who use it as an excuse — although an excuse is never lacking — to manhandle and fleece the peasants. The sanctity of the home does not exist for them; not long ago they entered a house . . . through the window and beat up a peaceful inhabitant to whom their commanding officer owed money and favors. There is no security for the individual: when they want their barracks or their houses cleaned, they go out and seize anyone who does not resist and make him work the whole day. Do you want to hear more? During these days of the fiesta they have permitted gambling, but have brutally disturbed the celebrations which were duly authorized. You saw yourself what the people think about them. What good has it done them to swallow their anger and place their hopes on human justice? If this, sir, is what you call maintaining peace and order . . ."

"I agree that there are evils," replied Ibarra, "but let us accept the evils for the sake of the good things that go with them. The Constabulary may not be perfect, but, believe me, the fear it inspires prevents an increase in the number of criminals."

"Say rather that this fear increases their number," Elias corrected him. "Before the creation of this organization almost all criminals, with the exception of a very few, were driven to crime by hunger; they looted and robbed to stay alive, but when times were easier, the highways were once more safe. . . . Now outlaws are outlaws for life. One misdemeanor, one felony punished with inhumanity, one gesture of resistance against the excesses of authority, is enough, with the fear of atrocious tortures, to exile them forever from society, and condemn them to kill or be killed. The Constabulary's terrorism shuts the doors of repentance, and, since an outlaw fights and defends himself in the mountains better than the soldier whom he flouts, the result is that we cannot extinguish the evil we have created. . . . A regime of terror is useful when a people are enslaved, when there are no caves in the mountains, when the ruling power can place a sentry behind every tree, and when the body of the slave has only a stomach and intestines! But when a desperate man fighting for his

life feels his arm stiffen, his heart beat, and his whole body fill up with spleen, can terrorism extinguish the fire on which it pours more fuel?" . . .

Elias was speaking with passion and enthusiasm; his eyes were flashing and his voice vibrant. An impressive pause followed. The boat, undisturbed by the paddle, seemed to float motionless on the water; the moon shone splendidly in the dark blue sky; on the distant shore a few lights gleamed.

"And what else do they ask?" Ibarra wanted to know.

"The reformation of the clergy," replied Elias with glum discouragement. "The unfortunate ask for greater protection from . . ."

"From the religious Orders?"[1]

"From their oppressors."

"Has the Philippines forgotten what she owes to these Orders? Has she forgotten her immense debt of gratitude to those who redeemed her from error and gave her the True Faith, to those who shielded her from the tyranny of civil power? This is the evil result of not teaching the history of our country."

Elias, surprised, could scarcely believe what he heard.

"Sir," he answered gravely, "you accuse the people of ingratitude. Permit me, one of the suffering people, to defend them. If favors are to be acknowledged, they should be disinterested. We need not talk about such commonplaces as duty or Christian charity. Let us put history aside and forbear from asking what Spain did to the Jews who gave all Europe one Book, one Faith, and one God, or what she did to the Arabs who gave her culture, who themselves tolerated her religion,

---

1. The five religious orders in the Philippines were the Dominicans, Franciscans, Jesuits, Augustinians, and Recollects; to prevent squabbling, the Spanish government had allotted to each one of them a specific area of jurisdiction.

and who awakened her national self-consciousness, dormant, almost dead, under Roman and Visigothic rule.[2] But you say that the religious Orders gave us the True Faith and redeemed us from error. Do you call external practices the True Faith, or the commerce in girdles and scapulars,[3] religion; or the stories of miracles and other fairy tales that we hear every day, the truth? Is this the law of Jesus Christ? God did not have to be crucified for this, nor we assume the obligation of eternal gratitude; superstition existed long before this, all that was needed was to organize it and raise the price of the merchandise. You will tell me that imperfect as our present religion may be, it is preferable to the one we had before; I believe you and I agree with you, but it is too expensive, for we have paid for it with our national identity, with our independence. For its sake we have given to its priests our best towns, our fields, and even our savings, which are spent on the purchase of religious trinkets. A product of foreign manufacture has been imported here; we have paid for it; and we are even. . . ."

"I love our country, Elias, as you may love her; I understand somewhat of what is wanted; I have listened attentively to what you have said. Yet, my friend, for all that, I think we have been rather carried away by emotion. I see less need for reforms in this field than anywhere else."

"Is it possible?" asked Elias throwing up his hands despondently. "You do not see the need for reforms, you, whose family misfortunes . . ."

"I do not consider myself and my own misfortunes when it comes to the security of the Philippines and the interests of Spain," Ibarra interrupted him hotly. "To keep the Philippines for Spain it is necessary for the friars to continue as they are, and the good of our country lies in her union with Spain."

Elias seemed to be listening still even when Ibarra had stopped; his face was grim, and his eyes had lost their brightness. . . .

"Forgive me, sir," answered Elias, shaking his head. "I am not eloquent enough to convince you. Although I have had a little schooling, I am only a native. You will always doubt my right to say anything, and whatever I may say will always be suspect. Those who have given a contrary opinion are Spaniards, and, as such, although they may spout trivialities and stupidities, their accent, their titles, and their race make what they say sacred, and give them such authority that I shall never try again to argue with them. Then again, when I see that you, who love our country, whose own father rests beneath these quiet waters, who have found yourself provoked, insulted, and persecuted, maintain such opinions in spite of everything, in spite of your education, I begin to doubt my own convictions and to admit the possibility that the people may be wrong. I must tell those unfortunates who have placed their faith in men to place it in God and their own strength. I thank you again; tell me where you want me to take you."

"Elias," said Ibarra, "your bitter words touch my heart and make me doubt in turn. Well, how can I help it? I was not brought up among the people, and perhaps I do not know what they need. I spent my childhood in the Jesuit school and grew up

---

2. Elias is referring to the Spanish persecution of the Jews and Muslims on the Iberian Peninsula from the fifteenth through the seventeenth centuries.

3. Part of the attire worn by friars.

in Europe. My opinions were formed by books, and I know only what men have brought to light; I know nothing of the things that remain hidden, that have not been written about. For all that, I love our country like you do, not only because it is the duty of every man to love the country that gave him life and which will perhaps be his last refuge, not only because my father taught me to, because my mother was a native and because all my most beautiful memories are alive in it, but also because I owe it and will owe it my happiness."

"And I, because I owe it my misfortunes," Elias murmured.

PART IV

The Emergence of a New Global Order, 1914 to the Present

Although it is difficult to predict how future historians will interpret our own century, it would be surprising if their accounts did not stress the dramatic contrasts between its first and second halves. Until the 1940s, imperialist nations — Great Britain, Germany (until its defeat in World War I), France, Russia, the Netherlands, Portugal, Belgium, Italy, Spain, the United States, and Japan — ruled Africa, India, most of Southeast Asia, and parts of the Middle East, East Asia, the Caribbean, and South America. By the end of the century these colonial empires had all but disappeared. Between 1914 and 1945, while nationalist demands for independence swept through the colonial world, two world wars and the Great Depression of the 1930s exhausted the imperialist powers, leaving them with neither the will nor the resources to maintain their empires. During the second half of the twentieth century, almost 100 former colonies gained their independence, sometimes after bitter and protracted struggles, sometimes after peaceful negotiations.

But if the late twentieth century saw a successful worldwide revolt of colonial peoples against the dominance of the West, it also witnessed the dissemination of Western science, technology, education, and political ideologies throughout the globe. As a result, modernization, a term used by social scientists and historians to describe the process of industrialization, urbanization, growth in government, secularism, and the acceptance of science, ceased to be a unique Western and Japanese phenomenon.

In most of the non-Western world, the seeds of modernization had been planted during the age of colonialism, when Westerners introduced railroads, modern communications, and Western-style schools. After World War II, when colonial empires disappeared, leaders of the newly independent nations eagerly sought entry into the ranks of the "developed nations" and fashioned policies to accelerate industrialization, increase agricultural production, and encourage secular, scientific education.

For many of the newly independent states, modernization has proved to be slow, frustrating, controversial, and painful. Low educational levels, lack of capital, political instability, corruption, public lethargy, and foreign interference have all retarded hoped-for economic development. Some African and Asian nations have lacked the resources to take even the first step toward successful industrialization. Others have taken that first step, then faltered. For them, modernization in the late twentieth century is symbolized by half-finished or half-occupied skyscrapers, surrounded by shantytowns filled by people with no money, no prospects, and no hope. Yet even in these partially modernized areas, traditional values and social relationships have been undermined. Populations have soared, cities have mushroomed, old patterns of rural life have disappeared, and traditional political and religious elites have been challenged and overthrown.

What does the future hold? Optimists affirm their faith in progress, holding fast to the dream that reasonable human beings are capable of shaping a future of peace, harmony, and a just sharing of the world's wealth. Pessimists ponder population projections, inevitable oil shortages, worsening pollution, perhaps even nuclear winter, and warn of the coming of a new "dark age." However things may develop, the twentieth century has launched humankind on paths that will determine its future for years to come.

The Industrialized World in Crisis

*I*n 1922 the French intellectual Paul Valéry spoke these words to a university audience in Switzerland:

> The storm has died away, and still we are restless, uneasy, as if the storm is about to break. Almost all the affairs of men remain in terrible uncertainty. We think of what has disappeared, we are almost destroyed by what has been destroyed; we do not know what will be born, and we fear the future, not without reason. We hope vaguely, we dread precisely; . . . we confess that the charm of life is behind us, abundance is behind us, but doubt and disorder are in us and with us. There is no thinking man, however shrewd or learned he may be, who can hope to dominate this anxiety, to escape this darkness, to measure the probable duration of this period when the vital relations of humanity are disturbed profoundly.[1]

How stark a contrast between Valéry's despondency and the buoyant optimism of the previous generation! Before World War I, the West's wealth, political power, and scientific achievements reached unimagined heights, and most Americans and Europeans were optimistic, self-satisfied, and proud to the point of arrogance. No one questioned the superiority of Western values and institutions or doubted that Western world domination would continue indefinitely. Similarly, the Japanese, new entrants into the ranks of industrialized nations, confidently looked forward to a future of expanding trade, prosperity, and national glory. Only a few years later assurance gave way to doubt, hope to despair, and optimism to dread.

The turning point, especially for Europe, was World War I — the four-year exercise in death that resulted in 30 million casualties, billions of squandered dollars, and a sobering realization that technological "progress" had a dark and demonic side. World War I and the treaties that followed set the stage for three decades of turmoil, which included uncontrolled inflation, global depression, the rise of totalitarianism, diplomatic failure, growing disregard for human rights, and, finally, a second world war, whose legacy was 50 or 60 million deaths, the attempted annihilation of Europe's Jews, and the dropping of the first atomic bombs.

Commentators of the 1950s and 1960s wrote of the decline and disappearance of Western civilization, suggesting that human history had reached a crossroads similar to that of the fourth and fifth centuries, when the Western Roman Empire collapsed. From the perspective of the late twentieth cen-

---

[1] Paul Valéry, *Variety* (New York: Harcourt Brace, 1927), p. 252.

tury, however, such views were overstated. The industrialized nations, even devastated Germany and Japan, have recovered from wars and depression and managed to retain many of their distinctive characteristics. What has changed is their role in the world. Empires have disappeared, and many former colonial peoples have re-established control of their wealth and resources. For these changes, the traumatic events that began in 1914 and continued into the 1940s are largely responsible.

World War I

In the summer of 1914, the armies of Great Britain, France, Germany, Austria-Hungary, and Russia marched off to war, and the world has never been the same. All the belligerents expected a short war, and everyone was confident that "the boys would be home by Christmas." This was not to be. By the time the war ended in November 1918, thirty-two nations had declared war, hundreds of billions of dollars had been spent, close to 75 million men had been mobilized, 10 million soldiers had been killed, and 20 million had been wounded.

By 1914 the European powers were locked into two major alliances — the Triple Alliance, which included Germany, Austria-Hungary, and Italy, and the Triple Entente, composed of France, Great Britain, and Russia. Since the 1880s, economic rivalries, a continent-wide arms race, colonial disputes, conflicts in the Balkans, and growing nationalism had created an unhealthy atmosphere of insecurity and suspicion. Politicians and generals prepared for a war they assumed was inevitable. In 1905, 1908, and 1911, diplomats managed to settle peace-threatening crises. After June 28, 1914, when a Serbian terrorist assassinated the Austrian Archduke Francis-Ferdinand and his wife at Sarajevo, Europe faced another crisis. This time the diplomats failed. As armies mobilized and crowds cheered, Sir Edward Grey, the British Secretary of State for Foreign Affairs, proclaimed, "The lights are going out in Europe; we shall not see them lit again in our lifetime."

The inspiration for military thinking before the war was still the French commander Napoleon Bonaparte, whose many brilliant victories suggested that rapid troop movement, surprise, massive use of artillery, and huge infantry and cavalry charges would result in overwhelming and decisive victories. Elan and spirit could conquer all obstacles. On the western front, however, after the Germans nearly took Paris in the early weeks of fighting, the war became a stalemate. "Defense" — a combination of deeply dug trenches, barbed wire, land mines, poison gas, and machine guns — proved superior to "offense" — massive artillery barrages followed by the charges of troops who were sent "over the top," across "no man's land," to overrun enemy lines. Such offensive tactics rarely resulted in anything except appallingly long casualty lists.

The economic crises and diplomatic conflict of the postwar years made such human sacrifice seem meaningless. Germany and its allies deeply resented the harsh treaties imposed upon them. Japan and Italy (which ended up fighting with the Entente powers, not Germany and Austria-Hungary), although on the winning side, were angry because their territorial gains fell short of expectations. The Arabs, who had fought against Germany's ally, the Turks, in the hope of achieving nationhood, were embittered when Great Britain and France denied their independence. The United States, disillusioned with foreign war and great power wrangling, withdrew into diplomatic isolation, leaving Great Britain and France to enforce the treaties and deal with the fearsome problems caused by the reordering of Europe and Russia's

Bolshevik Revolution. Great Britain and France added to their empires in Africa and the Middle East, but such territorial gains were scant compensation for the loss of life, the war's huge costs, and the host of new problems they now faced. Even for them, the word "victory" in World War I is inappropriate.

Erich Maria Remarque

ALL QUIET ON THE WESTERN FRONT

So great was the carnage of World War I that no historian has captured its horror as effectively as poets and writers of fiction. Every major belligerent nation had writers who evoked the desolation and inhumanity of trench warfare. Among the most powerful was Erich Maria Remarque (1898–1970). Drafted at the age of eighteen into the German army, Remarque was wounded on the western front. After the war he was a sportswriter and race-car driver while establishing his literary career. In 1929 he published his worldwide best-seller, known to English readers as *All Quiet on the Western Front.* It chronicles the horrors of World War I through the experiences of the novel's main character, Paul Bäumer, a young recruit who survives the war until its final weeks, and then is killed just before the armistice. Repelled by the Nazis' growing strength, Remarque left Germany in 1932 for Switzerland and became an American citizen in 1947. His powerful indictment of war was one of many books the Nazis banned.

Questions
for Analysis

1. Why do the German soldiers find the cries of the wounded horses so disturbing?
2. What point about the war is Remarque making in the episode of the abandoned wounded man?
3. How does Remarque describe the condition of the young recruits? Why, according to Paul, are they "almost more trouble than they are worth"?
4. Does Paul seem to blame the enemy for the plight of the German soldiers?

*A*t last it grows quiet. The fire has lifted over us and is now dropping on the reserves. We risk a look. Red rockets shoot up to the sky. Apparently there's an attack coming.

Where we are it is still quiet. I sit up and shake the recruit by the shoulder. "All over, kid! It's all right this time."

He looks round him dazedly. "You'll get used to it soon," I tell him. . . .

He goes off. Things become quieter, but the cries do not cease. "What's up, Albert?" I ask.

"A couple of columns over there got it in the neck."

The cries continued. It is not men, they could not cry so terribly.

"Wounded horses," says Kat.

It's unendurable. It is the moaning of the world, it is the martyred creation, wild with anguish, filled with terror, and groaning.

We are pale. Detering stands up. "God! For God's sake! Shoot them."

He is a farmer and very fond of horses. It gets under his skin. Then as if deliberately the fire dies down again. The screaming of the beasts becomes louder. One can no longer distinguish whence in this now quiet silvery landscape it comes; ghostly, invisible, it is everywhere, between heaven and earth it rolls on immeasurably. Detering raves and yells out: "Shoot them! Shoot them, can't you? damn you again!"

"They must look after the men first," says Kat quietly.

We stand up and try to see where it is. If we could only see the animals we should be able to endure it better. Müller has a pair of glasses. We see a dark group, bearers with stretchers, and larger black clumps moving about. Those are the wounded horses. But not all of them. Some gallop away in the distance, fall down, and then run on farther. The belly of one is ripped open, the guts trail out. He becomes tangled in them and falls, then he stands up again.

Detering raises up his gun and aims. Kat hits it in the air. "Are you mad — ?"

Detering trembles and throws his rifle on the ground.

We sit down and hold our ears. But this appalling noise, these groans and screams penetrate, they penetrate everywhere.

We can bear almost anything. But now the sweat breaks out on us. We must get up and run no matter where, but where these cries can no longer be heard. And it is not men, only horses.

From the dark group stretchers move off again. Then single shots crack out. The black heap convulses and then sinks down. At last! But still it is not the end. The men cannot overtake the wounded beasts which fly in their pain, their wide open mouths full of anguish. One of the men goes down on one knee, a shot — one horse drops — another. The last one props itself on its forelegs and drags itself round in a circle like a merry-go-round; squatting, it drags round in circles on its stiffened forelegs, apparently its back is broken. The soldier runs up and shoots it. Slowly, humbly, it sinks to the ground.

We take our hands from our ears. The cries are silenced. Only a long-drawn, dying sigh still hangs on the air.

Then only again the rockets, the singing of the shells and the stars there — most strange.

Detering walks up and down cursing: "Like to know what harm they've done." He returns to it once again. His voice is agitated, it sounds almost dignified as he says: "I tell you it is the vilest baseness to use horses in the war."

. . .

The days go by and the incredible hours follow one another as a matter of course. Attacks alternate with counter-attacks and slowly the dead pile up in the field of craters between the trenches. We are able to bring in most of the wounded that do not lie too far off. But many have long to wait and we listen to them dying.

For one of them we search two days in vain. He must be lying on his belly and unable to turn over. Otherwise it is hard to understand why we cannot find him;

for it is only when a man has his mouth close to the ground that it is impossible to gauge the direction of his cry.

He must have been badly hit — one of those nasty wounds neither so severe that they exhaust the body at once and a man dreams on in a half-swoon, nor so light that a man endures the pain in the hope of becoming well again. Kat thinks he has either a broken pelvis or a shot through the spine. His chest cannot have been injured otherwise he would not have such strength to cry out. And if it were any other kind of wound it would be possible to see him moving.

He grows gradually hoarser. The voice is so strangely pitched that it seems to be everywhere. The first night some of our fellows go out three times to look for him. But when they think they have located him and crawl across, next time they hear the voice it seems to come from somewhere else altogether.

We search in vain until dawn. We scrutinized the field all day with glasses, but discover nothing. On the second day the calls are fainter; that will be because his lips and mouth have become dry.

Our Company Commander has promised next turn of leave with three days extra to anyone who finds him. That is a powerful inducement, but we would do all that is possible without that for his cry is terrible. Kat and Kropp even go out in the afternoon, and Albert gets the lobe of his ear shot off in consequence. It is to no purpose, they come back without him.

It is easy to understand what he cries. At first he called only for help — the second night he must have had some delirium, he talked with his wife and his children, we often detected the name Elise. To-day he merely weeps. By evening the voice dwindles to a croaking. But it persists still through the whole night. We hear it so distinctly because the wind blows toward our line. In the morning when we suppose he must already have long gone to his rest, there comes across to us one last gurgling rattle.

The days are hot and the dead lie unburied. We cannot fetch them all in, if we did we should not know what to do with them. The shells will bury them. Many have their bellies swollen up like balloons. They hiss, belch, and make movements. The gases in them make noises.

The sky is blue and without clouds. In the evening it grows sultry and the heat rises from the earth. When the wind blows toward us it brings the smell of blood, which is very heavy and sweet. This deathly exhalation from the shell-holes seems to be a mixture of chloroform and putrefaction, and fills us with nausea and retching.

. . .

Although we need reinforcement, the recruits give us almost more trouble than they are worth. They are helpless in this grim fighting area, they fall like flies. Modern trench-warfare demands knowledge and experience; a man must have a feeling for the contours of the ground, an ear for the sound and character of the shells, must be able to decide beforehand where they will drop, how they will burst, and how to shelter from them.

The young recruits of course know none of these things. They get killed simply because they hardly can tell shrapnel from high-explosive, they are mown down because they are listening anxiously to the roar of the big coal-boxes falling in the rear, and miss the light, piping whistle of the low spreading daisy-cutters. They flock together like sheep instead of scattering, and even the wounded are shot down like hares by the airmen.

Their pale turnip faces, their pitiful clenched hands, the fine courage of these poor devils, the desperate charges and attacks made by the poor brave wretches, who are so terrified that they dare not cry out loudly, but with battered chests, with torn bellies, arms and legs only whimper softly for their mothers and cease as soon as one looks at them.

Their sharp, downy, dead faces have the awful expressionlessness of dead children.

It brings a lump into the throat to see how they go over, and run and fall. A man would like to spank them, they are so stupid, and to take them by the arm and lead them away from here where they have no business to be. They wear grey coats and trousers and boots, but for most of them the uniform is far too big, it hangs on their limbs, their shoulders are too narrow, their bodies too slight; no uniform was ever made to these childish measurements.

Between five and ten recruits fall to every old hand.

. . .

Bombardment, barrage, curtain-fire, mines, gas, tanks, machine-guns, hand-grenades — words, words, but they hold the horror of the world.

Our faces are encrusted, our thoughts are devastated, we are weary to death; when the attack comes we shall have to strike many of the men with our fists to waken them and make them come with us — our eyes are burnt, our hands are torn, our knees bleed, our elbows are raw.

How long has it been? Weeks — months — years? Only days. We see time pass in the colorless faces of the dying, we cram food into us, we run, we throw, we shoot, we kill, we lie about, we are feeble and spent, and nothing supports us but the knowledge that there are still feebler, still more spent, still more helpless ones there who, with staring eyes, look upon us as gods that escape death many times.

We show them how to take cover from aircraft, how to simulate a dead man when one is overrun in an attack, how to time hand-grenades so that they explode half a second before hitting the ground; we teach them to fling themselves into holes as quick as lightning before the shells with instantaneous fuses; we show them how to clean up a trench with a handful of bombs; we explain the difference between the fuse-length of the enemy bombs and our own; we put them wise to the sound of gas shells; — show them all the tricks that can save them from death.

They listen, they are docile — but when it begins again, in their excitement they do everything wrong.

Haie Westhus drags off with a great wound in his back through which the lung pulses at every breath. I can only press his hand; "It's all up, Paul," he groans and he bites his arm because of the pain.

We see men living with their skulls blown open; we see soldiers run with their two feet cut off, they stagger on their splintered stumps into the next shell-hole; a lance-corporal crawls a mile and a half on his hands dragging his smashed knee after him; another goes to the dressing station and over his clasped hands bulge his intestines; we see men without mouths, without jaws, without faces; we find one man who has held the artery of his arm in his teeth for two hours in order not to bleed to death. The sun goes down, night comes, the shells whine, life is at an end.

Still the little piece of convulsed earth in which we lie is held. We have yielded no more than a few hundred yards of it as a prize to the enemy. But on every yard there lies a dead man.

■ **Woodrow Wilson**

FOURTEEN POINTS

The United States entered World War I on the side of Great Britain, France, and Russia on April 6, 1917. This decision resulted from the effectiveness of Allied propaganda, concern within the U.S. banking community about the safety of loans to Great Britain and France, and, most important, the dramatic rise in anti-German feeling after Germany's resumption of unrestricted submarine warfare on February 1, 1917.

In his speech of April 2, 1917, President Woodrow Wilson asked Congress to declare war on Germany and its allies, disclaiming territorial ambitions and explaining the American entry as a crusade "to make the world safe for democracy." Then, in January 1918, before American troops began to arrive at the front in substantial numbers, he delivered another speech to Congress in which he reiterated American motives for entering the war and outlined his plans for a postwar settlement. His outline, which came to be known as the Fourteen Points, gave hope to the war-weary on both sides that despite the war's brutalities, once the fighting stopped, leaders could forge a world "fit and safe to live in."

Questions
for Analysis

1.   What principles does Wilson want to serve as the basis for the peace settlement?
2.   According to the introduction to the Fourteen Points, what are the American reasons for entering the war?
3.   Based on his vision of the world after the war, what can you deduce about Wilson's thinking on its causes?
4.   If the Fourteen Points had been put into effect, how would the Central Powers — Germany, Austria-Hungary, Bulgaria, and Turkey — have been punished?
5.   How concerned is Wilson with the future of peoples living under colonialism?

We entered this war because violations of right had occurred which touched us to the quick and made the life of our own people impossible unless they were corrected and the world secured once for all against their recurrence. What we demand in this war, therefore, is nothing peculiar to ourselves. It is that the world be made fit and safe to live in; and particularly that it be made safe for every peace-loving nation which, like our own, wishes to live its own life, determine its own institutions, be assured of justice and fair dealing by the other peoples of the world as against force and selfish aggression. All the peoples of the world are in effect partners in this interest, and for our own part we see very clearly that unless justice be done to others it will not be done to us. The program of the world's peace, therefore, is our program; and that program, the only possible program, as we see it, is this:

I. Open covenants of peace, openly arrived at, after which there shall be no private international understandings of any kind but diplomacy shall proceed always frankly and in the public view.

II. Absolute freedom of navigation upon the seas, outside territorial waters, alike in peace and in war, except as the seas may be closed in whole or in part by international action for the enforcement of international covenants.

III. The removal, so far as possible, of all economic barriers and the establishment of an equality of trade conditions among all the nations consenting to the peace and associating themselves for its maintenance.

IV. Adequate guarantees given and taken that national armaments will be reduced to the lowest point consistent with domestic safety.

V. A free, open-minded, and absolutely impartial adjustment of all colonial claims, based upon a strict observance of the principle that in determining all such questions of sovereignty the interests of the populations concerned must have equal weight with the equitable claims of the government whose title is to be determined.

VI. The evacuation of all Russian territory[1] and such a settlement of all questions affecting Russia as will secure the best and freest cooperation of the other nations of the world in obtaining for her an unhampered and unembarrassed opportunity for the independent determination of her own political development and national policy and assure her of a sincere welcome into the society of free nations under institutions of her own choosing; and, more than a welcome, assistance also of every kind that she may need and may herself desire. The treatment accorded Russia by her sister nations in the months to come will be the acid test of their good will, of their comprehension of her needs as distinguished from their own interests, and of their intelligent and unselfish sympathy.

VII. Belgium,[2] the whole world will agree, must be evacuated and restored, without any attempt to limit the sovereignty which she enjoys in common with all other free nations. No other single act will serve as this will serve to restore confidence among the nations in the laws which they have themselves set and determined for the government of their relations with one another. Without this healing act the whole structure and validity of international law is forever impaired.

VIII. All French territory should be freed and the invaded portions restored, and the wrong done to France by Prussia in 1871 in the matter of Alsace-Lorraine,[3] which has unsettled the peace of the world for nearly fifty years, should be righted, in order that peace may once more be made secure in the interest of all.

---

1. When Wilson delivered his speech, Russia had been through a year of revolution. In March 1917, a moderate, liberal provisional government replaced the tsarist regime; in November the Bolsheviks, followers of Karl Marx, overthrew the provisional government and seized power. In March 1918, the Bolsheviks accepted the Treaty of Brest-Litovsk, resulting in Russia's loss of over a million square miles of territory.

2. Germany had invaded neutral Belgium in the first days of the war; this was the stated reason for Great Britain's entry into the war.

3. France had lost Alsace-Lorraine in 1871 after the Franco-Prussian War; all French nationalists dreamed of its recovery.

IX. A readjustment of the frontiers of Italy should be effected along clearly recognizable lines of nationality.

X. The peoples of Austria-Hungary,[4] whose place among the nations we wish to see safeguarded and assured, should be accorded the freest opportunity of autonomous development.

XI. Rumania, Serbia, and Montenegro[5] should be evacuated; occupied territories restored; Serbia accorded free and secure access to the sea; and the relations of the several Balkan states to one another determined by friendly counsel along historically established lines of allegiance and nationality; and international guarantees of the political and economic independence and territorial integrity of the several Balkan states should be entered into.

XII. The Turkish portions of the present Ottoman Empire should be assured a secure sovereignty, but the other nationalities which are now under Turkish rule should be assured an undoubted security of life and an absolutely unmolested opportunity of autonomous development, and the Dardanelles should be permanently opened as a free passage to the ships and commerce of all nations under international guarantees.[6]

XIII. An independent Polish state should be erected which should include the territories inhabited by indisputably Polish populations, which should be assured a free and secure access to the sea, and whose political and economic independence and territorial integrity should be guaranteed by international covenant.

XIV. A general association of nations must be formed under specific covenants for the purpose of affording mutual guarantees of political independence and territorial integrity to great and small states alike.

TREATY OF VERSAILLES

Although the representatives of all the victorious powers sent delegations to the postwar peace conference in Paris, the so-called Council of Four, consisting of U.S. President Woodrow Wilson and the prime ministers of Great Britain (David Lloyd George), France (Georges Clemenceau), and Italy (Vittorio Orlando) made all the important decisions. From January 1919 to the middle of 1920, they devised separate treaties, each named after a different Paris suburb, which they handed over to the defeated Central Powers for their signatures. The most controversial was the Treaty of Versailles, dictated to and grudgingly accepted by Germany in the summer of 1919 (see the map on page 398). The treaty reflected the views of Clemenceau, whose wish to punish Germany was well known, and Lloyd George, who was under pres-

---

4. The Austro-Hungarian Empire included substantial numbers of Slavs who sought independence.

5. Lands held by Austria-Hungary at the time of Wilson's speech.

6. The Turks controlled Arab lands in the Middle East. The Dardanelles was the strait connecting the Aegean Sea with the Sea of Marmama; it afforded access between the Black Sea and the Mediterranean.

sure to make good his recent campaign promise that at the peace table "he would squeeze Germany until the pips squeak." Wilson opposed Clemenceau and George, but, hoping to gain support for his brainchild, the League of Nations, he approved provisions in a treaty more vindictive than he had wished. The humiliated Germans bitterly resented their government's forced acceptance of the treaty, and many of them listened carefully and approvingly to politicians like Adolf Hitler, who in the 1920s and 1930s promised to tear it up and lead Germany once more down a path of military glory.

Questions for Analysis

1. What steps in the treaty ensure that European states, especially France, will be protected from renewed German aggression?
2. What territorial losses did Germany suffer in Europe and in its colonies?
3. By what arguments does the treaty justify imposing reparations on Germany?
4. In what ways does the treaty compromise Wilson's principle of national self-determination?
5. Overall, to what extent do the provisions of the treaty reflect the principles of Wilson's Fourteen Points? To what extent do they differ?

PART III. POLITICAL CLAUSES FOR EUROPE

Article 42. Germany is forbidden to maintain or construct any fortifications either on the left bank of the Rhine or on the right bank to the west of a line drawn 50 kilometers to the East of the Rhine. . . .

Article 45. As compensation for the destruction of the coal-mines in the north of France and as part payment towards the total reparation due from Germany for the damage resulting from the war, Germany cedes to France in full and absolute possession, with exclusive rights of exploitation, unencumbered and free from all debts and charges of any kind, the coal-mines situated in the Saar Basin as defined in Article 48.[1] . . .

The High Contracting Parties, recognizing the moral obligation to redress the wrong done by Germany in 1871 both to the rights of France and to the wishes of the population of Alsace and Lorraine, which were separated from their country in spite of the solemn protest of their representatives at the Assembly of Bordeaux.[2]

Agree upon the following Articles:

Article 51. The territories which were ceded to Germany in accordance with the Preliminaries of Peace signed at Versailles on February 26, 1871, and the Treaty of Frankfurt of May 10, 1871, are restored to French sovereignty as from the date of the Armistice of November 11, 1918.

The provisions of the Treaties establishing the delimitation of the frontiers before 1871 shall be restored. . . .

---

1. Article 48 defined the boundaries.

2. The recovery of Alsace and Lorraine had been one of France's major goals since the two

provinces were lost after the Franco-Prussian War (1870–1871).

Article 80. Germany acknowledges and will respect strictly the independence of Austria, within the frontiers which may be fixed in a Treaty between that State and the Principal Allied and Associated Powers; she agrees that this independence shall be inalienable, except with the consent of the Council of the League of Nations.

Article 81. Germany, in conformity with the action already taken by the Allied and Associated Powers, recognizes the complete independence of the Czecho-Slovak State which will include the autonomous territory of the Ruthenians to the south of the Carpathians. Germany hereby recognizes the frontiers of this State as determined by the Principal Allied and Associated Powers and the other interested States. . . .

Article 84. German nationals habitually resident in . . . the Czecho-Slovak State will obtain Czecho-Slovak nationality *ipso facto* and lose their German nationality. . . .

Article 87. Germany, in conformity with the action already taken by the Allied and Associated Powers, recognizes the complete independence of Poland. . . .

Article 89. Poland undertakes to accord freedom of transit to persons, goods, vessels, carriages, wagons and mails in transit between East Prussia and the rest of Germany over Polish territory, including territorial waters, and to treat them at least as favorably as the persons, goods, vessels, carriages, wagons and mails respectively of Polish or of any other more favored nationality, origin, importation,

starting-point, or ownership as regards facilities, restrictions and all other matters.[3] . . .

Article 116. Germany acknowledges and agrees to respect as permanent and inalienable the independence of all the territories which were part of the former Russian Empire on August 1, 1914.

PART IV. GERMAN RIGHTS AND INTERESTS OUTSIDE GERMANY

Article 119. Germany renounces in favor of the Principal Allied and Associated Powers all her rights and titles over her oversea possessions. (This renunciation includes Germany's concessions in China.) . . .

PART V. MILITARY, NAVAL, AND AIR CLAIMS

Article 159. The German military forces shall be demobilized and reduced as prescribed hereinafter.

Article 160. (1) By a date which must not be later than March 31, 1920, the German Army must not comprise more than seven divisions of infantry and three divisions of cavalry.

After that date the total number of effectives in the Army of the States constituting Germany must not exceed one hundred thousand men, including officers and establishments of depots. The Army shall be devoted exclusively to the maintenance of order within the territory and to the control of the frontiers.

The total effective strength of officers,

---

3. The establishment of an independent Poland separated the German province of East Prussia from the rest of the nation.

including the personnel of staffs, whatever their composition, must not exceed four thousand. . . .

(3) The German General Staff and all similar organizations shall be dissolved and may not be reconstituted in any form. . . .

Article 180. All fortified works, fortresses and field works situated in German territory to the west of a line drawn fifty kilometers to the east of the Rhine shall be disarmed and dismantled. . . .

Article 181. After the expiration of a period of two months from the coming into force of the present Treaty the German naval forces in commission must not exceed: 6 battleships of the *Deutschland* or *Lothringen* type, 6 light cruisers, 12 destroyers, 12 torpedo boats, or an equal number of ships constructed to replace them as provided in Article 190.

No submarines are to be included.

All other warships, except where there is provision to the contrary in the present Treaty, must be placed in reserve or devoted to commercial purposes. . . .

Article 198. The armed forces of Germany must not include any military or naval air forces. . . .

PART VIII. REPARATION

Article 231. The Allied and Associated Governments affirm and Germany accepts the responsibility of Germany and her allies for causing all the loss and damage to which the Allied and Associated Governments and their nationals have been subjected as a consequence of the war imposed upon them by the aggression of Germany and her allies.

Article 232. The Allied and Associated Governments recognize that the resources of Germany are not adequate, after taking into account permanent diminutions of such resources which will result from other provisions of the present Treaty, to make complete reparation for all such loss and damage.

The Allied and Associated Governments, however, require, and Germany undertakes, that she will make compensation for all damage done to the civilian population of the Allied and Associated Powers and to their property during the period of the belligerency of each as an Allied or Associated Power against Germany by such aggression by land, by sea and from the air, and in general all damages as defined in Annex I hereto. . . .

Article 233. The amount of the above damage for which compensation is to be made by Germany shall be determined by an Inter-Allied Commission, to be called the *Reparation Commission* and constituted in the form and with the powers set forth hereunder and in Annexes II to VII inclusive hereto.

This Commission shall consider the claims and give to the German Government a just opportunity to be heard.

The findings of the Commission as to the amount of damage defined as above shall be concluded and notified to the German Government on or before May 1, 1921, as representing the extent of that Government's obligations.[4]

---

4. That total demand on Germany was placed at $33 billion, a huge sum, especially given the value of the U.S. dollar in 1921.

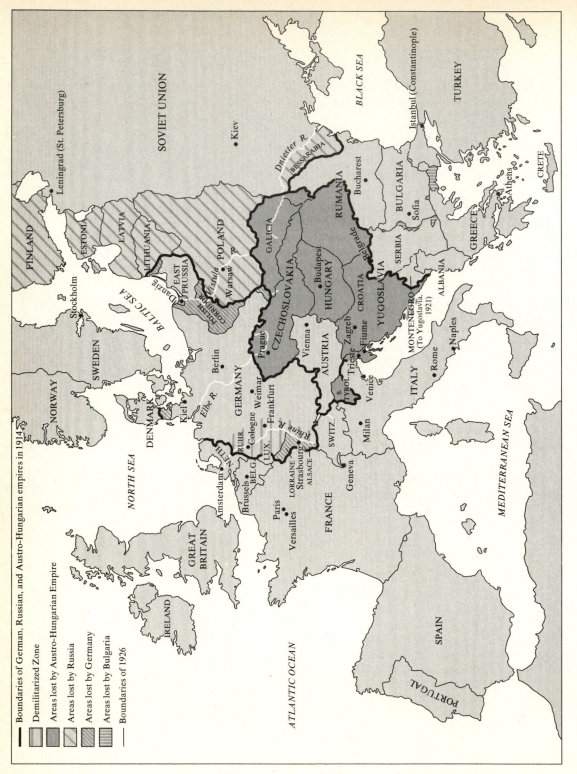

SOVIET UNION

FINLAND

Leningrad (St. Petersburg)

ESTONIA

LATVIA

LITHUANIA

Kiev

BLACK SEA

TURKEY

Istanbul (Constantinople)

Dniester R.

BESSARABIA

RUMANIA

Bucharest

BULGARIA

Sofia

CRETE

GREECE

Athens

SWEDEN

Stockholm

BALTIC SEA

Danzig

EAST PRUSSIA

POLISH CORRIDOR

Vistula R.

Warsaw

POLAND

GALICIA

CZECHOSLOVAKIA

Prague

Belgrade

SERBIA

YUGOSLAVIA

ALBANIA

NORWAY

Kiel

DENMARK

Berlin

Elbe R.

GERMANY

Weimar

Cologne

Frankfurt

RUHR

LUX.

Rhine R.

Budapest

HUNGARY

Vienna

AUSTRIA

Zagreb

CROATIA

Trieste

Fiume

S. TYROL

Venice

MONTENEGRO
(To Yugoslavia, 1921)

ITALY

Rome

Naples

NORTH SEA

NETH.

Amsterdam

Brussels

BELG.

LORRAINE

Strasbourg

ALSACE

SWITZ.

Geneva

Milan

Paris

Versailles

FRANCE

GREAT BRITAIN

IRELAND

ATLANTIC OCEAN

SPAIN

PORTUGAL

MEDITERRANEAN SEA

Map 3   Post–World War One: Broken Empires and Changed Boundaries

The Russian Revolution and the Foundation of the Soviet State

Among the many results of World War I, the downfall of Russia's tsarist government and its replacement by a Bolshevik dictatorship stands as one of the most important. In March 1917, facing military defeat, defections within the army, and riots in St. Petersburg, Tsar Nicholas II abdicated and was succeeded by a provisional government, which sought to govern Russia on liberal principles until a constituent assembly could meet and devise a new constitution. Seven months later, the Marxist-inspired Bolsheviks wrested power from the provisional government, and, despite four years of foreign intervention and civil war, managed to establish the world's first Communist state.

Before the revolution, Russia was full of discontent. Peasants and the growing new class of factory workers lived in wretched poverty, relieved only by drinking bouts and frequent acts of violence against government officials and the wealthy. At the same time, many intellectuals, members of the small middle class, and even a few aristocrats, most of whom were acquainted with Western European political developments, became deeply alienated from the tsarist regime and espoused political causes that ranged from anarchism to constitutional monarchy. With the fervor of religious zealots, they argued, organized, hatched plots, planned revolution, assassinated government officials (including Tsar Alexander II in 1881), issued pamphlets by the thousands, and tried, not always successfully, to stay a step ahead of the secret police.

Nicholas II briefly raised his subjects' hopes in 1905, when, after riots in St. Petersburg, he promised a parliament and other constitutional reforms. Soon, however, Russians realized that their tsar had no intention of abandoning control of such crucial areas as finance, defense, and the appointment of ministers. Meanwhile, discontent among workers and peasants festered and revolutionaries continued to plot. World War I provided the final push to a regime that for decades had been teetering on the brink of collapse.

After the Bolsheviks seized power in 1917 and survived the civil war that lasted until 1921, they faced the challenge of establishing a state on Marxist principles. A decade of experiment and controversy ensued, but by the early 1930s Soviet leaders had created a framework of government and economic policy that remained in place until the 1980s. In politics, the Soviet Union became a highly centralized, one-party dictatorship that tolerated no debate or dissent. In economics, it was characterized by agricultural collectivization and rapid industrialization in which the state made all economic decisions. Freedom and individual initiative played no role in this new society, based, so their leaders claimed, on the principles of Karl Marx.

▨ Vladimir Ilyich Lenin

"WHAT IS TO BE DONE?"

The greatest Russian revolutionary, and the founder of Soviet Russia, was Vladimir Ilyich Ulyanov (1870–1924), better known by his adopted revolutionary name, Lenin. The son of a government bureaucrat, Lenin became a dedicated revolutionary after his brother was executed for plotting the assassination of Tsar Alexander III. He embraced Marxism and became active in the Marxist-inspired Social-Democratic party, founded in 1898. In 1903 he became the leader of the "majority men," or Bolsheviks, who, in opposition to the "minority men," or Mensheviks, demanded highly centralized party leadership, noncooperation with bourgeois liberals, and single-minded devotion to revolution. He described his ideas about revolutionary tactics and organization in 1902 in the long polemical pamphlet, "What Is to Be Done?," directed against ideological enemies Lenin dubbed "Economists," Social Democrats who sought short-term economic gains for workers rather than revolution. Its appearance marks the beginning of that distinctive variant of Marxism known as Leninism.

Questions for Analysis

1. What dangers to the international socialist movement does Lenin see in the "critical Marxism" of men like Bernstein?
2. Why does Lenin feel that "ideology," or "revolutionary theory," is so important for the revolutionary movement?
3. What does Lenin mean when he says that the workers themselves are not capable of developing "revolutionary consciousness"? What must be done to change this?
4. What, according to Lenin, are the advantages of restricting the party to a small corps of dedicated professional revolutionaries?

*I*n fact, it is no secret for anyone that two trends have taken form in present-day international Social-Democracy. The conflict between these trends now flares up in a bright flame and now dies down and smolders under the ashes of imposing "truce resolutions." The essence of the "new" trend, which adopts a "critical" attitude towards "obsolete dogmatic" Marxism, has been clearly enough *presented* by Bernstein and *demonstrated* by Millerand.[1]

Social-Democracy must change from a

---

1. Eduard Bernstein (1850–1932) was a German socialist leader identified with the cause of "revisionism," the idea that socialists should seek their goals not by revolution, but by working peacefully through the democratic process. Alexandre Millerand (1859–1943) was the first French socialist to take a cabinet seat in a government dominated by nonsocialists.

party of social revolution into a democratic party of social reforms. Bernstein has surrounded this political demand with a whole battery of well-attuned "new" arguments and reasonings. Denied was the possibility of putting socialism on a scientific basis and of demonstrating its necessity and inevitability from the point of view of the materialist conception of history. Denied was the fact of growing impoverishment, the process of proletarization, and the intensification of capitalist contradictions; the very concept, "*ultimate aim,*" was declared to be unsound, and the idea of the dictatorship of the proletariat was completely rejected. Denied was the antithesis in principle between liberalism and socialism. Denied was *the theory of the class struggle,* on the alleged grounds that it could not be applied to a strictly democratic society governed according to the will of the majority, etc. . . .

Without revolutionary theory there can be no revolutionary movement. This idea cannot be insisted upon too strongly at a time when the fashionable preaching of opportunism[2] goes hand in hand with an infatuation for the narrowest forms of practical activity. Yet, for Russian Social-Democrats the importance of theory is enhanced by three other circumstances, which are often forgotten: first, by the fact that our Party is only in process of formation, its features are only just becoming defined, and it has as yet far from settled accounts with the other trends of revolutionary thought that threaten to divert the movement from the correct path.

Secondly, the Social-Democratic movement is in its very essence an international movement. This means, not only that we must combat national chauvinism, but that an incipient movement in a young country can be successful only if it makes use of the experiences of other countries. . . .

Thirdly, the national tasks of Russian Social-Democracy are such as have never confronted any other socialist party in the world. We shall have occasion further on to deal with the political and organizational duties which the task of emancipating the whole people from the yoke of autocracy imposes upon us. At this point, we wish to state only that the *role of vanguard fighter can be fulfilled only by a party that is guided by the most advanced theory.* . . .

We have said that *there could not have been* Social-Democratic consciousness among the workers. It would have to be brought to them from without. The history of all countries shows that the working class, exclusively by its own effort, is able to develop only trade-union consciousness, i.e., the conviction that it is necessary to combine in unions, fight the employers, and strive to compel the government to pass necessary labor legislation, etc. The theory of socialism, however, grew out of the philosophic, historical, and economic theories elaborated by educated representatives of the propertied classes, by intellectuals. By their social status, the founders of modern scientific socialism, Marx and Engels, themselves belonged to the bourgeois intelligentsia. In the very same way, in Russia, the theoretical doctrine of Social-Democracy arose altogether independently of the spontaneous growth of the working-class movement; it arose as a natural and inevitable outcome of the development of thought among the revolutionary socialist intelligentsia. . . .

The question arises, what should political education consist in? Can it be confined to the propaganda of working-class

---

2. Lenin used the word "Opportunism" as a general term of opprobrium, against any oppo-nent who compromised principles for short-term gains.

hostility to the autocracy? Of course not. It is not enough *to explain* to the workers that they are politically oppressed (any more than it is *to explain* to them that their interests are antagonistic to the interests of the employers). Agitation must be conducted with regard to every concrete example of this oppression (as we have begun to carry on agitation round concrete examples of economic oppression). Inasmuch as *this* oppression affects the most diverse classes of society, inasmuch as it manifests itself in the most varied spheres of life and activity — vocational, civic, personal, family, religious, scientific, etc., etc. — is it not evident that *we shall not be fulfilling our task* of developing the political consciousness of the workers if we do not *undertake* the organization of the *political exposure* of the autocracy *in all its aspects?* In order to carry on agitation round concrete instances of oppression, these instances must be exposed (as it is necessary to expose factory abuses in order to carry on economic agitation). . . .

Why do the Russian workers still manifest little revolutionary activity in response to the brutal treatment of the people by the police, the persecution of religious sects, the flogging of peasants, the outrageous censorship, the torture of soldiers, the persecution of the most innocent cultural undertakings, etc.? Is it because the "economic struggle" does not "stimulate" them to this, because such activity does not "promise palpable results," because it produces little that is "positive"? To adopt such an opinion, we repeat, is merely to direct the charge where it does not belong, to blame the working masses for one's own philistinism (or Bernsteinism). We must blame ourselves, our lagging behind the mass movement, for still being unable to organize sufficiently wide, strik-

ing, and rapid exposures of all the shameful outrages. When we do that (and we must and can do it), the most backward worker will understand, *or will feel*, that the students and religious sects, the peasants and the authors are being abused and outraged by those same dark forces that are oppressing and crushing him at every step of his life. Feeling that, he himself will be filled with an irresistible desire to react, and he will know how to hoot the censors one day, on another day to demonstrate outside the house of a governor who has brutally suppressed a peasant uprising, on still another day to teach a lesson to the gendarmes in surplices who are doing the work of the Holy Inquisition,[3] etc. As yet we have done very little, almost nothing, *to bring* before the working masses prompt exposures on all possible issues. Many of us as yet do not recognize this as our *bounden duty* but trail spontaneously in the wake of the "drab everyday struggle," in the narrow confines of factory life. . . .

"A dozen wise men can be more easily wiped out than a hundred fools." This wonderful truth (for which the hundred fools will always applaud you) appears obvious only because in the very midst of the argument you have skipped from one question to another. You began by talking and continued to talk of the unearthing of a "committee," of the unearthing of an "organization," and now you skip to the question of unearthing the movement's "roots" in their "depths." The fact is, of course, that our movement cannot be unearthed, for the very reason that it has countless thousands of roots deep down among the masses; but that is not the point at issue. As far as "deep roots" are concerned, we cannot be "unearthed" even now, despite all our amateurism,

---

3. The reference is to the clergy of the Russian Orthodox Church; "gendarmes" means police; "surplices" refers to the robes worn by clergy.

and yet we all complain, and cannot but complain, that the "*organizations*" are being unearthed and as a result it is impossible to maintain continuity in the movement. But since you raise the question of *organizations* being unearthed and persist in your opinion, I assert that it is far more difficult to unearth a dozen wise men than a hundred fools. This position I will defend, no matter how much you instigate the masses against me for my "anti-democratic" views, etc. As I have stated repeatedly, by "wise men," in connection with organization, I mean *professional revolutionaries*, irrespective of whether they have developed from among students or working men. I assert: (1) that no revolutionary movement can endure without a stable organization of leaders maintaining continuity; (2) that the broader the popular mass drawn spontaneously into the struggle, which forms the basis of the movement and participates in it, the more urgent the need for such an organization, and the more solid this organization must be (for it is much easier for all sorts of demagogues to side-track the more backward sections of the masses); (3) that such an organization must consist chiefly of people professionally engaged in revolutionary activity; (4) that in an autocratic state, the more we *confine* the membership of such an organization to people who are professionally engaged in revolutionary activity and who have been professionally trained in the art of combating the political police, the more difficult will it be to unearth the organization; and (5) the *greater* will be the number of people from the working class and from the other social classes who will be able to join the movement and perform active work in it.

I shall deal only with the last two points. The question as to whether it is easier to wipe out "a dozen wise men" or "a hundred fools" reduces itself to the question, above considered, whether it is possible to have a mass *organization* when

the maintenance of strict secrecy is essential. We can never give a mass organization that degree of secrecy without which there can be no question of persistent and continuous struggle against the government. To concentrate all secret functions in the hands of as small a number of professional revolutionaries as possible does not mean that the latter will "do the thinking for all" and that the rank and file will not take an active part in the *movement*. On the contrary, the membership will promote increasing numbers of the professional revolutionaries from its ranks; for it will know that it is not enough for a few students and for a few working men waging the economic struggle to gather in order to form a "committee," but that it takes years to train oneself to be a professional revolutionary; and the rank and file will "think," not only of amateurish methods, but of such training. Centralization of the secret functions of the *organization* by no means implies centralization of all the functions of the *movement*. . . . The active and widespread participation of the masses will not suffer; on the contrary, it will benefit by the fact that a "dozen" experienced revolutionaries, trained professionally no less than the police, will centralize all the secret aspects of the work — the drawing up of leaflets, the working out of approximate plans; and the appointing of bodies of leaders for each urban district, for each factory district, and for each educational institution. . . . Centralization of the most secret functions in an organization of revolutionaries will not diminish, but rather increase the extent and enhance the quality of the activity of a large number of other organizations, that are intended for a broad public and are therefore as loose and as non-secret as possible, such as workers' trade unions; workers' self-education circles and circles for reading illegal literature; and socialist, as well as democratic, circles among *all* other sections of the population; etc., etc. We must have such circles, trade unions, and organizations everywhere in *as large a number as possible* and with the widest variety of functions; but it would be absurd and harmful *to confound* them with the organization of *revolutionaries,* to efface the border-line between them, to make still more hazy the all too faint recognition of the fact that in order to "serve" the mass movement we must have people who will devote themselves exclusively to Social-Democratic activities, and that such people must *train* themselves patiently and steadfastly to be professional revolutionaries.

Yes, this recognition is incredibly dim. Our worst sin with regard to organization consists in the fact that *by our primitiveness we have lowered the prestige of revolutionaries in Russia.* A person who is flabby and shaky on questions of theory, who has a narrow outlook, who pleads the spontaneity of the masses as an excuse for his own sluggishness, who resembles a trade-union secretary more than a spokesman of the people, who is unable to conceive of a broad and bold plan that would command the respect even of opponents, and

who is inexperienced and clumsy in his own professional art — the art of combating the political police — such a man is not a revolutionary, but a wretched amateur!

Let no active worker take offense at these frank remarks, for as far as insufficient training is concerned, I apply them first and foremost to myself. I used to work in a study circle[4] that set itself very broad, all-embracing tasks; and all of us, members of that circle, suffered painfully and acutely from the realization that we were acting as amateurs at a moment in history when we might have been able to say, varying a well-known statement: "Give us an organization of revolutionaries, and we will overturn Russia!" The more I recall the burning sense of shame I then experienced, the bitterer become my feelings towards those pseudo-Social-Democrats whose preachings "bring disgrace on the calling of a revolutionary," who fail to understand that our task is not to champion the degrading of the revolutionary to the level of an amateur, but *to raise* the amateurs to the level of revolutionaries.

REPORT OF THE PETROGRAD SECURITY POLICE

Lenin, in exile in Switzerland in 1917, played no direct role in fomenting the disorders that caused Nicholas II's abdication. They began in Petrograd (its former name, St. Petersburg, was dropped when the war began because it was too German-sounding) on March 8, when workers demonstrated, then rioted, and finally called for the tsar's resignation. They were angry about food shortages, but, like Russians of every class, they were also bitter over war casualties and the bungling of the war effort. In October 1916 — five months before the March revolution — the tsar's secret police submitted the following report on conditions in Petrograd.

---

4. A group that met regularly to discuss solutions to Russia's problems.

Questions for Analysis

1. According to this report, what are the signs of deterioration on the Russian home front? To what extent are the problems related to the weakness of the tsarist government?
2. According to this report, what explains the growing alienation of the Russian masses?
3. How had the war years affected the economic situation of the Russian workers?
4. On the basis of this report, what steps will the government have to take to decrease discontent?

The brilliant results of the offensive by General Brusilov's armies in the spring of this year, 1916,[1] and the present state of the work of supplying the active front definitely indicate that the tasks undertaken in these directions by the government and by wide sections of the public have been more than successfully fulfilled. The problem of providing the army with military supplies may be considered solved and properly taken care of . . . But the gradually increasing disorganization of the rear — in other words, of the entire country — which has become chronic and is ever worsening, has at this moment achieved such an extreme and monstrous stage that it is even now beginning to threaten results achieved at the front and promises in the very near future to plunge the country into the destructive chaos of catastrophic and elemental anarchy.

The systematically growing disorganization of transport; the unrestrained orgy of pillaging and swindling of every kind by shady operators in the most diverse branches of the country's commercial, industrial, and socio-political life; the unsystematic and mutually contradictory orders of representatives of state and local administrations; the unconscientiousness of minor and lower agents of the government in the provinces; and, as a result of all the foregoing, the inequitable distribution of food products and essential goods, the incredible rise in prices, and the lack of sources and means of procuring food among the presently starving populations of the capitals and large population centers . . . all this, taken together . . . shows categorically and definitely that a dire crisis is already upon us which must inevitably be resolved in one direction or another.

The above summary may be confirmed by the particularly troubled mood now observable among the masses of the people. By the beginning of September of this year an exceptional intensification of the feelings of opposition and animosity was distinctly noted among the most diverse sections of the residents of the capitals. Ever more frequent complaints against the administration and harsh and merciless condemnations of government policy have begun to be expressed.

By the end of September, according to

---

1. In the spring of 1916, Russian armies under General Aleksei Brusilov launched an offensive designed to divert the Germans from their massive assault on the allied fortress at Verdun; it turned into a 200-mile advance when Austrian resistance collapsed.

well-informed sources, this spirit of opposition reached an exceptional scale, which it had not attained — in any case among the broad masses — even during the period 1905–06.[2] Open and unconstrained complaints against "venality in the administration," against the enormous burdens of the war, and against the intolerable conditions of daily existence have begun to be heard. The outcries of radical and left-wing elements about the need "first to destroy the German here in our own country, and then to tackle the German abroad," have begun to elicit more and more sympathy.

Despite the great increase in wages, the economic condition of the masses is worse than terrible. While the wages of the masses have risen 50 percent, and only in certain categories 100 to 200 percent (metal workers, machinists, electricians), the prices on all products have increased 100 to 500 percent. According to the data collected by the sick benefit fund of the "Triangle" plant,[3] a day's wages for a worker before the war were as follows, in comparison with current wages:

[Type of Worker]	[Prewar Wages]
Unskilled	1 to 1 rub. 25 kop.[4]
Metal worker	2 to 2 rub. 50 kop.
Electrician	2 to 3 rub.

[Type of Worker]	[Present Wages]
Unskilled	2 rub. 50 kop. to 3 rub.
Metal worker	4 to 5 rub.
Electrician	5 to 6 rub., etc.

At the same time, the cost of consumer goods needed by the worker has changed in the following incredible way:

[Item]	[Prewar Cost]
Rent for a corner[5]	2 to 3 rub. monthly
Dinner (in a tearoom)	15 to 20 kop. (at the same place)
Tea (in a tearoom)	7 kop.
Boots	5 to 6 rub.
Shirt	75 to 90 kop.

[Item]	[Present Cost]
Rent for a corner	8 to 12 rub.
Dinner (in a tearoom)	1 rub. to 1 rub. 20 kop.
Tea	35 kop.
Boots	20 to 30 rub.
Shirt	2 rub. 50 kop. to 3 rub., etc.

Even if we estimate the rise in earnings at 100 percent, the prices of products have risen, on the average, 300 percent. The impossibility of even buying many food products and necessities, the time wasted standing idle in queues to receive goods, the increasing incidence of disease due to malnutrition and unsanitary living conditions (cold and dampness because of lack of coal and wood), and so forth, have made the workers, as a whole, prepared for the wildest excesses of a "hunger riot." . . .

If in the future grain continues to be

---

2. The reference is to the rioting during the Revolution of 1905.

3. A large factory in the Narva district of Petrograd.

4. Rub. is the abbreviation for ruble, the basic unit of Russian currency; kop. is the abbreviation for kopeck, 100 of which make a ruble.

5. A Russian term to describe any tiny room that could be rented out to a family.

hidden, the very fact of its disappearance will be sufficient to provoke in the capitals and in the other most populated centers of the empire the greatest disorders, attended by pogroms[6] and endless street rioting. The mood of anxiety, growing daily more intense, is spreading to ever wider sections of the populace. Never have we observed such nervousness as there is now. Almost every day the newspapers report thousands of facts that reflect the extremely strained nerves of the people in public places, and a still greater number of such facts remains unrecorded. The slightest incident is enough to provoke the biggest brawl. This is especially noticeable in the vicinity of shops, stores, banks, and similar institutions, where "misunderstandings" occur almost daily.

Joseph Stalin

THE TASKS OF BUSINESS EXECUTIVES

Joseph Stalin (1879–1953), the son of a shoemaker in the province of Georgia, was a candidate for the priesthood in the Russian Orthodox Church before he abandoned Christianity for Marxism and became a loyal follower of Lenin in 1903. By 1917 he was secretary of the Bolshevik party, an office he continued to hold after the revolution. After Lenin's death in 1924, Stalin's position within the party enabled him to win the power struggle with Leon Trotsky (1879–1940), the leader of the Red Army during the civil war and Lenin's heir apparent. Shortly after he assumed power in 1928, Stalin launched a fundamental restructuring of the Soviet economy.

In 1928 the New Economic Policy (NEP), which Lenin had adopted in 1921, dictated Soviet economic life. The NEP was Lenin's solution to the problem of restoring agricultural and industrial production after seven years of war, revolution, and anarchy. Although the state maintained control of banks, foreign trade, and heavy industry, peasants could sell their goods on the open market and small businessmen could hire labor, operate small factories, and keep their profits.

Although the NEP saved the U.S.S.R. from economic collapse, its capitalist features troubled Marxist purists, and it did little to spur industrialization. Thus, in 1928, shortly after taking power, Stalin abandoned the NEP and replaced it with the first Five-Year Plan, a program that established a highly centralized planned economy in which Moscow bureaucrats regulated agriculture, manufacturing, finance, and transportation. In agriculture, he ordered massive collectivization, that is, the abolition of individual peasant holdings and their amalgamation into large collective

---

6. A massacre of innocent people, usually Jews; since the late nineteenth century discontented Russians had often expressed their frustration by attacking Jewish communities. It is unclear if the author of this report meant pogrom in the sense of specific anti-Jewish violence.

and state farms. In manufacturing, Stalin emphasized heavy industry and the production of goods such as tractors, trucks, and machinery. He launched second and third Five-Year Plans in 1933 and 1938.

In a speech delivered in 1931 to a conference of industrial managers, or "business executives," Stalin succinctly spelled out the motives that led him to initiate the first Five-Year Plan.

Questions for Analysis

1. What factors convince Stalin that the Soviet Union has the capacity to reach its industrial goals in 1931?
2. In what ways does Stalin feel the Soviet system is superior to capitalism? How do his views of capitalism's weaknesses resemble those of Marx and Engels in *The Communist Manifesto*?
3. By what arguments does Stalin seek to inspire the industrial managers to work for industrialization?
4. What does he mean by the Soviet Union's responsibility to the "world proletariat"?

Comrades! The deliberations of your conference are drawing to a close. You are now about to adopt resolutions. I have no doubt that they will be adopted unanimously. In these resolutions — I know something about them — you approve the control figures of industry for 1931 and pledge yourselves to fulfil them.

A Bolshevik's word is his bond. Bolsheviks are in the habit of fulfilling their pledges. But what does the pledge to fulfil the control figures for 1931 mean? It means ensuring a general increase of industrial output by 45 percent. And this is a very big task. More than that. Such a pledge means that you not only promise to fulfil our Five-Year Plan in four years — that is decided, and no more resolutions are needed on that score — *it means that you promise to fulfil it in three years in all the basic, decisive branches of industry.*

It is good that the conference gives a promise to fulfil the plan for 1931, to fulfil the Five-Year Plan in three years. But we have been taught by "bitter experience." We know that promises are not always kept. In the beginning of 1930, also, a promise was given to fulfil the plan for the year. At that time it was necessary to increase the output of our industries by 31 to 32 percent. But that promise was not kept to the full. Actually, the increase in industrial output in 1930 amounted to 25 percent. We must ask ourselves: will not the same thing occur again this year? The directors and managers of our industries now promise to increase the industrial output in 1931 by 45 percent. But what guarantee have we that this promise will be kept? . . .

In the history of states and countries, in the history of armies, there have been cases when every opportunity for success and for victory was on hand, but these opportunities were wasted because the leaders did not see them, did not know how to make use of them, and the armies suffered defeat.

Have we all the possibilities that are needed to fulfil the control figures for 1931?

Yes, we have these possibilities.

What are these possibilities? What are the necessary factors that make these possibilities real?

First of all, adequate *natural resources* in the country: iron ore, coal, oil, grain, cotton. Have we these resources? Yes, we have. We have them in larger quantities than any other country. . . .

What else is needed?

A *government* capable and willing to utilize these immense natural resources for the benefit of the people. Have we such a government? We have. . . .

What else is needed?

That this government should enjoy the *support* of the vast masses of workers and peasants. Does our government enjoy such support? Yes, it does. You will find no other government in the world that enjoys such support from the workers and peasants as does the Soviet government. . . .

What else is needed to fulfil and over-fulfil the control figures for 1931?

A *system* which is free of the incurable diseases of capitalism and which is greatly superior to capitalism. Crises, unemployment, waste, poverty among the masses — such are the incurable diseases of capitalism. Our system does not suffer from these diseases because power is in our hands, in the hands of the working class; because we are conducting a planned economy, systematically accumulating resources and properly distributing them among the different branches of national economy. . . .

The capitalists are cutting the ground from under their own feet. And instead of emerging from the crisis they aggravate it; new conditions accumulate which lead to a new, and even more severe crisis. The superiority of our system lies in that we have no crises of over-production, we have not and never will have millions of unemployed, we have no anarchy in production; for we are conducting a planned economy. . . .

It is sometimes asked whether it is not possible to slow down the tempo a bit, to put a check on the movement. No, comrades, it is not possible! The tempo must not be reduced! On the contrary, we must increase it as much as is within our powers and possibilities. This is dictated to us by our obligations to the workers and peasants of the U.S.S.R. This is dictated to us by our obligations to the working class of the whole world.

To slacken the tempo would mean falling behind. And those who fall behind get beaten. But we do not want to be beaten. No, we refuse to be beaten! One feature of the history of old Russia was the continual beatings she suffered for falling behind, for her backwardness. She was beaten by the Mongol Khans. She was beaten by the Turkish beys. She was beaten by the Swedish feudal lords. She was beaten by the Polish and Lithuanian gentry. She was beaten by the British and French capitalists. She was beaten by the Japanese barons. All beat her — for her backwardness: for military backwardness, for cultural backwardness, for political backwardness, for industrial backwardness, for agricultural backwardness. She was beaten because to do so was profitable and could be done with impunity. . . . They beat her, saying: "You are abundant," so one can enrich oneself at your expense. They beat her, saying: "You are poor and impotent," so you can be beaten and plundered with impunity. Such is the law of the exploiters — to beat the backward and the weak. It is the jungle law of capitalism. You are backward, you are weak — therefore you are wrong; hence, you can be beaten and enslaved. You are mighty — therefore you are right; hence, we must be wary of you.

That is why we must no longer lag behind.

In the past we had no fatherland, nor could we have one. But now that we have overthrown capitalism and power is in the hands of the working class, we have a fatherland, and we will defend its independence. Do you want our Socialist fatherland to be beaten and to lose its independence? If you do not want this you must put an end to its backwardness in the shortest possible time and develop genuine Bolshevik tempo in building up its Socialist system of economy. There is no other way. That is why Lenin said during the October Revolution: "Either perish, or overtake and outstrip the advanced capitalist countries."

We are fifty or a hundred years behind the advanced countries. We must make good this distance in ten years. Either we do it, or they crush us.

This is what our obligations to the workers and peasants of the U.S.S.R. dictate to us.

But we have other, still more serious and more important obligations. They are our obligations to the world proletariat. They coincide with our obligations to the workers and peasants of the U.S.S.R. But we place them higher. The working class of the U.S.S.R. is part of the world working class. . . . We must march forward in such a way that the working class of the whole world, looking at us, may say: "This is my vanguard, this is my shock-brigade, this is my working-class state, this is my fatherland; they are promoting their cause, which is our cause, and they are doing this well; let us support them against the capitalists and spread the cause of the world revolution." Must we not justify the hopes of the world's working class, must we not fulfil our obligations to them? Yes, we must if we do not want utterly to disgrace ourselves.

Such are our obligations, internal and international.

The Impact of the Great Depression

For five gaudy, glorious years of prosperity from 1925 to 1929, most people of the industrialized nations believed they had solved the economic problems that followed World War I. Inflation had been curbed, even in Germany, where the mark, exchanged at four to the dollar before the war, fell to two and a half trillion to the dollar in 1923. Fueled by U.S. loans and investments, Europe's economy revived and the industrialized nations experienced higher employment, increased output, and expanded foreign trade. Despite lagging worldwide agricultural prices and the checkered performance of the Japanese economy, optimism reigned, and stock prices, especially on the New York Stock Exchange, skyrocketed.

Things darkened in September 1929, when prices on the Exchange began a decline that in some cases caused a loss of stock values of 90 percent over the next several months. As personal fortunes evaporated, banks failed by the thousands, investment plummeted, factories closed, prices fell, and unemployment lines became a feature of the urban landscape. The crash caused United States bankers to call in short-term loans from European creditors, and, in the spring of 1931, major banks in Austria and Germany failed. Worse, the crash stopped the flow of investment dollars to Europe, where soon the number of boarded-up factories and unemployed workers reached horrifying proportions.

Industrialized nations were not alone in feeling the effects of the Great Depression. Because Europeans and Americans no longer needed or could afford the world's raw materials and agricultural products, Asians, Latin Americans, and Africans had no means to purchase manufactured goods from the industrialized nations. Between 1929 and 1933, international trade declined more than 50 percent.

The Great Depression added immeasurably to the post-war dissatisfaction gnawing at the nations of the West. It had political repercussions everywhere, most notably in Germany, where it contributed to the Nazi triumph in 1933, and the United States, where it gave rise to dozens of new government-sponsored programs to blunt its impact. Most important, it crushed the economic prospects of millions of human beings, leaving them lives with little hope or dignity.

Ed Paulsen and Louis Banks

RECOLLECTIONS OF THE GREAT DEPRESSION

Ed Paulsen, born into a South Dakota farm family in 1912, finished high school in 1930 and headed west, where he picked apples in Washington, lived briefly in Los Angeles, and arrived in San Francisco in 1931. Louis Banks, the son of a black Arkansas farmer, was born in 1915. At some point he and his mother moved to Chicago, where in 1929, at age 14, he lost his job as a kitchen helper and also headed west.

Studs Terkel, a Chicago radio journalist and author, interviewed both men in the late 1960s and in 1970 published their recollections in his book, *Hard Times: An Oral History of the Great Depression.*

Questions
for Analysis

1. Based on Paulsen's and Banks's recollections, how would you characterize the unemployed men's attitude toward each other and the government?
2. How would you characterize society's response to the unemployed men?
3. In what ways do the experience and views of Banks, a black, differ from those of Paulsen?
4. In what ways were the men's lives affected by the legislation Congress passed between 1933 and 1935?

[*Ed Paulsen*]

I'd get up at five in the morning and head for the waterfront. Outside the Spreckles Sugar Refinery, outside the gates, there would be a thousand men. You know dang well there's only three or four jobs.

The guy would come out with two little Pinkerton cops:[1] "I need two guys for the bull gang. Two guys to go into the hole." A thousand men would fight like a pack of Alaskan dogs to get through there. Only four of us would get through. I was too young a punk.

So you'd drift up to Skid Row. There'd be thousands of men there. Guys on baskets, making weird speeches, phony theories on economics. About eleven-thirty, the real leaders would take over. They'd say: O.K., we're going to City Hall. The Mayor was Angelo Rossi, a dapper little guy. He wore expensive boots and a tight vest. We'd shout around the steps. Finally, he'd come out and tell us nothing.

I remember the demands: We demand work, we demand shelter for our families, we demand groceries, this kind of thing. . . . Half the guys up there making the demands were Negroes. Now there wasn't a big black colony in San Francisco in those days. But they were pretty cagey, the leaders — they always kept a mixture of black and white.

I remember as a kid how courageous this seemed to me, the demands, because you knew that society wasn't going to give it to you. They'd demand that they open up unrented houses and give decent shelters for their families. But you just knew society wasn't yielding. There was nothing coming.

This parade would be four blocks long, curb to curb. Nobody had a dime. There were guys on the corner trying to sell apples to this moneyless wonder. (Laughs.)

The guys'd start to yell and there come some horses. They used to have cops on horseback in those days. Then there'd be

some fighting. Finally it got to killing. I think they killed three people there that day, besides the wounded. It really got rough because the guys had brought a bunch of marbles and threw them on the street, and the horses were slipping and sliding around. This made the cops mad and they got rough.

There'd be this kind of futile struggle, because somehow you never expected to win. We had a built-in losing complex. That's the way those crowds felt. A lot of them would drift back into the Sally.[2] By now it's one o'clock, and everybody's hungry. We were a gentle crowd. These were fathers, eighty percent of them. They had held jobs and didn't want to kick society to pieces. They just wanted to go to work and they just couldn't understand. There was a mysterious thing. You watched the papers, you listened to rumors, you'd get word somebody's gonna build a building.

So the next morning you get up at five o'clock and you dash over there. You got a big tip. There's three thousand men there, carpenters, cement men, guys who knew machinery and everything else. These fellas always had faith that the job was gonna mature, somehow. More and more men were after fewer and fewer jobs. So San Francisco just ground to a halt. Nothing was moving. . . .

We weren't greatly agitated in terms of society. Ours was a bewilderment, not an anger. Not a sense of being particularly put upon. We weren't talking revolution; we were talking jobs.

We'd grown up in small-town high schools. There wasn't much expression, in the press, of the intelligentsia. It was just

---

1. Employees of the Pinkerton Detective Agency, founded by a Scottish immigrant, Allan Pinkerton (1819–1884), in 1850; frequently hired by employers to break up strikes and labor demonstrations.

2. The Salvation Army.

a tough world, and you had been born into it. . . .

By this time, Roosevelt was President. There was the NRA[3] . . . mystical things were going on we didn't understand at all. People were talking price-fixing and what have you. Very, very weird world. It didn't mean a damn to us. There were three brothers of us, we got a freight and went down to Portland. They'd started to work on the Bonneville Dam. Beautiful sight down that river. On a decent day, if you set on top of a boxcar, it was beautiful. . . .

We make an orange freight. We rode in the reefer.[4] Clear to Kansas City. It goes like a bat out of hell, a rough ride. We broke through the wire netting and ate the oranges. We got vitamins like mad. (Laughs.) But your mouth gets burnt by that acid juice and your teeth get so damn sore from that ride. By the time we got off at K.C., I could hardly close my mouth.

We catch a train into Kansas City, that night. At the stops, colored people were gettin' on the trains and throwin' off coal. You could see people gatherin' the coal. You could see the railroad dicks[5] were gettin' tough.

Hal and I are ridin' on the top of the boxcar, it's a fairly nice night. All of a sudden, there's a railroad dick with a flashlight that reaches a thousand miles. Bam! Bam! He starts shooting. We hear the bullets hitting the cars, bam! like that. I throw my hands up and start walking towards that light. Hal's behind me. The guy says, "Get off." I said, "Christ, I can't." This

thing's rollin' fifty miles an hour or more. He says, "Jump." I says, "I can't." He says, "Turn around and march ahead." He marches us over the top. There's a gondola, about eight feet down. He says, "Jump." So I jumped and landed in wet sand, up to my knees.

We come to a little town in Nebraska, Beatrice. It's morning. I'm chilled to the bone. We crawl into a railroad sandbox, almost frozen to death. We dry out, get warmed up, and make the train again. We pull into Omaha. It's night. All of a sudden, the train is surrounded by deputies, with pistols. The guy says, "Get in those trucks." I said, "What for? We haven't done anything." He said, "You're not going to jail. You're going to the Transient Camp."

They drive us up to an old army warehouse. They check you in, take off your clothes, run them through a de-louser, and you take a bath. It's midnight. We come out, and here's a spread with scrambled eggs, bacon, bread, coffee and toast. We ate a great meal. It was wonderful. We go upstairs to bed. Here's a double-decker, sheets, toothbrush, towels, everything. I sat down on this damn bed, I can't tell you, full of wonderment. We thought we'd gone to heaven. . . .

The next morning, they called us up to a social worker. By this time, there's a thousand guys in there. They're playing baseball, some guys are washing down walls — bums, bindlestiffs,[6] cynical rough guys who've been on the road for years. It's kind of like a playhouse. It's unbelievable.

---

3. The National Recovery Administration, established in 1933 by an act of Congress to deal with a range of economic problems, such as ruinous competition, overproduction, labor-management disputes, and price fluctuations.

4. A refrigerator car.

5. Slang for detective.

6. Slang for hobo.

————————— ✍ —————————

Through a social worker, he is assigned to a job with the National Youth Administration [an organization established by Congress in 1935 to provide jobs for youth], at "a little cold-water college" in Aberdeen, South Dakota.

————————— ✍ —————————

And then the good life began for me.

Before Roosevelt, the Federal Government hardly touched your life. Outside of the postmaster, there was little local representation. Now people you knew were appointed to government jobs. Joe Blow or some guy from the corner.

It came right down to Main Street. Half of them loved it, half of them hated it. There was the immediacy of its effect on you. In Aberdeen, Main Street was against it. But they were delighted to have those green relief checks cashed in their cash registers. They'd have been out of business had it not been for them. It was a split thing. They were cursing Roosevelt for the intrusion into their lives. At the same time, they were living off it. Main Street still has this fix.

The NYA was my salvation. I could just as easily have been in Sing Sing as with the UN.[7] Just every bit a chance. Hell, yes. Everybody was a criminal. You stole, you cheated through. You were getting by, survival. Stole clothes off lines, stole milk off back porches, you stole bread. I remember going through Tucumcari, New Mexico, on a freight. We made a brief stop. There was a grocery store, a supermarket kind of thing for those days. I beat it off the train and came back with rolls and crackers. This guy is standing in the window shaking his fist at you.

It wasn't a big thing, but it created a coyote mentality. You were a predator. You had to be. The coyote is crafty. He can

be fantastically courageous and a coward at the same time. . . . A coyote is nature's victim as well as man's. We were coyotes in the Thirties, the jobless.

No, I don't see the Depression as an ennobling experience. Survivors are still ridin' with the ghost — the ghost of those days when things came hard.

[*Louis Banks*]

I'd ride atop a boxcar and went to Los Angeles, four days and four nights. The Santa Fe, we'd go all the way with Santa Fe. I was goin' over the hump and I was so hungry and weak. . . . I was sayin', "Lord, help me, Oh Lord, help me," until a white hobo named Callahan, he was a great big guy, looked like Jack Dempsey, and he got a scissors on me, took his legs and wrapped 'em around me. Otherwise, I was about to fall off the Flyer into a cornfield there. I was sick as a dog until I got into Long Beach, California.

Black and white, it didn't make any difference who you were, 'cause everybody was poor. All friendly, sleep in a jungle. We used to take a big pot and cook food, cabbage, meat and beans all together. We all set together, we made a tent. Twenty-five or thirty would be out on the side of the rail, white and colored. They didn't have no mothers or sisters, they didn't have no home, they were dirty, they had overalls on, they didn't have no food, they didn't have anything.

Sometimes we sent one hobo to walk,[8] to see if there were any jobs open. He'd come back and say: Detroit, no jobs. He'd say: they're hirin' in New York City. So we went to New York City. Sometimes ten or fifteen of us would be on the train. . . .

I was in chain gangs and been in jail all over the country. I was in a chain gang in

---

7. Sing Sing is a prison in Ossining, New York; UN stands for the United Nations, where Paulsen worked at the time of the interview.

8. To travel.

Georgia. I had to pick cotton for four months, for just hoboin' on a train. Just for vag.[9] They gave me thirty-five cents and a pair of overalls when I got out. Just took me off the train, the guard. 1930, during the Depression, in the summertime. Yes, sir, thirty-five cents, that's what they gave me.

I knocked on people's doors. They'd say, "What do you want? I'll call the police." And they'd put you in jail for vag. They'd make you milk cows, thirty or ninety days. Up in Wisconsin, they'd do the same thing. Alabama, they'd do the same thing. California, anywhere you'd go. Always in jail, and I never did nothin'.

A man had to be on the road. Had to leave his wife, had to leave his mother, leave his family just to try to get money to live on. But he think: my dear mother, tryin' to send her money, worryin' how she's starvin'.

The shame I was feeling. I walked out because I didn't have a job. I said, "I'm goin' out in the world and get me a job." And God help me, I couldn't get anything. I wouldn't let them see me dirty and ragged and I hadn't shaved. I wouldn't send 'em no picture.

I'd write: "Dear Mother, I'm doin' wonderful and wish you're all fine." That was in Los Angeles and I was sleeping under some steps and there was some paper over me. This is the slum part, Negroes lived down there. And my ma, she'd say, "Oh, my son is in Los Angeles, he's doin' pretty fair."

I had fifteen or twenty jobs. Each job I would have it would be so hard. From six o'clock in the morning till seven o'clock at night. I was fixin' the meat, cookin', washin' dishes and cleaning up. Just like you throwed the ball at one end and run down and catch it on the other. You're jack of all trade, you're doin' it all. White chefs were gettin' $40 a week, but I was gettin' $21 for doin' what they were doin' and everything else. The poor people had it rough. The rich people was livin' off the poor.

'Cause I picked cotton down in Arkansas when I was a little bitty boy and I saw my dad, he was workin' all day long. $2 is what one day the poor man would make. A piece of salt pork and a barrel of flour for us and that was McGehee, Arkansas.

God knows, when he'd get that sack he would pick up maybe two, three hundred pounds of cotton a day, gettin' snake bit and everything in that hot sun. And all he had was a little house and a tub to keep the water. 'Cause I went down there to see him in 1930. I got tired of hoboing and went down to see him and my daddy was all gray and didn't have no bank account and no Blue Cross. He didn't have nothin', and he worked himself to death. (Weeps.) And the white man, he would drive a tractor in there. . . . It seems like yesterday to me, but it was 1930.

'33 in Chicago they had the World's Fair. A big hotel was hirin' colored fellas as bellboys. The bellboys could make more money as a white boy for the next ten or fifteen years. I worked as a bellhop on the North Side at a hotel, lots of gangsters there. They don't have no colored bellboys at no exclusive hotels now. I guess maybe in the small ones they may have some.

Jobs were doing a little better after '35, after the World's Fair. You could get dishwashin' jobs, little porter jobs.

Work on the WPA,[10] earn $27.50. We just dig a ditch and cover it back up. You thought you was rich. You could buy a

9. Vagrancy.

10. The Works Progress Administration was created by Congress in 1935 to provide work for the unemployed; by 1941 it had supplied jobs to 40 percent of the nation's unemployed, pumping $11 billion into the economy.

suit of clothes. Before that, you wanted money, you didn't have any. No clothes for the kids. My little niece and my little kids had to have hand-down clothes. Couldn't steal. If you did, you went to the penitentiary. You had to shoot pool, walk all night and all day, the best you could make was $15. I raised up all my kids during the Depression. Scuffled . . . a hard way to go.

H. Hessel Tiltman

SLUMP! A STUDY OF STRICKEN EUROPE TODAY

H. Hessel Tiltman (1897–1977) was a British author-journalist best known for his coverage of East Asia during the 1930s and '40s. During 1931 and 1932 as European correspondent for the Manchester *Guardian*, he traveled across Europe to observe the effects of the Great Depression. On his return, he recorded his impressions in his widely read book, *Slump! A Study of Stricken Europe Today* (1932). In the following selection he describes the impact of the depression on two German families.

Questions
for Analysis

1. How has the Great Depression affected the economic situation of the former baker and former clerk and salesman?
2. How does the situation of the laborer's family differ from those of the former baker and salesman?
3. What does Tiltman's account suggest about the psychological impact of unemployment?
4. What connection does Tiltman make between Germany's economic woes and the appeal of Nazism?

*I*n the course of those two days beneath the surface of Berlin life I saw overcrowding, because those living on relief can rarely afford more than one room, however large the family. . . . I saw hunger, because, as I have said, these victims cannot escape that horror. I saw rags, because the welfare centers can no longer supply anyone with even secondhand shoes until *both* the soles of the existing pair have been worn to nothing. The mass need is now so great that it has swamped every channel along which relief trickles. . . .

But more painful than any of these things, I saw utter despair. Some of the wives could still hold up their heads and be interested in the life about them, but most of the men were shattered in spirit and breaking in health. They had fought despair for one year, two years, maybe even three years. But it got them in the end. . . .

The first house I entered was still supported by the second category "dole,"[1] the husband, a baker, having been out of work only seven months.

The family comprised husband, wife, and four children, and the total income amounted to 94/-[2] a month, made up of 82/- unemployment benefit, and 12/- a month orphans' pension received for one of the children.

For one room and a kitchen in a large tenement building, with a wall blocking out both view and light, they paid 20/- a month rent, leaving a balance of 74/-.

Electric light and gas cost about 7/- a month, soap 6d. a month, and a burial insurance policy for the family another 1/6 a month. Payments on this policy were being discontinued on the week that I called.

The rest of the income, amounting to 15/- a week, went to buy food for six people, a task made easier by the fact that three of the children were supplied with a midday meal — and a good meal — at the school they attended.

The weekly menus in this home consisted of oatmeal, potato soup, herrings and bread. Only in the case of the husband was there any sign of physical strain, and he was well below the standard of fitness enforced in the German Army in which he had served in what, tragically enough, he spoke of as "happier days." . . .

In another home a family of seven — man, wife, and five children — were living in two rooms. The man, workless since the beginning of 1931, had formerly been employed, first as a clerk, and later as a salesman in a store, his wage in the latter occupation being 42/- a week.

The total income of the family, from the "second category" dole, had amounted to about 30/- a week, but this sum was subject to a cut of 20 percent on June 27, 1932. On the same date the rent of 10/- a week was raised to 12/6, or nearly half their total income, by the reimposition of a rent tax formerly waived in the case of the workless. Thus the relentless march of the crisis forces the living standards of its victims down and down.

Sitting on the only sound chair in that home, in which a sewing machine was the sole article of furniture which would have sold for more than a few pence, I listened while the wife, a woman of twenty-five whose face bore clear marks of strain, explained to me how they managed to feed seven people on 15/- a week.

A loaf of bread a day cost 6d. A pound of dripping[3] a week cost the same sum. They bought one liter (pint and a quarter) of milk a day for the two youngest children, and 1/4 lb. of butter a week for the youngest child. Three lbs. of sugar a week, two tins of condensed milk for the baby, aged nine months, and five cigarettes a day for the man, costing one penny a packet, completed the list of "luxuries." For the rest, they had 8 lbs. of potatoes a day and, twice a week, 3 lbs. of cabbage costing 3d., boiled into a soup to which, on Sundays, was added a pennyworth of bones. Occasionally — not more frequently than once a month — they bought half a pound of pork at the specially reduced prices charged, under government supervision, to those in receipt of "doles." . . .

From that home I went to another near by — two rooms occupied by a builders'

1. The English term for government payments to the unemployed.

2. Tiltman, an Englishman, expresses income and expenditures in units of English money rather than German. In the amounts he lists, the number left of the slash represents shillings, twenty of which made up a British pound; the number on the right represents pence, twelve of which made a shilling. The symbol for pence is d.

3. A term for animal fat.

laborer, unemployed for over two years. The rooms were in a cellar below the level of the street, and approached through quarters occupied by another family. The income for a family of three was 16/- a week, "a little higher than the average," as the man explained to me. The rent, including the new tax, was 6/- a month. The wife produced the rent book, showing that they owed two months' rent, and in view of the new law, already mentioned, which rendered them liable to eviction at any time upon twelve hours' notice, it worried them. If that happened, they explained, there would be no alternative to a shed somewhere on the outskirts of the city, which would mean living like pigs, and necessitate a long walk for the man every time he had to report to the relief officer.

The husband had just drawn 32/-, two weeks' relief payment, and I went out with the wife to spend it.

The first 9/- went to pay a debt at the grocer's. A cwt.[4] of coal cost another 1/6½; 12/- went to pay the fortnight's rent; 2/6 liquidated a debt for potatoes eaten during the previous week. Seven shillings were left, and the wife spent this on eggs, dripping, bread, potatoes and cabbage — which may be described as the universal diet of the German workless. On that menu, they had to exist for another week at least.

When we returned, the husband was sitting on a box, his head in his hands — gazing fixedly into space. Looking for what? As a trade unionist, he had been a member of the Social Democratic Party,[5]

the bulwark of the German Republic. Now he was nothing — too broken in spirit to care. Sitting there, a picture of dejection, he might have been looking back to the pre-war days, when the Junkers[6] thundered forth claims to a "place in the sun," and at least found work for their people. If he was, who will blame him? It is one of the misfortunes of these years that troubles have crowded in upon Germany under the republican regime.

A moment later two young men, clad in leather jackets, burst into that cellar-room with a stamp of feet, to provide another glimpse of the curses which afflict Germany today. This time the curse, not of poverty, but of Hitlerism.

It could not truthfully be said that the visitors entered that room. Their domineering manners and assertive attitude somehow preceded them through the door, which they slammed after entering. Compared with the Socialist worker, wearied by waiting for the turn of the tide, these two members of the Nazi "S.A."[7] . . . represented another world — a Germany which has lost its patience and demands the impossible under threat of instant reprisals. . . .

Those two young workless men were walking evidence, seen beside that Socialist, of the fact that whatever else Adolf Hitler has, or has not, done, he has enabled a large number of Germans to keep up their spirits — the great demagogue would himself call it "saving the soul of Germany" — at a time when Germany's spirits were in danger of sinking to zero.

---

4. Abbreviation for a hundredweight, 100 pounds.

5. The Social Democrats were Marxist in inspiration but sought to achieve socialism through legislation rather than revolution.

6. German aristocrats from Prussia, who for

centuries dominated the Prussian and, after unification, the German army's officer corps.

7. *Sturmabteilung*, a paramilitary organization attached to the Nazi party and noted for violent methods; also known as Brown Shirts and Storm Troopers.

Ultranationalism in Italy, Germany, and Japan

Nationalism, depite its role in causing World War I, became even more powerful and poisonous during the 1920s and 1930s, leading humankind into a second world war many times more costly and horrifying than the struggle between 1914 and 1918. In Italy and Germany, fanatical nationalism became the hallmark of right-wing, anti-democratic movements personified by Benito Mussolini, whose Fascists seized power in Italy in 1922, and Adolf Hitler, whose Nazis gained domination over Germany in 1933. In Japan, ultranationalists never subverted the limited democracy established by the 1890 constitution, but in the 1930s their views of Japan's past and future inspired millions and became dogma within the Japanese military.

The three nations in which nationalism ran wild were similar in several ways. They were, in a sense, new political entities: Italy had gained national unity between 1859 and 1870, Germany achieved the same in 1871, and Japan did not emerge from its feudal past until the Meiji Restoration of 1868. All three had weak parliamentary governments and populations with little experience in democratic politics. All three resented their treatment in the post–World War I treaties: the Germans hated the humiliating Treaty of Versailles and the Italians and Japanese were insulted by Great Britain's and France's refusal to recognize their territorial claims. Finally, all three had real or imagined economic problems that extreme nationalists claimed could be solved by expansion and conquest.

Although ultranationalism in each country differed in certain important respects, it had the same results: it led all three into catastrophic wars. Japan, after conquering Manchuria in 1931, invading China in 1937, and attacking the United States at Pearl Harbor in 1941, was brought to its knees after atomic bombs devastated Hiroshima and Nagasaki in August 1945. Germany launched World War II in Europe with its attack on Poland in September 1939, but after conquering much of Western Europe and plunging into the Soviet Union in 1941, the Allies steadily pushed back its armies until the leaders of a devastated land surrendered in May 1945. Italy entered World War II on the side of Nazi Germany in 1940, but its armies performed poorly, and only massive military support from the Germans prevented its rapid collapse. Anti-fascists captured Mussolini and shot him without trial on April 28, 1945, just a few days before Adolf Hitler committed suicide in his bunker under the streets of Berlin.

Benito Mussolini

THE POLITICAL AND SOCIAL DOCTRINE OF FASCISM

Benito Mussolini (1883–1945), Europe's first fascist dictator, was the son of a black-smith and a schoolteacher who as a youth actively participated in socialist and revolutionary political movements. He discarded radicalism for nationalism during World War I when, as a journalist, Mussolini called for Italy's entry into the war against Austria to pursue territorial expansion. After the war, he founded his own private army of some forty unemployed veterans, which he called the *Fascio di Combattimento*, or "combat group." The Fascists adopted a strong nationalist stance and portrayed themselves as Italy's only protection from Socialists and Communists, with whom they battled in the streets. Many Italians, dismayed by inflation, high taxes, widespread unemployment, strikes, peasant revolts, corruption, and ineffectual leadership, looked to the Fascists for Italy's salvation. Party membership soared to 300,000 by 1921. In 1922, even though the Fascists and their supporters controlled less than one tenth of the seats in the Italian parliament, Mussolini demanded that the king name him premier. When the king hesitated, Mussolini organized a March on Rome, in which thousands of Fascists converged on the capital, prompting the resignation of the cabinet and causing the king to name "Il Duce" premier. He and his henchmen quickly suppressed opposition and undermined the Italian parliamentary regime. By 1924 Italy's fascist dictatorship was secure.

Claiming that fascism was based on "action," not ideology, Mussolini at first declined to explain fascist doctrine. In 1932, however, he wrote (or had published under his name) the following statement for the *Enciclopedia Italiana*.

Questions for Analysis

1. Why, according to Mussolini, does fascism glorify war and oppose pacifism?
2. To Mussolini, what are the flaws of Marxian socialism?
3. Why does fascism oppose democracy?
4. What is the relationship between the individual and the state, according to Mussolini?
5. What does Mussolini mean when he says that "the State is a spiritual and moral fact"?
6. Most of what Mussolini wrote describes what fascism opposed. Are there positive features in its ideology?

*F*ascism, the more it considers and observes the future and the development of humanity quite apart from political considerations of the moment, believes neither in the possibility nor the utility of perpetual peace. It thus repudiates the doctrine of Pacifism — born of a renunciation of the struggle and an act of cowardice in the face of sacrifice. War alone brings up to its highest tension all human energy and puts the stamp of nobility upon the peoples who have the courage to meet it. All other trials are substitutes, which never really put men into the position where they have to make the great decision — the alternative of life or death. Thus a doctrine which is founded upon this harmful postulate of peace is hostile to Fascism. And thus hostile to the spirit of Fascism, though accepted for what use they can be in dealing with particular political situations, are all the international leagues and societies which, as history will show, can be scattered to the winds when once strong national feeling is aroused by any motive — sentimental, ideal, or practical. This anti-pacifist spirit is carried by Fascism even into the life of the individual; the proud motto of the Squadrista,[1] *"Me ne frego"* (I do not fear), written on the bandage of the wound, is an act of philosophy not only stoic, the summary of a doctrine not only political — it is the education to combat, the acceptance of the risks which combat implies, and a new way of life for Italy. . . .

Such a conception of life makes Fascism the complete opposite of that doctrine, the base of the so-called scientific and Marxian Socialism, the materialist conception of history; according to which the history of human civilization can be explained simply through the conflict of interests among the various social groups and by the change and development in the means and instruments of production. That the changes in the economic field — new discoveries of raw materials, new methods of working them, and the inventions of science — have their importance no one can deny; but that these factors are sufficient to explain the history of humanity excluding all others is an absurd delusion. Fascism, now and always, believes in holiness and in heroism; that is to say, in actions influenced by no economic motive, direct or indirect. . . . And above all Fascism denies that class war can be the preponderant force in the transformation of society. These two fundamental concepts of Socialism being thus refuted, nothing is left of it but the sentimental aspiration — as old as humanity itself — towards a social convention in which the

sorrows and sufferings of the humblest shall be alleviated. But here again Fascism repudiates the conception of "economic" happiness, to be realized by Socialism and, as it were, at a given moment in economic evolution to assure to everyone the maximum of well-being. Fascism denies the materialist conception of happiness as a possibility, and abandons it to its inventors, the economists of the first half of the nineteenth century: that is to say, Fascism denies the validity of the equation, well-being = happiness, which would reduce men to the level of animals, caring for one thing only — to be fat and well-fed — and would thus degrade humanity to a purely physical existence.

After Socialism, Fascism combats the whole complex system of democratic ideology, and repudiates it, whether in its theoretical premises or in its practical application. Fascism denies that the majority, by the simple fact that it is a majority, can direct human society; it denies that numbers alone can govern by means of a periodical consultation, and it affirms the immutable, beneficial, and fruitful inequality of mankind, which can never be permanently leveled through the mere operation of a mechanical process such as universal suffrage. The democratic regime may be defined as from time to time giving the people the illusion of sovereignty, while the real effective sovereignty lies in the hands of other concealed and irresponsible forces. Democracy is a regime nominally without a king, but it is ruled by many kings — more absolute, tyrannical, and ruinous than one sole king, even though a tyrant. . . .

The foundation of Fascism is the conception of the State, its character, its duty, and its aim. Fascism conceives of the State as an absolute, in comparison with which

---

1. Fascists who did much of the street fighting against Socialists and Communists during their struggle for power.

all individuals or groups are relative, only to be conceived of in their relation to the State. . . . In 1929, at the first five-yearly assembly of the Fascist regime, I said:

"For us Fascists, the State is not merely a guardian, preoccupied solely with the duty of assuring the personal safety of the citizens; nor is it an organization with purely material aims, such as to guarantee a certain level of well-being and peaceful conditions of life; for a mere council of administration would be sufficient to realize such objects. Nor is it a purely political creation, divorced from all contact with the complex material reality which makes up the life of the individual and the life of the people as a whole. The State, as conceived of and as created by Fascism, is a spiritual and moral fact in itself, since its political, juridical, and economic organization of the nation is a concrete thing: and such an organization must be in its origins and development a manifestation of the spirit. The State is the guarantor of security both internal and external, but it is also the custodian and transmitter of the spirit of the people, as it has grown up through the centuries in language, in customs, and in faith. And the State is not only a living reality of the present, it is also linked with the past and above all with the future, and thus transcending the brief limits of individual life, it represents the immanent spirit of the nation. . . . The individual in the Fascist State is not annulled but rather multiplied, just in the same way that a soldier in a regiment is not diminished but rather increased by the number of his comrades.

The Fascist State organizes the nation, but leaves a sufficient margin of liberty to the individual; the latter is deprived of all useless and possibly harmful freedom, but retains what is essential; the deciding power in this question cannot be the individual, but the State alone." . . .

Fascism is the doctrine best adapted to represent the tendencies and the aspirations of a people, like the people of Italy, who are rising again after many centuries of abasement and foreign servitude. But empire demands discipline, the co-ordination of all forces and a deeply felt sense of duty and sacrifice: this fact explains many aspects of the practical working of the regime, the character of many forces in the State, and the necessarily severe measures which must be taken against those who would oppose this spontaneous and inevitable movement of Italy in the twentieth century, and would oppose it by recalling the outworn ideology of the nineteenth century — repudiated wheresoever there has been the courage to undertake great experiments of social and political transformation: for never before has the nation stood more in need of authority, of direction, and of order. If every age has its own characteristic doctrine, there are a thousand signs which point to Fascism as the characteristic doctrine of our time. For if a doctrine must be a living thing, this is proved by the fact that Fascism has created a living faith; and that this faith is very powerful in the minds of men, is demonstrated by those who have suffered and died for it.

■ **Adolf Hitler**

MEIN KAMPF

Born the son of a minor Austrian customs official in 1889, Hitler moved at the age of nineteen to Vienna, where he sought a career as an artist or architect. His efforts failed, however, and for the next four years he lived at the bottom of Viennese society, moving from one low-paying job to another. In 1912 he moved to Munich, where his life fell into the same pattern of purposeless drifting. In a sense, World War I rescued Hitler, giving him comradeship and a sense of direction that had been lacking. After the war, the shattered Hitler returned to Munich, where in 1919 he joined the small German Workers' Party, which in 1920 changed its name to the National Socialist German Workers' Party.

After becoming leader of the National Socialists, Hitler led an abortive coup d'état against the government of Bavaria in 1923. For this he was sentenced to a five-year prison term (of which he served only nine months). During this time he wrote the first volume of his major political work, *Mein Kampf* (*My Struggle*), which centers on his theories about the superiority of the "Aryan" race, most purely represented in modern history by Germans and other Nordic peoples. To a remarkable degree, this work, completed in 1925, provided the basic framework of ideas that inspired his millions of followers and guided the National Socialists until their destruction in 1945.

Questions
for Analysis

1. In what ways do Hitler's views of life and politics resemble Mussolini's? In what ways do they differ?
2. What broad purpose does Hitler see in human existence?
3. How have Hitler's ideas been influenced by his understanding of Charles Darwin's theories (Chapter 8)?
4. In Hitler's view, what are the basic dissimilarities between Aryans and Jews?
5. What does Hitler fear most from the Jews?
6. What is Hitler's view of political leadership? What role should parliaments play in a "folkish" state?
7. How does Hitler plan to reorient German foreign policy? What goals does he set for Germany, and how are they to be achieved?

NATION AND RACE

There are some truths which are so obvious that for this very reason they are not seen or at least not recognized by ordinary people. They sometimes pass by such truisms as though blind and are most astonished when someone suddenly discovers what everyone really ought to know. . . .

Thus men without exception wander about in the garden of Nature; they imagine that they know practically everything and yet with few exceptions pass blindly by one of the most patent principles of Nature's rule: the inner segregation of the species of all living beings on this earth. . . .

Any crossing of two beings not at exactly the same level produces a medium between the level of the two parents. This means: the offspring will probably stand higher than the racially lower parent, but not as high as the higher one. Consequently, it will later succumb in the struggle against the higher level. Such mating is contrary to the will of Nature for a higher breeding of all life. The precondition for this does not lie in associating superior and inferior, but in the total victory of the former. The stronger must dominate and not blend with the weaker, thus sacrificing his own greatness. Only the born weakling can view this as cruel, but he after all is only a weak and limited man; for if this law did not prevail, any conceivable higher development of organic living beings would be unthinkable. . . .

Nature looks on calmly, with satisfaction, in fact. In the struggle for daily bread all those who are weak and sickly or less determined succumb, while the struggle of the males for the female grants the right or opportunity to propagate only to the healthiest. And struggle is always a means for improving a species' health and power of resistance and, therefore, a cause of its higher development.

No more than Nature desires the mating of weaker with stronger individuals, even less does she desire the blending of a higher with a lower race, since, if she did, her whole work of higher breeding, over perhaps hundreds of thousands of years, night be ruined with one blow. . . .

Blood mixture and the resultant drop in the racial level is the sole cause of the dying out of old cultures; for men do not perish as a result of lost wars, but by the loss of that force of resistance which is contained only in pure blood.

All who are not of good race in this world are chaff.

And all occurrences in world history are only the expression of the races' instinct of self-preservation, in the good or bad sense.

. . .

All the human culture, all the results of art, science, and technology that we see before us today, are almost exclusively the creative product of the Aryan. This very fact admits of the not unfounded inference that he alone was the founder of all higher humanity, therefore representing the prototype of all that we understand by the word "man." He is the Prometheus of mankind from whose bright forehead the divine spark of genius has sprung at all times, forever kindling anew that fire of knowledge which illumined the night of silent mysteries and thus caused man to climb the path to mastery over the other beings of this earth. Exclude him — and perhaps after a few thousand years darkness will again descend on the earth, human culture will pass, and the world turn to a desert.

If we were to divide mankind into three groups, the founders of culture, the bearers of culture, the destroyers of culture, only the Aryan could be considered as the representative of the first group. From him originate the foundations and walls of all human creation, and only the outward form and color are determined by the changing traits of character of the various peoples. He provides the mightiest building stones and plans for all human progress and only the execution corresponds to the nature of the varying men and races.

. . .

The mightiest counterpart to the Aryan is represented by the Jew. In hardly any people in the world is the instinct of self-preservation developed more strongly than in the so-called "chosen." Of this, the mere fact of the survival of this race may be considered the best proof. Where is the people which in the last two thousand years has been exposed to so slight changes of inner disposition, character, etc., as the

Jewish people? What people, finally, has gone through greater upheavals than this one — and nevertheless issued from the mightiest catastrophes of mankind unchanged? What an infinitely tough will to live and preserve the species speaks from these facts! . . .

Since the Jew — for reasons which will at once become apparent — was never in possession of a culture of his own, the foundations of his intellectual work were always provided by others. His intellect at all times developed through the cultural world surrounding him. . . .

For if the Jewish people's instinct of self-preservation is not smaller but larger than that of other peoples, if his intellectual faculties can easily arouse the impression that they are equal to the intellectual gifts of other races, he lacks completely the most essential requirement for a cultured people, the idealistic attitude.

In the Jewish people the will to self-sacrifice does not go beyond the individual's naked instinct of self-preservation. Their apparently great sense of solidarity is based on the very primitive herd instinct that is seen in many other living creatures in this world. It is a noteworthy fact that the herd instinct leads to mutual support only as long as a common danger makes this seem useful or inevitable. The same pack of wolves which has just fallen on its prey together disintegrates when hunger abates into its individual beasts. . . .

It is similar with the Jew. His sense of sacrifice is only apparent. It exists only as long as the existence of the individual makes it absolutely necessary. . . . The Jew is only united when a common danger forces him to be or a common booty entices him; if these two grounds are lacking, the qualities of the crassest egoism come into their own, and in the twinkling of an eye the united people turns into a horde of rats, fighting bloodily among themselves.

If the Jews were alone in this world, they would stifle in filth and offal; they would try to get ahead of one another in hate-filled struggle and exterminate one another, in so far as the absolute absence of all sense of self-sacrifice, expressing itself in their cowardice, did not turn battle into comedy here too. . . .

No, the Jew possesses no culture-creating force of any sort, since the idealism, without which there is no true higher development of man, is not present in him and never was present. Hence his intellect will never have a constructive effect, but will be destructive. . . . Not through him does any progress of mankind occur, but in spite of him. . . .

—————— ⁓ ——————

Hitler describes the process by which the European Jews in concert with Bolsheviks have come close to subverting and controlling other races and peoples of Europe.

—————— ⁓ ——————

Here he stops at nothing, and in his vileness he becomes so gigantic that no one need be surprised if among our people the personification of the devil as the symbol of all evil assumes the living shape of the Jew. . . .

How close they see approaching victory can be seen by the hideous aspect which their relations with the members of other peoples takes on.

With satanic joy in his face, the black-haired Jewish youth lurks in wait for the unsuspecting girl whom he defiles with his blood, thus stealing her from her people. With every means he tries to destroy the racial foundations of the people he has set out to subjugate. . . .

Around peoples who offer too violent a resistance to attack from within he weaves a net of enemies, thanks to his international influence, incites them to war, and finally, if necessary, plants the flag of revolution on the very battlefields.

In economics he undermines the states until the social enterprises which have become unprofitable are taken from the state and subjected to his financial control.

In the political field he refuses the state the means for its self-preservation, destroys the foundations of all national self-maintenance and defense, destroys faith in the leadership, scoffs at its history and past, and drags everything that is truly great into the gutter.

Culturally he contaminates art, literature, the theater, makes a mockery of natural feeling, overthrows all concepts of beauty and sublimity, of the noble and the good, and instead drags men down into the sphere of his own base nature.

Religion is ridiculed, ethics and morality represented as outmoded, until the last props of a nation in its struggle for existence in this world have fallen.

PERSONALITY AND THE CONCEPTION OF THE FOLKISH[1] SLATE

The folkish philosophy is basically distinguished from the Marxist philosophy by the fact that it not only recognizes the value of race, but with it the importance of the personality, which it therefore makes one of the pillars of its entire edifice. These are the factors which sustain its view of life.

The folkish state must care for the welfare of its citizens by recognizing in all and everything the importance of the value of personality, thus in all fields preparing the way for that highest measure of productive performance which grants to the individual the highest measure of participation.

And accordingly, the folkish state must free all leadership and especially the highest — that is, the political leadership — entirely from the parliamentary principle of majority rule — in other words, mass rule — and instead absolutely guarantee the right of the personality.

From this the following realization results:

The best state constitution and state form is that which, with the most unquestioned certainty, raises the best minds in the national community to leading position and leading influence. . . .

From the smallest community cell to the highest leadership of the entire Reich, the state must have the personality principle anchored in its organization.

There must be no majority decisions, but only responsible persons, and the word "council" must be restored to its original meaning. Surely every man will have advisers by his side, but *the decision will be made by one man.*

The principle which made the Prussian army in its time into the most wonderful instrument of the German people must some day, in a transferred sense, become the principle of the construction of our whole state conception: *authority of every leader downward and responsibility upward.* . . .

This principle — absolute responsibility unconditionally combined with absolute authority — will gradually breed an élite of leaders such as today, in this era of irresponsible parliamentarianism, is utterly inconceivable.

---

1. The original German word, *volkisch*, is based on the word *Volk*, meaning "people" or "nation," a word Hitler defined in a racial sense; thus, a "folkish state" is one that expresses the characteristics of and furthers the interests of a particular race, in this case the Aryans.

EASTERN ORIENTATION OR EASTERN POLICY

If the National Socialist movement really wants to be consecrated by history with a great mission for our nation, it must be permeated by knowledge and filled with pain at our true situation in this world: boldly and conscious of its goal, it must take up the struggle against the aimlessness and incompetence which have hitherto guided our German nation in the line of foreign affairs. Then, without consideration of "traditions" and prejudices, it must find the courage to gather our people and their strength for an advance along the road that will lead this people from its present restricted living space to new land and soil, and hence also free it from the danger of vanishing from the earth or of serving others as a slave nation.

The National Socialist movement must strive to eliminate the disproportion between our population and our area — viewing this latter as a source of food as well as a basis for power politics — between our historical past and the hopelessness of our present impotence. And in this it must remain aware that we, as guardians of the highest humanity on this earth, are bound by the highest obligation, and the more it strives to bring the German people to racial awareness so that, in addition to breeding dogs, horses, and cats, they will have mercy on their *own* blood, the more it will be able to meet this obligation. . . .

National Socialists must hold unflinchingly to our aim in foreign policy, namely, to secure for the German people the land and soil to which they are entitled on this earth. . . .

State boundaries are made by man and changed by man.

The fact that a nation has succeeded in acquiring an undue amount of soil constitutes no higher obligation that it should be recognized eternally. At most it proves the strength of the conquerors and the weakness of the nations. And in this case, right lies in this strength alone. If the German nation today, penned into an impossible area, faces a lamentable future, this is no more a commandment of Fate than revolt against this state of affairs constitutes an affront to Fate. No more than any higher power has promised another nation more territory than the German nation, or is offended by the fact of this unjust distribution of the soil. Just as our ancestors did not receive the soil on which we live today as a gift from Heaven, but had to fight for it at the risk of their lives, in the future no folkish grace will win soil for us and hence life for our people, but only the might of a victorious sword. . . .

But we National Socialists must go further. *The right to possess soil can become a duty if without extension of its soil a great nation seems doomed to destruction.* And most especially when not some little nigger nation or other is involved, but the Germanic mother of life, which has given the present-day world its cultural picture. *Germany will either be a world power or there will be no Germany.* And for world power she needs that magnitude which will give her the position she needs in the present period, and life to her citizens.

. . .

And so we National Socialists consciously draw a line beneath the foreign policy tendency of our pre-War period. We take up where we broke off six hundred years ago. We stop the endless German movement to the south and west, and turn our gaze toward the land in the east. At long last we break off the colonial and commercial policy of the pre-War period and shift to the soil policy of the future.

If we speak of soil in Europe today, we can primarily have in mind only *Russia* and her vassal border states.

THE WAY OF SUBJECTS

In the summer of 1941, only a few months before the bombing of Pearl Harbor, the Japanese Ministry of Education issued a pamphlet entitled *The Way of Subjects,* which became required reading for all students in secondary schools and universities. The authors present a view of the world and of Japan's past and future that reflects the basic principles of Japanese ultranationalism, a growing force during the 1920s and 1930s.

National pride had characterized the Japanese for hundreds of years and had been a decisive factor in the success of Japanese modernization during the Meiji period. During the 1930s and 1940s, however, nationalism intensified, and, as in Germany and Italy, it became identified with reactionary antidemocratic and antisocialist political movements. Japanese ultranationalism grew in response to several developments, including resentment against the West for its treatment of Japan after World War I, fears of a reunified China under the leadership of Chiang Kai-shek's Nationalists, concerns over economic fluctuations and social tensions caused by the Great Depression, opposition to "dangerous" ideologies such as socialism and communism, and anxiety over the increasing influence of the West on Japanese society.

In response, the ultranationalists denounced democracy, socialism, and the pernicious influence of big business on Japanese life. They praised traditional Japanese virtues of harmony and duty, demanded absolute obedience to the emperor, and called for the revival of ancient warrior values. They also clamored for Japanese expansion to the Asian mainland, claiming that only this could save Japan from overpopulation and economic isolation.

With widespread support in the rural population and the army, ultranationalism peaked between 1931 and 1936, when its disciples assassinated business leaders and government officials, including a prime minister, and hatched plots to overthrow the government. The most serious attempted coup took place in February 1936, when officers and troops of the Fifteenth Division attacked and held downtown Tokyo for three days before authorities suppressed their rebellion. The government survived, but to placate the extremists, it cracked down on leftist politicians and generally acceded to the army's demands. The delicate balance of Japanese politics had shifted to the right-wing militarists, setting the stage for the invasion of China in 1937 and the bombing of Pearl Harbor in 1941.

Questions for Analysis

1. What is the stated purpose of *The Way of Subjects*?
2. According to the authors, what are the distinguishing characteristics of Western nations? In what ways do Western attitudes and ideologies threaten Japan?

3. According to the authors, how do the Japanese differ from other peoples? What do they see as Japan's special mission? To what extent do their views resemble Hitler's racial views?
4. What is the purpose of the Great East Asia Coprosperity Sphere?
5. What is the role of individual Japanese in fulfilling the nation's mission? How does their role resemble that of the individual in fascist Italy?

PREAMBLE

The way of the subjects of the Emperor issues from the polity of the Emperor, and is to guard and maintain the Imperial Throne coexistent with the Heavens and the Earth. This is not in the sphere of the abstract, but a way of daily practices based on history. The life and activities of the nation are all attuned to the task of giving great firmness to the foundation of the Empire.

In retrospection, this country has been widely seeking knowledge in the world since the Meiji Restoration, thereby fostering and maintaining the prosperity of the state. With the influx of European and American culture into this country, however, individualism, liberalism, utilitarianism, and materialism began to assert themselves, with the result that the traditional character of the country was much impaired and the virtuous habits and customs bequeathed by our ancestors were affected unfavorably.

With the outbreak of the Manchurian Affair[1] and further occurrence of the China Affair,[2] the national spirit started to be elevated gradually, but there is still more or less to be desired in point of understanding the fundamental principle of polity by the people as a whole and their consciousness as subjects of the Emperor. It is to be deeply regretted that, well knowing the dignity of the polity of the Empire, people are likely to be satisfied with making it a mere conception, and fail to let it be manifest in their daily lives.

If this situation is left unremedied, it will be difficult to eradicate the evils of European and American thought that are deeply penetrating various strata of the national life of Japan, and to achieve the unprecedentedly great tasks by establishing a structure of national solidarity of guarding and maintaining the prosperity of the Imperial Throne. Herein lies an urgent need of discarding the self-centered and utilitarian ideas and of elevating and practicing the way of the subjects of the Emperor based on state services as the primary requisite.

PART I

The thoughts that have formed the foundation of the Western civilization since the early period of the modern age are individualism, liberalism, materialism, and so on. These thoughts regard the strong preying on the weak as reasonable, unstintedly promote epicurean desires, seek a highly expanded material life, and stimulate the competition for acquiring colonies and securing trade, thereby leading the world to a veritable hell of fighting and bloodshed through complicated causes and effects. The self-destruction in the shape of the World War finally followed. It was only natural that cries were

---

1. The Japanese invasion of Manchuria in 1931.

2. The invasion of China in 1937.

raised even among men of those countries after the war that the Occidental civilization was crumbling. A vigorous movement was started by Britain, France, and the United States to maintain the status quo by all means. Simultaneously, a movement aiming at social revolution through class conflict on the basis of thoroughgoing materialism like Communism also was developed with unremitting vigor. On the other hand, Nazism and Fascism arose with great force. The basic theories of these new racial principles and the totalitarianism in Germany and Italy are to remove and improve the evils of individualism and liberalism.

That these principles show great concern for Oriental culture and spirit is a noteworthy fact that suggests the future of the Occidental civilization and the creation of a new culture. Thus, the orientation of world history has made the collapse of the world of the old order an assured conclusion. Japan has hereby opened the start for the construction of a new world order based on moral principles.

The Manchurian Affair was a violent outburst of Japanese national life long suppressed. Taking advantage of this, Japan in the glare of all the Powers stepped out for the creation of a world based on moral principles and the construction of a new order. This was a manifestation of the spirit, profound and lofty, embodied in the Empire-founding, and an unavoidable action for its national life and world mission. Japan's position was raised suddenly to the world's forefront as a result of the Russo-Japanese War of 1904–05. . . .

The general tendency of world domination by Europe and America has begun to show signs of a change since then. Japan's victory attracted the attention of the entire world, and this caused a reawakening of Asiatic countries, which had been forced to lie prostrate under British and American influence, with the result that a situation in which an independence movement was started has developed.

Hopes to be free of the shackles and bondage of Europe and America were ablaze among the nations of India, Turkey, Arabia, Thailand, Annam, and others. This also imparted a stimulus to a new racial movement in China. Amid this swelling atmosphere of Asia's reawakening, Japan has come to be keenly conscious of the fact that the stabilization of East Asia is her mission, and that the emancipation of East Asiatic nations rests solely on her efforts. . . .

PART III

Viewed from the standpoint of world history, the China Affair is a step toward the construction of a world of moral principles by Japan. The building up of a new order for securing lasting peace of the world will be attained by the disposal of the China Affair as a steppingstone. In this regard the China Affair would not and should not end with the mere downfall of the Chiang Kai-shek regime. Until the elimination of the evils of European and American influences in East Asia that have led China astray is realized, until Japan's cooperation with New China as one of the links in the chain of the Great East Asia Coprosperity Sphere yields satisfactory results, and East Asia and the rest of the world are united as one on the basis of moral principles, Japan's indefatigable efforts are sorely needed. . . .

Japan has a political mission to help various regions in the Great East Asia Coprosperity Sphere,[3] which are reduced to a state of quasi-colony by Europe and

---

3. The Japanese term for their Asian empire.

America, so as to rescue them from their control. Economically, this country will have to eradicate the evils of their exploitation and then set up an economic structure for coexistence and coprosperity. Culturally, Japan must strive to fashion East Asiatic nations to change their following of European and American culture and to develop Oriental culture for the purpose of contributing to the creation of a right world. The Orient has been left to destruction for the past several hundred years. Its rehabilitation is not an easy task. It is natural that unusual difficulties attend the establishment of a new order and the creation of a new culture. The conquest of these difficulties alone will do much to help in establishing a morally controlled world, in which all nations can co-operate and all people can secure their proper positions. . . .

It is an urgent matter for Japan to realize the establishment of a structure of national unanimity in politics, economy, culture, education, and all other realms of national life. Defense is absolutely necessary for national existence. A nation without defense is one that belongs to a visionary world. Whether defense is perfect or not is the scale that measures the nation's existence or ruin. National growth and development can hardly be expected without perfection of defense. . . .

With the change of war from a simple military to a complicated total affair, distinction between wartime and peacetime has not been made clear. When the world was singing peace, a furious warfare was staged behind the scenes in economy, thought, and so on, among nations. Unless a country is systematized even in time of peace, so that the total war of the state and the people is constantly concentrated on the objective of the country, and the highest capacity is displayed, the country is predestined to be defeated before taking to arms. . . .

PART IV

The cardinal objective of strengthening the total war organism is solely to help the Imperial Throne, and this can be attained by all the people fulfilling their duty as subjects through their respective standpoints. The Soviet Union has world domination through Communism as its objective, and for this that country follows the policy of using compulsory rights through class dictatorship.

Standing on the national principle of blood and soil, Germany aims at destroying the world domination of the Anglo-Saxon race and the prevailing condition of pressure brought to bear upon Germany. She rests on the gravity of her voice for the right of national existence, and for this she has succeeded in achieving thoroughgoing popular confidence in, and obedience to, the dictatorship of the Nazis, and is adopting totalitarianism. Italy's ideals are the restoration of the great Roman Empire, and her policy for realizing them is not different from that of Germany. This country stands on the dictatorial totalitarianism of the Fascists. . . .

The ideals of Japan are to manifest to the entire world the spirit of her Empire-founding represented by the principle that "the Capital may be extended so as to embrace the six cardinal points, and the eight cords may be covered so as to form a roof." There is virtually no country in the world other than Japan having such a superb and lofty mission bearing world significance. So it can be said that the construction of a new structure and a defense state is all in order that Japan may revive her proper national structure and come back to her original status of supporting the Throne by the myriad subjects, thereby perfecting the workings of national strength and leaving no stone unturned in displaying her total power to the fullest extent.

PART V

The Imperial Family is the fountain source of the Japanese nation, and national and private lives issue from this. In the past, foreign nationals came to this country only to enjoy the benevolent rule of the Imperial Family, and became Japanese subjects spiritually and by blood. The Imperial virtues are so great and boundless that all are assimilated into one. Here is the reason for the present glorious state, in which the Emperor and his subjects are harmonized into one great unit. That the myriad subjects with one mind are glad to be unified to the Throne is the substance of the Imperial subjects.

The way of the subjects is to be loyal to the Emperor in disregard of self, thereby supporting the Imperial Throne coextensive with the Heavens and with the Earth. All the Rulers of Japan respected their subjects, calling them "honorable treasures." The subjects are conscious of their being the Imperial subjects. . . .

The great duty of the Japanese people to guard and maintain the Imperial Throne has lasted to the present since the Empire-founding and will last forever and ever. To serve the Emperor is its key point. Our lives will become sincere and true when they are offered to the Emperor and the state. Our own private life is fulfillment of the way of the subjects; in other words, it is not private, but public, insofar as it is held by the subjects supporting the Throne.

"As far as the clouds float and as far as the mountains and valleys expand," the land is Imperial territory and the people living there are subjects of the Emperor. It is not correct to observe, therefore, that private life has nothing to do with the state and is quite free. Every action has not only a private side, but has more or less connection with the state. All must be unified under the Emperor. Herein lies the significance of national life in Japan.

The Legacy of World War II

In terms of cost, number of belligerent nations, casualties, and, arguably, impact, World War II surpassed every war in human history. As if World War I had not already done so sufficiently, the Second World War revealed again the awesome power of science and technology when utilized by large modern states to obliterate human enemies. Modern communications and transportation systems enabled generals to plan and execute massive, complicated campaigns such as the German invasion of the Soviet Union in 1941 and the Allies' Normandy invasion of 1944. The airplane, only a curiosity in World War I, became a major instrument of destruction in World War II, making possible the German assault on English cities in 1940, the Japanese attack on Pearl Harbor in 1941, the around-the-clock bombing of Germany by Britain and the United States from 1943 to 1945, and the American fire bombing of Tokyo in 1945.

Only the closing months of the war, however, revealed fully the terrible potential inherent in modern science and large bureaucratic states. As the armies of the Soviet

Union and the Western powers liberated Europe in the spring of 1945, they discovered in the Third Reich's concentration camps and extermination camps the full horror of the Nazi assault on humanity, especially on Europe's Jews, some 6 million of whom they massacred. Then, on August 6, the United States opened a new chapter in human history when it dropped the first atomic bomb on Hiroshima. It killed close to 140,000 people, caused 300,000 casualties, and obliterated 90 percent of the city.[1] On August 9, Nagasaki suffered the same fate.

More than four decades later, these casualty figures still evoke nightmares in a world awash with nuclear weapons. Similarly, the Holocaust, the Nazi attempt to exterminate Europe's Jews, continues to haunt the imagination of humankind. On gaining power, the Nazis implemented the anti-Jewish policies Hitler had demanded in his speeches and writings. Police looked the other way when Jewish shops were plundered, Jewish physicians were excluded from hospitals, Jewish judges lost their posts, and limits were placed on Jewish enrollment at universities. In 1935 the Nazis promulgated the Nuremberg Laws, which deprived German Jews of citizenship and outlawed marriage between Jews and "Aryans." In November 1938, the regime organized nation-wide violence against Jewish synagogues and shops.

Once the war began, Germany's conquest of Poland and much of the Soviet Union gave the Nazis new opportunities to deal with the "Jewish problem." In early 1941, they began to deport German Jews to Poland and Czechoslovakia, where, along with Jews from conquered territories, they were forced into large urban ghettos and employed as slave laborers. In June 1941 the Nazis organized special army units to exterminate Jews in territories conquered by the advancing German armies. In eighteen months, they gunned down over one million Jews and threw them into open pits. As high as these numbers are, they do not compare with the mass slaughter after the Nazis approved the Final Solution to the Jewish problem in January 1942. They constructed special camps, all in conquered territory, designed to systematically exterminate European Jewry. The gas chambers and ovens at Auschwitz could handle 10,000 victims per day; an estimated 2.5 million persons, mostly Jews, were killed there by poison gas; and another 500,000 perished from disease, malnutrition, and torture.

When World War II ended, the Nazis had still not achieved their Final Solution — the annihilation of all 11 million European Jews. They did, however, slaughter 6 million, thus earning themselves a permanent, and perhaps the leading, place in the long history of man's inhumanity to man.

---

[1] Early estimates that 78,000 died are now considered low; recent studies suggest that the bomb caused 140,000 deaths in 1945 and, as a result of radiation sickness and other bomb-related diseases, 200,000 by 1950. On the difficulty of computing casualties, see The Committee for Compilation of Materials on Damage Caused by the Atomic Bomb, *Hiroshima and Nagasaki: The Physical, Medical, and Social Effects of the Atomic Bomb*, Elsei Ishikawa, and David Swain, trans. (New York: Basic Books, 1981), pp. 363–384.

▪ "B.F."

RECOLLECTIONS OF THE HOLOCAUST

"B.F." was a Jew born in Warsaw, Poland, in 1925. In 1935 he and his family moved to Lódź, also in Poland, where he was captured after the German conquest. He was sent to the Warsaw ghetto, escaped, was recaptured, and finally sent to Sobibór, one of the Nazis' extermination camps, at which approximately 250,000 Jews were executed in 1942 and 1943. In the fall of 1943, just before the camp closed, he participated in a breakout in which several hundred Jewish prisoners turned on their captors and escaped. He survived the war and recounted his experiences in an interview recorded in 1945.

. . .

The authors offer no Questions for Analysis for this reading and the reading that follows. To do so would trivialize two events that raise profound and disturbing questions about human nature and humanity's future.

. . .

*A*fter our train moved in, the doors were thrown open and armed Germans and Ukrainians, cracking whips, drove us out of the wagons. We had bloody welts all over our bodies. The day we came to Sobibór was May fifth in the year '42. We were led through a second tower to an assembly point which was ringed by barbed-wire fences, with posts on the wire perimeters capped by some sort of metal hoods. They split us up here — men to one side and women and children to the other. Soon, SS squads came in and led the women with the children away. Where they were being taken to we didn't know, but off in the distance we heard screams of people being beaten and stripped and then we heard the rumblings of motors being started. It was the women and children being killed. We could sense

in the air that, locked up like this between the wires, we'd be slaughtered right here. Night fell and we fell into a panic. We'd been told that in Belżec, people were burned alive in pits. We wouldn't believe this while we were in the ghetto, but here, when we saw a fire in the distance, we were sure they were burning people. We were overcome with fear and started saying our *viduyim*.[1]

It was a nightmare. The Ukrainians beat us and wouldn't let us out to relieve ourselves. People evacuated on the spot. Later, they told us they wouldn't do anything to us, that the women had only been taken off to work. . . .

There were thirty men in our group. They divided us up right away. Some were used to sort our belongings. The bundles were lying in ditches surrounded

---

1. A prayer of confession said by Jews before their death.

by wires and vines, with the same metal-hooded perimeter posts. The whole camp looked like this. I was taken into the second group and set to work digging a latrine. I never held a shovel in my life and a German who guarded us at work noticed my "skill" and let fly such a blow over my head that he nearly split my skull. That was when I learned how to work.

We worked from daybreak till nine, then they gave us breakfast. Bread and fingerbowls of fat was all we got and afterwards, they put us to work till late evening. As night fell, we were all lined up and an SS man informed us nothing would happen to us if we behaved well. If we didn't — they'd "make us a gift" of a bullet to the head. . . . Then, simply because he had the urge, he picked two men out — one who had stomach pains and the other who just wasn't to his liking — and led them off into the woods where he shot them. Most of the time, the men returned from work beaten, bloodied, and injured all over the body. . . .

This is what the system of going into the "bath" was like: As soon as a train with a transport of people arrived, everyone was either pulled off violently or made to jump. They were all forced to march into that sealed area. Later, the people were led off in groups of thousands, sometimes groups of hundreds. An SS[2] man addressed them, saying since there was a war on, everyone had to work and they were about to be transported somewhere else for labor. They'd be well taken care of. Children and the old wouldn't have to work, but wouldn't lack food either. So great attention must be

paid to cleanliness and we had to take a bath first. Those from the West would always applaud at this point. Later, when the Polish Jews arrived, they knew all this ended in death and screamed and made an uproar. So he said to them: "*Ruhe,*[3] I know you long for death already, but you won't be obliged so easily. First, you must work." And he kept punishing them and demoralizing them like this.

Inside the first barrack, they had their coats, jackets, and pants taken off and in the second barrack, had to strip down completely nude. They were told in that first speech that they wouldn't need any towel or soap — they'd find all that in the bath. All this led to them being brought naked into the third barrack near the bath. There was a special cell there where they were kept on arranged benches, guarded by Germans. Not a sound was permitted. Twenty barbers cut off the women's hair.[4] When the women came in naked and saw the men there, they pulled back, but the Germans dragged them and beat them forward. They had to sit naked. I was one of the barbers. To shave someone's head lasted half a minute. We held the long hair out from the head and snipped it off all along the scalp so that "stairs" were left — tufts of hair sticking out from the scalp. The foreign Jews[5] didn't suspect anything, they were just sorry about losing their hair. The Germans said it didn't matter — in half a year, the hair'd grow back. But on the other side, the Polish Jews screamed and wouldn't let us cut their hair, and they were beaten, and tortured. From there, they went straight through a corridor into a chamber. . . .

I was in the camp eighteen months al-

2. SS stands for Schutzstaffel (Guard Detachment), Hitler's elite corps, which under Heinrich Himmler staffed police posts and concentration camps; SS members played a central role in exterminating the Jews.

3. German for, "Be calm."

4. The hair was used to make felt footwear for German submarine personnel and highway workers.

5. Jews from outside Poland.

ready. The next day, a transport of Czech Jews was brought to the camp. They came at three in the morning and we were chased out of the bunks in the dead of night. We hauled the bundles off the train, running between two rows of Ukrainians who did nothing but beat us savagely. We worked like this without stop until ten the next night because there was so much cargo. . . .

That evening, SS man Paul harangued us as usual. He says he has to have five men for the *Lazarett*. What's a *Lazarett*? Well, a *Lazarett* is a place you don't have to work, you can sleep without interruption and don't have to bear any more burdens. But the real *Lazarett*, which means field hospital, was a small structure with a cross and icon of Jesus inside — probably from before the war — and there was a pit there where he'd lower people down and shoot them. This was his own *Lazarett*. The people he got to bury the dead there didn't come back either — they were dragged off to the third camp and burned there. Every day, that monster had to have from three to five Jews in his *Lazarett* and he'd pick them out himself or just ask, "*Ja*, well, who's sick today? Who doesn't want to work anymore?" Or he just grabbed them at random. If he hated someone, he simply pointed his finger at them and said, "*Komm, komm*,[6] you look like you don't want to work anymore," and then led them away. They were times when some Jews had heard before what the *Lazarett* meant, and they came forward to die voluntarily, because this life had driven them mad with despair. Victims succumbed like this every day. At the beginning of the work we did, we had 250 men. A month later, around eighty of us were left. Death came in many ways: sometimes by shooting, sometimes being bludgeoned to death with clubs. Some

committed suicide. There were times we got up in the barrack in the morning, and before our eyes, saw several Jews hanging from the rafters.

The most cruel death was at the jaws of Paul's dog, "Bari." Paul would yell at him: "Bari! Be my deputy!" and the dog tore people into pieces and devoured them. As soon as he got his jaws on you, there was no way out. He snapped you around, whirling you and tearing at you so long, till there was nothing left for his jaw to clamp down on. . . .

Wagner — he was the worst murderer — broke a shovel over my head. My face was completely disfigured. The eyes were pulp. No matter on which side I tried to lie down, I couldn't. I stayed up whole nights and howled and wept in pain. They tortured us unbelievably. . . .

In the year '43, our group kept growing till it reached 600 people — 120 women and 480 men.

Paul the murderer fell bewitched of a Czech Jewish girl. She cleaned up in his barrack and his attitude to us now became less sadistic. The other Germans realized this. One time, they waited till he left for the day, then came and shot the girl. When he got back, they teased him: "Well, Paul, where's your Jewish girl now?" He was so enraged, he persecuted us even more than before. He'd stand by the barrack door through which we hauled the packs, with a hatchet in his hand, and whenever the urge took him, he just swung away till he hacked someone down in a pool of blood. When the new latrines were dug and he came upon some impurity, he threatened all of us with execution. Once, he walked into the latrine area and saw two Jews stooping over the ditch, but there was a pile nearby so he dragged the two Jews over and made them eat it. They fell into a swoon,

---

6. German for "Come, come."

begging to be shot instead. But he wouldn't call back his order. They had to keep eating and then heaved up for the rest of the day. . . .

Once, he ordered a Jew over fifty to crawl like a dog and imitate all a dog's actions, making him tug at everyone's pants with his teeth, run after them and bite them. Wherever we walked, he had to run after us on all fours and tear at our pants, pounce on us and bark. When we were marched from the labor sites and forced to sing, he had to run alongside and bark, and he was whipped, to keep this up all day long. . . .

Sometimes, naked women hid out under the garbage, under rags. One time, I was about to sort through the rags when I take a look and see a woman lying among them. What do I do? I can't pull the rags away because a German will spot her immediately, so I went off to another pile of rags, but it didn't work — she was found out. She was led off and clubbed to death.

Another time, after one of the disinfections,[7] we found a child, one and a half years old, among the rags. But a Ukrainian immediately ordered me to take the child to the garbage pit, where he said: "*Ach*, a waste of a bullet!" and took

a garbage shovel and split open the baby into pieces. The child hardly let out a whimper.

Often, mothers bore children during the night. Whenever found, the babies were thrown straight into the garbage pits or were torn apart down the middle by their legs, or just flung up and shot in the air or wherever they landed. They made no fuss over children. Finally, the women rebelled. While stripping, they would scream out and attack the Germans, clawing at them and yelling. "You've lost the war anyway! Your death will be a lot crueller than ours! We're defenseless, we have to go to our death — but your women and children will be burned alive!!!" And they screeched and wailed. . . .

While we cut their hair, we stole some conversation with the women — as long as no German was watching, of course. They asked, "Tell us, can you? Will this death be painless? Does it last long?"

They asked us how we were still able to work for "them" while everyone else was dead. We answered, "You have it better. You're going to die soon — but we have to keep working, getting beaten all the time, till we're finally exterminated too."

Iwao Nakamura and Atsuko Tsujioka

RECOLLECTIONS OF AUGUST 6, 1945

In 1951 Dr. Arata Osada, a professor of education at the University of Hiroshima, sponsored a research project in which young Japanese from primary grades through the university were asked to write down their memories of the events of August 6 and their aftermath. Deeply moved by the children's recollections, he published a representative sample of their compositions in 1951 in Japanese. His stated purpose was to reveal the full horrors of nuclear war and thereby encourage nuclear disar-

---

7. Disinfection of clothes.

mament. The first English translation appeared in 1980. The recollections of two children follow.

Iwao Nakamura

11th Grade Boy (5th Grade at the Time)

Today, as I begin to write an account of my experiences after five years and several months have passed, the wretched scenes of that time float up before my eyes like phantoms. And as these phantoms appear, I can actually hear the pathetic groans, the screams.

In an instant it became dark as night, Hiroshima on that day. Flames shooting up from wrecked houses as if to illuminate this darkness. Amidst this, children aimlessly wandering about, groaning with pain, their burned faces twitching and bloated like balloons. An old man, skin flaking off like the skin of a potato, trying to get away on weak, unsteady legs, praying as he went. A man frantically calling out the names of his wife and children, both hands to his forehead from which blood trickled down. Just the memory of it makes my blood run cold. This is the real face of war. To those who knew nothing of the pitiful tragedies of Hiroshima's people, the scene would seem like a world of monsters, like Hades itself. A devil called war swept away the precious lives of several hundred thousand citizens of Hiroshima.

I, who cannot forget, was in the fifth year of primary school when it happened. To escape the frequent air raids, I and my sisters had been evacuated to the home of our relatives in the country, but on August 21 returned to my home at Naka Kakomachi (near the former Prefectural Office) during the summer vacation, to recover from the effects of a summer illness that had left me very weak. At the time, there were five of us living in Hiroshima: my parents, two younger brothers (aged

five and two) and myself. I used to drag myself along to the nearby Prefectural Hospital every morning at eight.

It was after eight on August 6 and the midsummer sun was beginning to scorch down on Hiroshima. An all-clear signal had sounded and with relief we sat down for breakfast a little later than usual. Usually by this time, my father had left the house for the office and I would be at the hospital for treatment.

I was just starting on my second bowl of rice. At that moment, a bluish-white ray of light like a magnesium flare hit me in the face, a terrific roar tore at my eardrums and it became so dark I could not see anything. I stood up, dropping my rice bowl and chopsticks. I do not know what happened next or how long I was unconscious. When I came to, I found myself trapped under what seemed like a heavy rock, but my head was free. It was still dark but I finally discovered that I was under a collapsed wall. It was all so sudden that I kept wondering if I was dreaming. I tried very hard to crawl free, but the heavy wall would not budge. A suffocating stench flooded the area and began to choke me. My breathing became short, my ears began to ring, and my heart was pounding as if it were about to burst. "I can't last much longer," I said to myself, and then a draft of cold air flowed past me and some light appeared. The taste of that fresh air is something I shall never forget. I breathed it in with all my might. This fresh air and the brighter surroundings gave me renewed vigor and I somehow managed to struggle out from under the wall. Where were my parents? Where were my brothers? I looked around in the dim light and glimpsed the hazy figures of my parents looking for me. I hurried over to them. Their hair was disheveled and their faces pale. When they saw me, they sighed with relief, "Oh you're safe, you're safe." . . .

Nothing was left of the Hiroshima of a few minutes ago. The houses and buildings had been destroyed and the streets transformed into a black desert, with only the flames from burning buildings giving a lurid illumination to the dark sky over Hiroshima. Flames were already shooting out of the wreckage of the house next door. We couldn't see my two brothers. My mother was in tears as she called their names. My father went frantic as he dug among the collapsed walls and scattered tiles. It must have been by the mercy of God that we were able to rescue my brothers from under the wreckage before the flames reached them. They were not hurt, either. The five of us left our burning home and hurried toward Koi. Around us was a sea of flames. The street was filled with flames and smoke from the burning wreckage of houses and burning power poles which had toppled down blocked our way time after time, almost sending us into the depths of despair. It seems that everyone in the area had already made their escape, for we saw no one but sometimes we heard moans, a sound like a wild beast. I began to shudder as I thought that everyone on earth had perished, leaving only the five of us here in an eerie world of the dead. As we passed Nakajima Primary School area and approached Sumiyoshi Bridge, I saw a damaged water tank in which a number of people had their heads down, drinking. I was so thirsty and attracted by the sight of people that I left my parents' side without thinking, and approached the tank. But when I got near and was able to see into the tank, I gave an involuntary cry and backed away. What I saw reflected in the blood-stained water were the faces of monsters. They had leaned over the side of the tank and died in that position. From

the burned shreds of their sailor uniforms, I knew they were schoolgirls, but they had no hair left and their burned faces were crimson with blood; they no longer appeared human. After we came out on the main road and cross Sumiyoshi Bridge, we finally came across some living human beings — but maybe it would be more correct to say that we met some people from Hell. They were naked and their skin, burned and bloody, was like red rust and their bodies were bloated up like balloons. Nevertheless, since we had not seen any living person on the way, we felt better seeing them and soon joined this group in our attempt to escape from Hiroshima. The houses on both sides of this street, which was several dozen yards wide, were in flames so that we could only move along a strip in the center about three or four yards wide. This narrow passage was covered with seriously burned and injured people, unable to walk, and with dead bodies, leaving hardly any space for us to get through. At places, we were forced to step over them callously, but we apologized in our hearts as we did this. Among them were old people pleading for water, tiny children seeking help, students unconsciously calling for their parents, brothers, and sisters, and there was a mother prostrate on the ground, moaning with pain but with one arm still tightly embracing her dead baby. But how could we help them when we ourselves did not know our own fate?

When we reached the Koi First Aid Station, we learned that we were among the last to escape from the Sumiyoshi Bridge area. After my father had received some medical treatment, we hurried over Koi Hill to our relatives at Tomo Village in Asa County. When we were crossing the hill late that evening, we could see Hiroshima lying far below, now a mere smoldering desert. After offering a silent prayer for the victims, we descended the hill toward Tomo.

ATSUKO TSUJIOKA

Student, Hiroshima Women's Junior College

It happened instantaneously. I felt as if my back had been struck with a big hammer, and then as if I had been thrown into boiling oil. I was unconscious for a while. When I regained my senses, the whole area was covered with black smoke. It seemed as if it were a bad dream or something. I felt stifled, I could hardly breathe. I thought I was going to die! I lay on the ground with my arms pressed against my chest, and called for help, again and again: "Mother! Mother! Father!"

But, of course, neither Mother nor Father answered me. As I was lying there quietly, accepting now the thought of death, an image of the smiling face of my little sister, who is no longer alive, came into my mind. Oh! Now I was really conscious! I could hear the other girls shouting for their mothers in the hellish darkness, and I sensed that they were getting away. I got up and just ran after them desperately. Near Tsurumi Bridge, a red hot electric wire got wrapped around my ankles. I pulled free of it somehow, without thinking, and ran to the foot of the Tsurumi Bridge. By that time, there was white smoke everywhere. I had been working in a place called Tanaka-cho, about 600 yards from the blast center. I seemed to have been blown quite a bit north and had to take a completely different route to the bridge, which would have been straight ahead of me if I was where I should have been.

There was a large cistern at the foot of the bridge. In the tank were some mothers, one holding her naked, burned baby above her head, and another crying and trying to give her baby milk from her burned breast. Also in the tank were schoolchildren, with only their heads, and their hands clasped in prayer, above

the surface of the water. They were sobbing for their parents, but everyone had been hurt, so there was no one to help them. People's hair was white with dust, and scorched; they did not look human. "Surely not me," I thought, and I looked down at my own hands. They were bloody and what looked like rags hung from my arms, and inside was freshlooking flesh, all red, white and black. I was shocked and reached for the handkerchief I carried in the pocket of my trousers, but there was no handkerchief or pocket. The lower part of the trousers had been burned away. I could feel my face swelling up, but there was nothing I could do about it. I and some friends decided to try to get back to our houses in the suburbs. Houses were blazing on both sides of the street as we walked along, and my back started hurting worse.

We heard people calling for help inside wrecked buildings, and then saw the same buildings go up in flames. A boy of about six, covered in blood, was jumping up and down in front of one of the burning houses, holding a cooking pot in his hands and yelling something we could not understand. It was as much as I could do to take care of myself, so I had to go on by without offering any help. I wonder what happened to those people? And the ones trapped in the buildings. In our rush to get home quickly, the four of us were proceeding toward the center of the atomic explosion, in the opposite direction from everyone else. However, when we reached Inari-machi, we could not go any further because the bridge had been destroyed, so we headed for Futaba Hill, instead. My legs gave out near Futaba, and I almost crawled the last part of the way to the foot of the hill, saying, "Wait for me! Please wait for me!"

Luckily for us, we met some kind soldiers in white coats there, who took us to a place we could lie down and rest, and treated our wounds. They dug around and told me that they had removed pieces of tile from the back of my head. They bandaged my head for me and tried to console us by saying, "Rest here now. Your teacher is bound to come and get you soon." . . .

That first night ended. There were cries for water from early morning. I was terribly thirsty. There was a puddle in the middle of the barracks. I realized that the water was filthy, but I scooped up some of it with my shoe and drank it. It looked like coffee with milk. I had always been very healthy. Perhaps that was the reason why I was still in possession of all my senses, although I had been badly injured. I found out that there was a river just behind the barracks and went out with my shoes and drank to my heart's content. After that, I went back and forth many times to get water for those lying near me, and for the injured soldiers. My underpants got soaking wet each time, but they soon dried out in the hot sun. Mercurochrome had been painted on my burns once, and they got black and sticky. I tried to dry them out in the sun. My friends and the other people were no longer able to move. The skin had peeled off of their burned arms, legs and backs. I wanted to move them, but there was no place on their bodies that I could touch. Some people came around noon on the second day and gave us some rice balls. Our faces were burned and swollen so badly that we could hardly open our mouths, so we got very little of the rice into them. My eyes had swollen up by the third day, and I could not move around. I lay down in the barracks with my friends. I remember being in a kind of dream world, talking on and on with my delirious friends. . . .

Another time, I must have been dreaming: I thought that my father and sister were coming up the hill to get me. I was so glad that I forced my eyes open with my fingers to see, but it was dark and I could not see anything. People who came to the barracks would call out the names and addresses of the people they were looking for. My father and four or five of our neighbors had been searching for me since the bombing. They found me in a corner of the barracks at the foot of Futaba Hill, on the evening of the third day. They were able to find me because the wooden name tag my father had written for me was on my chest. The writing on the tag had been burned all the way through it, as if it had been etched.

"Atsuko! This is your father!"

I was so happy I couldn't speak. I only nodded my head. My eyes were swollen closed. I could not see my father, but I was saved.

I still have the scars from that day; on my head, face, arms, legs and chest. There are reddish black scars on my arms and the face that I see in the mirror does not look as if it belongs to me. It always saddens me to think that I will never look the way I used to. I lost all hope at first. I was obsessed with the idea that I had become a freak and did not want to be seen by anyone. I cried constantly for my good friends and kind teachers who had died in such a terrible way.

My way of thinking became warped and pessimistic. Even my beautiful voice, that my friends had envied, had turned weak and hoarse. When I think of the way it was then, I feel as if I were being strangled. But I have been able to take comfort in the thought that physical beauty is not everything, that a beautiful spirit can do away with physical ugliness. This has given me new hope for the future. I am going to study hard and develop my mind and body, to become someone with culture and inner beauty.

C H A P T E R

12

Anticolonialism and Revolution in Asia, Africa, and Latin America, 1900–1945

*I*n the first half of the twentieth century, turmoil and change were not limited to the industrialized nations of Europe, North America, and Japan but also characterized the experience of the less developed areas of Africa, Asia, and the Americas. Given the wide differences in these societies, the nature of that turmoil varied greatly. Anticolonialism, for example, was an important force throughout those parts of the world still under the domination of European nations or the United States, but everywhere it had different traits and impact. In Africa, subjugated only in the late 1800s, anticolonialism was still weak. In India, opposition to British rule intensified and spread from educated members of the middle class to the Indian masses despite growing religious conflict among Hindus, Muslims, and Sikhs. In Southeast Asia, ethnic and religious rivalries and the Japanese conquest in World War II complicated the struggle for political independence, while in the Middle East, dynastic and religious antagonism and tension between "traditionalists" and "modernizers" hindered the formation of united anti-imperialist movements. Despite these differences, nationalism was a growing force in all these regions.

While people in colonial areas directed their political energies largely against the dominant foreigner, the independent nations of the "underdeveloped" world debated their political and economic futures. In Turkey, the debate was brief. Mustafa Kemal assumed dictatorial control in 1923 and single-mindedly pushed his subjects toward secularization and modernization. In China, the fall of the Ch'ing Dynasty after the 1911 revolution initiated thirty-five years of conflict in which military strong men, Nationalists, and Communists fought among themselves and against the Japanese. The nations of Latin America, though independent since the early 1800s, continued to experience political instability, vast disparities in wealth, and foreign control of much of their industry and commerce. The Great Depression of the 1930s severely damaged their economies and intensified political struggles between entrenched elites often supported by foreign governments and populist leaders who appealed to the masses through promises of social reform.

By the end of World War II, most issues that emerged in the first half of the twentieth century in Africa, Asia, and the Americas were still unresolved. Nonetheless, developments in these decades set the stage for the far-reaching postwar transformations that shape much of the global community in the late twentieth century.

Nationalism and Modernization in Turkey and the Middle East

When World War I ended, the leaders of Ottoman Turkey and their subjects faced a bleak future. After entering the war on the side of Germany in 1914, the Turks fought bravely but were hampered by equipment shortages, poor leadership, and the revolt of their Arab subjects in 1916. Now defeated, they could expect the final dismemberment of their empire and perhaps even territorial losses in Asia Minor itself. In 1920, the Treaty of Sèvres, which ended Turkish control of the Arab Middle East and proposed to hand over Turkish territory to Italy, Greece, and the new Christian republic of Armenia, confirmed their worst fears.

In only a few years, however, humiliation turned to pride. Under the leadership of Turkey's hero, Mustafa Kemal, the Turks rallied to drive out the Italians and Greeks and smash the nascent Armenian Republic. As a result, in 1923 the European powers agreed to replace the harsh Treaty of Sèvres with the Treaty of Lausanne, which recognized the existence of an independent Turkey. Kemal now had the opportunity to transform his country into a modern secular state.

In contrast to the Turks, the Arabs greeted the end of World War I with celebration. Lured by Great Britain's deliberately vague promises of political independence, the Arabs under Hussein ibn-Ali (1856–1931), the sharif of Mecca and the ruler of the eastern lands of the Arab Peninsula, revolted against the Ottomans in 1916. Buoyed by their success in battle, they now looked forward to controlling their own political fortunes for the first time in hundreds of years. As they soon learned, however, the British had secretly agreed with the French in 1916 to divide the Arab portions of the Ottoman Empire between themselves. This, rather than the vague promises to Hussein, became the basis for the post–World War I settlement. The French received control of Syria and Lebanon, while the British gained authority over Palestine and Iraq. Equally disturbing to the Arabs was the revelation that in 1917 Great Britain, through the Balfour Declaration, had pledged to support the establishment of a "National Home for the Jewish People" in Palestine. The Arab sense of betrayal was intense, and hostility to the West became an enduring part of the region's politics.

ARTICLE 22 OF THE COVENANT OF THE LEAGUE OF NATIONS

Although the statesmen who fashioned the peace treaties following World War I attempted to apply the principle of national self-determination in redrawing the political map of Europe, old-style imperialism was still the order of the day when dealing with colonies. Technically, Germany's former colonies and the non-Turkish regions of the defunct Ottoman Empire became "mandates" of the League of Nations, the international organization founded as part of the general peace settlement. These mandates were to be administered, however, by Great Britain, France, Japan, Australia, and South Africa, and the whole system was correctly viewed as a thinly veiled version of traditional imperialism. Article 22 of the League of Nations Covenant, adopted in 1919 at the Paris Peace Conference, outlined the basis for the mandate system and its goals.

Questions for Analysis

1. How does the spirit of Article 22 differ from that of Wilson's Fourteen Points (see Chapter 11)?
2. What is the "sacred trust" referred to in the first paragraph of Article 22? In what ways does it resemble Kipling's views in "The White Man's Burden" (see Chapter 8)?
3. What distinctions does the article make among the different territories that are to come under the authority of mandates?
4. What provisions does the article make to ensure that the mandatory powers carry out their responsibilities?

To those colonies and territories which as a consequence of the late war have ceased to be under the sovereignty of the States which formerly governed them and which are inhabited by peoples not yet able to stand by themselves under the strenuous conditions of the modern world, there should be applied the principle that the well-being and development of such peoples form a sacred trust of civilization and that securities for the performance of this trust should be embodied in this Covenant.

The best method of giving practical effect to this principle is that the tutelage of such peoples should be entrusted to advanced nations who by reason of their resources, their experience or their geographical position can best undertake this responsibility, and who are willing to accept it, and that this tutelage should be exercized by them as Mandatories on behalf of the League.

The character of the mandate must differ according to the stage of the development of the people, the geographical situation of the territory, its economic conditions and other similar circumstances.

Certain communities formerly belonging to the Turkish Empire have reached a stage of development where their existence as independent nations can be provisionally recognized subject to the rendering of administrative advice and assistance by a Mandatory until such time as they are able to stand alone. The wishes of these communities must be a principal consideration in the selection of the Mandatory.

Other peoples, especially those of Central Africa, are at such a stage that the Mandatory must be responsible for the administration of the territory under conditions which will guarantee freedom of conscience and religion, subject only to the maintenance of public order and morals, the prohibition of abuses such as the slave trade, the arms traffic and the liquor traffic, and the prevention of the establishment of fortifications or military and naval bases and of military training of the natives for other than police purposes and the defense of territory, and will also secure equal opportunities for the trade and commerce of other Members of the League.

There are territories, such as South-West Africa and certain of the South Pacific Islands, which, owing to the sparseness of their population, or their small size, or their remoteness from the centers of civilization, or their geographical contiguity to the territory of the Mandatory, and other circumstances, can be best administered under the laws of the Mandatory as integral portions of its territory, subject to the safeguards above mentioned in the interests of the indigenous population.

In every case of mandate, the Mandatory shall render to the Council an annual report in reference to the territory committed to its charge.

The degree of authority, control or administration to be exercized by the Mandatory shall, if not previously agreed upon by the Members of the League, be explicitly defined in each case by the Council.

A permanent Commission shall be constituted to receive and examine the annual reports of the Mandatories and to advise the Council on all matters relating to the observance of the mandates.

▨ General Syrian Congress at Damascus

RESOLUTION OF JULY 2, 1919

At the urging of U.S. President Wilson, who had reservations about the Anglo-French plan to control the Arab Middle East, England and France agreed in March 1919 to participate with the United States in an Inter-Allied Commission to investigate conditions in Syria in order to reach, in Wilson's words, the "most scientific basis" for a settlement. The French, however, refused to name a representative, and the British soon withdrew, so the Inter-Allied Commission became a U.S. enterprise, led by educator Henry C. King and industrialist and diplomat Charles R. Crane. In response, Syrian nationalists called a general Syrian congress, which Palestinian and Lebanese delegates also attended, and adopted the following resolution on July 2, 1919.

The King-Crane Commission included the resolution in its report, but Britain and France ignored it and proceeded with their plans. In March 1920, a second Syrian congress declared Syria independent. Four months later, however, on July 24, the French defeated the poorly equipped Syrian army and on the following day abolished the newly independent state.

Questions
for Analysis

1. In what ways does the resolution reject the premises of Article 22 of the League of Nations Covenant?
2. Why do the delegates prefer the United States and Great Britain over France as the nations to offer Syria economic and technical aid?
3. What arguments do the delegates offer to convince the great powers of the justice of their cause?

We the undersigned members of the General Syrian Congress, meeting in Damascus on Wednesday, July 2nd, 1919 . . . provided with credentials and authorizations by the inhabitants of our various districts, Muslims, Christians, and Jews, have agreed upon the following statement of the desires of the people of the country who have elected us to present them to the American Section of the International Commission; the fifth article was passed by a very large majority; all the other articles were accepted unanimously.

1. We ask absolutely complete political independence for Syria within these boundaries. The Taurus System on the North; Rafah and a line running from Al Jauf to the south of the Syrian and the Hejazian line to Akaba on the south; the Euphrates and Khabur Rivers and a line extending east of Abu Kamal to the east of Al Jauf on the east; and the Mediterranean on the west.[1]

2. We ask that the Government of this Syrian country should be a democratic civil constitutional Monarchy on broad decentralization principles, safeguarding the rights of minorities, and that the King

be the Emir Feisal, who carried on a glorious struggle in the cause of our liberation and merited our full confidence and entire reliance.[2]

3. Considering the fact that the Arabs inhabiting the Syrian area are not naturally less than other more advanced races and that they are by no means less developed than the Bulgarians, Serbians, Greeks, and Roumanians at the beginning of their independence, we protest against Article 22 of the Covenant of the League of Nations, placing us among the nations in their middle stage of development which stand in need of a mandatory power.

4. In the event of the rejection by the Peace Conference of this just protest for certain considerations that we may not understand, we, relying on the declarations of President Wilson that his object in waging war was to put an end to the ambition of conquest and colonization, can only regard the mandate mentioned in the Covenant of the League of Nations as equivalent to the rendering of economical and technical assistance that does not prejudice our complete independence.

---

1. The region described includes the present nations of Syria, Lebanon, Israel, and Jordan.

2. Prince Feisal (1881–1933; also spelled Feysel and Faysel), the son of Hussein ibn-Ali, was an Arab military hero in the Anglo-Arab struggle against the Turks. After the French drove him from Syria in 1920, the British installed him as Iraq's first king in 1921.

And desiring that our country should not fall a prey to colonization and believing that the American Nation is farthest from any thought of colonization and has no political ambition in our country, we will seek the technical and economical assistance from the United States of America, provided that such assistance does not exceed 20 years.

5. In the event of America not finding herself in a position to accept our desire for assistance, we will seek this assistance from Great Britain, also provided that such assistance does not infringe the complete independence and unity of our country and that the duration of such assistance does not exceed that mentioned in the previous article.

6. We do not acknowledge any right claimed by the French Government in any part whatever of our Syrian country and refuse that she should assist us or have a hand in our country under any circumstances and in any place.

7. We oppose the pretentions of the Zionists to create a Jewish commonwealth in the southern part of Syria, known as Palestine, and oppose Zionist migration to any part of our country; for we do not acknowledge their title but consider them a grave peril to our people from the national, economical, and political points of view. Our Jewish compatriots shall enjoy our common rights and assume the common responsibilities.

8. We ask that there should be no separation of the southern part of Syria, known as Palestine, nor of the littoral western zone, which includes Lebanon, from the Syrian country. We desire that the unity of the country should be guaranteed against partition under whatever circumstances.

9. We ask complete independence for emancipated Mesopotamia[3] and that there should be no economic barriers between the two countries.

10. The fundamental principles laid down by President Wilson in condemnation of secret treaties impel us to protest most emphatically against any treaty that stipulates the partition of our Syrian country and against any private engagement aiming at the establishment of Zionism in the southern part of Syria; therefore we ask the complete annulment of these conventions and agreements.[4]

The noble principles enunciated by President Wilson[5] strengthen our confidence that our desires emanating from the depths of our hearts, shall be the decisive factor in determining our future; and that President Wilson and the free American people will be our supporters for the realization of our hopes, thereby proving their sincerity and noble sympathy with the aspiration of the weaker nations in general and our Arab people in particular.

We also have the fullest confidence that the Peace Conference will realize that we would not have risen against the Turks, with whom we had participated in all civil, political, and representative privileges, but for their violation of our national rights, and so will grant us our desires in full in order that our political rights may not be less after the war than they were before, since we have shed so much blood in the cause of our liberty and independence.

---

3. The region of modern Iraq.

4. This passage refers to the Balfour Declaration of 1917 and the Sykes-Picot Agreement of 1916, in which Great Britain and France agreed to divide former Ottoman territories between them.

5. Wilson's "Fourteen Points" (see Chapter 11).

We request to be allowed to send a delegation to represent us at the Peace Conference to defend our rights and secure the realization of our aspirations.

Mustafa Kemal

SPEECH TO THE CONGRESS OF THE PEOPLE'S REPUBLICAN PARTY

Mustafa Kemal (1881–1938), the son of a government official, became a Turkish national hero during World War I, when he directed the defense of the Dardanelles against the British. Disgusted that the sultan acquiesced to the Greek occupation of the Turkish port city of Smyrna (Izmir), in 1919 Kemal moved to central Turkey to lead a resistance movement against both the sultan's government and the Allies. His determined leadership led the Turks to military victory over Greece and the subsequent dropping of the punitive Sèvres treaty in 1923. One year earlier, Kemal had convened a National Assembly, which deposed the sultan and set the stage for a decade and a half of revolutionary change. Exercising as president near dictatorial powers, he sought to transform Turkey into a modern secular nation-state. To accomplish this, he broke the power of the Islamic clergy over education and the courts, encouraged industrialization, accorded women full legal rights, mandated the use of a new Turkish alphabet, and, in a fashion reminiscent of Peter the Great, ordered the Turks to adopt Western-style dress.

Having consolidated his control of the country, Kemal in 1927 decided to review his accomplishments and to impress on the Turks the need to accept his policies. He chose as the occasion the 1927 meeting of the People's Republican party, founded by Kemal and Turkey's only legal political party. The result was an extraordinary speech. Having worked intensively on it for three months (and in the process exhausting dozens of secretaries), Kemal delivered the speech over a period of six days, from October 15 to 20. In the excerpts that follow, he expresses his view of Turkish nationalism and explains why he supported abolishing the caliphate, the ancient office by virtue of which Turkish sultans were the theoretical rulers of all Muslims.

Questions
for Analysis

1. What, according to Kemal, are the "erroneous ideas" that had guided the Ottoman state?
2. Why does Kemal argue that nation-states, not empires, are the most desirable form of political organization?
3. Like Hitler and Mussolini, Kemal speaks of life as a struggle and is clearly a

nationalist. What then differentiates Kemal's position from that of the fascist dictators?

4.   What arguments does Kemal offer against the continuation of the caliphate?
5.   What seems to be Kemal's attitude toward Islam? Toward religion in general?

You know that life consists of struggles and conflicts. Success in life is only possible by overcoming difficulties. All depends upon strength, upon moral and material energy. Further than that, all the questions that engage the attention of mankind, all the dangers to which they are exposed and all the successes which they achieve arise from the turmoil of the general combat which is raging throughout human society. The conflicts between the Eastern and Western races mark some of the most important pages in history. It is a generally accepted fact that among the peoples of the Orient the Turks were the element who bore the brunt and who gave evidence of the greatest strength. In fact, both before and after the rise of Islam, the Turks penetrated into the heart of Europe and attacked and invaded in all directions. We must not omit to mention the Arabs also, for they attacked the Occident and carried their invasion as far as Spain and across the frontiers of France.[1] But in every offensive we must always be prepared for a counter-attack. The end that awaits those who act without considering this possibility and without taking the necessary precautionary measures against it is defeat, annihilation, extinction. . . .

Passing over the Empire of Attila[2] which extended as far as France and the territory of the West-Roman Empire, we will turn our minds to the times when the Ottoman State in Istanbul, founded on the ruins of the Seljuk State,[3] was master of the crown and the throne of the East-Roman Empire. Among the Ottoman rulers there were some who endeavored to form a gigantic empire by seizing Germany and West-Rome. One of these rulers hoped to unite the whole Islamic world in one body, to lead it and govern it. For this purpose he obtained control of Syria and Egypt and assumed the title of Caliph.[4] Another Sultan pursued the twofold aim, on the one hand of gaining the mastery over Europe, and on the other of subjecting the Islamic world to his authority and government. The continuous counterattacks from the West, the discontent and insurrections in the Mohamedan world, as well as the dissensions between the various elements which this policy had artificially brought together within certain limits, had the ultimate result of burying the Ottoman Empire, in the same way as many others, under the pall of history.

What particularly interests foreign pol-

---

1. In the century after Muhammad's death in A.D. 632, Arab armies conquered Northern Africa and Spain.

2. Attila the Hun, a conqueror of legendary cruelty, established a sizable empire during his reign from A.D. 434 to 453; but by 500 the Hun empire had collapsed.

3. The Seljuks (or Seljuqs) were a Turkish people who established themselves in Asia Minor before they were absorbed into the Ottoman Empire in the 1300s and 1400s.

4. The reference is to Selim I, who conquered Egypt and Syria in 1515–1516; it is doubtful that he actually considered himself caliph in the sense of leader of all Muslims.

icy and upon which it is founded is the internal organization of the State. Thus it is necessary that the foreign policy should agree with the internal organization. In a State which extends from the East to the West and which unites in its embrace contrary elements with opposite characters, goals and culture, it is natural that the internal organization should be defective and weak in its foundations. In these circumstances its foreign policy, having no solid foundation, cannot be strenuously carried on. In the same proportion as the internal organization of such a State suffers specially from the defect of not being national, so also its foreign policy must lack this character. For this reason, the policy of the Ottoman State was not national but individual. It was deficient in clarity and continuity.

To unite different nations under one common name, to give these different elements equal rights, subject them to the same conditions and thus to found a mighty State is a brilliant and attractive political ideal; but it is a misleading one. It is an unrealizable aim to attempt to unite in one tribe the various races existing on the earth, thereby abolishing all boundaries. Herein lies a truth which the centuries that have gone by and the men who have lived during these centuries have clearly shown in dark and sanguinary events.

There is nothing in history to show how the policy of Panislamism[5] could have succeeded or how it could have found a basis for its realization on this earth. As regards the result of the ambition to organize a State which should be governed by the idea of world-supremacy and include the whole of humanity without distinction of race, history does not afford examples of this. For us, there can be no question of the lust of conquest. . . .

The political system which we regard as clear and fully realizable is national policy. In view of the general conditions obtaining in the world at present and the truths which in the course of centuries have rooted themselves in the minds of and have formed the characters of mankind, no greater mistake could be made than that of being a utopian. This is borne out in history and is the expression of science, reason and common sense.

In order that our nation should be able to live a happy, strenuous and permanent life, it is necessary that the State should pursue an exclusively national policy and that this policy should be in perfect agreement with our internal organization and be based on it. When I speak of national policy, I mean it in this sense: To work within our national boundaries for the real happiness and welfare of the nation and the country by, above all, relying on our own strength in order to retain our existence. But not to lead the people to follow fictitious aims, of whatever nature, which could only bring them misfortune, and expect from the civilized world civilized human treatment, friendship based on mutality.

. . .

I must call attention to the fact that Hodja Shukri, as well as the politicians who pushed forward his person and signature, had intended to substitute the sovereign bearing the title of Sultan or Padishah by a monarch with the title of

---

5. The program of uniting all Muslims under one government or ruler.

Caliph.[6] The only difference was that, instead of speaking of a monarch of this or that country or nation, they now spoke of a monarch whose authority extended over a population of three hundred million souls belonging to manifold nations and dwelling in different continents of the world. Into the hands of this great monarch, whose authority was to extend over the whole of Islam, they placed as the only power that of the Turkish people, that is to say, only from 10 to 15 millions of these three hundred million subjects. The monarch designated under the title of Caliph was to guide the affairs of these Mohamedan peoples and to secure the execution of the religious prescriptions which would best correspond to their worldly interests. He was to defend the rights of all Mohamedans and concentrate all the affairs of the Mohamedan world in his hands with effective authority. . . .

The absurd ideas which ignorant people like Shukri Hodja and his companions were disseminating about the actual condition prevailing in the world under the power of "religious prescriptions" with the intention of abusing our nation, are not worthy of being repeated here. In the course of centuries there have been people and there are still people today in the interior as well as in foreign countries who profited by the ignorance and fanaticism of the nations and try to make use of religion as a tool to help them in their political plans and personal interests. The fact that there are such individuals unfortunately compels us again to go into this question. . . .

If the Caliph and Caliphate, as they maintained, were to be invested with a dignity embracing the whole of Islam, ought they not to have realized in all justice that a crushing burden would be imposed on Turkey, on her existence; her entire resources and all her forces would be placed at the disposal of the Caliph?

According to their declarations, the Caliph-Monarch would have the right of jurisdiction over all Mohamedans and all Mohamedan countries, that is to say, over China, India, Afganistan, Persia, Iraq, Syria, Palestine, Hedjas, Yemen, Assyr, Egypt, Tripolis, Tunis, Algeria, Morocco, the Sudan. It is well known that this Utopia has never been realized. . . .

I made statements everywhere, that were necessary to dispel the uncertainty and anxiety of the people concerning this question of the Caliphate. I formerly declared: "We cannot allow any person, whatever his title may be, to interfere in questions relating to the destiny, activity and independence of the new State which our nation has now erected. The nation itself watches over the preservation and independence of the State which they have created, and will continue to do so for all time." I gave the people to understand that neither Turkey nor the handful of men she possesses could be placed at the disposal of the Caliph so that he might fulfill the mission attributed to him, namely, to found a State comprising the whole of Islam. The Turkish nation is incapable of undertaking such an irrational mission.

For centuries our nation was guided under the influence of these erroneous ideas. But what has been the result of it? Everywhere they have lost millions of men. "Do

---

6. The events Kemal describes here took place in January 1923. After Mehmed V was deposed as sultan on November 1, 1922, his cousin, Abdul Mejid, was designated caliph. Because of their long rule and vast territories, the Ottoman sultans by the nineteenth century were viewed by many Muslims as caliphs, that is,

"successors" of the prophet Muhammad, with spiritual jurisdiction over all Islam. Shukri was a hodja (or hojja), a Turkish religious leader, who hoped that the new Turkish state would continue to support the caliphate, even though the sultanate no longer existed. In 1924, however, Kemal successfully abolished the caliphate.

you know," I asked, "how many sons of Anatolia have perished in the scorching deserts of the Yemen? Do you know the losses we have suffered in holding Syria and the Iraq and Egypt and in maintaining our position in Africa? And do you see what has come out of it? Do you know?

"Those who favor the idea of placing the means at the disposal of the Caliph to brave the whole world and the power to administer the affairs of the whole of Islam must not appeal to the population of Anatolia alone but to the great Mohamedan agglomerations which are eight or ten times as rich in men.

"New Turkey, the people of New Turkey, have no reason to think of anything else but their own existence and their own welfare. She has nothing more to give away to others." . . .

I asked the people: "Will Persia or Afganistan, which are Mohamedan States, recognize the authority of the Caliph in a single matter? Can they do so? No, and this is quite justifiable, because it would be in contradiction to the independence of the State, to the sovereignty of the people."

I also warned the people by saying that "the error of looking upon ourselves as masters of the world must cease."

Let us put an end to the catastrophes into which the people had been dragged by following those who deceive themselves and misjudge our real rank and position in the world. We cannot conscientiously permit this tragedy to continue. The English author Wells has written an historical work which was published two years ago.

The last pages of this work contain some contemplations under the heading of "History of Mankind in the Future."[7]

These contemplations relate to the question of the establishment by the Governments of a World League. . . .

I will by no means deny the beauty of the idea of the "United States of the World" the establishment of which would produce the result that the experience, knowledge and conceptions of mankind at large would be developed and uplifted, that mankind would abandon Christianity, Islam, Buddhism, and that a pure, spotless, simplified religion, understood by all and of a universal character, will be established, and that men will understand that they have lived hitherto in a place of misery amidst disputes and ignominy, their desires and gross appetites, and that they will decide to eradicate all infectious germs which have hitherto empoisoned both body and soul.

Anticolonialism in India and Southeast Asia

During the nineteenth century, while the Indians were already in a full-scale debate about their relationship with Britain and thinking seriously of independence, Southeast Asians were just beginning to feel the brunt of European imperialism. Nonetheless, developments in both areas showed some marked similarities in the first half of the twentieth century. Nationalism swept through the Indian population, and, de-

---

7. H. G. Wells (1866–1946) was a prolific English journalist, novelist, and historian; Kemal is undoubtedly referring to Wells's *The Outline of* *History* (1920), the last chapter of which is entitled "Possible Unification of the World into One Community of Knowledge and Will."

spite their many differences in religion, education, and caste status, millions of Indians came to agree that the British should "quit India" and allow Indian self-rule. The British responded to this with minor concessions but mostly with armed repression. Similarly, nationalism grew in Southeast Asia, especially in Vietnam and the Dutch East Indies, where the French and Dutch forcefully suppressed anticolonial movements in the 1920s and 1930s.

Many reasons account for this upsurge of anti-European sentiment in south Asia, including religious revivals of Hinduism in India, Buddhism in Burma, and Islam in Southeast Asia, all of which heightened peoples' consciousness of their differences from the West; the emergence of Japan, which proved that an Asian nation could become a great power; the carnage of World War I, which raised doubts about the "superiority" of Europeans; and the spread of Western education and political ideologies. Above all others was anger over the disparity between the Europeans' expressions of good intentions about their colonies' futures and the actual record of economic exploitation, racial prejudice, and refusal to consider seriously the possibility of self-rule.

To this was added the extraordinary influence of charismatic leaders such as Mohandas Gandhi, who drew the Indian masses into the natonalist movement; Jawaharlal Nehru, who guided the Indian Congress party in the 1930s and 1940s; Ho Chi Minh, who built a strong nationalist coalition in Vietnam in the face of French persecution; and Sukarno, who did the same in Indonesia despite resistance from the Dutch.

World War II was the catalyst for the creation of independent nations throughout the region in the late 1940s and 1950s. But events and leaders of the first half of the twentieth century had provided the foundation for independence.

Mohandas Gandhi

INDIAN HOME RULE

Mohandas Gandhi, the outstanding figure in modern Indian history, was born in 1869 in a village north of Bombay on the Arabian Sea. His father was an important government official who presided over an extended family with strict Hindu religious practices. Gandhi studied law in England and, after failing to establish a legal practice in Bombay, in 1893 moved to South Africa to serve the area's large Indian population.

Here, he became incensed over the many discriminatory laws against Indians, many of whom were exploited indentured servants employed by whites. During his struggle to improve the lot of South Africa's Indian population, Gandhi developed his theory of Satyagraha, usually translated into English as "soul force" (*Satya* means "spiritual truth," *agraha* means "insistence upon"). Based on his own Hindu beliefs and some insights from Christianity, Satyagraha sought social justice not through violence or force, but through love, a willingness to suffer, and conversion of the oppressor. Central to his strategy was massive nonviolent resistance: his followers would disobey unjust laws and accept the consequences — even beatings and imprisonment — without violence.

Gandhi first wrote down his theories of Satyagraha in 1908, after meeting a group of Indian nationalists in England who proposed to use force to oust the British. On his return voyage he composed a pamphlet, *Hind Swaraj*, or *Indian Home Rule*, in which he explained his theories of nonresistance and expressed his reservations about the "benefits" of modern civilization. Written in the form of a dialogue between a "reader" and an "editor" (Gandhi), *Indian Home Rule* was printed in hundreds of editions and still serves as the best summary of Gandhi's philosophy.

Questions for Analysis

1. What does Gandhi see as the major deficiency of modern civilization? What have human beings lost through the influence of civilization? How has civilization affected women?
2. Why might Gandhi's attack on civilization have gained him support among the Indian masses?
3. How does Gandhi's view of the West compare with the comments on Western civilization in *The Way of Subjects* (see Chapter 11)?
4. On what basis does Gandhi hope that Hindus and Muslims will be able to live in peace in India?
5. What, according to Gandhi, has been India's role in preserving true civilization?
6. What leads Gandhi to his conviction that love is stronger than force?
7. Why does he reject the assertion that passive resistance is a weapon only for the weak?

CHAPTER VI

Civilization

Reader: Now you will have to explain what you mean by civilization. . . .

Editor: Let us first consider what state of things is described by the word "civilization." Its true test lies in the fact that people living in it make bodily welfare the object of life. We will take some examples: The people of Europe today live in better-built houses than they did a hundred years ago. This is considered an emblem of civilization, and this is also a matter to promote bodily happiness. Formerly, they wore skins, and used as their weapons spears. Now, they wear long trousers, and for embellishing their bodies they wear a variety of clothing, and, instead of spears, they carry with them revolvers containing five or more chambers. If people of a certain country, who have hitherto not been in the habit of wearing much clothing, boots, etc., adopt European clothing, they are supposed to have become civilized out of savagery. Formerly, in Europe, people plowed their lands mainly by manual labor. Now, one man can plow a vast tract by means of steam-engines, and can thus amass great wealth. This is called a sign of civilization. Formerly, the fewest men wrote books, that were most valuable. Now, anybody writes and prints anything he likes and poisons people's minds. Formerly, men traveled in wagons; now they fly through the air, in trains at the rate of four hundred and more miles per day. This is considered the height of civilization. It has been stated that, as men progress, they shall be able to travel in airships and reach any part of the world in a few hours. Men will not need the use of their hands and feet. They will press a button, and they will have their clothing by their side. They will press another button, and they will have their newspaper. A third, and a motor-car will be in waiting for them. They will have a variety of delicately dished up food. Everything will be done by machinery. Formerly, when people wanted to fight with one another, they measured between them their bodily strength; now it is possible to take away thousands of lives by one man working behind a gun from a hill. This is civilization. Formerly, men worked in the open air only so much as they liked. Now, thousands of workmen meet together and for the sake of maintenance work in factories or mines. Their condition is worse than that of beasts. They are obliged to work, at the risk of their lives, at most dangerous occupations, for the sake of millionaires. Formerly, men were made slaves under physical compulsion, now they are enslaved by temptation of money and of the luxuries that money can buy. There are now diseases of which people never dreamed before, and an army of doctors is engaged in finding out their cures, and so hospitals have increased. This is a test of civilization. Formerly, special messengers were required and much expense was incurred in order to send letters; today, anyone can abuse his fellow by means of a letter for one penny. True, at the same cost, one can send one's thanks also. Formerly, people had two or three meals consisting of homemade bread and vegetables; now, they require something to eat every two hours, so that they have hardly leisure for anything else. What more need I say? All this you can ascertain from several authoritative books. These are all true tests of civilization. And, if any one speaks to the contrary, know that he is ignorant. This civilization takes note neither of morality nor of religion. . . .

This civilization is irreligion, and it has taken such a hold on the people in Europe that those who are in it appear to be half mad. They lack real physical strength or courage. They keep up their energy by intoxication. They can hardly be happy in solitude. Women, who should be the queens of households, wander in the streets, or they slave away in factories. For the sake of a pittance, half a million women in England alone are laboring under trying circumstances in factories or similar institutions. This awful fact is one of the causes of the daily growing suffragette movement.

This civilization is such that one has only to be patient and it will be self-destroyed.

CHAPTER X

The Condition of India (Continued) The Hindus and the Mahomedans

Reader: But I am impatient to hear your answer to my question. Has the introduction of Mahomedanism not unmade the nation?

Editor: India cannot cease to be one nation because people belonging to different religions live in it. The introduction of foreigners does not necessarily destroy the nation, they merge in it. A country is one nation only when such a condition obtains in it. That country must have a faculty for assimilation. India has ever been such a country. In reality, there are as many religions as there are individuals, but those who are conscious of the spirit of nationality do not interfere with one another's religion. If they do, they are not fit to be considered a nation. If the Hindus believe that India should be peopled only by Hindus, they are living in dreamland. The Hindus, the Mahomedans, the Parsees[1] and the Christians who have made India their country are fellow-countrymen, and they will have to live in unity if only for their own interest. In no part of the world are one nationality and one religion synonymous terms; nor has it ever been so in India.

Reader: But what about the inborn enmity between Hindus and Mahomedans?

Editor: That phrase has been invented by our mutual enemy.[2] When the Hindus and Mahomedans fought against one another, they certainly spoke in that strain. They have long since ceased to fight. How, then, can there be any inborn enmity? Pray remember this too, that we did not cease to fight only after British occupation. The Hindus flourished under Muslim sovereigns and Muslims under the Hindu. Each party recognized that mutual fighting was suicidal, and that neither party would abandon its religion by force of arms. Both parties, therefore, decided to live in peace. With the English advent the quarrels recommenced. . . .

Hindus and Mahomedans own the same ancestors, and the same blood runs through their veins. Do people become enemies because they change their religion? Is the God of the Mahomedan different from the God of the Hindu? Religions are different roads converging to the same point. What does it matter that we take different roads, so long as we reach the same goal? Wherein is the cause for quarreling?

CHAPTER XIII

What Is True Civilization?

Reader: You have denounced railways, lawyers and doctors. I can see that you will discard all machinery. What, then, is civilization?

Editor: The answer to that question is not difficult. I believe that the civilization India has evolved is not to be beaten in the world. Nothing can equal the seeds sown by our ancestors. Rome went, Greece shared the same fate, the might of the Pharaohs was broken, Japan has become westernized, of China nothing can be said, but India is still, somehow or other, sound at the foundation. The people of Europe learn their lessons from the writings of the men of Greece or Rome, which exist no longer in their former glory. In trying to learn from them, the Europeans imagine that they will avoid the mistakes of Greece and Rome. Such is their pitiable condition. In the midst of all this, India remains immovable, and that is her glory. It is a charge against India that her people are so uncivilized, ignorant and stolid, that it is not possible to induce them to adopt any changes. It is a charge really against our merit. What we have tested and found true on the anvil of experience, we dare not change. Many thrust their advice upon India, and she remains steady. This is her beauty; it is the sheet-anchor of our hope.

Civilization is that mode of conduct which points out to man the path of duty. Performance of duty and observance of

---

1. Members of a religious sect in India descended from Persian refugees of the seventh and eighth centuries.

2. The British.

morality are convertible terms. To observe morality is to attain mastery over our mind and our passions. So doing, we know ourselves. The Gujarati[3] equivalent for civilization means "good conduct."

If this definition be correct, then India, as so many writers have shown, has nothing to learn from anybody else, and this is as it should be.

CHAPTER XVII

Passive Resistance

Reader: Is there any historical evidence as to the success of what you have called soul-force or truth-force? No instance seems to have happened of any nation having risen through soul-force. I still think that the evil-doers will not cease doing evil without physical punishment.

Editor: . . . The force of love is the same as the force of the soul or truth. We have evidence of its working at every step. The universe would disappear without the existence of that force. But you ask for historical evidence. It is, therefore, necessary to know what history means. . . .

The fact that there are so many men still alive in the world shows that it is based not on the force of arms but on the force of truth or love. Therefore the greatest and most unimpeachable evidence of the success of this force is to be found in the fact that, in spite of the wars of the world, it still lives on.

Thousands, indeed, tens of thousands, depend for their existence on a very active working of this force. Little quarrels of millions of families in their daily lives disappear before the exercise of this force. Hundreds of nations live in peace. History

does not and cannot take note of this fact. History is really a record of every interruption of the even working of the force of love or of the soul. . . . Soul-force, being natural, is not noted in history.

Reader: According to what you say, it is plain that instances of the kind of passive resistance are not to be found in history. It is necessary to understand this passive resistance more fully. It will be better, therefore, if you enlarge upon it.

Editor: Passive resistance is a method of securing rights by personal suffering; it is the reverse of resistance by arms. When I refuse to do a thing that is repugnant to my conscience, I use soul-force. For instance, the government of the day has passed a law which is applicable to me: I do not like it, if, by using violence, I force the government to repeal the law, I am employing what may be termed body-force. If I do not obey the law and accept the penalty for its breach, I use soul-force. It involves sacrifice of self.

Everybody admits that sacrifice of self is infinitely superior to sacrifice of others. Moreover, if this kind of force is used in a cause that is unjust only the person using it suffers. He does not make others suffer for his mistakes. Men have before now done many things which were subsequently found to have been wrong. No man can claim to be absolutely in the right, or that a particular thing is wrong, because he thinks so, but it is wrong for him so long as that is his deliberate judgment. It is, therefore, meet that he should not do that which he knows to be wrong, and suffer the consequence whatever it may be. This is the key to the use of soul-force. . . .

Reader: From what you say, I de-

---

3. An Indian dialect spoken in the northwest region of Gujarat.

duce that passive resistance is a splendid weapon of the weak but that, when they are strong, they may take up arms.

Editor: This is gross ignorance. Passive resistance, that is, soul-force, is matchless. It is superior to the force of arms. How, then, can it be considered only a weapon of the weak? Physical-force men are strangers to the courage that is requisite in a passive resister. Do you believe that a coward can ever disobey a law that he dislikes? Extremists are considered to be advocates of brute-force. Why do they, then, talk about obeying laws? I do not blame them. They can say nothing else. When they succeed in driving out the English, and they themselves become governors, they will want you and me to obey their laws. And that is a fitting thing for their constitution. But a passive resister will say he will not obey a law that is against his conscience, even though he may be blown to pieces at the mouth of a cannon.

What do you think? Wherein is courage required — in blowing others to pieces from behind a cannon or with a smiling face to approach a cannon and to be blown to pieces? Who is the true warrior — he who keeps death always as a bosom-friend or he who controls the death of others? Believe me that a man devoid of courage and manhood can never be a passive register.

This, however, I will admit: that even a man, weak in body, is capable of offering this resistance. One man can offer it just as well as millions. Both men and women can indulge in it. It does not require the training of an army; it needs no Jiu-jitsu. Control over the mind is alone necessary, and, when that is attained, man is free like the king of the forest, and his very glance withers the enemy.

Passive resistance is an all-sided sword; it can be used anyhow; it blesses him who uses it and him against whom it is used. Without drawing a drop of blood, it produces far-reaching results.

Jawaharlal Nehru

TOWARD FREEDOM

During his first nationwide campaign of nonresistance in 1921, Gandhi touched the life of a young lawyer, Jawaharlal Nehru, who in 1947 became independent India's first prime minister. Coming from a prestigious upper-class family, Nehru was educated in British schools and, like Gandhi, received legal training in London. On his return to India in 1912, he joined the Congress party, the largely middle-class, moderate organization that since 1885 had been working toward increased Indian participation in government and, ultimately, independence (see Chapter 9). After meeting Gandhi, Nehru was inspired to devote himself to the causes of Indian independence and improving the lives of India's poor. After a trip to Europe, in which he developed admiration for socialism and some features of the new Soviet regime, Nehru returned to the political struggle and, with Gandhi's support, was elected president of Congress in 1930.

On January 26, 1930, Congress voted a resolution in favor of complete independence from Britain and made plans for a second campaign of nonresistance. This time the target was the hated salt tax, which Gandhi proposed to avoid by encouraging Indians to make their own salt. He dramatized his campaign by leading 50,000 followers to the sea to do this. Nehru describes the events of 1930 and reflects on Gandhi's power in the following excerpts from his 1941 autobiography.

Questions for Analysis

1. Why did Gandhi and the other Indian leaders believe that 1930 was a good time for another campaign of nonresistance?
2. What do the events of the salt boycott tell us about Gandhi's influence on the Indian people?
3. What does Nehru's description of events reveal about women's role in the nonresistance campaign?
4. Nehru was a secular-minded socialist and a strong supporter of industrialization. Nonetheless, he deeply admired Gandhi and willingly followed him. How does he explain Gandhi's hold on him and others?

*I*ndependence Day came, January 26, 1930, and it revealed to us, as in a flash, the earnest and enthusiastic mood of the country. There was something vastly impressive about the great gatherings everywhere, peacefully and solemnly taking the pledge of independence without any speeches or exhortation. This celebration gave the necessary impetus to Gandhiji,[1] and he felt, with his sure touch on the pulse of the people, that the time was ripe for action. Events followed then in quick succession, like a drama working up to its climax.

As civil disobedience approached and electrified the atmosphere, our thoughts went back to the movement of 1921–22 and the manner of its sudden suspension after Chauri Chaura.[2] The country was more disciplined now, and there was a clearer appreciation of the nature of the struggle. The technique was understood to some extent, but more important still from Gandhiji's point of view, it was fully realized by everyone that he was terribly in earnest about nonviolence. . . . The great question that hung in the air now was — how? How were we to begin? What form of civil disobedience should we take up that would be effective, suited to the circumstances, and popular with the masses? And then the Mahatma[3] gave the hint.

Salt suddenly became a mysterious word, a word of power. The salt tax was to be attacked, the salt laws were to be broken. We were bewildered and could not quite fit in a national struggle with common salt. . . .

We had no time to argue, for events

---

1. The *ji* added as a suffix to Indian names is an expression of respect for the person's accomplishments.

2. Gandhi called off his first nationwide campaign of nonresistance when twenty-two policemen were killed and rioting took place in Chauri Chaura.

3. Gandhi.

were on the move. They were moving politically before our eyes from day to day in India; and, hardly realized by us at the time, they were moving fast in the world and holding it in the grip of a terrible depression. Prices were falling, and the city dwellers welcomed this as a sign of the plenty to come, but the farmer and the tenant saw the prospect with alarm.

Then came Gandhiji's correspondence with the Viceroy and the beginning of the Salt March. . . . As people followed the fortunes of this marching column of pilgrims from day to day, the temperature of the country went up. A meeting of the All-India Congress Committee was held at Ahmedabad to make final arrangements for the struggle that was now almost upon us. . . .

And so, having made our final preparations, we bade good-by to our comrades of the All-India Congress Committee at Ahmedabad, for none knew when or how we would meet again, or whether we would meet at all. We hastened back to our posts to give the finishing touches to our local arrangements, in accordance with the new directions of the All-India Congress Committee, and . . . to pack up our toothbrushes for the journey to prison.

April came, and Gandhiji drew near to the sea, and we waited for the word to begin civil disobedience by an attack on the salt laws. For months past we had been drilling our volunteers, and Kamala and Krishna (my wife and sister) had both joined them and donned male attire for the purpose. The volunteers had, of course, no arms or even sticks. The object of training them was to make them more efficient in their work and capable of dealing with large crowds. The 6th of April

was the first day of the National Week, which is celebrated annually in memory of the happenings in 1919[4]. . . . On that day Gandhiji began the breach of the salt laws at Dandi beach, and three or four days later permission was given to all Congress organizations to do likewise and begin civil disobedience in their own areas.

It seemed as though a spring had been suddenly released; all over the country, in town and village, salt manufacture was the topic of the day, and many curious expedients were adopted to produce salt. We knew precious little about it, and so we read it up where we could and issued leaflets giving directions; we collected pots and pans and ultimately succeeded in producing some unwholesome stuff, which we waved about in triumph and often auctioned for fancy prices. It was really immaterial whether the stuff was good or bad; the main thing was to commit a breach of the obnoxious salt law, and we were successful in that, even though the quality of our salt was poor. As we saw the abounding enthusiasm of the people and the way salt-making was spreading like a prairie fire, we felt a little abashed and ashamed for having questioned the efficacy of this method when it was first proposed by Gandhiji. And we marveled at the amazing knack of the man to impress the multitude and make it act in an organized way. . . .

Those were days of stirring news — processions and lathee charges[5] and firing, frequent *hartals*[6] to celebrate noted arrests, and special observances. . . . For the time being the boycott of foreign cloth and all British goods was almost complete. When I heard that my aged mother and, of course, my sisters used to stand

---

4. The reference is to the Amritsar Massacre.
5. A lathee or lathi, was a bamboo stick often filled with lead and used as a weapon, especially by police attempting to quell riots.
6. Work stoppages and business closings.

under the hot summer sun picketing before foreign cloth shops, I was greatly moved. Kamala did so also, but she did something more. She threw herself into the movement in Allahabad city and district with an energy and determination which amazed me, who thought I had known her so well for so many years. She forgot her ill-health and rushed about the whole day in the sun, and showed remarkable powers of organization. . . .

Many strange things happened in those days, but undoubtedly the most striking was the part of the women in the national struggle. They came out in large numbers from the seclusion of their homes and, though unused to public activity, threw themselves into the heart of the struggle. The picketing of foreign cloth and liquor shops they made their preserve. Enormous processions consisting of women alone were taken out in all the cities; and, generally, the attitude of the women was more unyielding than that of the men. Often they became Congress "dictators" in provinces and in local areas.

The breach of the Salt Act soon became just one activity, and civil resistance spread to other fields. This was facilitated by the promulgation of various ordinances by the Viceroy prohibiting a number of activities. As these ordinances and prohibitions grew, the opportunities for breaking them also grew, and civil resistance took the form of doing the very thing that the ordinance was intended to stop. The initiative definitely remained with the Congress and the people; and, as each ordinance law failed to control the situation from the point of view of government, fresh ordinances were issued by the Viceroy.

Gandhiji had been arrested on May 5. After his arrest big raids on the salt pans and depots were organized on the west coast. There were very painful incidents of police brutality during these raids.

Bombay then occupied the center of the picture with its tremendous *hartals* and processions and lathee charges. Several emergency hospitals grew up to treat the victims of these lathee charges. Much that was remarkable happened in Bombay, and, being a great city, it had the advantage of publicity. Occurrences of equal importance in small towns and the rural areas received no publicity.

. . .

Whether Gandhiji is a democrat or not, he does represent the peasant masses of India; he is the quintessence of the conscious and subconscious will of those millions. It is perhaps something more than representation; for he is the idealized personification of those vast millions. Of course, he is not the average peasant. A man of the keenest intellect, of fine feeling and good taste, wide vision; very human, and yet essentially the ascetic who has suppressed his passions and emotions, sublimated them and directed them in spiritual channels; a tremendous personality, drawing people to himself like a magnet, and calling out fierce loyalties and attachments — all this so utterly unlike and beyond a peasant. And yet withal he is the greatest peasant, with a peasant's outlook on affairs, and with a peasant's blindness to some aspects of life. But India is peasant India, and so he knows his India well, reacts to her slightest tremors, gauges a situation accurately and almost instinctively, and has a knack of acting at the psychological moment.

What a problem and a puzzle he has been not only to the British Government but to his own people and his closest associates! Perhaps in every other country he would be out of place today, but India still seems to understand, or at least appreciate, the prophetic-religious type of man, talking of sin and salvation and nonviolence. Indian mythology is full of stories of great ascetics, who, by the rigor of their sacrifices and self-imposed penance, built up a "mountain of merit" which threatened the dominion of some of the lesser gods and upset the established order. . . .

India, even urban India, even the new industrial India, had the impress of the peasant upon her; and it was natural enough for her to make this son of hers, so like her and yet so unlike, an idol and a beloved leader. He revived ancient and half-forgotten memories, and gave her glimpses of her own soul. Crushed in the dark misery of the present, she had tried to find relief in helpless muttering and in vague dreams of the past and the future, but he came and gave hope to her mind and strength to her much-battered body, and the future became an alluring vision. Two-faced like Janus,[7] she looked both backward into the past and forward into the future, and tried to combine the two.

Many of us had cut adrift from this peasant outlook, and the old ways of thought and custom and religion had become alien to us. We called ourselves moderns and thought in terms of "progress," and industrialization and a higher standard of living and collectivization. We considered the peasant's viewpoint reactionary; and some, a growing number, looked with favor toward socialism and communism. How came we to associate ourselves with Gandhiji politically, and to become, in many instances, his devoted followers? The question is hard to answer, and to one who does not know Gandhiji, no answer is likely to satisfy. Personality is an indefinable thing, a strange force that has power over the souls of men, and

he possesses this in ample measure, and to all who come to him he often appears in a different aspect. He attracted people, but it was ultimately intellectual conviction that brought them to him and kept them there. They did not agree with his philosophy of life, or even with many of his ideals. Often they did not understand him. But the action that he proposed was something tangible which could be understood and appreciated intellectually. . . .

All this shows that we were by no means clear or certain in our minds. Always we had the feeling that, while we might be more logical, Gandhiji knew India far better than we did, and a man who could command such tremendous devotion and loyalty must have something in him that corresponded to the needs and aspirations of the masses. . . .

How he disciplined our lazy and demoralized people and made them work — not by force or any material inducement, but by a gentle look and a soft word and, above all, by personal example! In the early days of *Satyagraha* in India, as long ago as 1919, I remember how Umar Sobani of Bombay called him the "beloved slave-driver." Much had happened in the dozen years since then. Umar had not lived to see these changes, but we who had been more fortunate looked back from those early months of 1931 with joy and elation. Nineteen-thirty had, indeed, been a wonder year for us, and Gandhiji seemed to have changed the face of our country with his magic touch. No one was foolish enough to think that we had triumphed finally over the British Government. Our feeling of elation had little to do with the Government. We were proud of our people, of our womenfolk, of our youth, of our children for the part they

---

7. In Roman mythology, the guardian of portals and the patron of beginnings and ends; Janus was represented with two faces, one in the front and one behind.

had played in the movement. It was a spiritual gain, valuable at any time and to any people, but doubly so to us, a subject and downtrodden people. And we were anxious that nothing should happen to take this away from us.

■ Sukarno

INDONESIA ACCUSES

Extreme economic exploitation marked Dutch control of Indonesia in the nineteenth century, when administrators enforced what was known as the Culture System, which required farmers, especially in Java, to reduce the cultivation of rice and concentrate on crops such as coffee, tea, spices, and cotton that the Dutch could sell on the international market. The Dutch made enormous profits, while low wages and food shortages became the lot of Indonesians.

In 1900 the Dutch government adopted a new Ethical Policy to compensate for decades of oppression and neglect by promoting improvements in education and welfare. An early graduate of one of the new schools established by the Dutch was Sukarno (1901–1970), the leader of Indonesia's struggle for independence and the first president of the Republic of Indonesia. The son of a schoolteacher, Sukarno received an engineering degree in 1925 but soon became involved in nationalist politics, founding in 1927 the *Partai Nasional Indonesia* (Indonesian Nationalist Association), usually known as the PNI, an organization pledged to noncooperation with the colonial regime.

In 1930 the Dutch moved to crush the PNI by arresting and trying Sukarno and other leaders. During his trial, Sukarno delivered a long speech in his defense (December 1, 1930). Known as "Indonesia Accuses," it is a classic statement of Indonesian grievances and hopes. It did not, however, prevent his conviction, which came only a few days later.

Questions
for Analysis

1. How does Sukarno define imperialism?
2. What aspects of imperialism does he most deeply oppose?
3. What is Sukarno's strategy for deepening the Indonesian nationalist consciousness?
4. According to Sukarno, how would Indonesia have developed without Western interference?

And the word "Imperialism"? This too designates a concept. . . . It designates a tendency, a striving, to dominate or influence the affairs of another nation, of another country. It designates a system of economic control or domination of another nation or people. It is a social phenomenon that owes its origin to an economic necessity in the development of the affairs of a country or a nation. For as long as there has been a "social system," a "national economy," has the world beheld imperialism. We find it in the endeavor of the Roman Eagle to subjugate all countries on the Mediterranean and even those beyond its shores. We find it in the endeavor of the Spanish nation to conquer the Netherlands to enable it to vanquish England.

We find it in the endeavor of the Empire of Çrivijaya[1] to bring under its rule the peninsula of Malacca as well as the Malay Realm, the endeavor to dominate the economy of Cambodia and Champa. We find it in the endeavor of the Empire of Majapahit[2] to control and influence all the islands of Indonesia, from Bali to Borneo, from Sumatra to the Moluccas. We find it again in the endeavor of the Japanese Empire to occupy the peninsula of Korea, to obtain influence in Manchuria, to dominate the Pacific Islands. We find imperialism again at all times and in all periods of established "social systems," we find it with all nations whose economy of necessity propels them to imperialism. Imperialism is not a quality peculiar to the white races; it occurs among the yellow, the black, and among the brown races, as exemplified at the time of Çrivijaya and at the time of Majapahit. Imperialism is an "economically determined necessity."

. . . And, as we have already said, imperialism is not only a system or a tendency to subjugate other countries and peoples, but it can also find expression in the endeavor to dominate the economy of another country and people. It need not

necessarily be carried out by means of the sword, the machine gun, the cannon or the "dreadnought"; . . . it can also take place by means of a peaceful penetration.

Which roads must we follow? The Partai Nasional Indonesia answers to this question with full conviction: those roads that lead to Free Indonesia![3] Behind Free Indonesia the P.N.I. sees the magnificence of the motherland of prosperity and the motherland of grandeur, behind Free Indonesia the P.N.I. sees the glowing brilliance of the future!

This is the essence of the conviction of the P.N.I. as it was written in the declaration of principle: "The Partai Nasional Indonesia has the conviction that the most important precondition for the reconstruction of Indonesian Society is National Freedom, and therefore the endeavor of the whole of the Indonesian nation must be directed first of all to National Freedom."

Deviating from the point of view of many other political parties which teach: "Reconstruct your economy, then freedom will come automatically"; deviating from the point of view of many other political parties which are of the opinion that freedom is the fruit of the reconstruction of the economy, the P.N.I. says: "Be zealous in the cause of national freedom, for only through national freedom can the Indonesian people bring about complete national reconstruction"; thus it says that complete national reconstruction is possible only after the return of national independence. . . .

Almost every important measure in a colonial country is taken for the benefit of imperialism. This is why the measures taken by a country for its economy bear

---

1. Or Sri Vijaya, one of the first kingdoms of Island Southeast Asia, centered on Sumatra; it controlled areas mentioned by Sukarno until its decline in the fourteenth century.

2. Succeeded Sri Vijaya as the dominant power in the region during the fourteenth and fifteenth centuries; centered on Java.

3. The motto of the P.N.I.

partially or completely the imprint of imperialism as long as it is still a colony, indeed as long as a country is a "protectorate" or a "mandated territory," in short, as long as a country cannot regulate its national economy completely on its own. That is to say: As long as a nation does not wield political power in its own country, part of its potential, economic, social or political, will be used for interests which are not *its* interests, but contrary to them. *It is bound hands and feet, prevented from combating the imperialism by which it is harmed;* it is not capable of preventing the use of its potential for the interests of others, not capable of applying its potential to its own economic, social, and political life. *In short, it is not capable of exerting itself in the struggle against, and the annihilating of, imperialism; it is not capable of helping itself.*

A colonial nation is a nation that cannot be itself, a nation that in almost all its branches, in all of its life, bears the mark of imperialism, a mark it owes to the great influence of imperialism. There is no community of interests between the subject and the object of imperialism. Between the two there is only a contrast of interests and a conflict of needs. All interests of imperialism, social, economic, political, or cultural, are opposed to the interests of the Indonesian people. The imperialists desire the continuation of colonization, the Indonesians desire its abolition. The regulations that came into being under the influence of imperialism are therefore contrary to the interests of the Indonesian people.

And yet it accepts the regulations without ado, you ask? Oh certainly, the people accept the regulations. The people respect those regulations. But they accept them and they respect them because they are forced to do so! . . .

What are the roads to promote Indonesian nationalism? Those roads are of three kinds:

first: we point out to the people that they have had a great past;

second: we reinforce the consciousness of the people that the present is dark;

third: we show the people the pure and brightly-shining light of the future and the roads which lead to this future so full of promises.

In other words, the P.N.I. awakens and reinforces the people's consciousness of its "grandiose past," its "dark present" and the promises of a shining, beckoning future. . . .

Our grandiose past! Oh, much honored judges, what Indonesian does not feel his heart shrink with sorrow when he hears the stories about the beautiful past, who among us does not regret the disappearance of that departed glory! What Indonesian does not feel his national heart beat with joy when he hears about the greatness of the empires of Melayu[4] and Çrivijaya . . . Mataram,[5] . . . and Majapahit and Pajajaran[6]. . . . What Indonesian does not feel his heart shrink with sorrow when he realizes that his flag was formerly seen even as far away as Madagascar, Persia and China. But on the other hand, in whom is hope not rekindled that a nation with such a grandiose past must *surely* have sufficient natural aptitude to have a beautiful future, must *surely* have in itself the possibilities to attain again that level of greatness in the future? Who of us is not imbued by new strength when he reads the history of those past times? And thus among the people, too, again con-

---

4. Or Malayu, an east Sumatran state, that rose at the expense of Sri Vijaya in the thirteenth century.

5. A Javanese kingdom that succumbed to the Dutch in the eighteenth century.

6. A Javanese kingdom at its height in the sixteenth and seventeenth centuries.

scious of their great past, national feeling is revived, and the fire of hope blazes in their hearts! Through this the people regain a new soul and new strength.

To be sure, that past is a feudal past, the present is a modern present. We do not wish to revive that feudal past; we are not at all in favor of a new feudal period. We know the bad aspects of the feudal system for the people. We only point out to the people that the feudalism of the past was a living, a healthy and not a sickly feudalism, a feudalism full of possibilities for development, that, had it not been disturbed by, for instance, foreign imperialism, would surely have achieved its evolution, *would in the end surely have brought forth an equally healthy modern society.*

Africa: Colonialism and the Origins of Black Nationalism

Compared with India's experience, the unfolding of African colonialism resembles a film shown at high speed. The Europeans arrived in force at the end of the nineteenth century and, after squabbling among themselves over who controlled what, gave serious thought to what they wanted to do with their new acquisitions and how they wanted to govern them. Not long after they resolved these issues, World War II was fought, India gained independence, and nationalist movements swept through Africa. In 1957 the Gold Coast, a British colony, became the independent nation of Ghana, sparking a chain of events that in the next decade and a half resulted in the establishment of dozens of new independent states.

European colonialism in Africa was a fleeting episode that in many ways only touched the surface of society, but it did bring enough changes to complicate the efforts of the new African nations to form stable and prosperous states.

Frederick Lugard

THE DUAL MANDATE IN BRITISH TROPICAL AFRICA

Lord Frederick Lugard (1858–1945) served in the Indian army before arriving in Africa in 1888. In the following two decades, he played a central role in establishing British control in the colonies of Nyasaland, Uganda, and Nigeria. He served in several important administrative posts, including high commissioner of northern Nigeria and governor general of a united Nigeria from 1914 to 1919.

After crushing native opposition to British rule in northern Nigeria between 1900 and 1903, Lugard faced the task of establishing an administration in a vast region with few European settlers and with only limited funds. His solution was to leave intact traditional native authorities and use their elaborate hierarchy of officials to carry out day-to-day affairs of government under the direction of the British. Many British administrators adopted Lugard's system of "indirect rule" in Africa, thus standing in contrast to the French system of direct rule through appointed officials, both European and African. The following excerpt is drawn from Lugard's book, *The Dual Mandate in British Tropical Africa*, published in 1926, in which he describes the principles of "indirect rule."

Questions for Analysis

1. What types of government activities are placed in the hands of native administrators?
2. Note how the construction of highways, schools, and hospitals is to be financed. What may this plan suggest about the British commitment to improving the lives of their African subjects?
3. Lugard outlines six areas in which the power of African authorities is limited. What seems to have been the purposes of these limitations?
4. What role, according to Lugard, is the system of indirect rule to play in the historical development of the African people?
5. What overriding assumptions affect Lugard's thinking about African affairs? How close is it to Kipling's notion of "The White Man's Burden" (see Chapter 8)?
6. How might the restrictions on the political responsibilities of native chiefs have presented problems for the African states after independence?

*T*he object in view is to make each "Emir"[1] or paramount chief, assisted by his judicial Council, an effective ruler over his own people. He presides over a "Native Administration" organized throughout as a unit of local government. The area over which he exercizes jurisdiction is divided into districts under the control of "Headmen," who collect the taxes in the name of the ruler, and pay them into the "Native Treasury," conducted by a native treasurer and staff under the supervision of the chief at his capital. Here, too, is the prison for native court prisoners, and probably the school.[2] . . . Large cities are divided into wards for purposes of control and taxation. . . .

The tax — which supersedes all former "tribute," irregular imposts, and forced labor — is, in a sense, the basis of the whole system, since it supplies the means to pay the Emir and all his officials. The district and village heads are effectively supervised and assisted in its assessment by the British staff. The native treasury retains the proportion assigned to it (in advanced communities a half), and pays the remainder into Colonial Revenue.

The surplus is devoted to the construction and maintenance of dispensaries,

---

1. Arabic for leader or chief; many of the tribes under Lugard's jurisdiction were Muslim.

2. Lugard and the British assumed erro-

neously that such a scheme would suit all African tribes, but many were ruled democratically and had no "paramount chief."

leper settlements, schools, roads, court-houses, and other buildings. Such works may be carried out wholly or in part by a Government department, if the native administration requires technical assistance, the cost being borne by the native treasury.

The native treasurer keeps all accounts of receipts and expenditure, and the Emir, with the assistance of the Resident, annually prepares a budget, which is formally approved by the Lieut.-Governor.

Subject, therefore, to the limitations which I shall presently discuss, the native authority is thus *de facto* and *de jure* ruler over his own people. He appoints and dismisses his subordinate chiefs and officials. He exercises the power of allocation of lands, and with the aid of the native courts, of adjudication in land disputes and expropriation for offenses against the community; these are the essential functions upon which, in the opinion of the West African Lands Committee, the prestige of the native authority depends. The lawful orders which he may give are carefully defined by ordinance, and in the last resort are enforced by Government. . . .

The limitations to independence which are frankly inherent in this conception of native rule — not as temporary restraints to be removed as soon as may be, but as powers which rightly belong to the controlling Power as trustee for the welfare of the masses, and as being responsible for the defense of the country and the cost of its central administration — are such as do not involve interference with the authority of the chiefs or the social organization of the people. They have been accepted by the Fulani[3] Emirs as natural and proper

to the controlling power, and their reservation in the hands of the Governor has never interfered with the loyalty of the ruling chiefs, or, so far as I am aware, been resented by them. The limitations are as follows —

1. Native rulers are not permitted to raise and control armed forces, or to grant permission to carry arms. To this in principle Great Britain stands pledged under the Brussels Act.[4] The evils which result in Africa from an armed population were evident in Uganda before it fell under British control, and are very evident in Abyssinia[5] today. No one with experience will deny the necessity of maintaining the strictest military discipline over armed forces or police in Africa if misuse of power is to be avoided, and they are not to become a menace and a terror to the native population and a danger in case of religious excitement — a discipline which an African ruler is incapable of appreciating or applying. For this reason native levies should never be employed in substitution for or in aid of troops.

2. The sole right to impose taxation in any form is reserved to the Suzerain[6] power. This fulfils the bilateral understanding that the peasantry — provided they pay the authorized tax (the adjustment of which to all classes of the population is a responsibility which rests with the Central Government) — should be free of all other exactions whatsoever (including unpaid labor), while a sufficient proportion of the tax is assigned to the native treasuries to meet the expenditure of the native administration. . . .

3. The right to legislate is reserved.

---

3. A mostly Muslim people of northwest and central Africa.

4. The Brussels Act (1892), accepted by the European powers, prohibited the export of firearms and certain alcoholic beverages to Africa.

5. Lugard may be referring to the chronic disorder that plagued Abyssinia (Ethiopia) at the time he wrote the book or to the fact that, of all the areas of Africa, only here was slave trading still practiced.

6. The sovereign power, that is, the British.

That this should remain in the hands of the Central Government — itself limited by the control of the Colonial Office, as I have described — cannot be questioned. The native authority, however, exercises very considerable power in this regard. A native ruler, and the native courts, are empowered to enforce native law and custom, provided it is not repugnant to humanity, or in opposition to any ordinance. . . .

4. The right to appropriate land on equitable terms of public purposes and for commercial requirements is vested in the Governor. . . .

5. In order to maintain intact the control of the Central Government over all aliens, and to avoid friction and difficulties, it has been the recognized rule that the employees of the native administration should consist entirely of natives subject to the native authority. . . .

6. Finally, in the interests of good government, the right of confirming or otherwise the choice of the people of the successor to a chiefship, and of deposing any ruler for misrule or other adequate cause, is reserved to the Governor.

. . .

There are some who consider that however desirable it may be to rule through the native chiefs of advanced communities, such a policy is misplaced, if not impossible, among the backward tribes. . . . To attempt to adapt such methods — however suitable to the Muslim communities — to the conditions of primitive tribes, would be to foist upon them a system foreign to their conceptions. . . .

Let us realize that the advanced communities form a very minute proportion of the population of British Tropical Africa. The vast majority are in the primi-

tive or early tribal stages of development. To abandon the policy of ruling them through their own chiefs, and to substitute the direct rule of the British officer, is to forgo the high ideal of leading the backward races, by their own efforts, in their own way, to raise themselves to a higher plane of social organization, and tends to perpetuate and stereotype existing conditions.

We must realize also two other important facts. First, that the British staff, exercising direct rule, cannot be otherwise than very small in comparison to the area and population of which they are in charge. . . .

The changed conditions of African life is the second important fact for consideration. The advent of Europeans cannot fail to have a disintegrating effect on tribal authority and institutions, and on the conditions of native life. . . . And with the rapid changes the native character has deteriorated. Stealing and burglary are rife, and the old village discipline and respect for chiefs has gone. In the West we find the mine manager with his wife and flower-garden established in a district which only a few years ago was the inaccessible fastness of a cannibal tribe. Ladies in mission schools teach nude savage children the elements of geography and arithmetic. The smattering of knowledge and caricature of the white man's ways acquired by these children react on their village, and upset tribal customs and authority. A few years ago one would find communities in which no individual had ever been twenty miles from his home. Today the young men migrate in hundreds to offer their labor at the mines or elsewhere, and return with strange ideas. Some perhaps have even been overseas from West to East Africa during the war.

The produce of the village loom, or dye-pit, or smithy, is discounted by cheap imported goods, and the craftsman's calling is not what it was. Traders, white and black, circulate under the *pax Britannica* among tribes but recently addicted to head-hunting, and bring to them new and strange conceptions. The primitive African is called upon to cope with ideas a thousand years in advance of his mental and social equipment. "He cannot proceed leisurely along the road to progress. He must be hurried along it, or the free and independent savage will sink to the level of the helot and the slave."

Here, then, in my view, lies our present task in Africa. It becomes impossible to maintain the old order — the urgent need is for adaptation to the new — to build up a tribal authority with a recognized and legal standing, which may avert social chaos. It cannot be accomplished by superseding — by the direct rule of the white man — such ideas of discipline and organization as exist, nor yet by "stereotyping customs and institutions among backward races which are not consistent with progress."

MANIFESTO OF THE SECOND PAN-AFRICAN CONGRESS

African nationalist movements before World War II were impeded by the slow growth in the pool of educated Africans and by the multiplicity of Africa's tribal and ethnic groups. Thus, it is not surprising that the original inspiration for African nationalism came largely from blacks living in the United States and the British West Indies. Of the early prophets of African nationalism, the most prominent was W. E. B. Du Bois. Born in Massachusetts in 1868, he became in 1895 the first black to receive a Ph.D. from Harvard University. After achieving prominence among American blacks for his writings and his involvement in the establishment of the National Association for the Advancement of Colored People, in 1919 Du Bois helped to organize the first Pan-African Congress in Paris in the hope of influencing decisions being made at the Paris Peace Conference. One hundred and thirteen delegates from Africa, the West Indies, the United States, and Europe attended a second meeting, which met sequentially in London, Brussels, and Paris in 1921. At the close of the 1921 congress, the delegates adopted the following manifesto.

Questions for Analysis

1. What is the manifesto's position on the relationship of the world's races?
2. What do the authors regard as the main obstacle to African advancement?
3. According to the manifesto, why should "advanced" people aid the Africans?
4. Do the authors of the manifesto feel Africa is ready for self-government? Why or why not?

*T*he absolute equality of races, — physical, political and social — is the founding stone of world peace and human advancement. No one denies great differences of gift, capacity and attainment among individuals of all races, but the voice of science, religion and practical politics is one in denying the God-appointed existence of super-races, or of races naturally and inevitably and eternally inferior.

That in the vast range of time, one group should in its industrial technique, or social organization, or spiritual vision, lag a few hundred years behind another, or forge fitfully ahead, or come to differ decidedly in thought, deed and ideal, is proof of the essential richness and variety of human nature, rather than proof of the co-existence of demi-gods and apes in human form. The doctrine of racial equality does not interfere with individual liberty, rather, it fulfils it. And of all the various criteria by which masses of men have in the past been prejudged and classified, that of the color of the skin and texture of the hair, is surely the most adventitious[1] and idiotic.

It is the duty of the world to assist in every way the advance of the backward and suppressed groups of mankind. The rise of all men is a menace to no one and is the highest human ideal; it is not an altruistic benevolence, but the one road to world salvation.

For the purpose of raising such peoples to intelligence, self-knowledge and self-control, their intelligentsia of right ought to be recognized as the natural leaders of their groups.

The insidious and dishonorable propaganda, which, for selfish ends, so distorts and denies facts as to represent the advancement and development of certain races of men as impossible and undesirable, should be met with widespread dissemination of the truth. . . .

If it be proven that absolute world segregation by group, color or historic infinity is best for the future, let the white race leave the dark world and the darker races will gladly leave the white. But the proposition is absurd. This is a world of men, of men whose likenesses far outweigh their differences; who mutually need each other in labor and thought and dream, but who can successfully have each other only on terms of equality, justice and mutual respect. They are the real and only peacemakers who work sincerely and peacefully to this end.

The beginning of wisdom in interracial contact is the establishment of political institutions among suppressed peoples. The habit of democracy must be made to encircle the earth. Despite the attempt to prove that its practice is the secret and divine gift of the few, no habit is more natural or more widely spread among primitive people, or more easily capable of development among masses. . . .

Surely in the 20th century of the Prince of Peace,[2] . . . there can be found in the civilized world enough of altruism, learning and benevolence to develop native institutions for the native's good, rather than continue to allow the majority of mankind to be brutalized and enslaved by ignorant and selfish agents of commercial institutions, whose one aim is profit and power for the few.

And this brings us to the crux of the matter: It is the shame of the world that today the relation between the main groups of mankind and their mutual estimate and respect is determined chiefly

---

1. Accidental.

2. Jesus.

by the degree in which one can subject the other to its service, enslaving labor, making ignorance compulsory, uprooting ruthlessly religion and customs, and destroying government, so that the favored Few may luxuriate in the toil of the tortured Many. . . .

The day of such world organization is past and whatever excuse be made for it in other ages, the 20th century must come to judge men as men and not as material and labor. . . .

What do those wish who see these evils of the color line and racial discrimination and who believe in the divine right of suppressed and backward peoples to learn and aspire and be free?

The Negro race through its thinking intelligentsia is demanding:

I. The recognition of civilized men as civilized despite their race or color

II. Local self-government for backward groups, deliberately rising as experience and knowledge grow to complete self-government under the limitations of a self-governed world

III. Education in self-knowledge, in scientific truth and in industrial technique, undivorced from the art of beauty

IV. Freedom in their own religion and social customs, and with the right to be different and non-conformist

V. Co-operation with the rest of the world in government, industry and art on the basis of Justice, Freedom and Peace

VI. The ancient common ownership of the land and its natural fruits and defense against the unrestrained greed of invested capital

VII. The establishment under the League of Nations of an international institution for the study of Negro problems

VIII. The establishment of an international section in the Labor Bureau of the League of Nations, charged with the protection of native labor.

The world must face two eventualities: either the complete assimilation of Africa with two or three of the great world states, with political, civil and social power and privileges absolutely equal for its black and white citizens, or the rise of a great black African state founded in Peace and Good Will, based on popular education, natural art and industry and freedom of trade; autonomous and sovereign in its internal policy, but from its beginning a part of a great society of peoples in which it takes its place with others as co-rulers of the world.

In some such words and thoughts as these we seek to express our will and ideal, and the end of our untiring effort. To our aid we call all men of the Earth who love Justice and Mercy. Out of the depths we have cried unto the deaf and dumb masters of the world. Out of the depths we cry to our own sleeping souls.

The answer is written in the stars.

Political Disintegration and Revolution in China

The overthrow of the Manchu, or Ch'ing, Dynasty in 1911 resulted not in the dreamed-of national revival but close to four decades of political conflict, foreign invasion, and enormous human suffering. After the death of General Yüan Shih-k'ai, who ruled the new Chinese "republic" as dictator between 1912 and 1916, the country was divided among dozens of generally unscrupulous and greedy warlords, military men whose control of private armies was the basis of their local authority.

Under warlord rule China's political deterioration reached a low point, but out of the nation's humiliation were born two new revolutionary parties — the National People's party, or Kuomintang (KMT; Chinese for National People's Party) and the Chinese Communist party (CCP) — each of which in the 1920s and 1930s sought to unify China and govern it according to its principles. The KMT, founded in 1912 by Sun Yat-sen, was dedicated in theory to his "three principles of the people" — Democracy, Nationalism, and Livelihood (see Chapter 10). The Kuomintang's collaborator and later its bitter enemy was the Chinese Communist party, founded in 1921 and dedicated to Marxism-Leninism.

Aided by agents of the Soviet Union, the Kuomintang and the Communists formed an alliance in 1922 to rid China of the warlords. It lasted only until 1927, when the Kuomintang, now under the leadership of General Chiang Kai-shek (1887–1975), purged the Communists from the KMT and killed many of their leaders. Removed from the coastal cities, their original centers of support, Communist troops and leaders fled to the countryside, where under the leadership of Mao Zedong (1893–1976), they rebuilt the party into a formidable military and revolutionary force. After a long struggle against the Japanese, who invaded China in 1937, and the Kuomintang, the Communists took control of China in 1949.

THE CAREER OF WARLORD GENERAL CHANG TSUNG-CH'ANG

Warlord politics of the 1920s were as confusing to the Chinese who experienced them as they are to modern historians. With no legitimate sanction for their rule, the warlords relied on force and were almost always fighting someone, either other warlords or the Kuomintang. Their unfortunate subjects paid the price in extortionate taxes, insecurity, and death.

The following account, printed in the Chinese journal *I ching* and based on its readers' recollections, tells the story of Chang Tsung-ch'ang (1881–1932), a notorious warlord of the 1920s in the Shantung region, in northeast China on the Yellow Sea. Kuomintang forces expelled him in 1928, and he went to Manchuria and then Japan. He was assassinated by the son of one of his former victims when he returned to Shantung in 1932. One should not assume that Chang's policies were typical of all the warlords, some of whom were reasonable men who sought to establish sound government and worked for social reform. Chang's career does, however, offer insight into the chaos that ruled China in the 1920s.

Questions
for Analysis

1. By what process did Chang become governor of the Shantung region? What qualities did he have that contributed to his rise to power?
2. As a ruler, what seem to have been Chang's major priorities and concerns?
3. In what ways did life deteriorate in the Shantung region during his rule? Did anyone benefit from his rule?

Chang Tsung-ch'ang, nicknamed "Dog-meat General" and "Lanky General," was from I county in Shantung. His father was a trumpet-player (hired for funeral processions, etc.) and barber, and his mother was a shamaness.[1] At the age of twelve or thirteen, Chang started helping his father by playing the cymbals. When he was fifteen or sixteen he went with his mother to Yin-k'ou, and worked as a servant in a gambling house, mixing with pickpockets and thieves. The gentry of the town, annoyed, drove him away. He then fled to Kuan-tung (in Manchuria) to join the "bearded bandits."[2] His mother stayed on at Yin-k'ou, and lived with the proprietor of a bathhouse, then with a cobbler, then with a cloth vendor. . . .

—————— ✤ ——————

The account details Chang's maneuverings after the 1911 revolution that led to his rise to power.

—————— ✤ ——————

Chang was very brave in battle, but he had no mind for strategy. His soldiers were mostly bandits, and therefore very valiant warriors, which by and large accounted for his success in military ventures. But he also had an advisor who assisted him in military maneuvers, the fortune-teller T'ung Hua-ku. During the Feng-tien-Chihli[3] warfare, Chang was stationed to the east of the Hsi-feng Pass. One day, Chang came across T'ung and went up to him for advice. T'ung told him that his physiognomy[4] revealed that he would achieve great distinction. He also predicted that the next day, when the Chihli troops passed by train, the train would derail, and if Chang would take this opportunity, he could attack them and win a big victory. The next day, Chang stationed his troops to wait for the Chihli troops. Just as T'ung had predicted, the train derailed, and Chang routed the enemies. At the time of the battle T'ung paced back and forth on top of a hill, his hair untied, his mouth uttering words of magic. After the battle, Chang asked T'ung to step down from the hill, and with utmost deference appointed him

---

1. A person who had the power to contact the spirits of the dead and who would be consulted on matters such as health and business.

2. The identity of the "bearded bandits" is not clear; one can only guess that they stole for their living and had facial hair.

3. After the death of Yuan Shih-k'ai, the Chihli clique, supporters of warlord Feng Kuo-chang, struggled with the Anhwei clique, supporters of Tuan Ch'i-jui; war between the cliques broke out in 1920.

4. The practice of trying to judge one's mental qualities and characteristics by observing bodily, especially facial, features.

as his military advisor. From then on, Chang followed T'ung's words to the letter where military action was concerned.

It turned out that the fortune-teller was rather shrewd. The night that he met Chang, he hired a few peasants to remove the screws connecting the rails over a bridge, thereby causing the derailment. Because he knew Chang could easily be fooled, he used a fairytale as a steppingstone to a career. At any rate, on account of Chang's military distinctions, he was finally appointed as Governor of Shantung. . . .

Not long after Chang became Governor, two phrases were heard all over the cities: "Cut apart to catch light," and "listen to the telephone." The former referred to the human heads which were treated like watermelons, cut in halves to bask in the sun; the latter referred to the same, except the heads were hung from telephone poles, and from afar they seemed to be listening on the telephone. At the same time, at the train stations . . . people started to hear the strange expression "My head is my passport; my ass is my ticket." This was because people were being regularly kicked, beaten up, abused in vile language, and spat in the face by the soldiers. . . . Living in Shantung at this time, one could really feel the truth in the saying "A man's life is less valuable than that of a chicken."

Soon after Chang Tsung-ch'ang came to his post, he unveiled his ugly nature and started his vile deeds. Under his . . . policy, the once-flourishing academies disappeared, the better students fled, and the provincial assembly was silenced. On the other hand, clever people moved with the current and began buttering Chang up. Upholding the philosophy that "In an age of chaos, don't miss the chance to loot during the fire," they went after offices. From circuit Intendants and county Magistrates to bureau Chiefs, all positions

were refilled with much pomp. Whenever these henchmen went to a local district, their first priority was to extort and exploit, so that they could repay past favors and secure future ones, whereas the people were becoming skinnier daily. Too true was the proverb "In the official's house, wine and meat are allowed to rot, but on the roads are the bones of those who starved to death."

Chang Tsung-ch'ang came to Shantung in June of 1925, and he fled on the 30th of April, 1928. In these three years he took a total of 350,000 dollars of the people's blood money. . . .

After each battle, the field was strewn with bodies. The loss of the soldiers required replacement, which in turn required military funds, which resulted in higher taxes. When funds were raised, more soldiers were drafted, and another war was in the making. This cycle was repeated again and again. This was the way Chang Tsung-ch'ang ruled the province of Shantung from 1925 to 1928. The white banners of recruitment flew all over the province, and young people were driven straight into their graves. In such a situation, how could the people of Shantung escape hardship and poverty? . . .

In order to raise funds to pay his soldiers and buy arms, Chang Tsung-ch'ang frequently "borrowed" from various banks and commercial unions. Though these were loans in name, they were extortions in fact. The Kung-li Banking House, which had operated in Shantung for over a decade, went out of business because of such extortions, and its manager went into exile. . . .

To manifest his own "merits and distinctions," Chang planned to build a living shrine and a bronze statue for himself. . . . The expenses were extorted from the people. He shipped a full trainload of granite from Mount T'ai for the construction. But because of the rapid advance of the troops of the Northern Expedition,[5] there was not enough time for the actual work to begin. However, the "donations" for these purposes had been collected in full. . . .

In the summer of 1927, there was a severe drought in Shantung. Not a drop of rain fell, and the crops were all dying. Chang Tsung-ch'ang ordered a general fast and personally went to the "Dragon King Temple" to pray for rain. But the Dragon King was apparently not impressed, and the drought continued. In a rage, Chang slapped the Dragon King's face many times. He then went to the Chang-chuang Arsenal and fired cannon balls into the sky for hours, so as to vent his anger at Heaven. Nevertheless, it still did not rain.

◼ Mao Zedong

STRATEGIC PROBLEMS OF CHINA'S REVOLUTIONARY WAR

Mao Zedong (1893–1976) was born into a well-to-do peasant family in Hunan province and as a university student participated in the anti-Manchu revolution of 1911. During the next several years, while serving as a library assistant at Peking University, he was converted to Marxism and became one of the first members of the Chinese Communist party. Originally given responsibility for organizing urban labor unions, Mao gradually concluded that in China the peasants, a class whose capacity for revolution was discounted by orthodox Marxist-Leninists, would be the force to lead China to socialism. In 1927 he summarized his ideas in his "Report on an Investigation of the Peasant Movement in Hunan."

After the break from the Kuomintang, Mao established his small army in the remote and hilly region on the Hunan-Kiangsi border, where in 1931 he proclaimed the Chinese Soviet Republic. In 1934 Chiang Kai-shek's troops surrounded Mao's forces, but over 100,000 Communist troops and officials broke out of the Kuomintang encirclement and embarked on the Long March. This legendary trek lasted more than a year and covered 6,000 miles before a small remnant found safety in the distant mountains of Kansu province. Here Mao established unchallenged control over the party, rebuilt his army, and readied himself and his followers for what would be fourteen more years of struggle against the Japanese and the Kuomintang.

In 1936 Mao explained how this struggle was to be won in a series of lectures presented to the Red Army College and subsequently published under the title. *Strategic Problems of China's Revolutionary War.* The following excerpts summarize Mao's basic ideas.

---

5. The Kuomintang military campaign of 1928 that succeeded in taking Peking (Beijing).

Questions for Analysis

1. According to Mao, what is the role of the Communist party in China's revolutionary struggle? In what way is it similar to Lenin's conception of the party's role (see Chapter 11)?
2. According to Mao, what are the four unique characteristics of China's revolutionary war? How do they affect Mao's theories of military strategy?
3. What is the peasantry's role in revolutionary war? What is the proletariat's role?
4. What does Mao mean by a policy of "active defense"? In his view, what are its advantages?

THE CHINESE COMMUNIST PARTY AND CHINA'S REVOLUTIONARY WAR

The chief enemies in China's revolutionary war are imperialism and the feudal forces. Although the Chinese bourgeoisie may take part in the revolutionary war on certain historical occasions, yet owing to its selfish character and its lack of political and economic independence, it is neither willing nor able to lead China's revolutionary war to complete victory. The masses of the Chinese peasantry and of the urban petty bourgeoisie are willing to take part actively in the revolutionary war and to bring about its complete victory. They are the main forces in the revolutionary war, yet small-scale production, which is their characteristic and limits their political outlook, renders them unable to give correct leadership in the war. Thus, in an era when the proletariat has already appeared on the political stage, the responsibility of leadership in China's revolutionary war inevitably falls on the shoulders of the Chinese Communist Party. At such a time any revolutionary war will certainly end in defeat if the lead-

ership of the proletariat and the Communist Party is lacking or is forsaken. For of all the social strata and political groups in semicolonial China only the proletariat and the Communist Party are the most open-minded and unselfish, possess the most farsighted political outlook and the highest organizational quality, and are also the readiest to learn with an open mind from the experiences of the advanced proletariat of the world and its parties as well as to apply what they have learned in their own undertakings. . . .

CHARACTERISTICS OF CHINA'S REVOLUTIONARY WAR

1. The Importance of the Subject

People who will not admit, who do not know, or who do not care to know that China's revolutionary war has its own characteristics have treated the war waged by the Red Army against the Kuomintang forces as similar in nature to wars in general or the civil war in the Soviet Union.[1] The experience of the civil war in the Soviet Union directed by Lenin and Stalin has indeed a world-wide significance. All Com-

---

1. The reference is to the postrevolutionary struggle between the Bolsheviks and their opponents from 1917 to 1921.

munist Parties, including the Chinese Communist Party, regard this experience and its theoretical summing-up by Lenin and Stalin as their guiding compass. Yet this does not mean that we are to make use of this experience mechanically under our own conditions. China's revolutionary war is distinguished by many characteristics from the civil war in the Soviet Union. Failure to reckon with these characteristics or denial of them is of course erroneous. This point has been fully proved in the ten years of our war. . . .

2. What Are the Characteristics of China's Revolutionary War?

What then are the characteristics of China's revolutionary war?

I think there are four.

The first is that China is a vast semi-colonial country which is unevenly developed both politically and economically. . . .

The unevenness of political and economic development in China — the coexistence of a frail capitalist economy and a preponderant semi-feudal economy; the coexistence of a few modern industrial and commercial cities and the boundless expanses of stagnant rural districts; the coexistence of several millions of industrial workers on the one hand and, on the other, hundreds of millions of peasants and handicraftsmen under the old régime; the coexistence of big warlords controlling the Central government and small warlords controlling the provinces; the coexistence of two kinds of reactionary armies, i.e., the so-called Central army under Chiang Kai-shek and the troops of miscellaneous brands under the warlords in the provinces; and the coexistence of a few

railway and steamship lines and motor roads on the one hand and, on the other, the vast number of wheel-barrow paths and trails for pedestrians only, many of which are even difficult for them to negotiate. . . .

The second characteristic is the great strength of the enemy.

What is the situation of the Kuomintang, the enemy of the Red Army? It is a party that has seized political power and has relatively stabilized it. It has gained the support of the principal counter-revolutionary countries in the world. It has remodeled its army, which has thus become different from any other army in Chinese history and on the whole similar to the armies of the modern states in the world; its army is supplied much more abundantly with arms and other equipment than the Red Army, and is greater in numerical strength than any army in Chinese history, even than the standing army of any country in the world. . . .

The Chinese Red Army is confronted with such a powerful enemy. This is the second characteristic of China's revolutionary war. This characteristic inevitably makes the war waged by the Red Army different in many ways from wars in general, from the civil war in the Soviet Union and from the Northern Expedition.[2]

The third characteristic is that the Red Army is weak and small. . . .

Our political power is dispersed and isolated in mountainous or remote regions, and is deprived of any outside help. In economic and cultural conditions the revolutionary base areas are more backward than the Kuomintang areas. The revolutionary bases embrace only rural districts and small towns. They were

---

2. The military campaign the Kuomintang pursued between 1926 and 1928 to break the hold of the warlords on central north China.

extremely small in the beginning and have not grown much larger since. Moreover, they are often shifted and the Red Army possesses no really consolidated bases. . . .

The fourth characteristic is the Communist Party's leadership and the agrarian revolution.

This characteristic is the inevitable result of the first one. It gives rise to the following two features. On the one hand, China's revolutionary war, though taking place in a period of reaction in China and throughout the capitalist world, can yet be victorious because it is led by the Communist Party and supported by the peasantry. Because we have secured the support of the peasantry, our base areas, though small, possess great political power and stand firmly opposed to the political power of the Kuomintang which encompasses a vast area; in a military sense this creates colossal difficulties for the attacking Kuomintang troops. The Red Army, though small, has great fighting capacity, because its men under the leadership of the Communist Party have sprung from the agrarian revolution and are fighting for their own interests, and because officers and men are politically united.

On the other hand, our situation contrasts sharply with that of the Kuomintang. Opposed to the agrarian revolution, the Kuomintang is deprived of the support of the peasantry. Despite the great size of its army it cannot arouse the bulk of the soldiers or many of the lower-rank officers, who used to be small producers, to risk their lives voluntarily for its sake. Officers and men are politically disunited and this reduces its fighting capacity. . . .

STRATEGIC DEFENSIVE

Military experts of new and rapidly developing imperialist countries like Germany and Japan positively boast of the advantages of strategic offensive and condemn strategic defensive. Such an idea is fundamentally unsuitable for China's revolutionary war. Such military experts point out that the great shortcoming of defense lies in the fact that, instead of gingering up the people, it demoralizes them. But that applies only to countries where class contradictions are sharp and the war benefits only the reactionary ruling strata or the reactionary groups in power. Our case is different. Under the slogan of safeguarding the revolutionary base areas and safeguarding China, we can rally the greatest majority of the people to fight single-mindedly, because we are the victims of oppression and aggression. The Red Army of the Soviet Union defeated its enemies also by defensive warfare during the civil war. It not only carried on the war under the slogan of defending the Soviets when the imperialist powers organized the Whites[3] for an onslaught, but also carried out military mobilization under the slogan of defending the capital when the October Uprising was being prepared. Defensive battles in a just war can not only exercise a lulling influence on the politically alien elements but mobilize the backward sections of the masses to join in the war.

When Marx said that once an armed uprising is started there must not be a moment's pause in the attack, he meant that the masses, having taken the enemy by surprise in an uprising, must not allow the reactionary ruling classes any chance

3. In the Russian civil war, the opponents of the "Reds," or Bolsheviks.

to retain or recover their political power, but must seize this moment to spring a surprise attack on the nation's reactionary ruling forces, and that they must never feel satisfied with the victories they have won, underrate the enemy, relent in their attacks on the enemy, or hesitate to go forward so as to miss the chance of annihilating the enemy and court failure for the revolution. This is correct. This does not mean, however, that we revolutionaries should not adopt defensive measures even when we are already locked in a battle with an enemy stronger than ourselves and are hard pressed by him. Anyone who thinks so would be a prize idiot.

Our past war was on the whole an offensive against the Kuomintang, though militarily it assumed the form of smashing the enemy's campaigns of "encirclement and annihilation."

In military terms, our warfare consists in the alternate adoption of the defensive and the offensive. It makes no difference to us whether our offensive is regarded as following the defensive or preceding it, because the turning-point comes when we smash the campaigns of "encirclement and annihilation." It remains a defensive until a campaign of "encirclement and annihilation" is smashed, and then it immediately begins as an offensive; they are but two phases of the same thing, as one campaign of "encirclement and annihilation" of the enemy is closely followed by another. Of the two phases, the defensive phase is more complicated and more important than the offensive phase. It involves numerous problems of how to smash the campaign of "encirclement and annihilation." The basic principle is for active defense and against passive defense.

In the civil war, when the Red Army surpasses the enemy in strength, there will no longer be any use for strategic defensive in general. Then our only directive will be strategic offensive. Such a change depends on an overall change in the relative strength of the enemy and ourselves. The only defensive measures that remain will be of a partial character.

Economic Nationalism and Reform in Latin America

During the second half of the nineteenth century, most Latin American economies experienced rapid growth, based largely on exports of petroleum, agricultural products, copper, tin, and nitrates. But developments in the first half of the twentieth century revealed the weak foundations of this seemingly spectacular expansion. It had, first of all, brought few benefits to the vast majority of the population. Profits from railroading, banking, mining, and oil drilling went into the pockets of European and North American investors, and money earned from the area's agricultural exports enriched a small number of wealthy landowners. Furthermore, the slump in demand for Latin America's products immediately following World War I, and, to a greater extent, during the Great Depression revealed the dangers of the region's heavy dependence on exports. With little money coming in from foreign customers, the region could not buy manufactured goods, and real economic hardship resulted.

The disasters of the 1920s and 1930s convinced many Latin American leaders of the need to limit foreign control of their nations' economies and to encourage native-owned industries through tariffs and other incentives. The economic problems also sharpened concern about a variety of social issues, most of which stemmed from mass poverty and illiteracy. Because the wealthy and powerful were generally whites of Portuguese or Spanish descent and the poorest were Indian or black, these issues had racial connotations. Spokesmen for the poor generally were journalists, academics, lawyers, and politicians, mostly drawn from the middle class and often inspired by socialism and the European and U.S. labor movement.

Mexico offers the best example of a Latin American nation that combined economic nationalism with social reform in the first half of the twentieth century. Under the dictatorship of Porfirio Díaz (1877–1911), railroad construction, rising agricultural exports, the establishment of the oil industry, and increased output from mining all seemed to suggest growing prosperity. But the number of landless peasants increased, factory workers and miners were exploited unmercifully, and foreigners controlled much of Mexico's natural wealth. In 1910 and 1911 widespread popular demonstrations took place against Díaz's heavy-handed government, and rather than stand and fight, the aging dictator sailed to France and died as an exile in 1915. The Mexican revolution of 1910 and 1911, which has never formally ended, led to the foundation of the Mexican republic and allowed the Mexican people and their leaders to deal head-on with their problems of social inequality and foreign economic domination.

Developments in Peru were more typical of the experiences of most Latin American nations. A small elite of landowning and mercantile families, with close connections to the army and foreign business interests, controlled the country, but the overwhelming majority of the population, 50 percent of whom were Indians who spoke Indian dialects rather than Spanish, were peasants and farm laborers, miners, and factory workers. Labor protest against long hours, child labor, and low pay began early, and a general strike in 1919 resulted in a rarely enforced eight-hour-day law. In the 1920s Peru produced two influential leaders, José Maria Mariátegui (1895–1930), the "father of Latin American Marxism" and a strong spokesman for Indian rights, and Victor Raúl Haya de la Torre (1895–1979), the founder of the American Popular Revolutionary Alliance (APRA), an organization dedicated to anti-imperialism and the nationalization of land and industry.

Peru seemed close to revolution between 1930 and 1933, as members of APRA, Communists, disgruntled miners, and laborers clashed with government authorities. The army remained loyal to the traditional oligarchy, however, and in 1933 Oscar Benavides established himself as dictator. No serious effort to deal with Peru's economic and social problems took place until the 1970s, by which time they had reached such a scale that progress has been difficult.

José Maria Mariátegui

SEVEN INTERPRETIVE ESSAYS ON PERUVIAN REALITY

José Maria Mariátegui was raised in poverty by his mother, a seamstress, and, after only a few years of schooling, at the age of 14 went to work as a printer's assistant for a newspaper in Lima, Peru's largest city. Self-taught, by age 20 he was writing news stories, verse, and reviews for his newspaper and a number of independent journals, and when he was 21 his first full-length poetic drama was performed on the Lima stage. Much of his writing sharply criticized the Peruvian military, political, and ecclesiastical establishments for their disregard for the poor, especially the Indians, and Peru's dictator, Augusto B. Leguía, exiled Mariátegui to Europe. Returning to Peru as a convinced Marxist, he worked, despite government harassment, to strengthen the labor movement, wrote hundreds of articles, and founded the Socialist party of Peru in 1928. His most widely read work, *Seven Interpretive Essays on Peruvian Reality,* from which the following excerpt is taken, is a collection of previously published newspaper and journal articles. Before he died at age 35, he was involved in discussions leading to the formation of the Peruvian Communist party, formally organized a month after his death from cancer in 1930.

Questions for Analysis

1. Mariátegui rejects previous "solutions" to Peru's Indian problem. What were they, and why in his view have they failed?
2. What is the only viable solution to Peru's Indian problem?
3. Mariátegui considered himself a Marxist. What is Marxist about his ideas? It what ways do his ideas differ from orthodox Marxism expressed in *The Communist Manifesto* (see Chapter 8)?
4. Are Mariátegui's ideas closer to those of Lenin (see Chapter 11) or Mao?
5. Does Mariátegui indicate how he hopes to accomplish his goals? How might this process have affected the pace of social reform in Peru?

THE PROBLEM OF THE INDIAN

All approaches to the Indian problem that ignore or evade its socioeconomic essence are so many sterile theoretical exercises — sometimes on a purely verbal level — that are doomed to absolute discredit. The sincerity of some of these approaches does not save them. In practice, they serve only to conceal or distort the reality of the problem. A socialist critique discloses and illuminates that reality, because it seeks its causes in the country's economy, not in its administrative, juridical, or ecclesiastical mechanism or in the duality or plurality of its races or in its cultural and moral conditions. The Indian question derives from our economy. It has its roots in the system of land tenure. Every effort to solve it with administrative or protective measures, with educational methods or road-building projects, represents a superficial labor as long as the feudalism of the great landowners exists.

Gamonalismo[1] inevitably invalidates every law or ordinance for the protection of the Indian. The landowner, the *latifundista*,[2] is a feudal lord. Against his authority, supported by the milieu and by custom, the written law is impotent. The law forbids unpaid labor, yet unpaid labor and even forced labor survive on the latifundio. The judge, the subprefect, the commissary, the teacher, the tax-collector, are vassals of the great landowners. The law cannot prevail against the gamonales. The official who should obstinately strive to impose it would be abandoned and sacrificed by the central government, over which the influence of gamonalismo, acting directly or through Parliament, ever with the same efficacy, is always omnipotent.

The new approach to the Indian problem, therefore, is much less concerned with devising Indian protective legislation than with the consequences of the system of land tenure. . . .

This critique rejects as invalid the various approaches that evaluate the question according to one or another of the following unilateral and exclusive criteria: administrative, juridical, ethnic, moral, educational, ecclesiastical.

The first and most evident rout has been suffered by those who would reduce the protection of the Indian to a problem of ordinary administration. Since the days of Spanish colonial legislation, wise

and comprehensive ordinances, framed after conscientious inquiries, have proven totally fruitless. The Republican era[3] has been particularly fecund in the production of decrees, laws, and provisions directed toward the protection of the Indians against extortion and abuse. But the gamonal of today, like the encomendero[4] of yesterday, has very little to fear from administrative theory. He knows that the practice is different.

The individualistic character of the Republican legislation unquestionably favored the absorption of Indian property by the latifundio. In this respect Spanish legislation viewed the situation of the Indian with greater realism.[5] But juridical reform has no more value than administrative reform, given the existence of a feudalism intact in its economic structure. The expropriation of the greater part of Indian individual and communal property has already been completed. For the rest, the experience of all countries that have emerged from their feudal age shows that without the dissolution of the feudal estate a liberal legal system cannot function anywhere.

The view that the Indian problem is an ethnic problem draws on the most ancient repertory of imperialist ideas. The concept of inferior races served the white West in its work of expansion and conquest. To expect Indian emancipation to result from an active crossing of the aboriginal race with white immigrants is an example of sociological naiveté that could only arise

---

1. A term used in Latin America referring to the social and political dominance of wealthy landowners; sometimes simply translated as "feudalism."

2. The owner of a latifundio, a great landed estate worked by farm laborers in a state of partial serfdom.

3. The period since Peruvian independence in 1824.

4. On the Spanish colonial encomienda system, see Chapter 1.

5. Early republican leaders decreed the end of Indian communal property in favor of individual property rights; unfortunately for most Indians, their private plots were taken over by wealthy latifundio owners. The Spaniards had sought to preserve Indian communal property.

in the rudimentary brain of an importer of merino sheep. The Asiatic peoples, to whom the Indian people is not at all inferior, have admirably assimilated the most dynamic and creative elements in Western culture without transfusions of European blood. The degeneracy of the Peruvian Indian is a cheap invention of legal lickspittles at the feudal table.

The tendency to consider the Indian problem as a moral problem embodies a liberal, humanitarian, eighteenth-century enlightened conception that in Europe finds expression in the organization of "Leagues of the Rights of Man." This view, which has always placed excessive faith in its appeal to the moral sense of civilization, inspired the European anti-slavery conferences and societies that more or less fruitlessly denounced the crimes of the colonizers. . . . The experiment has been carried out far enough, in Peru and throughout the world. Humanitarian preachments have not restrained or abashed European imperialism, or improved its methods. The struggle against imperialism now relies solely on the solidarity and strength of the emancipation movements of the colonial masses. . . .

In the field of reason and morality, the religious approach was applied centuries ago, with greater energy, or at least with greater authority, than today. . . .

But today the hope of an ecclesiastical solution is indisputably the most obsolete and unhistoric of all. The individuals who represent it do not even concern themselves, like their distant — ever so distant! — teachers, with obtaining a declaration of Indian rights, or with the appointment of qualified officials and the adoption of just laws, but instead propose to entrust to the missionary the function of mediating between the Indian and the gamonal.

If the Church could not accomplish its task in a medieval social order — in which its intellectual and spiritual capacity could be measured by friars of the stature of Father Las Casas[6] — what chance of success does it have now? . . .

The pedagogical solution, advanced by many persons with perfect sincerity, is now discarded even in official quarters. The educators, I repeat, are the last people to think of asserting their independence of the socio-economic reality. There remains, then, in effect, nothing but a vague and formless suggestion for which no group or body of doctrine assumes responsibility.

The new approach consists in identifying the Indian problem with the problem of land.

We who study and define the Indian problem from a socialist point of view begin by declaring that the old humanitarian and philanthropic points of view are absolutely superseded. Our first concern is to establish its character as an essentially economic problem. We revolt, in the first place, against the instinctive — and defensive — tendency of the creole or misti[7] to reduce it to an exclusively administrative, pedagogic, ethnic, or moral problem, in order to escape at all costs from the economic plane. . . .

The agrarian problem appears, above all, as the problem of liquidating feudalism in Peru. This liquidation should have been accomplished by the democratic-bourgeois regime formally established by the revolution of independence. But in Peru, in a century of the Republic, we have not had a true bourgeois or capitalist class. The ancient feudal class —camouflaged or masked as a republican bourgeoisie — has preserved its positions. . . .

The expressions of our surviving feu-

---

6. Bartolomé de Las Casas (1474–1566) was a Spanish Franciscan friar who denounced the enslavement of Indians by early Spanish settlers.

7. People of mixed Spanish and Indian ancestry; mestizos.

dalism are two: latifundio and serfdom. These are related and consubstantial expressions, whose analysis leads to the conclusion that the serfdom that weighs down the Indian race cannot be liquidated without liquidating the latifundio.

The agrarian problem in Peru, posed in this way, does not lend itself to equivocal distortions. It appears in all its magnitude as a socio-economic — and therefore political — problem, in the domain of men who concern themselves with social and economic facts and ideas. And it is vain, for example, to try to convert it into a technical-agricultural problem in the domain of agronomists.

Everyone knows that the liberal solution for this problem, in conformity with individualist ideology, would be to break up the latifundio in order to create small landed properties. So great is the ignorance of the elementary principles of socialism among us that it is not stating the obvious or unnecessary to emphasize that this formula — the break-up of the latifundio in favor of small landed property — is neither utopian, heretical, nor revolutionary, neither Bolshevik nor advanced, but orthodox, constitutional, democratic, capitalist, and bourgeois. And that it has its origin in the liberal ideology which underlies the constitutions of all the bourgeois-democratic states. And that in the countries of Central and Eastern Europe — where the war crisis brought down with a crash the last ramparts of feudalism with the consent of the capitalist West (which henceforth opposed to Russia this bloc of anti-Bolshevik lands) — in Czechoslovakia, Rumania, Poland, Bulgaria, etc., agrarian laws have been passed that in principle limit the ownership of land to a maximum of 500 hectares.

In conformity with my ideological position, I think that in Peru the hour for trying the liberal method, the individualist formula, has already passed. Leaving doctrinal reasons aside, I regard as fundamental an indisputable and concrete factor that gives a peculiar stamp to our agrarian problem: the survival of the Indian community and of elements of practical socialism in Indian life and agriculture.

Lázaro Cárdenas

SPEECH TO THE NATION

Instability and conflict among various aspiring leaders marked the first decade of Mexico's revolution, and it was unclear if the revolutionary movement would survive. In 1917, however, a constitutional convention drafted a new charter for the nation that confirmed the principles of free speech, religious toleration, universal manhood suffrage, the separation of powers, and the inviolability of private property. It also sought to give the nation greater control over its economy and committed the government to serious social reform on behalf of the masses.

Little reform took place until the presidency of Lázaro Cárdenas from 1934 to 1940. In a series of bold steps he confiscated millions of acres of land from the large estates for redistribution to peasants, introduced free and compulsory elementary education, and sponsored legislation that provided medical and unemployment insurance. His most audacious step, however, was the nationalization of Mexico's oil industry in 1938, which he accomplished after a dispute between the unions and the American and British oil companies erupted into a strike in 1936. In the legal battle that followed, seventeen oil companies refused to accept the pro-union ruling of an arbitration board appointed by Cárdenas and the decision of the Mexican Supreme Court that upheld the ruling. This repudiation led Cárdenas to announce on national radio on March 18, 1938, that in the national interest the government had expropriated the property of the oil companies. In the following excerpt from his speech, Cárdenas, after recounting the events in the labor dispute, comments on the role of the oil companies in Mexico's development.

Questions
for Analysis

1. According to Cárdenas, in what ways have the actions of the foreign oil companies been "immoral"?
2. Who does he blame for the actions of the oil companies?
3. In what ways is Cárdenas's speech an appeal to Mexican nationalism?

*I*n each and every one of the various attempts of the Executive to arrive at a final solution of the conflict within conciliatory limits . . . the intransigence of the companies was clearly demonstrated.

Their attitude was therefore premeditated and their position deliberately taken, so that the Government, in defense of its own dignity, had to resort to application of the Expropriation Act, as there were no means less drastic or decision less severe that might bring about a solution of the problem.

For additional justification of the measure herein announced, let us trace briefly the history of the oil companies' growth in Mexico and of the resources with which they have developed their activities.

It has been repeated *ad nauseam* that the oil industry has brought additional capital for the development and progress of the country. This assertion is an exaggeration. For many years throughout the major period of their existence, the oil companies have enjoyed great privileges for development and expansion, including customs and tax exemptions and innumerable prerogatives; it is these factors of special privilege, together with the prodigious productivity of the oil deposits granted them by the Nation often against public will and law, that represent almost the total amount of this so-called capital.

Potential wealth of the Nation; miserably underpaid native labor; tax exemptions; economic privileges; governmental tolerance — these are the factors of the boom of the Mexican oil industry.

Let us now examine the social contributions of the companies. In how many of the villages bordering on the oil fields is there a hospital, or school or social center, or a sanitary water supply, or an athletic field, or even an electric plant fed by the millions of cubic meters of natural gas allowed to go to waste?

What center of oil production, on the other hand, does not have its company police force for the protection of private, selfish, and often illegal interests? These organizations, whether authorized by the Government or not, are charged with innumerable outrages, abuses, and murders, always on behalf of the companies that employ them.

Who is not aware of the irritating discrimination governing construction of the company camps? Comfort for the foreign personnel; misery, drabness, and insalubrity for the Mexicans. Refrigeration and protection against tropical insects for the former; indifference and neglect, medical service and supplies always grudgingly provided, for the latter; lower wages and harder, more exhausting labor for our people.

The tolerance which the companies have abused was born, it is true, in the shadow of the ignorance, betrayals, and weakness of the country's rulers; but the mechanism was set in motion by investors lacking in the necessary moral resources to give something in exchange for the wealth they have been exploiting.

Another inevitable consequence of the presence of the oil companies, strongly characterized by their anti-social tendencies, and even more harmful than all those already mentioned, has been their persistent and improper intervention in national affairs.

The oil companies' support to strong rebel factions against the constituted government in the Huasteca region of Veracruz and in the Isthmus of Tehuantepec during the years 1917 to 1920 is no longer a matter for discussion by anyone. Nor is anyone ignorant of the fact that in later periods and even at the present time, the oil companies have almost openly encouraged the ambitions of elements discontented with the country's government, every time their interests were affected either by taxation or by the modification of their privileges or the withdrawal of the customary tolerance. They have had money, arms, and munitions for rebellion, money for the anti-patriotic press which defends them, money with which to enrich their unconditional defenders. But for the progress of the country, for establishing an economic equilibrium with their workers through a just compensation of labor, for maintaining hygenic conditions in the districts where they themselves operate, or for conserving the vast riches of the natural petroleum gases from destruction, they have neither money, nor financial possibilities, nor the desire to subtract the necessary funds from the volume of their profits.

Nor is there money with which to meet a responsibility imposed upon them by judicial verdict, for they rely on their pride and their economic power to shield them from the dignity and sovereignty of a Nation which has generously placed in their hands its vast natural resources and now finds itself unable to obtain the satisfaction of the most elementary obligations by ordinary legal means.

As a logical consequence of this brief analysis, it was therefore necessary to adopt a definite and legal measure to end this permanent state of affairs in which the country sees its industrial progress held back by those who hold in their hands the power to erect obstacles as well as the motive power of all activity and who, instead of using it to high and worthy purposes, abuse their economic strength to the point of jeopardizing the very life of a Nation endeavoring to bring about the elevation of its people through its own laws, its own resources, and the free management of its own destinies.

With the only solution to this problem thus placed before it, I ask the entire Nation for moral and material support sufficient to carry out so justified, important, and indispensable a decision.

The Government has already taken suitable steps to maintain the constructive activities now going forward throughout the Republic, and for that purpose it asks the people only for its full confidence and backing in whatever dispositions the Government may be obliged to adopt.

Nevertheless, we shall, if necessary, sacrifice all the constructive projects on which the Nation has embarked during the term of this Administration in order to cope with the financial obligations imposed upon us by the application of the Expropriation Act to such vast interests; and although the subsoil of the country will give us considerable economic resources with which to meet the obligation of indemnization which we have contracted, we must be prepared for the possibility of our individual economy also suffering the indispensable readjustments, even to the point, should the Bank of Mexico deem it necessary, or modifying the present exchange rate of our currency, so that the whole country may be able to count on sufficient currency and resources with which to consolidate this act of profound and essential economic liberation of Mexico.

It is necessary that all groups of the population be imbued with a full optimism and that each citizen, whether in agricultural, industrial, commercial, transportation, or other pursuits, develop a greater activity from this moment on, in order to create new resources which will reveal that the spirit of our people is capable of saving the nation's economy by the efforts of its own citizens.

And, finally, as the fear may arise among the interests now in bitter conflict in the field of international affairs[1] that a deviation of raw materials fundamentally necessary to the struggle in which the most powerful nations are engaged might result from the consummation of this act of national sovereignty and dignity, we wish to state that our petroleum operations will not depart a single inch from the moral solidarity maintained by Mexico with the democratic nations, whom we wish to assure that the expropriation now decreed has as its only purpose the elimination of obstacles erected by groups who do not understand the evolutionary needs of all peoples and who would themselves have no compunction in selling Mexican oil to the highest bidder, without taking into account the consequences of such action to the popular masses and the nations in conflict.

---

1. World War II in Europe was still over a year away, but the Japanese invasion of China was in full swing, Spain was in the midst of its civil war, and Hitler had just annexed Austria.

C H A P T E R

13

The Global Community Since 1945

*S*ince the end of World War II, human beings have walked on the moon, invented deadly atomic weapons, created powerful computers, transformed agriculture through the "green revolution," conquered diseases such as polio, and developed sophisticated machines for instant worldwide communication. The communications revolution is just one of the unique examples of late-twentieth-century existence — the ever-greater interaction and interdependence among the world's peoples. International organizations such as the United Nations, international sporting events such as the Olympic Games, and worldwide attempts to coordinate activities such as postal services, disease control, whale hunting, and the preservation of the ozone layer are taken for granted by human beings whose ancestors only 500 years ago lived in a "world" that barely extended beyond their agricultural village.

It is easy, however, to exaggerate the uniqueness of humankind's present state. Many of our problems are age-old. The past half century has seen the dissolution of Western colonial empires and the establishment of new independent nations in much of the world, a movement that has immeasurably changed global politics from what they were 100 years ago. But the breakup of empires is nothing new. Every empire that has ever existed has disappeared, leaving in its wake challenges inherent in any new political order. Similarly, the cold war, the post–World War II competition between the United States and the Soviet Union, is only one more chapter in the long story of rivalries between and among political units. Today's religious conflicts in the Middle East, India, and Northern Ireland confirm that throughout history religion has been something for which humans have been willing to fight and die. The current struggle for justice by oppressed groups such as racial minorities, homosexuals, and women also has many historical precedents in movements to improve the lot of slaves, workers, and peasants.

Perhaps the most unique feature of the modern condition is the vast power now in human hands. The question is how to use that power. The miracles of modern science and medicine, combined with the organizational capacities of modern states, have given human beings the ability to alleviate many of the problems that have always diminished their condition — poverty, hunger, ignorance, premature death from disease. At the same time nuclear weapons have provided them with a means to bring about their destruction — literally in a flash. Another possibility is that human beings will lack the courage or vision to face and solve creatively the many daunting problems before them — environmental damage, resource depletion, Third World poverty, overpopulation, to name only a few. In this case, humanity will continue but in such a way as to mock those modern thinkers who saw limitless progress in humankind's future.

As human beings strive in the late twentieth century to build a world of peace, justice, and environmental responsibility, one thing is certain. Just as the problems they face are worldwide, their solutions will also have to be global in scope. After thousands of years of earthly existence, human beings in the late twentieth century have established a true global community.

The Origins of the Cold War

In February 1945, with victory over Germany in World War II in sight, the Allied leaders, Joseph Stalin, Winston Churchill, and Franklin Roosevelt, met at Yalta, a Soviet city on the Black Sea and agreed that the Soviet Union would have preponderance in the Eastern European nations liberated from the Nazis but that each nation would hold free elections to determine its political future. Instead, within a year after fighting ended, Communist regimes were established in Albania, Yugoslavia, Hungary, Bulgaria, Rumania, and eastern Germany, and in most instances Soviet troops, not free elections, determined the issue. The Soviet Union incorporated the Baltic nations of Latvia, Lithuania, and Estonia. Poland and Czechoslovakia still had coalition governments that included Communist and non-Communist parties, but the presence of numerous Soviet troops in both countries foretold of Communist takeovers.

In the West, these developments confirmed old fears about communism and its presumed goal of world domination. In the Soviet Union, Western opposition to the new pro-Soviet regimes reinforced convictions that capitalist nations were determined to destroy communism. From these mutual fears emerged the conflict between the Soviet Union and the United States that has dominated diplomacy in the second half of the twentieth century. Competition between the two superpowers has taken many forms — propaganda campaigns, espionage, efforts to gain influence in developing nations, the "space race," success in international athletics, votes in the United Nations, and an arms race that has created huge armies and nuclear arsenals. Although thousands of lives have been lost on each side in Korea, Vietnam, and Afghanistan, the ultimate Soviet-American showdown has never occurred. Technically, this has remained a "cold war."

Within the past forty years, cold war tensions have relaxed, but only temporarily. The "peaceful coexistence" of the mid-1950s gave way to renewed acrimony in the early 1960s after the shooting down of a U.S. spy-plane on Soviet soil, the building of the Berlin Wall, and the Cuban missile crisis. Soviet–United States relations improved again in the 1970s during the era of *détente* but deteriorated after the Soviet invasion of Afghanistan in 1979 and the election in 1980 of U.S. president Ronald Reagan, who at first branded the Soviet Union an "evil empire" and sponsored a huge U.S. arms buildup. In the mid-1980s, however, the atmosphere of détente returned, when the new Soviet leader, Mikhail Gorbachev, sought to improve East-West relations. Since 1987 the Soviet Union has withdrawn troops from Eastern Europe and Afghanistan, and the United States and the Soviet Union have agreed to limit their arsenals of intermediate range missiles. Once more people hoped that the cold war was over.

■ **Winston Churchill**

IRON CURTAIN SPEECH

Many Soviet historians claim the cold war began on March 5, 1946, when Winston Churchill, Britain's wartime leader, delivered a speech at Westminster College in Fulton, Missouri, in which he warned of the dangers of Soviet expansionism. Many listened carefully, for the speaker had distinguished himself as one of the twentieth century's outstanding statesmen. Born in 1874 into an aristocratic family, Churchill entered politics at an early age and held many cabinet posts, including First Lord of the Admiralty during World War I. Known for his outspoken views and pugnacious personality, he was one of the few politicians in the 1930s who denounced his government for "appeasing" Hitler to avoid war. In 1940, after Germany defeated France, he was named prime minister to lead his country in what seemed a hopeless struggle against the Nazis. His unwavering determination and inspiring words rallied the nation and contributed to Germany's defeat.

After the war, Churchill feared the Western nations would ignore Soviet expansionism just as they had tolerated Nazi aggression. That the Soviet Union was an enemy, no longer a wartime ally, was the message of the Iron Curtain Speech (also known by Churchill's title, "The Sinews of Peace"), delivered to an audience that included the president of the United States, Harry S. Truman.

Questions
for Analysis

1. How does Churchill characterize the Soviet Union? What does he perceive as its goals?
2. What seems to be the basis of Churchill's fear of communism?
3. How does Churchill view the future role of the United States in world affairs? Of Great Britain?
4. What does Churchill consider the best way to deal with the Russians?

*T*he United States stands at this time at the pinnacle of world power. It is a solemn moment for the American Democracy. For with primacy in power is also joined an awe-inspiring accountability to the future. If you look around you, you must feel not only the sense of duty done but also you must feel anxiety lest you fall below the level of achievement. Opportunity is here now, clear and shining for both our countries. To reject it or ignore it or fritter it away will bring upon us all the long reproaches of the after-time. . . .

A shadow has fallen upon the scenes so lately lighted by the Allied victory. Nobody knows what Soviet Russia and its Communist international organization intends to do in the immediate future, or what are the limits, if any, to their expansive and proselytizing tendencies. . . . We understand the Russian need to be secure on her western frontiers by the removal of all possibility of German aggression. We welcome Russia to her rightful place among the leading nations of the world. We welcome her flag upon the seas. Above all, we welcome constant, frequent and growing contacts between the Russian people and our own people on both sides of the Atlantic. It is my duty however, for I am sure you would wish me to state the facts as I see them to you, to place before you certain facts about the present position in Europe.

From Stettin in the Baltic to Trieste in the Adriatic, an iron curtain[1] has descended across the Continent. Behind that line lie all the capitals of the ancient states of Central and Eastern Europe. Warsaw, Berlin, Prague, Vienna, Budapest, Belgrade, Bucharest and Sofia, all these famous cities and the populations around them lie in what I must call the Soviet sphere, and all are subject in one form or another, not only to Soviet influence but to a very high and, in many cases, increasing measure of control from Moscow. Athens alone — Greece with its immortal glories — is free to decide its future at an election under British, American and French observation. . . . The Communist parties, which were very small in all these Eastern States of Europe, have been raised to pre-eminence and power far beyond their numbers and are seeking everywhere to obtain totalitarian control. Police governments are prevailing in nearly every case, and so far, except in Czechoslovakia, there is no true democracy. . . .

In front of the iron curtain which lies across Europe are other causes for anxiety. In Italy the Communist Party is seriously hampered by having to support the Communist-trained Marshal Tito's[2] claims to former Italian territory at the head of the Adriatic. Nevertheless the future of Italy hangs in the balance. Again one cannot imagine a regenerated Europe without a strong France. All my public life I have worked for a strong France and I never lost faith in her destiny, even in the darkest hours. I will not lose faith now. However, in a great number of countries, far from the Russian frontiers and throughout the world, Communist fifth columns[3] are established and work in complete unity and absolute obedience to the directions they receive from the Communist center. Except in the British Commonwealth and in the United States where Communism is in its infancy, the Communist parties or fifth columns constitute a growing challenge and peril to Christian civilization. These are somber facts for anyone to have to recite on the morrow of a victory gained by so much splendid comradeship in arms and in the cause of freedom and democracy; but we should be most unwise not to face them squarely while time remains. . . .

I have felt bound to portray the shadow which, alike in the west and in the east, falls upon the world. I was a high minister at the time of the Versailles Treaty[4] and a close friend of Mr. Lloyd-George, who was the head of the British delegation at Versailles. . . . In those days there were high hopes and unbounded confidence that the wars were over, and that the

---

1. If one were to draw a line from Stettin, a city in northwestern Poland, to Trieste in northeast Italy, the lands to the east were under Soviet domination; this is Churchill's "iron curtain."

2. Born Josip Broz, Tito (1892–1980) was the Communist leader of Yugoslavia.

3. A term first used during the Spanish Civil War (1936–1939), when a general announced he was besieging Madrid with four columns of troops from the outside and a "fifth column" of supporters inside the city; by extension, any group inside a country that aids the enemy.

4. See Chapter 11.

League of Nations would become all-powerful. I do not see or feel that same confidence or even the same hopes in the haggard world at the present time.

On the other hand I repulse the idea that a new war is inevitable; still more that it is imminent. It is because I am sure that our fortunes are still in our own hands and that we hold the power to save the future, that I feel the duty to speak out now that I have the occasion and the opportunity to do so. I do not believe that Soviet Russia desires war. What they desire is the fruits of war and the indefinite expansion of their power and doctrines. But what we have to consider here today while time remains, is the permanent prevention of war and the establishment of conditions of freedom and democracy as rapidly as possible in all countries. Our difficulties and dangers will not be removed by closing our eyes to them. They will not be removed by mere waiting to see what happens; nor will they be removed by a policy of appeasement. What is needed is a settlement, and the longer this is delayed, the more difficult it will be and the greater our dangers will become.

From what I have seen of our Russian friends and Allies during the war, I am convinced that there is nothing they admire so much as strength, and there is nothing for which they have less respect than for weakness, especially military weakness. For that reason the old doctrine of a balance of power is unsound. We cannot afford, if we can help it, to work on narrow margins, offering temptations to a trial of strength. If the Western Democracies stand together in strict adherence to the principles of the United Nations Charter,[5] their influence for furthering

those principles will be immense and no one is likely to molest them. If however they become divided or falter in their duty and if these all-important years are allowed to slip away then indeed catastrophe may overwhelm us all.

Last time I saw it all coming and cried aloud to my own fellow-countrymen and to the world, but no one paid any attention. Up till the year 1933 or even 1935, Germany might have been saved from the awful fate which has overtaken her and we might all have been spared the miseries Hitler let loose upon mankind. There never was a war in all history easier to prevent by timely action than the one which has just desolated such great areas of the globe. It could have been prevented in my belief without the firing of a single shot, and Germany might be powerful, prosperous and honored today; but no one would listen and one by one we were all sucked into the awful whirlpool. We surely must not let that happen again. . . .

If the population of the English-speaking Commonwealths be added to that of the United States with all that such cooperation implies in the air, on the sea, all over the globe and in science and in industry, and in moral force, there will be no quivering, precarious balance of power to offer its temptation to ambition or adventure. On the contrary, there will be an overwhelming assurance of security. If we adhere faithfully to the Charter of the United Nations and walk forward in sedate and sober strength seeking no one's land or treasure, seeking to lay no arbitrary control upon the thoughts of men; if all British moral and material forces and convictions are joined with your own in

5. Signatories of the United Nations Charter in 1945 pledged to work toward the peaceful settlement of all disputes.

fraternal association, the high-roads of the future will be clear, not only for us but for all, not only for our time, but for a century to come.

▨ Joseph Stalin

PRAVDA INTERVIEW ON CHURCHILL'S IRON CURTAIN SPEECH

On March 14, 1946, only a week and a half after Churchill's speech at Westminster College, *Pravda*, the official newspaper of the Soviet Union and the only source of news for most Soviet citizens, published a response by Premier Joseph Stalin in the form of an interview with an unidentified correspondent.

Questions for Analysis

1. What is Stalin's view of Churchill? Why does he equate him with Hitler? What does he see as Churchill's ultimate goals?
2. Which of Churchill "facts" does Stalin challenge as false?
3. How, according to Stalin, did the course of World War II justify Soviet predominance in Eastern Europe after the war?
4. How does Stalin explain the popularity of Communist regimes in Eastern Europe?

Q. How do you assess the last speech of Mr. Churchill which was made in the United States?

A. I assess it as a dangerous act calculated to sow the seed of discord among the Allied governments and hamper their cooperation.

Q. Can one consider that the speech of Mr. Churchill is damaging to the cause of peace and security?

A. Undoubtedly, yes. In substance, Mr. Churchill now stands in the position of a fire-brand of war. And Mr. Churchill is not alone here. He has friends not only in England but also in the United States of America.

In this respect, one is reminded remarkably of Hitler and his friends. Hitler began to set war loose by announcing his racial theory, declaring that only people speaking the German language represent a fully valuable nation. Mr. Churchill begins to set war loose also by a racial theory, maintaining that only nations speaking the English language are fully valuable nations, called upon to decide the destinies of the entire world.

In substance, Mr. Churchill and his friends in England and the United States present nations not speaking the English language with something like an ultimatum: "Recognize our lordship voluntarily and then all will be well. In the contrary case, war is inevitable."

But the nations have shed their blood during five years of cruel war for the sake of liberty and the independence of their countries, and not for the sake of exchanging the lordship of Hitler for the lordship of Churchill.

It is, therefore, highly probable that the nations not speaking English and which, however, make up an enormous majority of the world's population, will not consent to go into a new slavery. The tragedy of Mr. Churchill lies in the fact that he, as a deep-rooted Tory,[1] cannot understand this simple and obvious truth.

There is no doubt that the set-up of Mr. Churchill is a set-up for war, a call to war with the Soviet Union. . . .

Q. How do you assess that part of Mr. Churchill's speech in which he attacks the democratic regime of the European countries which are our neighbors and in which he criticizes the good neighborly relations established between these countries and the Soviet Union?

A. This part of Mr. Churchill's speech is a mixture of the elements of libel with the elements of rudeness and lack of tact. Mr. Churchill maintains that Warsaw, Berlin, Prague, Vienna, Budapest, Belgrade, Bucharest and Sofia, all these famous cities and the populations of those areas, are within the Soviet sphere and are all subjected to Soviet influence and to the increasing control of Moscow.

Mr. Churchill qualifies this as the "boundless expansionist tendencies of the Soviet Union." It requires no special effort to show that Mr. Churchill rudely and shamelessly libels not only Moscow but also the above-mentioned states neighborly to the U.S.S.R.

To begin with, it is quite absurd to speak of the exclusive control of the U.S.S.R. in Vienna and Berlin, where there are Allied control councils with representatives of four States, where the U.S.S.R. has only one-fourth of the voices.

It happens sometimes that some people are unable to refrain from libel, but still they should know a limit.

Secondly, one cannot forget the following fact: the Germans carried out an invasion of the U.S.S.R. through Finland, Poland, Rumania, Bulgaria[2] and Hungary. The Germans were able to carry out the invasion through these countries by reason of the fact that these countries had governments inimical to the Soviet Union.

As a result of the German invasion, the Soviet Union has irrevocably lost in battle with the Germans, and also during the German occupation and through the expulsion of Soviet citizens to German slave labor camps, about 7,000,000 people.[3] In other words, the Soviet Union has lost in men several times more than Britain and the United States together.

It may be that some quarters are trying to push into oblivion these sacrifices of the Soviet people which ensured the liberation of Europe from the Hitlerite yoke.

But the Soviet Union cannot forget them. One can ask, therefore, what can be surprising in the fact that the Soviet Union, in a desire to ensure its security for

---

1. A member of Britain's Conservative party, which Stalin uses here to designate a person of reactionary views.

2. Stalin's facts are incorrect. The Soviet Union and Bulgaria do not share a common border and were not at war until the Russian army occupied Bulgaria in 1944.

3. Stalin underestimates the Soviet peoples' sacrifice; more likely, 15 to 20 million died during World War II.

the future, tries to achieve that these countries should have governments whose relations to the Soviet Union are loyal? How can one, without having lost one's reason, qualify these peaceful aspirations of the Soviet Union as "expansionist tendencies" of our Government? . . .

Mr. Churchill further maintains that the Communist parties were very insignificant in all these Eastern European countries but reached exceptional strength, exceeding their numbers by far, and are attempting to establish totalitarian countries everywhere; that police-government prevailed in almost all these countries, even up to now, with the exception of Czechoslovakia, and that there exists in them no real democracy. . . .

The growth of the influence of communism cannot be considered accidental. It is a normal function. The influence of the Communists grew because during the hard years of the mastery of fascism in Europe, Communists showed themselves to be reliable, daring and self-sacrificing fighters against fascist regimes for the liberty of peoples. . . .

It is they, millions of these common people, having tried the Communists in the fire of struggle and resistance to fascism, who decided that the Communists deserve completely the confidence of the people. Thus grew the Communists' influence in Europe. Such is the law of historical development.

Of course, Mr. Churchill does not like such a development of events. And he raised the alarm, appealing to force. But he also did not like the appearance of the Soviet regime in Russia after the First World War. Then, too, he raised the alarm and organized an armed expedition of fourteen states against Russia with the aim of turning back the wheel of history.[4]

But history turned out to be stronger than Churchill's intervention and the quixotic antics of Churchill resulted in his complete defeat. I do not know whether Mr. Churchill and his friends will succeed in organizing after the Second World War a new military expedition against Eastern Europe. But if they succeed in this, which is not very probable, since millions of common people stand on guard over the peace, then one man confidently says that they will be beaten, just as they were beaten twenty-six years ago.

NATIONAL SECURITY COUNCIL REPORT-68

The United States wasted little time in heeding Churchill's advice to oppose Soviet expansion. The Truman Doctrine (1947) pledged military aid to Greece and Turkey and any other country resisting a Communist takeover; the Marshall Plan (1947) allocated millions of dollars to rebuild the economies of Western Europe; and the

---

4. Stalin refers to Churchill's energetic efforts to organize a military campaign by Britain, the United States, Japan, and other former allies to stamp out the young Bolshevik regime after World War I. Fourteen nations were technically involved, but their impact on the Russian civil war was negligible.

North Atlantic Treaty Organization was established in 1949 to counter Soviet military strength in Eastern Europe. Although no European countries adopted communism after Czechoslovakia in 1947, American anxiety over international communism sharpened in 1949, when the Communists under Mao Zedong triumphed in China and the Soviets detonated their first atomic bomb.

Against this background, President Truman commissioned the State and Defense departments to prepare a position paper on suitable American response to the Soviet "menace." The result was National Security Council Report-68 (NSC-68), released in April 1950, several months before the Korean War began. The report, which remained classified until the 1970s, provided a blueprint for the United States' cold war strategy.

Questions for Analysis

1. According to this document, how did World War II fundamentally alter world diplomatic relationships?
2. What view of the Soviet Union does this document present?
3. What is the Soviet strategy for subverting the "Free World"?
4. What does "containment" mean? What must be done to ensure its effectiveness?
5. To what extent do the authors express views similar to Churchill?

Within the past thirty-five years the world has experienced two global wars of tremendous violence. . . . During the span of one generation, the international distribution of power has been fundamentally altered. For several centuries it had proved impossible for any one nation to gain such preponderant strength that a coalition of other nations could not in time face it with greater strength. The international scene was marked by recurring periods of violence and war, but a system of sovereign and independent states was maintained, over which no state was able to achieve hegemony.

Two complex sets of factors have now basically altered this historical distribution of power. First, the defeat of Germany and Japan and the decline of the British and French Empires have interacted with the development of the United States and the Soviet Union in such a way that power has increasingly gravitated to these two centers. Second, the Soviet Union, unlike previous aspirants to hegemony, is animated by a new fanatic faith, antithetical to our own, and seeks to impose its absolute authority over the rest of the world. Conflict has, therefore, become endemic and is waged, on the part of the Soviet Union, by violent or non-violent methods in accordance with the dictates of expediency. . . .

On the one hand, the people of the world yearn for relief from the anxiety arising from the risk of atomic war. On the other hand, any substantial further extension of the area under the domination of the Kremlin would raise the possibility that no coalition adequate to confront the

Kremlin with greater strength could be assembled. It is in this context that this Republic and its citizens in the ascendancy of their strength stand in their deepest peril.

The issues that face us are momentous, involving the fulfillment or destruction not only of this Republic but of civilization itself. They are issues which will not await our deliberations. With conscience and resolution this Government and the people it represents must now take new and fateful decisions. . . .

Our overall policy at the present time may be described as one designed to foster a world environment in which the American system can survive and flourish. It therefore rejects the concept of isolation and affirms the necessity of our positive participation in the world community.

This broad intention embraces two subsidiary policies. One is a policy which we would probably pursue even if there were no Soviet threat. It is a policy of attempting to develop a healthy international community. The other is the policy of "containing" the Soviet system. . . .

As for the policy of "containment," it is one which seeks by all means short of war to (1) block further expansion of Soviet power, (2) expose the falsities of Soviet pretentions, (3) induce a retraction of the Kremlin's control and influence and (4) in general, so foster the seeds of destruction within the Soviet system that the Kremlin is brought at least to the point of modifying its behavior to conform to generally accepted international standards.

It was and continues to be cardinal in this policy that we possess superior overall power in ourselves or in dependable combination with other like-minded nations. One of the most important ingredients of power is military strength. In the concept of "containment," the maintenance of a strong military posture is deemed to be essential for two reasons: (1) as an ultimate guarantee of our national security and (2) as an indispensable backdrop to the conduct of the policy of "containment.". . .

At the same time, it is essential to the successful conduct of a policy of "containment" that we always leave open the possibility of negotiation with the U.S.S.R. A diplomatic freeze — and we are in one now — tends to defeat the very purposes of "containment" because it raises tensions at the same time that it makes Soviet retractions and adjustments in the direction of moderated behavior more difficult. It also tends to inhibit our initiative and deprives us of opportunities for maintaining a moral ascendancy in our struggle with the Soviet system. . . .

It is quite clear from Soviet theory and practice that the Kremlin seeks to bring the free world under its dominion by the methods of the cold war. The preferred technique is to subvert by infiltration and intimidation. Every institution of our society is an instrument which it is sought to stultify and turn against our purposes. Those that touch most closely our material and moral strength are obviously the prime targets, labor unions, civic enterprises, schools, churches, and all media for influencing opinion. The effort is not so much to make them serve obvious Soviet ends as to prevent them from serving our ends, and thus to make them sources of confusion in our economy, our culture and our body politic. The doubts and diversities that in terms of our values are part of the merit of a free system, the weaknesses and the problems that are peculiar to it, the rights and privileges that free men enjoy, and the disorganization and destruction left in the wake of the last attack in our freedoms, all are but opportunities for the Kremlin to do its evil work. Every advantage is taken of the fact that our means of prevention and retaliation are limited by those principles and scruples which are precisely the ones that give our freedom and democracy its meaning for us. None of our scruples deter those whose only code is, "morality is that which serves the revolution."

At the same time the Soviet Union is seeking to create overwhelming military force, in order to back up infiltration with intimidation. In the only terms in which it understands strength, it is seeking to demonstrate to the free world that force and the will to use it are on the side of the Kremlin, that those who lack it are decadent and doomed. In local incidents it threatens and encroaches both for the sake of local gains and to increase anxiety and defeatism in all the free world.

The possession of atomic weapons at each of the opposite poles of power, and the inability (for different reasons) of either side to place any trust in the other, puts a premium on a surprise attack against us. It equally puts a premium on a more violent and ruthless prosecution of its design by cold war, especially if the Kremlin is sufficiently objective to realize the improbability of our prosecuting a preventive war. It also puts a premium on piecemeal aggression against others, counting on our unwillingness to engage in atomic war unless we are directly attacked. We run all these risks and the added risk of being confused and immobilized by our inability to weigh and choose, and pursue a firm course based on a rational assessment of each. . . .

Our position as the center of power in the free world places a heavy responsibility upon the United States for leadership. We must organize and enlist the energies and resources of the free world in a positive program for peace which will frustrate the Kremlin design for world domination by creating a situation in the free world to which the Kremlin will be compelled to adjust. Without such a cooperative effort, led by the United States, we will have to make gradual withdrawals under pressure until we discover one day that we have sacrificed positions of vital interest. . . .

In summary, we must, by means of a rapid and sustained build-up of the political, economic, and military strength of the free world, and by means of an affirmative program intended to wrest the initiative from the Soviet Union, confront it with convincing evidence of the determination and ability of the free world to frustrate the Kremlin to the new situation. Failing that, the unwillingness of the determination and ability of the free world to frustrate the Kremlin design of a world dominated by its will. Such evidence is the only means short of war which eventually may force the Kremlin to abandon its present course of action and to negotiate acceptable agreements on issues of major importance.

The whole success of the proposed program hangs ultimately on recognition by this Government, the American people, and all free peoples, that the cold war is in fact a real war in which the survival of the free world is at stake. Essential prerequisites to success are consultations with Congressional leaders designed to make the program the object of nonpartisan legislative support, and a presentation to the public of a full explanation of the facts and implications of the present international situation. The prosecution of the program will require of us all the ingenuity, sacrifice, and unity demanded by the vital importance of the issue and the tenacity to persevere until our national objectives have been attained.

The End of Colonialism

After World War I, the major imperialist powers, despite their crushing losses, actually expanded their colonial holdings as a result of the mandate system established under the League of Nations (see Chapter 11). History did not repeat itself after World War II. Between 1944 and 1985, no less than ninety-six new nations, most of them in Africa and Asia, won their independence, and old-style political colonialism disappeared. Many factors contributed to this reorientation in global politics, including the military and financial exhaustion of postwar Great Britain and France, the destruction of Japan's empire, strengthened nationalist movements in colonial areas, and the emergence of such strong, Western-educated leaders as Nehru in India, Sukarno in Indonesia, Kwame Nkrumah in Ghana, and Jomo Kenyatta in Kenya (see Chapter 12).

Independence for most of the former colonies came peacefully, even if, as in India, the struggle against colonialism had been long and frequently bloody. It took no military confrontation to make France and Great Britain abandon most of their colonies in sub-Saharan Africa. For the British the major exceptions were Kenya and Southern Rhodesia, where relatively large white populations resisted black nationalist movements. Kenya won independence in 1963, but only after the bloody Mau-Mau uprising (1952–1956), while in Southern Rhodesia the white minority illegally declared its independence from Britain in 1965 to protect its property and political rights, thus setting the stage for a protracted guerrilla war before the independent African state of Zimbabwe was born in 1980.

Outside tropical Africa, the British relinquished their former colonies without a struggle, but the French attempted the military occupation of Syria in 1945 before withdrawing at British urging, struggled ten years against nationalists in Vietnam before they were forced out in 1954, granted independence to Tunisia in 1956 only after a two-year guerrilla war, and recognized Algerian independence in 1962 after pouring thousands of men and billions of dollars into a military effort to maintain their hold. The Dutch attempted to reoccupy their former East Indian colonies after World War II, granting independence to the United States of Indonesia in 1949 only after two years of fighting.

As independent nations, many former colonies have floundered. Most began with Western-style constitutions, but wars, social conflict, and inexperience caused democracy, with the major exception of India, to give way to dictatorships. Nor have most of the newly independent nations successfully dealt with economic modernization or overpopulation. None of these problems could have been foreseen at those deeply emotional moments when, in the midst of an armed struggle, a people declared its independence or when during formal and peaceful ceremonies the flag of the new nation was raised for the first time.

DECLARATION OF INDEPENDENCE OF THE DEMOCRATIC REPUBLIC OF VIETNAM

After gaining control of Vietnam in the 1870s and 1880s, France used military force to maintain a firm grip on Vietnam despite widespread dissatisfaction among the Vietnamese. Then, in 1940, France fell to Germany and Vietnam came under the control of the Vichy government, a French puppet regime loyal to Germany. Later in the year, the Vichy administration in Vietnam itself became a puppet of the Japanese, who forced the French to place military facilities and resources at their disposal in return for their continued recognition of French authority. In response, the Vietnamese Communist party, which had maintained a tenuous existence since the 1930s, decided to deemphasize agrarian reform and class warfare and work to organize all Vietnamese in a national struggle for independence. The renamed Viet Minh (Vietnamese Defense League) organized an army and by 1944 controlled three northern provinces. In March 1945, the Japanese forcefully took direct administrative control of Vietnam, ending almost a century of French rule. In August, the Japanese surrender created a political vacuum, which the Viet Minh quickly moved to fill. On August 26, they took Hanoi, and on September 2, their leader Ho Chi Minh proclaimed the Democratic Republic of Vietnam in the following document. The French refused to recognize the new government, setting the stage for almost thirty more years of war before Ho and his supporters achieved their goal of a united and independent Vietnam.

Questions for Analysis

1. By what "right" does this declaration proclaim Vietnamese independence?
2. According to this document, what have been the major "crimes" of the French?
3. Why does the declaration assert that the Vietnamese have won their independence from the Japanese, not the French?
4. Does the declaration seem primarily inspired by nationalism or a desire for social reform?

"*A*ll men are created equal. They are endowed by their Creator with certain inalienable Rights; among these are Life, Liberty and the pursuit of Happiness."

This immortal statement was made in the Declaration of Independence of the United States of America in 1776. In a broader sense, this means: All the peoples on the earth are equal from birth, all the peoples have a right to live and to be happy and free.

The Declaration, made in 1791 at the time of the French Revolution, on the Rights of Man and the Citizen, also states:

"All men are born free and with equal rights, and must always remain free and have equal rights."[1]

Those are undeniable truths.

Nevertheless, for more than eighty years, the French imperialists, abusing the standard of Liberty, Equality and Fraternity, have violated our Fatherland and oppressed our fellow-citizens. They have acted contrary to the ideals of humanity and justice.

In the field of politics, they have deprived our people of every democratic liberty.

They have enforced inhuman laws; they have set up three distinct political regimes in the North, the Center and the South of Viet Nam in order to wreck our national unity and prevent our people from being united.[2]

They have built more prisons than schools. They have mercilessly slain our patriots; they have drowned our uprisings in rivers of blood. They have fettered public opinion; they have practised obscurantism against our people. To weaken our race they have forced us to use opium and alcohol.

In the field of economics, they have fleeced us to the bone, impoverished our people and devastated our land.

They have robbed us of our ricefields, our mines, our forests, our raw materials. They have monopolized the issue of banknotes and the export trade.

They have invented numerous unjustifiable taxes, and reduced our people, especially our peasantry, to a state of extreme poverty.

They have hampered our national bourgeoisie from prospering; they have mercilessly exploited our workers.

In the autumn of 1940, when the Japanese fascists violated Indochina's territory to establish new bases against the Allies, the French imperialists went down on their bended knees and handed over our country to them.

Thus, from that date, our people were subjected to the double yoke of the French and the Japanese. Their sufferings and miseries increased. The result was that from the end of last year to the beginning of this year, from Quang Tri province to the North of Viet Nam, more than two million of our fellow-citizens died from starvation.[3] On the 9th of March, French troops were disarmed by the Japanese. The French colonialists either fled or surrendered, showing that not only were they incapable of "protecting" us, but that, in the span of five years, they had twice sold our country to the Japanese.

On several occasions before the 9th of March, the Viet Minh league had urged the French to join forces with it against the Japanese. Instead of agreeing to this proposal, the French colonialists so intensified their terrorist activities against the Viet Minh members that before fleeing they massacred a great number of political prisoners detained at Yen Bay and Cao Bang.

Notwithstanding all this, our fellow-citizens have always manifested a tolerant and humane attitude towards the French. Even after the Japanese coup de force of March 1943, the Viet Minh League helped

---

1. The date 1791 is not accurate; the Declaration of the Rights of Man and of the Citizen was adopted in 1789 (see Chapter 7).

2. The French had divided Vietnam into Tongking in the north, Annam in the center, and Cochin-China in the south.

3. The starvation was partly the result of Japanese confiscations, but hoarding by Vietnamese and heavy rainfall in the previous autumn also contributed.

many Frenchmen to cross the frontier, rescued some of them from Japanese jails and protected French lives and property.

From the autumn of 1940, our country had in fact ceased to be a French colony and had become a Japanese possession.

After the Japanese had surrendered to the Allies, our whole people rose up to regain our national sovereignty and to found the Democratic Republic of Viet Nam.

The truth is that we have wrested our independence from the Japanese and not from the French.

The French have fled, the Japanese have capitulated. Emperor Bao Dai[4] has abdicated. Our people have broken the chains which for nearly a century have fettered us, and have won independence for the Fatherland. Our people at the same time have overthrown the monarchic regime that has reigned supreme for tens of centuries. In its place has been established the present Democratic Republic.

For these reasons, we, members of the Provisional Government, representing the whole Vietnamese people, declare that from now on we break off all relations of a colonial character with France; we repeal all the international obligations that France has so far subscribed to on behalf of Viet Nam and we abolish all the special rights the French have unlawfully acquired in our Fatherland.

The whole Vietnamese people, animated by a common purpose, are determined to fight to the bitter end against any attempt by the French colonialists to reconquer our country.

We are convinced that the Allied nations, which at Teheran and San Francisco[5] have acknowledged the principles of self-determination and equality of nations, will not refuse to recognize the independence of Viet Nam.

A people that has courageously opposed French domination for more than eighty years, a people that has fought side by side with the Allies against the fascists during these last years, such a people must be free and independent.

For those reasons, we, members of the Provisional Government of the Democratic Republic of Viet Nam, solemnly declare to the world that Viet Nam has the right to be free and independent, and in fact it is so already. The entire Vietnamese people are determined to mobilize all their physical and mental strength, to sacrifice their lives and property in order to safeguard their freedom and independence.

▨ Patrice Lumumba

INDEPENDENCE DAY SPEECH

Among the many independence-day ceremonies that occurred after World War II, few matched the drama of June 30, 1960, when Belgian rule ended in the Congo. By previous arrangement, speeches were to be delivered by young King Baudouin of Belgium and the president-elect of the new Congo Republic, Joseph Kasavubu. The

---

4. Vietnam's figurehead emperor.

5. Churchill, Roosevelt, and Stalin attended the Teheran Conference of 1943; the San Fran-

cisco Conference of April 1945 established the United Nations.

king's speech, paternalistic and patronizing to the extreme, praised King Leopold II, the greedy founder of the Belgian Congo, and congratulated the Belgians for their contributions to Congolese development. Baudouin's speech angered the Congolese, and in his speech Kasavubu skipped over the parts where he had planned to compliment the Belgians. Then the microphone was handed over to Patrice Lumumba, the nationalist leader who had been chosen to be the Congo's first prime minister. His fiery words stunned his listeners and revealed the deep emotional wounds caused by eight decades of colonial rule.

Lumumba, born in 1925 and educated in Stanleyville, had been a postal clerk and a sales manager for a brewery before entering politics in the late 1950s. Founder of the *Mouvement National Congolais* in 1958, Lumumba was the sole Congolese leader who could claim a truly national rather than regional following. Tragically, only months after delivering his speech, Lumumba was dead, one of the many Congolese who died in the civil wars that followed independence.

Questions for Analysis

1. What does Lumumba find to be the most repugnant aspect of Belgian imperialism?
2. What basic disagreements does he have with the Belgian king?
3. After achieving independence the new nation almost immediately disintegrated into chaos. What in Lumumba's speech hints of this imminent political turmoil?

Your Majesty,
Excellencies, Ladies and Gentlemen,
Congolese men and women,
fighters for independence who today are victorious,
I salute you in the name of the Congolese government.

I ask of you all, my friends who have ceaselessly struggled at our side, that this thirtieth of June, 1960, may be preserved as an illustrious date etched indelibly in your hearts, a date whose meaning you will teach proudly to your children, so that they in turn may pass on to their children and to their grandchildren the glorious story of our struggle for liberty.

For if independence of the Congo is today proclaimed in agreement with Belgium, a friendly nation with whom we are on equal footing, yet no Congolese worthy of the name can ever forget that it has been by struggle that this independence has been gained, a continuous and prolonged struggle, an ardent and idealistic struggle, a struggle in which we have spared neither our strength nor our privations, neither our suffering nor our blood.

Of this struggle, one of tears, fire, and blood, we are proud to the very depths of our being, for it was a noble and just struggle, absolutely necessary in order to bring to an end the humiliating slavery which had been imposed upon us by force.

This was our fate during eighty years of colonial rule; our wounds are still too fresh and painful for us to be able to erase them from our memories.

We have known the back-breaking

work exacted from us in exchange for salaries which permitted us neither to eat enough to satisfy our hunger, nor to dress and lodge ourselves decently, nor to raise our children as the beloved creatures that they are.

We have known the mockery, the insults, the blows submitted to morning, noon and night because we were "nègres."[1] Who will forget that to a Negro one used the familiar term of address, not, certainly, as to a friend, but because the more dignified forms were reserved for Whites alone?

We have known that our lands were despoiled in the name of supposedly legal texts which in reality recognized only the right of the stronger.

We have known the law was never the same, whether dealing with a White or a Negro; that it was accommodating for the one, cruel and inhuman to the other.

We have known the atrocious suffering of those who were imprisoned for political opinion or religious beliefs: exiles in their own country, their fate was truly worse than death itself.

We have known that in the cities there were magnificent houses for the Whites and crumbling hovels for the Negroes, that a Negro was not admitted to movie theaters or restaurants, that he was not allowed to enter so-called "European" stores, that when the Negro traveled, it was on the lowest level of a boat, at the feet of the White man in his de luxe cabin.

And, finally, who will forget the hangings or the firing squads where so many of our brothers perished, or the cells into which were brutally thrown those who escaped the soldiers' bullets — the soldiers whom the colonialists made the instruments of their domination?

From all this, my brothers, have we deeply suffered.

But all this, however, we who by the vote of your elected representatives are directed to guide our beloved country, we who have suffered in our bodies and in our hearts from colonialist oppression, we it is who tell you — all this is henceforth ended.

The Republic of the Congo has been proclaimed, and our beloved country is now in the hands of its own children.

Together, my brothers, we are going to start a new struggle, a sublime struggle, which will lead our country to peace, prosperity and greatness.

Together we are going to establish social justice and ensure for each man just remuneration for his work.

We are going to show the world what the black man can do when he works in freedom, and we are going to make the Congo the hub of all Africa.

We are going to be vigilant that the lands of our nation truly profit our nation's children.

We are going to re-examine all former laws, and make new ones which will be just and noble.

We are going to put an end to suppression of free thought and make it possible for all citizens fully to enjoy the fundamental liberties set down in the declaration of the Rights of Man.[2]

We are going to succeed in suppressing all discrimination — no matter what it may be — and give to each individual the just place to which his human dignity, his work and his devotion to his country entitle him.

---

1. *Nègres*, the French word for Negroes, when used in certain contexts or phrases had racist, derogatory connotations.

2. The statement of political principles written early in the French Revolution (see Chapter 6).

We shall cause to reign not the peace of guns and bayonets, but the peace of hearts and good will.

And for all this, dear compatriots, rest assured that we shall be able to count upon not only our own enormous forces and immense riches, but also upon the assistance of numerous foreign countries whose collaboration we shall accept only as long as it is honest and does not seek to impose upon us any political system, whatever it may be.

In this domain, even Belgium, who finally understanding the sense and direction of history has no longer attempted to oppose our independence, is ready to accord us its aid and friendship, and a treaty to this effect has just been signed between us as two equal and independent countries. This cooperation, I am sure, will prove profitable for both countries. For our part, even while remaining vigilant, we shall know how to respect commitments freely consented to.

Thus, in domestic as well as in foreign affairs, the new Congo which my government is going to create will be a rich country, a free and prosperous one. But in order that we may arrive at this goal without delay, I ask you all, legislators and Congolese citizens, to help me with all your power.

I ask you all to forget tribal quarrels which drain our energies, and risk making us an object of scorn among other nations.

I ask the parliamentary minority to help my government by constructive opposition, and to remain strictly within legal and democratic bounds.

I ask you all not to demand from one day to the next unconsidered raises in salary before I have had the time to set in motion an over-all plan through which I hope to assure the prosperity of the nation.

I ask you all not to shrink from any sacrifice in order to assure the success of our magnificent enterprises.

I ask you all, finally, to respect unconditionally the life and the property of your fellow citizens and of the foreigners established in our country. If the behavior of these foreigners leaves something to be desired, our justice will be prompt in expelling them from the territory of the Republic; if, on the other hand, their conduct is satisfactory, they must be left in peace, for they also are working for the prosperity of our country.

And so, my brothers in race, my brothers in conflict, my compatriots, this is what I wanted to tell you in the name of the government, on this magnificent day of our complete and sovereign Independence.

Our government — strong, national, popular — will be the salvation of this country.

Homage to the Champions of National Liberty!

Long Live Independent and Sovereign Congo!

Religious Conflict

Although gradual secularization has characterized world history since 1500, religion remains a vital force in the lives of millions of human beings. In several parts of the world, religious tensions, usually in concert with social and political conflict, have caused bloodshed and violence. In India, Hindu-Muslim clashes have resurfaced, and the Sikhs (see Chapter 2), who were responsible for the assassination of Prime Minister Indira Gandhi in 1984, have resorted to violence to gain greater autonomy. In Northern Ireland the list of deaths resulting from Protestant-Catholic hatreds grows longer each year.

Religious conflicts have been most damaging in the Middle East. The establishment of the Jewish state of Israel in Palestine in 1948 was an affront to the region's pious Muslims, who immediately declared war on the new country. Israel's survival and subsequent expansion only exacerbated tensions that have resulted in three more wars, millions of refugees, countless acts of terrorism, and the disintegration of Lebanon. Resolution of the Arab-Israeli conflict seems no closer today than forty years ago.

Tensions within the Islamic faith itself have also convulsed the Middle East. Sunni-Shiite hostility (see Chapter 2) contributed to the demise of Lebanon and was the root of the costly and debilitating war between largely Sunni Iraq and Shiite Iran from 1980 to 1988. Since the 1920s, Muslims have also deeply disagreed over how to come to terms with Western-inspired science and secularism. As seen in Chapter 12, Mustafa Kemal, in his campaign to modernize Turkey, severely limited Islam's role in education, government, and people's everyday lives. Progress and secularization, he believed, went hand in hand. Kemal's policies had many imitators, most notably the Pahlavi rulers of Iran, Reza Shah (1925–1941) and Muhammad Reza Shah (1941–1979), and the current president of Iraq, Saddam Hussein.

Other Muslims, however, found such "progress" profoundly disturbing. Fundamentalists deplored the drift toward secularism and materialism and urged Muslims to renew their devotion to Islamic values. During the 1960s and 1970s, Islamic fundamentalism helped cause the demise of secularist rulers in Indonesia, Libya, Pakistan, and Iran and is a destabilizing element in many predominantly Muslim states. It has fostered terrorism and intensified both the Arab-Israeli conflict and anti-Western animosity throughout the region.

Palestine Liberation Organization

THE PALESTINE NATIONAL CHARTER

In 1947, faced with the impossible task of reconciling Jewish demands for complete freedom to settle in Palestine with the implacable opposition of Palestinian Arabs, the British announced their intention to leave Palestine in 1948, handing the problem to the newly founded United Nations. In a nonbinding resolution late in 1947, the UN recommended partitioning Palestine into separate states, one Jewish and one Arab. After nearly a year of Arab-Jewish violence, the Jews proclaimed the independent state of Israel when the British formally departed on May 14, 1948. The Arab states immediately sent in their armies to destroy it.

Israel won the war but in so doing created a problem that more than any other has poisoned their relations with the Arabs. During the fighting 750 to 900 thousand Palestinian Arabs fled to Egypt, Jordan, and Syria, most of them assuming they would return to their homes after the war ended. Israel, however, refused to permit their return and confiscated their property. During the 1950s the refugees, most of them living in camps in Egypt and Jordan, formed a number of organizations to give them a political voice and to work toward winning back their homeland. In 1964, with the approval of the major Arab states, these groups formed the Palestine Liberation Organization (PLO), whose goals were spelled out in the Palestine National Charter, approved at the meeting of the Fourth Palestine National Council in November 1968.

Questions for Analysis

1. How does the National Charter define who is a Palestinian?
2. Why does the charter compare Zionism (the drive to establish an independent Jewish state in Palestine) with imperialism? Why does it compare Zionism with racism?
3. Why does the charter argue that the partition of Palestine in 1947 was "fundamentally invalid"?
4. How does the charter propose to achieve Palestine's liberation?

1. Palestine, the homeland of the Palestinian Arab people, is an inseparable part of the greater Arab homeland, and the Palestinian people are a part of the Arab Nation.

2. Palestine, within the frontiers that existed under the British Mandate, is an indivisible territorial unit.

3. The Palestinian Arab people alone have legitimate rights to their homeland, and shall exercise the right of self-determination after the liberation of their homeland, in keeping with their wishes and entirely of their own accord.

4. The Palestinian identity is an authentic, intrinsic and indissoluble quality that is transmitted from father to son. Neither the Zionist occupation nor the dispersal of the Palestinian Arab people as a result of the afflictions they have suffered can efface this Palestinian identity.

5. Palestinians are Arab citizens who were normally resident in Palestine until 1947. This includes both those who were forced to leave or who stayed in Palestine. Anyone born to a Palestinian father after that date, whether inside or outside Palestine, is a Palestinian.

6. Jews who were normally resident in Palestine up to the beginning of the Zionist invasion are Palestinians.

7. Palestinian identity, and material, spiritual and historical links with Palestine are immutable realities. It is a national obligation to provide every Palestinian with a revolutionary Arab upbringing, and to instill in him a profound spiritual and material familiarity with his homeland and a readiness for armed struggle and for the sacrifice of his material possessions and his life, for the recovery of his homeland. All available educational means and means of guidance must be enlisted to that end, until liberation is achieved.

8. The Palestinian people is at the stage of national struggle for the liberation of its homeland. For that reason, differences between Palestinian national forces must give way to the fundamental difference that exists between Zionism and imperialism on the one hand and the Palestinian Arab people on the other. On that basis, the Palestinian masses, both as organizations and as individuals, whether in the homeland or in such places as they now live as refugees, constitute a single national front working for the recovery and liberation of Palestine through armed struggle.

9. Armed struggle is the only way of liberating Palestine. . . . The Palestinian Arab people hereby affirm their unwavering determination to carry on the armed struggle and to press on towards popular revolution for the liberation of and return to their homeland. They also affirm their right to a normal life in their homeland, to the exercise of their right of self-determination therein and to sovereignty over it.

10. Commando action[1] constitutes the nucleus of the Palestinian popular war of liberation. This requires that commando action should be escalated, expanded and protected, and that all the resources of the Palestinian masses and all scientific potentials available to them should be mobilized and organized to play their part in the armed Palestinian revolution. . . .

12. The Palestinian Arab people believe in Arab unity. To fulfill their role in the achievement of that objective, they must,

at the present stage in their national struggle, retain their Palestinian identity and all that it involves, work for increased awareness of it and oppose all measures liable to weaken or dissolve it. . . .

14. The destiny of the Arab nation, indeed the continued existence of the Arabs, depends on the fate of the Palestinian cause. This interrelationship is the point of departure of the Arab endeavor to liberate Palestine. The Palestinian people are the vanguard of the movement to achieve this sacred national objective.

15. The liberation of Palestine is a national obligation for the Arabs. It is their duty to repel the Zionist and imperialist invasion of the greater Arab homeland and to liquidate the Zionist presence in Palestine. The full responsibility for this belongs to the peoples and governments of the Arab nation and to the Palestinian people first and foremost. For this reason, the task of the Arab nation is to enlist all the military, human, moral and material resources at its command to play an effective part, along with the Palestinian people, in the liberation of Palestine. . . .

16. On the spiritual plane, the liberation of Palestine will establish in the Holy Land an atmosphere of peace and tranquility in which all religious institutions will be safeguarded and freedom of worship and the right of visit guaranteed to all without discrimination or distinction of race, color, language or creed. For this reason the people of Palestine look to all spiritual forces in the world for support.

17. On the human plane, the liberation of Palestine will restore to the Palestinians their dignity, integrity and freedom.

---

1. Commandos are small, usually well-trained forces operating inside enemy territory.

For this reason, the Palestinian Arab people look to all those who believe in the dignity and freedom of man for support.

18. On the international plane, the liberation of Palestine is a defensive measure dictated by the requirements of self-defense. This is why the Palestinian people, who seek to win the friendship of all peoples, look for the support of all freedom, justice and peace-loving countries in restoring the legitimate state of affairs in Palestine, establishing security and peace in it and enabling its people to exercise national sovereignty and freedom.

19. The partition of Palestine, which took place in 1947, and the establishment of Israel, are fundamentally invalid, however long they last, for they contravene the will of the people of Palestine and their natural right to their homeland and contradict the principles of the United Nations Charter, foremost among which is the right of self-determination.

20. The Balfour Declaration, the Mandate Instrument, and all their consequences, are hereby declared null and void.[2] The claim of historical or spiritual links between the Jews and Palestine is neither in conformity with historical fact nor does it satisfy the requirements for statehood. Judaism is a revealed religion; it is not a separate nationality, nor are the Jews a single people with a separate identity; they are citizens of their respective countries.

21. The Palestinian Arab people, expressing themselves through the Palestinian armed revolution, reject all alternatives to the total liberation of Palestine. . . .

22. Zionism is a political movement that is organically linked with world imperialism and is opposed to all liberation movements or movements for progress in the world. The Zionist movement is essentially fanatical and racialist; its objectives involve aggression, expansion and the establishment of colonial settlements, and its methods are those of the Fascists and the Nazis. Israel acts as cat's paw for the Zionist movement, a geographic and manpower base for world imperialism and a springboard for its thrust into the Arab homeland to frustrate the aspirations of the Arab nation to liberation, unity and progress. Israel is a constant threat to peace in the Middle East and the whole world. Inasmuch as the liberation of Palestine will eliminate the Zionist and imperialist presence in that country and bring peace to the Middle East, the Palestinian people look for support to all liberals and to all forces of good, peace and progress in the world, and call on them, whatever their political convictions, for all possible aid and support in their just and legitimate struggle to liberate their homeland.

23. The demands of peace and security and the exigencies of right and justice require that all nations should regard Zionism as an illegal movement and outlaw it and its activities, out of consideration for the ties of friendship between peoples and for the loyalty of citizens of their homelands. . . .

26. The Palestine Liberation Organization, as the representative of the forces of the Palestinian revolution, is responsible for the struggle of the Palestinian Arab people to regain, liberate and return to

---

2. The Balfour Declaration of 1917 pledged the British government to work for the establishment of a Jewish state in Palestine; after World War I, Palestine became a British mandate (see Chapter 12).

their homeland and to exercise the right of self-determination in that homeland, in the military, political and financial fields, and for all else that the Palestinian cause may demand, both at Arab and international levels.

Chaim Herzog

SPEECH TO THE UNITED NATIONS GENERAL ASSEMBLY

In the mid-1970s, the Palestine Liberation Organization, with the support of most Arab states, launched a campaign to discredit the state of Israel in international forums. In August 1975, for example, the Organization of African Unity grouped Israel with the white-dominated regimes of South Africa and Rhodesia when it condemned racism and imperialism, and later in the year, the Conference of Non-Aligned Nations, meeting in Peru, also condemned Zionism as a racist and imperialist ideology. In November, an anti-Israeli resolution was proposed in the General Assembly of the United Nations.

Chaim Herzog, Israeli ambassador to the UN, denounced the anti-Zionist resolution in the following speech on November 10, 1973. Despite his efforts, later in the day a coalition of Muslim, Arab, Third World, and Soviet-bloc nations approved the resolution that "Zionism is a form of racism and racial discrimination."

Questions for Analysis

1. What does Herzog mean when he says, "Zionism is to the Jewish people what the liberation movements of Africa and Asia have been to their own people"?
2. How does Herzog's historical perspective on Palestine differ from that of the 1968 Palestine National Charter?

*I*t is symbolic that this debate, which may well prove to be a turning point in the fortunes of the United Nations and a decisive factor in the possible continued existence of this organization, should take place on November 10. Tonight, thirty-seven years ago, has gone down in history as Kristallnacht, the Night of the Crystals. This was the night in 1938 when Hitler's Nazi storm-troopers launched a coordinated attack on the Jewish community in Germany, burned the synagogues in all its cities and made bonfires in the streets of the Holy Books and the Scrolls of the Holy Law and Bible. It was the night when Jewish homes were attacked and heads of families taken away, many of them never to return. It was the night when the windows of all Jewish businesses and stores were smashed, covering the streets in the cities of Germany with a film of broken glass which dissolved into the millions of crystals which gave the night its name. It was the night which led eventually to the crematoria and the gas chambers, Auschwitz, Birkenau, Dachau, Buchenwald, Teresienstadt and others. It was the night which led to the most terrifying holocaust in the history of man.

It is indeed befitting, Mr. President, that this debate, conceived in the desire to deflect the Middle East from its moves towards peace and born of a deep pervading feeling of anti-Semitism, should take place on the anniversary of this day. It is indeed befitting, Mr. President, that the United Nations, which began its life as an anti-Nazi alliance, should thirty years later find itself on its way to becoming the world center of anti-Semitism. Hitler would have felt at home on a number of occasions during the past year, listening to the proceedings in this forum, and above all to the proceedings during the debate on Zionism.

It is sobering to consider to what level this body has been dragged down if we are obliged today to contemplate an attack on Zionism. For this attack constitutes not only an anti-Israeli attack of the foulest type, but also an assault in the United Nations on Judiasm — one of the oldest established religions in the world, a religion which has given the world the human values of the Bible, and from which two other great religions, Christianity and Islam, sprang. Is it not tragic to consider that we here at this meeting in the year 1975 are contemplating what is a scurri-

lous attack on a great and established religion which has given to the world the Bible with its Ten Commandments, the great prophets of old, Moses, Isaiah, Amos; the great thinkers of history, Maimonides, Spinoza, Marx, Einstein,[1] many of the masters of the arts and as high a percentage of the Nobel Prize-winners in the world, in sciences, in the arts and in the humanities as has been achieved by any people on earth? . . .

The resolution against Zionism was originally one condemning racism and colonialism, a subject on which we could have achieved consensus, a consensus which is of great importance to all of us and to our African colleagues in particular. However, instead of permitting this to happen, a group of countries, drunk with the feeling of power inherent in the automatic majority[2] and without regard to the importance of achieving a consensus on this issue, railroaded the U.N. in a contemptuous maneuver by the use of the automatic majority into bracketing Zionism with the subject under discussion.

I do not come to this rostrum to defend the moral and historical values of the Jewish people. They do not need to be defended. They speak for themselves. They have given to mankind much of what is great and eternal. They have done for the spirit of man more than can readily be appreciated by a forum such as this one.

I come here to denounce the two great evils which menace society in general and a society of nations in particular. These two evils are hatred and ignorance. These two evils are the motivating force behind

---

1. Maimonides (1135–1204) and Baruch Spinoza (1632–1677) were prominent philosophers; Albert Einstein (1879–1955) was a giant of modern physics. There is some irony in the mention of Karl Marx, given that all the Communist and pro-Marxist governments would vote in favor of the anti-Zionist resolution.

2. The coalition of Communist, "unaligned," and Third World states had the votes to win a majority on any issue that was meaningful to them.

the proponents of this resolution and their supporters. These two evils characterize those who would drag this world organization, the ideals of which were first conceived by the prophets of Israel, to the depths to which it has been dragged today.

The key to understanding Zionism is in its name. The eastern-most of the two hills of ancient Jerusalem during the tenth century B.C.E. was called Zion. In fact, the name Zion, referring to Jerusalem, appears 152 times in the Old Testament. The name is overwhelmingly a poetic and prophetic designation. The religious and emotional qualities of the name arise from the importance of Jerusalem as the Royal City and the City of the Temple. "Mount Zion" is the place where God dwells. Jerusalem, or Zion, is a place where the Lord is King, and where He has installed His King, David.

King David made Jerusalem the capital of Israel almost three thousand years ago, and Jerusalem has remained the capital ever since. During the centuries the term "Zion" grew and expanded to mean the whole of Isreal. The Israelites in exile could not forget Zion. The Hebrew Psalmist sat by the waters of Babylon and swore: "If I forget thee, O Jerusalem, let my right hand forget her cunning." This oath has been repeated for thousands of years by Jews throughout the world. It is an oath which was made over seven hundred years before the advent of Christianity and over twelve hundred years before the advent of Islam, and Zion came to mean the Jewish homeland, symbolic of Judaism, of Jewish national aspirations.

While praying to his God every Jew, wherever he is in the world, faces towards Jerusalem. For over two thousand years of exile these prayers have expressed the yearning of the Jewish people to return to their ancient homeland, Isreal. In fact, a continuous Jewish presence, in larger or smaller numbers, has been maintained in the country over the centuries.

Zionism is the name of the national movement of the Jewish people and is the modern expression of the ancient Jewish heritage. The Zionist ideal, as set out in the Bible, has been, and is, an integral part of the Jewish religion.

Zionism is to the Jewish people what the liberation movements of Africa and Asia have been to their own people.

Zionism is one of the most dynamic and vibrant national movements in human history. Historically it is based on a unique and unbroken connection, extending some four thousand years, between the People of the Book and the Land of the Bible.

In modern times, in the late nineteenth century, spurred by the twin forces of anti-Semitic persecution and of nationalism, the Jewish people organized the Zionist movement in order to transform their dream into reality. Zionism as a political movement was the revolt of an oppressed nation against the depredation and wicked discrimination and oppression of the countries in which anti-Semitism flourished. It is no coincidence that the co-sponsors and supporters of this resolution include countries who are guilty of the horrible crimes of anti-Semitism and discrimination to this very day.

Support for the aim of Zionism was written into the League of Nations Mandate for Palestine and was again endorsed by the United Nations in 1947, when the General Assembly voted by overwhelming majority for the restoration of Jewish independence in our ancient land.

The re-establishment of Jewish independence in Israel, after centuries of struggle to overcome foreign conquest and exile, is a vindication of the fundamental concepts of the equality of nations and of self-determination. To question the

Jewish people's right to national existence and freedom is not only to deny to the Jewish people the right accorded to every other people on this globe, but it is also to deny the central precepts of the United Nations.

Ayatollah Ruhullah Khomeini

IN COMMEMORATION OF THE FIRST MARTYRS OF THE REVOLUTION

Ayatollah Ruhullah Khomeini, whose name is synonymous with Islamic fundamentalism and Iran's Islamic Revolution, was born in 1902 in Khumayn, a small Iranian village sixty miles southwest of Teheran, and died early in 1989. Following the example of his father and grandfather, he became a religious scholar who by the late 1930s directed a prestigious Islamic school in the city of Qum. In the late 1950s he became a vocal opponent of Shah Muhammad Reza Pahlavi, attacking the shah's pro–U.S. policies, dictatorial rule, and efforts to diminish Islam's role in Iranian life. In 1963 widespread rioting, inspired in part by the Qum scholars, was suppressed by the shah's troops, and Khomeini was arrested and sent into exile. While living in Turkey, Iraq, and France, he continued to denounce the shah, whose heavy-handed rule, corrupt government, and ill-conceived economic policies were causing widespread discontent. On January 8, 1978, rioting again broke out in Qum, this time sparked by articles in the state-controlled press insulting Khomeini. In the following months, millions of Iranians, spurred on by Khomeini and other Islamic clergy, took to the streets, chanting, "death to the shah." In early 1979, events moved quickly. In January the shah left the country; in February Khomeini returned from exile; and in March a national referendum approved the establishment of the Islamic Republic of Iran.

Khomeini delivered the following speech at a mosque in Najaf, Iraq, in February 1978. Later printed and distributed in Iran, it is a good example of the ayatollah's anti–United States, anti-shah rhetoric in the early days of the Iranian Revolution.

Questions for Analysis

1. What are Khomeini's stated reasons for denouncing the United States? Does he hate the Americans simply because of their support for the shah? What do Americans represent to Khomeini?
2. What in Khomeini's view is the proper relationship between Islam and politics? What are the major points of disagreement with Mustafa Kemal (see Chapter 12)?
3. What is Khomeini's view of the shah's efforts to modernize and industrialize Iran?

4. What in his speech suggests some of the reasons for Khomeini's popularity among the Iranian masses?
5. Why does Khomeini insist at the end of his speech on the necessity of reading the Qur'an?

*A*ll the miseries that we have suffered, still suffer, and are about to suffer soon are caused by the heads of those countries that have signed the Declaration of Human Rights,[1] but that at all times have denied man his freedom. Freedom of the individual is the most important part of the Declaration of Human Rights. Individual human beings must all be equal before the law, and they must be free. They must be free in their choice of residence and occupation. But we see the Iranian nation, together with many others, suffering at the hands of those states that have signed and ratified the Declaration.

The U.S. is one of the signatories to this document. It has agreed that the rights of man must be protected and that man must be free. But see what crimes America has committed against man. As long as I can remember — and I can remember back further than many of you, for you are younger than I — America has created disasters for mankind. It has appointed its agents in both Muslim and non-Muslim countries to deprive everyone who lives under their domination of his freedom. The imperialists proclaim that man is free only in order to deceive the masses. But people can no longer be deceived. All these declarations they make, supposedly in favor of human rights, have no reality; they are designed to deceive. . . . What we have said is true not only of America

but also of Britain, another power that signed and ratified the Declaration of Human Rights — Britain, whose civilization and democracy everybody praises so much without realizing that they are repeating the propaganda slogans Britain is cunningly feeding people; Britain, which is meant to practice true constitutionalism! But have we not seen, despite all this propaganda, what crimes Britain has committed in India, Pakistan, and its other colonies?

The imperialist states, like America and Britain, brought Israel into existence, and we have seen what misery they have inflicted on the Muslim peoples by means of Israel, and what crimes they are now committing against the Muslims, particularly the Shi'a. . . .

As for America, a signatory to the Declaration of Human Rights, it imposed this Shah upon us, a worthy successor to his father. During the period he has ruled, this creature has transformed Iran into an official colony of the U.S. What crimes he has committed in service to his masters!

What crimes that father and this son have committed against the Iranian nation since their appointment by the signatories to the Declaration of Human Rights. All they have to offer humanity is repression; we have witnessed part of it, and we have heard of part of it. But hearing is not enough truly to understand. You may have heard what happened to the people

---

1. The reference is to the Universal Declaration of Human Rights, adopted by the United Nations on December 10, 1948.

in the time of Riza Khan,[2] but you cannot perceive what the people themselves actually went through. You cannot yourselves experience what this man is doing now. You can understand what has happened to the Iranian people during the last few days as a result of recent events, but you cannot actually experience it. . . .

The Iranian government granted absolute immunity to the American advisers and got a few dollars in exchange. How many American officers there are in Iran now, and what huge salaries they receive! That is our problem — everything in our treasury has to be emptied into the pockets of America, and if there is any slight remainder, it has to go to the Shah and his gang. They buy themselves villas abroad and stuff their bank accounts with the people's money, while the nation subsists in poverty. At the same time, they say constantly, "Iran is one of the most advanced countries in the world. It is now on a par with America, or at least Japan (maybe a bit more advanced than Japan)." But the absurdity of these words and the corrupt frame of mind that underlies them have become apparent to everyone. Even the corner grocer will tell you, "The Shah is talking nonsense." But he's quite unashamed and goes right on talking. We can't do anything about it. . . .

We are faced with so many difficulties; I cannot possibly tell you all of them. God knows, the problems that are referred to me by the people! They tell me, for example, "We want to build a water-storage tank at such-and-such a place, because there the people have no water." Now if people don't have water, do they have electricity? Do they have paved roads? They have nothing!

Ignore the northern sections of Tehran where they have put things in order; go take a look at the south of the city — go look at those pits, those holes in the ground where people live, dwellings you reach by going down about a hundred steps into the ground; homes people have built out of rush matting or clay so their poor children can have somewhere to live. I am talking about Tehran, not some distant village or town; that is the way Tehran is. When you enter Tehran, you see all the cars and that deceptive exterior, but you haven't gone to the other side of Tehran to see what state that is in. They don't have any drinking water. They have to take their pitchers and climb up those hundred steps until they come to a water faucet, then fill their pitchers, and climb down again. Picture some poor woman in the middle of the biting winter climbing up and down those steps to fetch water for her children. A reliable informant told me that some poor woman who was living in one of those holes brought her children and sat down right in the middle of Paminar Avenue, until finally people gathered around and helped her find a place to live. That is our highly advanced country with its capital city, Tehran.

In one of their own newspapers they wrote that in some part of the country — I can't remember exactly where; I think it was somewhere in the region of Shushtar — when the people wake up in the morning, they wash the trachoma-infected eyes of their children with urine so they can open their eyes. That is the state of our country, our advanced and progressive country!

What happens to all that money? Is our country poor? Our country has an ocean of oil. It has iron; it has precious metals. Iran is a rich country. But those so-called

---

2. Riza (or Reza Shah), the founder of the Pahlavi Dynasty, was Shah of Iran from 1925 until 1941. In imitation of Mustafa Kemal, he sought the modernization and secularization of Iran.

friends of humanity have appointed their agent to rule this country in order to prevent the poor from benefiting from its riches. Everything must go into his masters' pockets and be spent on their enjoyment. . . .

The religious center in Qum has brought Iran back to life; it has performed a service to Islam that will endure for centuries. This service must not be underestimated; pray for the religious center in Qum and pray that we will come to resemble it. The name of the religious center in Qum will remain inscribed in history for all time. By comparison with Qum, we here in Najaf are dead and buried; it is Qum that has brought Islam back to life. It is the center in Qum and the preaching of its *maraji'* and *'ulama*[3] that have awakened the universities, those same places where we religious scholars used to be accused of being the opium of the people and the agents of the British and other imperialists. . . .

The imperialists know full well how active the religious scholars are, and what an activist and militant religion Islam is. So they drew up a plan to bring the religious scholars into disrepute, and for several centuries propagated the notion that religion must be separated from politics. Some came to believe it and began asking, "What business do we have with politics?" The posing of this question means the abandonment of Islam; it means burying Islam in our cells in the *madrasa!*[4] . . .

They kill our young men, and we shouldn't care? They kill our *'ulama*, and we shouldn't care? They kill the believers and the Muslims, and we shouldn't care? We are supposed to agree to all this, or do something that suggests our agreement? Then we must become different human beings! . . .

We have not read the Qur'an properly and have not understood the logic of the Qur'an. Above all else, we must study the Qur'an; the Qur'an has given instructions for everything and made clear what our duties are. . . .

The Qur'an constantly discusses warfare against the unbelievers, and mentions the question of the hypocrites; is this purely for the purpose of telling us a story? Is the Qur'an a book of stories? The Qur'an is a book designed to produce true human beings; it is a book intended to create active human beings; it is a book that deals with everything in this world, from beginning to end, and all the stages in man's development. It is a book that regulates man's spiritual life and orders his government. Everything is there, in the Qur'an . . . but careful study . . . is needed in order for us to understand what we must do. We constantly read in the Qur'an that the Pharaoh acted in a certain way and Moses in another way, but we don't think about why the Qur'an tells us all this. It tells us this so that we may act like Moses toward the Pharaoh of our age; let us pick up our staffs and oppose this vile Shah. At the very least, let no one support this regime.

May God Almighty grant all of you success. May God Almighty remove this evil from rule over the Muslims. May God, Exalted and Almighty, preserve our people in the midst of their tribulation. May God, Exalted and Almighty, grant the Muslims a favorable result in this, their struggle.

And peace be upon you, and the mercy and blessings of God.

---

3. Muslim clergy, noted for their legal and religious learning, who at the local level made judgments on private and public matters.

4. Schools for teaching Islamic law, theology, and Arabic literature.

The Struggle for Racial Equality

Racism, a belief that one ethnic group is inherently superior to others, has existed throughout history and has been used repeatedly to justify the conquest, enslavement, and exploitation of "inferior peoples" by their self-proclaimed betters. In the past 500 years, racism has contributed to the enslavement of Black Africans, Western imperialism, the Nazi assault on the Jews, the near destruction of American Indian culture, Japanese expansionism, and the legally sanctioned discrimination against persons of color in colonial India and Africa, the United States, and South Africa.

Despite the universal revulsion against Nazi racist doctrines, the end of colonialism in Africa and Asia, and the recent economic accomplishments of Asian peoples in Taiwan, Korea, and Japan, racism continues to warp human relationships at many levels and in many parts of the world. Thus, an important theme in recent world history has been the continuing struggle by suppressed peoples, especially in Africa and the United States, to end racial prejudice and gain full acceptance and equality. Victories have been won, but many battles are still being fought, and at this point in history it is unclear if human beings can build a world in which a person's skin color truly does not matter.

Nelson Mandela

THE RIVONIA TRIAL SPEECH TO THE COURT

Although the South African government has practiced legally sanctioned racial segregation since gaining independence from Great Britain in 1910, only in 1948, under the leadership of the National party, did the nation officially adopt the policy of "apartheid." Apartheid, which means "apartness" in Afrikaans, the Dutch dialect of South Africa, classifies all South Africans as Bantu (all Black Africans), Colored (those of mixed race), Asians (Indians and Pakistani), and White. In a series of laws passed in the 1950s, the government established separate business and residential areas in cities for each race, forbade most social contact among races, authorized segregated public facilities, established separate educational systems and standards, restricted each race to certain kinds of jobs, denied non-White participation in the national government, and forced all Blacks to live in Black "homelands," or Bantustans.

Blacks have fought racism in South Africa since 1910, the nation's year of independence. In 1913 they formed the African National Congress (ANC), whose goal was to foster unity among Africans and work peacefully for political rights. At first, the ANC sought to reach its goals through petitions and appeals to White politicians, but after the adoption of apartheid, it sponsored Gandhi-inspired campaigns of passive resistance and supported strikes by Black labor unions. Violence often resulted, leading to more government repression and measures to stifle Black political activity.

Predictably, frustration over their deteriorating condition caused some Blacks to abandon moderation for sabotage and terrorism. Among them was Nelson Mandela, a Black lawyer who had been active in the ANC since the 1940s. After the ANC was outlawed in 1960 and he organized a three-day stay-at-home protest in 1961, Mandela went underground and, while avoiding a nationwide manhunt, helped establish *Umkonto we Sizwe* ("Spear of the Nation" in Zulu), a branch of the ANC that carried out bombings in several South African cities. Turned in by an informer in 1963, he was convicted of treason and sent to Robben Island, the notorious prison forty miles south of Capetown, where he remained until 1982, when he was returned to a mainland prison. In summer 1989, Mandela met with South Africa's prime minister P. W. Botha for reasons that are unclear.

The following excerpt comes from Mandela's speech of April 20, 1964, by which he opened his defense before an all-White court.

Questions
for Analysis

1. Why did Mandela decide that the ANC must resort to violence to achieve its goals? What distinction does he draw between sabotage and terrorism?
2. What attractions did Mandela and other ANC leaders see in communism?
3. What aspects of apartheid does Mandela find most degrading?
4. Compare Mandela's speech with Lumumba's at the time of Congolese independence. To what extent does their anger result from similar feelings?
5. According to Mandela, how does apartheid affect the daily lives of Africans?

*I*n my youth . . . I listened to the elders of my tribe telling stories of the old days. Amongst the tales they related to me were those of wars fought by our ancestors in defense of the fatherland. . . . I hoped then that life might offer me the opportunity to serve my people and make my own humble contribution to their freedom struggle. This is what has motivated me in all that I have done in relation to the charges made against me in this case. . . .

I have already mentioned that I was one of the persons who helped to form Umkonto. I, and the others who started the organization, did so for two reasons. Firstly, we believed that as a result of Government policy, violence by the African people had become inevitable, and that unless responsible leadership was given to canalize and control the feelings of our people, there would be outbreaks of terrorism which would produce an intensity of bitterness and hostility between the various races of this country which is not produced even by war. Secondly, we felt that without violence there would be no way open to the African people to succeed in their struggle against the principle of White supremacy. All lawful modes of expressing opposition to this principle had been closed by legislation, and we were placed in a position in which we had either to accept a permanent state of inferiority, or to defy the Government. . . .

But the violence which we chose to adopt was not terrorism. We who formed Umkonto were all members of the African National Congress, and had behind us the ANC tradition of non-violence and negotiation as a means of solving political disputes. We believed that South Africa belonged to all the people who lived in it, and not to one group, be it Black or White. We did not want an interracial war, and tried to avoid it to the last minute. . . .

The African National Congress was formed in 1912 to defend the rights of the African people which had been seriously curtailed by the South Africa Act, and which were then being threatened by the Native Land Act.[1] For thirty-seven years — that is until 1949 — it adhered strictly to a constitutional struggle. It put forward demands and resolutions; it sent delegations to the Government in the belief that African grievances could be settled through peaceful discussion and that Africans could advance gradually to full political rights. But White Governments remained unmoved, and the rights of Africans became less instead of becoming greater. . . .

Even after 1949, the ANC remained determined to avoid violence. At this time, however, there was a change from the strictly constitutional means of protest which had been employed in the past. The change was embodied in a decision which was taken to protest against apartheid legislation by peaceful, but unlawful, demonstrations against certain laws. Pursuant to this policy the ANC launched the Defiance Campaign, in which I was placed in charge of volunteers. This campaign was based on the principles of passive resistance. More than 8,500 people defied apartheid laws and went to jail. Yet there was not a single instance of violence in the course of this campaign on the part of any defier. . . .

During the Defiance Campaign, the Public Safety Act and the Criminal Law Amendment Act were passed. These Statutes provided harsher penalties for offenses committed by way of protests against laws. Despite this, the protests continued and the ANC adhered to its policy of non-violence.

In 1960 there was the shooting at Sharpeville,[2] which resulted in the proclamation of a state of emergency and the declaration of the ANC as an unlawful organization. My colleagues and I, after careful consideration, decided that we would not obey this decree. The African people were not part of the Government and did not make the laws by which they were governed. We believed in the words of the Universal Declaration of Human Rights,[3] that "the will of the people shall be the basis of authority of the Government," and for us to accept the banning was equivalent to accepting the silencing

---

1. The South Africa Act (1910) was the act of Parliament that established the Union of South Africa; the Native Land Act (1913) was a South African law restricting the areas where non-Whites could own land.

2. In the 1960 Sharpeville Massacre police killed 69 and wounded 178 anti-apartheid demonstrators.

3. The Universal Declaration of Human Rights was adopted by the United Nations on December 10, 1948.

of the Africans for all time. The ANC refused to dissolve, but instead went underground. . . .

It must not be forgotten that by this time violence had, in fact, become a feature of the South African political scene. . . . Each disturbance pointed clearly to the inevitable growth among Africans of the belief that violence was the only way out — it showed that a Government which uses force to maintain its rule teaches the oppressed to use force to oppose it. . . .

The avoidance of civil war had dominated our thinking for many years, but when we decided to adopt violence as part of our policy, we realized that we might one day have to face the prospect of such a war. This had to be taken into account in formulating our plans. We required a plan which was flexible and which permitted us to act in accordance with the needs of the times; above all, the plan had to be one which recognized civil war as the last resort, and left the decision on this question to the future. We did not want to be committed to civil war, but we wanted to be ready if it became inevitable.

Four forms of violence were possible. There is sabotage, there is guerrilla warfare, there is terrorism, and there is open revolution. We chose to adopt the first method and to exhaust it before taking any other decision.

In the light of our political background the choice was a logical one. Sabotage did not involve loss of life, and it offered the best hope for future race relations. Bitterness would be kept to a minimum and, if the policy bore fruit, democratic government could become a reality. . . .

Attacks on the economic life lines of the country were to be linked with sabotage on Government buildings and other symbols of apartheid. These attacks would serve as a source of inspiration to our people. In addition, they would provide an outlet for those people who were urging the adoption of violent methods and

would enable us to give concrete proof to our followers that we had adopted a stronger line and were fighting back against Government violence. . . .

. . .

Another of the allegations made by the State is that the aims and objects of the ANC and the Communist Party are the same. I wish to deal with this and with my own political position, because I must assume that the State may try to argue from certain Exhibits that I tried to introduce Marxism into the ANC. . . .

It is true that there has often been close cooperation between the ANC and the Communist Party. But cooperation is merely proof of a common goal — in this case the removal of White supremacy — and is not proof of a complete community of interests. . . .

It is perhaps difficult for White South Africans, with an ingrained prejudice against communism, to understand why experienced African politicians so readily accept communists as their friends. But to us the reason is obvious. Theoretical differences amongst those fighting against oppression is a luxury we cannot afford at this stage. What is more, for many decades communists were the only political group in South Africa who were prepared to treat Africans as human beings and their equals; who were prepared to eat with us; talk with us, live with us, and work with us. They were the only political group which was prepared to work with the Africans for the attainment of political rights and a stake in society. Because of this, there are many Africans who, today, tend to equate freedom with communism. . . .

It is not only in internal politics that we count communists as amongst those who support our cause. In the international field, communist countries have always come to our aid. In the United Nations and other Councils of the world the communist *bloc* has supported the Afro-Asian struggle against colonialism and often seems to be more sympathetic to our plight than some of the Western powers. Although there is a universal condemnation of apartheid, the communist *bloc* speaks out against it with a louder voice than most of the White world. In these circumstances, it would take a brash young politician, such as I was in 1949, to proclaim that the communists are our enemies.

. . .

Our fight is against real, and not imaginary, hardships or, to use the language of the State Prosecutor, "so-called hardships." Basically, we fight against two features which are the hallmarks of African life in South Africa and which are entrenched by legislation which we seek to have repealed. These features are poverty and lack of human dignity, and we do not need communists or so-called "agitators" to teach us about these things.

South Africa is the richest country in Africa, and could be one of the richest countries in the world. But it is a land of extremes and remarkable contrasts. The Whites enjoy what may well be the highest standard of living in the world, whilst Africans live in poverty and misery. Forty percent of the Africans live in hopelessly overcrowded and, in some cases, drought-stricken Reserves, where soil erosion and the overworking of the soil makes it impossible for them to live properly off the land. Thirty percent are laborers, labor tenants, and squatters on White farms and work and live under conditions similar to those of the serfs of the Middle Ages. The other 30 percent live in towns where they have developed economic and social habits which bring them closer in

many respects to White standards. Yet most Africans, even in this group, are impoverished by low incomes and high cost of living.

The complaint of Africans, however, is not only that they are poor and the Whites are rich, but that the laws which are made by the Whites are designed to preserve this situation. There are two ways to break out of poverty. The first is by formal education, and the second is by the worker acquiring a greater skill at his work and thus higher wages. As far as Africans are concerned, both these avenues of advancement are deliberately curtailed by legislation. . . .

The lack of human dignity experienced by Africans is the direct result of the policy of White supremacy. White supremacy implies Black inferiority. Legislation designed to preserve White supremacy entrenches this notion. Menial tasks in South Africa are invariably performed by Africans. When anything has to be carried or cleaned the White man will look around for an African to do it for him, whether the African is employed by him or not. Because of this sort of attitude, Whites tend to regard Africans as a separate breed. They do not look upon them as people with families of their own; they do not realize that they have emotions — that they fall in love like White people do; that they want to be with their wives and children like White people want to be with theirs; that they want to earn enough money to support their families properly, to feed and clothe them and send them to school. And what "house-boy" or "garden-boy" or laborer can ever hope to do this? . . .

Poverty and the breakdown of family life have secondary effects. Children wander about the streets of the townships because they have no schools to go to, or no money to enable them to go to school, or no parents at home to see that they go to school, because both parents (if there be two) have to work to keep the family alive. This leads to a breakdown in moral standards, to an alarming rise in illegitimacy, and to growing violence which erupts, not only politically, but everywhere. Life in the townships is dangerous. There is not a day that goes by without somebody being stabbed or assaulted. And violence is carried out of the townships in the White living areas. People are afraid to walk alone in the streets after dark. Housebreakings and robberies are increasing, despite the fact that the death sentence can now be imposed for such offenses. Death sentences cannot cure the festering sore. . . .

During my lifetime I have dedicated myself to this struggle of the African people. I have fought against White domination, and I have fought against Black domination. I have cherished the ideal of a democratic and free society in which all persons live together in harmony and with equal opportunities. It is an ideal which I hope to live for and to achieve. But if needs be, it is an ideal for which I am prepared to die.

Malcom X

SPEECH TO THE ORGANIZATION OF AFRICAN UNITY

Born Malcolm Little in 1925 in Omaha, Nebraska, Malcom X became a militant spokesman for Black pride and nationalism in the late 1950s and early 1960s. After living for a time in Lansing, Michigan, he moved to Boston, where he was arrested in 1946 for robbery. In prison he converted to Islam and dropped his family name as a sign of his break from the past ("X" represents his unknown African name). After his release, he moved to Chicago, where he became a follower of Elijah Muhammed, the leader of the Black Muslims, an organization founded in 1930 that taught blacks to overcome "white slavery" by devotion to Islam. Malcom X urged blacks to practice vigilant self-defense against white violence and asserted that the differences between the races were irreconcilable. In 1964 he made a pilgrimage to Mecca, an experience that caused him to become more optimistic about the possibility of racial harmony. In 1965 he was assassinated in New York City by followers of Elijah Muhammed, with whom he had broken two years earlier.

The following selection is from a speech delivered to a meeting of the Organization of African Unity on July 17, 1964, in Egypt on his return from Mecca.

Questions
for Analysis

1. What arguments does Malcom X use to convince African leaders that they should help American Blacks in their struggle for equality?
2. Why does he argue that the United States is "worse than South Africa"?
3. In what specific ways does Malcom X's speech differ from the 1921 Manifesto of the Second Pan-African Congress (see Chapter 12)?

The Organization of Afro-American Unity[1] has sent me to attend this historic African Summit Conference as an observer to represent the interests of 22 million African-Americans whose *human rights* are being violated daily by the racism of American imperialists.

The Organization of Afro-American Unity has been formed by a cross section of America's African-American community, and is patterned after the letter and spirit of the Organization of African Unity.

Just as the Organization of African Unity has called upon all African leaders to submerge their differences and unite on common objectives for the common good of all Africans, in America the Organization of Afro-American Unity has called upon Afro-American leaders to submerge their differences and find areas of agreement wherein we can work in unity for the good of the entire 22 million African-Americans.

Since the 22 million of us were originally Africans, who are now in America, not by choice but only by a cruel accident in our history, we strongly believe that African problems are our problems and our problems are African problems.

We also believe that as heads of the independent African states you are the shepherds of *all* African peoples everywhere, whether they are still at home here on the mother continent or have been scattered abroad.

Some African leaders at this conference have implied that they have enough problems here on the mother continent without adding the Afro-American problem.

With all due respect to your esteemed positions, I must remind all of you that *the Good Shepherd* will leave ninety-nine sheep who are safe at home to go to the aid of the one who is lost and has fallen into the clutches of the imperialist wolf.[2]

We in America are your long-lost brothers and sisters, and I am here only to remind you that our problems are your problems. As the African-Americans "awaken" today, we find ourselves in a strange land that has rejected us, and, like the prodigal son, we are turning to our elder brothers for help. We pray our pleas will not fall upon deaf ears.

We were taken forcibly in chains from this mother continent and have now spent over three hundred years in America, suffering the most inhuman forms of physical and psychological tortures imaginable.

During the past ten years the entire world has witnessed our men, women, and children being attacked and bitten by vicious police dogs, brutally beaten by police clubs, and washed down the sewers by high-pressure water hoses that would rip the clothes from our bodies and the flesh from our limbs.[3]

And all of these inhuman atrocities have been inflicted upon us by the American governmental authorities, the police themselves, for no reason other than that we seek the recognition and respect granted other human beings in America.

The American Government is either unable or unwilling to protect the lives and property of your 22 million African-American brothers and sisters. We stand defenseless, at the mercy of American racists who murder us at will for no reason other than we are black and of African descent. . . .

---

1. Malcom X founded the Organization of Afro-American Unity in 1964 after his break with Elijah Muhammed.

2. The reference is to the New Testament teaching of Jesus, found in Matthew 18:10–14.

3. All these tactics were used to break up civil-rights demonstrations; the most notorious episode took place in the spring of 1963 in Birmingham, Alabama.

Last week an unarmed African-American educator was murdered in cold blood in Georgia; a few days before that three civil rights workers disappeared completely, perhaps murdered also, only because they were teaching our people in Mississippi how to vote and how to secure their political rights.[4]

Our problems are your problems. We have lived for over three hundred years in that American den of racist wolves in constant fear of losing life and limb. Recently, three students from Kenya were mistaken for American Negroes and were brutally beaten by the New York police. Shortly after that two diplomats from Uganda were also beaten by the New York City police, who mistook them for American Negroes.

If Africans are brutally beaten while only visiting in America, imagine the physical and psychological suffering received by your brothers and sisters who have lived there for over three hundred years.

Our problem is your problem. No matter how much independence Africans get here on the mother continent, unless you wear your national dress at all time when you visit America, you may be mistaken for one of us and suffer the same psychological and physical mutilation that is an everyday occurrence in our lives.

Your problems will never be fully solved until and unless ours are solved. You will never be fully respected until and unless we are also respected. You will never be recognized as free human beings until and unless we are also recognized and treated as human beings.

Our problem is your problem. It is not a Negro problem, nor an American problem. This is a world problem, a problem for humanity. It is not a problem of civil rights, it is a problem of human rights. . . .

We pray that our African brothers have not freed themselves of European colonialism only to be overcome and held in check now by American *dollarism*.[5] Don't let American racism be "legalized" by American dollarism.

America is worse than South Africa, because not only is America racist, but she is also deceitful and hypocritical. South Africa preaches segregation and practices segregation. She, at least, practices what she preaches. America preaches integration and practices segregation. She preaches one thing while deceitfully practicing another.

South Africa is like a vicious wolf, openly hostile toward black humanity. But America is cunning like a fox, friendly and smiling, but even more vicious and deadly than the wolf.

The wolf and the fox are both enemies of humanity, both are canine, both humiliate and mutilate their victims. Both have the same objectives, but differ only in methods.

If South Africa is guilty of violating the human rights of Africans here on the mother continent, then America is guilty of worse violations of the 22 million Africans on the American continent. And if South African racism is not a domestic issue, then American racism also is not a *domestic* issue. . . .

We beseech independent African states to help us bring our problem before the

---

4. Lemuel Penn was killed in Georgia on July 11, 1964, while driving back to Washington, D.C., after summer army reserve duty. The civil rights workers had indeed been murdered; two weeks after Malcolm X's speech, the bodies of James E. Chaney, Michael H. Schwerner, and Andrew Goodman were found buried in an earthen dam outside Philadelphia, Mississippi.

5. Malcom X's term for what he viewed as the U.S. effort to buy the support of African nations through economic and military aid.

United Nations, on the grounds that the United States Government is morally incapable of protecting the lives and the property of 22 million African-Americans. And on the grounds that our deteriorating plight is definitely becoming a threat to world peace.

Out of frustration and hopelessness our young people have reached the point of no return. We no longer endorse patience and turning the other cheek. We assert the right of self-defense by whatever means necessary, and reserve the right of maximum retaliation against our racist oppressors, no matter what the odds against us are.

We are well aware that our future efforts to defend ourselves by retaliating — by meeting violence with violence, eye for eye and tooth for tooth — could create the type of racial conflict in America that could easily escalate into a violent, worldwide, bloody race war.

In the interests of world peace and security, we beseech the heads of the independent African states to recommend an immediate investigation into our problem by the United Nations Commission on Human Rights.

One last word, my beloved brothers at this African Summit: "No one knows the master better than his servant." We have been servants in America for over three hundred years. We have a thorough inside knowledge of this man who calls himself "Uncle Sam." Therefore, you must heed our warning. Don't escape from European colonialism only to become even more enslaved by deceitful, "friendly" American dollarism.

May Allah's blessings of good health and wisdom be upon you all.

Women in the Modern World

During the twentieth century, political leaders of industrialized nations, communist revolutionaries such as Lenin and Mao, and nationalist heroes as different as Kemal and Gandhi have all pledged to work toward equality between men and women. The 1945 charter of the United Nations is committed to the same purpose, and the United Nations Universal Declaration of Human Rights of 1948 reaffirms the goal of ending all forms of discrimination based on sex.

It would be an understatement to say that progress toward the goal of sexual equality has been uneven. With the exception of a few conservative Islamic nations, women have attained legal equality with men and have won basic political rights such as the right to vote. In the past forty years educational and vocational opportunities for women in many societies have increased. Nonetheless, even in developed industrial societies, women usually earn lower wages than men and lack access to managerial positions in business. Although current prime ministers such as Margaret Thatcher of Britain and Benazir Bhutto of Pakistan and former ones such as Golda Meir of Israel and Indira Gandhi of India are notable exceptions, politics has continued to be a male-dominated activity, as have professions in engineering, computers, and science. In developing nations progress toward sexual equality has been even more elusive. Even in nations such as China and India, which have adopted strong antidiscrimination laws, it has proved difficult to modify, let alone eradicate, centuries-old customs and attitudes that maintain female subservience.

▨ Betty Friedan

THE FEMININE MYSTIQUE

In the mid-1950s Betty Friedan, a 1942 graduate of Smith College, was a housewife in a suburb of New York City, a mother of three, and a writer for popular women's magazines such as *McCall's, Redbook,* and *Ladies' Home Journal.* By the standards of the day she was a successful woman, yet she was troubled by "a nameless, aching dissatisfaction" and became convinced that "there was something very wrong about the way American women were trying to lead their lives." After five years of research and self-analysis, in 1963 Friedan published *The Feminine Mystique,* in which she rejected the American consensus that women's lives should focus solely on home, husband, and family. Highly impressionistic, the book had great impact, causing millions of women and men throughout the United States and elsewhere to rethink the role of middle-class women in industrialized societies. In 1966 Friedan co-founded the National Organization for Women (NOW) and served as its first president.

Questions
for Analysis

1. According to Friedan, what was the problem of American middle-class women in the 1950s? Why did it have no name?
2. What does this excerpt reveal about Friedan's research, and what may it suggest about the book's limitations?
3. Based on Friedan's description of the problem of post–World War II women, what solution do you think she would propose?

THE PROBLEM THAT HAS NO NAME

The problem lay buried, unspoken, for many years in the minds of American women. It was a strange stirring, a sense of dissatisfaction, a yearning that women suffered in the middle of the twentieth century in the United States. Each suburban wife struggled with it alone. As she made the beds, shopped for groceries, matched slipcover material, ate peanut butter sandwiches with her children, chauffeured Cub Scouts and Brownies, lay beside her husband at night — she was afraid to ask even of herself the silent question — "Is this all?"

For over fifteen years there was no word of this yearning in the millions of words written about women, for women, in all the columns, books and articles by experts telling women their role was to seek fulfillment as wives and mothers. . . . Experts told them how to catch a man and keep him, how to breastfeed children and handle their toilet training, how to cope with sibling rivalry and adolescent rebellion; how to buy a dishwasher, bake bread, cook gourmet snails, and build a swimming pool with their own hands; how to dress, look, and act more feminine and make marriage more exciting; how to keep their husbands from dying young and their sons from growing into delinquents. They were taught to pity the neurotic, unfeminine, unhappy women who wanted to be poets or physicists or presidents. They learned that truly feminine women do not want careers, higher education, political rights — the independence and the opportunities that the old-fashioned feminists fought for. Some women, in their forties and fifties, still remembered painfully giving up those dreams, but most of the younger women no longer even thought about them. A thousand expert voices applauded their femininity, their adjustment, their new maturity. All they had to do was devote their lives from earliest girlhood to finding a husband and bearing children. . . .

In the fifteen years after World War II, this mystique of feminine fulfillment became the cherished and self-perpetuating core of contemporary American culture. Millions of women lived their lives in the image of those pretty pictures of the American suburban housewife, kissing their husbands goodbye in front of the picture window, depositing their station-wagonsful of children at school, and smiling as they ran the new electric waxer over the spotless kitchen floor. . . . Their only dream was to be perfect wives and mothers; their highest ambition to have five children and a beautiful house, their only fight to get and keep their husbands.

They had no thought for the unfeminine problems of the world outside the home; they wanted the men to make the major decisions. They gloried in their role as women, and wrote proudly on the census blank: "Occupation: housewife.". . .

If a woman had a problem in the 1950's and 1960's, she knew that something must be wrong with her marriage, or with herself. Other women were satisfied with their lives, she thought. What kind of a woman was she if she did not feel this mysterious fulfillment waxing the kitchen floor? She was so ashamed to admit her dissatisfaction that she never knew how many other women shared it. If she tried to tell her husband, he didn't understand what she was talking about. She did not really understand it herself. For over fifteen years women in America found it harder to talk about this problem than about sex. Even the psychoanalysts had no name for it. When a woman went to a psychiatrist for help, as many women did, she would say, "I'm so ashamed," or "I must be hopelessly neurotic." "I don't know what's wrong with women today," a suburban psychiatrist said uneasily. "I only know something is wrong because most of my patients happen to be women. And their problem isn't sexual." . . .

Gradually I came to realize that the problem that has no name was shared by countless women in America. As a magazine writer I often interviewed women about problems with their children, or their marriages, or their houses, or their communities. But after a while I began to recognize the telltale signs of this other problem. I saw the same signs in suburban ranch houses and split-levels on Long Island and in New Jersey and Westchester County; in colonial houses in a small Massachusetts town; on patios in Memphis; in suburban and city apartments; in living rooms in the Midwest. Sometimes I sensed the problem, not as a reporter, but as a suburban housewife, for during this time I was also bringing up my own three children in Rockland County, New York. I heard echoes of the problem in college dormitories and semi-private maternity wards, at PTA meetings and luncheons of the League of Women Voters, at suburban cocktail parties, in station wagons waiting for trains, and in snatches of conversation overheard at Schrafft's. The groping words I heard from other women, on quiet afternoons when children were at school or on quiet evenings when husbands worked late, I think I understood first as a woman long before I understood their larger social and psychological implications.

Just what was this problem that has no name? What were the words women used when they tried to express it? Sometimes a woman would say "I feel empty somehow . . . incomplete." Or she would say, "I feel as if I don't exist." Sometimes she blotted out the feeling with a tranquilizer. Sometimes she thought the problem was with her husband, or her children, or that what she really needed was to redecorate her house, or move to a better neighborhood, or have an affair, or another baby. Sometimes, she went to a doctor with symptoms she could hardly describe: "A tired feeling . . . I get so angry with the children it scares me . . . I feel like crying without any reason." (A Cleveland doctor called it "the housewife's syndrome.") . . .

Most men, and some women, still did not know that this problem was real. But those who had faced it honestly knew that all the superficial remedies, the sympathetic advice, the scolding words and the cheering words were somehow drowning the problem in unreality. A bitter laugh was beginning to be heard from American women. They were admired, envied, pitied, theorized over until they were sick of it, offered drastic solutions or silly choices that no one could take seriously. They

got all kinds of advice from the growing armies of marriage and child-guidance counselors, psychotherapists, and armchair psychologists, on how to adjust to their role as housewives. No other road to fulfillment was offered to American women in the middle of the twentieth century. Most adjusted to their role and suffered or ignored the problem that has no name. It can be less painful for a woman, not to hear the strange, dissatisfied voice stirring within her.

It is no longer possible to ignore that voice, to dismiss the desperation of so many American women. This is not what being a woman means, no matter what the experts say. For human suffering there is a reason; perhaps the reason has not been found because the right questions have not been asked, or pressed far enough. I do not accept the answer that there is no problem because American women have luxuries that women in other times and lands never dreamed of; part of the strange newness of the problem is that it cannot be understood in terms of the age-old material problems of man: poverty, sickness, hunger, cold. The women who suffer this problem have a hunger that food cannot fill. It persists in women whose husbands are struggling internes and law clerks, or prosperous doctors and lawyers; in wives of workers and executives who make $5,000 a year or $50,000. It is not caused by lack of material advantages; it may not even be felt by women preoccupied with desperate problems of hunger, poverty or illness. And women who think it will be solved by more money, a bigger house, a second car, moving to a better suburb, often discover it gets worse. . . .

If I am right, the problem that has no name stirring in the minds of so many American women today is not a matter of loss of femininity or too much education, or the demands of domesticity. It is far more important than anyone recognizes. It is the key to these other new and old problems which have been torturing women and their husbands and children, and puzzling their doctors and educators for years. It may well be the key to our future as a nation and a culture. We can no longer ignore that voice within women that says: "I want something more than my husband and my children and my home."

WHAT SHOULD I DO WHEN MY WIFE AND MOTHER-IN-LAW DO NOT GET ALONG?

In traditional China, when a young woman married, connections with her natal family and friends ended and she joined the family of her husband, where she was expected to be subservient and obedient, especially to her mother-in-law, who often treated her like a domestic servant. It was expected that elderly parents' children, but especially the daughter-in-law, should devote themselves to their elders' happiness and welfare.

In the 1950s, the Chinese Communist government issued laws limiting the dictatorial power of mothers-in-law over daughters-in-law, and since then the movement of women into the labor market has made it difficult for young married women to care for their elderly relatives. As the following selection shows, tension and conflict have resulted. The letter and the response by Liu Tao were first published in *Zhongguo ginnian bao (China Youth News)* in 1980.

Questions for Analysis

1. How do the conflicts this letter describes and the response reflect changes in Chinese society?
2. According to Liu Tao, who is usually to blame for conflicts between daughters-in-law and mothers-in-law?
3. Consider the proposed solution to this problem. Which member of the family needs to make the greatest changes? The daughter-in-law or mother-in-law?

Dear Editors:

Since my father passed away in 1960, my mother has raised me. We supported each other until I got married. Then she retired from her job and has helped me raise my child and prepare meals every day. My family life should be very happy. But recently I have dreaded going home. Each time I enter the door my wife looks at me with a long face and asks: "Who do you want, your mother or me? If you want me, you had better find a separate home for us soon." My mother then tells me how her daughter-in-law avoids doing housework and offends her. She complains that I have forgotten her ever since I got married. I am being attacked by both sides. What should I do?

Huang Chun, Xinyang, Henan

Dear Huang Chun:

I was asked by the editors to write to you about my own experiences and to tell you my opinions about how to handle conflicts between a mother-in-law and daughter-in-law. I will tell you frankly what I know.

My family is very similar to yours. My wife is a texile worker and my mother is retired. The conflict within my family worried me, too. After a little thinking I realized that the conflict had several causes. First, the daughter-in-law was annoyed by the mother-in-law's lack of understanding of the hardships she had to deal with; she was annoyed by the mother-in-law's pampering of the grandson, and by her habit of talking too much. The mother-in-law complained about the daughter-in-law's failure to take the initiative in doing housework, her habit of spending money freely, and her lack of respect for the aged.

What was the main cause of this conflict? In the old society, the mother-in-law ruled the family. People believed that "the daughter-in-law is like a purchased horse: you can ride or beat her as you please." But things are different now. The daughter-in-law has an independent income; she is literate and articulate. When there is conflict, the daughter-in-law is the

main cause of it. Take my home, for example. My wife is a high-level worker in her workshop. Naturally she thought that after walking sixty li^1 back and forth during the day she deserved a break. Therefore she did less housework. Of course she also believed that since she earned her own money, she should be able to spend it however she liked. Thus she seldom consulted her mother-in-law.

To solve this conflict I patiently tried to make my wife realize that she should see more of the positive aspects of the old woman, and appreciate the hardships she had to go through in doing the housework and raising our child. I also told her how difficult it had been for my mother to raise me all by herself after my father died. Even if my mother could not do anything useful, it was still our responsibility to take care of her in her old age. My mother had been thrifty her whole life, and that was a virtue we lacked. As for her habit of talking too much, I said it was common among old people. We would probably talk even more when we were old. My wife laughed at my joke. Later, each time we received our pay, we gave it to my mother to keep. After work I would take care of our child while my wife would help my mother do the cooking. Actually we did not help all that much. But when my mother saw that the younger generation could understand and respect her, she was so happy that she would finish the cooking very early every day. As for spending money — my wife and I actually always had our way. The more the younger generation respects the old, the more love they will give us.

Certainly we should not give in to certain old ideas, such as pampering the grandson. Our experience is that usually

---

1. A Chinese measure of distance, equal to about one-third of a mile.

it is better for the son to talk to his mother than for the daughter-in-law to talk to her. It is even better if when some gifts such as tonics or clothes are bought for the mother-in-law, the daughter-in-law gives them to her. By the same token, it would be better for me to send gifts to my mother-in-law. When I am with my mother, I often tell her how tiring my wife's work in the factory is. On holidays or weekends we try to share more of the housework so that my mother can go to the theater or visit relatives. Now my mother praises my wife in front of everyone. To sum up, when there is a conflict between the mother-in-law and the daughter-in-law, the husband should be the mediator.

Liu Tao, Wuxi

EDITORIAL AGAINST DOWRY

Although women's place in Hindu society had improved slightly before independence, major steps were not taken until India reached self-government in 1947. Women were given full political rights and the right to hold property and divorce their husbands; child marriage and polygamy were outlawed; and intercaste marriages were encouraged. In 1961 dowries, the gifts of property a new bride was expected to bring to her husband's family, were also outlawed. The new law resulted from the government's belief that such practices caused hardship for families with daughters and prevented lower-caste women from marrying men from higher castes. As the following editorial shows, however, the practice of dowries continues, often with tragic results for young married women. This anonymous editorial was originally published in 1979 in *Manushi*, an Indian magazine for women.

Questions
for Analysis

1. According to this editorial's author, to what extent is the giving and taking of dowries the result of recent developments? Of long-standing Indian traditions?
2. According to the author, why have efforts to end the practice of dowries failed?
3. What does the author see as the solution to the problem?

Most people are not even aware that the giving and taking of dowry is a legal offense. Since the Prohibition of Dowry Act was passed in 1961, the custom has flowered and flourished, invading castes and communities among whom it was hitherto unknown — sprouting new forms and varieties. It is percolating downwards and becoming so widespread even among the working classes that it is no longer possible to consider it a problem of the middle class alone.

With the entire bourgeois mass media oriented towards viciously promoting the religion of mindless consumerism, demands for dowry are becoming more and more "modernized." Marriages are made and broken for such items as cars, scooters, TVs, refrigerators and washing machines, wedding receptions in five-star hotels or an air ticket plus the promise of a job for the son-in-law in a foreign country.

In India, we have a glorious heritage of systematic violence on women in the family itself, sati and female infanticide being the two better-known forms. Today, we do not kill girl-babies at birth. We let them die through systematic neglect — the mortality rate among female children is 30-60% higher than among male children. Today, we do not wait till a woman is widowed before we burn her to death. We burn her in the lifetime of her husband so that he can get a new bride with a fatter dowry.

"Woman burnt to death. A case of suicide has been registered. The police are enquiring into the matter." For years, such three-line news items have appeared almost every day in the newspapers and gone unnoticed. It is only lately that dowry deaths are being given detailed coverage. It is not by accident that fuller reporting of such cases has coincided with a spurt of protest demonstrations.

We, as women, have too long been silent spectators, often willing participants in the degrading drama of matrimony — when girls are advertised, displayed, bargained over, and disposed of with the pious injunction: "Daughter, we are sending you to your husband's home. You are not to leave it till your corpse emerges from its doors." It is significant that in all the cases of dowry murders recently reported, the girls had on previous occasions left the in-laws' houses where they were being tortured and felt insecure.

Their parents had insisted on their going back and "adjusting" there.

Death may be slow in coming — a long process of killing the girl's spirit by harassment, taunts, torture. It may be only too quick — fiery and sudden. Dousing the woman with kerosene and setting her on fire seems to have become the most popular way of murdering a daughter-in-law because with police connivance it is the easiest to make out as a case of suicide or accident.

And for every one reported murder, hundreds go unreported, especially in rural areas where it is almost impossible to get redress unless one is rich and influential. For years, the police and the administration have hushed up these cases under the plea that people are not willing to appear as witnesses, that they are indifferent.

Why is it that gifts have to be given with the daughter? Hindu scriptures proclaim that the girl herself is the most precious of gifts "presented" by her father to her husband. Thus the money transaction between families is bound up with the marriage transaction whereby the girl becomes a piece of transferable property. So little is a woman worth that a man has literally to be paid to take her off her father's hands. The dramatic increase in dowry-giving in the post-independence period reflects the declining value of women in our society. Their only worth is as reproducers who provide "legitimate" heirs for their husbands' property.

Most people opposing dowry feel that the problem can be solved by giving girls an equal share in their fathers' property. This was one of the reasons why daughters were given near-equal rights in the Hindu Succession Act, 1956. And yet the law has been reduced to a farce because in most cases, daughters are pressurized to, or even willingly sign away their rights in favor of their brothers. In any case, it is the woman's husband who usually controls any property she inherits. So the property transaction remains between men, women acting only as vehicles for this transaction.

This will continue to be so as long as the majority of women remain economically dependent on men and as long as this dependence is reinforced by our social values and institutions so that even those women who earn seldom have the right to control their own income. . . .

What is needed is a widespread movement against dowry and allied social evils. A number of women's organizations have recently been galvanized around this issue. But they have been working without proper co-ordination with each other, in fact often at cross-purposes with each other. This is most unfortunate as it will only dissipate the movement before it has even got off the ground. We appeal, therefore, to all the women's organizations to undertake a broad-based united action on this issue and launch an intensive, concerted campaign instead of the isolated, sporadic protests which have so far been organized, and which can have only a short-term, limited impact.

Perhaps even more urgent is the need to begin the movement from our own homes. Are we sure that none of us who participated so vociferously in these demonstrations will take dowry from our parents or give it to our daughters in however veiled a form? That we will rather say "No" to marriage than live a life of humiliations and compromises? Do we have the courage to boycott marriages where dowry is given? Even the marriage of a brother or sister or of a dear friend? Will we socially ostracize such people, no matter how close they are to us? All the protest demonstrations will be only so much hot air unless we are prepared to create pressures against dowry beginning from our own homes.

Zand Dokht

THE REVOLUTION THAT FAILED WOMEN

Although the Pahlavi regimes of Reza Shah (1925–1941) and Muhammad Reza Shah (1941–1979) gave women political rights, allowed them to abandon the veil for Western-style dress, and encouraged female literacy and higher education, millions of women became disgusted with their government's autocracy and corruption, and they played an important role in the massive public demonstrations that preceded the shah's downfall in 1979. Many of these women were bitterly disappointed when Khomeini's Islamic Republic revoked the shah's legislation on women and the family and reinstated traditional Islamic practices.

In response, in 1979 representatives from various women's organizations founded the Women's Solidarity Committee, an organization dedicated to the protection of women's rights in Iran. Although subsequently banned in Iran itself, Iranian women still maintain a branch of the organization in London. Known as the Iranian Women's Solidarity Group, it publishes pamphlets and newsletters publicizing women's issues in Iran. The following selection appeared in one of their publications in 1981.

Questions for Analysis

1. In what specific ways did Iran's Islamic Revolution affect women?
2. How does the author explain the fact that so many Iranian women supported the revolution that toppled the shah?

When Khomeini created his Islamic Republic in 1979, he relied on the institution of the family, on support from the women, the merchants, and the private system of landownership. The new Islamic constitution declared women's primary position as mothers. The black veil, symbol of the position of women under Islam, was made compulsory. Guards were posted outside government offices to enforce it, and women were sacked from their jobs without compensation for refusing to wear the veil. The chairman of the Employment Office, in an interview with the government's women's magazine said, "We can account for 100,000 women government employees being sacked as they resisted the order of the revolutionary government when it was demanded of them to put the veil on."

Schools were segregated, which meant that women were barred from some technical schools, even from some religious schools, and young girls' education in the villages was halted. Lowering the marriage age for girls to 13, reinstating polygamy and *Sighen* (temporary wives), the two major pillars of Islam, meant that women did not need education and jobs, they only needed to find husbands.

The Ayatollahs in their numerous public prayers, which grew to be the only possible national activity, continuously gave sermons on the advantages of marriage, family, and children being brought up on their mother's lap. They preached that society would be pure, trouble free, criminal-less (look at the youth problem in the West) if everybody married young, and if men married as many times as possible (to save the unprotected women who might otherwise become prostitutes). The government created a marriage bank at a time when half the working population was unemployed, whereby men were given huge sums — around £3,500 — to get married. Another *masterpiece* of the revolutionary Islamic government was to create a system of arranged marriages in prisons, between men and women prisoners, to "protect" women after they leave prison.

Because abortion and contraception are now unobtainable, marriage means frequent pregnancy. If you are 13 when you get married, it is likely that you will have six children by the time you are 20. This, in a country where half the total population are already under 16, is a tragedy for future generations.

Religious morality demands that all pleasures and entertainments be banned. Wine, music, dancing, chess, women's parts in theater, cinema and television — you name it, Khomeini banned it. He even segregated the mountains and the seas, for male and female climbers and swimmers.

But compulsory morality, compulsory marriage, and the compulsory wearing of the veil did not create the Holy Society that Khomeini was after; but public lashings, stonings, chopping of hands and daily group executions sank Iran into the age of Barbarism.

Perhaps nowhere else in the world have

women been murdered for walking in the street open-faced. The question of the veil is the most important issue of women's liberation in Muslim countries. The veil, a long engulfing black robe, is the extension of the four walls of the home, where women belong. The veil is the historical symbol of woman's oppression, seclusion, denial of her social participation and equal rights with men. It is a cover which defaces and objectifies women. To wear or not to wear the veil, for Muslim women is "the right to choose." . . .

Why do women, workers and unemployed, support this regime which has done everything in its power to attack their rights and interests? The power of Islam in our culture and tradition has been seriously underestimated . . . and it was through this ideology that Khomeini directed his revolutionary government. The clergy dealt with everyday problems and spoke out on human relationships, sexuality, security and protection of the family and the spiritual needs of human beings. It was easy for people to identify with these issues and support the clergy, although nobody knew what they were later to do. When Khomeini asked for sacrifices — "we haven't made the Revolution in order to eat chicken or dress better" — women (so great in the art of sacrifice) and workers accepted these antimaterialist ideas. . . .

Women's attraction to Khomeini's ideas was not based simply on his Islamic politics, but also on the way he criticized the treatment of women — as secretaries and media sex objects — under the Shah's regime. Women were genuinely unsatisfied and looking for change. Some educated Iranian women went back to Iran from America and Europe to aid the clergy with the same messages, and became the government's spokeswomen. They put on the veil willingly, defended Islamic virtues and spiritual values while drawing from their own experiences in the West. They said it was cold and lonely, Western women were only in pursuit of careers and self-sufficiency, and that their polygamous sexual relationships had not brought them liberation, but confusion and exploitation. These women joined ranks with an already growing force of Muslim women, to retrieve the tradition of true/happy Muslim women — in defense of patriarchy.

The mosque is not just a place of prayer, it is also a social club for women. It provides a warm, safe room for women to meet, chat or listen to a sermon, and there are traditional women-only parties and picnics in gardens or holy places. Take away these traditional and religious customs from women is the Shah — with his capitalist and imperialist reforms, irrelevant to women's needs — tried to do and a huge vacuum is left. Khomeini stepped in to fill that vacuum. The reason why Khomeini won was that the Shah's social-economic program for women was dictatorial, bureaucratic, inadequate (especially in terms of health education) and therefore irrelevant to women's needs. What little the Shah's reform brought to women was just a token gesture. Women dissatisfied with the Shah's reform felt that they had benefited little from him and would not miss it if it was taken away.

New Directions in the Communist World

Two developments stand out in the history of world communism since the end of World War II. One has been the increase in the number of states officially committed to the ideology of Marxism. In 1945 the only communist state was the Soviet Union. By the early 1960s, eight European nations, China, North Korea, North Vietnam, and, most shockingly to the United States, Cuba, also had become communist states. Subsequently, Yemen, Cambodia, Angola, Nicaragua, Afghanistan, and Ethiopia officially adopted Marxism.

The second notable development has been the recent reorientation, or "restructuring," of communism in the Soviet Union, China, Poland, and Hungary. Throughout the 1950s most observers assumed that all communist states were destined to follow the Leninist-Stalinist path of one-party dictatorship, state control of the economy, suppression of civil liberties, and general antagonism toward the United States and other "imperialist" powers. The death of Stalin in 1953, however, opened new possibilities. Nikita Khrushchev (1894–1971), who became the Soviet leader in 1953, initiated a policy of "De-Stalinization," a name applied to a broad range of reforms designed to rejuvenate the Communist party, to shift resources from heavy industry to agriculture, and to encourage open discussion among intellectuals and political leaders. De-Stalinization had its Chinese analogue in Chairman Mao Zedong's 1957 decision to "let one hundred flowers bloom," that is, to tolerate free and critical opinion.

In the 1960s and 1970s, Soviet leadership stopped further liberalization and "re-Stalinized" Soviet society. In the 1980s, however, a new leader, Mikhail Gorbachev, initiated a policy of *perestroika*, or "restructuring," which has scrapped some of the apparatus of the state-controlled economy, encouraged public debate, and even led to free democratic elections for a new Soviet parliament. Hungary and Poland have also moved toward democratization and liberalization during the 1980s.

China's experience has been erratic. The late 1960s and early 1970s were characterized by radicalization and upheaval, followed in the 1980s by a sharp break from Maoism and a move toward greater economic freedom and political openness. In the spring of 1989, however, the Chinese leadership brutally suppressed large-scale popular demonstrations for democracy, and for now, the door to political reform has been closed.

Fidel Castro

SPEECH OF APRIL 17, 1966

After gaining its independence from Spain in 1899, Cuba experienced the same problems other Latin American states faced — maldistribution of wealth, foreign ownership of major agricultural and industrial enterprises, racial discrimination against blacks, and widespread illiteracy. Corrupt politicians, usually with ties to wealthy Cubans and the United States government, made little headway against these problems, and revolutions such as that of 1933 failed. This situation changed in the 1950s, when Fidel Castro, the son of a wealthy farmer, led a successful guerrilla war that toppled the dictatorship of General Fulgencio Batista in 1959. In the following months, Castro, backed only at the last minute by the small Cuban Communist party, radicalized the regime by nationalizing U.S. plantations and businesses, accepting aid from the Soviet Union, and redistributing land to the peasants. Historians continue to debate whether Castro had always been a Communist at heart (which Castro claims is true) or whether early U.S. opposition to his regime pushed him into the arms of the Soviets.

In a speech delivered in April 1966, Castro provided a historical perspective on the Cuban Revolution and outlined its challenges. The occasion was the fifth anniversary of the Battle of Girón Beach on the Bay of Pigs, when Castro's forces repulsed an ill-planned invasion by Cuban exiles supported by the U.S. Central Intelligence Agency.

Questions for Analysis

1. According to Castro, what factors inhibited Cuban economic development before the revolution?
2. Why, according to Castro, have Cuba's needs for teachers, doctors, agronomists, and engineers increased since the revolution? What progress has been made in these areas? Why is he convinced that Cuba will succeed in reaching its economic goals?
3. What is Castro's view of the significance of the Cuban Revolution? What contribution will it make to human history?

While many nations were developing, were becoming industrialized, our Latin American nations straggled behind and became poorer and poorer. And the gap separating the industrialized countries from Latin America grew wider. Population also grew. But resources, wealth, and industry did not grow; the population increased more than did food production.

A hundred and fifty years of accumulated misery! During that century and a half, Cuba spent one hundred years toiling and struggling to free herself from Spanish colonialism. And then during more than half a century, we worked for the Yankee imperialists, the corrupt politicians, and the privileged few who squandered the resources of this country for almost sixty years.

They built few factories. The privileged of this country and the corrupt politicians bought country estates, built mansions, deposited millions in foreign banks. And meanwhile, in the countryside, the men who cut the cane and produced the sugar, the men who, in other words, produced the country's foreign exchange, lived in huts and hovels. They never saw cement, nor electric lights, nor running water, nor streets, nor parks. They worked for such a long time and received such an insignificant share of the national product, while our capital city grew and grew. A drive along Fifth Avenue is sufficient to see where a good part of the sweat of the workers of this country was invested.

And undoubtedly we are making the best possible use of those palatial mansions; it is a fact that today we have tens of thousands of students living in those houses. But what we lack are cement factories; what we lack are fertilizer factories; what they did not leave us were industries, except for a few entirely dependent upon imported raw materials, and the sugar mills, the newest of which is more than thirty years old, because in the last thirty years not a single new sugar mill has been built. And many of those industries are old and almost dilapidated.

They did not even leave us an advanced mechanized agriculture. They did not, nor could they, because the workers had opposed mechanization, since under capitalism the introduction of machinery is opposed by the workers as it takes away their jobs and leaves them to starve. Neither cane-loading machines, nor cane harvesters, nor cane-conditioning centers, nor bulk loading facilities; not one of these modern labor-saving techniques would they have been able to introduce into our country.

. . .

It is a fact that there is practically not a single corner of our country without a school, nor is there a region of our country without a hospital. We are now, in education as well as in medical care, without doubt the foremost country of this continent, including the U.S.

But there is still much poverty; there still exist many inadequate dwellings. Thousands of kilometers of roads and hundreds of thousands of houses must be built, as well as electrical installations and water supplies. And that, naturally, cannot be achieved in a few years, especially in a country that produces about one-third of the cement it could use at this time.

The road is long and patience is needed. This is the road of any underdeveloped country. But at least since the triumph of

the Revolution, well done or not, better or worse, our work no longer benefits the foreigner. We no longer work for a privileged class. Even though it has been necessary to create everything, to begin everything from zero, it was necessary to overthrow the rotting bourgeois state in order to build anew. The country had to be completely revolutionized. It was necessary to do away with the old and to rebuild. And this task had to be carried out with new men, the great majority of whom lacked experience. . . .

Our country suffered from a true poverty of technical personnel. And part of the technical personnel — of what little technical personnel this country had — was identified with the interests affected by the Revolution. It was necessary to begin to prepare cadres. And this also takes years. In spite of the efforts made, legions of new technicians have not yet entered production; it will take us a few years but we will get there. We will reach the goal because we have not wasted time, having set about this task from the very beginning. In some activities in some fields, tens of thousands are already prepared. . . .

Where do we stand today? We strive to have the greatest possible number of young people in our universities. If 10,000 enroll, it seems few to us; if 20,000 enroll, they are still too few. Nevertheless, when one reads the news reports about the situation in the universities in other countries of Latin America, the case is different. The number of university students is limited, and problems exist in many countries of Latin America because of this limitation on the number of students who can enter the universities. What future can these economically underdeveloped, technically backward countries have if they close the doors of their universities? For not only do the university graduates have difficulties in getting jobs, but a large number of them emigrate to the United States seeking employment. How can these countries overcome their underdevelopment and their poverty if they close the doors of their universities?

Who can know this better than we? Who can better understand the enormous need for technicians?

Of course a social system which is totally unconcerned with the health of its people does not need many doctors. In countries where practically no medical service exists, there are more than enough doctors, who always tend to concentrate in the big cities.

In countries full of large land-holdings, where agriculture is under a feudal-type regime, agronomists are not needed, veterinarians are not needed, mechanical engineers are not needed.

Our need for mechanical engineers is constantly present. Why? Because the need constantly arises for machines, machines of every kind: machines for fertilizing, clearing, and cultivating; machines for cutting, cleaning, and transporting sugar cane. And our need for mechanical engineers is evident; our need for hydraulic engineers is evident; for civil engineers, electrical engineers, architects, chemists, and research workers. Our need for pedagogues, university professors, professors for pre-university and technological institutes; our need for skilled workers in industry, in production, for the development of the country, for the fulfilling of its social needs, is constantly arising. Because that is precisely the task of the Revolution; to develop the country in every way, to develop the country materially and culturally.

In our system no one works to make profits for any individual; we work to satisfy the needs of the people, to enrich the country, to raise the productivity of labor; every citizen of this country is today concerned with increasing labor productivity; every citizen in this country is, logically, interested in raising and multiplying the productivity of a rural worker, of a cane-worker, of a construction worker, of a mineworker, a transport worker, a fisherman, because our resources will increase and it will be possible to take care of the most pressing needs of the people in the same measure as labor productivity increases.

These are the things that make our case different from that of the other Latin American nations. We are ahead of them. And in a world where the population increases more rapidly than the output of foodstuffs, how will the underdeveloped nations be able to face this tremendous problem without Revolution, without doing precisely what we are doing? . . .

And when we say the Cuban Revolution, we are speaking of the Revolution in Latin America. And when we speak of the revolution in Latin America we are speaking of revolution on a universal scale, the revolution of the peoples of Asia, Africa and of Europe. . . .

We are not denying the heroism of any people. The heroic peoples of the world are many, both of large and small nations. But naturally we look with great sympathy upon those men who at a given hour taught the peoples of the world that, regardless of size, it is possible to fight against the imperialists and to withstand the imperialists' aggressions.

The imperialists are cowards. They like to be merciless with small nations, while at the same time they tremble at the possibility of coming to blows with the great powers.

In the United States there are many senators and leaders who talk every day about aggressions against Cuba and invasions of Cuba, because they imagine they are going to have "easy pickings" here. And really, we are not interested in persuading them to the contrary.

We know that aggressions are not defeated by words but by weapons. We know that we are not going to save ourselves from the dangers of an invasion by scaring the imperialists. We confront the dangers of an invasion, or the consequences of any invasion, by preparing ourselves, constantly preparing ourselves! And we will not stop preparing ourselves for one single minute. . . .

And we are a small country but against this country, against its dignity, against its integrity . . . this country which is the first one to conquer true independence, the vanguard of America, an example for all the other countries of this Continent; this country which defies imperialism and all its might and marches forward, does so because it is ready to do so, because it is ready to march ahead, because it is certain that it will march ahead, because no one can prevent us from doing so. And if they attack us, they will be smashed by that integrity and that heroism. Because we will be martyrs, like those of Girón, rather than the slaves of anyone!

Our Country or Death! We will triumph!

COMMUNIQUÉ ON THE FOUR MODERNIZATIONS BY THE CENTRAL COMMITTEE OF THE CHINESE COMMUNIST PARTY

During the 1950s, China's leaders adopted a plan of economic development inspired by Stalin's Five-Year Plans (see Chapter 11), emphasizing the development of heavy industry, agricultural collectivization, and centralized planning. Although China experienced impressive industrial progress, Mao Zedong became disturbed that the emerging elite of educated industrial managers and government planners was destroying the Party's commitment to egalitarianism. Thus, in 1958 he sought to accelerate economic growth and end central bureaucratic control of the economy by instituting the Great Leap Forward. In a little more than two years, some 24,000 people's communes were established, each containing approximately 30,000 people who performed industrial and agricultural work, received political indoctrination, and participated in a variety of social experiments. The Great Leap Forward was an economic disaster, and in 1960 Mao lost influence in government to moderates such as Deng Xiaoping, who dismantled the communes and reintroduced incentives and centralized planning.

In 1966, however, Mao made another bold attempt to revive revolutionary vigor and rescue the Party from the "capitalist road" of Soviet-style bureaucratization. The result was the Cultural Revolution, in which Chinese young people were urged to rise up and smash "bourgeois" elements in the Party and society. By early summer millions of school-aged youth organized into Red Guards and devoted themselves to full-time political activity.

Although the intensity of the Great Cultural Revolution abated after 1969, Mao retained control of the Party until his death in 1976. As his health deteriorated, a struggle began between his radical disciples, led by his wife Jiang Qing, and moderates discredited during the Cultural Revolution, led by Deng Xiaoping. Deng's faction gradually gained ascendancy, and by 1978 the Central Committee had officially abandoned Maoist extremism in favor of a moderate, pragmatic policy designed to achieve the "Four Modernizations" in agriculture, industry, science and technology, and the military. To encourage economic growth the government fostered the return of free markets, private incentives, and limited competition, and Deng claimed that China had entered its "second revolution." It was to be an economic revolution only, however. When millions of Chinese demonstrated for democracy in Beijing in the spring of 1989, the government crushed the demonstrators with soldiers and tanks and reinstituted the old methods of a police state.

Questions for Analysis

1. What position does the communiqué take on the following issues: (a) the importance of ideology, (b) egalitarianism, (c) the purpose of education, and (d) the importance of economic development?
2. How does the communiqué judge Mao and the Cultural Revolution?

*I*n the early years after the founding of the People's Republic, especially after the socialist transformation was in the main completed, Comrade Mao Tse-tung instructed the whole party time and again to shift the focus of our work to the field of the economy and the technical revolution. Under the leadership of Comrade Mao Tse-tung and Comrade Chou En-lai[1] our party did a great deal for socialist modernization and scored important achievements. But the work was later interrupted and sabotaged by Lin Piao and the gang of four.[2] Besides, we had some shortcomings and mistakes in our leading work because we lacked experience in socialist construction, and this also hampered the transition in the focus of our party's work. Since the nation-wide mass movement to expose and criticize Lin Piao and the gang of four has fundamentally come to a successful conclusion, though in a small number of places and departments the movement is less developed and still needs some time to catch up and so cannot end simultaneously, on the whole there is every condition needed for that transition.

Therefore the plenary session unanimously endorsed the policy decision put forward by Comrade Hua Kuo-feng[3] on behalf of the Political Bureau of the Central Committee that, to meet the developments at home and abroad, now is an

---

1. Chou En-lai was a long-time associate of Mao, serving as premier of China until his death in 1976.

2. Lin Piao fell from Mao's favor when he resisted the Chinese rapprochement with the United States in 1971 and 1972; the "gang of four" refers to four disciples of Mao who sought to continue his policies after his death and fought with the moderates led by Deng Xiaoping.

3. The premier of China.

appropriate time to take the decision to close the large-scale nation-wide mass movement to expose and criticize Lin Piao and the gang of four and to shift the emphasis of our party's work and the attention of the whole people of our country to socialist modernization. . . . The general task put forward by our party for the new period reflects the demands of history and the people's aspirations and represents their fundamental interests. Whether or not we can carry this general task to completion, speed socialist modernization and on the basis of a rapid growth in production improve the people's living standards significantly and strengthen national defense — this is a major issue which is of paramount concern to all our people and of great significance to the cause of world peace and progress. Carrying out the four modernizations requires great growth in the productive forces, which in turn requires diverse changes in those aspects of the relations of production and the superstructure not in harmony with the growth of the productive forces, and requires changes in all methods of management, actions and thinking which stand in the way of such growth. Socialist modernization is therefore a profound and extensive revolution. . . .

The session points out that one of the serious shortcomings in the structure of economic management in our country is the over-concentration of authority, and it is necessary boldly to shift it under guidance from the leadership to lower levels so that the local authorities and industrial and agricultural enterprises will have greater power of decision in management under the guidance of unified state planning; big efforts should be made to simplify bodies at various levels charged with economic administration and transfer most of their functions to such enterprises as specialized companies or complexes . . . it is necessary, under the

centralized leadership of the party . . . , to institute a division of responsibilities among different levels, types of work and individuals, increase the authority and responsibility of administrative bodies and managerial personnel, reduce the number of meetings and amount of paperwork to raise work efficiency, and conscientiously adopt the practices of examination, reward and punishment, promotion and demotion. These measures will bring into play the initiative, enthusiasm and creativeness of four levels, the central departments, the local authorities, the enterprises and the workers, and invigorate all branches and links of the socialist economy. . . .

The plenary session holds that the whole party should concentrate its main energy and efforts on advancing agriculture as fast as possible because agriculture, the foundation of the national economy, has been seriously damaged in recent years and remains very weak on the whole. The rapid development of the national economy as a whole and the steady improvement in the living standards of the people of the whole country depends on the vigorous restoration and speeding up of farm production. . . . This requires first of all releasing the socialist enthusiasm of our country's several hundred million peasants, paying full attention to their material well-being economically and giving effective protection to their democratic rights politically. Taking this as the guideline, the plenary session set forth a series of policies and economic measures aimed at raising present agricultural production. The most important are as follows: The right of ownership by the people's communes, production brigades and production teams and their power of decision must be protected effectively by the laws of the state: it is not permitted to commandeer the manpower, funds, products and material of any production team; the economic organizations at various levels of the people's commune must conscientiously implement the socialist principle of "to each according to his work," work out payment in accordance with the amount and quality of work done, and overcome egalitarianism; small plots of land for private use by commune members, their domestic side-occupations, and village fairs are necessary adjuncts of the socialist economy, and must not be interfered with. . . .

The plenary session also discussed strengthening of education in agricultural science, the drafting of regional programs for developing agriculture, forestry and animal husbandry, the establishment of modern farming, forestry, livestock-breeding and fishing centers, the active expansion of rural industry and side-occupations run by people's communes and production brigades and other important questions, and decided upon relevant measures.

The plenary session points out that it is imperative to improve the livelihood of the people in town and country step by step on the basis of the growth of production. The bureaucratic attitude of paying no attention at all to urgent problems in the people's livelihood must be resolutely opposed. On the other hand, since our economy is still very backward at present, it is impossible to improve the people's livelihood very rapidly and it is essential to keep the people informed on the relevant state of affairs and to intensify education in the revolutionary ideas of self-reliance and hard struggle among the youth and other sectors of the people, and leading comrades at all levels must make themselves examplars in this regard. . . .

The session emphatically points out that the great feats performed by Comrade Mao Tse-tung in protracted revolutionary struggle are indelible. Without his outstanding leadership and without Mao Tse-tung Thought, it is most likely that the Chinese revolution would not have been victorious up to the present. The Chinese people would still be living under the reactionary rule of imperialism, feudalism and bureaucrat-capitalism and our party would still be struggling in the dark. Comrade Mao Tse-tung was a great Marxist. He always adopted a scientific attitude of dividing one into two toward everyone, including himself. It would not be Marxist to demand that a revolutionary leader be free of all shortcomings and errors. It also would not conform to Comrade Mao Tse-tung's consistent evaluation of himself. The lofty task of the party Central Committee on the theoretical front is to lead and educate the whole party and the people of the whole country to recognize Comrade Mao Tse-tung's great feats in a historical and scientific perspective, comprehensively and correctly grasp the scientific system of Mao Tse-tung Thought and integrate the universal principles of Marxism-Leninism-Mao Tse-tung Thought with the concrete practice of socialist modernization and develop it under the new historical conditions.

The session holds that the Great Cultural Revolution should also be viewed historically, scientifically and in a down-to-earth way. Comrade Mao Tse-tung initiated this great revolution primarily in the light of the fact that the Soviet Union had turned revisionist and for the purpose of opposing revisionism and preventing its occurrence.

As for the shortcomings and mistakes in the actual course of the revolution, they should be summed up at the appropriate time as experience and lessons so as to unify the views of the whole party and the people of the whole country. However, there should be no haste about this. Shelving this problem will not prevent us from solving all other problems left over from past history in a down-to-earth manner, nor will it affect our concentration of efforts to speed up the four modernizations, the greatest historic task of the time.

Mikhail Gorbachev

PERESTROIKA

Since becoming general secretary of the Communist party in March 1985, Mikhail Gorbachev has initiated what appears to be the most decisive period of change in the Soviet Union since Stalin's early years. Born of peasant parents, Gorbachev received training in law and agricultural economics. After holding a variety of positions in the Communist party and becoming a member of the Politburo in 1979, he took power at age 54. Gorbachev has characterized his sweeping program of redefining Soviet society as *perestroika* ("restructuring"). The following selection comes from his 1987 book, *Perestroika*, in which he explains his ideas about the Soviet Union's future.

Questions
for Analysis

1. What developments in the Soviet Union led Gorbachev to conclude that Soviet society and government needed reform?
2. In Gorbachev's view, how will the "individual" in Soviet society be affected by his reforms?
3. To what extent is *perestroika* democratic?
4. What similarities and differences do you see between Gorbachev's statements about *perestroika* and the Chinese "Communiqué on the Four Modernizations"?

Russia, where a great Revolution took place seventy years ago, is an ancient country with a unique history filled with searchings, accomplishments and tragic events. It has given the world many discoveries and outstanding personalities.

However, the Soviet Union is a young state without analogues in history or in the modern world. Over the past seven decades — a short span in the history of human civilization — our country has traveled a path equal to centuries. One of the mightiest powers in the world rose up to replace the backward semi-colonial and semi-feudal Russian Empire. . . .

At some stage — this became particularly clear in the latter half of the seventies — something happened that was at first sight inexplicable. The country began to lose momentum. Economic failures became more frequent. Difficulties began to accumulate and deteriorate, and unresolved problems to multiply. Elements of what we call stagnation and other phenomena alien to socialism began to appear in the life of society. A kind of "braking mechanism" affecting social and economic development formed. And all this happened at a time when scientific and technological revolution opened up new prospects for economic and social progress. . . .

Analyzing the situation, we first discovered a slowing economic growth. In the last fifteen years the national income growth rates had declined by more than a half and by the beginning of the eighties had fallen to a level close to economic stagnation. A country that was once quickly closing on the world's advanced nations began to lose one position after another. . . .

It became typical of many of our economic executives to think not of how to build up the national asset, but of how to put more material, labor and working time into an item to sell it at a higher price. Consequently, for all "gross output," there was a shortage of goods. We spent, in fact we are still spending, far more on raw materials, energy and other resources per unit of output than other developed nations. Our country's wealth in terms of natural and manpower resources has spoilt, one may even say corrupted, us. . . .

The presentation of a "problem-free" reality backfired: a breach had formed between word and deed, which bred public passivity and disbelief in the slogans being proclaimed. It was only natural that this situation resulted in a credibility gap: everything that was proclaimed from the rostrums and printed in newspapers and textbooks was put in question. Decay began in public morals; the great feeling of solidarity with each other that was forged during the heroic times of the Revolution, the first five-year plans, the Great Patriotic War[1] and postwar rehabilitation was weakening; alcoholism, drug addiction and crime were growing; and the penetration of the stereotypes of mass culture alien to us, which bred vulgarity and low tastes and brought about ideological barrenness increased.

Political flirtation and mass distribution of awards, titles and bonuses often replaced genuine concern for the people, for their living and working conditions, for a favorable social atmosphere. An atmosphere emerged of "everything goes," and fewer and fewer demands were made on discipline and responsibility. Attempts were made to cover it all up with pompous campaigns and undertakings and celebrations of numerous anniversaries centrally and locally. The world of day-to-day realities and the world of feigned prosperity were diverging more and more. . . .

An unbiased and honest approach led us to the only logical conclusion that the country was verging on crisis. This conclusion was announced at the April 1985 Plenary Meeting of the Central Committee,[2] which inaugurated the new strategy of perestroika and formulated its basic principles. . . .

By saying all this I want to make the reader understand that the energy for revolutionary change has been accumulating amid our people and in the Party for some time. And the ideas of perestroika have been prompted not just by pragmatic interests and considerations but also by our troubled conscience, by the indomitable commitment to ideals which we inherited from the Revolution and as a result of a theoretical quest which gave us a better knowledge of society and reinforced our determination to go ahead.

Today our main job is to lift the individual spiritually, respecting his inner world and giving him moral strength. We are seeking to make the whole intellectual potential of society and all the potentialities of culture work to mold a socially active

---

1. The Soviet name for World War II.

2. The Central Committee of the Communist Party, the body that sets broad policy for the Soviet government.

person, spiritually rich, just and conscientious. An individual must know and feel that his contribution is needed, that his dignity is not being infringed upon, that he is being treated with trust and respect. When an individual sees all this, he is capable of accomplishing much.

Of course, perestroika somehow affects everybody; it jolts many out of their customary state of calm and satisfaction at the existing way of life. Here I think it is appropriate to draw your attention to one specific feature of socialism. I have in mind the high degree of social protection in our society. On the one hand, it is, doubtless, a benefit and a major achievement of ours. On the other, it makes some people spongers.

There is virtually no unemployment. The state has assumed concern for ensuring employment. Even a person dismissed for laziness or a breach of labor discipline must be given another job. Also, wage-leveling has become a regular feature of our everyday life: even if a person is a bad worker, he gets enough to live fairly comfortably. The children of an outright parasite will not be left to the mercy of fate. We have enormous sums of money concentrated in the social funds from which people receive financial assistance. The same funds provide subsidies for the unkeep of kindergartens, orphanages, Young Pioneer[3] houses and other institutions related to children's creativity and sport. Health care is free, and so is education. People are protected from the vicissitudes of life, and we are proud of this.

But we also see that dishonest people try to exploit these advantages of socialism; they know only their rights, but they do not want to know their duties: they work poorly, shirk and drink hard. There are quite a few people who have adapted the existing laws and practices to their own selfish interests. They give little to society, but nevertheless managed to get from it all that is possible and what even seems impossible; they have lived on unearned incomes.

The policy of restructuring puts everything in its place. We are fully restoring the principle of socialism. "From each according to his ability, to each according to his work," and we seek to affirm social justice for all, equal rights for all, one law for all, one kind of discipline for all, and high responsibilities for each. Perestroika raises the level of social responsibility and expectation.

. . .

It is essential to learn to adjust policy in keeping with the way it is received by the masses, and to ensure feedback, absorbing the ideas, opinions and advice coming from the people. The masses suggest a lot of useful and interesting things which are not always clearly perceived "from the top." That is why we must prevent at all costs an arrogant attitude to what people are saying. In the final account the most important thing for the success of perestroika is the people's attitude to it.

Thus, not only theory but the reality of the processes under way made us embark on the program for all-round democratic changes in public life which we presented at the January 1987 Plenary Meeting of the CPSU[4] Central Committee.

The Plenary Meeting encouraged exten-

---

3. A youth organization sponsored by the Soviet regime.

4. Communist Party of the Soviet Union.

sive efforts to strengthen the democratic basis of Soviet society, to develop self-government and extend glasnost, that is openness, in the entire management network. We see now how stimulating that impulse was for the nation. Democratic changes have been taking place at every work collective, at every state and public organization, and within the Party. More glasnost, genuine control from "below," and greater initiative and enterprise at work are now part and parcel of our life. . . .

The adoption of fundamental principles for a radical change in economic management was a big step forward in the program of perestroika. Now perestroika concerns virtually every main aspect of public life. . . .

Perestroika means overcoming the stagnation process, breaking down the braking mechanism, creating a dependable and effective mechanism for the acceleration of social and economic progress and giving it greater dynamism.

Perestroika means mass initiative. It is the comprehensive development of democracy, socialist self-government, encouragement of initiative and creative endeavor, improved order and discipline, more glasnost,[5] criticism and self-criticism in all spheres of our society. It is utmost respect for the individual and consideration for personal dignity.

Perestroika is the all-round intensification of the Soviet economy, the revival and development of the principles of democratic centralism in running the national economy, the universal introduction of economic methods, the renunciation of management by injunction and by admin-

istrative methods, and the overall encouragement of innovation and socialist enterprise.

Perestroika means a resolute shift to scientific methods, an ability to provide a solid scientific basis for every new initiative. It means the combination of the achievements of the scientific and technological revolution with a planned economy.

Perestroika means priority development of the social sphere aimed at ever better satisfaction of the Soviet people's requirements for good living and working conditions, for good rest and recreation, education and health care. It means unceasing concern for cultural and spiritual wealth, for the culture of every individual and society as a whole.

Perestroika means the elimination from society of the distortions of socialist ethics, the consistent implementation of the principles of social justice. It means the unity of words and deeds, rights and duties. It is the elevation of honest, highly-qualified labor, the overcoming of leveling tendencies in pay and consumerism. . . .

I stress once again: perestroika is not some kind of illumination or revelation. To restructure our life means to understand the objective necessity for renovation and acceleration. And that necessity emerged in the heart of our society. The essence of perestroika lies in the fact that *it unites socialism with democracy* and revives the Leninist concept of socialist construction both in theory and in practice. Such is the essence of perestroika, which accounts for its genuine revolutionary spirit and its all-embracing scope.

The goal is worth the effort. And we are sure that our effort will be a worthy contribution to humanity's social progress.

---

5. Russian for "openness"; describes Gorbachev's policy of encouraging open debate of Soviet problems.

Pondering the Future

In 1793 the French *philosophe*, the Marquis de Condorcet, wrote in his *Sketch of the Progress of the Human Mind*:

> Nature has set no term to the perfection of the human mind; . . . the perfectibility of man is truly indefinite; . . . the progress of this perfectibility has no other limit than the duration of the globe upon which nature has cast us; this progress will doubtless vary in speed, but it will never be reversed as long as the earth occupies its present place in the system of the universe, and as long as the general laws of this system produce neither a general cataclysm nor such changes as will deprive the human race of its present faculties and present resources.[1]

Thus did Condorcet express the Enlightenment belief in the power of reason and science to lead humanity to future perfection, a belief that many peoples of the West enthusiastically embraced during the nineteenth century.

In 1974 U.S. economist Robert L. Heilbroner also assessed the future in his *An Inquiry into the Human Prospect*:

> I do not pose the question . . . — "Is there hope for man?" — as a mere rhetorical flourish, a straw figure to be dismantled as we proceed to more "serious" matters. The outlook for man, I believe, is painful, difficult, perhaps desperate, and the hope that can be held out for his future prospect seems very slim indeed. Thus . . . to answer the question whether we can conceive of the future other than as a continuation of the darkness, cruelty, and disorder of the past seems to me to be no; and the question of whether worse impends, yes.[2]

Thus did Heilbroner express the despair of many human beings in the late twentieth century and their disillusionment with the premise that industrialization, technology, and science guarantee limitless progress.

Although the mass destruction of World Wars I and II dimmed the optimism of many of the world's peoples, the rapid postwar economic recovery and high expectations engendered by the end of colonialism sparked renewed hopes for humanity's future in the 1950s and 1960s. By the 1970s, however, nuclear proliferation, environmental damage, resource depletion, soaring population rates, and growing poverty and famine in underdeveloped nations inspired the profound pessimism of Heilbroner and many others. Their dark vision of the future attracted numerous critics, and the debate over humanity's prospects continues to the present day. The issues have more than academic interest, for our view of the future shapes both the policies of governments and our behavior as individuals.

---

1. Marquis de Condorcet, *Sketch for a Historical Picture of the Progress of the Human Mind,* June Barraclough, trans. (London: Weidenfield & Nicolson, 1955), pp. 4–5. See Chapter 5.

2. Robert L. Heilbroner, *An Inquiry into the Human Prospect* (New York: Norton & Company, 1974), 22.

▨ World Bank

WORLD DEVELOPMENT REPORT

A basic disagreement between optimists and pessimists concerning humanity's future centers on the prospects of underdeveloped nations. Pessimists see their continuing decline into mass poverty and social disintegration; optimists predict a future in which all nations will prosper. Statistics provided by the World Bank allow an assessment of the two positions based on recent developments and short-range projections.

The World Bank, also known as the International Bank for Reconstruction and Development, was founded in 1944 and shortly thereafter became affiliated with the newly established United Nations. Using funds subscribed by UN members, it advances loans to nations and private businesses for projects that further economic development. Although most loans at first went for postwar reconstruction projects, since the 1950s the bank has mainly supported loans for power projects and agricultural development in developing areas. Since 1978 it has published annually its *World Development Report*, with articles on development strategies and statistics on economic, demographic, and educational trends. The following statistics are drawn from the 1988 edition.

Questions
for Analysis

1. In what areas have the low-income nations made the greatest progress in the past two decades?
2. Is the gap between rich and poor nations getting larger or smaller?
3. What do these statistics suggest about changes in a nation's population make-up as it becomes more "developed"?
4. What do these statistics reveal about conditions that have slowed down development of poorer nations?

World Bank Statistics

Nation	Population (millions)			GNP per capita		Fertilizer consumption (hundreds of grams plant nutrient/hectare[1] arable land)		Energy consumption/ capita (kilograms of oil equivalent)	
	1986	1990	2000	Dollars 1986	Av. annual growth rate (%) 1965–1986	1970	1985	1965	1986
Ethiopia	43	49	65	120	0.0	4	47	10	21
Zaire	32	36	48	160	-2.2	8	10	74	73
India	781	846	1002	290	1.8	114	504	100	208
China	1054	1117	1279	300	5.1	384	1692	178	532
Pakistan	99	113	150	350	2.4	168	736	135	205
Ghana	13	15	20	390	-1.7	9	44	76	131
Indonesia	166	178	207	490	4.6	119	947	91	213
Philippines	57	62	76	560	1.9	214	358	160	180
Bolivia	7	7	9	600	-0.4	13	17	155	255
Nigeria	103	118	164	640	1.9	3	108	34	134
Egypt, Arab. Rep.	50	55	67	760	3.1	1282	3473	313	577
Nicaragua	3	4	5	790	-2.2	184	494	172	259
Turkey	51	56	67	1100	2.7	166	538	258	750
Jordan	4	5	6	1540	5.5[2]	20	369	226	767
Brazil	138	150	180	1810	4.3	169	425	286	830
Mexico	80	87	107	1860	2.6	246	693	604	1235
Hungary	11	11	11	2020	3.9	1485	2527	1825	2985
Korea, Rep. of	41	44	49	2370	6.7	2466	3764	237	1408
Greece	10	10	10	3680	3.3	858	1739	615	1932
Israel	4	5	5	6210	2.6	1394	2203	1574	1944
Iran, Islamic Rep.	46	52	69	—	—	76	609	537	958
Saudi Arabia	12	14	20	6950	4.0	44	2926	1759	3336
United Kingdom	57	57	58	8870	1.7	2521	3566	3481	3802
Japan	121	124	129	12,840	4.3	3849	4273	1474	3186
Canada	26	27	28	14,120	2.6	192	497	6007	8945
United States	242	249	263	17,480	1.6	800	939	6535	7193
Switzerland	7	6	6	17,680	1.4	3842	4362	2501	4052
USSR	281	291	312	—	—	437	1093	2603	4949

555

Nation	Population/physician 1965	Population/physician 1981	% Total age group enrolled in primary ed.[3] 1965	1985	% Labor force in Agriculture 1965	1980	Industry 1965	1980	Services 1965	1980
Ethiopia	70,190	88,150	11	36	86	80	5	8	9	12
Zaire	35,130	13,430	70	98	82	72	9	13	9	16
India	4880	3700	74	92	73	70	12	13	15	17
China	3790	1730	89	124	81	74	8	14	11	12
Pakistan	—	2910	40	47	60	55	18	16	22	30
Ghana	13,740	6680	69	66	61	56	15	18	24	26
Indonesia	31,740	12,330	72	118	71	57	9	13	21	30
Philippines	—	6850	113	106	58	52	16	16	26	33
Bolivia	3300	2000	73	91	54	46	20	20	26	34
Nigeria	29,530	9400	32	92	72	68	10	12	18	20
Egypt, Arab. Rep.	2300	760	75	85	55	46	15	20	30	34
Nicaragua	2560	2230	69	101	57	47	16	16	28	38
Turkey	2900	1530	101	116	75	58	11	17	14	25
Jordan	4710	1190	95	99	37	10	26	26	37	64
Brazil	2500	1300	108	104	49	31	20	27	31	42
Mexico	2080	1210	92	115	50	37	22	29	29	35
Hungary	630	390	101	98	32	18	40	44	29	38
Korea, Rep. of	2700	1390	101	96	55	36	15	27	30	37
Greece	710	390	110	106	47	31	24	29	29	40
Israel	400	400	95	99	12	6	35	32	53	62
Iran, Islamic Rep.	3800	2900	63	112	49	36	26	33	25	31
Saudi Arabia	9400	1800	24	69	68	48	11	14	21	37
United Kingdom	870	680	92	101	3	3	47	38	50	59
Japan	970	740	100	102	26	11	32	34	42	55
Canada	770	550	105	105	10	5	33	29	57	65
United States	670	500	—	101	5	4	35	31	60	66
Switzerland	710	390	87	—	9	6	49	39	41	55
USSR	480	270	103	106	34	20	33	39	33	41

1. One hectare equals 10,000 square meters, or 2.47 acres.
2. Figures in italics are for years other than those specified.
3. Age group for primary school-age children is 6 to 11 years. Some nations with universal primary education show gross enrollment ratios in excess of 100% because of the enrollment of younger or older students in primary school.

■ Herman Kahn

THE NEXT 200 YEARS: A SCENARIO FOR AMERICA AND THE WORLD

Born in 1922 in New Jersey, Herman Kahn, a mathematician and physicist, worked as a defense analyst from 1946 to 1961 for the RAND Corporation, a nonprofit research institute employed primarily by the U.S. Department of Defense. In 1961 he co-founded the Hudson Institute, a research group that concentrates on broad public policy issues related to defense, national security, health, transportation, food supply, and future planning. In 1976 Kahn, along with co-authors William Brown and Leon Martel, published *The Next 200 Years: A Scenario for America and the World*, in which they attempt to counter what they call the "doomsday literature" of the early 1970s. They advance the thesis that humanity's problems are solvable and that in 200 years human beings everywhere will be "numerous, rich, and in control of the forces of nature."

At the beginning of the book, the authors present the following table, which compares four different scenarios about the future. The name of one of these groups, "neo-Malthusian," derives from Thomas Malthus (1766–1834), an Englishman who argued that population growth always tends to outrun food supply, thus making poverty and famine humanity's inescapable lot. His name has come to symbolize pessimism about the future. The authors call their scenarios "earth-centered," meaning they assume that human exploration and exploitation of space will not lead to significant migration from earth to space colonies.

Questions
for Analysis

1. According to the four points of view represented, what is the future of the less developed nations? How will further population growth affect human existence? Is the depletion of basic natural resources truly a problem for humanity?
2. How do the positions differ on the question of industrialization's impact on the earth and human existence?
3. To what extent is the position of the "optimists" based on a faith in continued scientific and technological innovation? Why do the "pessimists" reject such a faith?
4. How do basic attitudes toward human nature and human capabilities affect the four points of view represented?
5. Based on the four scenarios, what policies should governments adopt to promote the best possible future for humanity?

Four Views of the Earth-Centered Perspective

A. Convinced Neo-Malthusian

B. Guarded Pessimist

C. Guarded Optimist

D. Technology-and-Growth Enthusiast

1. BASIC WORLD MODEL

Finite pie. Most global nonrenewable resources can be estimated accurately enough (within a factor of 5) to demonstrate the reality of the running-out phenomenon. Whatever amounts of these resources are consumed will forever be denied to others. Current estimates show we will be running out of many critical resources in the next 50 years. The existing remainder of the pie must be shared more fairly among the nations of the world and between this generation and those to follow. Because the pie shrinks over time, any economic growth that makes the rich richer can only make the poor poorer.

Uncertain pie. The future supply and value of both old and new materials are necessarily uncertain. Past projections of the future availability of materials usually have been gross underestimates. One can concede this could happen again, but current estimates seem relatively reliable. Current exponential growth clearly risks an early exhaustion of some critical materials. Prudence requires immediate conservation of remaining resources. Excessive conservation poses small risks while excessive consumption would be tragic.

Growing pie. Past technological and economic progress suggests that increasing current production is likely to increase further the potential for greater production and that progress in one region encourages similar developments everywhere. Thus as the rich get richer, the poor also benefit. Higher consumption in the developed world tends to benefit all countries. Excessive caution tends to maintain excessive poverty. Some caution is necessary in selected areas, but both the "least risk" and the "best bet" paths require continued and rapid technological and economic development.

Unlimited pie. The important resources are capital, technology and educated people. The greater these resources, the greater the potential for even more. There is no persuasive evidence that any meaningful limits to growth are in sight — or are desirable — except for population growth in some LDCs.[1] If any very long-term limits set by a "finite earth" really exist, they can be offset by the vast extraterrestrial resources and areas that will become available soon. Man has always risen to the occasion and will do so in the future despite dire predictions from the perennial doomsayers who have always been scandalously wrong.

2. TECHNOLOGY AND CAPITAL

Largely illusory or counterproductive. Proposed technological solutions to problems of pollution or scarce resources are shortsighted illusions that only compound

Mostly diminishing returns. Generally, despite many exceptions, the future will bring diminishing marginal returns from new investments, and the effort required for

Required for progress. Despite some dangers, only new technology and capital investment can increase production; protect and improve the environment; hold

Solves almost all problems. Some current problems have resulted from careless application of technology and investment, but none is without a remedy. It is

---

1. Less-developed countries.

A. Convinced Neo-Malthusian

the difficulties. Even on a moderate scale this approach would only further deplete crucial resources while avoiding the real problems and prolonging the poverty of the LDCs. Any future economic development should be restricted to the Third World and should include some transfer of existing capital assets from the over-developed nations. A completely new approach is needed for the long term.

B. Guarded Pessimist

economic gains will increase dramatically. The technology, capital equipment and other efforts required to obtain minerals and food in increasingly marginal situations will accelerate the approaching exhaustion of many resources and substantially increase pollution and shortages — possibly to lethal levels. Until practical solutions to these problems have appeared, we must turn away from technology and investment.

C. Guarded Optimist

down the cost of energy, minerals and food; provide economic surpluses with which to improve living standards in the LDCs; and prepare prudently for any potential unexpected catastrophes. We must be alert for problems resulting from inadequately understood innovations, inappropriate growth and/or natural causes. However, we should proceed with energy and confidence even while exercising great caution and constantly reassessing future risks and benefits.

D. Technology-and-Growth Enthusiast

not paradoxical that technology which caused problems can also solve them — it only requires mankind's attention and desire. There is little doubt that sufficient land and resources exist for continual progress on earth. Most current problems are the result of too little technology and capital, not too much. In any case man's desire for expansion into new frontiers will lead eventually to the colonization of the solar system and effectively cunlimited *lebensraum.*[2]

3. MANAGEMENT AND DECISION-MAKING

Failure is almost certain. The complexities, rigidities and ideological differences among nations and their institutions make it inconceivable that present human organizations, even with computer assistance, could sufficiently comprehend and effectively act to solve our most important problems. A drastic redesign is needed to circumvent the thrust toward big-

Likely failure. The rapidity of change, growing complexity and increasing conflicting interests make effective management of resources, control of pollution and resolution of social conflicts too difficult. Some slowdown and simplification of issues are imperative — even if they require drastic actions. If we don't reform voluntarily, more painful political and eco-

Moderately successful. Systematic internalization of current external costs and normal economic mechanisms can make most private organizations adequately responsive to most problems. A practical degree of public regulation and a low degree of international cooperation can handle the rest, if somewhat awkwardly. Outstanding management is rare

Not a serious problem. We flatter ourselves that current issues are more important and difficult than ever. Actually there is usually nothing very special happening. Mankind always has faced difficult and dangerous problems and poor solutions resulted in high costs. Sometimes there is even a Darwinian selection — the successes surviving and the failures

---

2. German for "living space."

A. Convinced Neo-Malthusian	B. Guarded Pessimist	C. Guarded Optimist	D. Technology-and-Growth Enthusiast
ness, to permit much more local and decentralized decision-making, and to live and work on a manageable human scale. More emphasis is needed on the community and regional level — much less on big business, big government and big organizations generally.	nomic changes may be imposed on us by the catastrophic events made inevitable by failure to act soon. (Note that there is a wide range of attitudes here toward central planning and local decision-making, but almost all of them mistrust the current "unfree market.")	but usually not essential as most institutions learn from experience — if often slowly and painfully. (But good management can reduce the number and intensity of painful experiences.) Except for wars, shocks as great as the oil shock and other 1973–74 experiences are rare, and yet existing systems reacted adequately — and survived.	disappearing. Progress has made the stakes today less dramatic. Modern communication and information systems and sophisticated organizations provide a capability for rapid adjustments to reality whenever changes are required and government interference is not counterproductive.

4. RESOURCES

| *Steady depletion.* Mankind is steadily, and often rapidly, depleting the earth's potential resources for foods, fuels and minerals, and overwhelming its capability to absorb or recycle pollutants. Catastrophic results for some of these resources may be postponed until the 21st century, but food, energy and some minerals already appear to be critically short for the near term. All signs point to catastrophe for the medium- and long-term future. | *Continual difficulties.* The basic problem of limited resources may be insoluble. Even when sufficient resources exist, politics, incompetent management, poor planning and slow responses make effective solutions difficult under conditions of exponentially increasing demand. Where resources are becoming scarce and unrelenting demands for growth are coupled with incompetence, intolerable pressures are generated and disaster becomes probable. A | *Generally sufficient.* Given slow but steady technological and economic progress and an ultimate world population below 30 billion, it should be feasible to attain economic living standards markedly better than current ones. With rapid progress and good management generally, even higher economic levels and an outstanding quality of life become possible. Economic success enhances national capabilities to resolve specialized resource issues as they arise. | *Economics and technology can provide superb solutions.* The earth is essentially bountiful in all of the important resources. Sudden large price fluctuations tend to be "self-correcting" within a few years although they can be misinterpreted as basic shortages (as in 1973–74).[3] Near-term prices are certainly important, but we have often lived with short-term problems. Trust in the economics of the market system, confidence in emerging technologi- |

---

3. In the wake of the so-called Yom Kippur War between Israel and the Arab states in 1973, Muslim nations that were members of OPEC curtailed oil production and declared an embargo on oil exports to the United States. Before the embargo ended in 1974, oil prices had quadrupled in the United States.

A. Convinced Neo-Malthusian	B. Guarded Pessimist	C. Guarded Optimist	D. Technology-and-Growth Enthusiast
	more cautious approach to growth seems clearly desirable.	However, the tendency toward cartels coupled with political conflicts could create short-term problems in maintaining adequate supplies at reasonable prices.	cal solutions and a little patience will remedy the current resource issues just as they have in the past.

5. CURRENT GROWTH

A. Convinced Neo-Malthusian	B. Guarded Pessimist	C. Guarded Optimist	D. Technology-and-Growth Enthusiast
Carcinogenic. Current population and economic production are akin to a spreading cancer. They are already more than the earth can sustain in a steady state. Future economic or population growth will hasten and increase the magnitude of the future tragedy. The current demand for continued economic growth and the likelihood of a greatly increased world population only imply a steady worsening of the present extremely dangerous conditions.	*Large potential for disaster.* Even if roughly current levels of production could be indefinitely sustained, continued exponential growth in population and production eventually must lead to exhausted resources and hazardous pollution. Few positive human values would be served by continued mindless growth. We must learn that demand is not need. Unless drastic voluntary reforms limit future growth, catastrophes stemming from limited resources and high pollution levels are likely to make these reforms mandatory before long.	*Probable transition to stability.* Although current projections are uncertain, social and cultural forces inherent in both developing and affluent societies appear likely to limit the world population to about three times the current level and average per capita production to about two or three times the current U.S. level. There seems to be more than enough energy, resources and space for most populations, assuming that a relatively small number of people put forth the necessary efforts and others do not interfere.	*Desirable and healthy.* No obvious limits are apparent. Even with current technological potential, growth (except perhaps in a few of the poorest nations) is and will be purely a matter of human choice, not of natural limitations. Problems always exist, but solutions always emerge — often as a result of the dynamism of growth. We do not know man's ultimate fate, but truly fantastic economic and technological capabilities are likely to be included as both a means and an end (e.g., they probably include self-reproducing automation and space colonization in the next century).

6. INNOVATION AND DISCOVERY

A. Convinced Neo-Malthusian	B. Guarded Pessimist	C. Guarded Optimist	D. Technology-and-Growth Enthusiast
A trap. New discoveries of resources, new technologies and new projects may	*Increasingly ineffective.* The basic solution is to increasingly limit demands, not to	*Usually effective.* New resources, new technology and economic growth often	*Mankind's greatest hope.* New and improving technologies (agronomy, electron-

A. Convinced Neo-Malthusian	B. Guarded Pessimist	C. Guarded Optimist	D. Technology-and-Growth Enthusiast
postpone the immediate need for drastic actions, but not for long. Such postponement will make eventual collapse earlier and more severe. Prudence demands immediate restraint, cutbacks and a basic change in values and objectives. The time for short-run palliatives is past.	encourage a desperate search for new inventions that might suffice temporarily but would exacerbate long-run problems by increasing environmental damage and depletion of resources, while encouraging current growth and deferring hard decisions. Although technological solutions may buy some time, it has become increasingly important to use this time constructively and avoid the undue economic expansion that new discoveries encourage.	produce new problems, but they still do solve current problems, improve efficiency and upgrade the quality of life. Also, they increase the toughness and flexibility of the economy and society (i.e., provide insurance against bad luck or incompetency). With good management, they also can help to reduce population growth, conserve expensive minerals, improve nutrition within the poorer countries and generally improve future prospects.	ics, genetics, power generation and distribution, information processing, etc.) aided by fortuitous discoveries (e.g., ocean nodules) further man's potential for solving current perceived problems and for creating an affluent and exciting world. Man is now entering the most creative and expansive period of his history. These trends will soon allow mankind to become the "master" of the solar system.

7. INCOME GAPS AND POVERTY

Destined to tragic conclusions. The major consequences of industrialization and economic growth have been to enrich the few while exploiting and impoverishing the many. The gap between rich and poor as well as the total misery in the world are at all-time highs — and growing. Meanwhile natural resources, the heritage of the poor countries, are being consumed by the rich, thereby denying the poor any	*Increasing and threatening.* Income gaps have been increasing and may lead to dangerous responses. A drastic decrease in income among the poor may even be likely soon. Worldwide class warfare may emerge following a series of desperate political crises. These are not only possible but may be imminent as a consequence of the gaps and the exploitation of the mineral resources of the	*Declining absolute poverty.* Worldwide, the threat of absolute povery (i.e., possible large-scale famine) is likely soon to be forever abolished. Some income gaps may increase during the next century, but some will decrease. Generally, incomes of both rich and poor will increase. Both the gaps and improving technology will tend to accelerate development in poor countries. Attempts to force a rapid equali-	*A misformulated problem.* Western civilization required about 200 years to change from general poverty to general affluence. Because of their success and continuing advances in technology, many of the current LDCs will be able to make a similar transition within 50 years. All countries can be expected to become wealthy within the next 200 years. Any lesser scenario would be unreasonable or

A. Convinced Neo-Malthusian	*B. Guarded Pessimist*	*C. Guarded Optimist*	*D. Technology-and-Growth Enthusiast*
real hope for better living conditions — even temporarily.	LDCs. A more equitable income distribution has become a most urgent matter.	zation of income would guarantee only failure and tragic consequences.	an expression of very bad luck and/or bad management.

. . .

9. QUALITY OF LIFE

Ruined. Through excessive growth, mankind has become the most destructive species in history and may yet increase the extent of this damage manyfold. Indeed, a point of no return may have been passed already, mostly because of the persistent and growing potential for nuclear warfare. In any event, the values that lead toward a satisfying and wholesome life have already been largely destroyed in the developed nations.	*In conflict with much growth.* Continued economic development or population growth might well mean further deterioration of the environment, overcrowding, suburban sprawl and a society suitable more for machines than human beings. Priorities must change; market demand is not the same as need; GNP is not wealth, high technology not the same as a good life; automation and appliances do not necessarily increase human happiness.	*More gains than losses.* If environmental protection, health, safety and other considerations are neglected, growth would be accompanied by an unnecessary destruction of important values. However, much of what some elites claim to be destructive others consider constructive (e.g., a pipeline). With adequate internalization of the appropriate costs (by society's criteria), complaints from unhappy factions might still be loud or visible but would be generally inappropriate.	*A meaningless phrase and issue.* Disgruntled or unhappy people often oppose real progress for romantic, class, selfish or other reasons. They are not representative of the nation and need not be taken at face value. In a changing world, some elites may not benefit much or may even lose somewhat. But most people would benefit and gain expectations for an even better future.

NOTES ON THE CHAPTER-OPENING ILLUSTRATIONS

Chapter 1
Wooden Incan beaker (ca 1650) illustrating Peru's multiracial society. Shown in procession are an Amerindian, a Spaniard, and a black.

Chapter 2
Early seventeenth-century engraving of the Copernican system. The Polish astronomer Copernicus (1473–1543) proposed a heliocentric theory of the world: the Sun is the center of the cosmos, and the Earth is one of its planets.

Chapter 3
Painting (artist unknown) of the Tokugawa chief, Iesayu, who in 1603 established his rule at Edo.

Chapter 4
Seventeenth-century engraving of the port of Amsterdam, from Caspar Commelin et al., *Beschryving der Stad Amsterdam* (1665).

Chapter 5
Allegorical painting by Jeaurat de Bertry, *Tableau allégorique révolutionnaire* (1794). A portrait of Jean-Jacques Rousseau, the spiritual father of the French Revolution, is shown suspended over symbols of the revolution.

Chapter 6
Patriotic banner of the Jeffersonian era (1800–1808) in the United States.

Chapter 7
Engraving of a row of slaves sifting for diamonds in mineral-rich Minas, Brazil, in the early nineteenth century. At that time Brazil was one of the world's largest slave-holding nations.

Chapter 8
W. Louis Sontag, *The Bowery at Night* (1895). As this painting illustrates, the new inventions of the late nineteenth century, particularly those of George Westinghouse, contributed to the growth of cities.

Chapter 9
Photograph of Emat Bey, a leader of the Young Turks, in conference with the British military attaché and a correspondent of the French periodical *L'Illustration,* following the Young Turks' coup of January 23, 1913.

Chapter 10
Wood block print by Ando Hiroshige II or III (ca 1873; part of triptych) of Japan's first commercial bank, located in a building owned by the Mitsui family in the center of Edo.

Chapter 11
François Flameng's painting, *Trenches in Winter, 1915–1916,* conveys the horror and bleakness of World War I trench warfare.

Chapter 12
Photograph of Mohandas Gandhi and a handful of followers in 1930 as they embarked on the Salt March. The procession quickly grew to a length of two miles, and Gandhi's act of civil disobedience attracted worldwide attention.

Chapter 13
Chinese students mill around the student-built "Goddess of Liberty." The statue, which stood in Beijing's Tienanmen Square for five days during the spring of 1989, was razed at the time of the government's violent repression of the protesters.

SOURCES

Chapter 1

Pages 7–10: Gomes Eannes de Azurara, *The Chronicle of the Discovery and Conquest of Guinea*, trans. Charles Raymond Beazley and Edgar Prestage, 2 vols. (London: Hakluyt Society, 1896), Vol. 1, pp. 27–29, 83–85. Pages 11–13: Extracts from Letters of King Afonso to King of Portugal, 1526. Translated and published in THE AFRICAN PAST by Basil Davidson. Copyright © Basil Davidson, 1964. Reproduced by permission of Curtis Brown Ltd, London. Page 14: Reproduced by Courtesy of the Trustees of the British Museum. Pages 16–19: Bernardino de Sahagun, *The War of Conquest: How It Was Waged Here in Mexico*, tr. by Arthur J. O. Anderson and Charles E. Dibble (Salt Lake City: Utah, 1978), pp. 16–17, 19–23. Copyright 1976. Used by permission of the publisher. Pages 20–23: *The Laws of Burgos of 1512–1513: Royal Ordinances for the Good Government and Treatment of the Indians*, Lesley B. Simpson, trans. (San Francisco: John Howell, 1960), pp. 11–47, passim. Pages 24–26: David Pieterzen DeVries, *Voyages from Holland to New York* (New York: 1853), pp. 114–117. Pages 28–30: Charles T. Forster and F. H. Blackburne Daniell, eds., *The Life and Letters of Ogier Ghiselin de Busbecq*, 2 vols. (London: Hakluyt Society, 1881), Vol. 1, pp. 162, 369, 405–407. Pages 31–33: *The Akbar Nama of Abu-1-Fazl*, trans. Henry Beveridge, 3 vols. (New Delhi: Ess Ess Publications, 1902–1939), Vol. 1, pp. 37, 207, 322–323, 368–370, 410–411. Pages 35–39: From CHINA IN THE SIXTEENTH CENTURY: THE JOURNALS OF MATTHEW RICCI: 1583–1610, translated by Louis J. Gallagher, S. J. Copyright 1953 by Louis J. Gallagher, S. J. Reprinted by permission of Random House, Inc. Pages 40–41: David John Lu, ed. and tr., *Sources of Japanese History* (New York: McGraw-Hill, 1974), vol. 1, pp. 207–209. Copyright 1974. Used by permission of McGraw-Hill Publishing Company.

Chapter 2

Pages 46–50: Niccolò Machiavelli, *The Prince*, tr. by George Bull (London: Penguin Classics, 1961), pp. 61–66, 90–102. Copyright © George Bull, 1961, 1975, 1981 (revised edition). Reproduced by permission of Penguin Books Ltd. Pages 52–56: William Hazlitt, ed. and trans., *The Tabletalk of Martin Luther* (London: H. G. Bohn, 1857), pp. 72–73, 117, 294, 28, 45, 54–55, 25–27, 198, 199, 205–206, 219, passim. Pages 56–58: Excerpts from THE SPIRITUAL EXERCISES OF ST. IGNATIUS. Copyright © 1964 by Doubleday, a division of Bantam Doubleday Dell Publishing Group, Inc. Reprinted by permission of the publisher. Pages 59–61: Nicholas Copernicus, *On the Revolutions*, ed. by Jerry Dobrzycki, tr. by Edward Rosen (Baltimore: Johns Hopkins, 1978), pp. 3–6. Copyright 1978. Used by permission of Macmillan, London and Basingstoke. Pages 64–66: John J. Saunders, ed., *The Muslim World on the Eve of Europe's Expansion* (Englewood Cliffs, NJ: Prentice-Hall, 1966), pp. 40–43. © 1966. Reprinted by permission of the publisher, Prentice-Hall, Inc., Englewood Cliffs, NJ. Pages 67–70: Abul Fazl, *The Ain-i-Akbari*, trans. H. S. Jarrett, 3 vols. (Calcutta: Baptist Mission Press, 1868–1894), Vol. 3, pp. 8, 114–119, 159–160, 225–232, 279, 284, 285–286, 291–292. Pages 72–74: Extract taken from THE SACRED WRITINGS OF THE SIKHS, translated by Kushwant Singh and others, reproduced by kind permission of Unwin Hyman Ltd. © George Allen & Unwin, 1960.

Pages 76–79: From CHINA IN THE SIXTEENTH CENTURY: THE JOURNALS OF MATTHEW RICCI: 1583–1610, translated by Louis J. Gallagher, S. J. Copyright 1953 by Louis J. Gallagher, S. J. Reprinted by permission of Random House, Inc. Pages 80–82: Ryusaku Tsunoda, William Theodore de Bary, Donald Keene, and others, eds. and trs., *Sources of Japanese Tradition*, pp. 340–342, 364–366. Copyright © 1927 and 1958 Columbia University Press. Used by permission. Pages 83–85: Inca Garcilaso de Vega, *Royal Commentaries of the Incas*, trans. Clements R. Markham (London: Hakluyt Society, 1869–1871), Vol. 2, pp. 155–164. Pages 85–86: John W. Blake, tr., *Europeans in West Africa, 1450–1560* (London: Hakluyt Society, 1942), Vol. 1, pp. 150–151. Copyright 1942. Used by permission of the Hakluyt Society.

Chapter 3

Pages 93–95: Reprinted with permission of Macmillan Publishing Company from *Constitutionalism and Resistance in the Sixteenth Century* by Julian H. Franklin. Copyright © 1969 by The Bobbs-Merrill Company. Pages 96–99: Lloyd E. Berry and Robert O. Crummey, eds., *Rude and Barbarous Kingdom: Russia in the Accounts of Sixteenth-Century English Voyagers* (Madison: Wisconsin, 1968), pp. 132–135, 138–140, 146–153. Copyright 1968. Used by permission of University of Wisconsin Press. Pages 100–102: Leo Africanus, *The History and Description of Africa*, trans. John Pory (1600). Reprinted in 3 vols by the Hakluyt Society, London, 1896. Vol. 3, pp. 824–827, passim. Modernized by A. J. Andrea. Pages 102–104: John Dos Santos, "Eastern Ethiopia," in *Hakluytus Posthumus* (Glasgow: Hakluyt Society, 1901), pp. 203–214. Pages 106–108: C. T. Foster and F. H. Blackburne Daniell, eds., *The Life and Letters of Ogier Ghiselin de Busbecq*, 2 vols. (London: Hakluyt Society, 1881), Vol. 1, pp. 152–156, 219–221. Pages 109–112: David Price, trans., *Memoirs of the Emperor Jahangueir Written by Himself* (London: Oriental Translation Committee, 1928), pp. 13–20, 33–36, 51–53, 65–66. Pages 114–117: Ryusaku Tsunoda, William Theodore de Bary, Donald Keene, and others, eds. and trs., *Sources of Japanese Tradition*, pp. 335–338. Copyright © 1958 Columbia University Press. Used by permission. Pages 117–120: Jonathan D. Spence, *Emperor of China: Self-Portrait of K'ang-hsi* (New York: Knopf, 1974), pp. 29–34, 40, 41, 50, 51. Copyright 1974. Used by permission of Jonathan D. Spence. Pages 121–123: Excerpts from THE WORLD OF SOUTHEAST ASIA by Harry J. Benda and John A. Larking. Copyright © 1967 by Harry J. Benda and John A. Larking. Reprinted by permission of Harper & Row, Publishers, Inc.

Chapter 4

Pages 127–133: Tomé Pires, *The Suma Oriental*, ed. and tr. by Arando Cortesao (London: Hakluyt Society, 1944), 2nd series, pp. 89, 90. Copyright 1944. Used by permission of The Hakluyt Society. Pages 134–137: Reprinted with permission of The Free Press, a Division of Macmillan, Inc. from CHINESE CIVILIZATION AND SOCIETY: A Sourcebook by Patricia Buckley Ebrey. Copyright © 1981 by The Free Press. Pages 138–142: Shephard B. Clough and Carol Gayle Moodie, eds. and trs., *European Economic History* (Princeton: Van Nostrand, 1965), pp. 233–256. Copyright 1965. Used by permission of Wadsworth Publishing Company. Pages 143–145: Pieter van Dam, *Beschryvinge van de Oostindische Com-*

pagnie, trans. Herbert H. Rowen in Herbert H. Rowen, ed., *The Low Countries in Early Modern Times* (New York: Walker, 1972), pp. 144–149. Pages 147–149: Heinrich Kramer and James Sprenger, *The Malleus Maleficarum*, ed. and tr. by Montague Summers (New York: Dover, 1971), pp. 41–48. Pages 150–151: Katherine Usher Henderson and Barbara F. McManus, *Half Humankind: Contexts and Texts of the Controversy About Women in England, 1540–1640* (Champaign: Illinois, 1985), pp. 336–342. Copyright 1985. Used by permission of University of Illinois Press. Pages 151–152: Thomas Hodgkin, *Nigerian Perspectives* (London: Oxford, 1975), pp. 162–164, 170. Copyright 1975. Used by permission of Oxford University Press. Pages 153–154: C. T. Foster and F. H. Blackburne Daniell, eds., *The Life and Times of Ogier Ghiselin de Busbecq*, 2 vols. (London: Hakluyt Society, 1881), Vol. 1, pp. 228–231. Pages 154–155: Sigismund von Herberstein, *Notes upon Russia*, ed. R. H. Majo (London: Hakluyt Society, 1851), Vol. 1, pp. 91–94. Pages 157–158: Benjamin Keen, ed. and tr., *Readings in Latin American Civilization* (Boston: Houghton Mifflin, 1955), pp. 17–18. Copyright 1955. Used by permission of Benjamin Keen. Pages 159–161: Richard Hellie, trans., in Thomas Rhia, ed., *Readings in Russian Civilization* (Chicago: Chicago, 1969), Vol. 1, pp. 155–162. Copyright 1969. Used by permission of the publisher. Pages 162–163: David John Lu, ed. and tr., *Sources of Japanese History* (New York: McGraw-Hill, 1974), Vol. 2, pp. 216–218. Copyright 1974. Used by permission of McGraw-Hill Publishing Company.

Chapter 5

Pages 169–171: Excerpts from DISCOVERIES AND OPINIONS OF GALILEO translation by Stillman Drake. Copyright translation © 1957 by Stillman Drake. Reprinted by permission of Doubleday, a division of Bantam Doubleday Dell Publishing Group, Inc. Pages 172–175: James Spedding, R. L. Ellis, and Douglas Heath, eds., *The Works of Francis Bacon* (New York: Hurd and Houghton, 1864), Vol. 10, pp. 67–69, 72–75, 131–132, 140–142. Pages 176–178: Reprinted by permission of The Putnam Publishing Group from LES PHILOSOPHES edited by Norman L. Torrey. Copyright © 1960 by Norman L. Torrey. Pages 179–181: Jean-Jacques Rousseau, *The Social Contract and Discourses*, tr. by G. D. H. Cole (New York: Dutton, 1950), pp. 3–4, 6–7, 13–16, 97–102. Copyright 1950. Used by permission of Everyman Library (J. M. Dent & Sons). Pages 182–186: Condorcet, *Sketch for the Historical Picture of the Progress of the Human Mind*, ed. and tr. by June Barraclough (London: Weidenfeld & Nicolson, 1955), pp. 173–176, 196–202. Copyright 1955. Used by permission of George Weidenfeld & Nicolson Limited. Pages 187–189: Henry M. Elliot and John Dowson, eds., *The History of India as Told by Its Own Historians*, 8 vols. (London: Truebner, 1867–1877), Vol. 7, pp. 157–162. Pages 191: Chester Beatty Library, Dublin. Page 192: Courtesy, Freer Gallery of Art, Smithsonian Institution, Washington, D.C. Page 193: Private Collection of Gavin Hambly. Courtesy, Paul Elek, London. Pages 195–196, 197–199: William Theodore de Bary, *Sources of Chinese Tradition*, pp. 608; 515–520. Copyright © Columbia University Press 1966. Used by permission. Pages 200–201: David John Lu, ed. and tr., *Sources of Japanese History* (New York: McGraw-Hill, 1974), Vol. 1, pp. 253–255. Copyright 1974. Used by permission of McGraw-Hill Publishing Company.

Chapter 6

Pages 206–207, 207–208: George Vernadsky, ed., *A Source Book for Russian History from Early Times to 1917* (New Haven: Yale, 1972), p. 347. Copyright 1972. Used by permission of Yale University Press. Pages 207, 208–209: From the book PETER THE GREAT (Great Lives Observed), edited by L. Jay Oliva. © 1970. Used by permission of the publisher, Prentice-Hall, Inc., Englewood Cliffs, NJ. Pages 211–213: Andrew Browning, ed., *English Historical Documents* (London: Eyre & Spottiswoode, 1953), Vol. 7, pp. 122–124, 126. Copyright 1953. Used by permission of Eyre & Spottiswoode. Pages 214–216: James Harvey Robinson, ed., "The French Revolution, 1789–1791," in *Translations and Reprints from the Original Sources of European History* (Philadelphia: University of Pennsylvania, 1898), Vol. 1, no. 5, pp. 6–8. Pages 216–219, 220–222: D. I. Wright in *The French Revolution: Introductory Documents*, University of Queensland Press, 1974. Used by permission of University of Queensland Press. Pages 223–224: Jedidiah Morse, *Annals of the American Revolution* (Hartford, Ct.: 1824), pp. 251–254. Pages 225–228: Benjamin Keen, ed. and tr., *Readings in Latin American Civilization* (Boston: Houghton Mifflin, 1955), pp. 225–227. Copyright 1955. Used by permission of Benjamin Keen. Pages 229–232: François Bernier, *Travels in the Mogul Empire*, ed. and tr. by Archibald Constable (London: Oxford, 1914), pp. 205, 208–209, 220–221, 223–225. Copyright 1914. Used by permission of Oxford University Press.

Chapter 7

Pages 240–243: R. Campbell, *The London Tradesman* (London: T. Gardner, 1747), pp. 284–292. Pages 244–248: Adam Smith, *An Inquiry into the Nature and Causes of the Wealth of Nations*, ed. William Playfair (Hartford: Cooke and Hall, 1818), pp. 299–302, 306, 312–313, 315–317, 319–321, 330–331. Pages 249–251: From THE LOW COUNTRIES IN EARLY MODERN TIMES, translated and edited by Herbert H. Rowen. Copyright © 1972 by Herbert H. Rowen. Reprinted by permission of Walker and Company, from their Documentary History of Western Civilization. Pages 252–256: Paul Edwards, ed. and tr., *Equiano's Travels*, pp. 25–42. Heinemann Educational Books (Oxford). Used by permission. Pages 257–258: Virginia Thompson, *Dupleix and His Letters* (Ballou: 1933), pp. 801–822. Pages 259–261: John Malcolm, *The Life of Robert, Lord Clive* (London: John Murray, 1836), Vol. 2, pp. 119–125. Pages 262–264: E. Backhouse and J. O. P. Brand, *Annals and Memoirs of the Court of Peking* (Boston: Houghton Mifflin, 1914), pp. 325–331. Pages 265–267: From *China in Transition*, ed. by Dun J. Li. © 1969. (New York: Van Nostrand), pp. 64–67. Used by permission of Wadsworth Publishing Company. Pages 268–271: *The Maritime Customs of China, Treaties, Conventions, etc., Between China and Foreign States*, 2nd ed. (Shanghai: 1917), pp. 351–356, 393.

Chapter 8

Pages 277–278: Arthur Young, *Tours in England and Wales* (London: London School of Economics, 1932), pp. 255–258. Pages 280–281: Report from Committee on the Bill To Regulate the Labour of Children in the Mills and Factories in the United Kingdom. *British Sessional Papers*, Vol. XV, pp. 195, 196. London, 1832. Pages 281–282: Second Report of the Commission for Inquiry into the Employment of Children in Factories. *British Sessional Papers*, Vol. XXI, Part D.3, pp. 26–28. London, 1833. Pages 282–284: First Report of the Commissioners for Inquiry into the Employment of Children in Mines. *British Sessional Papers*, Vol. XVI, pp. 149, 230, 258, 263–264. London, 1842. Pages 285–286: Sidney Pollard and Colin Holmes, eds. and trs., *Documents of European Economic History* (New York: St. Martin's, 1972), pp. 478–481. Used by permission of Edward Arnold, a division of Hodder & Stoughton Publishers. Pages 293–295: W. Stephen Sanders, *The Socialist Movement in Germany* (London: The Fabian Society, 1913), pp. 24–26. Copyright 1913. Used by permission of The Fabian Society. Pages 296–297: Gerda Lerner, *The Female Experience: An American Documentary* (Indianapolis: Bobbs-Merrill, 1977), pp. 343–347. Pages 298–300: E. Sylvia Pankhurst, *The Suffragette: The History of the Women's Militant Suffrage Movement, 1905–1910* (London: Gay and Hancock, 1911), pp. 483–487. Pages 302–306: Charles Darwin, *The Origin of the Species* (New York: Appleton and Company, 1896), Vol. I, pp. 75–78, 162, 163; *The Descent of Man* (New York: Appleton and Company, 1886), pp. 62–63, 164–165, 613, 616–617. Pages 307–310: Ralph A. Austen, ed. and tr., *Modern Imperialism* (Lexington, Mass.: Heath, 1969), pp. 70–73. Copyright 1969. Used by permission of D. C. Heath & Co. Pages 310–311: "The White Man's Burden," *McClure's Magazine* 12(4): 290–291, 1899.

Chapter 9

Pages 316–318: *Papers Relating to Engagements Entered into by King Pepple and the Chiefs of the Bonny with Her Majesty's Navel Officers on the Subject of the Suppression of the Slave Trade*, in *Parliamentary Papers, 1847–1848* (London: T. A. Harrison, 1848), Vol. 44, pp. 3, 4. Pages 319–320: Edward Hertslet, ed., *The Map of Africa by Treaty*, 2nd ed. (London: Her Majesty's Stationery Office, 1896), Vol. 1, pp. 467–468. Pages 321–323: Edmund D. Morel, *King Leopold's Rule in Africa* (London: Heinemann Ltd., 1904), pp. 183–186. Pages 325–327: Edward Hertslet, ed., *The Map of Africa by Treaty* (London: Bitterworths, 1875–1891), Vol. 2, pp. 1243–1249. Pages 328–329: A. Sarrov, LA JEUNE-TURQUIE ET LA REVOLUTION (Paris: Bergier-Leviault, 1912), pp. 40–42, tr. as "Young Turks" in Rondo Cameron, ed. and tr., CIVILIZATION SINCE WATERLOO (Arlington Heights, Ill.: Harlan Davidson, 1971), pp. 245, 246. Reprinted with permission. Pages 330–332: Great Britain, *Parliamentary Papers* (London: 1908), Vol. CXXV, cmd. 3750. Pages 334–336: Rammohun Roy, *The English Works of Raja Rammohun Roy* (Allahabad, India: Panini Office, 1906), pp. 471–474. Pages 337–339: Edward Baines, Jr., *History of the Cotton Manufacture in Great Britain* (London: Fisher, Fisher and Jackson, 1835). Pages 340–342: Dadabhai Naoroji, *Essays, Speeches, Addresses and Writings* (Bombay: Caxton Printing Works, 1887), pp. 131–136.

Chapter 10

Pages 346–349: From *China in Transition*, ed. by Dun J. Li. © 1969. (New York: Van Nostrand), pp. 64–67. Used by permission of Wadsworth Publishing Company. Pages 350–352: Franz Michael, ed., *The Taiping Rebellion: History and Documents* (Seattle: Washington, 1971), pp. 312–320. Copyright 1971. Used by permission of University of Washington Press. Pages 353–354: Peking and Tientsin *Times*, May 5, 1900, in *The Boxer Rising*, 2nd ed. (Shanghai: 1901), p. 24. Pages 354: Chien Po-tsan, ed., *I-ho-t'uan* (Shanghai: Shenchou kuo-kang-she, 1951), vol. 4, pp. 148–149, trans. in Ssu-

yu Teng and John K. Fairbank, *China's Response to the West* (Cambridge, Mass.: Harvard University Press, 1954), p. 190. Pages 355–357: Sun Yat-sen, *Fundamentals of National Reconstruction* (Chungking: Chinese Ministry of Information, 1945), pp. 37–40. Pages 359–361, 365–368: David John Lu, ed. and tr., *Sources of Japanese History* (New York: McGraw-Hill, 1974), Vol. 2, pp. 7–8, 42–45. Copyright 1974. Used by permission of McGraw-Hill Publishing Company. Pages 362–364: Ryusaku Tsunoda, William Theodore de Bary, Donald Keene, and others, eds. and trs., *Sources of Japanese Tradition*, pp. 609–615. Copyright © Columbia University Press, 1958. Used by permission. Pages 372–374: Michael Symes, *Journal of His Second Embassy to the Court of Ava in 1802* (London: Allen & Unwin, 1955), pp. 253–257. Copyright 1955. Used by permission of Unwin Hyman, Ltd. Pages 375–376: From WE THE VIETNAMESE by François Sully and Donald Kirk. Copyright © 1971 Praeger Publishers Inc. Reprinted by arrangement with Henry Holt and Company, Inc. Pages 378–381: Jose Rizal, *The Lost Eden*, ed. and tr. by Leon M. Guerrero (Bloomington: Indiana, 1961), pp. 306–315. Copyright 1961. Used by permission of Indiana University Press.

Chapter 11

Pages 388–391: *All Quiet on the Western Front* by Erich Maria Remarque. "Im Westen Nichts Neues," copyright 1928 by Ullstein A. G.; Copyright renewed © 1956 by Erich Maria Remarque; "All Quiet on the Western Front," copyright 1929, 1930 by Little, Brown and Company; Copyright renewed © 1957, 1958 by Erich Maria Remarque. All Rights Reserved. Pages 392–393: *Congressional Record*, Vol. LVI (1918), part I, pp. 680–681. Pages 395–397: *Treaty of Peace with Germany*, 66th U.S. Congress, 1st Session, Senate Document No. 49, 1919. Pages 400–404: V. I. Lenin, *Collected Works* (Moscow: Progress, 1973), Vol. 5, pp. 352–353. Used by permission of Progress Publishers. Pages 405–407: George Verdnasky, ed., *A Source Book of Russian History from Early Times to 1917* (New Haven: Yale, 1972), pp. 867–868. Copyright 1972. Used by permission of Yale University Press. Pages 408–410: Joseph Stalin, "The Tasks of Business Executives" (speech), in *Problems of Leninism* (Moscow: 1940), pp. 359–360, 365–366. Pages 411–416: From HARD TIMES: AN ORAL HISTORY OF THE GREAT DEPRESSION, by Studs Terkel. Copyright © 1970 by Studs Terkel. Reprinted by permission of Pantheon Books, a Division of Random House, Inc. Reprinted by permission of Elaine Greene Ltd. Pages 416–418: H. H. Tiltman, *Slump: A Study of Stricken Europe Today* (London: Jarroids Limited, 1932), pp. 39–41. Copyright 1952. Used by permission of Marjorie Hessek Tiltman. Pages 420–422: *International Conciliation*, no. 306 (January 1935), pp. 5–17. Pages 423–427: Excerpts from MEIN KAMPF by Adolf Hitler, translated by Ralph Mannheim. Copyright 1943 and copyright © renewed 1971 by Houghton Mifflin Company. Reprinted by permission of Houghton Mifflin Company. Used by permission of Century Hutchinson Publishing Group Limited (London). Pages 429–432: Excerpts from *Tokyo Record* by Otto D. Tolischus, copyright 1943 by Otto D. Tolischus, reprinted by the permission of Harcourt Brace Jovanovich, Inc. Pages 434–437: Copyright © 1978 by Isaiah Trunk. From the book JEWISH RESPONSES TO NAZI PERSECUTION. Originally published by Stein & Day, Inc., reprinted with permission of Scarborough House/Publishers.

Chapter 12

Pages 445–446: Great Britain, *Parliamentary Papers, 1920.* Treaty Series no. 11, cmd. 964, pp. 11–12. Pages 447–449: *Foreign Relations of the United States: Paris Peace Conference 12:* 780–781, 1919. Pages 450–453: Mustafa Kemal, *A Speech Delivered by Ghazi Mustapha Kemal* (Leipzig: K. F. Hoehler, 1929), pp. 376–379, 589–594. Pages 455–459: Mohandas Gandhi, *Indian Home Rule* (Madras: Ganesh, 1922), pp. 30–35, 47–50, 63, 64, 85, 88, 90, 91. Copyright 1922. Used by permission of Ganesh & Company, Publishers. Pages 460–464: Excerpt from TOWARD FREEDOM by Jawaharlal Nehru. Copyright 1941 by The John Day Company, Inc.; copyright © renewed 1968 by Indira Gandhi. Reprinted by permission of Harper & Row, Publishers, Inc. Pages 464–467: Excerpts from THE WORLD OF SOUTHEAST ASIA by Harry J. Benda and John A. Larking. Copyright © 1967 by Harry J. Benda and John A. Larking. Reprinted by permission of Harper & Row, Publishers, Inc. Pages 468–471: Frederick Dealtry, *The Dual Mandate in British Tropical Africa* (London: Blackwood and Sons, 1922), pp. 200–207, 214–215, 217. Used by permission of Pillans & Wilson, Edinborough. Pages 472–473: *The Crisis* 23: 5–10, 1921. Pages 475–477: Reprinted with permission of The Free Press, a Division of Macmillan, Inc. from CHINESE CIVILIZATION AND SOCIETY, Patricia Buckley Ebrey, ed. Copyright © 1981 by The Free Press. Pages 478–481: Mao Zedong, *Selected Works* (New York: International Publishers, 1954), Vol. 1, pp. 192–196, 203–207. Pages 483–487, 487–489: Benjamin Keen, ed. and tr., *Readings in Latin American Civilization* (Boston: Houghton Mifflin, 1955), pp. 373–375; 362–364. Copyright 1955. Used by permission of Benjamin Keen.

Chapter 13

Pages 494–497: Winston Churchill, *His Complete Speeches,* ed. by R. R. James (New York: Bowker, 1974), cols. 7285–7293. Used by permission of Chelsea House Publishers. Pages 497–499: "Stalin Interview with *Pravda* on Churchill," March 14, 1946. Copyright © 1946 by The New York Times Company. Reprinted by permission. Pages 504–506: Information Service, Viet-Nam Delegation in France, *The Democratic Republic of Viet-Nam* (Paris: Imprimerie Centrale Commerciale, 1948), pp. 3–5. Pages 507–509: Patrice Lumumba, *Lumumba Speaks,* ed. by Jean la Lierde, tr. by Helen R. Lane (Boston: Little, Brown, 1972), pp. 220–224. Pages

511–514: Yehoshafat Herkabi, *The Palestine Covenant and Its Meaning* (London: Vallentine, Mitchell, 1979), pp. 119–124. Copyright 1979. Used by permission of Vallentine, Mitchell & Co., Ltd. Pages 514–516: From WHO STANDS ACCUSED?, by Chaim Herzog. Copyright © 1978 by State of Israel. Reprinted by permission of Random House, Inc. Pages 518–520: Ruhullah Khomeini, *Islam and Revolution,* tr. by Hamid Algar (Berkeley, Cal.: Mizan, 1981), pp. 269. Copyright 1981. Used by permission of Mizan Press. Pages 522–526: Nelson Mandela, *No Easy Walk to Freedom,* ed. by Ruth First (New York: Basic, 1965), pp. 163–168, 180–181, 184–189. Copyright 1965. Used by permission of Heinemann Educational Books Limited. Pages 527–529: Reprinted with permission of Macmillan Publishing Company from *Malcolm X: The Man and His Times,* by Malcolm X, edited by John Henrik Clarke. Copyright © 1969 John Henrik Clarke, Earl Grant and Peter Bailey. Used by permission of John Henrik Clarke. Pages 530–533: Betty Friedan, *The Feminine Mystique* (New York: Dell, 1962) pp. 11, 12, 13–16, 21, 22, 27. Copyright 1962. Used by permission of W. W. Norton & Company, Inc. Pages 533–535: Reprinted from PERSONAL VOICES: CHINESE WOMEN IN THE 1980'S by Emily Honig and Gail Hershatter with the permission of the publishers, Stanford University Press. © 1988 by the Board of Trustees of the Leland Stanford Junior University. Pages 535–537: Madhu Kishwar and Ruth Vanita, *In Search of Answers: Indian Voices from Manusha* (London: Zed, 1984), pp. 246–248. Copyright 1984. Used by permission of Zed Books Ltd. Pages 538–539: Miranda Davies, *Third World/Second Sex* (London: Zed, 1983), pp. 152–159. Copyright 1983. Used by permission of Zed Books Ltd. Pages 541–544: Martin Kenner and James Petras, eds., *Fidel Castro Speaks* (New York: Grove, 1969), pp. 191–199. Reprinted by permission of Grove Weidenfeld, a division of Wheatland Corporation. Copyright © 1969 by Martin Kenner and James Petras. Pages 545–547: *Peking Review,* August 12, 1966, pp. 6–11. Pages 548–551: Excerpt from PERESTROIKA by Mikhail Gorbachev. Copyright © 1987 by Mikhail Gorbachev. Reprinted by permission of Harper & Row, Publishers, Inc. Pages 554–555: *World Development Report, 1988* (New York: Oxford, 1988). Reprinted by permission of Oxford University Press, New York. Pages 556–562: Tables excerpted from pp. 10–16 of THE NEXT 200 YEARS by Herman Kahn. Copyright © 1976 by Hudson Institute. By permission of William Morrow and Company, Inc.